THE TERCENTENNIAL HISTORY OF
HARVARD COLLEGE AND UNIVERSITY
1636–1936

THE FOUNDING OF
HARVARD COLLEGE

BY

SAMUEL ELIOT MORISON
CLASS OF 1908

Cambridge, Massachusetts

HARVARD UNIVERSITY PRESS

PREFACE

IT IS amusing now to recall the disapproval of some of my friends when, seven or eight years ago, I proposed to devote myself to what they regarded as a 'narrow' subject. Actually, Harvard history has proved to be the most difficult, but at the same time the most stimulating and broadening, task that I have yet undertaken. For it soon became evident that this little institution 'in the wilderness' was no log-college for teaching the elements, or puritan divinity school. Narrow, if you will — a narrow gorge through which a stream of learning, the Arts and Sciences, Philosophies, and Humane Letters, poured from the Old World into New England, and thence spread through a large part of these United States. And so, slenderly equipped with but one of the 'learned tongues,' I had to breast the current and mount the stream to its origin. It could not have been done without the aid of friendly tow-ropes proffered by learned colleagues such as George Lyman Kittredge, Edward Kennard Rand, and Harry A. Wolfson. Then came a happy descent with the ancients and the humanists as my pilots, pausing to chart the spots where tributaries from the Alps and the Apennines entered the main stream. It has been an exciting cruise for an American historian, who now invites the reader to glide downstream with him and enjoy the sights. You may join the trip, if you wish, where the movement becomes rapid and the bottle-neck begins; but you must not expect me to carry you through the gorge into calm reaches in the space of a single volume. Although warned by the horrid example of Thomas Prince (A.B. 1707), who began his 'Chronological History of New-England' with the Creation, and died before he reached the year 1631, I have been unable to get beyond 1650 in the present tome. But the next, 'Harvard College in the Seventeenth Century' (now ready for the press), will include the organization of the College under the Charter of 1650, the curriculum and student life of the seventeenth century, and the history of the College from 1650 to 1708. This will be followed, *Deo volente*, by 'Harvard College in the Eighteenth Century,' and by

a fourth volume which will take the History of the University
down to President Eliot's administration, where the symposium
published in 1930, *The Development of Harvard University, 1869–
1929*, begins.

Alma mater Harvardiana may better be described as *digna*
than *illustris* in her young matronhood; but no less fair for
that, or significant.   Just as the practices and traditions of
English liberty would have been lost in the American wilderness
but for representative institutions; so scholarly traditions would
have perished, the English cultural heritage would have been
dissipated and the intellectual side of colonial life impoverished,
without a college to sustain them.   Hence the founding of Harvard College, and the struggle of the New England puritans to
maintain standards of excellence, form the first chapter of
higher education in the United States, and a vital part of American social history.

The Latin inscription facing the first page of text is from the
tympanum of Sanders Theatre, Memorial Hall.   It was written
by Professor George Martin Lane (A. B. 1846).

Of the many people who have helped me, I wish particularly
to thank Mr. Albert Matthews (A.B. 1882), Dr. Albert P.
Norris (M.D. 1903), Dr. Erwin Raisz, Mr. Harold R. Shurtleff
(A.B. 1906), Dr. Harold Bowditch (A.B. 1905), Mr. Robert
Dickson Weston (A.B. 1886), Dr. Peter Giles (Master of Em-
manuel), Dr. Clifford K. Shipton (S. B. 1926), Mr. Donald
H. Mugridge, and my secretary, Miss Florence Berlin (A.B. Rad-
cliffe 1926).

S. E. M.

Harvard University
January, 1935

CONTENTS

CONTENTS

LIST OF ILLUSTRATIONS
AND MAPS

LIST OF ARMS AND SEALS

THE blazons and bibliographical data for this list have been compiled with the assistance of members of the Committee on Heraldry, New England Historic Genealogical Society. Dr. Harold Bowditch (H.B.) and Robert Dickson Weston, Esq. (R.D.W.) have drawn most of the arms and seals. No personal arms have been inserted unless the Committee have passed on their authenticity, and the right of the person named to bear them. William Stoughton, for instance, used arms, and had them engraved on plate and carved on Stoughton College; but as he appears to have had no right to them they are not reproduced here. The Committee's principles of selection and rejection are explained in *A Roll of Arms* (hereinafter designated as *1st Roll*), published by the Society in 1928, and also printed in *N. E. H. G. R.*, LXXXII. 146–68; and in *A Second Roll of Arms*, 1932, also printed in *N. E. H. G. R.*, LXXXVI. 258–86. A third Roll has been prepared, but not yet published. Other members of the Committee who have been most generous in aid are Mr. G. Andrews Moriarty, Jr., of Bristol, Rhode Island, and Professor Arthur Adams of Trinity College, Hartford. Mr. Howard M. Chapin, Librarian of the Rhode Island Historical Society, has also assisted our researches.

Other abbreviations used in this list are *H. J.* for the *Heraldic Journal*, and *H. S.* for the *Harleian Society Publications*, containing the County Visitations of Heralds.

ABBREVIATIONS IN FOOTNOTES

A.A.S. .... American Antiquarian Society, Worcester. *Proc. A.A.S.* are the *Proceedings* of this Society, 1812–.

B.P.L. .... Boston Public Library.

C.S.M. .... *Publications of the Colonial Society of Massachusetts*, Boston, 1895–.
Vols. xv and xvi contain the Harvard College Books I, III, and IV from the University Archives, with an introduction by Albert Matthews.
Vol. xxxi will contain Chesholme's Steward's Book, the Laws of 1655, and other College Records.

D.A.B. .... *Dictionary of American Biography*, New York, 1928–.

D.N.B. .... *Dictionary of National Biography*, London.

Docs. U. Camb. ... *Documents relating to the University and Colleges of Cambridge*, 3 vols., London, 1852.

Eliot, *Sketch* ..... Samuel A. Eliot, *A Sketch of the History of Harvard College*, Boston, 1848.

H.C.L. .... Harvard College Library.

H.C.S.C. .... S. E. Morison, *Harvard College in the Seventeenth Century* (the next volume in this series).

H.U. Arch. ...... Harvard University Archives.

Magnalia .... Cotton Mather, *Magnalia Christi Americana: or, the Ecclesiastical History of New-England*, London, 1702.
Each of the seven 'books' of this volume is paged separately.

Mass. Archives ... Massachusetts Archives, State House, Boston.

Mass. Bay Recs. .. *Records of the Governor and Company of the Massachusetts Bay in New England*, 5 vols. in 6, N. B. Shurtleff ed., Boston, 1853–54.

M.H.S. .... Massachusetts Historical Society. *Coll. M.H.S.* are the printed *Collections* of this Society, 1792–. *Proc. M.H.S.* are the *Proceedings*, 1859–. Numerical prefixes indicate numbers of series.

Mullinger .... J. B. Mullinger's History of the University of Cambridge.
I. = *The U. of Camb. from Earliest Times to Royal Injunctions of 1535* (1873); II. = *The U. of Camb. from 1535 to Accession of Charles I* (1884); III. = *The U. of Camb. from 1626 to decline of Platonist Movement* (1911).

N.E.D. . . . . *The New English Dictionary*, Oxford, 1888–1928.

N.E.H.G.R. . . . . . . *New England Historical and Genealogical Register*, Boston, 1847–.

N.E.Q. . . . . *The New England Quarterly*, 1928–.

Paige . . . . Lucius R. Paige, *History of Cambridge* (Boston, 1877); *Supplement and Index* (1930).

Proc. . . . . *see* A.A.S.; M.H.S.

Quincy . . . . Josiah Quincy, *History of Harvard University*, 2 vols., Cambridge, 1840.

Rashdall . . . . Hastings Rashdall, *The Universities of Europe in the Middle Ages*, 2 vols. in 3, Oxford, 1895.

S.B. . . . . Chesholme's Steward's Book, printed in *C.S.M.*, xxxi.

Sibley . . . . J. L. Sibley, *Biographical Sketches of Graduates of Harvard University*, 4 vols., Cambridge, 1873–1933.

W.W.P. . . . . Edward Johnson, *Wonder-Working Providence of Sions Saviour in New England*, J. F. Jameson ed., New York, 1910.

THE FOUNDING OF
HARVARD COLLEGE

HIC IN SILVESTRIBVS ET INCVLTIS LOCIS ANGLI DOMO PROFVGI
ANNO POST CHRISTVM NATVM MDCXXXVI POST COLONIAM HVC
DEDVCTAM VI SAPIENTIAM RATI ANTE OMNIA COLENDAM
SCHOLAM PVBLICE CONDIDERVNT CONDITAM CHRISTO ET EC-
CLESIAE DICAVERVNT QVAE AVCTA IOHANNIS HARVARD MVNI-
FICENTIA A LITTERARVM FAVTORIBVS CVM NOSTRATIBVS TVM
EXTERNIS IDENTIDEM ADIVTA ALVMNORVM DENIQVE FIDEI
COMMISSA AB EXIGVIS PERDVCTA INITIIS AD MAIORA RERVM
INCREMENTA PRAESIDIVM SOCIORVM INSPECTORVM SENATVS
ACADEMICI CONSILIIS ET PRVDENTIA ET CVRA OPTVMAS ARTES
VIRTVTES PVBLICAS PRIVATAS COLVIT COLIT

I

THE ORIGIN OF UNIVERSITIES[1]

 'After God had carried us safe to *New England*, and wee had builded our houses, provided necessaries for our liveli-hood, rear'd convenient places for Gods worship, and setled the Civill Government: One of the next things we longed for, and looked after was to advance *Learning* and perpetuate it to Posterity; . . .'[2] So reads the earliest account of Harvard College at Cambridge in New England. Harvard it was named after the young man who, dying, gave the nascent college his library and half his estate. Cambridge recalled the English university which he and most of the founders owned as mother. *In Christi Gloriam* declared their continuity of purpose with the universities of the middle ages. *Veritas*, emblazoned on the three books of the College arms, proclaimed the principle that they held greater than knowledge. Near the Charles River a level site was chosen, and there, these three hundred years, 'the good and the great

1. Authorities for Chapters I and II: Hastings Rashdall, *The Universities of Europe in the Middle Ages* (2 vols. in 3, Oxford, 1895), the product of ripe but sometimes too imaginative scholarship, is the only extended work on this subject in the English language. The new edition being prepared by F. M. Powicke and A. B. Emden will contain emendations, some of which are supplied by H. E. Salter, 'The Medieval University of Oxford,' in *History*, n.s., xiv (1929). 57–61, by Gaines Post's chapter in *Anniversary Essays in Mediæval History, by Students of Charles H. Haskins* (Boston, 1929), and Stephen d'Irsay, *Histoire des Universités des Origines à nos jours* (tome i, Paris, 1933). The best brief treatment of the subject is Haskins' *Rise of Universities* (New York, 1923); his *Renaissance of the Twelfth Century* (Harvard University Press, 1927), and the appropriate chapters of Henry Osborn Taylor, *The Mediaeval Mind* (2 vols., New York, 1911), are the best works on the intellectual movement, on which there are some apposite remarks in L. J. Paetow's introduction to his edition of Henri d'Andeli, *La Bataille des VII Ars* (Memoirs of the University of California, iv. no. 1, 1914), and by E. K. Rand, 'The Classics of the Thirteenth Century,' in *Speculum*, iv (1929). 249–69.

2. *New Englands First Fruits*; see Appendix D.

in their beautiful prime' have dreamed the long dreams of youth.

Within a few years a timber building on the English collegiate model was erected; and there the traditional Arts and Philosophies and learned Tongues were taught, and the standards, forms, and amenities of English universities were reproduced, so far as the slender means and austere principles of New England would permit. Dark days followed, when the colonies were ravaged by Indian wars, and encroaching materialism all but quenched learning; but the torch never went out. The century of enlightenment brought fresh benefactions, a gradual change in curriculum and discipline, and a body of graduates who served their country in pulpit, senate, and the field. Yet how slight were the changes in the first half of the life of Harvard as compared with those of the last hundred and fifty years!

Under Kirkland, Harvard College blossomed into Harvard University, with schools of Medicine, Law, and Theology, and a national student body. The genius of an Eliot made Harvard the pacemaker of American universities, and one of the greatest of the world's universities; the devotion of a Lowell reëstablished certain values which had been lost in radical reform, restored an architectural distinction which had all but disappeared, and maintained academic freedom in an era of retreating liberty. Throughout her three centuries, because she has never called men to herself but to themselves, Harvard has grown through the generosity of her sons, asking only that she might offer even more to posterity. Old in wisdom but young at heart, she meets the three hundredth class as she met the first, eager to kindle in them that desire for truth which makes men free.

In these three centuries of Harvard history, two ages stand out. One is the Eliot era, which brought expansion and enrichment in every department of learning, and established the framework in which the University must live for many years to come. The other is the era of foundation, the age of Dunster, when a colony of a few thousand people, poor even by the modest standards of that day, had the audacity to plan and the energy to achieve a university college of equal status with the ancient foundations of England and Scotland. Yet we cannot begin the story of Harvard College with 1636, the year of foundation; her roots go far deeper into the past. Her founders had no new ideas on education. Although acutely conscious of living in a 'wilderness,' they stoutheartedly refused to yield an inch to pioneer prejudices or frontier values. They were determined to establish a new Cambridge as well as a New England. Yet, if Cambridge and her colleges were the immediate models, the ancestry of Harvard goes back through Oxford to Paris, the mother university of northern Europe. Certain forms, ceremonies, offices, and university methods which were first established in the Latin Quarter in the twelfth and thirteenth centuries are still flourishing on the banks of the Charles in the twentieth century.

Universities sprang up as a result of one of the most vital outbursts of intellectual activity in recorded history. As distinctive a product of the middle ages as Gothic architecture, the university bore a part in medieval life comparable only to that of the Empire and the Church. There had, indeed, been schools since the dawn of civilization, and classical antiquity was familiar with the noblest form of education, in which men of learning taught their pupils not merely as much as was conceived proper for the adolescent mind, but a method of attaining knowledge and wisdom. It flattered the men of the renaissance and the eighteenth century to call a school or group of learned men an academy, after the grove where Plato walked and argued. According to a medieval tradition which puritan Harvard accepted with uncritical alacrity, the prophet Samuel presided over the world's first university, consisting of 'Sons of the Prophets' organized in colleges at Bethel, Kirjath-sephir, and Kirjath-sannah.[1]

1. 2 Kings ii. 3, 5; Joshua xv. 15, 49; each place is translated πόλις γραμμάτων in the Septuagint; Cotton Mather refers to Newtown as 'the *Kiriath Sepher* appointed for the Seat of' Harvard College, in *Magnalia* (1702), book iv. 126. That this theory of the origin of universities was familiar in the middle ages is evident from a passage in a letter of Honorius III to the cathedral chapter of Paris, in 1219. Referring to the narrow quarters for students in the Ile de la Cité, he says, 'coangustatum est illic stratum et fere artus est locus ibidem filiis prophetarum' (Denifle and Châtelain, *Chartularium Univ. Parisiensis*, I. 92; cf. Rashdall, II. 691). Nathaniel Rogers, in his valedictory oration at the Harvard Commencement of 1652, paraphrasing a passage from the Commentary on Joshua by the Jesuit theologian Cornelius à Lapide, said, 'Kirjath-Sephir seems to have been a university of the Canaanites, the most ancient of all those which we read of in the sacred scriptures, where learned men taught all manner of literature and books. Three names of it occur: 1. Debir, as if the oracle of wisdom, or because therein eloquence and the art of right speaking was taught; 2. Kirjath-sephir, the city of literature or of books; 3. Kirjath-sanna, city of acuteness, in which matters were acutely discussed.' *C. S. M.*, xxxi. Cf. Jacobus Alting, *Hebræorum Respublica Scholastica: sive Historia Academiarum* (Amsterdam, 1652); Benjamin Colman, *The Master Taken up from the Sons of the Prophets* (Boston, 1724); Jacob Middendorp's

Between the last great academy of the ancient world at Alexandria and the first universities at Paris and Bologna there was a gap of six centuries, and a radical change in ideas and methods. The American whose notion of an efficient college was a student at one end of a log and Mark Hopkins at the other, unconsciously voiced a Greek, not a medieval, idea of education; for the men of the middle ages, like ourselves, could not conceive of higher learning apart from a society of scholars.

In the decay and destruction that overcame almost everything that we call civilization during the dark ages, it became necessary for men engaged in the same occupation, or living in the same community, to band together for self-protection. Hence the middle ages became the greatest institutionalizing era the world has ever known, and medieval man, like his American frontier descendant, became accustomed to merge his individuality in a gild, commune, fraternity, or corporation. He was an excellent 'joiner,' and one of the things he loved to join was a university.

A university [1] in the middle ages meant an institution of learning recognized as such by pope or king, where the teachers or students, or both, were united in gilds enjoying a certain privilege and autonomy, where some 'superior' study such as Law, Medicine, or Theology was taught in addition to the seven Arts and Philosophy, where a definite curriculum was marked out for each subject, and where at stated periods the students were examined and granted degrees.[2] All these attributes,

preface to his *Academiarvm Celebrivm Vniversi Terrarvm Orbis Libri viii* (Cologne, 1602), attributing the foundation of the first university to Noah, as a means of spreading 'bonarum literarum studia' and so preventing another flood!

1. The word used in the early thirteenth century for what we call a university was *studium generale*. *Universitas*, which simply meant 'the corporation,' 'the Assembly,' and carried no connotation of universal learning or teaching, was at first applied to the corporation of masters, or the agglomeration of students, or even to one of the faculties. But, quite early, *universitas* became applied to the *entire* university — the earliest instances noted by d'Irsay (*op. cit.*, pp. 127 n. 6, 148) are 1240 at Oxford and 1262 at Paris. Cf. Strickland Gibson, *Statuta Antiqua Vniv. Oxon.* (1931), pp. 72, 98. *Academia* was more commonly used for what we mean by 'university' from the renaissance to the eighteenth century; a University of Paris diploma of 1567, for instance, has *Parisiensis Academia*.

2. Denifle, *Die Universitäten des Mittelalters bis 1400*, I. 19, insists that a *studium generale* or university meant an institution of higher learning containing at least one of the superior faculties (Law, Medicine, Theology) besides a faculty of Arts; offering instruction to all who came, not merely to those of a city or gild; by pope, emperor, or king endowed with corporate individuality, and privileged with the power to exempt beneficed students from the canonical requirement to reside in their respective parishes;

which came into existence in the twelfth century, are still marks of the American university — except that the teachers have relinquished most of their administrative powers to external governing bodies.

What has this to do with Harvard, which made no serious claim to be a university before 1780? Much; for Harvard from the beginning was something more than an Old World college: it undertook to teach and to grant degrees. In medieval Europe, a college was a corporation established within a university to provide board and lodging to a small group of scholars. But by 1600 the colleges of Oxford and Cambridge had absorbed most of the teaching and other functions of those universities; and as the sentiments of the English university men who came to New England clustered around their respective colleges, it was a college that they established 'to advance Learning.' Hence, in the United States, the historical relationship between college and university is exactly the reverse of what it had been in Europe. There, the college grew up within the university; here, the college carried on the tradition of university learning, performed of necessity certain university functions, and finally, in some instances, expanded into a proper university. Hence, in American popular usage, a university is regarded merely as a big college, and a college as a small university. And, for the same reason, the ancestry of Harvard College must be sought in the medieval universities, as well as in the reformation colleges.

Indeed, one of the most persistently misunderstood features of early Harvard, the ecclesiastical flavor of the College, can only be rightly understood if we approach her history from the middle ages.

Since the Church had saved all that could be saved of learning from the wreck of the Roman Empire, she naturally took charge of education in the middle ages; universities grew up under her patronage; all masters and scholars were *clerici*, potential priests. Moreover, the Church fostered the universities in order to provide herself with a learned clergy, and to reconcile philosophy with theology. Medieval universities were distinctly 'purposeful'; they did not cultivate the Arts for their own sake,

and conferring the *ius ubique docendi* on its graduates. Rashdall, 1. 7–20, proves that *studium generale* meant different things at different times; indeed, the question 'When does an institution of learning become a university?' seems almost as incapable of exact solution for the middle ages as it does today.

as perhaps the ancients did, but as means toward a philosophical culture.[1] Yet their Arts curriculum was almost entirely taken over from classical antiquity. There was no special vocational training for the priesthood until after the reformation: the ecclesiastical seminary is a child of Trent. Theological faculties were intended to train doctors of the Church, the 'research scholars' of that age; one did not require a divinity degree to obtain even the highest ecclesiastical offices — nobody ever said to an ambitious priest, 'Go get a doctor's degree, and maybe you will become a bishop.' And the Protestant reformers had no new ideas in this respect; they merely wished to recall universities to their proper functions.

Early Harvard, from the point of view of nineteenth-century historians, seemed so shrouded in clerical black as to be later described as a 'divinity school.' No title could be more misleading. The sombre color of early Harvard was simply an inheritance of medieval tradition, to which in some respects the puritans reverted. Harvard College, to be sure, was founded *in Christi Gloriam* and later dedicated *Christo et Ecclesiae*. Her presidents and tutors insisted that there could be no true knowledge or wisdom without Christ.[2] Her founders dreaded 'to leave an illiterate Ministry to the Churches'; and but for the passionately sincere religion of these puritans, there would have been no Harvard. But the intellectual fare that she provided for young men was the old Liberal Arts course, with certain changes made in the renaissance and reformation.[3] Students destined for the ministry had to wait until after taking the bachelor's degree before receiving any specialized training in theology.

THE SEVEN LIBERAL ARTS

For more than a thousand years before Harvard College was founded, European boys studied in schools and universities the seven Liberal Arts as described by Martianus Capella in the fifth century: the *Trivium* (Grammar, Rhetoric, and Logic) and the *Quadrivium* (Music, Arithmetic, Geometry, and Astronomy). Six of the seven, together with the three Philosophies brought in by the twelfth-century renaissance, and the

1. Stephen d'Irsay, *Histoire des Universités*, I. 53.
2. See below, Chapter XVIII and *H. C. S. C.*, Chapter XXIII.
3. *H. C. S. C.*, Chapter VII.

Greek literature introduced by the later renaissance, remained the backbone of the undergraduate course in European and American universities well into the nineteenth century. To the immemorial prestige of the seven Liberal Arts [1] — the studies suitable for a *liber homo*, or free man — we pay unconscious homage whenever we speak of a 'Faculty of Arts and Sciences,' an 'Arts College,' or a 'liberal education.'

From one century to another the content and even the meaning of these subjects has changed. At all times Grammar [2] has been fundamental. When Latin was the language of law, of literature, of the Church, of learned conversation, and of international intercourse, a thorough grounding in it was essential for every educated man. Hence in the middle ages Latin grammar was almost the unique study of the schoolboy; and the tradition of it long outlasted the universality of the language. Even within the memory of men now living, boys in New England schools preparing for Harvard and Yale spent more time on Latin than on all other subjects combined.

Rhetoric, the art of persuasion, was studied through the ancient Latin authors in the twelfth century, when there took place a revival of classical learning comparable only to that of Greek learning in the Quattrocento. Virgil, Ovid, and Cicero had never been lost to sight, but in the twelfth century hundreds of classical manuscripts which had been treasured in monastic and cathedral libraries through the dark ages, and perhaps read by nobody since the confusion that followed Charlemagne, were now brought forth, copied, and established as the textbooks of the schools. For two or three generations educated men wrote better Latin than anyone had done during twenty generations past. In the cathedral schools of such towns as Canterbury, Salisbury, Chartres, Orleans, and Rheims there prevailed a harmonious and balanced type of literary culture; classical antiquity was studied in a true humanist spirit, for the sweetness that it gave to life.

One is tempted to conclude that the rise of universities stifled this classical revival with educational machinery. But that is not the historical sequence. Our young garden of humanities

1. Also called the Liberal Sciences, 'arts' and 'sciences' being used almost interchangeably in the middle ages. See *N. E. D.*, 'Science,' 3.
2. It will be understood that in the middle ages grammar, as an academic subject, meant Latin grammar.

was almost smothered in a dust-pall of dialectic before the universities fairly began. The circumstances of this era made Logic a 'practical' subject which drew off students from the study of belles-lettres; and the first universities of northern Europe were created in order to handle the vast throng of students who came to learn Logic, and the masters who came to teach Logic, as a stepping-stone to Theology and Law.

Around the year 1240 a trouvère named Henri d'Andeli wrote a satirical poem, *La Bataille des VII Ars*, deploring the decline of Rhetoric in much the same temper as a classicist of today bewails the loss of Latin and Greek. Dame Logic, in d'Andeli's poem, sends one of her pupils to parley with the enemy Grammar. As he has neglected his Latin for the 'practical' Logic, he cannot even make himself understood.

> In Grammar's Court there are more angles
> To check the lad, than Logic's jangles.

Returning to Dame Logic he is comforted and conducted to her high tower

> And told that she could make him fly
> Before to walk he 'gan to try.

Away with Grammar and Rhetoric and every art but Logic, cries the bitter-hearted poet. Logic for boys, logic for all! [1]

The outlook for belles-lettres was probably not quite so bad as d'Andeli made out. 'A humanist,' observes Edward Kennard Rand, 'generally lives in a period that is going to the dogs.' [2] But the mysteries of Logic had the same fascination for the medieval scholar's mind as have those of Economics and Sociology for his descendant in the twentieth century; and when new subjects press in, tradition must suffer. Young men, their minds sharpened by the 'old Logic' of Aristotle and Boethius' translation of Porphyry's *Isagoge*, began to apply themselves to reconciling ancient philosophy with Christian theology. Universities grew up, or were founded, to provide the appropriate facilities for this colossal effort of the human spirit. And within a little

1. L. J. Paetow (ed.), *The Battle of the Seven Arts, by Henri d'Andeli*, pp. 58-60.
2. *Speculum*, IV. 258. 'That the ruling passion of the age was dialectic, it would be absurd to deny,' he concludes (p. 266). 'Yet . . . along with the call of the practical, the revolutionary, and the modern, grammar and the old authors were still recognized as the portal of sound education.'

more than a century their prayers and pains were rewarded by one of man's most glorious achievements, Scholastic Philosophy, a system of thought and of nature at once rational and authoritative, which not only explained but integrated the universe.

Then time played one of her many jokes: scholasticism crumbled before fresh intellectual efforts; but the universities outlived the purpose that gave them birth. Like all human institutions they must one day disappear, and die they will and must when they cease to persuade mankind to value things of the spirit.

The University of Paris

Peter Abélard was the greatest, although not the first, of the teachers who applied the Aristotelian *organon* to the speculative problems of his age. Although the active part of his life preceded the birth of universities, it was as much the prestige of his teaching in the schools of Notre-Dame and Sainte-Geneviève as the physical advantages of Paris that fixed there the first *studium generale* in northern Europe. Among the great teachers of all time, Abélard stands in the front rank. A painstaking scholar who mastered the entire body of knowledge available to his generation, a fearless intellect that challenged the most sacred dogmas and time-honored formulas, a radiant personality that attracted youth to Paris from the furthest corners of the Christian world, and a born leader who fertilized a generation of scholars with a passion for knowledge, he was the very type of great teacher who is worshipped by pupils, hated by colleagues, suspected by the public, and crucified by authority. The story of his love for Héloïse remains the classic example of that pitfall which awaits radical thinkers who take insufficient heed of common prejudices. Even the identical problem upon which his brilliant intellect scored its most spectacular victories — the question stated in the *Isagoge* 'concerning genera and species': whether universals or general conceptions (such as genera and species) represent the only reality (the Realist and eventually the Idealist position), or whether these were names and sounds only which had no real existence apart from the things which the senses can perceive (the Nominalist position) — continued a major problem of the schools through the middle ages and remained to agitate

Harvard students.[1] The stream of pupils who came to learn under Abélard, the masters who remained after he had gone, and the increasing importance of Paris under Capetian kings fixed that city as seat of the first and greatest medieval university.

The process by which this congeries of teachers and pupils became the University of Paris began shortly after the death of Abélard in 1142, and was not completed within a century. There was no organization in Abélard's time, except that a teacher required a license from the Archbishop's representative before he was allowed to set up a school, or to lecture. Here is the first, or ecclesiastical, element in university government. Self-government, the second element, came when the teachers organized a gild to protect themselves and further their common interests, just as every trade and profession was then doing. Commencement (*Inceptio*), the oldest, most dignified, and widespread university institution, began simply as initiation to this gild of Masters of Arts. The candidate, having received his license to teach from the Chancellor, was ceremonially admitted to the masters' or teachers' gild, and confirmed in his new fellowship and title of Master of Arts by performing an appropriate 'Act.' If, eventually, he proceeded Doctor of Divinity, he was admitted to the gild of theologians with a different ceremonial, at a doctors' Commencement.

Most American universities, fearing to waste their presumably precious time, have telescoped all their commencements into one ceremony, at which the President admits candidates to sundry degrees that he does not himself possess. Yet even Thomas Aquinas might recognize in a Harvard Commencement of the twentieth century a lineal descent from the masters' *Inceptiones* which he had often witnessed. Our caps, gowns, and hoods have not greatly changed since the middle ages; our 'Commencement parts' are representative performances of the 'Act' formerly required of each candidate in order to prove himself worthy of his new fellowship.[2]

---

1. For example, 'Universalia non sunt extra intellectum,' Theses Logicae, 1642; 'Genus et species sunt notae causarum et effectorum,' Theses Logicae, 1643; 'Universalia sunt in se ἀειφανεῖς in re ἀφανεῖς Asterismi,' mock Theses Logicae, 1663. See also *H. C. S. C.*, Chapter XII.

2. Historically, commencement parts should be delivered *after* rather than *before* the conferment of degrees, since originally they were no part of the examination for the degree, but a proof of it. As Rashdall has shown (1. 286), the *Inceptio* consisted of two

From granting degrees and prescribing curricula, it was a natural step for the masters' gilds to reduce their unwritten customs to written by-laws. What we may call the earliest university statutes were passed by the masters of Paris about 1200. These prescribed an academic dress, enforced the observance of 'the accustomed order in lectures and disputations,' and required full attendance at members' funerals.[1] A few years later the Masters of Arts, formally recognized as a corporation by Pope Innocent III, chose their own *Rector* (ruler), who became the virtual President of the University. Things could not long go on like this without the University of masters and scholars coming into conflict with the City on the one side and the Diocese on the other. The Chancellor, as the Archbishop's superintendent of local schools, observed the growing numbers and power of masters with a jealous eye. It was for him, not this upstart gild of 'Artists,' to say who should be granted and who denied the teaching license. The masters, on the other hand, demanded for themselves a monopoly of teaching and examination; they insisted that the Chancellor must license all whom they had pronounced qualified to teach, and might license none other. If any scholar presumed to attend lectures of a licensed teacher not a Master of Arts, let him be disqualified for a degree. In other words, it was a clear issue of 'open shop' against 'closed shop.' Matters were aggravated because crimes and misdemeanors of *clerici* (who included students, masters, and their employes) were tried in the Chancellor's Court.

To Rome, the supreme court in such matters, these disputes were appealed. The popes, with that instinct for the winning horse which once characterized the Holy See, consistently snubbed the archiepiscopal authorities, and supported the growing pretensions of the University. The Chancellor was forbidden to take fees for his teaching license, which henceforth he must

elements: the incorporation of the newcomer into the society of masters, and his formal entrance upon his function by the actual performance of its duties, a condition which Roman law considered essential for all forms of investiture. Thus, in the Church, the newly ordained deacon proceeds to read the Gospel, and the newly ordained priest 'concelebrates' Mass with the bishop. But by the time Harvard College was founded, the original significance of the 'Act' had been forgotten.

1. Rashdall, I. 301. In spite of the multiplication of masters, the obligation to attend a member's funeral — still familiar in lodges and fraternal organizations — long remained. When John Stone, a Harvard graduate who proceeded M.A. at Cambridge, died in 1660, a 'Grace' had to be obtained from the University Senate in order to do business on the day of his funeral (Ms. Grace Book, Cambridge University Registry).

grant to all candidates recommended by the masters, saving objections on moral grounds; he might imprison clerks only for major offenses, and assess damages but not extort fines.

Other important privileges were secured by the University as a result of town-and-gown riots. In the last year of the twelfth century the manservant of a wealthy student — a German bishop-elect — adverted unfavorably to the quality of wine dispensed in a certain tavern, and was thrown out. After the German students had thrashed the innkeeper, a city mob led by the Provost of Paris attacked the German students and killed several, including the bishop-elect. The masters appealed for redress to the King, who demoted the Provost and issued a charter to 'The Scholars of Paris.' Therein he recognized the students' privilege of being tried by ecclesiastical courts, by virtue of their clerical character; he enjoined Parisians to respect scholastic privileges, and required future provosts to take oath before the masters to do likewise. Thirty years later, certain students on a holiday discovered 'vinum optimum in taberna quadam et ad bibendum suave' (in a certain tavern, most excellent and smooth wine). They drank more than was good either for their heads or their purses, disputed the reckoning, were driven out by the neighbors, returned with comrades to broach the wine-casks, and then, 'flown with insolence and wine,' took indecent liberties in the streets with peaceable *bourgeois* and *bourgeoises*. Queen Blanche ordered the Provost and his police to take summary punishment, which they did by wounding and killing the first students they came upon. No redress could be had from archbishop, regent, or papal legate. The masters then drew an irresistible weapon. With the scholars, in 1229 they dispersed from Paris to other centres of learning. Gregory IX peremptorily ordered the offending police to be punished, recalled his cardinal legate, and in 1231 granted the University of Paris her Magna Charta. Academic routine was resumed with the university statutes recognized by all parties, and with scholars exempt from the Chancellor's criminal jurisdiction.

Through conflict the University of Paris waxed strong. Her constitution, as it existed at the end of the thirteenth century, became the model for all other universities in northern Europe and the British Isles. Masters and scholars were organized into four 'nations,' according to the region of their origin. The

A FACULTY MEETING AT PARIS IN THE
SIXTEENTH CENTURY

Masters of Arts constituted the faculty of Arts; and there were three 'superior' faculties of Theology, Canon Law, and Medicine, to study in which the M.A. degree was normally a prerequisite.[1] Harvard, it will be observed, returned to this relation between the Liberal Arts and professional studies after experimenting with undergraduate schools of Law and Medicine — President Eliot in that respect was a good medievalist. Each faculty met regularly for legislation, under the presidency of its dean, and established its own curriculum and examinations. The Chancellor's license, conferred after examination by members of a faculty, carried with it the *ius ubique docendi*: the right to teach without further examination in the corresponding faculty of any other university in Christendom. All masters and scholars and their servants were exempt from taxation, from arrest by the royal police for anything short of capital offenses, and from the ordinary courts of justice. They enjoyed 'benefit of clergy' in criminal cases, and the offense was grave indeed for which a student was condemned to any penalty more severe than payment of damages and the exaction of an oath not to do so again.[2]

Thus, before she owned a single building or an acre of land or a penny of endowment, when her teachers' sole support came from lecture fees or outside sources, the University of Paris had become a commonwealth of learning, under the protection of the Universal Church; a centre from which were diffused the philosophical aspects of that splendid conception of unity which the middle ages contributed to human thought. That she reached this position is a tribute not only to the excellence of her teaching, the competence of her graduates, and the political acumen of her elected officials, but to the fresh intellectual vigor that was diffused through her entire body of masters and scholars. No other university has ever occupied such an exalted place in the world, or has so richly deserved it. Even in a remote sense to be the shoot from such a plant is a matter of pride to the universities of the British Empire and the United States.

1. Rashdall, 1. 324, 428–29, 465; Louis Halphen, in *Revue Historique*, CLXVI (1931). 231.

2. These privileges existed in more or less degree in every university in Europe; the taxation exemption crossed the ocean to Harvard, where the question also arose whether the village watch of Cambridge might invade the College Yard — a question not yet settled.

Before the thirteenth century was many decades old there had come into existence ten or twelve universities in northern Europe which were more or less closely modelled upon that of Paris. At Montpellier a university grew up around a medical school of the twelfth century.[1] The University of Toulouse was deliberately established by the papacy in 1229 as a check to the Albigensian heresy in that region. At Prague a university was founded in 1347 by papal bull and imperial charter; the University of Vienna (1365) was established by the House of Hapsburg as a rival to Prague. Erfurt, Heidelberg, and Cologne had universities before the end of the century. And in southern Europe, Bologna, fecund as her northern sister, had begun a different type of university.[2]

The two English universities grew up spontaneously, like Paris, and were very closely modelled on Paris; but it is still a matter of conjecture why Oxford and Cambridge pulled out ahead of the several cathedral and monastery schools in twelfth-century England, and reached university stature. Oxford was a central point for the south and west and Cambridge for the north and east of England; and both had the negative advantage of not being episcopal sees, with meddling bishops and chancellors. Oxford grew rapidly as a place of learning after 1165, but 'at what date it became recognized as a *studium generale*, no one can ever say.'[3] Cambridge University was founded in 1209 by a secession of scholars from Oxford, in consequence of a fatal town-and-gown riot; and twenty years later the great dispersal from Paris swelled its numbers.[4] But Cambridge was a relatively small and insignificant university

1. Rashdall, II. 126.
2. See Appendix A.
3. H. E. Salter, in *History*, n.s., XIV (1929). 58, disproves the theory of Rashdall (II. 329) that the University of Oxford dates definitely from 1167, when Henry II recalled the English students from Paris.
4. D'Irsay, *op. cit.*, p. 129, points out that Cambridge is the first university to which one can assign a precise date of foundation. It had a chancellor as early as 1226 (*English Historical Review*, XXXVI. 419–20), and received papal recognition as *studium generale* in 1318. The fabulous accounts of the origin of the universities of Oxford and Cambridge, which were invented by their medieval protagonists, were accepted at face value in early Harvard. In the chronologies prepared by Harvard students and appended to the New England almanacs, we find under August 16: '636. *Cambridge* University founded' (*An Almanack of Cœlestiall Motions for 1669*, by Joseph Browne, A.B. 1666), and on April 12: 'A C. 872. *Oxford* Univ. founded by K. *Alphred*' (*id.* for 1671, by Daniel Russell, A.B. 1669).

until the fifteenth century. Oxford, on the other hand, early acquired a European reputation, and throughout Christendom stood second only to Paris as a school of Philosophy and Theology.

Thus, by the middle of the thirteenth century, European education beyond the schoolboy stage had become institutionalized in the university, which for weal or woe has continued to dominate the upper levels of education throughout the Western World.

II

THE MEDIEVAL UNIVERSITY AT WORK AND PLAY [1]

 'Medieval' has so long been a literary synonym for obscurity and stagnation that, in spite of recent revaluations, one cannot altogether shake off the feeling that on the whole the middle ages form a dark chapter in the history of humanity. Hence many surprises await the lay reader who approaches the middle ages through a study of education. He will find piety, to be sure, but the wildest irreverence; stability, but an intellectual revolution; dogma, but free thought; tyranny, but democracy. In particular, he will find a freedom and flexibility in university life that seems almost unbelievable in our day of institutionalized higher education. Students came and went much as they pleased; for Latin was the language of instruction from St. Andrews to Salerno, and from Cracow to Coïmbra. There was no entrance examination; a student merely attached himself to any master who would accept him as a pupil, and thus obtained all the exemptions and privileges generously allotted to scholars by king and pope. If the student became dissatisfied he left without formality, and found his way to another university. Even the English Channel was no barrier— a fisherman would set him across, just as a householder would give him food and lodging, in return for the songs he could sing and the tales he could tell, and the masses he might promise to say for his benefactor's soul as soon as he received holy orders. Students like Chaucer's Clerke of Oxenforde were welcome in every company; the 'poor clerk' was a recognized feature of medieval life like the mendicant friar, and far more popular.[2]

1. For general authorities, see Chapter I; for the University of Cambridge, Chapter III; for Oxford, Chapter VIII. The two compilations of medieval Oxford documents are particularly useful: Strickland Gibson (ed.), *Statvta Antiqva Vniversitatis Oxoniensis* (1931); Henry Anstey (ed.), *Munimenta Academica* (2 vols., Rolls Series, 1868).

2. I am not speaking here of what we might call the professional wandering students of the middle ages, the learned vagabonds whose Goliardic verse or *Carmina Burana*

The situation of a graduate seems equally idyllic. Once you had obtained the master's degree at a *studium generale* like Paris, Bologna, or Oxford, you had the *ius docendi hic et ubique terrarum*, the right to hire a hall in any university of Christendom, and compete with the masters there for pupils and lecture fees. Competition was keen and savage, with no mercy to the weak; but a clever M.A., if he tired of lecturing to undergraduates, might attract the attention of some wealthy patron or kindly bishop, who would get him a benefice. While receiving the stipend, he could return to his chosen university to study for a higher degree in Theology or Canon Law; and having obtained that he was in line for a lucrative position in royal chancery or papal curia.

The very poverty of the early universities was a source of strength. At a time when the university as such owned no property, when lecture rooms and lodgings alike were hired, the townspeople had to beware of extortion, lest the university decamp over night, leaving vacant houses, empty taverns, and idle hands.[1] For in many a university town, as an Oxford scout remarked not long ago, the population was divided into 'them that lives off the young gentlemen, and them that lives off them that lives off the young gentlemen.' Scholars, unlike burghers, had no natural defense against excessive profiteering; their only recourse was violence or secession. 'Villa enim cara est et multa exigit' (the town is expensive and exacting), writes an Oxford student to his parents about the year 1220;[2] that wail has gone down the ages. Townspeople, on the other hand, found scholars insolent, lawless, and irresponsible; but not all of them.

have been charmingly translated in John Addington Symonds' *Wine, Women and Song*, and in Helen Waddell's *The Wandering Scholars* (1927).

1. Numbers in the larger medieval universities were large, even by modern standards; and considered in relation to the total population, much larger than today. Rashdall (II. 581–90) estimates that Paris and Bologna had 6000 to 7000 university students in residence at the same time in the thirteenth century — 400 were made Masters of Arts in a single year at Paris around 1284 — but the number dropped to 3000 or 2500 by the year 1450. At Oxford, the range was 1500 to 3000 in the middle ages, and around 1000 in the fifteenth century. Cambridge had only a few hundred students in the middle ages, but passed Oxford in the fifteenth century and attained 1267 in the year 1564. Prague may have had over 3000 before the dispersal in 1409. In the fifteenth century, when the numbers of students declined almost everywhere, the German universities had only a few hundred students, sometimes less than a hundred. In order to realize the relative importance of these numbers to the university towns, one would have to imagine a student population of twenty to thirty thousand in Oxford and Cambridge today, and fifty to a hundred thousand at Harvard.

2. Haskins, *Studies in Mediaeval Culture*, p. 10.

Many a young student from afar brought an irresistible flavor of romance to daughters of the staid burghers. His superior learning and address procured favors from the wenches which they denied to local swains, who retaliated with fist and cudgel; fellow-students came to the injured one's assistance; swords and daggers — strictly forbidden to scholars by all university statutes — appeared from somewhere; stones flew through the air and unsavory liquids descended from upper windows. Another town-and-gown riot was on.

METHODS OF INSTRUCTION

Harvard's heritage from the medieval university is most clearly traceable to the curriculum and the degree regulations. All degrees were originally teaching degrees; master, doctor, and professor meant one and the same thing — teacher.[1] Admission to the degree meant that you belonged to the gild of teachers, and began at once to teach the subjects you had just learned. But the same enthusiasm for learning which created the universities gave the master's degree a distinct 'cash value' both as the normal prerequisite for studying theology and as the gate to ecclesiastical preferment. Early in the thirteenth century we find the complaint that students want the sign without the substance, the degree without work; that a knack at logic-spinning has taken the place of the good old classical learning.[2] And be-

---

1. Every faculty had its bachelor's and its master's degree, but the masters in the higher faculties of Law, Medicine, and Theology were generally called *doctores* or *professores*. In Germany the Faculty of Arts was called the Faculty of Philosophy, and the *Magister Artium* was called *Philosophiae Doctor*. It was owing to the prestige of the German Ph.D. in the nineteenth century that American universities, and later Oxford and Cambridge, committed the historical solecism of conferring a doctor's and a master's degree in the same faculty.

2. This very modern complaint appears in a satirical poem of the thirteenth century:

Jam fiant baccalaurei	Now let us make these boys B.A.
pro munere denarii	as long as Dad their fees can pay
quam plures idiotae:	although they are but half-wits.
in artibus, et aliis	In all the noble Seven Arts
egregiis scientiis	and Sciences, in all their parts,
sunt bestiae promotae.	the candidates have calf-wits.
Jam fit magister artium	Now let him be a full M.A.
qui nescit quotas partium	who's nothing but an ignora-
de vero fundamento:	mus when it comes to knowledge.
habere nomen appetit,	To have the name he's O! so keen,
rem vero nec curat nec scit,	the substance neither had nor seen —
examine contento.	and seven years in College!

fore that century was many years old, it became necessary for the faculty of Arts to require that M.A.'s remain in the university to lecture for three years. The entire Arts instruction was given by these 'regent masters,' very few of whom could have been over twenty-five or thirty years old. Further, every regent master lectured in turn on every subject covered by his faculty — no specialists were wanted.[1] Harvard followed essentially the same system with her slender band of tutors until 1766.

Lectures were held in 'the Schools,' which were simply rooms in town houses hired by the university, or a faculty, or by individual masters, to whom they were allotted and who paid the rent.[2] In his school, each master lectured to such students as would pay his fees. These university lectures were almost invariably given on specified books. 'The authority of a textbook was in the Middle Ages something of which we have very little conception,' says Rashdall. 'To the medieval Doctor the *littera scripta* was an end of all strife not only on matters of faith but on matters of Science or speculation.' In medieval curricula, the student was required to have 'heard' such and such books, often to have heard them more than once. In early statutes there is evidently a conflict between the faculties, which required lectures to be delivered extempore and rapidly, and the students, who wished to take full notes, and who made a practice of interrupting fast lecturers by whistling,[3] shouting, and even throwing stones. A student came provided with ink-horn, goose-quill, and scraps of parchment or paper for taking

1. It is not clear how conflicts, and an oversupply of lecturers, were avoided. At Oxford, according to a statute of 1431, the Proctors divided the available regents into ten divisions according to seniority. The youngest lectured on Grammar, the lowest subject in the Trivium, and the oldest on Metaphysics, the highest of the three Philosophies. *Stat. Antiq. Univ. Oxon.*, pp. 235–36. The next term the juniors would move on to Rhetoric, and so on.

2. At Paris the Schools were in the Ile de la Cité and the rue du Fouarre (the *vico degli strami* of *Paradiso*, x. 137, so called from the straw-strewn floors on which the students sat). The statutes of 1452 forbid the soft modern improvement of benches, and require that students sit on the floor as of old, 'that all occasion of pride may be taken away from the young.' Rashdall, 1. 438. Medieval Oxford had two blocks of Schools, one built by Osney Abbey; the 'Old Schools Quadrangle' constructed by the University is of the early seventeenth century.

3. Rashdall, 1. 438, translates *sibilum* 'hissing'; and in Aberdeen the students still hiss a professor who speaks inaudibly, or too fast. But it seems more likely that *sibilum* meant whistling, that shrill, irritating *siffle* still used by students of the University of Paris in demonstrations against unpopular professors. When Marshall Joffre visited Harvard in 1917 he was disturbed by the crowds' whistling out of enthusiasm, which meant something very different to him.

notes, as he squatted on the straw of the crowded school. It would appear that in Oxford at least the students won, since the statutory instruction to Oxford lecturers in 1431 requires the regent master first to read the text in the proper order — no skipping. Next, he must explain the text, *secundum exigentiam materiæ*. Thirdly, he is to select notable passages from the text and repeat them. Finally, 'if necessary' he may raise points for discussion, but only such as are relevant, 'so that no prohibited sciences be taught.' [1]

It is generally assumed that the lecture became the favorite academic method because of the scarcity of books before printing was invented. This explanation is questionable. Medieval students had books, even though there were no public or university libraries. Every university town had officially regulated *scriptoria* where standard texts and glosses were copied, without unnecessary flourishes and illuminations, at a relatively low and fixed price, and let out as in a circulating library. The frequent requirement in university statutes that the student bring a copy of the text to the lecture, the warning against disturbing the lecturer by crackling the leaves of parchment (or by 'guttural sounds,' foot-shufflings, and other noises dear to students of all ages), indicate that some other reason than want of books dictated the lecture method. Indeed the fact that university lectures have survived through the centuries, despite the repeated outcries of educational reformers and the rivalry of cheap books, seems to prove that there is a value for young men in the spoken word that no written word can replace.

Medieval lectures were of two sorts: 'ordinary,' and 'extraordinary' or 'cursory.' The former seem to have been the official lectures by regent masters on set books; the latter, extra lectures for which an additional fee was required, and which might be given either by masters or bachelors. With a slight difference in meaning, and under the name of 'public' and 'private' lectures, the distinction was preserved in the English universities after the rise of colleges, and as such crossed the ocean to Harvard.[2] Lectures might be from one to three hours long.[3] Invariably the language was Latin, not only in the middle ages

1. *Stat. Antiq. Univ. Oxon.*, p. 236.
2. *C. S. M.*, xv. 136, 139.
3. At the University of Perpignan in the fourteenth century the statutes required morning lectures to last three hours. One is not surprised to learn that this university was a failure.

La tierce arz si ↄ logique
ke on appelle dyalectique
ceste si prove voir ⁊ faus
p quoi on conoist bien ⁊ uiffe
li bien samoro logiq̇ tonce
bien ⁊ mal ẽpuevoir sãc doute
p bĩ fu cieſt padrı
⁊ p mal enfer eſtablıſ

A tierce rethoriq̇ si nõ
li ↄ ſmiãc de raiſon
⁊ ordenãce de parole
hele ne ſoit tenue à fole
de ceſti ſont li droit aidié
p quoi li iugent ſont fait
li eſgardec ſont p raiſon
en tourt de roi ⁊ de baron
⁊ fort iugie dec toleſ malec
de ceſti arz furent decriſec
derret ⁊ decret ⁊ lois
li meſtier que entrent lois

ſi conoiſtront ⁊ tort ⁊ droit
la rethorique bĩ ſauron
p tort faire eſt li mar pō
⁊ p droit ſaume ſes vertuſ.

A quarte arz nõ Arrimetique
ceſte vient apſ rethorique
⁊ en mi lec am̃ arz eſt miſe
elle ſanſ lui ne puet eſtre aſſiſe
iſule dec arz pſrement
ſe bĩ ſeue entierement
denant ke on ſache ceſt arz
elle toneſ iprẽdent lec pars
ke ne porent eſtre ſanſ lui
pͬ che fu elle miſe en mi
Lec vij arz en qui aveit ſõ ombl
de ceſti mouuent tout li nõbre
p quoi tout creſt ⁊ tout neſt
car ſanſ nombre nule riens neſt
qͥlf peu voir omͭ che puet eſt
li dec vij arz n̄ eu maiſtre
ſãne qͥl enſache ſauoir rier dire

but well into the seventeenth century, and at Harvard as in Europe. To have delivered a lecture in the vernacular would have been contrary to the statutes and insulting to the auditors — much as if a university lecturer in modern New York should use Yiddish.[1]

After each lecture it appears to have been customary for some of the auditors to get together and hold a *resumptio*, each student contributing what he remembered, so that the lecture was substantially repeated.[2] In England the *resumptio* (also called *repetitio* and *recitatio*[3]) was presided over by a tutor, and became a required part of college discipline. The earliest Harvard recitations in the seventeenth century were of this nature; when one learned from lectures, it was as natural for teachers to 'check up' on them as on a text-book; indeed, a text-book was more often than not the substance of the lecture.

At the end of a course of lectures, it was the pleasant custom for masters and pupils to attend a special Mass. A manuscript of Odofredus, an early law professor at Bologna, preserves the concluding words of his course:

Gentlemen: We have begun and finished and gone through the middle of this book as you know who have been members of this course; for which we thank God, and the blessed Virgin and all His Saints. And it's an old custom in this university that a Mass shall be sung in honor of the Holy Ghost when the course is finished; and that's a good custom and ought to be kept up. But because it's also usual for professors at the end of a course to say something about their intentions next year, I will make a few announcements — but very few: I am telling you that next year I intend to give the ordinary required lectures well and properly just as I have always done, but I don't expect to give any extra lectures because students are not good payers; they wish to learn but not to loose their purse-strings:

> "To know, desire everybody
> To pay, desire nobody."

Now, I have nothing more to say, so begone with God's blessing — but you ought to come to the Mass, and I'm asking you.[4]

1. The first French lectures in the University of Paris were translations of Latin lectures in Medicine, authorized in 1491 with the precise intention of insulting the chirurgeons, who were pretending to equal privileges with doctors of medicine. This purpose fulfilled, the French lectures were dropped.
2. Rashdall, i. 493; ii. 649, 766–67.
3. *Id.*, ii. 772; *Stat. Antiq. Univ. Oxon.*, p. 195, l. 10.
4. Translated from the text in Fr. C. von Savigny, *Geschichte des Römischen Rechts im Mittelalter* (1834), iii. 264 n.

If the lecture, as an academic exercise, required only a passive process of assimilation on the student's part, the disputation offered him abundant opportunity to express himself, and to perform. A disputation, in the medieval university sense, was an oral discussion, without notes, of some *thesis* (proposition) or *quaestio* (question) by the recognized rules of logic: the major and minor premise, the syllogism, the fallacies, the refutation, and so on. Such was the only appropriate method for testing the student's powers in an age when enthusiasm ran high over the rediscovery of deductive or syllogistic logic. Aristotle's *organon* was considered the proper way to reach the truth in any conceivable subject. It was particularly applicable to the needs of the Church, for 'there was no *organon* of a fitness even comparable to Aristotle's for the task of drawing out the implications of dogmatic premises.'[1] Abélard taught the scholastic[2] method, brilliantly exemplified it himself, and left a manual of it to posterity in his famous *Sic et Non*. The Church needed to counter heretical propositions, not with mysticism — the fruitful mother of heresies — but with a logic against which, it was fondly assumed, neither the gates of hell nor the wit of heretics could prevail. From the time he ceased to be a freshman the medieval student was constantly practising this art, and at every important stage of his academic career he had to take part in public disputations, either as respondent[3] or opponent of some *thesis* or *quaestio*, which had been posted up beforehand.

These disputations were conducted wholly in Latin. Until the universities owned buildings, and sometimes for long after, they were held in a church especially allotted to such use — such as the St. Julien le Pauvre in Paris, St. Mary the Virgin in Oxford, or Great St. Mary's in Cambridge; and at all times they attracted a large scholarly audience. At their best, these exercises trained men in oratory and debate, taught them to think on their feet, stimulated the sluggard, and showed up the bluffer. At its worst, the disputation was a mere play on words, obscuring sound habits of thought and rewarding the superficially clever. Nevertheless, the method had such recognized pedagogic value that it long outlasted the scholastic philosophy

1. H. W. Blunt, in *Encyclopaedia Britannica*, 11th ed., XVI. 905.
2. So called because practised in the 'Schools' of the University; hence also scholastic theology and philosophy.
3. So called because disputations were begun by an opponent to the stated proposition, to whom the proponent then responded.

and manner of thinking to which it was peculiarly adapted. In seventeenth-century Harvard the disputation still received the medieval emphasis; and when it disappeared, in the nineteenth century,[1] there was left a void in the outgoing aspect of education that themes,[2] reports, and debating societies only partially filled. Indeed the recent advocacy of 'discussion groups,' 'socialized recitations,' and the like is a recognition that the middle ages were right in placing this active method of education beside the passive ones of hearing lectures and reading books.

Instruction of Freshmen

Having glanced at these methods, let us look at the matter of instruction, and follow the medieval arts student through his seven-year course to his license and his master's degree. It is impossible to strike an average age for entering freshmen. Rashdall will go no further than to say that 'as a rule the freshmen would be between thirteen and sixteen' at Paris;[3] but there were many who were much older and not a few who were even younger. In those universities which included grammar schools, as most did at one time or another, we find boys as young as eight — but they would be under the care of a grammar master, and for our purposes need not be considered. It seems probable that in every medieval university the bachelor's degree was normally taken between the ages of fifteen and nineteen.

The medieval student enjoyed almost complete liberty in a strange city, at a time when he was younger than most high school boys of today. On arriving at the university town towards Michaelmas,[4] the average *recens* (freshman), or *bejaunus* (bec-jaune, yellow-bill), as he was called on the Continent and in Scotland, joined a hall or hostel. These halls, ancestors of the colleges, were simply dwelling-houses hired by an enterprising Master of Arts, who proposed to make a living

1. Disputations are still held in many of the Catholic universities and colleges; see the description by Dr. James J. Walsh in *N. E. Q.*, v. 489.

2. The 'forensics' — written arguments — required of juniors at Harvard until 1900 may be considered as the last surviving relic of the medieval disputation with us, since all elements of dispute had long since vanished from the Commencement exercises.

3. II. 604.

4. September 29. The Paris statutes prescribed that lectures should begin on the feast of St. Remigius (Saint-Rémy), October 1, which even now marks the beginning of Michaelmas Term at the universities of Oxford and Cambridge.

by boarding and lodging students; they might even be started by a group of students who wished to mess together and who elected one of their number principal.[1] During the first week of term, the freshman visited the schools, sampling lectures on Grammar or Logic until he found a suitable master to take him as pupil. This master, if he remained there long enough, carried the boy through the entire seven years' Arts course.

Before many days elapsed the freshman discovered something far more exciting than lectures. In accordance with the most ancient of folkways, he must be initiated to his new status of *scholaris* and Artist. In vain did universities legislate against 'vexatores et tribulatores novellorum studentum quos *bejanos* vocant.' In vain did masters denounce the *receptores*, upperclassmen who took from each freshman 'magnam partem suae pecuniae.'[2] First the *bejaunus* is the victim of miscellaneous japes and tricks. In Paris he must be paraded through the streets on an ass; in England the obvious antidote to freshness was salt, administered internally and externally. But the really important part of the initiation was a feast at the freshman's expense to the comrades of his hall and to his new master. The next thing on his programme, no doubt, was to write home for more funds. 'A student's first song is a demand for money,' writes an irate father of the thirteenth century, 'and there will never be a letter which does not ask for cash.'[3]

With his master selected, his membership in a hall secured, and his purse replenished, our freshman is ready to get on with his education.

THE ARTS COURSE

The medieval Arts course consisted, in theory, of the seven Arts and the three Philosophies. In practice it was very nearly equivalent to a course on the works of Aristotle, in Latin translation. During the first five centuries of university history, Aristotle, 'the master of them that know,'[4] wielded an authority such as no one intellect has exerted before or since. About

---

1. Rashdall's dicta concerning the absence of discipline and supervision in the halls have been revised, as respects St. Edmund's Hall, Oxford, in A. B. Emden, *An Oxford Hall in Medieval Times* (1927), pp. 192–96; cf. H. E. Salter in *History*, n.s., xiv. 59–60.
2. Rashdall, ii. 628.
3. Haskins, *The Rise of Universities*, p. 103.
4. *Inferno*, iv. 131.

the year 1100, Christendom knew only the Aristotelian books called the 'Old Logic' — the Categories and *de Interpretatione*. One of the major excitements of the twelfth century was the rediscovery, largely through roundabout Arabic translations, of the 'New Logic': the Prior and Posterior Analytics, the Topics, and the 'Elenchs' or Sophistical Refutations. New and Old Logic together comprise the Aristotelian *organon*, the whole of which was thus absorbed into European thought by the year 1200.[1]

There soon followed — though not in this order — the rediscovery of Aristotle's works comprising the three Philosophies:

1. Natural Philosophy: the *Physica, de Coelo, de Mundo, de Anima, de Generatione et Corruptione*; four books on Animals; books on Colors, Plants, Acoustics, and Meteors; the *Parva Naturalia*; and several others.

2. Moral Philosophy: *Politica, Economica*, Nichomachæan and Eudemian Ethics, and *Magna Moralia*.

3. Mental Philosophy: the *Metaphysica*.

Thus Aristotle provided the medieval student with a logical *organon* for reaching the truth, and a corpus of secular knowledge in almost every subject outside Law and Medicine. Yet his works were only established in the schools against strenuous opposition. Hundred-percent Christians were not wanting to point out that Aristotle was a pagan, and his introducer and commentator Averroës an infidel; and there were some awkward contradictions between his views and those of Holy Writ. Conservatives were jubilant when Gregory IX, in 1231, forbade any work of Aristotle save the Old Logic to be read at Paris until an expurgated edition could be prepared. Yet just fourteen years later we find the whole of the proscribed books prescribed. There had happened what so often has occurred in the history of thought. Enthusiasm for Aristotle ran so high in Paris that the prohibition could not be enforced; the Church wisely decided to make an ally of this unconquerable enemy; 'apparent' contradictions were smoothed out and explained away by Albertus Magnus and St. Thomas Aquinas, and the Prince of Philosophers became a bulwark of the Church.[2]

---

1. Haskins, *Renaissance of the Twelfth Century* (1927), pp. 345–49. Several of the books hereinafter mentioned were not actually written by Aristotle, but were ascribed to him in the middle ages.

2. G. H. Luquet, *Aristote et l'Université de Paris* (1904).

Although the reformation gave birth to new logicians, these required a century or more to penetrate even Protestant universities, and the Aristotelian classification of knowledge long outlasted the revolution wrought by inductive methods and experimental science. Fifty years ago the academic name for Science was still Natural Philosophy, and laboratories were 'philosophical chambers.' Books on Economics were still classed with those on Ethics under 'Moral Philosophy' on the shelves of the Harvard College Library in 1880; and because Aristotle had written a book on the soul, Psychology at Harvard maintained until 1934 a formal and uncongenial alliance with Philosophy.[1]

Taking together the Arts course prescribed by the Paris statutes of 1252 and 1254 [2] and that of the Oxford statutes of 1268,[3] which probably represents the Cambridge course as well,[4] we find that the freshman began with what would nowadays be called Advanced Latin Grammar — using the textbooks of Donatus, who flourished in the fourth century, and Priscian, who wrote about fifty years later. For Rhetoric he had at Paris the *VI Principia* of Gilbert de la Porrée, Donatus' *Barbarismus*, and Boethius' Topics. It is probable that the Parisian undergraduate also found means to exercise the *Ars Dictaminis*, a course in Business Latin. *Dictamen* taught one how to write letters — including demands on one's parents for more money — and to draft charters, deeds, and notarial documents.[5]   As soon as his master thought proper and convenient, the freshman heard lectures on Logic, beginning with Boethius' translation of Porphyry's *Isagoge*, a book which remained in use well into the seventeenth century; [6] from that he proceeded through the entire Aristotelian *organon*.

1. *Development of Harvard University*, pp. 186 n., 216.

2. Cæsar du Boulay, *Hist. Vniv. Parisiensis* (1665–73), III. 280–89, and Denifle and Châtelain, *Chartularium Univ. Paris*, I. 227–32, 277–79; summarized in Rashdall, *op. cit.*, I. 435.

3. *Stat. Antiq. Vniv. Oxon.*, p. 26.

4. Stanley M. Leathes, introduction to *Grace Book A* (Cambridge Antiquarian Society, 1897), p. xxi; Mullinger, I. 345–52.

5. A student's letter of the thirteenth century strikes the modern note: 'The wise man takes honest subjects, and chiefly those which bring the greatest profit and honor.' Rhetoric, poetry, and that stuff lead only to the courtesans; whilst 'those who follow the science of *dictamen* come to kings and prelates, and are promoted to ecclesiastical honors.' Paetow, *op. cit.*, p. 29 n. See W. A. Pantin, in *Bulletin of the John Rylands Library*, XIII. 326–82.

6. See the early statutes of Trinity College, Dublin, where the *Isagoge* had to be read 'twice a year at least.' J. P. Mahaffy, *An Epoch in Irish History*, pp. 187, 351–52.

During his first two years, the undergraduate was required to 'frequent the Schools' where disputations were being held, but was not allowed to take part in them. About half way through his course, after he had acquired sufficient knowledge of Logic, he was created sophister,[1] which meant that he could take part in *sophismata* or public disputations, and wear an academic hood. It was equivalent to a preliminary degree on passing the Trivium.[2] Sophisters took themselves rather seriously, for in 1358 an Oxford friar who tried some dangerous punning on the word was forced to declare publicly that when he accused *sophistae* of seeming-wise, he did not mean 'those sophisters who study in Arts.'[3] By the fifteenth century we hear of *juniores sophistae* and *seniores sophistae* at Oxford.[4] These names for the last two years of the Arts course crossed the ocean to Harvard, where by ellipsis junior and senior sophisters became juniors and seniors.[5] Thus the names of the two upper classes in American colleges are derived from this long-forgotten medieval degree on the Trivium. Sophomore probably comes from the same root,[6] and freshman is merely the English equivalent of *recens*, the *becjaune* or yellow-beak of thirteenth-century Paris.

Having commenced sophister, the Arts student began in earnest his study of Aristotle, by hearing lectures on the prescribed books; and as he gathered knowledge his disputations probably improved in quality, while they lost the sophomoric freshness which set the schools in roars of laughter at his early appearances. It is difficult to gather from the statutes the exact order in which the different books were taken up, but we have a Paris curriculum of 1255 which shows the minimum time that lecturers were supposed to spend on each book. Six weeks sufficed for *Ethica*, but the course on the 'Old Logic,' including

1. From *sophista*, which was good medieval Latin for a learned or eloquent person, and, at least in the thirteenth century, carried no connotation of sophistical reasoning. See Rashdall, I. 445, and description of the ceremony in A. Clark, *Register Univ. Oxon.*, II. part I. 21–23.

2. William Harrison calls it a degree in his *Description* of Elizabethan England (1889 ed.), p. 254.

3. *Munimenta Academica*, I. 211.

4. Oxford Aularian Statutes, in Rashdall, II. 773.

5. Not until 1850–51 in the official catalogues (except for an earlier ellipsis which was corrected). In Oxford the two classes were lumped as *sophistae generales*, which was abbreviated to *generales*; in Cambridge they became *junior sophs* and *senior sophs*, terms which disappeared about 1870. The full names are still used at Trinity College, Dublin.

6. See below, Chapter IV.

the *Isagoge* and Boethius' Divisions and Topics, began on the day of Saint-Rémy (October 1), and must *not* be finished before Lady Day (March 25); lectures on the *de Anima* and *Parva Naturalia* must keep going until Ascension. A combined course on the *Physica*, *Metaphysica*, and *de Animalibus* required an entire academic year.[1] As the regent masters were supposed to lecture on the average about four times a week,[2] it is clear that plenty of time was allowed for the medieval student to grasp what he was supposed to learn.

Of course there was much idling and cutting of lectures in that era of student liberty. We hear much of cramming, placating one's neglected master with gifts, and entertainment of examiners, as means of 'getting by.' No doubt the medieval universities were full of earnest scholars; but the imprecatory sermons of the times have more to say about the boys who spent their time drinking, brawling, strumming guitars and casting dice, and wandering through the streets singing what might be the student's song of all ages:

> Le temps s'en vient,
> et je n'ai rien fait;
> le temps revient,
> et je ne fais rien.[3]

The next important degree of the academic career was the B.A. According to Cotton Mather, bachelors were so called because they 'battled' in public disputations;[4] but philology was not Mather's strong point, and the word, as we have seen, means simply 'apprentice.' There were bachelors of butchery and of bootmaking outside the University, as well as Bachelors of Arts and Theology within it. At Paris, the Arts candidate, after acquitting himself properly in his disputations, was examined by a board chosen by his own nation — an examination of which the more important part was checking records of his attendance at lectures. After the candidate had solemnly sworn that he had really 'heard' the books he was supposed to have heard, he was created Bachelor of Arts by the proctor of his nation. At Oxford and Cambridge the preliminaries,

---

1. Denifle and Châtelain, *Chartularium*, I. 278. These books were read for the master's, not the bachelor's, degree. Cf. Strickland Gibson, *op. cit.*, pp. 33–34.
2. Less at Oxford. See *Munimenta Academica*, I. cxlix.
3. *American Historical Review*, x. 21–26.
4. *Magnalia*, book iv. 128. Mather quotes this opinion from the learned Vossius.

devised for the purpose of preventing unfit candidates from getting farther, were so numerous and complicated that by the sixteenth century almost every candidate had to seek a 'grace' for exemption.[1] When all was in order, the senior sophister was 'created' or 'admitted' by the Vice-Chancellor a Bachelor of Arts, by a formula which allowed him 'to read any book of Aristotle's Logic, and of those Arts which by statute you are held to have heard.'[2]

Both at Paris and at the English universities, 'determinations' were the main ceremony connected with the B.A. These came *after* the granting of the degree, as the final stage of the investiture: 'doing your stuff.'[3] At Paris, determination was a sort of gala disputation, for which the determining bachelor hired his master's school on the rue du Fouarre. Fresh straw and free drinks were provided to attract an audience. Two friendly sophisters were selected to serve as foils to the young man's talents; and the determinant was stimulated to do his best by the knowledge that archdeacons, cathedral provosts, and even greater magnates were there to get a line on rising young talent. At the conclusion of this exhibition, the determining bachelor's friends escorted him in triumphal procession to his lodgings, where a banquet was held at his expense; after which they might get up a torchlight procession, or dance with wenches in the street.[4] At Oxford and Cambridge determinations early lost their hilarious character — there the main thing was *stare in quadragesima*, 'to stand' every day 'in Lent' in the university church to dispute both formally and informally with one's attendant sophisters, or with any senior member of the University who might drop in to take part in the battle of wits. The same practice was required in the first college hall at Harvard, where it was called 'sitting solstices.'

1. The Oxford process is described in detail in Andrew Clark, *Register Univ. Oxford*, II. part I. 27–66; for Cambridge, see Mullinger, I. 352–54, and below, Chapter IV.
2. That is, to read a 'cursory' lecture on a book. The bachelors' formula does not imply that before taking his B.A. the medieval student was not considered competent to read a book. It simply meant that he was no longer in a state of pupillage, and that he must begin to practise teaching, that is reading lectures, in preparation for his mastership. Cf., for early Harvard, *New Englands First Fruits* (Appendix D.)
3. See above, p. 12, n. 2.
4. Rashdall, II. 444 ff. Mullinger, I. 354, is in error in assuming that the determining bachelor presided over disputations instead of taking part in them. As Rashdall has shown, to 'determine' meant simply to maintain a thesis against an opponent. Determinations were presided over by bachelors admitted the previous year or earlier.

Only a small number of the students who attended medieval universities ever attained the bachelor's degree; and of these, not all reached the M.A., the proper goal of every Artist. The Bachelor of Arts was already somewhat of a person in the academic world, with the title *Dominus*, Englished as 'Sir,' prefixed to his last name. Thus, we are told in a 'parallel' between Cardinal Wolsey and Archbishop Laud that after taking their first degree 'Sir Wolsey was called the Boy Batchelor, and Sir Laud the little Batchelor.'[1] This usage also crossed the Atlantic. In the seventeenth and eighteenth centuries, bachelors who had not yet commenced M.A. always appear in the records of Harvard and Yale as *Dominus* or 'Sir.' In the seventeenth century this 'Sir' was used even in conversation and familiar correspondence.[2]

During the three years that normally elapsed between the two Arts degrees, our *Dominus Imberbis* or Sir Beardless did a good deal of disputing, and took an apprentice's part in the teaching of his faculty by reading 'cursory' lectures on books which he had heard. At the same time he continued his studies under a master. If attending an English or German university he acquired a smattering of the Quadrivium[3]; at Paris the Quadrivium appears to have been squeezed out by Aristotle. At this period of his course the Paris Artist heard the *Ethica*, *Physica*, *Metaphysica*, and *de Animalibus*; the *de Caelo*, *de Mundo*, *Meteorologica*, *de Generatione et Corruptione*, *Physica Auscultatio*, and a few of the *Parva Naturalia*.[4] It will be observed that this course covers fairly well the three Philosophies with the

---

1. *A Parallel between Cardinal Wolsey . . . and William Laud* (1641), quoted in *Gradus ad Cantabrigiam* (1824), pp. 45–46; earlier examples in *N. E. D.* 'Dominus' and 'Sir' appear at Harvard immediately after the first bachelors' Commencement and are found as late as 1801 (*C. S. M.*, xv. cxl, 5–8, 17). Dr. L. C. Purser writes me from Dublin that he remembers seeing 'Sir' prefixed to last names over the doors of resident bachelors at Trinity College in 1869. At Cambridge the first name on the Tripos list still has the prefix 'Ds.' It is placed against the resident bachelors' names in current buttery books at Oxford; and the late Provost of Queen's informed me in 1929 that he had often heard scouts in his college use the 'Sir.' For an instance at Yale, see F. B. Dexter, *Biographies and Annals of Yale*, iii. 467.

2. For example, *Diary of Samuel Sewall*, i. 51; *Winthrop Papers*, i. 342, 349–50. For the same reason, ministers were called 'Sir' in Shakspere's day.

3. The principal musical book used was Boethius' very elementary treatise on Notation. Boethius also answered for Arithmetic, the first six books of Euclid for Geometry. A little elementary drawing was learned from John of Pisa (Archbishop Peckham) and later Vitellio's book on *Perspective*. The *de Sphaera* of Johannes de Sacrobosco (John Holywood) or Ptolemy's *Almagest* sufficed for Astronomy. Rashdall, i. 442–43.

4. Denifle and Châtelain, *Chartularium*, i. 278–79.

PITAPHIVM GENEROSSIMI OPTIMÆO SPEI IV
VENIS IOANNIS PENDARVES CORNVBIENSIS
SAMVELIS PENDARVES ARMI-GERI
FILII NATV MAXIMI COLL EXON
COMMENSALIS

VIAS QVALIS ERAM NOTVM EST COGNOMINE CVIVS
ET PATRIAM ET STIRPEM SYLLABA PRIMA NOTAT

QVI IAM SVM PRÆNOMEN HABET NAM GRATIA DICOR
QVOD GRATVM SVMO ME NOTAT ESSE DEO

OBIIT XVIII die Junii
Anno Domini 1617.
Ætatis suæ: XVII

AN OXFORD UNDERGRADUATE DISPUTING IN THE SCHOOLS

notable omission of the *Politica* and *Economica*; these became possible substitutes for the *Ethica* in the Oxford statutes of 1408,[1] which were rather less exigent than the Paris requirements.

This Medieval Arts course was admirably adapted to the needs of the time. It was flexible: the Oxford statutes of 1267 distinctly state that other books than those prescribed may be substituted at the discretion of the masters.[2] This course put the student in touch with some of the greatest minds of antiquity; it placed at his disposal the cream of the world's knowledge in that happy day when one man could know all, and gave him the intellectural tools for using knowledge to good profit. In other words it was a *liberal* education — the education of a free man — bearing the same relation to life and to the professions as the undergraduate course is supposed to bear in English and American universities today. If a man wished to study Theology, Law, or Medicine he must first be admitted Master of Arts; he might then study under one of the higher faculties.[3] The English universities strove long and successfully to maintain this Arts prerequisite against the mendicant orders, who wished their members to proceed Bachelors of Divinity without a liberal education; and Harvard, after a temporary lapse in the early nineteenth century, still stoutly maintains this principle against the exponents of a 'practical' education.

The remaining exercises and ceremonies for the Arts candidate were the most important of his career. About two years after determinations came the examinations for the Chancellor's license. At Paris, owing to the continual friction between Chancellor and University, these examinations were oral, public, and two in number, one by a committee appointed by the Faculty, the other by the Chancellor himself. At Oxford, the candidate merely had to call upon every resident M.A. of a certain standing, and, if he were found 'at home,' put to him a formula which might be freely Englished as 'ask me another.' The master might, if he chose, privately question the candidate, and, if he found him unfit, appear at the proper assembly and 'pluck' him. Otherwise he was presented to the Vice-Chancellor

1. Rashdall, ii. 457–58.
2. Contenders among American university historians for the honor of establishing the 'first elective system' are respectfully referred to this statute.
3. See above, p. 15.

and received his license. On the Continent and in South America the license developed into a degree; at Oxford and Cambridge it early became merely a license to proceed to the master's degree, that is to incept.[1]

Inceptio, from which, as we have seen, our Commencement is derived, was the most formal of academic ceremonies. At Oxford and Cambridge it took place in early July, at the close of the academic year. An evening or two before, the candidates took part in a peculiarly solemn disputation called Vespers. Early in the morning of the great day, the University assembled to hear Mass. Immediately after, and in the same church, began the formal *disputationes in comitiis*, or 'the Act' as it was called in the English universities. An official jester, the *terrae filius* or *prevaricator*, acted as first respondent, and added to what would otherwise have been a very tedious and repetitious affair an element of humor, which tended to broad satire at the expense of university magnates. His opening speech was the ancestor of our Latin Salutatory Oration, with its time-honored invocation of *puellae pulcherrimae*, the only quip that a modern Commencement audience understands. When each inceptor's disputation was concluded, the presiding officer pronounced the prescribed formula, and presented him with the magisterial book, hood, and cap, together with a kiss on the cheek. This ceremony formally created him Master of Arts. 'The evening concluded with a banquet given at the expense of the inceptor or party of inceptors to the masters and others, at which it is probable that the prohibitions which we find in some universities against dancing or the introduction of actors and trumpeters were not always strictly complied with.'[2]

Medieval university students enjoyed far more liberty than their present-day successors. Law and custom denied to clerks the wholesome sports of laymen; but the hot blood of youth, after days of intellectual grind, found an outlet somewhere. Poaching in the royal forests and robbing orchards and hen-

1. The present M.A. degree ceremonies at Oxford and Cambridge are really vestiges of the license, the 'act' of the masters' *Inceptio* having been omitted long since.

2. Rashdall, I. 453 (for Paris); A. Clark, *Register Univ. Oxf.*, II. part I. 73–85; Mullinger, I. 355–58. Inceptions of Doctors of Law, Theology, Medicine, etc., were much more elaborate, including placing a ring on the inceptor's finger, and in the Spanish university investing him with gold spurs as a sign that the King considered doctors the equals of knights. The inception banquet survived at Harvard as the Commencement dinner down through 1904, and until about the middle of the nineteenth century the cost was assessed on the Commencers.

roosts were the mildest forms of what modern pedagogues call 'extra-curricular activity'; for the open country was not ten minutes' walk from the centre of any university town. Drinking bouts and feasts of song in taverns were frequent; and for these the youths had abundant example from their elders, since every stage in the long course from sophister to doctor was punctuated by official revelry of one sort or another. 'Fiant cerivisia honesta et moderata per incipientes primum cursum Biblie et tertium sententiarum' (let there be decent and moderate beer-drinking for those beginning the first course on the Bible and the third on the Sentences), reads a Paris statute for Theology students. For the rest, there were all the vices common where young men are congregated in large numbers, and frequent brawls between students of different nations, between town and gown, and between students and the armed retainers of abbot, lord, and king. This violence, the rhythm of the age, was considerably moderated in the sixteenth century both by a general softening of manners and by the establishment of colleges. Nevertheless, just as we inherit much of the medieval curriculum, ceremony, and organization, so the medieval student bequeathed a raffish tradition which persisted through the polished renaissance and the strict puritan age to our own day.

THE RISE OF COLLEGES

So far we have been considering the university in its earliest state, before there were enough colleges to impair the freedom of master and scholar, when all teaching was done by regent masters. The founding of colleges changed all this within two centuries. By the year 1500 not only in Oxford and Cambridge but in Paris and most of the Continental universities, the teaching was done largely by masters maintained by colleges, and the students lived either in a college under strict discipline or in a hall under close supervision.

The college, in its origin, was a hall endowed for special purposes, such as to support theological students during their long course of study for the divinity degrees, or to provide for the founder's kindred; and almost always the beneficiaries were required to celebrate masses for their benefactor's soul. The

Society of Fellows established at Harvard University in 1932 to support a certain number of relatively mature and gifted young men in their special researches is strikingly similar in purpose to the earliest colleges at Paris and Oxford. Until the renaissance, colleges were somewhat external to the university, and could have been swept away without being greatly missed; [1] but in the sixteenth century the colleges established an ascendancy over the universities of Oxford and Cambridge which they have maintained to this day. Harvard was founded at a period when colleges had absorbed the better part of English university life, and it was the colleges, rather than the university, that the founders of Harvard had in mind when framing their earliest laws and statutes.

Merton College, founded in 1264, was long the model for English university colleges. Walter de Merton, Bishop of Rochester, 'seeing that many scholars for want of temporalities, after they have incepted in Arts are forced to turn to material pursuits, that the Catholic Faith gathers strength from men "wound about" by knowledge of letters,'[2] — and seeing also that he had a number of nephews unprovided for — assigned certain lands and manors for the foundation of a college. At Oxford an uncompleted parish church was impropriated for the benefit of his scholars, and became the college chapel, around which the buildings were grouped. Merton College was a corporation, governed by the Warden and thirteen senior scholars, who filled all vacancies by coöptation, after examination. The founder's statutes prescribed for his scholars diligence, sobriety, chastity, the constant speaking of Latin, daily chapel attendance, and other virtues which recall the first laws of Harvard; and the 'Rule of Merton' was actually the model for almost every later college at Oxford and Cambridge. But no provision was made for instruction — that was to be had from the regent masters of the University. Merton, and all

1. H. E. Salter, in *History*, n.s., xiv. 58. The foundation of colleges began even earlier at Paris than at Oxford, and went further, but all were swept away at the Revolution, and the name of only one, the Sorbonne, survives. Almost all the Continental universities once contained colleges, but only one, the Collegio di Spagna at Bologna, still exists. D'Irsay, *op. cit.*, pp. 155–57.

2. The purposes ascribed to him — doubtless on his own statement — in a papal bull of 1280 confirming his foundation. P. S. Allen and H. W. Garrod, *Merton Muniments* (Oxford Historical Society, 1928), pp. 10–11.

the older colleges in the English universities, were intended for what we should call graduate study or research, not for teaching undergraduates. The founder's statutes of Queen's College, Oxford, provide stipends to the fellows (who corresponded to the scholars of Merton) only if they devote themselves to study; they are under no circumstances to be drawn aside 'to the care of pupils or other similar occupations.' [1] But when William of Wykeham, the founder of New College, Oxford (1379), required that the older fellows, in return for an extra stipend, take a certain responsibility for teaching the younger, a movement began that continued until the colleges had assumed entire responsibility for a student's education, leaving only the examining and degree-granting functions to the University. [2] As long as the colleges admitted only advanced students on scholarships, their teaching function was not very important. But Magdalen College (Oxford), founded in 1458, set a new fashion by inviting undergraduates to become *commensales* (commoners, boarders), [3] who paid well for the privilege, and in return received most of their instruction from college lecturers. Then began a flocking of undergraduates into the colleges, a fashion which, within a century and a half, ruined all but a few of the halls, and placed unattached students in somewhat the position of the modern 'commuter' at Harvard. [4]

As the colleges rose, university teaching declined; for although university statutes still required a certain number of regent masters to lecture on the seven Arts and three Philosophies, their audiences fell off, and their fees dwindled. From about 1450 on, the only means for a teacher to gain a living

1. J. R. Magrath, *The Queen's College*, i. viii–ix. Cf. H. E. Salter, *Registrum Mertonensis*, p. ix.

2. I think that it is misleading to trace the 'tutorial system,' as Mallet and Rashdall do, to this clause in the New College statutes; for the 'tutorial system,' at least in America, implies a certain method of teaching rather than college responsibility for teaching. There is no reason to suppose that the senior fellows of New College 'tutored' their juniors; there is every reason to suppose that they 'read lectures' like the regent masters.

3. It may be noted here that the word 'commoner' has no social connotation; it means simply 'table-fellow,' 'boarder'; the Cambridge equivalent was *pensionarius*, pensioner (cf. the French *pensionnaire*).

4. The 'chamber-deacons,' as the unattached students were called at Oxford, were legislated out of existence in 1581, and not legislated in again until 1868. Most of the halls at Oxford, and all those at Cambridge, had been put out of business by 1600, because they could not give their members the instruction that the endowed colleges afforded.

at Oxford or Cambridge or Paris was by becoming a college fellow.[1] Only the disputations, examinations, and commence-

ments remained to remind the student that there was a university over and above the colleges.

Equally striking was the change in student discipline. College gates enclosed the free cleric of the middle ages, and gave him security in return for liberty. The collegian's entire day was mapped out, with fixed hours for academic exercises, study, meals, prayers, and recreations — a system that lasted in some American colleges to the end of the nineteenth century. He was subject to schoolboy discipline, corrected by fines and whipping. Not only the crude horseplay of a rougher age was denied him, but pastimes like cards, dice, and playing such musical instruments as 'provoked levity and interfered with work.'[2] His social life was confined to a college of thirty or forty members, instead of a university of many hundred students. But the colleges provided the student with many good things to compensate for the robust liberty that he had lost. He was assured of lodging, meals, and *bibendia* — the 'bevers' of early Harvard. For recreation in summer college gardens, bowling greens, tennis courts, and fish ponds were provided; in winter, at stated seasons, there were mummers, comedies, and boy-bishops. Every evening after supper (says one college ordinance), the tutor shall lead an hour of 'honest joking' and 'light and humorous repartee,'[3] and so to bed 'post gloriose virginis antiphonam decantatam et biberium completum' (after singing the Antiphon of the Glorious Virgin and consuming the 'bever').[4] Bishop Fisher, founder of St. John's, Cambridge, would have his college hall cleared after supper; but 'whenever there is fire lighted in honor of God or His glorious Mother, or

1. Even the endowed university professorships, which began in the sixteenth century in the English universities, were generally held in connection with a college fellowship.

2. Queen's and Magdalen, Oxford (C. E. Mallet, *Hist. Univ. Oxf.*, I. 271, 388), and numerous other instances. An exception was almost always made for Christmastide, which, say the statutes of St. John's, Cambridge, should be celebrated 'honesta animi remissione et literariis exercitationibus cum laetitia et hilaritate.'

3. 'Interponet tutor jocum honestum per mediam horam et disputationem levem et jucundam per alteram mediam horam' (1476). Rashdall, II. 767.

4. Oxford Aularian Statutes, quoted in Rashdall, II. 655. The halls were placed by university enactment under much the same discipline as the colleges in the fifteenth century.

some other Saint,' the fellows, scholars, and college servants may sit up late singing songs, reciting poetry, telling tales, and such other honest recreations 'as becometh Scholars.'[1]

In two centuries the colleges transformed the universities.[2] Was more gained for learning than was lost? The answer depends on one's personal philosophy: whether with Jefferson and Eliot you would sail alone on the high seas of liberty with all their perils, or with Hamilton and Lowell you prefer the personally conducted cruise. Yet, if we find the intellectual flame burning low in the age of colleges as compared with the age of Aquinas, Occam, and Wyclif, it must be admitted that the colleges saved the universities. They not only made provision, which the medieval university did not, for poor students of intellectual promise; they supported teaching, at a time when instruction by regent masters had become so unremunerative that it was impossible to induce competent graduates to perform the duty. Several universities which once flourished under the system of regent masters had ceased to exist by 1500 for want of regular support. Others, such as the Spanish universities, were saved by endowed professorial chairs; but English and French benefactors were not interested in endowing chairs. It is true that after the lapse of centuries college fellowships were apt to be filled with wine-bibbers and absentees, and scholarships monopolized by idle and dissolute 'bloods,' and that it required vigorous parliamentary action to restore the English colleges to usefulness. But Harvard was founded when most of the colleges of Oxford and Cambridge were well performing their founders' intentions of providing financial support, discipline, and instruction for students of moderate means. American universities may take an equal pride in their college pedigree through Emmanuel, Trinity, and Christ's to New College and Merton as in their university descent, through Cambridge and Oxford, from glorious Paris, the 'First School of the Church.'

1. *Early Statutes of St. John's College* (J. E. B. Mayor, ed., 1859), p. 164. 'Tunc enim permittimus collegii sociis, discipulis et ministris post dictas refectiones et potationes gratia recreationis modestae, ut decet clericos, in canticis et aliis solaciis honestis in aula moram facere, necnon poemata ac historias et cetera huius generis litterata otia inter se exercere, conferre, legere et enarrare.'

2. Not only in England but on the Continent, save in universities devoted to Law and Medicine, lucrative professions whose students needed little pecuniary aid. The last of the regent master lectures in Paris were concluded by 1572, and college instruction in the Arts was given by a class system similar to that of early Harvard.

III

CAMBRIDGE, THE RENAISSANCE, AND THE PURITANS[1]

If we would know upon what model Harvard College was established, what were the ideals of her founders and the purposes of her first governors, we need seek no further than the University of Cambridge. It was there that the greater part of them had had their education. The puritan migration which established the colonies of Massachusetts Bay and Connecticut was led by alumni of Oxford and Cambridge. About a hundred Cambridge University men, and one third of that number from the University of Oxford, emigrated to New England before 1646;[2] and from these alumni[3] were recruited the founders and first governors of Harvard College; from their loins sprung most of the first generation of Harvard stu-

1. Authorities on the University of Cambridge: J. B. Mullinger, *History of the University of Cambridge*, published in three separate volumes with subtitles, is comprehensive and accurate, and pays more attention than most university histories to ideas. The contemporary Thomas Fuller's *History of the University of Cambridge* (1655, and Nichols ed., 1840) is full of flavor. Robert Willis and John W. Clark, *Architectural History of the University and Colleges of Cambridge* (3 vols. and one of plates, 1886), contains much information on other aspects of the University as well. Charles H. Cooper, *Annals of Cambridge* (vol. II, 1843; vol. III, 1845), presents an immense amount of information in the form of annals; and David Masson, *The Life of John Milton* (vol. I, 1859) is almost encyclopaedic for the years (1625–31) of Milton's residence at Cambridge. *Documents relating to the University and Colleges of Cambridge* (3 vols., published by the Cambridge University Commission, 1852) gives the Elizabethan statutes of the University, and the statutes of many colleges (but not of Trinity) as they existed in the early seventeenth century. Other documents of the period, in great variety, are published in James Heywood and Thomas Wright, *Cambridge University Transactions during the Puritan Controversies of the 16th and 17th Centuries* (2 vols., 1854). There is also a large amount of information in J. R. Tanner, *Historical Register of the University of Cambridge . . . to 1910* (1917), and John Venn (ed.), *Grace Book Δ* (1910). George Peacock, *Observations on the Statutes of the University of Cambridge* (1841), contains what is still the best description of the organization of the University around 1600.
2. See Appendix B.
3. *Alumnus* ('nursling') is here used, as in England, to include any student or past student, not merely a graduate, of a school or university.

dents. These university-trained emigrants were the people who founded the intellectual traditions and scholastic standards of New England. They created that public opinion which insisted on sound schooling, at whatever cost; and through their own characters and lives they inculcated, among a pioneer people, a respect for learning.

Founders of New England may be found in residence at the University of Cambridge over a period of fifty years. The first and oldest group was in college during the last seven years of Elizabeth and the first seven of James I (1596–1610). During this era, John Cotton was scholar of Trinity and fellow of Emmanuel, whence Nathaniel Ward had just gone down; John Winthrop was pensioner of Trinity; Sir Richard Saltonstall pensioner of Clare; Peter Bulkeley fellow of St. John's; and John Wilson fellow of King's. From 1610 to the end of James' reign in 1625, we find the largest number of future pioneers. John Humfrey, Hugh Peter, Thomas Weld, and Charles Chauncy were at Trinity; Thomas Hooker was fellow of Emmanuel, and Samuel Stone, Isaac Johnson, Thomas Shepard, and Nathaniel Rogers were students at the same college. Peter Hobart and John Knowles were at Magdalene, George Phillips at Caius, and John Eliot at Jesus. Shortly after the accession of Charles I there came up a group of young men who were destined to supply the vigor, the enthusiasm, and a large part of the funds which kept Harvard College alive during infancy: John Harvard, Nathaniel Eaton, Henry Dunster, the younger Saltonstall, and the two greatest headmasters of early New England, Ezekiel Cheever and Elijah Corlet.

The University and the Reformation

Before plunging into a description of that Cambridge which the founders of Harvard knew, let us briefly survey the history of the University during the previous century. Cambridge, after trailing Oxford for two centuries both as a place of learning and as an influence on the nation, suddenly pulled up in the fifteenth century, and by Queen Elizabeth's reign was a good length ahead — a lead which she long maintained. 'In intellectual activity, and in readiness to admit improvements, the superiority was then, as it has ever since been, on the side of the less ancient and splendid institution,' wrote Macaulay, in his Essay on Lord Bacon.[1] One would like to believe that Cambridge owed her rise to the intolerance of Oxford in banishing Wyclif and proscribing his followers;[2] unfortunately it is more likely that Oxford's dallying with Lollardry brought Cambridge 'into fashion with cautious parents and attracted the patronage of royal champions of orthodoxy and their ecclesiastical advisers.'[3] Both communities were hard hit by the reformation, but by the last half of Elizabeth's reign had recovered their numbers and prosperity.[4] Cambridge had never been so large as in 1623, with just short of three thousand members;[5] and not for another two centuries was she destined to pass that high point.

In the government and organization of the University as distinct from that of any college of the University, there was little that could profitably be copied by a small collegiate foundation such as Harvard, although much that portended the autocratic form that American university administration would eventually assume. Cambridge in the middle ages, like Oxford and Paris, had been a democracy of regent masters, which might defy the King by invoking the power of Rome and the prestige of the Republic of Letters. The reformation changed all that, and brought Oxford and Cambridge, Catholic at heart, trembling to their knees before the Tudor monarchs. No sooner had Henry VIII broken with Rome than he ordered the colleges to surrender their charters and the universities to alter their statutes. For a time it seemed likely that the colleges would suffer the fate of the monasteries; but when such a motion was made to the King, bluff Harry replied, 'Ah, sirra! I perceive the Abbey lands have fleshed you, and set your teeth on edge, to ask also those colleges.'[6] A royal commission — fortunately composed of Cambridge men — reported on the college revenues in such wise that the King declared 'he had not in his realme so

1. One does not have to be an Oxonian to question Macaulay's 'ever since.' Oxford has been more fertile than Cambridge in men of letters and statesmen; but Cambridge was intellectually the more active of the two in the sixteenth and seventeenth centuries, except in Science.

2. Albert Mansbridge, *The Older Universities of England*, pp. 41–42.

3. Rashdall, II. 552–53.

4. Cambridge granted 60 A.B. degrees in 1560, 114 in 1570, 277 in 1583. The numbers at Oxford were about one-third less. Mullinger, II. 214.

5. G. M. Edwards, *Sidney Sussex College*, p. 80.

6. William Harrison, *Description of England* (Withington ed., 1889), p. 261.

many persons so honestly mayntayned in lyvyng bi so little lond and rent.'[1] So the colleges were allowed to live. The King, himself no mean scholar, created (at others' expense) two noble foundations, Christ Church and Trinity, one at each university; and in each he established the Regius professorships of Divinity, Hebrew, Greek, Medicine, and Civil Law. These chairs[2] mark another stage in the transition from the medieval university, where all the instruction was by regent masters, to the modern university, where instruction is by endowed professors and college tutors.

PURITANISM

During the brief reign of Mary, the universities turned Catholic once more, only to be forcibly reconverted under Elizabeth. There now appeared in their midst the puritan party. As New England and Harvard College were founded by members of this party we may well pause to inquire what they wished to accomplish. On the religious side, the puritans proposed to carry out the reformation to a logical conclusion; to base the Church of England, both in doctrine and discipline, on the firm foundation of Sacred Scripture; or, in the words of Thomas Cartwright, to secure a church 'pure and unspotted' as in the apostolic age. On the moral side, puritanism was a reaction against the coarse manners and loose morals of the Elizabethan age, toward a strict observance of New Testament ethics.[3] These two aspects of puritanism were not always combined in the same person — the moral aspect was called 'preciseness' rather than 'puritanism,' and its supporters 'precisians.' We have puritans like the great Earl of Warwick who were swearers of great oaths and notorious loose livers; and, on the other side, precisians like Samuel Ward, Master of Sidney Sussex, who were Episcopalians; Charles I and Archbishop Laud yielded nothing to John Winthrop and Thomas Hooker in

1. Mullinger, II. 79.
2. They were the first professorial chairs in England, excepting the two Lady Margaret professorships of Divinity, founded in 1503 by the mother of Henry VII.
3. The political aspect of puritanism was secondary to the others, and hardly made its appearance before the meeting of the Long Parliament; until Charles I had very definitely taken a stand against their religious views the puritans were as royalist as anyone, and if the two first Stuart kings had adopted an ecclesiastical policy pleasing to the puritans, it is likely that they would have supported the Crown in its suppression of traditional English political liberties.

moral puritanism. But for the most part, both in the universities and in the nation, the two aspects were combined; and the men who lived or attempted to live as Christ taught leaned toward evangelistic rather than ritualistic religion, Presbyterian or Congregational rather than Episcopalian polity, and Calvinist rather than Lutheran or Arminian dogma. They preferred composing their own prayers to reading from the Book of Common Prayer.

The puritan party, both in the universities and the nation, was greatly strengthened in the early years of Elizabeth by the return of the Marian exiles — the 'wolves from Geneva'—from Switzerland and Germany, where they had been inspired by the leaders of Calvinism. Oxford at first was as deeply affected as Cambridge; but there was something in the 'less ancient and splendid institution,' possibly its situation in the ancient region of Lollardry, which made it more permanently receptive to puritanism.

In some respects, popular puritanism was an enemy to learning. For a man who 'hungered and thirsted for Christ', the Tyndale or Genevan translations of the Bible, written in the language of common speech, were sufficient food and drink. No need of a learned scholar to teach *him* religion! And as time went on, and strange, fierce little sects grew up around unlettered prophets, who found the 'plain words of God' perverted by university-educated prelates, many persons concluded that learning was a positive impediment to piety. This aversion of unlearned puritans was constantly being thrown up at the Cambridge puritans by their enemies. In 'The Pilgrimage to Parnassus,' a play acted in the Hall of St. John's College in 1597, the puritans are ridiculed in the person of Stupido, an undergraduate of that persuasion.

Stupido. You speake like a younge man indeede! . . . I have a good man to my uncle, that never wore capp nor surples in his life, nor anie suche popishe ornament, who sent mee yesterday a letter and this mandition, and a frize coate for a token, and the same counsell that he gave mee I, as I am bounde in charitie, will give you. 'Studie not these vaine arts of Rhetorique, Poetrie and Philosophie; there is noe sounde edifying knowledg in them.' Why, they are more vaine than a paire of organs or a morrice daunce! If you will be good men indeede, goe no further in this way; follow noe longer these profane artes that are the raggs and parings of learning; sell all these books, and by a good Martin, and twoo or three hundreth of chatechismes of Jeneva's printe, and I warrant you will have learning enoughe. Mr Martin and other good men tooke this course.

Philomusus.   Are then the artes foolish, profane and vaine,
That gotten are with studie, toile and paine?

Studioso.   Artistes belike then are phantastique fools,
That learne these artes in the laborious schools.

Stup. Artistes, fools; and that you may knowe by there undecent apparell. Why, you shall not see a Rhetorician, a rimer (a poet as you call it) but he wears such diabolicall ruffs and wicked great breeches full of sin, that it would make a zelous professor's harte bleed for grife. Well, Mr Wigginton and Mr Penorie never wore such profane hose, but such plaine apparell as I doe. Goe with mee, and you shall heare a good man exercise. I will get him to handle for youre better direction this pointe by the way; I would gladlie doe some good of you if I coulde.[1]

These taunts were quite beside the mark of Cambridge puritans, who had no quarrel with the Liberal Arts, and whose zeal both for popular education and higher learning is tested by such foundations as Emmanuel, the New England school system, and Harvard. From the beginning, to the end where it merged into Wesleyism, the main stem of English puritanism was kept straight by university-educated men; and the two cardinal principles of English puritanism which most profoundly affected the social development of New England and the United States were not religious tenets, but educational ideals: a learned clergy, and a lettered people.

In the matter of doctrine, the puritans had no complaint against the Established Church until the time of Laud. The Thirty-nine Articles of Religion were Calvinist;[2] the Lambeth Articles of 1595, promulgated by Archbishop Whitgift to suppress a few whispers of Anglo-Catholicism at Cambridge, were rigidly and harshly Calvinist. But all puritans were profoundly dissatisfied with the organization, liturgy, and ritual of the Church of England. It was not only episcopal government and ordination that they found unauthorized by Scripture, but ritual and vestments. The surplice appeared a symbol of the popery that they abhorred, and it became a standard around

1. W. D. Macray (ed.), *Pilgrimage to Parnassus* (1886), pp. 11–13.
2. Cotton Mather, in his *Ratio Disciplinae* (1726), p. 5, stated with truth that the Thirty-nine Articles were more faithfully observed in the puritan churches of New England than they had been for a century in the Church of England.

which the battle raged. It was probably the memories of this vestarian controversy that long prevented the adoption of formal academic dress at Harvard.

THE ELIZABETHAN STATUTES

In the fifteen-sixties, it seemed that the puritans might dictate the polity, as they had the doctrine, of the Church. Presbyterian ideas were sweeping the colleges. Beza, the successor of Calvin at Geneva, was in frequent correspondence with university divines, who looked on him almost as a pope.[1] Rubrics of the Book of Common Prayer were slighted in college services; fellows refused to wear the surplice; university preachers urged that all painted windows in the college chapels be smashed. Matters came to a head when Thomas Cartwright was elected by the regent masters to the Lady Margaret chair of Divinity, which he proceeded to make a rostrum for attacking the government and discipline of the Established Church. Great St. Mary's was filled with enthusiastic auditors; it was as if a new crusade was being preached. Cartwright's sermons brought on what Dr. Mullinger regards as 'the most important crisis in the whole history of the university.'[2] On June 29, 1570, the Vice-Chancellor of the University inflicted a public stigma on Cartwright by refusing to admit him to the degree of Doctor of Divinity, the crowning glory of a theologian's academic career. The regent masters, highly indignant, threatened at the next election of a vice-chancellor to choose a puritan. Sir William Cecil, the wise and wily Chancellor of the University, and John Whitgift, Master of Trinity College, put their heads together, and the result was the Code of Statutes of 12 Elizabeth, under which the University of Cambridge was governed for almost three centuries.[3] The immediate object was quickly attained. Whitgift *qua* Vice-Chancellor declared Cartwright's chair vacant, and *qua* Master of Trinity deprived him of his fellowship; Cartwright then retired to Geneva. It was a prophecy of the antinomian controversy in Massachusetts Bay in the next century; and the purpose of the persecuting authorities in both

1. Mullinger, II. 194–95.
2. II. 216–17.
3. Printed in *Docs. U. Camb.*, I. 454 ff. Comments in George Peacock, *Observations on the Statutes* (1841), and Mullinger, II. 223 ff.

PICTORIAL MAP OF CAMBRIDGE IN 1634

instances was the same: the preservation of religious and political unity in the face of a common enemy. For in 1570 the Council of Trent had lately adjourned; the counter-reformation was looming.

Like most heresy-hunts, whether religious or political or economic, the Cartwright incident had unforeseen effects. The Elizabethan statutes of 1570, devised primarily to get rid of one man, subjected the University to an autocracy of the Vice-Chancellor and the heads of colleges. As the regent masters complained, 'nothing can pass all the whole yeare' which the heads 'mislike, or any one of them'; and behind the heads stood the Crown.

Further, the Elizabethan statutes went into minute details regarding disputations, lectures, degrees, manner and dress of students, and every aspect of university affairs, except the very important one of the curriculum. Many of these regulations, taken over from the ancient statutes, were already obsolete in 1570; but there was no possible means of getting them repealed except by a completely new university constitution, which was not obtained until the middle of the nineteenth century. They might be added to by the Sovereign of his own free will, as for instance the Three Articles to which all candidates for degrees were compelled to subscribe by order of James I; [1] but they could only be dispensed with by a similar grace, which was seldom accorded. Every officer of the University and every holder of a Cambridge degree had to take solemn oath to obey every clause of the Elizabethan statutes; but as Dean Peacock remarked, several of its provisions were 'vehemently resisted at the period of their first promulgation.' They were destined, in fact, 'to experience the fate which has attended all systems of statutes or of laws which have attempted, by being themselves unchangeable, to fix immutably the changeable character of the wants and habits of mankind.' Even before 1640 the statute requiring M.A.'s to reside at the University as regents for five full years was systematically neglected; certain university lec-

1. 'I. That the king's majesty, under God, is the only supreme governor of this realm . . . as well in all spiritual or ecclesiastical things or causes, as temporal. . . . II. That the Book of Common Prayer . . . containeth in it nothing contrary to the word of God . . . and that he himself will use the form in the said book prescribed, in public prayer, and administration of the sacraments, and none other. . . . III. . . . That he acknowledgeth the Thirty-nine Articles . . . to be agreeable to the word of God.' Cooper, *Annals of Cambridge*, III. 9.

turers read scarcely four times a year, instead of the statutory four times a week; Latin-speaking was 'altogether neglected.' The academic dress so minutely prescribed in the statutes was discarded; instead, declared the Master of Peterhouse in 1636, 'we have fair roses upon the shoe, long frizled hair upon the head, . . . large merchant's ruffs about the neck, with fair and feminine cuffs at the wrist. Nay, although ruff-necked shirts be expressly forbidden by the statutes of the university, yet we use them without controul. Some of the heads and all, to the laudable example of others.' [1]

The example of all this was not lost on the founders of Harvard. They had had enough of irrepealable but unenforceable statutes, and of solemn oaths which were broken with impunity by laymen and ministers alike.[2] The early statutes of Harvard College were few and meagre; religious tests there were none.

On the University of Cambridge, the Elizabethan statutes had a very marked effect. Puritan objections to the establishment were in some cases satisfied by Hooker's 'Ecclesiastical Polity,' and in others forcibly silenced. The slightest suggestion in lecture or university sermon that the ways of the Church were not according to Scripture brought an inquisition by the heads of houses, followed by recantation or expulsion, even by imprisonment. But the prevalent Calvinist doctrine was not immediately affected. Until the Laudian period, any suggestions of revived Catholicism, or of non-Calvinist Protestantism, were treated with a like severity. The Sovereign was now the

---

1. Peacock, *op. cit.*, pp. 58, 61, 63; cf. the statutes, in *Docs. U. Camb.*, I. 482–83. This customary and connived-at breaking of solemn oaths was nothing new in academic history. The Arts candidate in thirteenth-century Paris by the time he had taken his master's degree had sworn a matter of fifty oaths that he had performed acts many of which he had left undone, and that he would perform acts many of which he had no intention of performing — and this at a time when the breaking of an oath was not only a social offense but a mortal sin, invoking the worldly punishment of excommunication, and eternal damnation. But as Rashdall observes (II. 689), 'We need not go back to medieval history to illustrate the fact that an unwavering acquiescence in the reality of supernatural terrors may at times exercise but little deterrent effect upon the ordinary life of believers.'

2. Cotton Mather records that John Sherman refused subscription to the Three Articles, and so lost his degree, and that John Wilson by pulling wires was allowed to take his M.A. without subscription. With these exceptions, the founders of New England cheerfully promised to use the Book of Common Prayer, which most of them had every intention of discarding as soon as they possibly could, and which they forbade others to use in New England. Their signatures to the Subscription Book in the University Registry appear in some of the illustrations to this and following chapters.

effective head of the universities, as of the Church. Royal mandates in matters which did not concern the royal prerogative, such as the election of certain persons to fellowships and headships of colleges, were evaded only by stealth — by filling the vacancy before it occurred. A natural result of this state of affairs [1] appears in the story of Lord Brooke's attempt to found in 1627 a long-desired chair of history at Cambridge.[2]

 As both universities had treated history somewhat lightly, no competent candidate could be found in England, and a rising young Dutchman named Dorislaus was imported from the University of Leyden. In his second lecture, the professor made bold to touch 'upon the Excesses of Tarquinius Superbus his infringing the Liberties of the People' and to vindicate his own countrymen against Spain. In short, as Samuel Ward informed the Lord Primate, 'he was conceived of by some, to speak too much for the defence of the Liberties of the People; though he spake with great moderation, and with an exception of such Monarchies as ours.' [3] Yet the more timid and subservient fellows began writing letters to important people about the 'dangerous tendency' of the lecturer. At Laud's instance, the professor was forbidden by a royal injunction to continue his course. Lord Brooke, in disgust, allowed the proposed endowment to lapse, and the professor returned to Holland.

This unwholesome attitude of timidity and subservience extended throughout the senior part of the University; and there was a constant pressure on fellows of colleges to expend their intellect on arid tracts of controversial divinity rather than on productive scholarship or creative writing. The obvious lesson of this state of affairs was learned by but one of the emigrating Cambridge puritans, Roger Williams, and not by him until he had become the victim of the puritan establishment in Massachusetts Bay.

1. Which also existed at Oxford, especially after Laud became Chancellor of the University in 1630. See Laud's *Works*, v. 48–63, and C. E. Mallet, *History Univ. Oxford*, II. chap. xvii.
2. Mullinger, III. 81–91. The Camden professorship of Ancient History was established at Oxford in 1622.
3. Richard Parr, *Life of James Usher*, p. 393.

The 'Polite Learning' of the Renaissance

 Parallel to this struggle for control of the University, the ideals and practices of university education were undergoing a profound modification. To the medieval ideal of a thorough training in logic and philosophy was added the renaissance ideal of a training no less thorough in Greek, and in what the humanists called *bonae litterae*, or polite letters.

The Cambridge Arts curriculum, around 1600, had become far more flexible than ever before, or than the Harvard curriculum would be for a matter of two centuries. University requirements in the Elizabethan statutes were so slender, and examinations for degrees had become so perfunctory, that infinite variations in the course were possible. It was a true 'elective system,' with this difference, that the election of subjects was by the tutor, who might or might not consult his pupil's tastes and aptitudes. One such course will be described in the next chapter; we may here trace the historical growth of the Arts curriculum during the century before Harvard was founded, and discover, if we can, what were the general ideas behind it.

If puritanism brought to the university an internal struggle for the control of opinion, it strengthened, if anything, the medieval conception of the university's function as a place for training a learned priesthood, from which the laity were expected to take their opinions. But in the meantime, another force had been operating to dissolve the solid clericalism of the university, and reform it into a school for practical affairs and polite letters.

This modern function had been forced on the university by the renaissance, which in education brought not only a revival of classical scholarship but the ideal of 'polite learning' — the education of a gentleman. It is true that the 'Liberal Arts' of the middle ages had originally meant just that: the arts suitable for a *liber homo*, free man, or gentleman;[1] but however suitable the seven Arts had been for a *liber homo* of the late Roman Empire, they made no appeal to the feudal nobility, nor to the merchants and magnates who at the renaissance began to dis-

---

1. Edward K. Rand, *Founders of the Middle Ages* (1929), chap. vii.

place ecclesiastics in the governing class. The medieval Arts course, with its overemphasis on Dialectic and Philosophy, served mainly those destined for the Church and the Law; it was too 'practical' an education to be of much value for anyone else. The English colleges of the thirteenth to the fifteenth centuries were founded in order to enable poor but deserving scholars to enter the Church, not for the general education of gentlemen's sons, who at that time were too earnestly engaged in exterminating one another to have time for study.

The Italian humanists of the Quattrocento despised the university education of that day. In their opinion it was equally unsuitable for a gentleman or a scholar, since there was no study of Greek or of classical texts, and the Latin was corrupt. Vergerio of Padua struck the Hellenic note when he defined a liberal education as one that 'calls forth, trains, and develops those highest gifts of body and of mind which ennoble men, and which are rightly judged to rank next in dignity to virtue only.' [1] We should be happy indeed if our present colleges fulfilled Vergerio's ideal.

Vittorino da Feltre realized this ideal of a gentleman's education in his own school, where the Christian spirit of devotion, the Greek ideal of physical perfection, and the study of ancient letters were harmoniously combined. The conception reached England through humanists such as Lily, Colet, and Erasmus; it was popularized by such works as Sir Thomas Eliot's 'Governour' (1531), Sir Thomas Hoby's translation of Baldassare Castiglione's 'Book of the Courtier' (1561), Laurence Humphrey's 'Nobles' (1563), and Roger Ascham's 'Scholemaster' (1570). The central principles of this new conception of education were unity, gentility, and public service. Education must develop the whole man — his body and soul as well as his intellect. It must teach manners to the boy of gentle or wealthy birth, and prepare him to take his place in the governing class. In other words, it must prepare him to be a gentleman and a man of action. Every item in the curriculum is weighed by these two standards. Latin and Greek literature remain central because they breed statesmanship, nobility, *virtus*. Logic may be admitted to 'whet the wit' and 'make the noble a good reasoner'; but Aristotle's logic is no longer suitable.

1. William H. Woodward, *Vittorino da Feltre*, p. 102.

History first appeared in English schools and colleges as a means of cultivating gentlemanly tastes and statesmanlike judgment. 'Amongst your other serious Studies,' says a dedication to Lord Brooke, 'History will be a recreation, and yet you will finde it exceeding usefull and profitable, and that which doth very much accomplish a Gentleman. *Cicero* saith, *Historia est testis temporum, Lux veritatis, Nuncia Vetustatis, Vitae magistra, etc.* Another saith, It's the Register of Honour . . . the Soveraign Judge of all men, and all exploits.'[1]

Education both in England and America was profoundly influenced by the fact that this ideal of a 'polite' or 'gentleman's' education appeared in England simultaneously with the humanistic ideal of classical scholarship, and with the reform of religion. All three were exemplified and propagated by Erasmus, during his five years' residence at Cambridge between 1509 and 1514. In a letter of 1516 he writes, 'It is scarcely thirty years ago, when all that was taught in the university of Cambridge, was Alexander, the *Parva Logicalia*, . . . those old exercises out of Aristotle, and *quaestiones* taken from Duns Scotus. As time went on, *bonae litterae* were introduced; to this was added a knowledge of mathematics; a new, or at least a regenerated, Aristotle sprang up; then came an acquaintance with Greek, and with a host of new authors . . .'[2] In the very year of this letter, Bishop Fox founded Corpus Christi College at Oxford, dedicated to the New Learning, and with the especial purpose of breeding knowledge of the Greek Fathers. A few years later the poet Skelton could declare,

> *In Academia* Parrot dare no problem keep,
> For *Graece fari* so occupieth the chair
> That *Latinum fari* may fall to rest and sleep,
> And *syllogisari* was drowned at Sturbridge Fair;
> Trivials and quatrivials so sore now they impair.[3]

Oxford, after passing through a period of violent opposition to the New Learning — in which scholars of Corpus Christi scarcely dared venture beyond college gates — accepted both it and the reform with almost fanatical zeal in 1535. The works

1. Samuel Clarke's dedication to his *Generall Martyrologie* (ed. 1651). The author, a puritan divine, was Thomas Shepard's contemporary at Emmanuel. His quotation is from *de Oratore*, ii. 9. 36.
2. Mullinger, 1. 515–16. Cf. Erasmus, *Epistles* (Allen ed.), ii. 328.
3. 'Speak, Parrot,' in *Complete Poems* (Henderson ed.), p. 265.

of 'the subtle doctor' Duns Scotus, the quintessence of ultra-refined scholasticism, were torn, burned, thrown out of libraries. New College quadrangle was 'full of the leaves of Dunce, the wind blowing them into every corner'; and the name of him who had once been the idol of the schools became the common English word for a school blockhead.

The association between these three ideas of Protestantism, classical scholarship, and a gentleman's education appears in the Royal Injunctions of 1535 to each and every member of the University of Cambridge. They must subscribe to the royal supremacy over the Church of England, and 'the extirpation of the papal usurpation.' Canon law shall no longer be read, nor any lecture in Peter Lombard, much less the 'frivolous questions and obscure glosses of Scotus.' Students should be encouraged to read the Scriptures. Each college must maintain 'two daily public lectures, one of Greek, the other of Latin.' And 'all ceremonies, constitutions, and observances that hinder *polite learning* should be abolished.' [1]

A Gentleman's Education

 By sweeping away the major portions of the medieval Arts curriculum, these Royal Injunctions opened the way at Cambridge to provide a gentleman's education. The very year after, the *Plutus* of Aristophanes was performed at St. John's College, in Greek.[2] In 1540 Henry VIII founded the Regius professorships, and his first appointment to the Greek chair was Sir John Cheke, 'the famous knight' and no less famous scholar, who had already lectured on Homer, Sophocles, Euripides, and Herodotus.[3] By 1547, according to Roger Ascham, the University was beginning to pick up. Many students were absorbed in the theological controversies of the day; but many, too, were reading Greek. And most of

1. Mullinger, I. 630.
2. *Id.*, II. 73. A statute of Queens' College in 1546 directs that any student refusing to take a part assigned to him in a play at College, or absenting himself from the performance, shall be expelled!
3. *Queene Elizabethes Achademy*, p. 2. Gilbert there reports that it was Cheke's intention to establish English orations and declamations in the University, which would have been a notable concession to the needs of the governing class. It was Cheke who introduced the new method of pronouncing Greek, which gave separate values to each vowel and diphthong.

the entering students were reported to be mere boys, the sons of wealthy parents, who were satisfied with superficial and elementary acquirements. Two years later, Latimer complained, 'There be none now but great men's sons in Colleges, and their fathers look not to have them preachers.'[1] William Harrison denounced the encroachment of the rich in even stronger terms.[2]

All these writers treat the influx of wealthy young men as something unnatural, unexpected, and undesirable. But what other result could be expected? A new upper class was arising. Enriched by the woolens trade or overseas commerce, glutted by spoils of the abbeys, families like the Cecils, Russells, Greshams, and Winthrops wished to educate their sons as gentlemen, and prepare them for active life. Oxford and Cambridge colleges were appropriate dwellings for such youths. They offered an opportunity, in luxurious surroundings and congenial company, to read the polite literature which Erasmus told them was necessary for a gentleman's education. It is true that the University did not admit the logic of the situation — Englishmen seldom do. All college students were supposed to be clerics, and behave as such. There was no objection to their smoking or drinking in moderation;[3] but they were forbidden to dress as men of rank, or to indulge in field sports such as hawking, hunting, and coursing with greyhounds, to keep dogs in college, bear arms, carouse in taverns, view bull- and bear-baitings, or visit 'bawdy Barnwell and Sturbridge Fair.' Of course all these forbidden things were done. When the Mitre, one of the most popular and prohibited taverns, burnt down in 1634, Thomas Randolph, the poet of Trinity College, thus offered to the host his fellows' aid on rebuilding:

> Wee'le be thy workemen day and night,
>   In spight of bugge-beare proctors,
> Before, we dranke like Freshmen all,
>   But now wee'le drinke like doctors.

---

1. Cooper, *Annals*, II. 26, quoting a sermon of Latimer.

2. *Description* (1889 ed.), p. 252. A similar complaint was voiced in 1579 in Lyly's *Euphues*.

3. It may be inferred that around 1600 smoking was well-nigh universal from the fact that it was forbidden in college halls while plays were being presented, and in St. Mary's Church at the time of disputations during the visit to the University of James I, whose aversion to tobacco was well known. Cooper, *Annals*, III. 27.

Yet lawbreaking, even in a university, had its inconveniences, since students if under the age of eighteen were subjected to flogging for cutting chapel or lectures, even for going in swimming.[1] It was largely because the University fell far short of the gentlemanly ideal that Sir Humphrey Gilbert drew up for the Queen's inspection a plan for an 'Achademy in London for educacion of her Maiestes Wardes, and others the youth of nobility and gentlemen.'[2]

Gilbert's scheme is a most interesting English adaptation of the Italian conception of polite learning. His purpose is to provide study in 'matters of accion meet for present practize, both of peace and warre,' and to exercise the pupils 'in qualities meet for a gentleman.' The young man shall study Greek and Latin Grammar, Hebrew, Logic, and Rhetoric, but his orations shall be in English. A professor of philosophy shall read lectures on Civil and Martial Polity, by which 'men shalbe taught more witt and pollicy then *Schole learninges* can deliuer. . . . For the greatest *Schole clarkes* are not alwayes the wisest men.' Mathematics shall be studied in application to fortification and ballistics; there shall be a riding academy to teach the knightly school of horsemanship, an old soldier to teach foot drill and the handling of arms. Another mathematical professor, equipped with a model ship, shall teach navigation, naval architecture, and cosmography; and a doctor of physic shall instruct in first-aid, chirurgerie, and the cure of wounds. Smatterings of law and divinity, French, Spanish, Italian and 'highe duche,' of music, dancing and vaulting, heraldry, and the blazonry of arms will be acquired. And it is significant that among the indirect advantages of his academy Sir Humphrey alleges that the 'vniuersities shall then better suffize to releiue poore schollers, where now the youth of nobility and gentlemen, taking up

1. 'Briefe of certain Statutes to be published in every severall College, by authority from Mr. Vicechancellor,' 1595, in Cooper, *Annals*, II. 538; for bathing, see *Cambridge Univ. Transactions during the Puritan Controversies* (Heywood and Wright, eds., 1854), I. 56. 'At Oxford (and I doe believe the like at Cambridge) the rod was frequently used by the tutors and deanes on his pupills, till bachelaours of Arts; even gentleman-commoners.' John Aubrey, *Brief Lives* (A. Clark ed., 1898), II. 171. There are instances of whipping in the Cambridge colleges as late as 1674. Rouse Ball, *Cambridge Papers*, pp. 212–13.

2. Printed as *Queene Elizabethes Academy*, in Early English Text Society, extra series no. viii (1869). For other attempts, as late as 1641, to found in England a courtly academy of the Continental type, see R. F. Young, *Comenius in England*, pp. 65–66.

their schollarshippes and fellowshippes, do disapoincte the poore of their livinges and avauncementes.'

Gloriana, doubtless from pecuniary considerations, gave no countenance to˙ her favorite's proposed academy, and Sir Humphrey sailed for Newfoundland. The 'great men's sons' continued to flock to Oxford and Cambridge, although never wholly to the exclusion of others. Mullinger probably exaggerates in declaring that around 1600 'the award of a fellowship on the ground of merit was the exception rather than the rule'; but it is certainly true that incumbents, instead of using fellowships to prepare themselves for the ministry, regarded colleges as their permanent homes. As Robert Wild, a Cambridge poet of this period, wrote in his 'Scholler's Complaint':

> Cambridge now I must leave thee
> And follow Fate,
> Colledge hopes do deceive me!
> I oft expected
> To have been elected
> But Desert is reprobate.
> Masters of colledges have no common Graces,
> And they that have Fellowships have but common Places,
> And those that Scholars are, they must have handsome faces.
> Alas, poor Scholar, whither wilt thou go? [1]

One can hardly exaggerate the importance of this intrusion of 'young gentlemen' into the English universities, for there they remained, and to Harvard they have come. Owing to the fact that England simultaneously received the reformation, the renaissance, and this notion of a gentleman's education, there was brought about an unwilling compromise between gentility and learning, a rubbing of shoulders between the poor scholar and the squire's son, that has made the English and American college what it is today: the despair of educational reformers and logical pedagogues, the astonishment of Continental scholars, a place which is neither a house of learning nor a house of play, but a little of both; and withal a microcosm of the world in which we live. To this sixteenth-century compromise, be-

---

1. *Iter Boreale and other Poems* (1668), p. 52; Mullinger (II. 387 n.) is misleading in calling Wild a poet of the restoration; he took his M.A. degree from St. John's in 1639, and this poem appears in John Rous's *Diary* for 1641 (Camden Society, 1856), p. 115. See also Fuller's amusing account (ed. 1840, p. 143) of the discussion among the Fellows of St. John's 'whether a religious dunce were to be chosen' for a fellowship or scholarship 'before a learned rakehell.'

come a tradition, we owe that common figure of the English-speaking world, 'a gentleman and a scholar.'

Such were several among the leading founders of New England, and of Harvard: both Winthrops and both Saltonstalls, Downing and Bradstreet, Bellingham, and Peter Bulkeley,[1] of whom Cotton Mather wrote, 'His Education . . . was Learned, it was Genteel, and . . . Pious.'[2] To Harvard they brought a new zeal for scriptural religion and the humanist tradition. From her opening day, Harvard has included a large proportion of young men who had no professional intentions. They have been complained of by their more serious preceptors, these three hundred years. They have committed every sort of folly and extravagance. New colleges such as Williams and Amherst have been founded in order to provide a place where poor but pious youths could be educated for the ministry, uncontaminated by the 'rakehells,' 'bloods,' and 'sports' of Harvard—and the same class of students have flocked to the new colleges. Even after countless examples of gentlemen who have become scholars and scholars who have become gentlemen by this illogical commingling, there are some people who would admit none to our colleges but serious students, and others who would set a standard of luxury and expense impossible for poor students. As long as Harvard remains true to her early tradition, rich men's sons and poor, serious scholars and frivolous wasters, saints and sinners, puritans and papists, Jews and Gentiles will meet in her Houses, her Yard, and her athletic fields, rubbing off each other's angularities, and learning from friendly contact what cannot be learned from books.

POLEMICAL DIVINITY

While a large part of undergraduate Cambridge was indulging in occupations altogether foreign to the main purpose of the University, controversial theology became the great intellectual preoccupation of their seniors. This fashion had a long and not altogether fortunate influence on Harvard College. The re-

---

1. See Appendix B. It will be noted that none of those here mentioned, save Bulkeley, who became a minister, took a degree. As Dr. Venn has observed in his introduction to *Alumni Cantabrigienses* the taking of an M.A. at Cambridge, in the early seventeenth century, was *prima facie* evidence that the candidate aspired to the ministry.

2. *Magnalia* (1702), book iii. 96.

proach has sometimes been made against colonial Harvard that she did not produce creative scholars; to this, if a pioneer environment were not deemed sufficient excuse, one might plead that a stream can rise no higher than its source. Neither at Oxford nor at Cambridge in 1630 was there any teacher to compare with the Italian humanists of the Quattrocento, or with the French school of classical scholars — men such as Scaliger, Casaubon, Lipsius, and Salmasius — or with Dutch university professors such as Heinsius and Grotius.[1] The distinctive intellectual achievements of the Elizabethan age were in creative literature, ever independent of universities. Even the great translators of the age were men of letters rather than scholars — to which doubtless they owe their continued vogue; for whilst the discoveries of a classical scholar like Casaubon are absorbed in another generation, rendering his works obsolete as those of pioneer scientists, Chapman's Homer and North's Plutarch, written by intellectual adventurers and masters of English speech in its golden age, have the promise of immortality.[2] The Bodleian Library was opened only in 1602, and a much longer time elapsed before Cambridge had a university library worthy of the name. The new learning of the renaissance was already old when Harvard was founded; and although Bacon had died and Selden had already won fame in several branches of knowledge, neither the one nor the other had ever been a college fellow or received the slightest countenance from his alma mater.

Harvard College, then, was founded after the new learning of the renaissance had been sifted into the old scholastic curriculum, but before the new scientific leaven had begun to work. Isaac Newton, from whom dates the scientific glory of Cambridge, was born in 1642, the year of Harvard's first Commencement. But there was one great, absorbing intellectual interest in the Oxford and Cambridge of the Harvard founders' day which they transplanted to the New World; that was the very ecclesiastical controversy which drove them forth to 'pitch new States as Old-World men pitch tents.'

During the century from 1540 to 1640 the contest between

1. See below, Chapter X.
2. The best English classical scholar of the age, the magnificent Sir Henry Savile, Warden of Merton College 1585–1622, tried a hand at translating Tacitus; but he was too good a scholar to produce a literary monument.

the Catholic and Protestant points of view, between Arminian and Calvinist theology, surpassed every other interest in the two universities; and no wonder, for this was no subject of abstract speculation, but a matter of immediate importance, of life and death for individuals, of glory or decay for England, of the triumph of English Protestantism or its extinction in blood, as across the Channel.

Almost all the teaching fellows in the English universities were clerics, who sought promotion and security from the Church; and a large proportion of their pupils looked forward to the same career. The Government regarded them as instruments of the State, whose duty it was to find arguments for whatever the dominant religious party wished to do. Accordingly, the literary output of both universities was confined largely to controversial divinity, works which then sold 'like hot cakes' but are completely useless today, save as sources for the history of thought. What, therefore, the English universities then lacked in learning they made up by warm contact with living issues; and if the average B.A. had never read a line of Bacon, and assumed that the ancients had apprehended all that a man might know of the mysteries of nature, he at least realized that sincere men differed in matters of high import in Church and State, and that he must shortly take his stand, if not draw his sword, either for Anglo-Catholicism and the royal prerogative, or for puritanism and the traditional liberties of Englishmen.

IV

CAMBRIDGE: THE ARTS COURSE
1600–1640

Having made this brief survey of the university from which most of the founders of Harvard came, let us examine the course for the two Arts degrees[1] that most of them had followed.

A young Englishman seeking a university education in the early seventeenth century had a much better opportunity of getting properly prepared for it than his forbears. To the pre-Elizabethan grammar schools and endowed colleges for secondary education such as Winchester, Eton, Westminster, and St. Paul's, many more such as Harrow, Repton, Rugby, and Uppingham were added in the reigns of Elizabeth and James.[2] The newly-rich of Tudor times were generous founders and liberal benefactors of schools. By 1600 'every boy, even in the remotest parts of the country, could find a place of education in his own neighborhood competent at any rate to fit him to enter College,'[3] and almost all these schools offered free tuition, board, and lodging to some at

---

1. The University conferred eight other degrees in the time of James I: the baccalaureates and doctorates in Divinity, Medicine, Civil Law, and Music. All but Divinity had very little importance in our period. There were no proper facilities for the study of 'physick' at Cambridge or Oxford; intending physicians either served an apprenticeship or studied at Leyden, Padua, or some other Continental university. The reformation made both the Civil and the Canon Law historical studies of no direct professional value; the common lawyers had what amounted to a law school of their own, at the Inns of Court. The music degrees, toward which no instruction was provided, were little regarded and seldom taken. At least nine-tenths of the time and energy at the University was bestowed on the Arts course, which is the only one which concerned the founders of Harvard. Only two of them, Chauncy and Cotton, proceeded B.D., and none went so far as D.D. The University provided no instruction for these Divinity degrees, other than the lectures of the Regius professor; but it required a residence of seven years after the M.A. before the B.D. could be taken, and five more for the D.D.

2. A. F. Leach, *The Schools of Mediaeval England* (1915) and *Educational Charters and Documents* (1911); Foster Watson, *The English Grammar Schools* (1908).

3. Venn, *Alumni Cantab.*, I. xv.

least of their scholars. Methods of teaching had been considerably improved since the renaissance, but the curriculum for the most part was still confined to Latin Grammar and Literature, with a smattering of Greek. Latin was the language of instruction; Lily's 'Grammar' and Colet's 'Accidence' the common text-books. With this classical equipment and a little elementary ciphering, the schoolboy went up to the University.

Despite these many years' training, Latin was no longer, in 1600, the sole language of instruction at Cambridge. The greater part of the text-books, many of the lectures, and all the disputations were in Latin, but English was the medium of communication between the tutor and his pupils. Sidney Sussex, founded in 1596, omitted the usual statutory prohibition of the mother tongue; [1] and a few years later it was reported to Archbishop Whitgift, among other common breaches of the university statutes, that Latin was 'altogether neglected.' [2] Curiously enough, the disuse of speaking Latin distressed not only Bishop Laud but the puritans, who both at Harvard and at Oxford during the protectorate made strenuous and largely ineffectual attempts to revive the medieval practice. [3]

Roger Ascham regarded seventeen as the proper age for a boy to enter the University; probably the average age in his time was somewhat lower. [4] There was no entrance examination: a boy could enter whenever he or his schoolmaster could convince a college tutor that he had enough Latin to go on with; and in the Stuart period there were not a few bright lads who were able to do this before adolescence. Of the future New Englanders whose birthdays are known, 45 were admitted to a college or matriculated in the University [5] under seventeen years of age:

1. G. M. Edwards, *Sidney Sussex College*, p. 39.

2. Peacock, *Observations*, p. 61 n.

3. Henry L. Thompson, *Christ Church*, pp. 76–77; Montagu Burrows, *Register of the Visitors of the University of Oxford* (Camden Society, 1881), pp. xcvi–xcviii, 249, 266, 320; Mullinger, III. 368.

4. Of 132 regent masters enumerated in 1572, the ages range from 21 to 28. As a regent must have been at least seven years in the University, and might have been twelve, it is clear that the average age of those men at entrance must have been nearer 15 than 17. Dr. Venn's introduction to *Grace Book* Δ (Cambridge, 1910), p. viii. Around 1550, the colleges allowed mere children of eleven and twelve to enter, and put them through a course of Latin Grammar before inducting them into higher studies; but as the University filled up again, this practice was discouraged.

5. The two things are not the same: a student was often 'admitted' before he actually came into residence, and if his preparation upon arrival was found defective, he might reside in college some time before matriculation in the University. But generally

24 were seventeen years old, 13 were eighteen, and 25, including John Harvard, were over eighteen.[1]

THE COLLEGE TUTOR

There was no fixed and rigid Arts curriculum at Cambridge in this period. Apart from certain books prescribed in the statutes, every tutor had liberty to make up his own programme. We are fortunate in having preserved one of these, the 'Directions for a Student in the Universitie,' drawn up by Dr. Richard Holdsworth for his own pupils.[2] The author, born in 1590, became fellow of St. John's in 1613, and remained a fellow and tutor in that college until 1637, when he was elected Master of Emmanuel. As that appointment indicates, Holdsworth was a moderate puritan,[3] who remained royalist when the issue was joined between loyalty and rebellion. Holdsworth's programme, therefore, must represent what many of the founders of Harvard studied, and what they doubtless wished to have studied by Harvard undergraduates.

A college tutor at that time had almost absolute control over his pupils, with whom his relation was more than paternal. He seldom had more than six pupils,[4] and usually less; for he was supposed to spend much time on his own studies. He might be

---

speaking he matriculated as soon as possible, in order to begin his statutory terms of residence for the B.A. Where both dates are known, I have used the earlier to calculate freshmen's ages.

1. See Appendix B for data on which this calculation is based.

2. Ms., Emmanuel College Library. The 'Directions' check up very closely with the account of a student's reading given in *Autobiography and Correspondence of Sir Simonds d'Ewes* (J. O. Halliwell ed., 2 vols., 1845), who was one of Holdsworth's pupils between 1619 and 1622. The manuscript appears to have been written between 1647 and the author's death in 1649, but to be the revision of a programme used by him when actively tutoring. Holdsworth was Master of Emmanuel College from 1637 to 1643, when he was ejected by the Roundheads and imprisoned for a year. He never returned to Cambridge, and died in 1649. It does not seem probable that he would have begun his 'Directions' after 1643, yet he could not have finished them before 1647, when one of the books mentioned, Ross's *Mystagogus Poeticus*, first appeared. Apart from that, the most recent book that I have noticed appeared in 1633. Another contemporary tutor's 'Advice on the Choice and Reading of Books' for a theological student is in the Mss. of St. John's College, Cambridge, 36-K, p. 197 (M. R. James, *Catalogue of Mss. in the Library of St. John's*, no. 347).

3. In addition to the evidence of his Emmanuel appointment, Holdsworth recommended the works of puritan divines such as Perkins and Sibbes to his pupils, and he was highly esteemed by his pupil Sir Simonds d'Ewes, a friend and connection of the Winthrops who sympathized with, while he did not take part in, the emigration to New England.

4. Mullinger, ii. 397–98. A very popular tutor might have as many as twenty.

highly conscientious, or otherwise. 'Most tutors I have known,' wrote a Cambridge graduate in 1646, 'if they read twice a day and took account of that,[1] held themselves sufficiently discharged of their trust; few did so much.' [2] He might teach his pupils in a class, or individually. But, in any case, one or more pupils shared his chamber, his compensation was a matter of personal arrangement with their parents, and he was responsible to the College for all their bills. Forth Winthrop, when a sophomore at Emmanuel College in 1627, wrote to his father, the future Governor of Massachusetts Bay: 'My Tutor beinge at London I hoped he had spoken with you, consearninge our quattridge . . . he tould me that we weare behinde with him 3 *li*. 13 *s*., and now another month is come in since, which maketh it vp 4 *li*. If you will send vs mony for him you may safly deliuer it to Hobson the Cambridge Carrier [3] by whome I send vp now markinge the letter for a mony letter.' [4] And Simonds d'Ewes, on leaving the University, notes: 'My loving and careful tutor Mr. Holdsworth, accompanied me home, not only to perform the last loving office to me, but to receive some arrearages due to him upon his bills.' [5]

THE DAILY PROGRAMME AND METHODS OF STUDY

Before examining the Arts programme of this loving and careful tutor, let us see how the student's day was divided, and where he found time for the five hours' reading which Holdsworth considered the minimum for a degree candidate. The day began at five with morning chapel, which was followed twice or thrice a week by commonplaces, ten- or fifteen-minute sermons delivered by candidates for the M.A. and B.D. degrees. At five-thirty or six came 'morning bever,' a breakfast of bread and

1. He means reading a lecture and holding a *repetitio* or quiz on it the same day.
2. J. E. B. Mayor (ed.), *Autobiography of Matthew Robinson*, p. 97.
3. Thomas Hobson, immortalized by Milton's epitaph, and by the phrase 'Hobson's choice,' referring to his custom of requiring a customer to take the freshest horse, which was placed nearest the stable door. He was the principal means of communication between Cambridge and the outside world and a noted character in the university town, and his stable was a favorite lounging place for the undergraduates. In a well-known Cambridge text-book, also used at Harvard, we find: 'God hath provided Speech, to be an *Hobson*, or Carrier, between man and man.' Alex. Richardson, *Logicians School-Master* (1657), Grammatical Notes, p. 1.
4. *Winthrop Papers*, I. 348.
5. *Autobiography*, I. 147–48.

beer consumed in the college buttery or in the student's chamber. The hours from breakfast to eleven o'clock dinner were devoted to lectures and study. Following dinner in hall came an hour for recreation. At one o'clock the student was supposed to retire to his study for two or three hours, unless he attended public disputations in the schools. At three or four he took another bite of bread and draught of beer, and then amused himself until supper at five or six o'clock. After supper came another period of relaxation, which would be spent around the hall fire in winter, or strolling in the garden or bowling on the green in summer. Students were not expected to read during the evening, in that era of crude lighting. At seven or eight o'clock the conscientious tutor assembled his pupils in his chamber for an hour's improving conversation, and packed them off to bed after leading them in evening prayer.[1]

Holdsworth offers good advice about methods of study. The student must take classified notes of everything he reads and of all lectures that he attends; and he should copy into notebooks any Latin and Greek idioms, epigrams, and turns of phrase which might be useful in themes and disputations. The Latin classics he should 'get without book,' that is without lexicon, reading them over several times in order to grasp the meaning and acquire the habit of thinking Latin; but he is not expected to read Greek thus. Almost all the Greek books used at Cambridge in his time were printed with a Latin translation facing every page of text.

In his curriculum, Holdsworth compromises between the old learning and the new by devoting his pupils' mornings to logic and the three philosophies; afternoons to humane letters and history. The morning programme offers no essential improvement over the medieval curriculum. There is no trace in it of the new science of the seventeenth century. In this respect, as Milton complained in his tractate 'Of Education' (1644), the universities were

not yet well recover'd from the Scholastick grosnesse of barbarous ages, that instead of beginning with Arts most easie, and those be such as are most obvious to the sence, they present their young unma-

---

1. This summary is based on Peacock's account of the Trinity College day given in his *Observations*, pp. 5–8, and on the manuscript Emmanuel College Order Book of *c.* 1600.

HOBSON THE CARRIER

triculated novices at first comming with the most intellective abstractions of Logick & metaphysicks: So that they having but newly left those Grammatick flats & shallows . . . to be tost and turmoild with their unballasted wits in fadomles and unquiet deeps of controversie, do for the most part grow into hatred and contempt of learning.[1]

Since they had to be got through, in order to satisfy the University statutes, these difficult and abstract studies were attacked by Holdsworth's students in the morning. Afternoons were reserved for *bonae litterae*: the pleasant arts of Rhetoric, History, Oratory, and Poetry:[2]

Studies not less necessarie than the first, if not more usefull, especialy Latine, and Oratory, without which all the other Learning, though never so eminent, is in a manner voide and useless. Without those you will be baffled in your disputes, disgraced and vilified in Publick examinations, laught at in speeches, and Declamations, you will never dare to appear in any act of credit in your University, nor must you look for Preferment by your Learning only.

TERMS AND 'YEARS'

Holdsworth's curriculum is divided into the four years required for the B.A., and subdivided into four quarters or terms. The four terms according to the Elizabethan statutes[3] were:

1. Michaelmas Term, October 10 to December 16.
2. Hilary, or Lent Term, January 13 to the decade before Easter.
3. Easter Term, eleventh day after Easter to Friday after Commencement, which came on the first Tuesday of July.
4. Vacation Term, from Friday after Commencement to October 10.

Of these, only the first three counted as residence for a degree. During the Vacation Term 'propter intemperiem coeli et pestis

1. 1644 ed., p. 2. And the complaint of another puritan educational reformer, John Hall, declares that freshmen are 'racked and tortured with a sort of harsh abstracted logicall notions, which their wits are no more able to endure, then their bodies the Strapado, and to be delivered over to a jejune barren Peripatetick Philosophy, suited onely (as *Mounsieur Des-Cartes* sayes) to wits that are seated below Mediocrity.' *An Humble Motion to the Parliament of England* (1649), p. 26.

2. This appears to have been the usual practice at Cambridge. Matthew Robinson, *c.* 1645, 'fixed upon a settled resolve, to study seven hours per day at least: four of these hours he spent in philosophy, his morning study; the afternoon hours he devoted *litteris amœnioribus*. . . .' *Autobiography* (1856 ed.), p. 19.

3. *Docs. Univ. Camb.*, 1. 455–56. The names (except Vacation Term) are not given in the Statutes, but are found in numerous contemporary accounts.

atque contagionis pericula' no university lectures or disputations were held; but the colleges continued to function, and all fellows and scholars on the foundation, together with such pensioners and others who chose to pay the fees, remained in residence, studying as usual.[1]

According to the *Quadriennium* memoir that President Dunster addressed to the Harvard Board of Overseers in 1654,[2] the four 'years' at Cambridge, corresponding to the four 'classes' at Harvard, began in Easter Term, in order to synchronize with the bachelors' commencement and determinations in Lent.[3] Hence it was at the beginning of Easter Term that the undergraduate had one, two, three, or four years to go. The students of these four 'years,' according to Dunster, were in his time called *recentes* (freshmen), *sophomori*[4] (sophomores), *juniores sophistae* (junior sophisters), and *seniores sophistae* (senior sophisters). Freshmen who matriculated at any time in Easter Term, even in the first week of July, were allowed to 'count' it for residence; hence that term was the most popular one for entering the University.[5] But Holdsworth's Directions presuppose that a freshman would enter by the first of January, as John Harvard did,[6] and therefore spend five regular terms and one summer vacation before he became a sophomore.

1. Several examples are given in Matthew Robinson's *Autobiography*.

2. *C. S. M.*, xxxi. 279–300.

3. This was the Paris custom (see Chapter II), and was doubtless kept up because the Schools were in use for other purposes later in the year. The 'Great' or proper Commencement in July was for the M.A. and higher degrees.

4. Dunster's is one of the earliest known uses of this word, the only earlier one known to me being a document of 1622 quoted in John Nichols, *Progresses, Processions of King James I*, iv. 1114: 'The young Scholars were placed from Jesus College gate next the street unto Trinity College gates in this manner: the Freshmen, Sophmoors, and Sophisters . . .; the Bachelors of Arts. . . .' Apparently *sophomore* was just coming into use in the early seventeenth century, and in England it died out by the early nineteenth. The literal meaning is probably 'one who is doing *sophismata* or sophomes,' a word which originally meant the public disputations of sophisters (see Chapter II), but by Elizabeth's reign was used for college disputations as well. Presumably the second-year student had to acquit himself well in these college sophomes before he was promoted.

5. Of the 79 Cambridge men in Appendix B whose dates of entry or matriculation are known, 17 entered in Michaelmas Term, 8 in Hilary Term, 51 in Easter Term, and 3 in the Vacation Term. Students generally matriculated in the University a few days after they entered their college; but there was no opportunity for matriculating during the vacation.

6. John Harvard was admitted in December, 1627, probably coming into residence after Christmas, and did not take his B.A. until February, 1631–32; Dunster, who had entered in Easter Term, 1627, was able to take his B.A. a whole year earlier than John Harvard.

HOLDSWORTH'S PROGRAMME FOR THE B.A.

Holdsworth's freshman begins his first winter term by copying a 'system' or synopsis of Logic, preferably one drawn up by his own tutor. This method of beginning one of the Liberal Arts went back at least to the thirteenth century, and was practised at Harvard well into the eighteenth. Having copied the 'system,' the freshman discusses it with his tutor. He then takes up a printed *systema majus Logicæ*, for which Holdsworth recommends *Burgersdicius,[1] a Dutch logician who was a great favorite at Harvard for a century. This text-book is to be read by the student without the help of his tutor; 'only as you read it you must gather some short notes out of it,' in this wise:

Ex Burgerdicij Logica

1. Unde dicitur logica? λόγος ἐνδιάθετος, et προφορικός.
2. Logica alio nomine Dialectica. Unde dicta? Dialectica universaliter et particulariter. Logica naturalis, habitualis systematica.
3. Quomodo probatur Logicam esse artem, et non scientiam? Quid est Ars?
4. ποιεῖν non semper significat actionem ex palpabili materia vel opus manens.
   Logicae finis duplex.
   Logica docens et utens. Quid sunt. Quaenam sunt officia docentis? utentis?
5. Objecta primaria et secundaria utriusque.
6. Pars Logicae Thematica, organica, etc.

By this time it is Easter Term, and the freshman logician must begin to study logical controversies out of authors such as †Brerewood, †Eustachius, the *Collecteana Complutense,* and the Coïmbra commentary on Aristotle's Logic. He is to select one question after another, and find out what each author says about it, and 'gather the sum, and substance of it in to your Paper-book.' The month of June 'I would have you to bestow in reading one Systeme more of Logick,' for 'by this time you will come to read Logick with more eas, and delite' (surely an

---

1. In order to avoid unnecessary annotation, I have marked with an asterisk those books in Holdsworth's list that we later find in use at Harvard College (see *H. C. S. C.*, Chapters VI–XII), and with a dagger those books that were in the library that John Harvard left to the College (*C. S. M.*, XXI, 190–230).

optimistic prediction); the authors recommended are *†Kecker-mann, Crackinthorp, *Pierre du Moulin, or Saunderson. Dur-ing the Vacation Term, 'begine to dispute by course in your Tutors Chamber, and so continue . . . as long as your Tutor shall think it necessarie.'

In Michaelmas Term the freshman takes up Ethics, after much the same method as in Logic. A minor system, which 'your Tutor will read . . . to you, and dispatch it in a fortnight, or three weeks time'; and a major system, for which *†Eusta-chius is recommended, with disputations in his tutor's chamber.

During the last term of this long freshman year, the student begins Physics by the same method: first 'a short Physick Sys-tem' with his tutor, then 'reading some other allone, as *†Ma-girus, †Eustachius, or the like,' taking notes as in *Burgers-dicius' Logic.

So much for the morning studies of freshman year. The *studia pomeridiana* are most interesting to us, as they doubtless were to our student. He begins with *Thomas Godwyn's *Ro-manae Historiae Anthologia*, in order to acquaint himself 'with the manners and Customes of the Romans'; that done, he goes through Justinus' epitome of general history. During the next term, 'towards the gaining of the purity of the Latine style,' he reads some of *†Cicero's Letters, *†Erasmus's Colloquies, and *†Terence's Comedies, spending a month on each; gathering phrases and epigrams into his 'paper-book,' and 'making Latine exercises' — writing letters when he is reading Tully, stories when doing Erasmus, and the like. During his summer after-noons, the freshman reads *Mystagogus Poeticus* [1] and Ovid's Metamorphoses as introduction to classical mythology, and spends one or two afternoons poring over maps of Greece and the Roman Empire in order to get classical geography clear in his mind. During September he warms up for the more serious studies of the academic year by reading the *Greek Testament. October and November afternoons are to be spent on such colloquies of Erasmus and 'Tullis Epistles' as he shall not have

---

1. 'Before you read Ovid's Metamorphoses it will be requisite to run over some book of Mythology. Natalis Comos is somewhat too large, and tedious Sir Francis Bacon too short. I direct to this as most convenient.' Alexander Ross's *Mystagogvs Poeticvs, Or The Muses Interpreter* was first published in 1647; the Harvard College Library has a copy of the 'second Edition much inlarged,' 1648. It is shot through with edifying com-ments; Ross could discover moral precepts even in the stories of Hermaphroditus and Priapus.

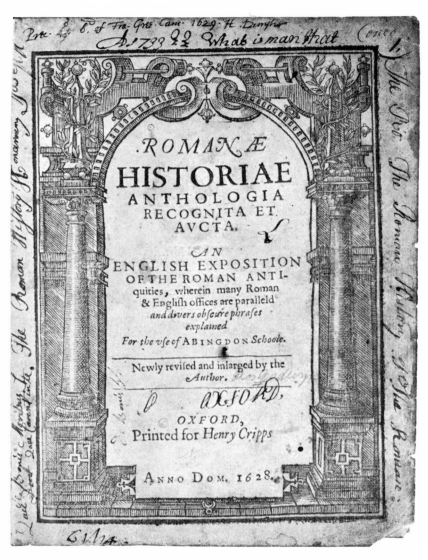

.ROMANÆ
HISTORIAE
ANTHOLOGIA
RECOGNITA ET
AVCTA.

AN
ENGLISH EXPOSITION
OF THE ROMAN ANTI-
quities, wherein many Roman
& English offices are paralleld
and divers obscure phrases
explained
For the vse of ABINGDON Schoole.

Newly revised and inlarged by the
Author.

OXFORD,
Printed for Henry Cripps

ANNO DOM. 1628.

TITLE-PAGE TO PRESIDENT DUNSTER'S COPY OF GODWYN'S
ROMANAE HISTORIAE ANTHOLOGIA

read during the summer; and in December he is to take up his Greek lexicon again and go through the poetry of *Theognis of Megara.

'Gramers must not be forgotten,' begin the instructions for January; 'it is now a year agoe or more since you came from schoole, and unless you look over them now and then, you shall perceave them to slip out of your memory.' How many of us have observed the same! 'After the Latine Gramer, read Valla' (†Lorenzo Valla's *de Elegantia*); the second half of the term is devoted to a Greek grammar, followed by François Viger's *de Idiotismis praecipuis Linguae Graecae*. And so we come to the sophomore year.

Since a principal duty of the sophomore was to develop his forensic powers in preparation for the sophomes, Holdsworth orders him to spend the mornings of his first two terms on controversies in Ethics, Physics, and Metaphysics, as he had spent the previous year on those in Logic. A variety of scholastic manuals containing the appropriate Aristotelian texts, with extensive glosses arguing almost every controversial point, are recommended: Burgersdicius, *†Eustachius, and Morisanus [1] in Ethics; †Egidio Colonna, Piccolomini,[2] *†Wendelin, Bento Pereira, and the *Doctors of Coïmbra in Physics; Pedro de Fonseca, †Eustachius, *Suarez, and †Christopher Scheibler in Metaphysics. Michaelmas Term is to be spent on all manner of controversies: the sophomes in college hall. *†Julius Caesar Scaliger's *de Subtilitate*, that abusively witty attack on the new science, is recommended for the last term of sophomore year.

The sophomore's afternoon studies are definitely classical: for Easter Term, †Cicero's *de Senectute, de Amicitia*, and *de Oratore*, and †Aesop's Fables; for Vacation, *Florus, *†Sallust, and Quintus Curtius; for Michaelmas Term, a heavy stint: Virgil's Eclogues and Georgics; Ovid's Heroides; Horace, Martial, *Hesiod, and *Theocritus.

Allow to each of these a fortnight, in which time I doe not expect you should read every one of them over, but . . . only as much as you can in the time alotted. I direct you to so many rather then one or

---

1. Bernardus Morisanus (a philosopher of Derry in Ireland), *in Aristotelis logicam, physicam, ethicam commentarii* . . . Francfort, 1625. There is a copy of this work in the Harvard College Library Catalogue of 1723.

2. Presumably Francesco Piccolomini, *Commentarii in libros Aristotelis de Coelo, Ortu et Interitu* (1608).

two, only because they are such books as no Scholar ought to be
ignorant of. . . . In them you will meet with many choice and witty
sayings, sentences, and passages, which you are to gather into your
paperbook, which you have for such things. . . . Use no Coment in
reading them, except some short one in Horace, and Martial: long
Comments spend much time, creat tediousness, and the benefit is not
answerable.

In Horace, after a day or two in the odes, spend the rest of the time
in the Sermons, Epistles, and *de Arte Poetica*, the Latine and Matter
both, being more useful then in the Odes. In Martial, take those Epigrams which are mark'd for good ones by *Farnaby, passing ouer the
obscene and scurrilous.

The sophomore is advised to spend the first hour of the afternoon in reading Horace and Martial at sight, which will 'raise
your fancie to a Poetick straine.' And, as a final preparation
for his public disputations, he is to spend the afternoons of
final term on *Causinus' *de Eloquentia*, which 'will give you the
grounds of Oratory a knowledge very usefull, and necessary, not
only in all professions of learning, but in any course of life whatsoever, though generaly neglected.' It will teach him how to
manage a discourse, how to move men's affections or quiet their
passions; the *Progymnasmata of Aphthonius may well be
used with Causinus. The sophomore must also practise orations — the declamations in hall required by most college
statutes.

If the undergraduate has proceeded so far to the satisfaction
of his tutor, he is created sophister by the head lecturer of his
college. This means that he may take part in the public or university disputations with members of other colleges.[1]

Holdsworth lays out a stiff programme for the junior sophister in the mornings of his first two terms, and his vacation:
*Aristotle's *organon*, *Physica*, and *Ethica*. 'The reading of
Aristotle will not only conduce much to your study of Controversy, being read with a Comentator but also help you in Greeke,
and indeed crown all your other learning, for he can hardly de-
serve the name of a Scholar, that is not in some measure acquainted with his works. Gather short memorial notes in Greek
out of him, and observe all his termes.' In Hilary Term, the
junior sophister is to read some work on natural science such as

1. According to Dunster's Quadriennium memoir, this privilege was withheld until
Hilary Term, doubtless for lack of space during a period of rising enrolment.

Seneca's *Naturales Quæstiones*, or Lucretius. 'The reading these books will furnish you with quaint and handsome expressions, for your Acts, to qualifie the harshnes and barbarisme of Philosophical termes.'

Afternoon studies of the junior sophister begin with *†Cicero's and Demosthenes' Orations, 'as many as you can with ordinary diligence and assiduity.' In July 'you come to some more raised and pollished' authors, 'the reading wherof will worke your fancy to such a kinde of expression when occasion is.' Begin with the *Prolusiones* [1] of Famiano Strada, and for variety's sake try *Barclay's *Argenis*, [1] *Euphormio*, or Petronius Arbiter's *Satyricon* [1] 'of the same kinde of stile, . . . for Latine as Sir Philip Sydnie is for English.' Robert Turner's *Orationes XVI* should be read in August, 'to acquaint you with Modern Oratorie,' Quintilian's Orations in September; Juvenal, Persius, Claudian, the Aeneid, and the *Iliad in Michaelmas Term. History, 'a most usefull and necesarie studie,' is begun in Hilary Term with the *Italia* and *Germania Antiqua* (1624) of Philip Cluvier; and as much of Livy and Suetonius 'as you have time to spare for after you have done Cluverius.'

It is not likely that the junior sophister will then have much time to spare, at least during the latter part of term; for during Lent, unless he be very stupid, he will be chosen by some determining Bachelor of his college as attendant sophister. He must spend every afternoon helping the determiner defend his theses, when attacked by arrogant Bachelors of Arts; and the proctors will set him disputing with the junior sophisters from other colleges. Since it was largely his performance in these exercises that determined his standing at graduation, and his chances of preferment, it is no wonder that so much of the student's training was pointed toward forensic skill.

The senior sophisters' own disputations, the medieval *sophismata*, began in the afternoons of Easter Term.[2] One of themselves moderated;[3] but of course there were M.A.'s present to criticize the performances. Each sophister must keep four 'Acts' — twice defending *quæstiones* which were posted up in advance

1. These works are found in the first catalogue of the Harvard College Library (1723).
2. Dunster's Memoir; the Elizabethan statutes, cap. xxii, say Michaelmas Term, but probably by Dunster's time the larger number of students required an earlier beginning.
3. The Moderator in 1623 was John Knowles (see Appendix B).

on the doors of the Sophister School; twice opposing them. In the meantime, he will be reading *Aristotle's *de Anima* and *de Coelo* in the mornings of Easter Term, the *Meteorologia* in summer (both with commentaries), and Wendelin's compendium of Divinity in Michaelmas Term. The ambitious tutor hopes he may also find time to 'run over some short Compendium of the Speculative part of Medecine, . . . as allso to read cursorily over Justinian's Institutions,' which 'might be done in a fortnight'; Aulus Gellius's *Noctes Atticae*, which will furnish him with 'handsome passages . . . usefull either for speeches, or common discourse among Scholars'; Macrobius' *Saturnalia*, and 'Plautus, or some part of him . . . but never immitate his latine'; †Cicero's *de Officiis* and *de Finibus*; a month on the *Iliad and Odyssey, and a fortnight each to *Seneca's Tragedies, †Lucan, and Statius.

BACCALAUREATE CEREMONIES

That brings the senior sophister to his final term, for which Holdsworth mercifully sets no reading. For it is now that he undertakes the many and (one would suppose) exhausting 'Acts,' ceremonies, and payments for his first degree. These were still much as they had been at Paris in the thirteenth century. One can only describe here the principal and essential steps, omitting the numerous litanies and sermons, fees, feasts, and tips (such as gloves, figs, and raisins to the bedels) with which every step was punctuated.

In his last Hilary Term, each senior sophister was examined by his college authorities, and if considered ready, presented to the Vice-Chancellor as a candidate. He was then given his oral university examination in the schools by the 'posers' (examiners) and other regent masters. If they were satisfied, he subscribed to the 'Three Articles' *in suo grege*,[1] and was then presented, with the proper *supplicat* from his college, to the University Senate, where he was passed by *placets* from the Masters in Arts — or, rarely, rejected by *non-placets*. At the conclusion of the voting, each senior sophister was presented kneeling to the Vice-Chancellor, who admitted him 'to the Question' with this formula:

1. The *grex* (flock) consisted of those students of the same college who graduated in the same year. Two photographs of the signatures of *greges* that included future founders of New England will be found among our illustrations.

In Dei Nomine, Amen. Authoritate nobis commissa admittimus Te ad respondendum Quæstioni; in nomine Patris, Filii, et Spiritus Sancti.[1]

The senior sophister now becomes a 'Questionist,' a term also used at Harvard in the early days;[2] and his B.A. degree was dated from his admission as a questionist; but he still had duties to perform before his baccalaureate would be considered full and complete.

First he must 'respond to the Question' or 'enter his Priorums,' that is, to answer a few perfunctory questions from Aristotle's Prior Analytics. He now ceases to be a questionist and becomes a determining bachelor. Determinations, the final exercises for the B.A., begin with a formal *sermo ad clerum* and assembly in the Schools on Ash Wednesday, and continue until Holy Week. Each determining bachelor must *stare in Quadragesima*, that is hold himself in readiness in the Schools during Lent, in order to dispute with any regent master who cares to take him on, or with any other questionist or sophister set upon him by the proctors. This rite, and the next, were observed at Harvard. Finally, at the 'latter Act' or second Tripos Day, which fell on the Thursday before Palm Sunday, there took place the bachelors' Commencement, a formal and public disputation which opened with a prearranged argument between the Tripos and a determining B.A. The Tripos was a Bachelor of Arts especially chosen for his wit, and the subject of the disputation was selected to give his wit play.[3] Frequently he or the corresponding Praevaricator at the masters' Commencement abused their license, and were reprimanded by the authorities. After a sufficient number of determiners had exhibited their

---

1. Peacock, *op. cit.*, pp. lxvii–lxviii. This formula was used at Cambridge until 1858.

2. Statutes of 1650, in *C. S. M.*, xv. 28, 190; and of 1655, in xxxi. 334.

3. These are sample subjects of Tripos verses between 1590 and 1640: 'Mulier est ingeniosior quàm vir.' 'Nihil est gravius argento vivo.' 'Tres mihi Convivae propè dissentire videntur' (Sel. Mss. 1. 11.ff. 26, 27, University Library, Cambridge). 'Multitudo librorum est studiorum impedimentum.' 'Uxores ex Maritorum personis nobilitatem sortiuntur' (theses for the M.A. and B.C.L., Wood Mss. 276a, ff. 439a, 441b, Bodleian Library, Oxford). The Tripos (so called because he sat on a three-legged stool) cast his opening arguments into Latin verse, which were printed on broadsheets and distributed among the audience. In the eighteenth century the names of the ranking candidates were printed on the backs of the Tripos verses, as an honor list; and by a series of ellipses the term Tripos in Cambridge has come to mean a system of examinations for honors at graduation. We shall find the equivalent of the Tripos verses on some of the masters' *quaestio* sheets at Harvard. They survived at Cambridge until about 1895.

talents, the presiding proctor said, 'In Dei nomine, Amen. Authoritate qua fungimur, decernimus, creamus et pronunciamus omnes hujus anni determinatores finaliter determinasse, et actualiter esse in Artibus Baccalaureos.'[1]

Studia Leviora and Studies for the Master's Degree

Following his programme for the degree candidate, Dr. Holdsworth suggests certain *studia leviora* for 'such as come to the University not with intention to make Scholarship their profession, but only to gett such learning as may serve for delight and ornament and such as the want whereof would speake a defect in breeding rather then Scholarship.' The list of works for this gentleman's course includes Earle's *Microcosmographie*, books of travel, Burton's Anatomy of Melancholy, Sandys' translation of Ovid, Erasmus' *Encomium Moriæ*, More's Utopia, Suarez' Civil Conversations, poems by Crashaw, Herbert, and Buchanan, and the famous new short cut to languages, the *Janua Linguarum* of Comenius, who would shortly be suggested for the Harvard presidency. This pleasant course must have been followed by many fellow-commoners and others who were not candidates for a degree.

Hebrew is absent from Holdsworth's list,[2] because the study of that language was a part of the programme for the M.A., not the B.A., and had been so prescribed as early as 1549. Since the cultivation of Hebrew in early Harvard has been generally ascribed to a supposed puritan predilection for the

1. Rashdall, II. 441–42 nn.; Peacock, *Observations*, pp. iv–xv, lxv–lxxiii; *Hist. Reg. Univ. Camb.* (1917), pp. 348–54.

2. Mullinger, II. 111. It is a little surprising that Holdsworth says nothing about Hebrew, because his own college, by exception, required a smattering of it for undergraduates: 'It was ordered and appoynted by ioynt consent of the Seniors thatt all the Bachelors of Arts and Senior Sophisters residing in the Colledge shold be tyed to be diligent auditors of the Hebrew lecture read within the said Colledge. And that in case of negligence the Lecturer may mulct them as the Greeke Lecturer hath vsed a penny for every absence. And in regard that theese auditors assigned may be ignorant of the Hebrew tounge It was therefore further ordered that it shalbe lawfull for the said Lecturer att the first entrance into his lecture to read over the Grammar vnto them before he proceed to interpprett any Autor in that tounge.' Records of St. John's College, January 19, 1630, printed in the *Eagle*, xxiv. 171, and in R. F. Scott, *Notes from the Records of St. John's College*, 2d series, p. 18. Holdsworth was also instrumental in persuading Thomas Adams to found the first chair of Arabic at Cambridge. Mullinger, III. 95–96.

Old Testament,[1] it is important to note that Hebrew was highly regarded by advocates of the new learning, both as a key to the textual study of the Bible and as the mother of all tongues.[2] The English divines who gave us the King James Bible were excellent Hebraists, well versed in the entire field of rabbinic literature. Hebrew and Aramaic verses were ground out by ambitious Cantabrigians to impress Queen Elizabeth on her visit to the University in 1564,[3] and Sir Humphrey Gilbert even found a place for Hebrew in his proposed Academy. A Regius professorship of Hebrew was established by Henry VIII along with the professorship of Greek; and 'of the two languages, Hebrew undoubtedly received the larger share of attention' at Cambridge, where such distinguished scholars as Tremellius, Chevallier, and Edward Lively filled the Regius chair. Oxford had as good or better Hebraists;[4] yet Archbishop Laud declared in 1630 that 'the study of that language is too much neglected, and not without the great prejudice both of the University and the Church.'[5] On this point the New England puritans agreed with their persecutor, though possibly for different reasons.[6] William Bedwell, fellow of Trinity in Chauncy's time, advocated the study of Arabic, not only for its relation to the language of the Scriptures, and for the wealth of Arabic scientific and philosophical literature, but also — a surprisingly modern note — for its practical value as a living tongue in the East.[7] A chair of Arabic was estab-

1. This notion about the puritans is quite unfounded in fact, as K. B. Murdock has shown in 'The Puritans and the New Testament,' *C. S. M.*, xxv, 239–43.
2. Mullinger, III. 92; cf. *H. C. S. C.*, Chapter IX.
3. Cooper, *Annals*, II. 198.
4. Mullinger, II. 416, speaking of the period 1575–1625. In Mark Pattison's *Casaubon*, pp. 411–16, is related the diverting episode of Richard Kilbye, the Regius Professor of Hebrew, encouraging a young Jew to teach Elementary Hebrew, and staging his public conversion to Christianity. But the Jew decamped the day before. He was imprisoned, and finally banished from the University. 'It will be long,' wrote Kilbye, 'before another jew of such attainments comes among us. Had he but put on Christ, what an aid he might have been to hebrew studies in this place!' This was in 1613; cf. the Monis episode of Harvard in 1722, *Proc. M. H. S.*, LII. 297.
5. *Works* (1853 ed.), v. 19.
6. Laud's interest in Oriental languages was not wholly unselfish; he hoped to engage the Oxford and Cambridge fellows in transcribing, collating, and elucidating Oriental texts as a substitute for their favorite intellectual pursuit of controversial divinity.
7. Mullinger, III. 93–94.

lished at Cambridge in 1632 with Abraham Wheelock of Clare as the first incumbent; and four years later Laud founded the professorship of Arabic at Oxford, with Edward Pococke, Bedwell's pupil, in the chair.

Aside from Hebrew, Bachelors of Arts reading for the M.A. studied Theology, since nobody proceeded to his second degree unless he looked for a career in the Church, or to a college fellowship for which holy orders were required.[1] Bachelors of Arts who already had fellowships or hoped to win them continued to reside in college; the others were encouraged to leave in order to make place for new men, and to pursue their studies at home. These paid a discontinuance fee to the College, and returned three years later to 'enter their posteriorums'[2] and perform other acts and formalities required for the master's degree — a system which was adopted at Harvard.

ESTIMATE OF THE COURSE

Noteworthy is the entire absence of even the most elementary mathematical or scientific studies, other than Aristotelian Physics, from Dr. Holdsworth's curriculum.[3] Such studies were then looked upon in the universities as suitable for merchants, mariners, and almanac-makers rather than gentlemen and scholars, and in those colleges where the tradition of the Quadrivium was kept up the text-books were medieval.

In the age of Galileo and Kepler, and nearly a century from the time when Copernicus caught from the fantastic page of Martianus Capella the hint which guided him to his great discovery, the student at Cambridge and Oxford was still deriving his notions of the celestial system from the Σύνταξις of Ptolemy; and although no less a period had elapsed since Magellan and Vasco da Gama rounded the southern continents, he still turned for his cosmical theory to the *Timaeus* of

1. Venn, *Alumni Cantab.*, I. xiv.
2. Perfunctory questions and answers from Aristotle's Posterior Analytics.
3. Sidney Sussex College in 1634 provides that those who are to commence M.A. 'shall sit in the chappel as Questionists used to do, 2 hours a day for 3 days, there to be examined for triall of their sufficiency. And because the University Statute *de Bacc. Art.* c. 7 requires that such be *auditores Philosophicæ lectionis, Astronomiæ Perspectivæ et Græcæ linguæ*; it is judged fit that triall be made of their skill therein, beside other things suited with their degree.' Ms. 'Extracts from the Collegii Dominæ Franciscæ Sidney Sussex Records,' Sidney Sussex muniment room. This exceptional gesture of respect to such relics of the quadrivium as were prescribed in the Elizabethan statutes was probably due to Samuel Ward, the conscientious Master of Sidney Sussex.

Plato, and for his geographical information to pagan writers of the first century.[1]

John Wallis, an eminent mathematician who was almost an exact contemporary of John Harvard at Emmanuel, never heard of the 'new or experimental philosophy' until 1645, when he left Cambridge and enjoyed, in London, the companionship of men who later formed the Royal Society.[2] This 'new philosophy' was first introduced in Cambridge by Isaac Barrow, who became fellow of Trinity in 1649, and was vigorously opposed by James Duport, one of the great men of John Harvard's day; whilst Edward Davenant 'could not endure to heare of the *New Philosophy*; "for," sayd he, "if a new philosophy is brought in, a new divinity will shortly follow."'[3] And Davenant was right.

Accordingly, the men who were educated at Cambridge by Holdsworth and his fellows came to New England with the most meagre and obsolete equipment in mathematics and natural science. Bacon's Essays and Advancement of Learning — but not his *Novum Organum* — came to Harvard College from her namesake's library; but it is doubtful if anyone who had to do with the founding of Harvard, except John Winthrop, Jr., had accepted Bacon's inductive and experimental method which was destined to revolutionize science and indeed all learning. Descartes' *Essais philosophiques* appeared at Leyden in 1637, and his views were being publicly taught, and attacked, in the Dutch universities within a year or two; but it is improbable that any of the university-trained founders of New England had studied Descartes. This was a serious handicap for a new college in the New World, whose means of communication with the centers of learning in the Old World were few.

According to our modern lights, Dr. Holdsworth's course afforded a severe training in Logic, Philosophy, the Latin and Greek Classics, and Latin Composition; but it was not calculated to breed inquiring minds. Only a creative intellect of the highest class, a Milton or a Newton, could rise superior to it.

1. Mullinger, II. 402.
2. John Ward, *Lives of the Professors of Gresham College* (1740), p. x. And it is noteworthy that John Pell, William Oughtred, and other good mathematicians who were educated at Cambridge in the late sixteenth or early seventeenth centuries did not obtain college fellowships, and had no further connection with the University.
3. John Aubrey, *Brief Lives* (1898 ed.), I. 201.

The great mass of Cambridge alumni probably assumed that the Ancients had said the last word on statecraft, the Schoolmen on philosophy, and the Reformers on divinity. It is gratifying to find in the opening statement of 'New Englands First Fruits'[1] the Baconian note that Harvard College was founded 'to advance *Learning* and perpetuate it to Posterity.' But the first generation at Harvard had no means or opportunity to advance learning, in the Baconian sense. They were too much engrossed in a desperate struggle to save for a transplanted society menaced by poverty, indifference, and materialism their cultural inheritance from the past. To establish *in silvestribus et incultis locis* a respect for learning was work enough for the first generation. Time and intelligence, the destroyers of all systems and certainties, could be trusted to render obsolete most of the doctrines that Dr. Holdsworth had inculcated in all sincerity and devotion. And so far as the University of Cambridge had introduced her children destined for New England to the best minds of antiquity, she had made them, through all wilderness toils and pains, companions of the deathless muses.

1. Appendix D.

V

THE FOUNDERS AND THEIR COLLEGES: TRINITY [1]
1600–1640

 Cambridge in 1600 was a University of Colleges: a federal Republic of Letters where no one questioned the superiority of states over the nation. It was impossible to become a member of the University without being accepted by a tutor in one of the sixteen colleges,[2] each of which was a self-contained and independent unit as to instruction, buildings, finance, and internal discipline. Externally, the colleges have altered little since 1640, in comparison with the overwhelming changes in American university architecture during the last century. New buildings have been added, but most of the more comely and conspicuous are still those that were seen by John Harvard.

An enchanting scene it was in which the young men of England pursued their studies of humane letters. Not chance alone

1. Authorities for Chapters V–VII: in addition to those mentioned under Chapter III, John and J. A. Venn, *Alumni Cantabrigienses, Part I* (4 vols., 1922–27), is a remarkable compendium of Cambridge biography from the earliest times to 1751. For brief sketches of Cambridge alumni who emigrated to New England, see Appendix B to this volume. Cotton Mather, *Magnalia*, is indispensable for the New England Cantabrigians. In the series of Cambridge College histories, E. S. Shuckburgh, *Emmanuel* (1904), G. M. Edwards, *Sidney Sussex* (1899), and John Peile, *Christ's* (1902), are the most useful for us. Unfortunately there is no proper history of Trinity College, only W. W. Rouse Ball's little sketch *Trinity College* (1906), largely reprinted in his *Cambridge Papers* (1918); and the statutes which were in force in the seventeenth century are to be found only in an edition printed in 1773. Thomas Baker, *History of the College of St. John The Evangelist* (J. E. B. Mayor ed., 2 vols., 1869), was written in the seventeenth century. For the atmosphere and the college politics of the time, see Thomas Ball, *Life of Doctor Preston*, first printed in Samuel Clarke's *Generall Martyrologie* (1651) and later in a separate edition by E. W. Harcourt (1885); William Dillingham, *Vita L. Chadertoni* (1700), also an English translation by Shuckburgh, 1884; and John Hacket, *Memorial of John Williams, D.D.* (1693).

2. Six of these had been founded since 1500; there have been but two more founded since 1596: one of them Downing College, founded by and named after a great-grandson of Sir George Downing of the first Harvard graduating class.

makes Cambridge a delight to the senses. The earlier colleges might have been built, like Harvard, on dry upland, at some distance from the river. Instead, they appropriated the space between the principal road and the river, shouldering each other for street frontage, but preserving ample 'backs,' which slope down to the placid Cam in gardens and lawns, through which an occasional pile of brick or masonry thrusts a way to the water's edge; and across the river the colleges acquired fields which preserved their rural outlook. If anyone doubt that the English race have an aesthetic sense, let him glide down the short reach of river from Queens' to Magdalene on a golden morning of October, or in the purple dusk of a June evening, when greensward, flowers, foliage, and ancient buildings are fused as on an antique vase. Here at last one can grasp the full meaning of the phrase *alma mater*: a mother fair as she is wise, ageless and timeless, pouring out love and beauty with learning to the countless generations of children who have laid their heads on her bosom.

COLLEGE ARCHITECTURE AND AMENITIES

Each college consisted of one or more quadrangles, or 'quadrants' as they were then called, the newer being open on one side to ensure an outlook and movement of air. None were over four stories high, including the ground floor, and most of them only three. The older or principal quadrant gave directly on a street, and was pierced by a more or less monumental gateway through which one entered the court. Usually on the opposite side of the court was the hall, separated from the kitchen, buttery, and pantries by a through-passage leading into a second court, or into the gardens. The hall was the heart and center of the college, where all the members assembled for commons, lectures, and disputations. One entered it from the through-passage by openings in a carved wooden screen. At the opposite end was a dais for the high table where the fellows dined, and which also served as a stage when plays were presented. In winter the hall had some of the chill taken from the air by a log fire on a hearth in the middle, the smoke, or some of it, escaping through louvres in the roof. The floor was strewn with rushes, which were periodically gathered up with the accumulated dirt, and burned.

The Master's Lodging, a self-contained dwelling house (since masters alone of college fellows were allowed to marry and keep a family), was generally adjoined to the dais end of the hall. On the ground floor of it, entered by a door behind the high table, was the parlor,[1] to which the fellows adjourned after commons to converse and warm themselves at the fire. Another side of the principal quadrant usually incorporated the college chapel, which (until Archbishop Laud forbade it) was also used for lectures, disputations, and even college plays. On a middle floor, to prevent damp, was the college library, where all the folios and other valuable books were chained, and to which undergraduates were granted only a grudging and occasional access. There were no laboratories and classrooms in the Oxford and Cambridge colleges until long after Harvard was founded; no administrative quarters other than small offices for the Bursar and Steward. The rest of the buildings were divided into chambers, arranged two to a floor on each side of a staircase, following a medieval tradition which has been continued at Harvard and other American universities.[2] An important principle, the neglect of which has made American imitations of English college architecture unsatisfactory, was to construct buildings only one room deep, so that every chamber had windows on opposite sides, and plenty of sunlight. Two, three, or even four students, one of them a fellow or B.A., slept in each chamber; but privacy was provided by small studies partitioned off from the ends, each lighted by at least part of a window.[3]

Colleges provided a place for recreation, as well as living quarters and instruction. In the courts a crude and rough game of football was played. When Oliver Cromwell entered Sidney Sussex College, in 1616, one of the older students was 'Sir Wheelwright,' who later became a famous minister in New England. Forty years later this gentleman visited England and waited on the Lord Protector at Whitehall. His Highness declared to the gentlemen about him 'that he could remember the time when he had been more afraid of meeting Whelewright at

1. Still so called at Emmanuel; but later called combination room at Cambridge and common room at Oxford.
2. In President Eliot's day the experiment was tried at Harvard of building dormitories, such as Weld and Perkins, with the rooms opening onto long corridors, as in hotels. The opportunities that this afforded for noise and disorder caused the authorities quickly to return to the traditional arrangement of separate staircases.
3. Cf. Chapter XX, below.

football, than of meeting any army since in the field; for he was infallibly sure of being tript up by him.' [1]

Several colleges had a tennis court on the model of the royal *jeux de paume* at Paris and Hampton Court; Emmanuel and Christ's built bathing pools in 1627; others had archery butts; and all but two or three enjoyed extensive lawns and gardens. A part of each garden was walled off as a bowling-green and orchard for the fellows' exclusive use. Christ's and Sidney Sussex by their situation were denied access to the Cam, but in compensation enjoyed an unobstructed view of open country; Jesus and Emmanuel were in the country itself, outside the town.

College Organization

At the head of the college was the Master,[2] a very important person in the academic world; in his own college, nothing could be done or concluded without his consent. Below him were the fellows, varying in number from six at St. Catharine's to sixty at Trinity; most of the colleges had from twelve to twenty. The Master and fellows in the smaller colleges, or the Master and a stated number of senior fellows in the larger, constituted the governing body, which controlled college property, discipline, studies, and the election of new members — except in so far as the King might interfere, or the University make inclusive regulations. Students' fees and rents or annuities from landed property constituted the colleges' revenues. Fellows enjoyed a small stipend, with free chamber and a fixed allowance for commons; and if there were any profits at the end of the year, they declared a dividend for their own benefit.[3] If they

1. Letter of Cotton Mather to George Vaughan, 1708, in Jeremy Belknap, *History of New Hampshire* (Boston, 1792), III. 339 (Ms. in M. H. S.). The records of Sidney Sussex show that Wheelwright was a resident bachelor from the date of Cromwell's entrance (April, 1616) until the summer of 1618.

2. The head of Queens' was called President, and the head of King's, Provost. At Oxford there was (and is) more variety in the titles of the heads of houses. The heads' stipends varied from £5 per annum for the Master of St. Catharine's to over £104 for the Master of Trinity College (Peacock, *Observations*, 113 n.); but they had many perquisites in addition. A curious one of the Master of Christ's was a 13s 6d 'fayring' or 'Sturbridge Fair money,' probably to buy books at that great summer fair of East Anglia. Samuel Ward, Master of Sidney Sussex, notes in his diary of personal shortcomings, 'My pride because so many at the Fayre asked my counsell in buying books.'

3. A fellow of St. John's in 1612 complains to the Master of poverty; he is getting only 26s 8d stipend and livery. St. John's cut no dividend until 1628. R. F. Scott, *Notes from Records*, no. III. 5–7.

CHARLES CHAUNCY'S NAME IN HIS 'ORDO SENIORITATIS,'
AND AT THE TOP OF HIS 'GREX'

did tutoring as well, they had their pupils' tuition fees. Fellows must take holy orders, and might if they chose retain their fellowships for life, even if they obtained lucrative benefices and resided far from Cambridge; but a fellowship was always vacated by marriage.

Below the fellows came the scholars or 'students on the foundation,' who received free lodging, about half the fellows' allowance for commons, and a small stipend. Some of the scholarships were tied to definite schools or counties; others were competed for by freshmen or other students already in the college. Next in importance, but taking precedence over scholars and even B.A.'s, were the fellow-commoners,[1] students whose fathers paid double fees for everything, and who dined at high table with the fellows. These 'university tulips' enjoyed many privileges, set the fashion, and seldom condescended to take degrees. Only five fellow-commoners emigrated to New England; yet the class was established at Harvard.

Most of our founders belonged to the next two classes of students: the pensioners or commoners,[2] who paid the normal fee; and the sizars or battelers,[3] who paid reduced fees. Sizars originally were students who performed the menial work in their colleges in return for free education; but the growth of wealth and luxury in the sixteenth century had largely replaced their somewhat inefficient ministrations by those of professional servants. This intrusion of paid menials was much resented, and the heads of houses issued a decree in 1625 to the effect that whereas 'boys and men ignorant of letters,' and even women, 'had crept within the college walls, to do those works which used to be done by indigent students to help to bear their charges; from whence great damage had accrued to poor scholars, and scandal to the University,' in the future none such

1. Called perhendinates (lit. 'tarriers') in some of the college statutes, and gentlemen-commoners or upper-commoners at Oxford, where some of the colleges had also recognized a separate class of 'noblemen.' Sidney Sussex in 1627 provided that noblemen should pay quadruple the normal pensioners' fees. Sir Simonds d'Ewes records that he, a studious fellow-commoner with no extravagant tastes, was just able to scrape through Cambridge on £50 a year. Presumably a pensioner could have done himself well on £40. Yet the high cost of college education was as much complained of then as now. See a father's lament in one of the college plays, *The Returne from Parnassus,* I. i.

2. For an explanation of these terms see above, p. 37 n.

3. The two words meant the same, and were derived from the word used at the respective universities for 'bevers' and other extras in the way of food and drink — the idea being that a sizar paid for his sizings, but not his commons.

were to be employed, unless personal body-servants, necessary cleaners, and sick-nurses; and they to 'be of mature age, good fame, and wives, or widows,' or if maids, at least fifty years old.[1] These efforts were unavailing, and the sizars were gradually displaced by the army of 'scouts,' 'bedders,' and 'gyps' who infest Oxford and Cambridge colleges today. The change was unfortunate, since it robbed poor boys who could not win a scholarship of opportunity for higher education, and made the colleges definitely aristocratic in tone. Both the name of sizar and his original functions were reproduced at Harvard, and although the name soon disappeared, American universities have fostered the tradition of student service.

We cannot, therefore, assume that a Cambridge sizar in 1600–40 performed menial service; but in most colleges, he still waited on the fellows' and scholars' tables in hall. In general, each fellow had a sizar, who served him as a *valet de chambre* and secretary, and in return received free tuition, at least part board, and perhaps 'livery' or clothing allowance. The Master was usually allowed two or more sizars to run his errands and write his letters — an institution that survived in the 'President's Freshman' at Harvard until 1870. At Trinity and St. John's there were subsizars who were similarly attached to fellow-commoners; but often one could find in the same college sizars who worked their way and others who were simply students paying half the normal pensioners' fees. As no stigma was attached to the rank at this period, and as a sizar had an equal chance with a pensioner of winning a scholarship or fellowship, youths of good family were apt to be entered sizars simply from economy. A good instance of this was that of the Davenport brothers at Oxford. Although members of an ancient family, and sons of an alderman of Coventry, they were entered battelers at Merton College, and dined in the kitchen. When the Warden, Sir Henry Savile, found out who they were, he offered them the alternative of becoming commoners, or leaving; their father chose the latter course, and entered them at Magdalen Hall. John in due course became vicar of a London parish, a convert to puritanism and, after emigrating to New England, a member of the first Harvard Board of Overseers, and founder of the New Haven Colony. Christopher went the other way, to Mother Church and Salamanca, whence he returned as chap-

1. Cooper, *Annals*, III. 181–82.

lain to Queen Henrietta Maria, and outraged Cambridge by entering a disputation with the Vice-Chancellor.[1]

Colleges were expected to dispense alms to outsiders, as well as charity to their own children. The 'Rewards and Extraordinaries' in the Stewards' accounts of Trinity College between 1622 and 1632 give a hint of the wretched misery abroad in that era of the Thirty Years' War, during which the English colleges seemed so peaceful and secure: —

Given unto a blind Irishman and his sonne toward their journey	ijs
Given unto 2 maymed souldiers of Bohemia	xviiid
Given unto 2 souldiers of the Palatinate	xviiid
Given unto Daniel Alexander a converted Jewe	xvs
Given unto a French gentleman schollar of Montaubon	vs
Given unto Eucharius Wilhelms a banished Minister of Bohemia	xiiis iiiid
Given unto a saylar redeemed from the Turkes	iis vid
Given to Mathew Newbold sometime of St Johns Coll. Mr. of Arts undone by the wilde Irish	xs
Given to a Muscovite that had suffered shipwrack	ijs
Given to James Coresey an Irish Gentn taken in a Duch bottome by the Dunkerks and landed at Douer	ijs
Given to 7 french men that were cast away in Frezeland	vs
Given to a poor old Joyner of this towne that had wrought in this college	vs
Given to Ann Parker an Irish ministers widdow whose Husband was slaine by the wood kernes	vs

In the social life of the students, there appear to have been no clubs or societies to destroy college solidarity. Privacy there was none, except in the tiny studies. In chapel, hall, and chamber, in college lectures, repetitions, and disputations, a Cambridge man was constantly rubbing shoulders with fellow-collegians; but he was not confined to his own college for friends. Forth Winthrop, for instance, kept in touch with several old

1. Anthony Wood, *Athenæ Oxon.* (1721 ed.), II. 460–62; *D. N. B.*; Cotton Mather, in *Magnalia*, book iii. 52, says that John Davenport was 'not a Brother (as a certain *Woodden* Historian, in his *Athenæ Oxonienses*, has reported) yet a Kinsman of that Sancta Clara,' and claims John Davenport for Brasenose College. The records bear Wood out.

schoolmates at different colleges; and Thomas Shepard, one morning after a drinking bout, woke up in Christ's College instead of his own Emmanuel. In the hours of recreation one might bowl or play tennis, stroll in college gardens or country fields, perhaps enjoy a surreptitious dip in the Cam, followed by ale at a country inn, or in a near-by village attend a forbidden show of strolling players, and indulge in leaping, wrestling, and throwing the bar.[1] Friday night was a great occasion for members of different colleges to get together. By a custom as old as the University, college kitchens furnished no supper that evening, when 'clerks' were supposed to fast. Although Friday fasting went out with the reformation, the cooks insisted on their hebdomadal rest; so the students had to buy supper with what pocket money they had, or could induce their tutors to advance. There was great crowding of the twopenny ordinaries, and much clubbing together to get up feasts at victualling houses and taverns. The sophisters' disputations and bachelors' determinations gave an opportunity for clever students to show off before the entire University; and the sermons at St. Mary's were university assemblies. We must remember that Cambridge around the year 1600 housed some three thousand students, hence we cannot assume that men resident at the same time knew one another. Still less are we justified in building fairy-tales of friendship — as between John Harvard and John Milton — on a mere coincidence of dates at different colleges.

TRINITY COLLEGE

In the year 1722 a loyal son of Harvard, Henry Newman (A.B. 1687), paid a visit to Cambridge, and was entertained at high table in Trinity College. Shortly after, he wrote to his friend Benjamin Colman (A.B. 1692), 'The Reverend Dr. Colebatch Senior Fellow of Trinity ... tells me they have some Memoires or Traditions in their College that our College sprang from them, or was found[ed] by Gent[lemen]

---

1. 'He never loved or used any games or ordinary recreations, either within doors, as cards, dice, tables, chess, or the like; or abroad, as buts, quoits, bowls, or any such: but his ordinary exercise and recreation was walking either alone by himself, or with some other selected companion, with whom he might confer and argue, and recount their studies.' *Two Answers to Cardinal Perron and other Miscellaneous Works of Lancelot Andrewes* (1854), p. vi.

educated there. I told him we should be glad to claim kindred with them, and by the name of Cambridge it is not to be doubted but our forefathers were Cantabrigians.'[1] Glad indeed to claim kindred with that noble and royal foundation which for three centuries led all the colleges of Cambridge, and in England was rivalled only by Christ Church, Oxford, for the splendor of her architecture and the distinction of her alumni. Moreover, there was a sound basis for this tradition cherished in Trinity during the better part of a century. The first head of Harvard College (Nathaniel Eaton) and the second President (Charles Chauncy) were Trinity men; and at Trinity were educated five of the first twelve Overseers of the College: Governor Winthrop, John Cotton, Hugh Peter, Thomas Weld, and John Humfrey.

Trinity College, founded in 1546 by Henry VIII, and sufficiently endowed with the spoils of the monasteries to support fifty fellows and sixty scholars, had already established a proud preëminence over her elder sisters under the mastership of Whitgift.[2] Thomas Nevile 'the Magnificent,' appointed Master in 1593, devoted energy and fortune to building up the College. In 1617 with 340 residents it was the largest in the University. The Great Court was completed under Nevile's direction. In 1604 the superb hall was begun. At that time one of the most promising scholars in residence was a certain John Cotton. The 'extraordinary charges' of building the hall were met only by dipping into fellowship funds; and this prevented Sir Cotton from being chosen fellow of Trinity.[3] Accordingly he migrated to Emmanuel, where we may follow him anon.

The most distinguished puritans connected with Trinity were the Winthrops of Suffolk. Adam Winthrop of Groton, the father of the Governor, had been a fellow-commoner at Magdalene. From 1593 to 1610 he made an annual visit to Cambridge to audit the accounts of St. John's and of Trinity,

1. Archives of the Society for the Promotion of Christian Knowledge (Northumberland House, London), New England Letters, 1, October 20, 1722. I am indebted to Mr. F. S. B. Gavin for calling my attention to these archives, and to the secretary of the S. P. C. K., Mr. W. K. Lowther Clarke, for allowing me to peruse them.

2. W. W. Rouse Ball, *Cambridge Papers*, p. 31; Mullinger, II. 470. In 1640 the College received from rents alone £3876, of which £1410 was in money, and the rest in wheat and malt. Ms. records, Trinity bursary.

3. *Magnalia*, book iii. 14–15.

an appointment which he doubtless owed to his double connection with John Still, Master successively of these two colleges.[1] In 1602, at the age of fourteen, John Winthrop entered pensioner at Trinity, where, if we may take literally his over-scrupulous record of spiritual experiences, he wasted precious time in vain pursuits. It is true that in his day the manners and customs of Trinity men were somewhat scandalous,[2] but the chapel services were puritan in character, and even Laud could not get the communion table moved to the east end until 1636. Trinity and the adjacent St. John's were keen rivals; when football matches between them were prohibited, they organized raids — in 1601 we hear of 'provision of stones layd up; and also of some bucketts to be provided to fetch water from her conduyt, to poure downne upon St. John's men.'[3] Living conditions appear to have been plain enough: the accounts for the scholars' and bachelors' table show 'boyld beafe' for dinner and 'rost mutton' for supper five days in the week — not until Friday and Saturday is there a change to buttered peas and spatchcocks. John Winthrop, like most gentlemen's sons who did not intend to take holy orders, left the College within two years; unlike most of them he married at the age of seventeen, and promptly experienced religion. His revulsion against youthful follies extended, apparently, to the scene of them, for John Winthrop, Jr. was sent to Trinity College, Dublin, and Forth, a younger son, to Emmanuel. Yet New England owes much to the elder Winthrop's education. Although not a learned man, and somewhat suspicious of 'heathen authors,' the Governor respected learning; as chief magistrate of Massachusetts Bay he was President of the Board of Overseers, and in both capacities had great influence over the rising college.

1. *Winthrop Papers*, I. 46 n. Cf. Rouse Ball, *Cambridge Papers*, pp. 128–31.

2. Samuel Ward's Diary for 1596: 'Oh the greivous sinnes of T[rinity] Colledg, which had a woman which was [carried] from chamber to chamber on the night tyme.' M. M. Knappen, *Two Puritan Diaries*, p. 111. Following the above-quoted decree of the heads on women in college, the fellows of Trinity voted that 'all young women shalbe banished and putt out of the Colledge,' and 'if any under any pretext bring any young women into the College to entertaine, maintaine, or employ them,' he shall be 'publickly corrected in the hall with the rodd' if *non-adultus*, fined 12d. if *adultus*, and 2s 6d if a fellow; there were double fines for second offenses. Ms. College Conclusion Book.

3. J. E. B. Mayor's edition of Baker's *History of St. John's*, II. 612.

Ten years after John Winthrop and John Cotton left Trinity, there came into residence four undergraduates, three of whom were destined to be on the first Harvard Board of Overseers, and the other to be President of the College for eighteen years. Thomas Weld, the son of a linen-draper at Sudbury in Suffolk, entered pensioner in 1611, and took his Arts degrees in due course. Ejected from his Essex vicarage in 1631, he emigrated to New England and became pastor of Roxbury, and a pillar of puritan orthodoxy. At the beginning of his junior sophister year there entered sizar an active youth of fifteen, son of a Cornwall squire, and known to fame as Hugh Peter, or Peters. Like Weld he took both Arts degrees and holy orders; like him he emigrated to become a puritan pastor in the Bay Colony, and with him returned to England to conduct what might be called Harvard's first drive for funds.[1] John Humfrey of Dorset, scholar of Trinity in 1614, left shortly for the Inns of Court. Within ten years of leaving college he became an important link between the West Country and the East Anglia puritans who brought the Massachusetts Bay Company into being. Like Weld and Peter he returned to England and took an active part in the Civil War.

CHARLES CHAUNCY

Easily the most distinguished of the Cantabrigians who emigrated to New England was Charles Chauncy, second President of Harvard College. His parents, who belonged to an ancient family of Hertfordshire, sent him to Westminster School at the exciting moment of Guy Fawkes' gunpowder plot. Westminster had the right of electing every year three of her boys as scholars of Trinity, and at Easter, 1609, when he was almost seventeen, Chauncy was so chosen, along with Edward Palmer, another Greek scholar like himself.[2] Chauncy's 'Westminster Book,' a handsome copy of *Historiæ Romanæ Scriptores Latini Veteres* presented to him by the School, is in the Harvard College Library.[3] A more substantial gain by this scholarship was free

---

1. See Chapter XXI.
2. *Alumni Westmonasterienses*, pp. 79–80.
3. The inscription in Chauncy's characteristically crabbed handwriting is: 'My Westminster book given me by the Colledge there when I was chosen from that schoole to Trinity Colledge in Camb. anno domini 1605.' The date is an obvious mistake for 1609, the date of the imprint and of Chauncy's scholarship.

commons and a quarterly stipend of 3s 4d.[1] Four years later Chauncy took his B.A., appearing next to the top of the *ordo senioritatis*. That was a list drawn up at the conclusion of the B.A. examinations by the presiding proctor; and although it is not quite clear to the Cambridge historians how far social considerations weighed in the scale with scholastic attainments, 'some notion of merit, in the sense of intellectual superiority must have been recognized.'[2] Chauncy's name stands second out of 176 commencing bachelors in 1614 — the same place taken the previous year by George Herbert. And in the M.A. *ordo senioritatis* three years later, which was more clearly an order of merit, Chauncy ranks fourth out of 121.[3] The inceptors' disputations at that Commencement were exceptionally brilliant; the Archbishop of Spalato, who attended, 'wept (it is saide) for joye' at them.[4]

Trinity was the first Cambridge college to provide complete instruction for her undergraduates. The college statutes declared that there should be appointed from among the fellows nine *lectores*, five on Dialectic and one each on Greek, Latin, Mathematics, and Greek Grammar. Chauncy, after he had been fellow a few years, was chosen *lector linguæ Græcæ*; his colleague George Herbert was the *lector Græcæ grammaticæ*. The Greek Lecturer's duty, we learn from the statutes, was to lecture on Isocrates, Demosthenes, Plato, Homer, and Hesiod. Lectures began immediately after morning prayer; *discupuli impubes* were whipped for cutting; *adulti*, fined a penny; the *lector* was fined 8d. if he cut his own lecture.[5]

When the statutory seven years had elapsed after his Master's Commencement, Chauncy took the degree of Bachelor of Divinity. He remained a fellow and tutor of the College until 1626. Not only a Greek but a Hebrew scholar,[6] Chauncy was

1. Ms. accounts, Trinity College. In 1615 he was promoted to the class of scholars receiving 10s a quarter; in 1618, as M. A. and fellow, he was receiving 13s 4d, beside the commons allowance.
2. John Venn, Introduction to *Grace Book* Δ, p. ix.
3. *Hist. Reg. Univ. Camb.*, p. 396; Grace Book E (Ms., University Register), p. 198.
4. *Calendar State Papers, Domestic, James I, 1611–1618*, p. 478, and Hackett, *Life of John Williams*, pp. 31–32. First on the Master's *ordo senioritatis* that year was John Cosin, Master of Peterhouse and Bishop of Durham, who became a strong partisan of Archbishop Laud and King Charles. The others became undistinguished clergymen. George Phillips of Caius, later minister of Watertown, took his M.A. at the same Commencement, but was not placed; the proctors often did not rank more than ten or twelve.
5. *Trinity College Statutes* (ed. 1773), cap. ix.
6. *Magnalia*, book iii. 134. Archbishop Ussher, in a letter of 1626 to Samuel Ward,

CHAUNCY'S INSCRIPTION ON TITLE-PAGE OF HIS 'WESTMINSTER BOOK'

nominated by the heads of houses to the Regius professorship of Hebrew, but a protégé of Bishop Williams the Lord Keeper obtained the chair. As evidence of his classical wit, we find Latin and Greek poems by Chauncy in the volumes of gratulatory or elegiac verse which the University got out at every birth, marriage, and death in the royal family.[1] In 1622 he pronounced a valedictory oration to the Spanish and Austrian ambassadors upon their departure from his college, where they had been entertained and presented for honorary degrees.[2] Chauncy was one of the best-known figures in the University of his day; even twenty-five years later, his name on a Harvard graduate's diploma was sufficient endorsement for an *ad eundem* degree at Cambridge.[3]

Between the years 1629 and 1636 we find another small group of future New Englanders at Trinity College: Abraham Pierson, father of the like-named Harvard graduate who became the first Rector of Yale; Thomas Rashley, elected a fellow upon taking his B.A., later the minister of Gloucester in Massachusetts; Thomas Hinckley, a yeoman's son who entered sizar in 1633, emigrated with his father two years later, and rose to be Governor of the Colony of New Plymouth. The most important of this younger group was Nathaniel Eaton, who entered scholar from Westminster School in 1630, and became the first head of Harvard College.

But in assessing what Harvard owes to Trinity we must write off Eaton as a bad debt!

Master of Sidney Sussex, asks to be remembered to Chauncy, from whom he would have the transcript of a verse in a Hebrew manuscript of the Psalter. He 'would willingly also hear how far he hath proceeded in the *Samaritan* Bible.' Ward replies, 'nor do I hear that Mr. *Chauncy* is come home.' Richard Parr, *Life of James Usher* (1686), pp. 340–41, 369.

1. To the *Lacrymae Cantabrigienses in obitum Serenissimae Reginae Annae* (1619) Chauncy contributes two Latin poems (pp. 39, 62), another contributor being George Herbert. He has three pages of Latin hexameter poetry in *Cantabrigiensium Dolor et Solamen, seu Decessio Beati Regis Jacobi Pacifici et Successio Anglorum Regis Caroli* (1625). To the *Epithalamium Illustrissimorum et Felicissimorum Principum Caroli Regis et Henriettae Mariae* (1625) he contributes a Latin and a Greek poem (p. 6), in company with Andrew Downes, Regius professor of Greek, and Thomas Randolph.

2. 'Oratio Valedictoria per Carolum Chauncy, Mag. Art.,' in *True Copies of all the Latine Orations made and pronounced at Cambridge by the Vice-Chancellor and others* (1623). Most of these effusions are reprinted, not with scrupulous accuracy, in William Chauncey Fowler, *Memorials of the Chaunceys* (1858), pp. 3–10. This author errs in ascribing to Chauncy a poem signed 'C. C.   C. P.' in another *Gratulatio* of 1623. The 'C. P.' indicates that the author was a member of Pembroke College.

3. *Diary and Correspondence of Dr. John Worthington*, I. 101.

VI

EMMANUEL COLLEGE AND JOHN HARVARD
1584–1635

 Emmanuel College, a puritan foundation established for the special purpose of providing the Church with a preaching ministry, is where John Harvard became imbued with that love of learning which inspired his famous benefaction;[1] and with Emmanuel no less than thirty-five of the university emigrants to New England were connected. The first governing body of the Bay Colony included two Emmanuel men, Isaac Johnson and Simon Bradstreet. When Johnson[2] alighted at Charlestown he found, living in lonely state across the Charles, William Blackstone, who had entered Emmanuel with him and taken his degrees at the same Commencements. The hermit of Beacon Hill invited Johnson to be his neighbor, the invitation was accepted, and Boston was founded.[3] Presently a famous fellow of Emmanuel, John Cotton, came over to be minister there. A similar friendship between two men of the same Emmanuel *grex*, Samuel Stone and Thomas Shepard, brought the latter, and eventually Harvard College, to Cambridge in Massa-

1. This connection between Emmanuel and Harvard has been acknowledged from the first. Thomas Ball refers in his 'Life of Preston' (Samuel Clarke, *Martyrologie*, p. 497) to a 'new plantation' which arose from the Emmanuel oak. Cotton Mather writes in *Magnalia*, book iii. 216, 'If *New-England* hath been in some Respects *Immanuel's Land*, it is well; but this I am sure of, *Immanuel-College* contributed more than a little to make it so.' In the windows of the college chapel John Harvard's image stands side by side with that of Dr. Chaderton, and there have been many interchanges of scholars and civilities between the two colleges.

2. The Johnsons of Rutland were an Emmanuel family. Isaac's grandfather Robert Johnson (1540–1625), fellow of Trinity College and Archdeacon of Leicester, founded Oakham and Uppingham Schools, as well as exhibitions for boys from those schools at Clare, St. John's, Emmanuel, and Sidney Sussex; he was a benefactor of Emmanuel and of the Cambridge University Library, and a neighbor and friend of Sir Walter Mildmay.

3. M. J. Canavan shows the close personal associations between Blackstone and the Johnson family, in *C. S. M.*, xxvii. 272–85, and the strong probability that this association led to the founding of Boston.

chusetts Bay. Of the same college were two famous school-masters of New England who fitted boys for Harvard, Daniel Maude and Ezekiel Cheever. Travelling north in the Bay Colony about the time Harvard College was opened, one would have found Samuel Whiting of Emmanuel in the parsonage at Lynn; William Walton of Emmanuel ministering to the fisher-men of Marblehead; and in the frontier town of Ipswich, the 'simple cobler of Aggawam,' magistrates Saltonstall and Brad-street, Giles Firmin practitioner of physic, and Major General Daniel Denison, Emmanuel alumni. Turn west and you would find Edmund Browne gracing the pulpit in the frontier set-tlement of Sudbury; follow the Bay Path to Connecticut and you would come under the domination of Thomas Hooker in the River Colony. Thus was fulfilled the prophecy of Sir Walter Mildmay, Emmanuel's founder, when Queen Elizabeth burst out with

'Sir Walter, I hear you have erected a Puritan Foundation?'

'No, Madam,' saith he. 'Farre be it from me to countenance any thing contrary to your established Lawes; but I have set an Acorn, which when it becomes an Oak, God alone knows what will be the fruit thereof.'[1]

Sir Walter Mildmay

 Elizabeth, too, was right. The term 'puritan' then was and long remained an opprobrious epi-thet implying disloyalty to Church and State. Since no puritan would admit the implication, he would not permit the term; it was a fighting matter to call a man a puritan before the 1640's — and a fighting matter to be a puritan then. But for all that, Emman-uel was palpably puritan by the name the founder chose,[2] and the declaration of his foundation statutes: 'I wish all to under-stand . . . who are to be admitted into the College, that the one object which I set before me in erecting this College was to ren-der as many as possible fit for the administration of the Divine Word and Sacraments; and that from this seed-ground the Eng-lish Church might have those that she can summon to instruct

1. Thomas Fuller, *Hist. Univ. Camb.* (1655), II. 147.

2. 'Emmanuel' (God with us) was often used as a superscription to letters by puri-tans and other pious persons.

the people and undertake the office of pastors, which is a thing necessary above all others.'[1] In other words, he intended to provide the Church with scholars to guard her from the intemperate prophesyings of the ignorant, and with preachers to instruct the people in the Word; preachers 'at once learned and zealous, instructed in all that scholars should know, but trained to use their learning in the service of the reformed faith.' Few founders have been so happy in fulfilling their dreams; graduates of Emmanuel like Cotton, Hooker, Harvard, and Shepard printed indelibly upon New England the stamp that Mildmay placed upon his college.

Walter Mildmay, a great officer of state under three Tudor sovereigns, and Queen Elizabeth's Chancellor of the Exchequer, 'saw that the new wine of the Reformation was finding an uneasy home in the old bottles' of Cambridge. Educated at Christ's College, he had later endowed it with a Greek lectureship and six scholarships. In his day Christ's had been the puritan stronghold in Cambridge; but the reaction signalized by the ejection of Cartwright was now in full tide, and Christ's in 1582 barely escaped having forced upon it an uncongenial Master by royal mandate.[2] Hence Mildmay required a new foundation to promote his pious objects. That Emmanuel succeeded even beyond his expectation was due in great part to his foresight. No scholarship or fellowship might be granted to anyone who did not intend to follow the sacred calling. That might easily have been evaded, as similar statutes of older foundations had been; but Mildmay insisted that fellowships be automatically vacated within twelve years of commencing M.A. His motive was to force the fellows into active ministry: 'we would not have any Fellow suppose that we have given him a permanent home in this college';[3] nor could a fellowship be held *in absentia*, as in other colleges.

Laurence Chaderton

The chief assurance that the founder's wishes would be carried out was his choice of an old fellow-student at Christ's as the first Master of Emmanuel. Laurence Chaderton, who was

1. E. S. Shuckburgh, *Emmanuel College*, p. 23.
2. Mullinger, II. 310, 472.
3. *Docs. Univ. Camb.*, III. 524–25.

SIR WALTER MILDMAY
Copyright *Country Life*

forty-eight years old when elected Master, eighty-six when he resigned his charge, and one hundred and two or three at his death, was the son of a Catholic gentleman in Lancashire, and a graduate and fellow of Christ's. There he was the tutor of William Perkins, who became one of the leading lights among puritan divines, and whose evangelical fervor is said to have been responsible for the notable crop of excellent preachers at Cambridge. This was 'Painful' Perkins, whose works were more highly esteemed by the New England puritans than those of any other modern theologian,[1] excepting Perkins's pupil, William Ames.

Ames had the most incisive, radical mind of any Cambridge puritan. Driven from Christ's in 1609 because he refused to wear the surplice, from the University for an imprecatory sermon against the 'pagan' revelries of Christmastide, and from England for taking charge of a Congregational church,[2] Ames found a congenial sphere of action in Holland as champion of the Calvinists against the Arminians, as puritan casuist, and compiler of that puritan *summa*, the 'Marrow of Theology.' He intended to migrate to New England; the opportunity was lost, but his influence passed overseas.[3]

So much for Chaderton's effect on Harvard and New England through his original college of Christ's; later, as Master of Emmanuel his power was incalculable. He combined, as no other man in the puritan movement, sound scholarship, a gift for popular preaching, and a vigorous personality. A taste for manly sports — archery, tennis, and boxing — unusual in scholars of that era, established his ascendancy over young men. During undergraduate days he saved the life of Richard Bancroft in a town-and-gown riot, fighting his way into the crowd and rescuing his chum from a gang of ruffians, at the cost of a crushed right hand. Chaderton supported the Millenary Petition of the puritans in 1603. The following year Bancroft became Archbishop of Canterbury, and vigorously opposed the

---

1. *Magnalia*, book iv. 145, and *D.N.B.*; not to be confused with the William Perkins of Emmanuel who emigrated to New England. 'Painful,' in the sense of painstaking and zealous, was a favorite adjective of commendation among puritans.

2. Mullinger, II. 510–11; but Nethenus, in the biographical introduction of his edition of Ames' *Works* (Amsterdam, 1658), says that Ames and Robert Parker were sent to Holland by some generous merchants, in order to give them opportunity to write against the English hierarchy.

3. See index to this volume, and to the next.

puritans; but the two always remained friends.[1] Once, when the Master of Emmanuel called on the Archbishop, they argued at length, then stripped and had it out with bare fists. 'Now I know this is mine own Laurence!' cried the Archbishop when the Master had him down.[2] In every respect, Chaderton was an upstanding, independent man. 'Master of his own thoughts, he refused to adapt himself to the habits of other people, or to live under an assumed character; for he thought that what most became a man was what he really was.'[3]

In 1576 Chaderton married, and therefore had to resign his fellowship at Christ's. Eight years later Sir Walter, his old college-mate, called him to be Master of Emmanuel. Some half-ruined buildings which had formerly belonged to a suppressed Dominican college were purchased by the founder; repairs were made and new buildings begun; and in 1584 the College opened with eight fellows, four scholars, and a number of fellow-commoners, pensioners, and sizars.

THE PURITAN COLLEGE

From its very opening, the puritan character of Emmanuel was signalized by the devotion of her fellows to teaching and preparation for the ministry, by evangelical services in the chapel, without surplice or prayer-book ritual, and by the members' receiving the elements seated around a communion table. According to the college orders adopted in 1588, the fellows were to meet periodically after supper for a 'mutuall conference and communication of giftes,' to be opened by the Master with prayer, in which all 'Prophets and Sonnes of the Prophets' should speak their thoughts; and all students should 'resort unto their Tutors prayers at viij of the clock.'[4] Yet so strong was the demand for education under puritan auspices that by 1617 Emmanuel had over two hundred undergraduates, more than any other college of the University save Trinity,[5] although but twelve or thirteen fellows were available for teaching, as compared with fifty or sixty at Trinity and St. John's. The

1. William Dillingham, *Vita L. Chadertoni* (1700), p. 7.
2. A college tradition at Emmanuel, related to me by the present Master, Dr. Peter Giles.
3. Shuckburgh's translation of Dillingham's *Vita*, p. 26.
4. Emmanuel Order Book (Ms.) for 1589 and 1605.
5. Mullinger, II. 472.

college buildings could not contain her members; many had to live out, contrary to university statutes; the new Brick Building was constructed in 1633–34, just before John Harvard left, 'for the bringing of them all to keepe and lodge within the walls.'[1]

The robust Christianity of Chaderton was diffused throughout the College; and his disciples gave the English puritan movement a stout morale. Emmanuel bred stiff-backed Christians who had the moral courage to withstand social pressure, and the physical courage to brave ocean and wilderness for the faith that was in them. Your whining, canting, unhealthy puritan found no encouragement there. Moreover, Chaderton protected his college from the jealousy of others. When King James I visited Cambridge in 1615, as that witty Oxonian, Richard Corbet, wrote:[2]

> Their colledges were new be-painted,
> Their founders eke were new be-sainted;
> Nothing escap'd, nor post, nor door,
> Nor gate, nor rail, nor bawd, nor whore:
> You could not know (Oh strange mishap!)
> Whether you saw the town or map.

> But the pure house of Emmanuel
> Would not be like proud Jesabel,
> Nor shew her self before the king
> An hypocrite, or painted thing:
> But, that the ways might all prove fair,
> Conceiv'd a tedious mile of prayer.

Yet Emmanuel came to no harm by this. Someone observed to the King, in Chaderton's presence, that the chapel of Emmanuel was oriented wrong. James answered, 'God will not turn away his face from the prayers of any holy and pious man, to whatever region of heaven he directs his eyes. So, doctor, I beg you to pray for me.'[3] James I always trusted Chaderton. In the next reign, the College was not so happy. The surplice was forced on the fellows. Bishop Laud rebuked the venerable

1. Ms. Order Book, 1633. The Brick Building is shown at the extreme right of the illustration. One of the corner chambers, with two large studies, is now reserved for the holders of the Lionel de Jersey Harvard scholarship, since John Harvard may have roomed there his last year. Note also the pool and tennis court at left rear.

2. Cooper, *Annals*, iii. 76.

3. Shuckburgh, *Emmanuel*, p. 37.

retired Master because the chapel was not consecrated. Chaderton answered that it had been consecrated by prayer and devotion for thirty years. There was no possible meeting ground of these two points of view.

Although a serious purpose was assumed of Emmanuel students, they were provided with the amenities of English college life. There was none of that harsh asceticism and material ugliness which nineteenth-century puritans were apt to regard as the proper frame for a parson's education. Mildmay's buildings were as fair as could be without extravagance. Behind them were a spacious garden with shady walks, a pool where students might bathe without incurring the awful penalties of the law, a tennis court, where Sir Worthington 'had a dangerous blow on the eye,' and a fellows' orchard, where Samuel Ward strutted before visitors from St. John's, played bowls, and ate too many damsons.[1] Like other colleges Emmanuel had her brewhouse, and no one had occasion to complain of her beer (as did Erasmus of another college brew) that it was 'raw, small and windy.' Students' commons were eaten from wooden trenchers, as in the other colleges; but the Emmanuel high table was well provided with silver: each fellow had his tankard, wine-bowl, stoop, salt, and spoon — forks were unknown as yet save in noblemen's houses, and one provided one's own knife. Certainly the masters and fellows of Emmanuel were none of that sort of puritan who

> Fetch their precepts from the Cynic tub,
> Praising the lean and sallow Abstinence.

A Book of Punishments, still preserved in the college muniments, records the usual undergraduate misdemeanors, and singularly mild punishments, with but one instance of whipping. Students were merely admonished for neglect of prayers and lectures, and for 'making and letting off squibbs' on Candlemas Eve. Thomas Dudley, son of the future Governor of the Massachusetts, is admonished for quarrelling and fighting; Sir Shewbury for 'notorious quarrellinge with and beatinge of Sir Dixy tearinge his gowne and ruffe, and kickinge him'; others for 'distempering' themselves with drink at the Falcon, the Dolphin, the Cock, and the Bird Bolt; Sir Meadows 'for his frequent

---

1. M. M. Knappen, *Two Elizabethan Puritan Diaries*, pp. 110, 113–14.

EMMANUEL COLLEGE

From a painting, c. 1670, in the Master's Lodge.   Copyright *Country Life*

going abroad to hunte with greyhounds, and for disorderly carriage in that exercise'; six other B.A.'s for staying out after the gates were locked, 'riding Mr. Wolfe's horses and letting them into his corn, and coming in over the college walls.' Sir Harlakenden, particular friend of Thomas Shepard, is admonished for 'notorious negligence at chappel, and for other loose and idle behaviour.' Thomas Shepard was more fortunate in his escapades; for it is from his autobiography, not the college records, that we learn how during his first two years he neglected prayers, as junior sophister became foolish and proud, 'yet still restraynd from the grosse act of whoordom' which some of his 'familiars were to their horrour and shame ouertaken with'; how he 'dranke so much on day' that he was 'dead drunke and that vpon a saturday night'; how he woke up on the Sabbath morn in Christ's College, and spent the day sobering up in the corn fields; and how a sermon from the Master set him in the way to salvation.[1] Emmanuel College youths were full of high spirits — fortunately for New England.

Yet this collegiate oak bore not only puritan acorns. Emmanuel nurtured the neo-Platonic divines who sought truth in a different direction — almost a different dimension — from that of Cotton and Hooker. Within the very decade that nurtured the men who went forth to found a puritan commonwealth in the New World, Emmanuel became 'the cradle of a movement animated by the spirit of Plato and devoted to the golden mean in every sphere of thought and life.'[2] These were men who believed that the Church, however corrupt, and human reason, however fallible, might yet be roads to truth; that 'to seek our Divinity meerly in Books and Writings is to seek the living among the dead.'[3] Benjamin Whichcote, the father of the Cambridge neo-Platonists, came to Emmanuel just before John Harvard, and became a fellow and tutor in his time. Ralph Cudworth and Nathaniel Culverwel entered before Harvard commenced B.A.[4] In passing one may regret that the tolerant and

1. *C. S. M.*, xxvii. 360–62, 393.
2. F. J. Powicke, *Cambridge Platonists* (1926), p. 3.
3. E. T. Campagnac, *Cambridge Platonists* (1901), p. 81.
4. Although no influence of the neo-Platonists can be discerned in the writings of the early New England puritans, there were personal connections between them. Whichcote married in 1643 the widow of Matthew Craddock, the first Governor of the Massachusetts Bay Company, who assisted greatly the financing of the puritan migration. Ralph Cudworth was brought up by his stepfather, Dr. John Stoughton, brother

generous philosophy of these men, who believed in the nobility of human nature and the divine quality of human reason, could not have set the tone of Harvard College. But Harvard must have been puritan, or not have existed. A neo-Platonist could not be a man of action, a pioneer, an emigrant, any more than a Hindu. The Kingdom of God was within him, not in Massachusetts Bay. It was the very defects of the puritan — his fierce intolerance of 'idolatry' and unrighteousness, his unwearying intensity of purpose—which gave life to his ideal conception of a Christian commonwealth. His harsh temper was a part of his intense loyalty to God. His excessive reverence for the Scriptures was the root of his respect for learning. His firm grasp of the practical side of life was part of his middle-class heritage. But for these traits, which made him a successful pioneer, we could not have benefited by those qualities which made him an exceptional pioneer.

HOOKER, COTTON, AND PRESTON

The oldest Emmanuel man who emigrated to New England was the witty Nathaniel Ward, 'simple cobler of Aggawam' and author of the Massachusetts Body of Liberties. From 1603, when Ward took his M.A., to 1618, the men of greatest influence at Emmanuel besides the Master were two fellows, Hooker and Cotton. Hooker transferred from Queens' College in 1604, soon won a scholarship, and eventually a fellowship. A man of majestic port and searching glance, Hooker was destined to be a ruler; but it was not yet certain that he would be a puritan. Shortly after becoming fellow of Emmanuel the Spirit began to work, and in his harrowing experience of wrestling with the flesh and yearning in agony for assurance of God's regenerating grace, this proud intellectual had the help of a humble sizar who waited upon him 'and attended him with . . . discreet and proper Compassions.' [1] In 1616 he was Dean of the College; and two years later, in accordance with the founder's wishes, he left the College to seek a parish. After a short sojourn at Dedham with his friend John Rogers,[2] Hooker became

of Israel Stoughton, and early Overseer of Harvard College. Ralph's brother James emigrated to New England, and became a friend to President Dunster (see *H. C. S. C.*, Chapter XV). Jonathan Edwards and R. W. Emerson owed much to Ralph Cudworth.

1. Mather, *Magnalia*, book iii. 58.
2. Grandfather of President Rogers of Harvard; see Appendix B.

famous as town preacher at Chelmsford in Essex, as a writer on the psychology of conversion, and as leader in that growing school of puritan thought which favored the Congregational rather than the Presbyterian polity.

An associate fellow with Hooker was John Cotton, who came to Emmanuel from Trinity at the age of twenty, in 1604. In quick succession Cotton became fellow, Dean, Head Lecturer, and Catechist of his adopted college. In 1612 he resigned to become Vicar of St. Botolph's in Boston. But it was a different Cotton who went to Boston from the proud young man who had become fellow six years before, admired by all the 'sparkling wits of the University' for the spirited Latin of his university sermons. In those days he had hardened himself against the workings of the Spirit, 'through a vain Perswasion that if he became a Godly man, 'twould spoil him for being a Learned One.' At about his twenty-fifth year a sermon of Richard Sibbes opened his heart to the regenerating grace of God, and he became one of the twice-born. Shortly after came Cotton's turn to preach the university sermon at St. Mary's. Scholars crowded the church, expecting to hear a pretty play of wit in Ciceronian Latin. Instead, Master Cotton preached a plain sermon upon the doctrine of repentance. The wits openly showed their disgust. But the keenest wit in the congregation was 'pierced at the heart.'

This was John Preston, fellow of Queens', three years Cotton's junior and the outstanding figure among the younger tutors of Cambridge. Son of an ancient but impoverished family, Preston was determined to be a success. His 'firme, well-tempered constitution, brown, comely visage, vigorous and vivide eye,' his love of learning and grace in imparting it, caused young men to flock to Queens'; whilst his lively intelligence and flair for politics clearly marked him out for some great office of state — provided he steered clear of puritanism.[1] Yet John Cotton's sermon inflicted a wound that 'no cunning in Philosophy, or skill in Physick would suffice to heal.' Serious conferences with Cotton were followed by an intense study of

1. Thomas Ball, 'Life of Preston' (Clarke's *Martyrologie*), pp. 475–77; *Magnalia*, book iii. 15; Mullinger, ii. 480–83, 554–60. From about 1609, when things were made uncomfortable for puritans at Christ's, to the departure of Preston, Queens' College was second only to Emmanuel as a place of puritan education. No one who subsequently emigrated to New England, except the knightly Fenwick, entered Queens' after 1609, and two who were there before, Hobart and Hooker, migrated to other colleges.

Divinity; a colleague caught him reading Aquinas' *Summa* while the college barber cut his hair, impatiently blowing the shorn locks from the open page. In the end Preston was converted, and the puritans gained the choice young man of Cambridge for their own. He retained his prestige as a tutor, in one year alone entering twenty new pupils at Queens'; his college lectures were thronged by students from elsewhere, and his sermons at one of the town churches were so popular that he felt strong enough to defy the Bishop's commissary who ordered them suspended. Again and again Preston did what no other puritan dared; he had an instinct for eluding traps, and from each direct encounter he emerged stronger.

 The years 1618–22 were a turning-point in the history of puritanism at the University. Since their notable defeat at Cartwright's expulsion in 1570, the puritans had concealed and in some instances modified their views on discipline, but held their own in doctrine. In the University and the nation they bulked so large as to be courted by the Duke of Buckingham, who appointed Preston one of his chaplains. By 1619 the signs and portents of the coming storm began to be noticed. A fellow of Pembroke was imprisoned by royal mandate for a sermon hostile to the doctrine of non-resistance which Launcelot Andrewes and William Laud were quietly developing.[1] Oxford and Cambridge were ordered to condemn and burn the works of Pareus, the Calvinist theologian who taught resistance to tyrants; and they obeyed. Sermons adumbrating the doctrines of Anglo-Catholicism began to be heard in St. Mary's, and their authors received signal marks of royal favor. As puritan heads of colleges died, their successors were chosen by royal mandate, and their friends driven from the College. Puritanism was now on the defensive, in respect not only of church discipline but of the Augustinian doctrine developed by John Calvin and officially adopted by the Church of England. And in Europe the Thirty Years' War had begun.

1. Among those who got in trouble for 'subversive doctrines' in a university sermon was Charles Chauncy, who was required in 1624 to read a paper in Congregation declaring that he designed not to reflect upon any person or college. Cooper, *Annals*, III. 166.

It was in accordance with this trend that Queens' College had forced on her, about 1622, an anti-puritan president who made things uncomfortable for John Preston. At the same time, the fellows of Emmanuel decided for 'the good and welfare of that brave foundation' to persuade their octogenarian Master Chaderton to retire and make place for Preston. So close were the connections between academic and national politics that even after the fellows had received assurance from the Duke of Buckingham that he would promote his chaplain's candidacy, they held the election in deepest secrecy behind locked college gates, lest some rival be intruded by royal mandate. Thus John Preston at the age of thirty-two was elected Master of Emmanuel and inducted into office at a few hours' notice, the Queens' men trooping over to see him installed, and to be suitably feasted in Emmanuel hall.

In his six years as Master of Emmanuel, Preston left his stamp on the College, and on New England. He had the rare combination of social, moral, and intellectual distinction that always impresses undergraduates; no personality of old Cambridge was so often and affectionately mentioned by the founders of New England. It was during his mastership that the number of these founders reached its peak. Of important laymen there were Bradstreet, Denison, the younger Saltonstall, and William Perkins; of ministers, many more. Samuel Stone, inseparable colleague of Hooker, was 'instructed with the Light' and 'nourish'd with the Cup' at this time by his tutor Richard Blackerby,[1] Thomas Shepard, the greatest evangelist of early New England, was converted by a sermon of the Master's in the college chapel;[2] and it was during Preston's mastership that John Harvard entered pensioner.

JOHN HARVARD [3]

Until the two-hundred-and-fiftieth anniversary of Harvard College, nothing was known of John Harvard save his education at Emmanuel, his brief residence at Charlestown, and his benefaction to the College. The researches of Henry FitzGilbert Waters (A.B. 1855) and others have provided a few more facts,

1. Mather, *Magnalia*, book iii. 116.
2. *C. S. M.*, xxvii. 364.
3. For authorities, see the beginning of Chapter XVI.

mainly genealogical; [1] but not a single Harvard letter has been discovered, and the picture is still a mere outline. His family were fairly well-to-do tradespeople, who for a century [2] had followed the respectable calling of butcher in the roughest and bawdiest part of London: Southwark, on the right bank of the Thames, characterized by Leslie Hotson as 'that turbulent transpontine appendage of London which harbored the Bear Garden and Henslowe's Rose Theatre. In Southwark, too, were brothels — the notorious "stews" of the Bankside, near the elegant town house or palace of their landlord, the Bishop of Winchester; prisons — the King's Bench, the Clink, Marshalsea, and the White Lion; alehouses — three hundred of them; courts of justice. . . . A grim enough catalogue, exhibiting a very Elizabethan mixture of religion and crime.' [3]

Robert Harvard, John's father, was a butcher who owned his own shop and several pieces of property, including the Queen's Head tavern.[4] Katherine, the second wife of Robert and mother of John Harvard, was the thirteenth child of Thomas Rogers, cattle dealer and alderman of Stratford-on-Avon.[5] As Will Shakspere was also associated with Southwark and Stratford, it is almost more than human nature can bear to avoid dragging

1.
                    Thomas Rogers, alderman and
                    cattle dealer of Stratford, d. 1611

Robert Harvard of Southwark, butcher, d. Aug. 24, 1625
    m. (1) 1600 Barbara Descyn (d. 1603); (2) 1605 Katherine Rogers, b. 1584
                                                        d. July 9, 1635

Mary	Robert	Robert	John	Thomas	William	Katherine	Anne	Peter
b. 1601	b. 1602	b. 1606	bap. Nov.	b. 1609	b. 1610	b. 1612	b. 1613	b. 1615
d. 1625	d. infant	d. 1625	29, 1607	d. 1637	d. 1625?	d. 1625	d. ?	d. 1625
			d. Sept. 14, m. Eliz.					
			1638 King					

Katherine (Rogers) Harvard m. (2) on Jan. 19, 1626, John Elletson, cooper, who died in June, 1626; (3) Richard Yearwood, grocer, May, 1627. He died c. Oct. 1, 1632.

John Harvard m. April 19, 1636, Ann Sadler, daughter of Rev. John Sadler. She m. (2) Rev. Thomas Allen of Charlestown (see Appendix B).

2. One 'Thomas Hervy,' citizen and 'bocher' of London, who was living in the parish of St. Olave, Southwark, in 1505, was presumably an ancestor of our Harvards. H. F. Waters, *Gen. Glean.*, I. 184–85. A John Harvard is mentioned as participating in a 'common adventure . . . for Muscovie' in 1596, in a document in the Public Record Office, C 24/261, 2d bundle. He may have been the father or a brother of Robert Harvard and the one from whom our John was named.

3. *Atlantic Monthly*, CXLVIII. 27.

4. Will in Waters, *Gen. Glean.*, I. 118–19.

5. H. F. Waters, *John Harvard*, pt. II. 29–30.

SOUTHWARK CATHEDRAL IN 1647

THE PARISH CHURCH OF THE HARVARDS

S. Marie Ouers in Southwarke

in the Bard of Avon as matchmaker for Robert Harvard and Katherine Rogers.[1] But it seems much more likely that Robert's roving eye met Katherine's when visiting Stratford to buy cattle from Alderman Rogers. His house there, from which Katherine was married, has been restored as a Harvard memorial.

The Harvards were moderate puritans, content to conform so long as they had good preaching, and were not too much bothered by ceremonies. They were not members of Henry Jacob's Congregational meeting in the neighborhood, but faithful parishioners of St. Saviour's. It was in St. Saviour's Church (now Southwark Cathedral) that their second son John was baptized on November 29, 1607,[2] in a chapel that has since been restored through the piety of Harvard graduates.

We have no trace of John Harvard from his baptism to the year 1625, when a visitation of the plague took off his father and four of his brothers and sisters, almost wiping out the Harvard family. The butcher business was sold to John's cousin Thomas,[3] and a few months later his mother took for second husband John Elletson, 'citizen and cooper of London,' a man of some little property.[4] John Harvard was then in his eighteenth year. Presumably the ill wind of the plague made it possible for him to continue his education. And as the Harvard family had no university connections, it was obviously Nicholas Morton,[5] the rector of St. Saviour's, a man to whom they were all devoted, who gave John the proper credentials to enter his own college.

John was admitted to Emmanuel as a pensioner on December

---

1. This story is the creation of Mr. Shelley's imagination, in *John Harvard and His Times*, touched off by an incautious spark in Waters, *Gen. Glean.*, I. 617.

2. See the Harvard pedigree, above.

3. This Thomas Harvard is mentioned in the wills of both John Harvard's parents, and of his brother Thomas. He is undoubtedly the Thomas Harvard, 'of the parishe of St. Saviour, Butcher,' described as 'aged 51 yeares and upwarde' in a deposition dated 12 October 1608 (Public Record Office, C 24/345/78). For other Thomas Harvards see Waters, *Gen. Glean.*, I. 266–67, 117, and index; C. M. Clode, *Memorials of Guild of Merchant Taylors*, p. 594; Alexander Brown, *Genesis of the United States*, I. 304.

4. Subsequently she married for third husband, in May, 1627, Richard Yearwood, grocer, who is described as 'my good neighbour and friend' in her first husband's will (Waters, *Gen. Glean.*, I. 188, 119). He was cousin to and executor of Ralph Yeardley, merchant tailor, who was father of Sir George Yeardley, Governor of Virginia.

5. Scholar of Emmanuel, 1612; M.A. 1619. Most members of the Harvard family remembered him in their wills. For his son Charles Morton, Vice-President of Harvard College, see *H. C. S. C.*

19, 1627, at the unusually advanced age of twenty.[1] On his twenty-first birthday, the following November, he came in for a £300 legacy from his father's estate. He took his B.A. in 1631–32, and his M.A. in 1635. The College has no record of him except his admission;[2] his name never appears in the 'Book of Punishments'; the name of his tutor is not known. The University has no record of him except his signature to the subscription book for the Three Articles,[3] when he took his degrees. Orders of seniority for his bachelor's and his master's years are both wanting, so we have no evidence of his academic rank. We need not count against him the fact that he did not become a scholar or a fellow of his college; for John Milton was neither a scholar nor a fellow of Christ's. A student who entered pensioner and who inherited £300 the next year would not at that time have been awarded a scholarship; there may have been no vacant fellowship when he took his M.A., or he may not have desired one. Only one college contemporary is known to have been his friend: John Sadler, later an official under Cromwell, M.P., and Master of Magdalene College. John Harvard married Sadler's sister, Ann, on April 19, 1636, and with her emigrated to New England a little more than a year later. Of his scholarly tastes we have a hint in the catalogue of his library — of which more later — and in the generous act which made his name immortal.[4]

Preston's short and brilliant mastership was terminated by his death in July, 1628, at the age of forty. The usual electioneering followed; Nathaniel Ward wrote to William Sand-

1. According to his father's will (*Gen. Glean.*, i. 119), £200 was to be paid to him on his twenty-first birthday, and half of the share of his brother Peter, who died in the plague of 1625.

2. And an autograph — probably spurious — in a book in Emmanuel College Library.

3. See above, p. 47 n.

4. Of those who took the B.A. from Emmanuel with John Harvard, and whose signatures to the subscription book for the Three Articles are shown with his in the accompanying facsimile, the only one who attained any prominence was Samuel Winter, at the foot of the list. He had entered Emmanuel in 1623, but left in order to study for the ministry under John Cotton at Boston, returning to take his B.A. in 1632. He joined the Independent ministry, served as chaplain to several parliamentary commissions in Ireland, and was appointed Provost of Trinity College, Dublin, in 1652, a position in which he befriended young Increase Mather. K. B. Murdock, *Increase Mather*, pp. 60–62; W. MacNeile Dixon, *Trinity College, Dublin*, pp. 49–52. Ten others — the only ones of whom any information is obtainable — became clergymen; of these, seven were puritans of some sort, and one a Fifth Monarchy man.

JOHN HARVARD'S SIGNATURES IN THE SUBSCRIPTION
BOOK, CAMBRIDGE, WHEN TAKING HIS TWO
DEGREES *IN GREGE SUO*
On the B.A. list, sixth from the top; on the M.A., fifth from the top

croft declaring that Hooker and the whole College wished to make him Master, urging him to 'lay downe all fleshly pleas all private and personal respects, melancholy and super modest objections,' and accept. Ward has some friends 'powerfull with his Majesty and the Duke that shall trye theire strength faithfully and freely in the College behalfe.' Their strength evidently proved sufficient; for Sandcroft was elected Master, and Emmanuel held out as a puritan stronghold until the puritans were on top.[1]

In fifteen years that time would come. But the first fifteen years of Charles I's reign were unhappy ones for puritans. In 1625, just after his accession, appeared Richard Montagu's *Appello ad Caesarem*, explaining away the Thirty-nine Articles, and denying roundly that the Church of England was bound by the Calvinistic conclusions of the Synod of Dort. Laud and his two fellow-bishops of the rising school endorsed the 'Appeal,' which became a rallying-point for the new High Church party. Archbishop Williams, the Lord Keeper who had protected the Cambridge puritans, was forced to resign the Great Seal, and was denied any part in the coronation ceremonies. Buckingham abandoned his puritan friends to become the protector of the 'Montacutians,' and was elected Chancellor of the University of Cambridge in 1626 after a sharp contest. Interferences by the Crown in elections of heads of houses became more frequent. When Laud became Bishop of London in 1628, and parliament was dissolved in 1629, a group of Cambridge and East Anglia puritans felt that the time had come to establish a new England overseas; and New England must include a new Emmanuel.

1. *N. E. H. G. R.*, xxxvii. 59. There were two William Sandcrofts Masters of Emmanuel. The second, who usually spelled his name without the 'd,' was the former's nephew. He was Master 1662–65, and later as Archbishop of Canterbury defied James II.

VII

OTHER FOUNDERS AND THEIR COLLEGES

 When Dr. Preston left Queens' College, a freshman named Peter Hobart, of whom something was to be heard in New England, left with him. Instead of following the crowd to Emmanuel, Peter put his belongings in a boat and floated downstream to a little college at the other end of Cambridge. Magdalene College was founded in 1542 by Sir Thomas Audley, who had taken an active part in suppressing the monasteries, and profited accordingly. Magdalene was insufficiently endowed with but a small share of Audley's spoil, and held back by a succession of inefficient and corrupt masters.[1] There was not enough revenue to pay the tutors' salaries, and for many years the College was kept going by an annual loan from the senior fellow.[2] In 1617, with eighty-five members (of whom ten were fellows and twenty scholars), Magdalene was almost the smallest college in Cambridge, and probably the poorest. Yet even in those lean years she numbered among her alumni William Morrell, who wrote a poem on New England in Latin hexameters as a memorial of his short stay on our soil, and Robert Woodmancy, for seventeen years headmaster of the Boston Latin School.

Around 1620 Magdalene College began to pull out of her depression. Rents long in arrears were paid in; the number of pensioners and fellow-commoners increased, bringing the total membership up to 140 by 1635; instead of borrowing money, the fellows began to cut dividends of £5 to £40 per annum; and — certain sign of prosperity — a new brewhouse was erected at the cost of £207 9s 11½d.[3] Fuller writes that in his time

1. Mullinger, II. 65 ff., 286–87, 382 n., 494–95.
2. Ms. Accounts in Register, vol. I, Magdalene muniments.
3. Ms. Register, vol. I, Magdalene College muniments. In 1633, the most prosperous year before 1650, the college receipts amounted to £744 4s 1½d and the expenses to

QUADRANGLE OF MAGDALENE COLLEGE, CAMBRIDGE, IN DUNSTER'S DAY

In the centre, entrance to the through passage; to the left, the Hall;
to the right, the Kitchen and Butteries

(1628–35) 'The Scholars of this Colledge (though farthest from the Schools) were . . . observed first there, and to as good purpose as any. Every year this House produced some eminent Scholars, as living cheaper, privater, freer from Toun-Temtations by their remote situation.'[1]

Fuller's encomiums are well borne out by the later Magdalene contingent of New Englanders, of whom the most illustrious were John Rayner, Samuel Eaton, Peter Hobart, John Knowles, and Henry Dunster.[2] Rayner was a wealthy landowner of Yorkshire who later ministered to the Pilgrim Church at Plymouth, and whose son of the same name was the most brilliant young man of his generation at Harvard. Eaton, elder brother of the first head of Harvard College, had a distinguished career as a puritan controversialist under the Commonwealth, while pugnacious Peter Hobart, minister of Hingham in the Bay Colony, was making Governor Winthrop unhappy by his political assaults.

John Knowles of Lincolnshire entered the College a pensioner in 1620. Many years later an Emmanuel contemporary, Richard Saltonstall, proposed him for the presidency of Harvard College, writing:[3]

By his pregnant parts, and his Improovment thereof, in the Arts, and learned Languages, when he was a Senior Sophister in the University of Camebridge, he was thought fitt (as the flower of his year) to be Moderator of the Sophisters Schools where his worke was every day, each other weeke, in Terme time to make an Oration to the Sophisters, and other Auditors of all sorts, As also to moderate all Disputations, upon logicall and philosophicall questions . . . in which place, he gaue such proof of his ability, as that thereafter, he was chosen a Fellow of his Colledge, and after that (even all the time of his residence in Camebridge) being a Tutor, he was honoured not onely with more Pupils, but with Pupills more considerable than any of his senior fellows.

Knowles was placed eighteenth out of twenty-two, in the top of the *ordo senioritatis* of his bachelor's year.[4] After ten years as

---

£388 5s 5d, leaving a balance of £355 18s 8½d. Each of the nine fellows received a dividend of £39 10s 11d, leaving a balance of £45 7½d.

1. *Hist. Univ. Camb.*, II. 120.
2. See Appendix B.
3. *C. S. M.*, VIII. 197; but Knowles was never fellow of Magdalen.
4. *Hist. Reg. Univ. Camb.* (1917), p. 398.

fellow of St. Catharine's he emigrated to New England, and became colleague minister to George Phillips at Watertown; in 1651 he returned to England, where he became famous as a preacher, and was invited to become President Chauncy's successor at Harvard.

HENRY DUNSTER

But for his refusal, Magdalene would have scored twice in the Harvard presidency; as it is, she deserves eternal gratitude for having educated Henry Dunster, our first, youngest, and one of our greatest presidents.[1] He came of a family of small yeomen,[2] settled for at least four generations in the parish of Bury, Lancashire. Robert Dunster, the President's grandfather, who held a farm called Baleholt of the manor of Tottington, died in 1599, leaving an estate valued at £106, of which his son Henry (the President's father) was to have one-third, including the 'arks, chests, carts, husbandry gear, etc.' when he reached the age of twenty-one. That event came in 1601; the following year Goodman Dunster married, and his fifth child was baptized Henry on November 26, 1609.[3]

Henry Dunster was the 'whiteheaded boy' of this yeoman's family. At the age of four or five his curiosity was aroused by a roving puritan preacher, after whom many of the people flocked.[4] A new minister who came to Bury when he was twelve had him confirmed; but 'many faylings' followed as a schoolboy. In Easter Term, 1627, when he was seventeen years old, Henry matriculated in the University a sizar from Magdalene College. There were sixteen members of his year at Magdalene; of these he remembered best Henry Baker and

1. This gratitude has been recently expressed in substantial form by the erection of a Henry Dunster memorial gateway to the new buildings at Magdalene College, out of contributions from Harvard graduates, on the initiation of Charles Stewart Davison, Esq., an alumnus of both colleges.

2. They had no known connection with the arms-bearing family of Dunster in Somersetshire, whose arms have been appropriated by Dunster House. All the available information about the Dunster family will be found in the *N. E. H. G. R.*, LXI. 186–88 and LXXX. 86–95; and Ernest Axon, *Henry Dunster*, Transactions Lancashire and Cheshire Antiquarian Society, XXVII. 84–103.

3. Not in 1612, as frequently stated.

4. This account of Dunster's early life is taken from his confession on entering our Cambridge church Ms. in N. E. H. G. S.; photostat in M. H. S.; printed in Chaplin, *Life of Dunster*, pp. 262–65.

Phineas Muriall, possibly his chamber-fellows, and John Salt-marsh, who became a great figure in Commonwealth days, a preacher and pamphleteer for religious liberty.[1]

Like so many country boys who find themselves in a great university, Henry entered into the fascinating game of acquiring knowledge with more zeal than discretion — at least so he thought in later years. 'Growing more careless,' he ceased to think of Christ. Like Thomas Shepard and many another youthful sinner, he was 'quickened and revived' by a sermon of the magnetic Dr. Preston. Another sermon by Thomas Goodwin, fellow of St. Catharine's, convinced Henry that he 'had departed from God by folly in dissolute living'; but not for long: an 'inordinate love of humane learning' took possession of his heart. Our yeoman's son must have become something of a book-collector, since no less than three *ex libris*, printed for him while an undergraduate, have survived. The first, dated 1629, is in a pocket edition of the Justus Lipsius text of Tacitus, printed at Amsterdam in 1623.[2] The second is dated and printed in Greek:

῎ΕΡΡΙΚΟΣ ΔΟΥΝΣΤΗΡ,

ὁ ταύτης τῆς Βίβλου κτήτωρ ἐνιαυτῷ.

α. χ. λ. γ.

This label is pasted in the title-page of a miniature Hebrew Bible, beautifully printed by the Plantins at Antwerp in 1573, and handsomely bound at London in Dunster's time.[3] The third Dunster book-label, dated 1634, is in his copy of Thomas Godwyn's 'English Exposition of the Roman Antiquities,' that work on the manners and customs of the Romans so highly recommended by Dr. Holdsworth. Dunster bought it at Cambridge in his sophomore year for 4s 6d. Bound up with it is Godwyn's 'Moses and Aaron,' a corresponding work on Hebrew antiquities; on the back fly-leaf Dunster wrote and his grandson

---

1. Signatures of Dunster's *grex*, reproduced in *C. S. M.* xxxi. 296. For Saltmarsh, see *D. N. B.*; his signature is not found among the others because he graduated a year later. Simon Gunton, vicar and antiquary of Peterborough, is also in the *D. N. B.*; seven others, and John Luddington who joined the *grex* late, are known to have been ministers.

2. 'HENRY DUNSTER is the owner of this book, in the year 1633.' H. C. L.

3. The opinion of Mrs. Augustus P. Loring, Jr., expert on bindings. The Bible (no. 5102 in the Br. & For. Bible Soc. bibliography), is in the H. C. L.

copied a Virgilian verse, favorite of students and lovers in all ages:

Omnia vincit amor et nos cedamus amori.

Other volumes of Dunster's undergraduate library have come down to us with no book-label. Autographed front and back, and marked in his hand 'Pret. 8s 4d of Mr Moody. Cam. Statio,' [1] is an illustrated *Arithmetica et Geometria* of Petrus Ramus, of which he was to make good use later in a newer Cambridge.[2] The fly-leaf of Τῆς Ἑλλάδος φωνῆς ἐπιτομή by Antoine Laubegeois, S. J. (Douai, 1626),[3] bears the inscription 'Lib. Rich. Symons,' to which is added in Dunster's hand, 'quem dedit Henrico Dunstero.' Can this be Richard Symonds, the cavalier-archaeologist, who would shortly be defending the person of his king in Lord Litchfield's troop of horse? Or is it the Richard Symonds who fell fighting his king at Naseby? The one was Dunster's contemporary at Emmanuel, the other at Christ's. And, as evidence that belles-lettres were represented in the future President's library, his copy of the 1611 folio of the works of Edmund Spenser is still preserved.[4]

After sweetening his life in Old England, these books accompanied Dunster to new Cambridge, together with his college 'Paper-book' on the Holdsworthian model,[5] which is devoted to his morning readings in Aristotle. There is a digest of the first book of the *Physiologia* and the *Physica*, with references to Scotist and Thomist glosses, an outline of a syllogistic disputation *Utrum de rebus naturalibus sit Scientia*, definitions of thunder and lightning from the *Meteorologia*, and 'Mr Chappell's notes of especial use for a young preacher.' William Chappell, fellow of Christ's from before Dunster's birth to 1633, was one of the best known college tutors in Cambridge; Milton, among others, was his pupil. Chappell had the reputation of being an 'Arminian' or member of the High Church party.[6]

1. Henry Moody was a bookseller of Cambridge in 1637. Venn, *Admissions to Gonville & Caius College*, p. 196. The book is in the Prince Collection at the B. P. L.
2. See *H. C. S. C.*, Chapter IX.
3. Harvard College Library.
4. Now in the Yale University Library. See *C. S. M.*, vol. XXVIII.
5. Now in the M. H. S. The references to Dunster's books in his will (Chaplin, *Life of Dunster*, pp. 305–07) show that he possessed a considerable library; but these, with a few others mentioned in this volume, are the only ones that I have found with evidence of his ownership.
6. *D. N. B.*; Masson, *Life of John Milton*, I. 90–91. It was probably the same notes

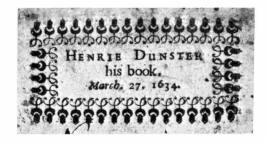

HENRY DUNSTER'S THREE BOOK-LABELS

The fact that Dunster copied down his advice to young preachers not only shows the profession which the future President
intended to follow, but suggests that he was not brought under
puritan influence at Magdalene — a supposition strengthened
by finding a Book of Common Prayer bound up in the same
covers with a black-letter King James Bible of 1634–36, which
became the family Bible of the Dunsters in New England.[1] It
must have been while studying for his M.A. that Dunster acquired that knowledge of Oriental languages which enabled him
to make them an integral part of the Harvard undergraduate
Arts course, and to carry on a learned correspondence from New
England with a German Hebraist. Yet in spite of his 'inordinate love of humane learning,' Dunster's academic career left
no impression of distinction on the records. He was neither
scholar nor fellow of his college, and in the *ordo senioritatis* of
1634 his name stands 115th out of 188 masters.[2] For one of so
low a rank he was probably fortunate in becoming schoolmaster
and curate in his native Bury, apparently 'the world forgetting,
by the world forgot.' But there was something about Dunster
that impressed itself on the college contemporaries who preceded him to New England.

KING'S COLLEGE AND JOHN WILSON

John Wilson, one of the most accomplished and
scholarly of New England divines, was the son of
an Oxonian, a successful pluralist (rector of Islip,
canon of Windsor, prebend of Rochester, chancellor
of St. Paul's) who married a niece of Archbishop
Grindal. John, when the tiniest scholar of Eton,
eight or nine years old, distinguished himself by delivering a
Latin address of welcome to a visiting ambassador. From Eton
he was promoted in due course to the 'scanty band of white-
robed Scholars' at King's College; and in 1608 he became fellow
of that royal foundation.

copied by Dunster which were published by Chappell in 1648 as *Methodus concionandi*,
and Englished as *The Preacher; or the Art and Method of Preaching* (London, 1656).
    1. Now in the Harvard College Library.
    2. Ms. Grace Book E, Cambridge University Registry. This low rank may merely
have indicated that for reasons of poverty he did not reside at college while studying for
the M.A., and was rather rusty when he came up to enter his 'posteriorums' and perform his acts.

'Eat at Trinity, sleep at Jesus, but pray at King's,' was a saying of James I. The chapel with its spreading fan-vault, lighted by the splendor of Flower's windows and supported by pillars bearing the sculptured achievements of Lancastrian and Tudor benefactors, is one of the glories of English architecture. The fellows of King's were a privileged class: university degrees were granted them without examination; they studied little, but spent much time writing poetry and playing music. They might remain fellows for life, unless they married or accepted a living in the Church. John Wilson, as a youth of good connections, studious habits, and a ready talent for Latin poetry, was on the certain road to ease or preferment, as he might choose, when the same spiritual force that deflected Cotton and Preston, and so many young men of that generation, from the primrose path of dalliance, wrenched him aside into rough and stony ways. A sermon of Dr. Chaderton made Wilson feel a want of something that no material comfort or amenity could supply. The 'Seven Treatises' of Richard Rogers [1] opened his heart to Christ; and a conference with William Ames completed the conversion of John Wilson to the puritan way of life. That led him far afield from the choice company and learned conversation in the scented dusk by the Cam, from comfortable sacraments under the

> branching roof
> Self-poised, and scoop'd into ten thousand cells
> Where light and shade repose, where music dwells
> Lingering . . .

to New England, a wooden meeting-house, bare maintenance, rude psalmody, and plain people.

All his values were now changed. The stately ritual of chapel was now a blasphemous mummery. The pleasant chat of his lute-playing fellows became tedious and repulsive. With chosen youths from other colleges who had also resolved to follow Christ, he formed a circle who met for serious discussion and prayer in his college chamber; and a stiff-backed refusal to bow or kneel in chapel lost him the fellowship of King's College. Family influence gained him admission to the Inns of Court, and opened a new path to success; but the law could not quench the flame in his heart. In a year or two Master Wilson had

---

1. Father of Ezekiel Rogers, M.A. Christ's, the pastor of Rowley, Massachusetts.

become a puritan minister, preaching Christ crucified to the poor and humble. We shall meet him later in this story, drawing on his boyhood memories of Eton to design the first Harvard building, resisting the excesses of the puritan spirit, and writing the stately Latin elegiac to our first benefactor.[1]

OTHER CAMBRIDGE COLLEGES

Wilson was one of the two ministers who crossed with Winthrop in 1630. The other, George Phillips, a student next door to him at Caius College, fell under the influence of the same 'old Mr. Rogers of Dedham' who had befriended Hooker, and whose grandson became President of Harvard College. After taking his M.A. in 1617, Phillips became Vicar of Bristed. When threatened with expulsion for non-conformity, a parishioner who was kinsman to the Winthrops recommended him to the Governor, with whom he sailed on the *Arbella* to become the first minister of Watertown. At Caius with him were John Allen, the future minister of Dedham in Massachusetts (so called because so many of old Master Rogers' admirers settled there), and Thomas Allen, who succeeded to John Harvard's office in the Charlestown church, and married his widow.

Pembroke College was the Cambridge home of Roger Williams, who exemplified the democratic and libertarian aspect of puritanism as Cotton and Hooker did the conservative and authoritarian.[2] 'I heartily acknowledge,' wrote Williams many years later, 'that among all the outward Gifts of God, humane learning and the knowledge of Languages and good Arts, are excellent . . . and therefore that Schools of humane Learning, ought to be maintained.'[3] But as he firmly believed that ministers need not be learned, the Colony of Rhode Island which he founded wanted the puritan passion for education, and became notorious for the illiteracy of her people, as she was notable for

1. Cotton Mather, *Johannes in Eremo* (1695), and in *Magnalia*, bk. iii, pt. 1, ch. iii; K. B. Murdock, *Handkerchiefs from Paul*, pp. xli–liii (biography) and 24–97 (poems). The sketch in Anthony Allen's manuscript history of fellows of King's, in the college library, is largely compiled from Mather, who says that Wilson took his M.A. from Emmanuel and sojourned there for a time; but there is no record of this at Emmanuel. As John Wilson was a rather common name, the New Englander is sometimes wrongly identified, for example by Mullinger, III. 179 n.

2. H. B. Parkes, 'Cotton and Williams,' *N. E. Q.*, IV. 735–56.

3. *The Hireling Ministry none of Christs* (1652), quoted in *Narragansett Club Publications*, III. 305–06.

religious and political liberty. Nevertheless, Roger Williams was the first New England pioneer to attempt the conversion of the natives.

The second, John Eliot, the 'Apostle to the Indians,' took his B.A. from Jesus College, Cambridge, in 1622. Forty years later his great Indian Bible was printed in the Indian College in the Harvard Yard; and in due course a copy reached the ancient library where he once had pored over chained books, inscribed 'For Jesus College. Accept, mother, I pray, what a most humble alumnus offers, a son ever having thy prayers.' [1] How often, amid the rough conditions and raw surroundings to which God called them in New England, must these university-bred pioneers have looked back with an aching nostalgia to the placid and mellow beauty of their Cambridge colleges, to the ardent friendships, and even the mad follies of their youth! How many prayers for their prosperity and welfare went up to God from the New England wilderness! There was little else these far-flung children could give to their alma mater. The best return that they could make for what she had given them was so to build that their children might not want the precious privilege of learning, in a society of scholars.

1. Morison, *Builders of the Bay Colony*, p. 291.

VIII

THE UNIVERSITIES OF OXFORD
AND OF DUBLIN[1]

1590–1640

 Since Oxford became royal headquarters in the Great Rebellion, whilst Cambridge early fell to the parliamentary army, too great a political contrast between them has been assumed (as between 'cavalier' Virginia and 'puritan' New England); their differences were circumstantial rather than innate. Under their respective Elizabethan statutes, the organization of the two universities was almost identical, and until a few years after Elizabeth's death it was a toss-up whether Oxford or Cambridge would be the intellectual center of the puritan movement. Robert Parker and Henry Jacob, whom the New Englanders revered only less than Ames and Perkins,[2] were Oxonians; but John Reinolds, last Oxford puritan advocate of the Cartwright school, died in 1607. The previous year an

1. There is no modern history of Oxford in the same class with Mullinger's *Cambridge*; the best is Charles E. Mallet, *History of the University of Oxford* (2 vols., 1924–27). But the contemporary works by Anthony Wood are priceless. His *History and Antiquities of the University of Oxford*, written before 1670, appeared in 1792–96 (John Gutch, ed.), over a century after the Latin translation. There are three editions of Wood's *Athenae Oxonienses*, the best being that of Philip Bliss (4 vols., 1813–20). Wood's *Life and Times*, an autobiography, was published in 5 volumes by the Oxford Historical Society, 1891–1900. William Laud's Diary, History of his Chancellorship, and History of his Troubles are in his *Works* (Oxford, 1847–60), vols. III, IV, and V. Andrew Clark's Introduction to the *Register of the University of Oxford*, vol. II (Oxford Historical Society, 1887), is a mine of information on the organization of the University. The Laudian statutes will be found in *Statutes of the University of Oxford Codified in the Year 1636* (Oxford, 1888, John Griffiths, ed.). Joseph Foster, *Alumni Oxonienses, 1500–1714* (4 vols., 1891–92), is a work similar in scope to Venn's *Alumni Cantabrigienses*, but inferior; the *Historical Register of the University of Oxford* (Oxford, 1900) is a valuable work of reference.

2. Perry Miller, *Orthodoxy in Massachusetts* (1933), *passim*. The first circumstance that pulled the two universities apart was geographic. Cambridge was situated in East Anglia, a region which took the Protestant reformation seriously; whilst Oxford drew on the south and west and on Wales, where Catholic sympathies lingered.

Oxford audience had been horrified when William Laud, fellow of St. John's, preached 'Arminianism' in a university sermon; but in 1611 Laud became President of St. John's. It was from Oxford that the new Anglo-Catholic offensive was launched, and Laud, with strong royal backing, was elected Vice-Chancellor of the University in 1630.[1] Under his able and energetic administration, Oxford became a somewhat more effective place of education than Cambridge, especially in Mathematics; but its intellectual life, like that of Cambridge, still revolved about the political and polemical aspects of theology.

Only one-third as many Oxonians as Cantabrigians emigrated to New England;[2] the Oxford contingent had an influence on early Harvard even less than their numbers would lead one to suppose. But we may not forget that Governor Vane, presiding officer of the General Court that founded Harvard College, was an Oxford man, or that Richard Mather, founder of a Harvard dynasty, had been a student at Brasenose College for a year.

The one Oxford society that sent more than four or five alumni to New England was Magdalen Hall,[3] the only puritan stronghold in that university. William Tyndale, a graduate of the Hall in 1515, there conducted his Bible readings which paved the way for the reformation. The severe discipline of Magdalen Hall appealed not only to puritans but to families like the Verneys, who had idle and frivolous sons needing discipline.[4] John Wilkinson, who became Principal in 1605, carried the fortunes of the Hall to so high a point that 113 students were admitted in one year. Edward Norris, the first schoolmaster of Salem, on whom President Dunster called to convince his Board of Overseers that the Oxford B.A. course lasted four years, migrated from Balliol College to Magdalen Hall, where one of his contemporaries was the great Thomas Hobbes (who

1. C. E. Mallet, *Oxford*, II. 235–37, 246–47, 303.
2. See Appendix B.
3. Not to be confused with Magdalen College. 'The College owned the site of the Hall, received its rent, and supplied most of its early rulers. But it had no jurisdiction over the Hall students.' Mallet, *Oxford*, II. 299–300, with illustration.
4. Wood, *Athenae* (1721 ed.), I. 459; *Memoirs of Verney Family during Civil War* (1892), I. 158 ff. The great Lord Clarendon took his B.A. from Magdalen Hall in 1625. In the nineteenth century the Hall was dissolved, its buildings annexed by Magdalen College, and its members incorporated as Hertford College.

MAGDALEN HALL, OXFORD

WITH HER DISTINGUISHED GRADUATES AND BENEFACTORS

according to his own account hated the puritan discipline, and passed his spare time snaring jackdaws). John Davenport took up residence in the Hall when expelled from Merton College for his father's misplaced economy. Harry Vane the younger sojourned there for a time, but gagged at the university oaths and took no degree. John Oxenbridge, minister of the South Church in Boston, took his B.A. from the Hall in 1628; and Benjamin Woodbridge left it in 1640 to enter Harvard, and head the roll of Harvard graduates.

The most important group of Oxonians in New England were the West Countrymen, whose interest in the New World had been aroused by John White of New College, and who with his blessing sailed from Plymouth in 1630 on the *Mary and John*. John Maverick and John Warham, the one educated at Exeter College (Oxford headquarters for men of Devon),[1] the other at St. Mary's Hall, were the two ministers on this vessel. Of Berkshire origin, the one probably of Magdalen College and the other of Brasenose, were the Damon and Pythias of the New England clergy, Thomas Parker and James Noyes. 'So unshaken was their Friendship, nothing but Death was able to part them. They taught in one School; came over on one Ship; were Pastor and Teacher of one Church; and Mr. Parker continuing always in Celibacy, they lived in one House, till Death separated them for a Time; but they are both now together in one Heaven.'[2]

In Thacher's Island and Avery's Rock off Cape Ann we have a permanent memorial of this Oxford habit of emigrating in couples — a natural precaution perhaps in a country so infested with Cantabrigians as New England. Peter Thacher took his B.A. from the Queen's College in 1608, became a fellow of Corpus Christi, and in due time Rector of St. Edmund's, Salisbury. His son Thomas had finished grammar school in 1635 and was ready for the University, but preferred emigrating to New England with uncle Anthony Thacher and cousin Joseph Avery, an alumnus of Queen's and of St. Edmund Hall. Avery and Anthony Thacher swore never to separate. First they went to

1. Dr. John Prideaux, later Rector of the College and a thorn in Laud's side, was his contemporary as an undergraduate. John Conant (B.A. Exeter, 1631), another famous rector of Exeter, was nephew of Roger Conant, for whose early connection with Harvard College see Chapter XII, below.

2. Memoir of Noyes and Parker by the former's nephew, Nicholas Noyes (A.B. 1667), incorporated in the *Magnalia*, book iii. 145–48.

Newbury, where Parker and Noyes ministered; but when Avery accepted a pastoral call from the fishermen of Marblehead, the Thachers must go too, by virtue of the young men's pact. One August day in 1635 the cousins embarked in an open pinnace, with their wives and numerous little Thachers and Averys and all their goods and chattels. At that season there was every prospect of a placid sail; but in the night 'it pleased the Lord to send so mighty a storm, as the like was never known in New-England since the English came.' The pinnace was driven hard and fast on a rock off Cape Ann. Anthony Thacher, though unable to swim, was washed up on a dry part of the island that now bears his name, and Mrs. Thacher floated ashore on the quarter-deck; but Mrs. Avery and all the children were drowned, and Parson Avery, after an eloquent prayer which heartened his cousins, was swept off the rock by a great wave to his death.[1]

Of such metal were the university-trained founders of New England. It was typical that Avery, little as he relished the prospect of shepherding the rough fisherfolk of Marblehead, accepted their call. If New England offered opportunities to English university men, they were opportunities for work and sacrifice.

Our debt to a class of men who more than any other gave New England her distinctive stamp and character can never be sufficiently acknowledged. These clerical alumni of Oxford and Cambridge were used to a way of life which offered at least security, that state most valued by a scholar, and which opened to ambitious youth many glittering prospects of prebends, deaneries, and bishoprics. All this they exchanged for a career that offered no material rewards, and for a world emphatically new, to which they felt summoned by the voice of God. These men took ill-paid pulpits, not only in the villages about Boston but in the most exposed and lonely wilderness settlements, where they were true pastors, ministers of healing besides performing the sacred office, maintaining standards of English culture amid the levelling influences of the frontier, and pitching their ambitions high in founding a college to educate their successors.

---

1. See Appendix B, and Whittier's sentimental rendering of Thacher's narrative of the shipwreck, 'The Swan Song of Parson Avery.' Thomas Thacher, who was not on board the pinnace, continued his education under the private tuition of Charles Chauncy, entered the ministry, and founded a dynasty of Harvard parsons.

A few became discouraged and returned to England; the majority lived and died serving their people, and played the gentleman's part bravely and well. Their example was a noble one for the Harvard graduates who came after; and nobly was it followed.

TRINITY COLLEGE, DUBLIN [1]

 Of peculiar interest to one searching for transatlantic origins is Trinity College, Dublin. Thomas Fuller of the 'Worthies' described the Irish college as *colonia deducta*, a colony derived from Cambridge; and her royal charter from Queen Elizabeth expressed the hope that Trinity might become *mater universitatis*, the mother of a university.[2] The one phrase might well be used to describe what Harvard was; and the other, her destiny. Harvard, like Trinity, was an English college *in partibus infidelium*; and despite good intentions to educate the native inhabitants, both colleges came to serve only the English colony.

Trinity College was founded in 1591 and established in 1593, largely through the efforts of Oxford and Cambridge graduates living in Ireland, with the double purpose of providing a university education for their sons and of civilizing the 'wild Irish.' A royal charter was obtained from Queen Elizabeth, a site from the Dublin corporation, and funds by public subscription. The early provosts and fellows were Cambridge alumni, the statutes were as near to those of a Cambridge college as the circumstances would permit, and the general tone and tendency of the College, until Archbishop Laud undertook to reform it, were

---

1. J. P. Mahaffy, *An Epoch in Irish History* (London, 1903), is one of the best college histories in existence. Further details about the early period may be found in William Urwick, *Early History of Trinity College* (London, 1892), and W. MacNeile Dixon, *Trinity College* (London, 1902). *The Particular Book of Trinity College, Dublin*, an early book of college records, is published in facsimile (London, 1904). Richard Parr, *The Life of James Usher* (London, 1686), contains much correspondence about the College. G. D. Burtchaell and T. U. Sadleir, *Alumni Dublinenses* (London, 1924), is the official catalogue of matriculates and graduates.

2. The meaning and intent of this last phrase have been much discussed by the historians of Trinity College. Mahaffy's explanation (pp. 63–64) seems the most reasonable: that the founders hoped that Trinity would be merely the first of several colleges like those of Cambridge, but in the meantime perforce clothed the one existing college with the university privilege of granting degrees.

predominantly puritan.¹ Although far more richly endowed than her transatlantic sister, and serving a large city and ancient kingdom, Trinity was very thinly attended for many years. On an average, only ten Bachelors of Arts were annually created during the years 1614–25;² Harvard at a corresponding age had but few less.

One might arrange universities in a descending series, of which Dublin was the next to the lowest, and Harvard at the foot. First comes the medieval university of masters and scholars, teaching all known subjects, and almost independent of the state within whose boundaries it lay. Colleges grew up in order to board and lodge poor scholars; and in England these colleges absorbed the teaching functions and even the administrative powers of the university. Next come universities like St. Andrews, from the first composed of colleges, and of little else; then universities like Glasgow, composed of a single Arts college with only a rudimentary university organization, which the college presently absorbs; and a term lower than Glasgow is Edinburgh.³ Next in the series is Trinity College, Dublin, a completely self-contained Arts college which grants an occasional degree in Divinity. The University of Dublin had no legal existence apart from the College; it was simply the degree-granting aspect of the College.⁴ Dublin degrees have always been granted, and the diplomas signed, by the Provost and Senior Fellows of Trinity College, and sealed with the college seal; just as Harvard degrees, under whatever faculty earned, are granted by, and the diplomas signed or sealed by, the President and Fellows of Harvard College.⁵ Harvard began as

1. Robert H. Murray, *Dublin University and the New World* (1921), p. 11. Cf. J. P. Mahaffy, *op. cit.*, p. 196. The first Provost was a graduate and fellow of Trinity, who had sojourned in Antwerp and Geneva; the second was of St. John's, the third of King's, and the fourth (William Bedell) had been a fellow of Emmanuel. In a letter to Dr. James Ussher, Provost Bedell defends several features of his new statutes as copied from those of Emmanuel, and adds, 'The Arts of dutiful Obedience, and just ruling also in part, I did for 17 years endeavour to learn, under that good Father Dr. Chaderton, in a well-temper'd Society; the cunning tricks of a packing, siding, bandying and skirmishing, with and between great Men, I confess my self ignorant in, and am now, I fear, too old to be taught.' Richard Parr, *Life of James Usher*, p. 392.

2. Mahaffy, *op. cit.*, p. 184 n. 3.

3. See Chapter IX. Rashdall, *op. cit.*, II. pt. I. 308, traces this evolution in the Scots universities and remarks, 'Only at S. Andrews does the existence of two Colleges remind Scotchmen that there was ever a difference between a College and a University.'

4. Mahaffy, *op. cit.*, pp. 63–64.

5. Originally the powers of the Provost and Fellows of Trinity were limited, as those

the last term of this descending series: a mere Arts college with neither the name nor the privileges of a university; and one might relate the three centuries of Harvard history in terms of an ascending series, retracing all the steps lost since the thirteenth century, until our colonial college reached the full stature of medieval Paris.

Trinity closely followed the University of Cambridge in her degree ceremonies, in her vertical classification of students (fellow-commoners, scholars, pensioners, and sizars), in disciplinary regulations, and in the general tone and temper of academic life.[1] But the Trinity undergraduates, as in Scotland and at Harvard, were also divided into four horizontal classes,[2] coincident with years. The names of these four classes were (and still are) junior and senior freshmen, junior and senior sophisters. Each class was taught exclusively by a praelector, or tutor, who was one of the college fellows. No endowed or salaried professorial chairs, excepting in Divinity, appear to have been established before 1656.

The Trinity curriculum, according to the statutes of 1628, is so meagre as to raise a doubt as to whether it includes all the requirements.

JUNIOR FRESHMEN: Dialectic, and a weekly 'Analysis of Invention and Rhetorical Elocution,' subject to the examination and correction of the prælector.

SENIOR FRESHMEN: The praelector explains and determines logical controversies; the students prepare corresponding analyses.

JUNIOR SOPHISTERS: The praelector shall interpret to his auditors precepts of Physiology; 'of the elements, or of mixed or imperfect bodies such as meteors, and of perfect bodies such as metals, plants and animals'; obviously Aristotle was the authority. Weekly disputations on logical theses.

SENIOR SOPHISTERS: Moral philosophy, presumably based on Aristotle. Weekly disputations on Physiology.

---

of the President and Fellows of Harvard are limited, by an outside Board of Visitors, composed of prelates and magnates like the Harvard Board of Overseers. But the fellows of Trinity, unlike those of Harvard, soon managed to get rid of this outside control.

1. As late as 1847, every candidate for a B.A. at Dublin had to deliver a Latin declamation *in laudem philosophiæ*, and act as respondent or defendant in a Latin disputation. D. C. Heron, *Constitutional History of the University of Dublin*, p. 118.

2. Both the Latin term *classis* and the English *class* are used, as at Harvard.

ALL UNDERGRADUATES: Weekly exercises in Latin composition. Archbishop Laud in 1637 required that the whole of Porphyry's *Isagoge* should be read twice a year at least, and that the text of Aristotle's *organon* should not be slighted. In 1659 a certificate of proficiency in Greek from the Greek lecturer, and certificates of 'considerable progress' from the Hebrew and Rhetoric lecturers, were required of all B.A. candidates.[1]

BACHELOR CANDIDATES for M.A.: Mathematics and Politics, commonplaces, and theological disputations.

Even supposing this to be but a skeleton outline of studies, it is clear that the Dublin curriculum was less modern and less ambitious than those of Oxford and Cambridge, the Scottish universities, or even Harvard. Of Mathematics there is none until after the baccalaureate; of Greek and Hebrew, only an elementary knowledge is required, and not even that when the College was first opened. Trinity College does not appear to have been a very effective place of learning — even Provost Bedell calls it a 'poor Colledg of Divines' [2] — until 1652, when two Emmanuel men, Henry Cromwell and Samuel Winter (the latter of John Harvard's year), became respectively Chancellor and Provost. Both worked valiantly to bring the College up to Cambridge standards; and it was during this era of progress that a recent Harvard graduate, Increase Mather, took his M.A. at Trinity, and was offered a fellowship by Provost Winter.

Between Dublin and Harvard there are several other personal links. Trinity may count among her alumni one of the worst and two of the best among the university-educated founders of New England. George Burdett, a bibulous and licentious parson, found New England uncongenial to his tastes, and returned to Ireland, where he obtained preferment under Charles II. Thomas Parker had two years at Dublin, under the tutorship of Dr. James Ussher, before proceeding to Oxford, Leyden, and Franeker. Later, as bachelor parson of Newbury in Massachusetts, he prepared many boys for Harvard. John Winthrop, Jr., Governor of Connecticut and Fellow of the Royal Society, experimental scientist and beloved physician, studied two years at Trinity before proceeding to the Inner Temple and the Near East. Whether his freshman reading of Ramus and Aristotle

1. W. MacN. Dixon, *Trinity College*, pp. 77–79.
2. Parr, *Life of James Usher*, p. 391.

bent his mind toward inquiry and experiment may be doubted; but his generous interest in Harvard is certain. As magistrate of the Bay Colony when the College was founded,[1] his counsel may well have carried weight in erecting a degree-granting college like his alma mater — but would a man who had passed but two years at Trinity have remembered much of its organization? After all, Cotton and Wilson, on the first Harvard Board of Overseers, had been fellows of their colleges, and several of their colleagues had spent seven years at Cambridge. Like circumstances often produce like results: the close institutional resemblance between Trinity College and Harvard seems evidence of a sisterly rather than a filial relation.

1. Winthrop was Assistant of the Massachusetts Bay from 1632 to 1649, and was present when the College was founded; but he was absent from New England between August, 1641, and September, 1643, and seldom in Massachusetts Bay after 1645.

IX

THE SCOTTISH UNIVERSITIES[1]

1574–1640

Any search for the origin of institutions such as universities is beset by many pitfalls. False analogies, distinctions without a difference, and mistaken notions of originality lie in wait for us. This is particularly true when we have to trace institutions overseas, as from England back to Germany and Normandy, or from America back to Europe. Records are scanty, often wanting altogether. At a certain date we find a church, court, town, college, or government in working order, with no direct evidence as to what model, if any, has been followed. As Americans, we naturally hope to find some fresh idea in our colonial institutions, and yield ground reluctantly before proof of European origin. And we need constantly to be on our guard against writers who, on the basis of some far-fetched or trifling resemblance, would provide us with a new pedigree.

1. Alexander Morgan, *Scottish University Studies* (Oxford University Press, 1933), and the *Report by a Royal Commission of Inquiry into the State of the Universities of Scotland* (Parliamentary Papers of 1831) are the best introductions to Scottish university history. A vivid contemporary authority for the sixteenth century, written in 'braid Scots,' is the *Diary of Mr James Melvill, 1556–1601* (Edinburgh, Bannatyne Club Publications, no. 34, 1829), the nephew of Andrew Melville.

Aberdeen. J. M. Bullock, *History of the University of Aberdeen* (London, 1895), and R. S. Rait, *The Universities of Aberdeen* (Aberdeen, 1895), are good short histories. P. J. Anderson, *Studies in the History and Development of the University of Aberdeen*, with bibliography (Aberdeen University Studies, no. 19, 1906), the *Record of the Celebration of the Quatercentenary* (Aberdeen, 1907), and W. Keith Leask, *Interamna Borealis* (Aberdeen, 1917), are collections of monographs and essays on the University's life and history. For King's College the *Fasti Aberdonenses, 1494–1854* (Aberdeen: Spalding Club, 1854), and for Marischal, Anderson's *Fasti Academiæ Mariscallanæ Aberdonensis, 1593–1860* (3 vols., Aberdeen: New Spalding Club, 1889–98), are comprehensive and valuable publications of the college records and muniments. Mr. Anderson also edited *Officers and Graduates of University and King's College Aberdeen, 1495–1860* (*ibid.*, 1893), and

The particular pitfall that awaits seekers for the origin of American educational institutions is the general family resemblance of all European universities in the seventeenth century, since they were all descended from Paris or Bologna, and were all concerned in the common task of inducing more or less reluctant youth to absorb learning. Search the statutes of whatever ,European university you will, and resemblances to the early laws and customs of Harvard and Yale will be found. But it would be a grave mistake to exalt what is at best a remote cousinage into direct parentage. In the absence of direct evidence, some personal connection between the old and the new must be found before even the probability of a causal relation can be plausibly claimed.

The men actively concerned in the foundation and early development of Harvard were, with few exceptions, Cambridge alumni; the phrase *pro modo Academiarum in Anglia* ('according to the manner of universities in England') is found in the first Harvard degree formula; President Dunster's *Quadriennium* memoir is founded on the maxim that Harvard should adopt Oxford and Cambridge standards. Hence it seems mere common sense to assume that whatever in early Harvard resembles old Cambridge was thence derived; and that, conversely, nothing in early Harvard was original, or elsewhere derived, unless it can be shown that nothing corresponding to it existed at the University of Cambridge. Nevertheless, we cannot close this survey without taking a glance at Scottish universities, of which certain founders of Harvard were well aware, and at those of the Low Countries, where a few of them had actually studied.

Roll of Alumni in Arts of the University and King's College of Aberdeen, 1596–1860 (Aberdeen University Studies, no. 1, 1900), which includes the matriculation rolls only; the Marischal College alumni and graduates are listed in the second volume of the *Fasti* and indexed in the third.

Edinburgh. Vol. 1 of Sir Alexander Grant's *Story of the University of Edinburgh* (London, 1884) is the best for our period of several short histories. The *Catalogue of the Graduates* appeared at Edinburgh in 1858.

Glasgow. James Coutts, *History of the University of Glasgow, 1451–1909* (Glasgow, 1909), is not satisfactory for the early period; but the *Munimenta Alme Universitatis Glasguensis* (Maitland Club Publications, no. 72, 3 vols., Glasgow, 1854) include a complete list of graduates for 1578–1695, and a rich collection of early records.

St. Andrews. There is no proper history. Early records, rolls, and statutes are in *Publications of the Scottish Historical Society* (3d ser., III [1926]), and St. Andrews University Publications, no. 7 (1910). R. K. Hannay and John Herkless, *The College of St. Leonard* (Edinburgh, 1905), contains documents with an introduction.

'Caledonia stern and wild' had five small universities in operation at the time Harvard was founded. Local pride and sectarian differences brought a dispersion of effort in a country which, like several of the American states in the last century, was neither large nor rich enough to support one good university.[1] The universities of St. Andrews and Glasgow, and 'The University and King's College of Aberdeen,' were of the fifteenth century, founded by energetic bishops, created *studia generalia* by papal bull, granted the customary privileges and exemptions by the reigning monarch, and endowed by the pious and faithful. 'The Marischal College and University of Aberdeen' and the University of Edinburgh were Presbyterian foundations of the same decade as Emmanuel College, Cambridge. All five claimed university standing, and occasionally granted degrees in Law, Medicine, and Theology.[2] But in general, each Scottish university in the sixteenth and early seventeenth centuries was simply a small [3] Arts college, whose teaching staff consisted of a principal, four young regent masters, and perhaps a professor of divinity who was the parson of some near-by parish.

Scottish and New England Puritans

Obviously, with such universities Harvard had much in common, as had New England with Scotland. Both countries were puritan in dogma, poor in material things, and zealous for education. Many American 'educational principles may be traced back through the Massachusetts School Act of 1647 to the Scottish reformers' 'Buke of Discipline' of 1560.[4] Un-

1. An extreme case of this was the two university colleges, King's and Marischal, situated within a mile of each other in Aberdeen, yet mutually independent. Each maintained a rudimentary university organization and granted its own degrees until 1860, when the two were forced by act of parliament to unite as the University of Aberdeen.

2. The first medical degree given by any Scottish university since the reformation was taken by John Glover, A.B. Harvard 1650, at King's College, Aberdeen, in 1654. St. Andrews alone included more than one college.

3. Marischal College, Aberdeen, granted degrees to only thirty-four men, although she was matriculating an average of nineteen in the same years (1616–19). Harvard, at her corresponding age (1659–62), granted degrees to thirty-six men; and the total enrolment in these four classes was sixty-two.

4. A few quotations from John Knox's 'Book of Discipline' will make this clear:
'Seing that God hath determined that his Churche heir in earth, shallbe tawght not be angellis but by men; and seing that men ar born ignorant of all godlynes; and seing,

doubtedly the founders of Harvard might have found in Scotland as much sympathy for their ideals as in England, and more light on their practical problems; but whether they actually sought help or obtained inspiration from that quarter is another matter. There was very little intercourse of any kind between Scotland and New England until late in the seventeenth century, and their two schools of Protestant theology hardly became aware of one another until the debates of the Westminster Assembly disclosed their differences in matters of polity. A continuous exchange of views between them began only in the lifetime of Jonathan Edwards. So far as we know, not a single Scotch university alumnus came to New England before 1660;[1] indeed, apart from an occasional mariner or merchant, the only New England Scotchmen before 1690 were those wretched captives whom John Cotton piously described to Cromwell as 'the Scots, whom God delivered into your hands at Dunbarre.'

Nor was there much contact between English and Scottish puritans before 1630. Such was the antipathy between the two nations that even after the union of the crowns we find Cam-

---

also, now God ceassith to illuminat men miraculuslie, suddanlie changeing thame, as that he did his Apostlis and utheris in the Primitive Churche: off necessitie it is that your Honouris be most cairfull for the virtuous educatioun, and godlie upbringing of the youth of this Realme.... Off necessitie thairfore we judge it, that everie severall Churche have a Scholmaister appointed, suche a one as is able, at least, to teache Grammer and the Latine toung, yf the Toun be of any reputatioun.... And farther, we think it expedient, that in everie notable toun ... be erected a Colledge, in whiche the Artis, at least Logick and Rethorick, togidder with the Tongues, be read be sufficient Maisteris, for whome honest stipendis must be appointed: as also provisioun for those that be poore, and be nocht able by them selfis, nor by thair freindis, to be sustened at letteris.... Last, The great Schollis callit Universiteis, shallbe repleanischit with those that be apt to learnyng; for this must be cairfullie provideit, that no fader, of what estait or conditioun that ever he be, use his children at his awin fantasie, especiallie in thair youth-heade; but all must be compelled to bring up thair children in learnyng and virtue.' John Knox, *Works* (ed. 1846), ii. 209-11.

1. Yet one of the most zealous advocates of education in the English colonies was Patrick Copland, an early graduate of Marischal College, Aberdeen. As 'preacher to the navie and fleit of the right worshipfull the East India company,' he made a voyage to India, and after his return, in 1617, gave 'the summe of Tua thowsand marks vsuall money of Scotland' to maintain 'a learned divine and Linguist skilfull in the Hebrew and Greeke tongues' in his old college. *Fasti Academiae Mariscallanae*, I. 158-80. Upon his return from a second voyage to India in 1621 he collected £70 from the passengers, in order to establish a free school in Virginia. The following year the Virginia Company appointed him Rector of the Indian College which they proposed to erect at Henricopolis (see Appendix C to this volume). When that project miscarried, Copland emigrated to Bermuda, took charge of a parish, and promoted a free school. For his later connection with Harvard, see the story of the Eleuthera donation (*H. C. S. C.*).

bridge colleges risking the wrath of James I and VI by refusing entrance to his countrymen. Until after the Royal Commission of 1858 had labored, no Scot could be a fellow of St. John's, Christ's, or Emmanuel College. A few sons of English puritan families were sent to Scottish rather than English universities because the discipline was supposed to be more strict, and the expense less burdensome.[1] The Scottish university student of the seventeenth century, younger than his English fellows, enjoyed fewer opportunities for dissipation, but indulged in frequent brawls and rebellions, like the Harvard students of a century ago. His distinctive mode of recreation was 'goff.' James Melvill, a St. Andrews student of pious family, enumerates among the 'necessars' which he had from his father 'bow, arrose, glub and bals' for 'archerie and goff';[2] and a reforming college principal of Aberdeen is said to have posted spies on the links during the hours prescribed for study.

As training schools for the ministry, Scottish universities had no advantage for puritans over Oxford and Cambridge, since by 1620 the policy of James VI had forced both the Church and the colleges of his native country into the Episcopalian mould. The three older universities, which liked not the manners of Scottish reformers (and who would?), were quite ready to fall into Episcopal arms; and this not unwilling union brought forth notable fruits in scholarship and letters. Hence many Presbyterians viewed learning as the scarlet woman; Andrew Cant regarded 'such as wer knowing in antiqwittie and in the wrytings of the Fathers' as men who 'smelled of Poperye.'[3] King's College, Aberdeen, scornfully rejected the Covenant of 1638, and in consequence was properly purged by the General Assembly, and well sacked by the Covenanters. Consequently, there was little in the general situation and atmosphere of the Scottish universities around 1640 to commend them to our founders as a model, and still less in their organization.

1. J. E. B. Mayor (ed.), *Life of Matthew Robinson*, p. 10. *Calendar State Papers, Domestic, 1638–39*, p. 543.

2. Melvill, *Diary*, p. 23. A rule made at Aberdeen in 1659 that bajans (freshmen) should 'furnis upon thair charges futeballs to the remanent classes' so closely resembles the old Harvard custom, 'The freshmen shall furnish . . . foot-balls for the use of the students,' that if one did not recall the antiquity of freshman contributions to the comfort and convenience of their elders and betters one would suspect a direct influence. Bulloch, *Aberdeen*, p. 127; Quincy, II. 540.

3. Bulloch, *Aberdeen*, pp. 103–04.

SCOTTISH ACADEMIC INSTITUTIONS

Small as these universities were, all save Edinburgh were closely modelled on Paris and Bologna — 'sicut in Parisiensi et Bononiensi studiis generalibus,' as the papal bull for Aberdeen prescribed. No attention whatever was paid to the English modifications of the Continental system; for Scots, when they went abroad to study, avoided Oxford and Cambridge, where they were ridiculed as uncouth barbarians, and flocked to Orleans or Paris.[1] In Scotland, university students were called 'supposts' instead of 'scholars.' As on the Continent, they were organized in nations, according to the place of their birth; and the nations annually elected a rector, the head of the university.[2] Continental universities were also followed in lowering the baccalaureate of Arts to an entering degree, or (as in Edinburgh) suppressing it altogether, and in making the M.A. the goal of the Arts course. All Scottish universities granted the M.A. at the end of four years' study, which was on about the same academic level as the B.A. course at Oxford and Cambridge.

The very curriculum was modelled on that of Paris. 'Regentes in artibus instruant et informent suos scolares in scientiis liberalibus prout regentes artium in alma Universitate Parisiensi . . .,' declares Bishop Elphinstone's foundation statute for King's College, Aberdeen.[3] Until after the reformation little was read by Arts students save the works of Aristotle, in Latin. James Melvill, who graduated M.A. from St. Andrews in 1574, notes 'the St. Andros axiom, Absurdum est dicere errasse Aristotelem'; and in his diary he declares, 'I wald haiff glaidlie bein at the Greik and Hebrew toungs, becauss I red in our Byble that it was translated out of Hebrew and Greik; bot tha langages war nocht to be gottine in the land.'

1. In both these universities there was a Collège des Ecossais; and in Paris, at one time, Scots made up a quarter of the English and Teutonic nations.

2. Bologna influence appears in the students, not merely the masters as at Paris, having a vote for Rector. This right is still retained, and the rectorial elections, carried on by political methods, are one of the distinguishing features of Scottish student life today.

3. *Fasti Aberdonenses*, p. 58.

Andrew Melville, the Geneva Academy, and the New Learning

 This want was soon remedied, shortly after Andrew Melville, 'the Scots Melanchthon,' returned to his native country in 1574. This remarkable character, the dominant figure in Scottish history for thirty years, learned his Greek from a French master at the grammar school of Montrose, and at St. Andrews studied Aristotle 'out of the Greik text, quhilk his maisters vnderstood nocht.' Leaving Scotland in 1564 at the age of nineteen, he perfected his knowledge of the Sacred Tongues at Paris, and became a disciple of Peter Ramus. After three years' teaching in the University of Poitiers, he fled before the storm of the counter-reformation to Geneva, walking all the way with no luggage but a Hebrew Testament, 'for he was small and light of body, but full of sprites, vigourus and cowragius.'[1]

When Andrew Melville reached Geneva, Calvin was but five years dead, and the famous academy which he founded was only ten years old. The Geneva Academy was not, strictly speaking, a university, since it enjoyed no corporate privileges and conferred no degrees; but it offered better instruction in Arts, Theology, and Law than many universities at the time. For Protestant youths, Geneva was the most stimulating educational center in Europe. Theodore Beza, who occupied the chair of Greek, at once inducted young Melville into a vacant chair of Humanity (Latin). Refugees from all parts of Europe came pouring in, especially after the tragic Bartholomew's Eve of 1572. Thomas Cartwright was there, gathering new ammunition for his struggle against prelacy. Peter Ramus offered a course in Dialectic; but as Calvinism was founded on Aristotelian Logic, he was not welcome. Cornelius Bertram, whose writings acquainted New England puritans with the polity of ancient Israel, occupied the chair of Hebrew, and taught Aramaic and Syriac to young Melville. Geneva was in a perpetual state of siege from the House of Savoy, and the students in the Academy, enrolled in the militia and liable to guard duty, felt themselves in a real sense soldiers of Christ, destined to

1. James Melvill, *Diary*, pp. 24, 31–33.

spread the reformed religion throughout the earth.[1] And through the dispersion of her alumni to Heidelberg, Leyden, and Scotland, Geneva proved a seed-bed of learning and of stout Protestant doctrine.

Full of knowledge and enthusiasm, Andrew Melville returned home in 1574, and was at once made principal regent of the college at Glasgow. 'Falling to work with a few number of capable heirars, sic as might be instructars of vthers thereafter,' he taught them Greek Grammar, the Ramean Dialectic, and Omer Talon's work on Rhetoric, in connection with classical authors like Homer, Virgil, Horace, Hesiod, Pindar, and Theocritus. 'From that he enterit to the Mathematiks,' and taught his class Euclid, Arithmetic, Geography, and Astronomy. Next he expounded Moral Philosophy, using Aristotle's Ethics and Politics with Cicero's *de Officiis* and some of Plato's Dialogues; then Natural Philosophy with Aristotle; and finally Universal History, supplemented by some practical instruction in the notarial art. In the meantime he was lecturing on Hebrew Grammar, with practical exercises in the Old Testament, and introduced his students to Aramaic and Syriac, using portions of Ezra and Daniel written in Aramaic, and the Syriac version of Galatians.[2]

'His learning and peacefulness was mikle admired,' writes his nephew, 'sa that the nam of that Collage within twa yeirs was noble throwout all the land, and in vther contreys also.' The high reputation of Scottish scholarship and of Scottish universities dates from that time. Melville carried his enthusiasm for Greek and Hebrew to St. Andrews, where he became Principal of St. Mary's College in 1580, and showed that Aristotle could err indeed. If the 'master of them that know' still reigned in Scotland, he was a constitutional and limited monarch; and if his works on Moral and Natural Philosophy still formed the backbone of the Arts course, his *organon* had to bear the competition of Melville's master Petrus Ramus, whose death on St. Bartholomew's Eve commended his work to ardent Protestants.[3] The other distinctive features of Melville's curricular influence

---

1. Charles Borgeaud, *Histoire de l'Université de Genève, L'Académie de Calvin* (Geneva, 1900), pp. 107–14, 132–74.

2. Melvill, *Diary*, pp. 38–39; paraphrased by Coutts, *Hist. Univ. Glasgow*, pp. 60–61.

3. For Ramus' influence at Harvard see *H. C. S. C.*, Chapter VIII.

are the mastering of Greek grammar in freshman year, so that Greek authors might be read in the original, the undergraduate study of Hebrew, and the study of History.

The Aberdeen Curriculum of 1640

 The list of prescribed books at King's College, Aberdeen, about 1640 [1] reflects Melville's influence twenty years after his death. This was undoubtedly the best 'Philosophy' or Liberal Arts curriculum in Scotland at the time Harvard College was founded.[2]

I Year. †Clenardus' entire Greek grammar with the *Scholia* of Antesignanus, selections from the syntaxis of Apollonius by Sylburg, the *de Hellenismo* of Angelo Canini, and constant practise in the analysis of the Greek Testament. The Epistle of St. Basil to St. Gregory of Nazianus; two orations of *†Isocrates and one of the *Philippics; the monitory poem attributed to *Phocylides; one book of *Hesiod's Works and Days, one of the *Iliad, two *Idylls of Theocritus; the first chapter of *Nonnus's Paraphrase of St. John. Elements of Hebrew from *Buxtorf's *Epitome*, with practise in five chapters of a certain catechism.

II Year. *†Ramus's Dialectic, *†Talaeus's or Vossius's Rhetoric; *Alsted's compendium of Arithmetic and Geometry; Porphyry's *Isagoge*, and almost the whole of the Aristotelian *organon*.

III Year. Aristotle: the rest of the *organon*, the first two books and half the third of the Nicomachean Ethics, the *de Virtutibus et Viciis*; the first five books of *de Physico Auditu*; 'A good synopsis of Economic and Political Science from *†Keckermannus, *Alstedius, or some other methodical writer of that kind.'

IV Year. Aristotle: *de Caelo*, books i, ii, iv; *de Ortu et Interitu*, two books; *de Anima*, books i–iii; an epitome of the *Parva Naturalia* and a synopsis of the *Meteorologia*; Elements of Astronomy, Geography, Optics, and Music from *Alsted's above-mentioned work, and elements of Metaphysics from *†Keckermann.

It will be observed that this curriculum, despite the admirable insistence on Greek, and the Ramean competition with

---

1. *Fasti Aberdonenses*, pp. 230–31; P. J. Anderson, *Notes on the Evolution of the Arts Curriculum in the Universities of Aberdeen*, p. 5. I have omitted the prescribed reading in catechisms.

2. In this list, * indicates books known to have been used at Harvard College in the seventeenth century (*H. C. S. C.*, Chaps. VII–XIII), and † indicates books in the College Library that were given by John Harvard (*C. S. M.*, XXI. 190–230).

Aristotle's logic, is still pretty much the old Trivium, Quadrivium, and three Philosophies. Hebrew and other Oriental languages have been deposed from the prominent place assigned by Melville to a freshman course which is not followed up. Of the 'new learning' of the renaissance there is but little; of the 'polite learning' of the same era, none. Greek authors like Nonnus and Phocylides were doubtless chosen, as at Harvard, for their edification rather than their style; and there is no place for History, the importance of which for men of affairs had been emphasized by the humanists. Both in omissions and inclusions, this Aberdeen curriculum bears a marked family resemblance to the early curricula of Harvard and Yale.

Edinburgh Commencement Theses

 A curriculum almost identical with that of Aberdeen was in force at Edinburgh about 1620.[1] This university grew out of an Arts college opened in 1583 by the town council, on land granted by the Crown. Edinburgh was at first a city college like the Academy of Geneva, without corporate independence; students for the most part lived at home or took lodgings; the municipal authorities had full powers 'imponendi et removendi' (of hiring and firing) professors. Yet the medieval university forms and standards of instruction were early established, masters' degrees were granted to students who completed the four years' Arts course,[2] a professor of Theology was appointed, and the 'Toun's College' at the Kirk-of-Field soon reached a modest university stature. Edinburgh Commencements were described as lasting 'de aurora ad vesperam'; and no wonder, since the local ministers and lawyers made a practice of attending, and taking issue with degree candidates in the Latin disputations.

These protracted Edinburgh Commencements provide the only proved link between a Scottish university and early Har-

1. Grant, *Edinburgh*, 1, 138, 148–50.
2. This assumption of authority appears to trouble the historians of the University of Edinburgh. Grant insists (1. 143) that there must have been either a provision in a royal charter, now lost, or oral permission from the authorities to grant degrees. It seems more likely that the Edinburgh city fathers, like the Harvard Overseers, simply assumed a function which by medieval usage could have come only from king or pope. This assumption was legalized in 1621.

vard. As in medieval universities, the Commencement 'Act' consisted of a series of disputations on philosophical and other theses, which had been posted up in advance. Neither at Oxford nor at Cambridge were the annual theses, or even the names of determining bachelors, printed. But at Aberdeen and Edinburgh, as early as 1596, the M.A. candidates [1] adopted the practice of publishing their theses in a quarto pamphlet, with a synopsis of the arguments. Each pamphlet opened with an elaborate dedication to the authorities by the graduating class, whose names followed, printed large and in Latin. From motives of economy, the Edinburgh students abandoned the quarto form of theses and began a broadside issue retaining the dedication and names, but omitting the arguments.[2] A comparison of the thesis sheet of 1641, earliest of this format which has been preserved, with the oldest Harvard thesis sheet (1643) [3] shows such striking resemblances in arrangement and typography as to leave no doubt that whoever arranged the first Harvard Commencement had seen a copy of an Edinburgh thesis sheet. Moreover there is a personal factor to clinch the connection. Francis Johnson, a younger brother of Isaac Johnson, one of the principal founders of the Massachusetts Bay Colony, proceeded from Emmanuel to Edinburgh, where he took his M.A. in 1640.[4] What would have been more natural than for young Master Johnson to have sent a copy of the theses, with his name proudly displayed as *Franciscus Johnsonus*, to some family connection in New England — such as his brother-in-law John Humfrey, Overseer of Harvard College? [5]

Through the same or other personal influences of which we

1. Corresponding to the B.A. candidates in England and at Harvard.

2. J. F. Kellas Johnstone, *Lost Aberdeen Theses* (Aberdeen, 1916), p. 10.

3. See illustrations. The 1642 Harvard theses as reprinted in *New Englands First Fruits* (Appendix D), proves that the arrangement of the 1643 sheet had been adopted the previous year.

4. Venn, *Al. Cantab.*, II. 477; *Catalogue of the Graduates of the University of Edinburgh* (1858), p. 57. No Edinburgh theses sheet for that year survives; but as the same motives of economy — the outbreak of civil war — which induced a change from the pamphlet to the broadside form would have been equally operative in 1640, it may be presumed that the theses sheet of that year resembled, typographically, the surviving example of 1641.

5. Humfrey married Lady Susan Fiennes, sister of Lady Arabella Johnson. He returned to England late in 1641; but that would not preclude his having communicated the Edinburgh theses to his fellow overseers. Lady Deborah Moody, another sister of Lady Arabella Johnson, was in Salem before April, 1640, purchased Humfrey's plantation at Lynn, and removed to Long Island in 1643.

Nobilissimo & Amplissimo Domino D. *Archibaldo Cambello* Argathelia Comiti,
Cambellae & Lorna Dynastae, Regi a secretioribus Consiliis: Adolescentes Magisterii Can-
didati, hasce Theses Philosophicas, quas Deo propitio ad diem *Julii* in Publico Academiae Jacobi Regis Auditorio Propugnabunt Praeside Duncano Forrestro D. C. Q.

Alexander Dickius	Gulielmus Crasordius	Jacobus Karus	Joannes Knoxius	Patricius Oliphantus
David Cunigamius	Gulielmus Oliphantus	Jacobus Lindesius	Joannes Makmillanus	Robertus Nisbetus
David Lindsius	Henricus Charteris	Joannet Galbrithus	Joannes Somervallus	Robertus Todus
David Peblius	Henricus Knoxius	Joannes H liburtonus	Michael Junius	Thomas Byrsius
Georgius Buchanaeus	Hugo Millarus	Joannes Jamisonus	Patricius Humius	Thomas Hamiltonus
				Thomas Pillanus

THESES LOGICAE.

THESES PHYSICAE.

THESES ETHICAE.

THESES SPHAERICAE.

EDINBURGI, Excudebat Jacobus Bryson, Anno Domini 1641.

EDINBURGH THESES OF 1641

NOBILISS· ET AMPLISS· DYNASTAE· D·

Joanni Lauduni Comiti, Machlyniæ & Taringlandiæ Baroni, &c.

Magno SCOTIÆ Cancellario

Theses has Philosophicas, pro quibus in diatriba solenni (Præsidente *Thoma Craufurdio* M. P.) in auditorio publico Academiæ J. R. Edinburgenab, die   Julii, pro virili stabimus

Adamus Silius.	*Clemens Litbiliæ.*
Alexander Forestato.	*Cuthbertus Cunigamius.*
Alexander Funisoni.	*Cuthbertus Grbarjonus.*
Andreas Haranditt.	*David Portisius.*
Archibaldus Turnatus.	*Georgius Buchaninus.*

Gulielmus Arnotus.	*Jacobus Somervdillus.*
Gulielmus Moraius.	*Marcus Duncanidus.*
Gulielmus Rollus.	*Philippus Niboræu.*
Jacobus Caldervodius.	*Robertus Cunigamius.*
Jacobus Calcadarius.	

Jacobus Xinolethus.	*Thomas Craufordius.*
Joannes Cambellus.	*Thomas Lermontius.*
Joannes Clappertonus.	
Joannes Graiæ.	D. DD. CQ.
Joannes Lermontius.	

THESES LOGICÆ.

THESES ETHICÆ.

THESES PHYSICÆ.

THESES MATHEMATICÆ.

Edinburgi, Excudebat Robertus Bryfonus 1642.

EDINBURGH THESES OF 1642

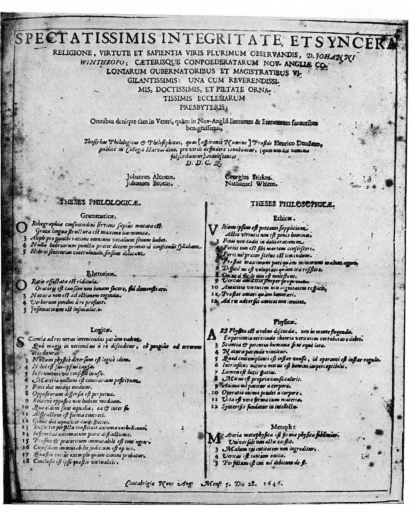

HARVARD THESES OF 1646

ILLVSTRISSIMIS PIETATE, ET VERA

RELIGIONE, VIRTVTE, ET PRVDENTIA HONORATISSIMIS VIRIS, D. IOHANNI Winthropo, cæterisque unitarum Nov-Angliæ Coloniarum Gubernatoribus, & Magiſtratibus Digniſſimis, Vna cum pientiſſimis, vigilantiſſimisque Eccleſiarum Presbyteris :

Nec non omnibus noſtræ Reip. literariæ, tam in Veteri quam in Nov-Anglia, Fautoribus benigniſſimis :

Has Theſes Philologicas & Philoſophicas, quas ſus Θεῶ, Præſide Henrico Dunſtero palam in Collegio Harvardino pro virili propugnare conabuntur (honoris, obſervantiæ et gratitudinis ergo) D. D. D. in artibus liberalibus initiandi Adoleſcentes.

Iohannes Ioneſius.
Samuel Matherus.

Samuel Danforthus.
Iohannes Allinus.

Theſis Philologic:

Grammatic.

L inguæ prius diſcendæ, quam artes .
  Linguæ fœlicius uſu, quam arte diſcuntur .
iij Linguarum Anglicana nulli ſecunda .
iiij Literæ diverſæ ſonum habent diverſum .
v   C. et T. efferre ut S. in latinis abſurdum .
vi Sheva nec vocalis eſt, nec eqnſona, nec ſyllabam efficit.
vij Nullæ diphthongi pronuntiandæ ut ſimplices vocales .
viij Syllabarum accentus non deſtruit tempus .
ix Verba valent ſicut nummus .
x   Syntheſis eſt naturalis Syntaxis .

Rhetoric :

R Hetorica eſt affectionum domina .
  Eloquentia naturalis excellit artificialem .
iij Apte loqui præſtat quam ornate .
iiij Vel geſtus fidem facit .

Logic :

D ialectica eſt omnium artium generaliſſima .
  Efficiens & finis non ingrediuntur rei eſſentiam .
iij Forma ſimul cum reipſa ingeneratur .
iv Poſita forma ponuntur eſſentia, differentia & actio.
v   Et motus et res motu factæ ſunt effecta
vj Oppoſitorum ex uno affirmato alterum negatur.
vij Relata ſunt ſibi mutuo cauſæ .
viij Contradictio topica negat ubique .
ix Privantia maxime diſſentiunt .
x   Genus et ſpecies ſunt notæ cauſarum et effectorum.
xi Omnis ſyllogiſmus eſt neceſſarius ratione formæ .
xii Omnis quæſtio non eſt ſubjectum ſyllogiſmi .
xiij Methodus procedit ab univerſalibus ad ſingularia .

Theſes Philoſophic :

Ethic :

F Oelicitas moralis eſt finis Ethices .
  Per unum actum non generatur habitus .
iij Habitus non pereunt ſola actuum ceſſatione .
iiij Virtus perfecta dari poteſt, vitium neutiquam .
v   Vitiorum cauſa eſt liberum arbitrium .
vi Nullus actus deliberatus in individuo eſt indifferens .
vij Mores non ſequuntur temperamentum corporis .
viij Vulgi mos non regeret nos .
ix Eſt abſtinens qui continens .
x   Honor ſequentem fugit, fugientem ſequitur .
xi Divitiæ nil conferunt fœlicitati morali .
xij Nulla eſt vera amicitia inter improbos .

Phyſic :

N ihil agit in ſeipſum .
  Omnis motus fit in tempore .
ij Non datur infinitum actu .
iiij Pura elementa, non ſunt alimenta .
v   Non datur proportio arithmetica in mixtis .
vi In uno corpore non ſunt plures animæ .
vii Anima eſt tota in toto, & tota in qualibet parte .
viij Status animæ in corpore eſt naturaliſſimus .
ix Viſio fit receptione ſpecierum .
x   Phantaſia producit reales effectus .
xi Primum cognitum eſt ſingulare materiale .

Metaphyſic :

E Ns qua ens, eſt objectum metaphyſices .
  Ente nihil prius, ſimplicius, melius, verius .
iij Datur diſcrimen inter ens et rem .
iv Eſſentia entis non ſuſcipit magis et minus .
v   Veritas eſt conformitas intellectus cum re .

Cantabrigiæ Nov. Ang. Menſ. 8. 1643.

have no trace, a knowledge of the Melville-inspired curricula of Aberdeen and Edinburgh may have reached President Dunster. It may well have been that example, if not the common source at Geneva, which encouraged President Dunster to make Hebrew, Aramaic, and Syriac subjects of undergraduate study.

CLASSES AND THE ROTATING REGENCY

A nearer parallel between Harvard and Scotland may be found in the class system, and the so-called rotating regency.

Cambridge undergraduates, as we have seen, were divided by 'years' into freshmen, sophomores, junior sophisters, and senior sophisters; but by reason of personal tutorial instruction, these 'years' were not organic; they did not constitute 'classes' in the American sense; it was the vertical classification of sizar, pensioner, scholar, and fellow-commoner which was significant at Cambridge. In Scotland these English categories did not exist; the undergraduates were divided into four organic classes, the bajans or bejans, semis, tertiands, and magistrands, with studies prescribed for each.[1] Teaching was organized by a system known as the 'rotating regency,' which was derived from the University of Paris.[2] Each bajan class was put in charge of one of the four regent (teaching) masters who made up the Faculty of Arts, and this regent master gave that class their entire instruction, in every subject, throughout their four undergraduate years. After that class had graduated, the regent, if he remained, took charge of the next entering bajans, and saw them through in turn. Andrew Melville, who observed the disadvantage of confiding an undergraduate's entire instruction to a single youthful tutor, abolished the rotating regency at Glasgow, and assigned each tutor to a subject; but it was restored as soon as he left. The system already had so strong a hold on Scottish university tradition that it lasted well into the eighteenth century.[3] It was adopted at Harvard as soon as

1. For these class names see Grant, *Edinburgh*, I. 144; *Fasti Aberdonenses*, pp. 326, 346; and the *N. E. D.* Bajan came from the Parisian *bec-jaune* (fledgling); semi was short for semi-bajan; the tertiands were called bachelors or determinands at Edinburgh, in memory of the B.A., which was not granted.

2. Rashdall, I. 455 n. 2, 509.

3. Abolished at Edinburgh in 1700, at Glasgow in 1727, at St. Andrews in 1747, at Marischal College in 1753, and at King's College in 1799. Bulloch, *Aberdeen*, pp. 149–50. At King's it was suspended from 1628 to 1641.

tutors were appointed, and continued until 1767, when each tutor was given a subject instead of a class to teach.

 Early in the nineteenth century, when Harvard classmates were beginning to hold reunions, compile records, and issue reports, Marischal College classmates began to do exactly the same things. Aberdeen is probably the only university outside North America where the term 'class of,' followed by a date, has any significance.[1]

The existence of this class system with the rotating regency both in Scotland and at Harvard suggests a causal connection. On the other hand, if Harvard had copied the system she would in all probability have adopted the names also. Instead of tutors and fellows instructing freshmen, sophomores, and sophisters, she would have had 'regents' instructing bejans, determinands, and magistrands; instead of President and Fellows, the college rulers would have been known as the Rector and Senatus Academicus.[2]   Further, the method as practised at Harvard may either have grown out of the tutorial system at Cambridge, where every college tutor took his pupils through their entire undergraduate course, or may simply have been an extension of the class system in secondary schools.[3]   Hence President Dunster needed no Scottish example to put each new

1. J. M. Bulloch, *Class Records in Aberdeen and America, with a Bibliography of Aberdeen Class Records by P. J. Anderson* (Aberdeen, 1916); W. Keith Leask, *Interamna Borealis* (1917). The earliest manuscript record is that of the Class of 1787; the first printed one, compiled by J. W. Barclay, is *Records of the Bageant Class of Marischal College, Session 1848–49* (Aberdeen, 1861). In America this would have been called the Class of 1852, for the distinguishing numeral of the Aberdeen classes is the year of entrance. A curious effect of the system at Aberdeen was a great difference in the size of classes; students would be kept out of college until they could obtain a popular regent.

2. *Senatus Academiae*, meaning the two governing boards, was first authorized on Harvard degree diplomas in 1733 (*C. S. M.*, XVI. 617), when it may well have been taken from Scotland.

3. 'This system,' writes Sir Alexander Grant (*op. cit.*, I. 147) of the rotating regency, 'had been commonly in use in mediaeval Colleges; it was a tutorial as distinguished from a Professorial system.' Rashdall states (II. 312) that there is no trace of a rotating regency outside Scotland. But elsewhere (I. 455 n. 2, 509) he shows that similar tutorial classes existed in Paris colleges in the sixteenth century. Or the rotating regency may equally well have been derived from later medieval university organization, where (for example at Oxford in the fifteenth century) the junior regent master had to lecture on the lowest subject in the prescribed Arts curriculum, through which he gradually worked his way as room was made at the top, and as younger regents came in at the bottom.

Harvard tutor in charge of a class, which he must carry through to their baccalaureate. If any outside suggestion was required for this economical practice, it more probably came from Trinity College, Dublin, where the class system also existed, and where the English names were used. Unless new and direct evidence is found, the verdict in the case of Scottish influence on the Harvard class system must be the Scottish one of 'not proven.'

X

THE UNIVERSITIES OF THE NETHERLANDS [1]
1575–1640

The case for Dutch influence on early Harvard rests on a basis directly contrary to that for the Scottish universities. Strong personal links are there; but institutional resemblances are wholly wanting.

During the century 1550–1650 there was much intellectual exchange between English and Dutch scholars; and the puritan party got aid and comfort from the Calvinists of the Low Countries. Before New England was even named, the Protestant Netherlands gave refuge to English puritans, who tried some of the first and most significant experiments in Congregationalist polity on Dutch soil.[2] John Robinson's congregation, in the words of William Bradford, 'removed to Leyden, a fair and bewtifull citie, and of a sweete situation, but made more famous by the universitie wherwith it is adorned, in which of late had been so many learned men.'[3]

---

1. *Leyden and Franeker.* N. C. Kist, *Bijdragen tot de Vroegste Geschiedenis en den Toekomstigen Bloei der Hoogeschool te Leiden* (Leyden, 1850), is a brief history incorporating extracts from the statutes and other documents. G. D. J. Schotel, *De Academie te Leiden* (Haarlem, 1875), is more detailed. *Pallas Leidensis* (Leiden, 1925) is a collection of monographs published on the occasion of the University's 350th anniversary. Several books of engravings, with brief biographies of the trustees and professors, were published in the early seventeenth century: *Illustris Academia Lugd.-Batava: id est Virorum Clarissimorum Icones, Elogia ac Vitæ* (Leyden, 1613); Joannes Meursius, *Illustrium Hollandiæ & Westfrisiæ Ordinum Alma Academia Leidensis* (Leyden, 1614) and *Athenæ Batavæ* (1625). There is a complete list of matriculations in *Album Studiosorum Academiæ Lugduno Batavæ, 1575–1875*, from which the English names have been collected in Edward Peacock, *Index to English Speaking Students who have graduated at Leyden University* (London, 1883). Everard van Bronkhorst, *Diarium* (The Hague, 1898), gives a vivid picture of university life from 1591 to 1627, in the diary of a professor of law. W. B. S. Boeles, *Frieslands Hoogeschool en het Rijks Athenaeum Te Franeker* (2 vols., Leeuwarden, 1878–89), is a comprehensive history of the University of Franeker, with documents.

2. R. P. Stearns, 'The New England Way in Holland,' *N. E. Q.*, VI. 747–92; Perry Miller, *Orthodoxy in Massachusetts* (1933), chap. v.

3. *History of Plymouth Plantation* (Comm. of Mass. ed.), p. 23.

There they remained ten years. The pilgrim fathers, to be sure, exerted no influence on the founding of Harvard;[1] but one of the most active members of the first Harvard Board of Overseers, Hugh Peter, and one of the most distinguished, John Davenport, had been pastors of English churches in the Low Countries; and the first head of Harvard College, Nathaniel Eaton, was an alumnus of Franeker. Thomas Hooker and Thomas Parker also carried to New England a knowledge of the young and vigorous universities of the Netherlands.

The indomitable Dutch, in the midst of their severe struggle for independence, found means and energy to establish five universities, of which the first and greatest was at Leyden. On October 3, 1574, William of Orange raised the siege of Leyden, whose population had been reduced to the utmost extremity by famine and pestilence. The Protestant provinces had not yet formed their federal union, and thirty-five years of warfare were ahead before even a truce would be won from Spain. But on December 28, 1574, the Prince of Orange requested the Estates of Holland to found a university. On the sixth day after, they formally decreed its foundation; on January 6, 1575, the charter was issued; and on February 5, the University of Leyden was inaugurated by a solemn procession and a classical pageant. Since that day it has never closed its doors.[2]

For a few years the number of students was small, but by the opening of the seventeenth century there were six hundred in residence. Well endowed with ecclesiastical revenues and supported by government grants, the University of Leyden attracted to her four faculties the most distinguished group of scholars in northern Europe. Among the earliest professors were Justus Lipsius, whose most productive period came during his twelve years as professor of History at Leyden, and his successor Joseph Justus Scaliger, the 'bottomless pit of erudition,' whose presence alone would have made a university famous. Among their pupils and successors were Daniel Heinsius, professor of History and Politics, whom Casaubon called 'le petit Scaliger'; Arminius, professor of Theology, whose theses of 1604

1. See Franklin B. Dexter's remarks on the intellectual poverty of the Plymouth Colony, in his *Miscellaneous Historical Papers*, pp. 107–08.
2. J. Lothrop Motley, *Rise of the Dutch Republic* (New York, 1856), ii. 551–82; A. Heynsius, *Discours Solennel pour le Jubilé de l'Université de Leiden* (1875).

against predestination shook Church and State; the Vorstii, professors of Medicine and directors of the anatomical amphitheatre and the botanical garden; Burgersdicius, professor of Philosophy and Golius, professor of Arabic, whose text-books in Logic and Ethics were later used at Harvard; Philip Cluvier, the leading geographer of his age; and Hugo Grotius, 'summus vir Batavae et seculi sui rarum decus.'[1]

Ten years younger than Leyden was the University of Franeker, founded in 1585 amid the din of warfare by the Estates of Friesland, and dedicated, as the Stadholders' proclamation declared, 'cum solenni Nominis Divini Invocatione, piaque ceremonia, non Palladi aut Musis, sed Christo et Ecclesiae.'[2] These last words are the third Harvard motto; and it is with Franeker rather than Leyden that we find our closest personal links. Thomas Parker, whom we have already traced from Dublin to Oxford, took his M.A. at Franeker in 1617, 'with the general Applause of all, and the special Esteem of *Maccovius.*'[3] Shortly after this young Parker, by publishing seventy theological theses with the approval of his master, involved Maccovius in a bitter controversy with a colleague. All theological Friesland joined in the fray; William Ames, who had been the companion in exile of Parker's father, was drawn into it; and finally the Synod of Dort pronounced a verdict.

During the decade before Harvard was founded, the most renowned professor of Theology at Franeker was William Ames, formerly of Christ's College, Cambridge. Ames resigned his chair in 1633 to become teacher of the English church at Rotterdam, as colleague to Hooker and Peter, but died before the year

---

1. So described in *Fundatoris, Curatorum et Professorum Effigies*, one of the illustrated *Athenae* of Leyden.

2. This disclaimer of invocations to Minerva and the Muses was probably meant as a reflection on the pagan ceremonial of the Leyden dedication. Clifford B. Clapp, 'Christo et Ecclesiæ,' *C. S. M.*, xxv. 60.

3. *Magnalia*, book iii. 144; *C. S. M.*, xxviii. 261–67. Johannes Maccovius (Makowski), a Polish nobleman by birth, was a theologian of some renown. The Harvard College Library has a copy of his *Loci Communes Theologici* (Amsterdam, 1658), a guide-book for theological disputations, with the autograph of Thomas Dudley (A.B. 1651) on the fly-leaf; also two copies of his *Metaphysica* edited by Heereboord (Amsterdam, 1651), which belonged to Thomas Goodridge (A.B. 1726).

Academia Lugdunensis

FVNDATIO ET INAVGVRATIO
Academiæ Leidensis.

O N D I T A est celeberrima hęc Academia anno cIɔ.Iɔ.LXXV. a GVLIELMO AVRIACO, magno Principe, & cujus in Belgium beneficia nulla ætas ignorabit. Obseſſa anno præterito quàm arctiſsimè Leida, admirabili Dei inprimis miſericoidiâ, & ſingulari civium virtute ac conſtantia eſt ſervata.

b   Itaq;

THE UNIVERSITY OF LEYDEN IN 1614

was out, and in Hugh Peter's arms.[1] There can be little doubt that if he had lived, Ames would have been offered the Harvard presidency. His widow and children emigrated to New England in 1637, when the General Court of Massachusetts promptly granted £40 to 'Mrs Ames, widow of Doctor Ames, of famos memory.'[2] His pupil Eaton became the first head of the College; his two sons studied at Harvard under Dunster. His portrait, painted at Franeker in 1633, is one of the oldest now owned by the University; his influence on the early Harvard curriculum probably exceeded that of any other scholar.[3]

These personal relations between Dutch scholars and New England puritans were never broken. For instance, Francis Higginson, son of the first minister of Salem, went to Leyden in 1639, bearing a letter from John Winthrop, Jr., to his old friend Professor Golius, and one from Hugh Peter to the pastor of the English church. Edmund Wilson, eldest son of the pastor of Boston, had preceded him; and two members of the first Harvard graduating class, Bellingham and Saltonstall, proceeded to Leyden for their medical education.[4] And Jeremiah Dummer (A.B. 1699), the first Harvard man to take a Ph.D., obtained it at Utrecht.

ORGANIZATION AND CURRICULUM

Everyone connected with the founding of Harvard revered Dutch scholars, and several had personal knowledge of the Dutch universities. Yet we find no resemblance in tone, cur-

---

1. When 'upon the Wing for this American Desart,' according to *Magnalia*, book iii. 8–9. Ames, who was connected by marriage with Governor Winthrop, wrote to him 'with his associates for N E' on December 29, 1629, expressing his love, his prayers for the success of their undertaking, and his intention 'to take the first convenient occasion of following after.' A year later John Humfrey wrote to Winthrop, 'Dr. Ames holds his first affections to you, and the worke,' but seemed to doubt whether 'his remove bee clearely warrantable' (*Winthrop Papers*, II. 180, 336, 340). Cf. Hugo Visscher, *Guilielmus Amesius*, pp. 74–75; George Lyman Kittredge in *C. S. M.*, XIII. 60–69.

2. *Mass. Bay Recs.*, I. 208.

3. See index to this volume, and Mr. Clapp's paper in *C. S. M.*, XXV. 59–83.

4. *Album Stud. Lug. Bat.*, pp. 278, 349, 368, 491; *Magnalia*, book iv. 136; D. Plooij, in *Harv. Grads. Mag.*, XXX. 201–09; Sibley, IV. 455. Winthrop's letter is in the Winthrop Mss. at the M. H. S. Peter's letter states that Higginson's purpose was to prepare himself for Harvard. Bellingham's 'M.D. Lugd.' has been dropped from the Catalogue of Harvard Graduates, since Dr. Plooij was unable to find any record of it at Leyden. Saltonstall proceeded to Padua for his medical degree.

riculum, or organization. Franeker, to be sure, was dedicated *Christo et Ecclesiæ*; but a contemporary reports the students as 'Sacrificing to Bacchus, fighting, and after the fashion of the most ferocious soldiers mutually and continually provoking one another to duels. . . . To Franeker I shall go, where the beer is praiseworthy as the wine is cheap, and the company so delightful that I shall spend all my money on conviviality.'[1] The foundation statutes of Leyden recommend divinity scholarships in words reminiscent of 'New Englands First Fruits': 'lest at any future time there be wanting a supply of fit men devoted to the government of State and Church.'[2] But Leyden and Franeker, in contrast with Harvard, made almost a clean breach with the middle ages, if not with Aristotle. They were of the modern type of Continental university, where all the effort and expense is applied to teaching and research. Little was done for the moral and material welfare of the students, who boarded and lodged in the town.[3] The university authorities prohibited student riots, expensive initiations, and degree banquets, but otherwise left the young men to their own devices, and provided no tutorial guidance. A travelling Englishman reported in 1634 that the students were 'apparelled some as gallants, some like soldiers, some like citizens, some like serving-men'; he saw 'no face or presence of an university' like Oxford.[4]

At Leyden one small building, containing lecture rooms, a library, and an anatomy theatre, sufficed for a university of four faculties, at least twelve professors, numerous associate professors, and several hundred students. Their organization differed fundamentally from that of early Harvard, but curiously resembles that of American state universities. A board of *Curatores* (Trustees) appointed by the government had the say

1. *C. S. M.*, xxviii. 263.
2. N. C. Kist, *Bijdragen*, p. 26. But there were similar formulae in the 'bidding prayers' of English universities.
3. Apart from a select group of divinity students at Leyden, who had scholarships from their home towns, and were boarded and lodged free in one of two small colleges — the Staten-College for Dutchmen, which was founded in 1591 and closed in 1807, and the Collegium Gallicum for Walloons, which was opened in 1606 and lasted about a century. These were colleges on the earliest Parisian, not on the English, model; they admitted no pensioners or commoners, and offered no instruction. William Ames was the second regent of the Staten-College, for whose students he wrote his famous *Medulla Theologiae*. Franeker also had a residential college for theological students.
4. Sir William Brereton, *Travels in Holland* (Chetham Society, 1844), pp. 39-40.

in most academic matters, including the appointment of professors. These were organized in a *Senatus Academicus,* which annually elected a rector and four assessors from among their number. There were frequent conflicts between Trustees and Senate, the latter repeatedly petitioning the Estates to permit no academic promotions or appointments to be made by the Trustees, except after consultation with the Senate.[1] At Franeker the Trustees kept careful watch on the professors' personal habits, noting down any evidence of the national failing, and even attended their lectures to see that they followed the prescribed books.[2]

Nor is there any resemblance between the Arts curriculum of Harvard, and that of Leyden or Franeker.

The Arts faculty took its students from a *pædagogium,*[3] where boys were supposed to enter at the age of seven, and where they studied Latin and Greek Grammar and Rhetoric. They then entered the University, studied Logic their first year, Mathematics the second, and Physics and Ethics the third.[4] By the age of fifteen the Dutch student was supposed to have finished his Arts course, and to have taken the degree of Master or Doctor of Arts.[5] From that point he might continue his linguistic and philosophical studies under one or more of the distinguished

1. Bronkhorst, *Diarium,* pp. 149, 153. One such demand, he says, was made 'especially to repel Vinnius, who, unwanted by the professors, was soliciting a readership in the Institutes, and moreover was speaking in no honorable manner of the Professor of Law' — the diarist himself. For the statutes of Leyden see N. C. Kist, *op. cit.,* pp. 26–29; *Statuta & Leges Academiæ Lugduno-Batavæ, quæ quotannis in ipsa novi Rectoris Inauguratione leguntur* (Lugd. Bat., 1654). Thomas Prince's copy is in the Boston Public Library.

2. Boeles, *Frieslands Hoogeschool,* I. 225. Neither the foundation statutes of Franeker (*ibid.,* I. 435–45) nor the *Statuta et Leges Fundamentales Academiæ Frisiorum quæ est Franequeræ* (1647) show anything suggesting imitation by Harvard.

3. This combination of the Faculty of Arts and a preparatory school was characteristic of the German universities in the fifteenth century, and is found also in Scotland. Rashdall, II. 299–300.

4. Physics is defined in a manner to delight the classicist. 'There is no position in physical doctrine, to which some poet or orator does not bring the fruit of a graceful and humane illustration. The whole of the Georgics are Physics: the whole of Lucretius is Physics. Seneca's *quaestiones* are natural history. That work of the divine Pliny is Physics.' These pleasant methods of teaching natural science were derived from Petrus Ramus (see Frank P. Graves, *Ramus,* p. 57). The Leyden statutes on the curriculum are in Kist, *op. cit.,* pp. 32–36.

5. Kist, pp. 14, 15, 30, 34. Leyden also followed the Continental universities, which depressed the B.A. and finally dropped it altogether; and in regarding master and doctor, Arts and Philosophy, as interchangeable terms. Later in the seventeenth century, the M.A. in Leyden, as in Germany, became known as the Ph.D.

professors in the Arts faculty, or begin a seven-year course leading to the doctorate in Law, Medicine, or Theology.

Here was another fundamental and organic difference between Harvard and the Dutch universities. They followed the
Continental practice in pushing general or 'liberal' education —
instruction in the *artes liberales* — down into the preparatory
school, and encouraging students to begin their professional
studies at the age of fifteen. Harvard followed the English universities in enriching the Arts curriculum at the expense of the
higher faculties, and making the last three years of the Arts
course in effect a professional course in Theology. In England
the great break in a student's life came when he left school and
went to the university. In the Netherlands, as elsewhere on the
Continent, the break came after he had taken his Arts degree,
on beginning professional studies. Leyden's fame rested on her
professors, who were not interested in educating gentlemen, but
in training scholars, lawyers, physicians, and theologians.
Several of them had already been affected by the modern scientific spirit, as René Descartes discovered, to his great delight.[1]
Scholasticism had been abandoned to the Jesuit colleges; Aristotle was no longer an authority, unless in Politics and Ethics.
A 'physic' (botanical) garden[2] and an anatomical theatre provided facilities for research which bore fruit in the seventeenth
and eighteenth centuries.

It would be pleasant, but unprofitable, to continue this exploration of the European background to Harvard. For the farther
we get from Cambridge, the more meagre is the result. The universities of the British Isles and of the Netherlands and Calvin's
Academy at Geneva exhaust all the probable or possible immediate sources of early Harvard institutions.[3] Research only
confirms the suggestion of common sense, that Oxford and

1. Elizabeth S. Haldane, *Descartes*, pp. 187–94. On the other hand, an academic
commission at Leyden decided in 1641 in favor of the Aristotelian as against the Car-
tesian philosophy. R. F. Young, *Comenius in England*, pp. 44–45 n.

2. H. Witte, *'S Rijks Academietuin te Leiden* (Haarlem, 1887). An interesting en-
graving of the University Library at Leyden about 1620 is reproduced in Georg Hirth,
Kulturgeschichtliches Bilderbuch aus drei Jahrhunderten, III. 999, pl. 1518.

3. It has been suggested to me that early Harvard owed something to Gresham College, London, and to the dissenting academies. Gresham College was simply a lecture
foundation for the citizens of London, like the Lowell Institute in Boston. It had no
incorporated students, and conferred no degrees. No dissenting academies were founded
until after the restoration.

THE UNIVERSITY OF FRANEKER

Cambridge alumni in establishing a college of the liberal arts in New England would have followed, as far as their means and circumstances would permit, those academic forms and institutions under which they had been reared, and of which they were justly proud.

XI

THE FOUNDING OF NEW ENGLAND
1630–1642

Harvard College was established at a place which had been a wilderness eight years before, in a colony whose history was less than ten years old,[1] and by a community of less than ten thousand people. The impulse and support came from no church, government, or individual in the Old World, but from an isolated people hemmed in between the forest and the ocean, who had barely secured the necessities of existence. No similar achievement can be found in the history of modern colonization; and in the eight centuries that have elapsed since Abélard lectured by the Seine, there have been few nobler examples of courage in maintaining intellectual standards amid adverse circumstances than the founding and early history of the puritans' college by the Charles.

The Commonwealth which so early established this college was no common plantation, and her inhabitants no ordinary people. They came out, to be sure, in an era of English migration. Barbados, in the first flush of her prosperity, and Virginia, the oldest English colony, where by costly trial and error the people had found security and well-being, attracted thousands of Englishmen who sought prosperity and freedom while caring little for religious disputes. But the main impulse in the emigration to Massachusetts Bay, as to Plymouth in 1620, was religious — in a broad rather than a narrow, sectarian sense.

The puritans, too, looked upon England as 'a lande ouer-burdened with people,' where 'thinges are growne, to suche a transcendente heighte of excess in all intemperance and ryotte, that no mans meanes are enoughe to keepe sayle with his

---

1. In 1630 the Plymouth Colony, founded by the Pilgrim Fathers in 1620, had no settlements within thirty miles of Cambridge, and a population of but 300.

equalls';[1] a land where the rich were growing richer and more insolent, and the poor, poorer and more desperate. Corruption had so demoralized manners and permeated trade that it was becoming difficult to bring up children decently, or to earn a living honestly. But these conditions were only a background to the picture. For twenty years, as we have seen, the position of the puritans had been growing steadily worse. All hope of simplifying the church organization according to their views of what was right had vanished with King James' flat rejection of the Millenary Petition; and the enemy was now sapping the Calvinist doctrine, which the puritans had thought an impregnable fortress of Thirty-nine Articles founded on the Scriptural Rock. Bishop Laud, the King's right-hand man, a High Churchman, a ritualist, and (it was unjustly suspected) a Roman at heart, was closing every vent through which puritan feeling might express itself. The colleges were being purged, the churches forced to conform to ritualistic observances; a people strangely hungry for sermons were given an emasculated version of the Mass, and a prayer-book. Dark clouds were on the European horizon. It was the Catholic period of the Thirty Years' War, when the Spanish infantry was invincible; the Huguenots' loss of La Rochelle and the presence of a Catholic junto at court seemed sinister omens. And during the decade after 1629, when the King attempted to govern England without a parliament, the puritan party began to draw into itself those deep English traditions that clustered about the word 'liberty.'

On the other side, there was the Utopian picture of what society might be if dedicated to the glory of God. For the puritans stripped down to the early Christian ideal that man's unique purpose on earth was to glorify God and obey his commandments. Theirs would be a society where men would be free to form churches on the apostolic pattern and worship according to the way that they (the puritans) thought best, a Christian commonwealth where everyone could exercise an honest calling, where the rulers would be good men, sworn to foster learning, to protect virtue, and to execute 'the punishment of wickedness and vice.' It was not to be a frontier society, where people were all on a level and the long gains of civilization were lost in a struggle to survive. The puritans were determined, if they emi-

1. *Winthrop Papers*, II. 123, 129.

grated, to transport society pure but whole, without corruption but with inequality and amenity. They found the most part of England good, and were quite as determined to reproduce that good as to exclude the evil remnant which had corrupted the rest — excepting the evil in human nature, which they could not hope to exclude but might control. To that end a cross-section of English society, with every valid trade and occupation, they must have, and both material and intellectual standards they must maintain, in order to attain a higher moral and spiritual level. And the puritans were wise enough to know that however difficult it might be to establish this society of their dreams, the task of keeping it going would be far more severe, and only possible with education. Children must learn to read the Bible, that they might know God's truth, and to write and cipher, as an aid to honest living; chosen boys must be taught the learned language in which the world's best thought and literature were still to be found; and a smaller selection of youths must be given university training, in order to furnish the State with competent rulers, the Church with a learned clergy, and society with cultured men.

A small joint-stock company composed largely of puritans had begun a plantation at Salem in 1628; and early in 1629, just as Charles I was dismissing his last parliament for eleven years, they obtained a royal charter as the Governor and Company of the Massachusetts Bay in New England. That region, glowingly described by Captain John Smith and other pioneers, seemed to have the necessary resources to support, with God's blessing, a Christian commonwealth. But it was essential that an enterprise of that sort be self-governing, and secured from interference by the Crown. The royal charter of the Massachusetts Bay Company omitted, whether by accident or intent, any stipulation that the courts of the Company should be held in England. Accordingly, it was possible to transfer the charter and the government to New England, where both would be safe from such vicissitudes as had destroyed the Virginia Company five years before.

THE PURITAN MIGRATION

On August 26, 1629, twelve officers and stockholders of the Company met at Cambridge. Four members of this group, John Winthrop, Sir Richard Saltonstall, Isaac Johnson, and

John Humfrey, were university men; William Pynchon was the son and brother of New College alumni, and Thomas Dudley, who was to sign the Harvard College charter, had two sons in Emmanuel. The twelve signed a compact 'to passe the seas (under God's protection) to inhabite and continue in New England,' provided the charter and government could legally be transferred thither. The General Court of the Company so voted a few days later, and elected John Winthrop governor of both Company and Colony. The word was spread about among puritan families, and by early spring enough had enlisted in the enterprise to fill, with their goods and chattels and supplies, sixteen vessels. The vanguard of this fleet, led by John Winthrop in the *Arbella*, sailed from Cowes on March 29, 1630, after John Cotton had preached a farewell sermon in which he warned the emigrants to 'have a tender care' to their children, 'that they doe not degenerate as the Israelites did.'

By the late autumn of 1630 about nine hundred passengers had been landed on the shores of Massachusetts Bay, and five settlements were rising on the shores of Boston Harbor and the valley of the Charles. The first winter was one of sickness, starvation, and discouragement; many died, including Isaac Johnson, wealthiest of the colonists, and many others returned to England, with gloomy tales of the New England climate. During the years 1631–32 the Colony just managed to hold its own; but in 1633 the great puritan emigration began in earnest; for by this time William Laud from a position of great influence had been promoted to one of great power — the archiepiscopal see of Canterbury — and the screws of conformity were pressed down hard. Ten or twelve passenger-ships arrived that summer, and on the first of October a thanksgiving day was decreed for 'plentifull harvest, ships safely arriued with persons of spetiall vse and quallity,' these last being John Cotton and Thomas Hooker, two of the most prominent nonconformists in England, John Haynes, 'a gentleman of great estate,' Thomas Leverett of Boston, 'and many other men of good estates.' [1] About seventeen emigrant ships came in 1634; thirty-two in 1635, including Thomas Shepard's company; eleven in 1637, including the vessel that brought John Harvard; and twenty in 1638. The influx then declined slightly, and had almost ceased by the beginning of 1641, when the Civil War stopped it alto-

---

1. *Mass. Bay Recs.*, I. 109; Winthrop's *Journal*, September 4, 1633.

gether. By that time there were at least seventeen or eighteen thousand English in New England, roughly twelve thousand in Massachusetts Bay, and five thousand divided between the 'Old Colony' of Plymouth and the three new colonies of Rhode Island, Connecticut, and New Haven.[1]

New England in 1640

This population was not compact or evenly spread, as colored maps misrepresent it, but divided into thirty or forty village communities in four or five district groups. The wealthiest and most populous group lay within the compass of a day's sail along the coast from Barnstable to Newbury, and within a day's march inland, as far as Concord and Sudbury. The second group included all the settlements in the Connecticut Valley, none of them older than 1634; a third, which was still younger, consisted of New Haven and the settlements on both sides of Long Island Sound.[2] It was still a raw, rough country, with long stretches of forest between the settlements. The villages were well seated and compactly laid out, and the houses neatly disposed about a training-field or town common; but the fields and roads were still full of stumps, and it would take time to develop the neat-gardened, white-painted, and steeple-crowned villages that we now associate with colonial New England. Yet the wattle-and-daub huts of the first settlers had already been replaced by houses of hewn and sawn timber, sheathed with unpainted clapboard, steep-roofed with thatch or cedar shingles, and lighted with casement windows. New England was well supplied with craftsmen in the medieval tradition, and the inventories of the time show that many houses were well furnished with oak and pine furniture, pewter and brass utensils, silver, hangings, and a few shelves of books. Public buildings there were none, save the meeting-house in each town, merely a large house 'as faire . . . as they can provide,' but without steeple or other adornment.[3]

Although divided into four distinct jurisdictions, the people of these three settlement groupings were a unit in race, culture,

1. See Appendix B.
2. A fourth group, the settlements about Narragansett Bay, and a fifth, the straggling fishing and trading communities along the Maine coast, had little in common save race with the rest of New England, and took little part or interest in New England educational development until the eighteenth century.
3. Lechford, *Plain Dealing* (1867 ed.), p. 43.

and religion. With very few exceptions, they were puritan or of puritan sympathies, and came to New England primarily to enjoy 'Gospel ordinances,' to maintain such standards and to work out such institutions as would make it possible for men and women to lead a Christian life. Many came in neighborhood companies, often with their pastor; conversely, few emigrating ministers failed to bring with them a band of parishioners and friends.[1] Class distinctions were jealously preserved by the puritans, and the title 'master' was accorded only to university graduates, to the better sort of merchant, to shipmasters or well-to-do tradesmen, and to the gentry, of whom there were sufficient to administer the government and set the tone. At the foot of the social ladder were indented servants — Jacks and Jills, Rogers and Joans — some of whom, to the leaders' great grief, smuggled into the Colony a pagan and merry-England note. But the great bulk of the New Englanders were 'goodmen' and 'goodwives,' artisans or yeoman farmers, of the class who made wills and devised property. These people had in most instances sold their farms and chattels in old England, in order to meet the expense of transportation, and of the first year or two in America.

It was a disappointment that no valuable staple could be grown or obtained in New England, except a small quantity of beaver. The puritans did not take kindly to fishing — one sea voyage was enough! Yet there was no difficulty in earning a living down to 1641, for the newcomers brought goods and money, which they were glad to exchange for the older settlers' corn and beef. As early as 1634 the General Court felt obliged to pass sumptuary legislation to check 'the greate, superfluous, and unnecessary expences occacioned by reason of some newe and immodest fashions' which were apparently becoming too interesting to the older settlers' wives.

This 'Great and General Court of the Governor and Company of the Massachusetts Bay in New England,' the body that founded Harvard College, was simply a stockholders' meeting of the old joint-stock corporation, adapted to the purpose of governing a colony. The government rested on a body of freemen, who must be communicants of a puritan church, and who were admitted individually to the franchise as to a club. These freemen annually elected a governor, deputy-governor and

1. See Appendix B.

assistants, who were known collectively as the magistrates, since they had conferred upon themselves the duties of the English justices of the peace, and exercised judicial as well as executive and legislative power. With them sat the deputies of the freemen.[1] The General Court (including both magistrates and deputies) cheerfully assumed complete authority over the jurisdiction, exercising not a few powers, such as coinage of money and chartering a college, that were by nature sovereign. The authors of 'New Englands First Fruits' could point with pride not only to spiritual and material achievements, but to the 'forme and face of a Commonwealth' appearing in the colony of Massachusetts Bay. The same could be said of New Plymouth, Connecticut, and New Haven, where political institutions developed in close resemblance to those of the Bay Colony.

The Religious and Moral Code

The New England churches were closely interwoven with College and Commonwealth. It so happened that most of the emigrating ministers in the first few years — notably Phillips, Wilson, Cotton, Hooker, and Mather — belonged to the Ames and Parker school of puritan thought, which argued that the primitive and apostolic church was Congregational rather than Presbyterian in polity. Moreover, Plymouth and Salem had already shown that the Congregational way did not necessarily (as most English publicists feared) lead to faction and anarchy. With the learned men and ministers in favor of it, there was no question but that a people 'who had lately stepped out of the Episcopal thraldom in England, to the free air of a new world' would adopt a way which held out to them 'so much liberty and honour.'[2]

It cannot be said that the State was superior to the Church in seventeenth-century New England, or vice-versa; they were parallel aspects of the same divine sovereignty. God's elect, organized in town meeting and court of elections, chose civil magistrates to conduct the Commonwealth; the same elect, organ-

1. From 1634, when the freemen asserted this right, until 1644, when the assistants separated into an upper house.

2. Robert Baillie, *A Dissuasive from the Errours of the Time* (1645), pp. 54–55; for a new study showing the rational development of New England Congregationalism from the school of Ames and Parker, see Perry Miller, *Orthodoxy in Massachusetts* (Harvard University Press, 1933); and cf. R. P. Stearns, 'The New England Way in Holland,' *N. E. Q.*, VI (1933), 747–92.

ized in churches, chose elders to conduct worship and teach the Word. Edward Johnson, when describing the settlement of New England, always speaks of 'the town and church of' such a place. A recent immigrant, writing home in 1638, says, 'Truely Sir, I like it very well, and soe I thinke any godly man God calls over will, when he sees Moyses and Aaron, I meane magistrate and minister, in church and commonwalthe to walke hand in hand, discountenancing and punishinge sinne in whomsoever, and standinge for the praise of them that doe well.' [1]

In New England there were many indented servants of no puritan leanings, in whom the spirit was willing but the flesh weak. For their benefit, the New England colonies passed stringent moral codes embodying in statute law what were supposed to be the commands of God, binding on all the faithful; and the most effective sanction for this code was the organized public opinion of village communities. Sabbatarian observance was most strict. The 'pagan' holidays of merry England were abolished as a waste of 'precious Time.' 'An hours Idleness is a sin, as well as an hours Drunkenness,' wrote Hugh Peter; [2] and the slogan was found useful in advising Harvard freshmen.[3] Thus, taverns were forbidden to provide games or tobacco, lest their clients hang about playing and smoking after having drunk their fill; and 'unprofitable fowlers' who roamed about with a gun were restrained, whilst professional pot-hunters were encouraged. Mercy and pity had a more distinct place in the puritan code than in the common law. Children and dumb animals were protected by legislation, and the punishments meted out by New England courts were not severe in comparison with those of contemporary England. First offenders commonly got off with an admonition or a small fine, and even serious offenders were often acquitted if they could convince the Court of their sincere penitence and make restitution to those injured.[4] New England was not merry. There were no routs and revels, masques and stage-plays, bull-baitings and Whitsun ales, maypoles and morris dances. But for all that, one gets

1. Letter of John Wiswall, September 27, 1638, *Fourteenth Report Hist. Mss. Commission*, Appendix, pt. IV. 56.
2. *A Dying Fathers Last Legacy to an Onely Child* (1660), p. 35. Cf. S. E. Morison, *Builders of the Bay Colony*, pp. 166–67.
3. *C. S. M.*, XIV. 193.
4. See introduction by Professor Zechariah Chafee, Jr., to the Suffolk Court Records, in *C. S. M.*, XXIX.

the impression of a healthy and hearty community, untroubled by the inhibitions and prohibitions that have made latter-day puritanism so unpopular.[1] People were busy building houses and ships, hewing farms out of the forest, consuming an abundance of palatable food and no small measure of exhilarating drink, marrying young and often, and getting large broods of children. They had found release from oppression, religious, political, and economic; and if their way of life would be far more oppressive to us than that from which they had fled, it was to them the way that they had crossed the ocean to enjoy. They were a free and a happy people.

Their right to that way of life they were determined to defend. In 1634 the King appointed a Commission for the Plantations, of which Archbishop Laud was chairman, with power to appoint governors and other officials, revoke charters, pass laws, and enforce religious conformity in all English colonies overseas. The Privy Council ordered Massachusetts Bay to produce her charter, and it was rumored that a royal governor for New England was on his way. The General Court promptly raised £600 for fortifications, ordnance was mounted on Castle Island, the militia system was stiffened up, and the trained bands were given frequent drills; musket balls were made legal tender; a beacon was erected in Boston to warn the country in case of attack; and every resident of or above the age of sixteen was required to swear 'by the greate and dreadfull name of the everliving God' to be true and faithful to the government of the Massachusetts Bay. In 1635 the Court of King's Bench, on a writ of *quo warranto* against the Company, gave judgment that the 'liberties privileges and franchises of the Massachusetts Bay Company' should be taken and seized into the King's hands. New England was divided up into a number of individual proprieties, for the benefit of John Mason, Sir Ferdinando Gorges, and others of the Court party. 'But the project took not effect. The Lord frustrated their design,' records Winthrop. Captain Mason died, Gorges' great ship collapsed on the ways, and the King was too busy with ship-money and with other protestants at home to spend his slender revenue in disciplining a colony overseas.

---

1. The strict code of 1630 represented a genuine striving after moral perfection, one that had the sanction of every normal man's conscience. What was left of the puritanic code in 1930 represented only a tradition, and respectability.

School, Church, and College

That danger past, it was time that education be seen to; for the puritans foresaw that without education to a relatively high level, their way of life could not be maintained. Hitherto, educational 'opportunities' in New England had been somewhat haphazard. No doubt the small boys who came over with their parents in the great emigration hoped to play Indian until they reached man's estate; but there is not much likelihood that many of them had their wish in a community so well provided with ministers, schoolmasters, and birch trees. The recorded history of New England schools begins with a vote of the town of Boston on April 13, 1635, that 'our brother Mr. Philemon Pormort, shalbe intreated to become scholemaster for the teaching and nourtering of children with us.' [1] There is no evidence whether or not Brother Pormort accepted; but it is certain that the 'richer inhabitants' of Boston raised about £40 by subscription on August 2, 1636, and for schoolmaster secured Daniel Maude, sometime of Emmanuel College; and that then, if not sooner, there opened the Boston Grammar or Latin School which has been sending well-equipped scholars to Harvard these three centuries.[2] Another Cambridge alumnus, William Wetherell, contracted with the town of Charlestown on June 3, 1636, 'to keepe a schoole for a twelve monthe' for a salary of £40; and shortly after, if not immediately, this school was free for all boys, and the expenses were raised by taxation. Dorchester provided for a free school out of the rents of Tompson's Island in 1639, with Thomas Waterhouse, late of Emmanuel, as master; Salem chose Master Edward Norris (*nuper de* Balliol and Magdalen Hall) 'to teach skoole' early in 1640; Master Thomas Willis, of Bishop Laud's own college, was teaching Latin at Lynn the same year; and New Haven gave the famous Ezekiel Cheever, whose career at Emmanuel overlapped John Harvard's, his first overseas appointment early in 1642.[3] In that year the General Court of Massachusetts declared that whereas many parents were neglectful 'in training up their children in learning, and labour,' the selectmen of every town must see to it

1. Ms. *Town Records, 1634–60*, printed in 2d Rep. of Record Commissioners, p. 5.
2. *Id.*, p. 160; H. F. Jenks, *Catalogue of Boston Latin School* (1886), pp. 17–19.
3. M. W. Jernegan, *Laboring and Dependent Classes in Colonial America, 1607–1783* (1931), pp. 73–80; for the schoolmasters mentioned, see Appendix B.

that children were at least taught to 'read and understand the principles of religion and the capital lawes of the country.' [1] Six years later this law was reënacted in more stringent terms, and in 1647 the General Court of the Bay Colony, declaring 'It being one chief project of that old deluder, Satan, to keep men from the knowledge of the Scriptures, . . . and that Learning may not be buried in the graves of our fore-fathers in Church and Commonwealth,' ordered that every township of fifty householders maintain a reading and writing master, and that towns of one hundred families or more 'shal set upon a Grammar-School, the Masters therof being able to instruct youth so far as they may be fitted for the Universitie.' [2] Within a few years the colonies of Connecticut and New Haven had passed similar laws, and by 1671 all New England excepting Rhode Island was under a system of compulsory education, with about twelve grammar or Latin schools that fitted lads for college.[3]

It might be expected that a system of primary and secondary schools would be sufficiently ambitious for a group of new, and by no means wealthy, colonies, and that fifty or a hundred years would be allowed to pass before there would be any real need for a university college. But the nature of the puritan church was such that New England could not afford to wait.

Strictly speaking, there was no New England Church, only churches in New England; for no central organization existed. The communicants were 'a royal priesthood, an holy nation, a peculiar people'; [4] each local group of them constituted a church, which had the right to censure, discipline, admit, expel, and excommunicate its members, and elect its officers. A church fully officered had two ministers, the pastor and the teacher, and two ruling elders. The pastor was supposed to exhort, the teacher to expound; but in practice their functions did not differ.[5] Both these 'teaching elders' were ordained by the laying-on of hands,

1. *Mass. Bay Recs.*, II. 8–9.

2. *The Laws and Liberties of Massachusetts* (reprinted from the 1648 edition, Harvard University Press, 1929), pp. 11–12, 47.

3. See *H. C. S. C.*, Chapter XVI, for the towns that had Latin schools.

4. 1 Peter ii. 9.

5. 'In general, pastoral visitation and friendly advice were expected from the pastor, while the teacher preached studied sermons and published treatises in elucidation of the truths of the Bible. In the church service the teacher expounded the meaning of a passage of the Bible, after which the pastor applied the truths to daily life and exhorted the congregation to conduct themselves accordingly. While the exposition of the

laymen and ministers from neighboring churches assisting; no ordination at large was considered valid by the puritans.[1] Services were held twice on the Lord's Day,[2] generally at nine and at two o'clock. The pastor began with a prayer, lasting fifteen minutes or more, the teacher read and expounded a chapter of the Bible;[3] one of the ruling or lay elders then 'lined out' a psalm in the Sternhold and Hopkins or the local Bay version, which the people sang after him, line by line. Then came the sermon, of at least an hour, the meat of the service; and finally a prayer and a blessing. Once a month Holy Communion (or, as they called it, the Lord's Supper) was administered in both kinds to the church members as they sat on their benches, or around the communion table with their Unseen Guest.

Every week each church provided an afternoon 'lecture,' or sermon, expounding the Law, the Gospel, and the Prophets, or applying them to daily life and conduct, as the case might be. And so popular were these lectures that people used to go from town to town in order to take in as many as possible. The General Court, believing this practice 'prejudiciall to the common good' by taking men away from work, attempted to legislate against the practice in 1633.[4] This prohibition was so unpopular that it could not be enforced, and when the Court approached the subject again, in 1639, the elders protested, pointing out that the bishops in England had tried to prevent people attending sermons in other parishes, and that 'liberty for the ordinances was the main end professed of our coming thither.' The Court saw the point, repealed its order, and merely resolved that weekday lectures ought to conclude in time for people to get home before dark.[5]

For a church of such nature, and a people of such tastes, an

teacher was carefully prepared, the application of the pastor had in the nature of the case to be extemporaneous. It was pre-eminently the business of the teacher to read and expound the Bible in the church service.' V. V. Phelps, 'The Pastor and Teacher in New England,' *Harvard Theological Review*, iv. 389. Cf. Lechford, *Plain Dealing* (1867 ed.), pp. 17–18 n.

1. Hence, in the Harvard Catalogues of Graduates from 1782, in which *Ecclesiarum Pastores literis Italicis exarantur*, only those graduates who were ordained over a particular church are recognized as having the clerical character.

2. A literal translation of *dies dominica* (*dimanche*). The New England puritans disliked the pagan term Sunday, and did not greatly relish the Jewish term Sabbath.

3. The puritans objected to what they called 'blind reading' of the Bible, reading with no remarks or explanations, as savoring of ritual.

4. *Mass. Bay Recs.*, i. 110.

5. *Id.*, p. 290; Winthrop, *Journal*, December 3, 1639.

adequate supply of learned clergy was an imperious necessity. In a ritualistic church, very little education would enable a priest to officiate successfully; but the reformation and the puritan movement were in great measure the protests of hungry sheep who were not fed. In evangelistic churches, the 'meer motion of the spirit' was the desired quality in a preacher; but the puritans abhorred 'spiritual drunkenness' and 'gospel wantons.'[1] Neither the weekday lectures nor the Lord's Day assemblies of the puritans were services of worship, as worship is understood by Catholics; they were, literally, *meetings* of the faithful to offer up prayers in matters of common concern, and to hear the Sacred Scripture read, interpreted, and expounded by an expert.[2] Glorifying God by the singing of psalms was incidental; even the Lord's Supper was not conceived of as a sacrament or act of worship, but as a commemorative observance. Hence the teaching function, implicit in every Christian ministry, was explicit and almost exclusive in the puritan ministry. And in those simple days teachers were supposed to know the subject they professed, not merely to be trained in teaching methods. Hence no amount of godliness, good will, or inspiration could compensate for want of learning. Down to the American Revolution and beyond, only a 'learned' minister could qualify for a Congregational church in the puritan colonies. He must be 'learned' not only in the Sacred Tongues, but in the vast literature of exegesis and interpretation that had grown up around the Scripture. There was nothing more dangerous and detestable, in the eyes of orthodox puritans, than an unlearned preacher presuming to interpret Scripture out of his own head.

Thus, in the oft-quoted words of 'New Englands First Fruits,' 'After God had carried us safe to *New England*, and wee had builded our houses, provided necessaries for our liveli-hood, rear'd convenient places for Gods worship, and setled the Civill Government: One of the next things we longed for, and looked after was to advance *Learning* and perpetuate it to Posterity; dreading to leave an illiterate Ministery to the Churches, when our present Ministers shall lie in the Dust.'

1. Title of a famous sermon by Thomas Shepard. See also Chapter XIII.
2. Cf. George Foot Moore's description of the Jewish Synagogue, in his *Judaism* (1927), I. 114–15. The primitive Church of the Acts and the Epistles, which the puritans attempted to restore, followed very closely the programme and purpose of the synagogue.

XII

THE FOUNDING OF HARVARD COLLEGE
1636

'Thus the Lord,' recorded Thomas Shepard, 'was pleased to direct the harts of the magistrates (then keeping court ordinarily in our town because of ther stirs at Boston) to thinke of erecting a Schoole or Colledge, and that speedily to be a nursery of knowledge in these deserts and supply for posterity.'[1]

A project of such relevance to the puritan purpose, and requiring so great an effort to accomplish, must have been the subject of long and earnest discussion. But few records of that time have come down to us, and the most important contemporary chronicler, Governor Winthrop, only mentions the College after it was established.

There was, indeed, a stillborn project for an Indian college in New England, similar in scope and purpose to an earlier plan of the Virginia Company.[2] Dr. John Stoughton, Rector of St. Mary Aldermanbury, London, and sometime fellow of Emmanuel College, a friend of Master John White of Dorchester and a promoter of the Massachusetts Colony, was ambitious to convert the natives. When he was up before the Court of High Commission in 1635, Dr. Stoughton's study was searched for incriminating matter,[3] and an undated subscription paper was found for 'erecting a place where Some may be maintained for learninge the language and instructing heathen and our owne and breeding up as many of the Indians children as providence shall bringe into our hands.'[4]

---

1. Autobiography, in *C. S. M.*, xxvii. 389.
2. See Appendix C.
3. Frances Rose-Troup, *John White*, pp. 297–304; cf. *Diary of John Rous* (1865), pp. 79–80.
4. Printed in Appendix C.

THE SALEM-MARBLEHEAD SITE

Nothing appears to have been done to further this scheme, which was not what the New Englanders wanted. The earliest allusion that I have found to a plan for an English university college in New England is in the town records of Salem for May 2, 1636:[1]

In the reading of an order for the division of Marble head neck; A motion was brought in by Cp. Endicott in behalfe of mr. John Humphries for some Land beyond Forest River, moved by spetiall argument one whereof was, Least that should hinder the building of a Colledge which would be manie [mens] losse.

It was agreed upon this motion that six men should be nominated by the towne to view these Lands, and to consider of the premisses, and for that end was named

mr Thomas Scrugs	Cp Trask
mr Roger Conant [2]	mr Townsen Bishop [4]
John Woodbery [3]	Peter Palfrey.[5]

This record needs interpretation. On May 6, 1635, the General Court had granted the land in question to John Humfrey, provided that no prior rights were claimed by inhabitants of Salem.[6] These Salem rights appear to have been firmly asserted, for on November 11, 1635, the town meeting granted the

1. *Essex Inst. Hist. Coll.*, IV. 93, ix. 16. Mr. William H. Bowden (A.B. 1931) has given me much assistance on this subject.

2. Roger Conant (1592–1679), son of Richard Conant of East Budleigh, Devon, was uncle to John Conant, Rector of Exeter College, Oxford. After a short sojourn in Plymouth Colony in 1623–24, Roger became overseer of the Dorchester Adventurers' plantation at Cape Ann, which removed in 1627 to Nahum-Keike (Salem). After the Endecott party arrived, Conant and his friends (the 'Old Planters') removed to Cape Ann Side (Beverly). Conant frequently served in Salem town offices, as deputy to the General Court, and as local magistrate. President Conant is his descendant. *D. A. B.*; F. O. Conant, *Conant Family*.

3. 'Goodman Woodbery' of Somersetshire joined the Cape Ann settlement in 1624, and followed Conant; he was a town officer and deputy; died *c.* 1643. Ancestor of the poet George Edward Woodberry.

4. Townsend Bishop was in Salem by 1634; a town officer, commissioner in the first Salem Quarterly Court, and deputy to the General Court.

5. Peter Palfrey was in Salem by 1626; a town officer and deputy. Removed to Reading, where he died in 1663.

6. *Mass. Bay Records*, I. 147. It adjoined a grant made to Humfrey at the same time by the General Court, which lay in the town of Saugus (Lynn), the boundary between Lynn and Salem dividing the two grants. On the other side, toward Marblehead, was Hugh Peter's grant of three hundred acres.

same land to Thomas Scruggs.[1] During the following winter, it occurred to some local resident interested in the future college, probably Master Hugh Peter, that this Humfrey-Scruggs grant would be a suitable site for the new seat of learning — as indeed it was.

The tract contained three hundred acres, and extended from Forest River, a tidal inlet of Salem harbor, to the outer coast between Phillips Beach and Marblehead Neck, where it had a frontage of about three-quarters of a mile. It included two small ponds, and consisted for the most part of a level plain suitable for college buildings, of which thirty acres were already 'fitt to be mowed'; for that reason it is referred to in early records as 'the Plains Farm.'[2] The village center of Salem was only two and a half miles away, and Boston fifteen or sixteen miles distant, by way of Lynn and the Charlestown ferry. The Plains Farm contained ample room for Harvard's expansion, even to this day, and it is still remote from main roads such as those which now hem in the Yard and the Houses by lines of roaring motor traffic. For scenic beauty and outdoor sports on land and water there was no better site on the shores of Massachusetts Bay. But our founders were not interested in that sort of scenery or in any sort of sporting possibilities.

The somewhat obscure wording of the town vote quoted above means that Captain Endecott, at the instance of Humfrey (who as a Lynn man could not vote in Salem meeting), proposed that the Plains Farm be reserved for the future College, if Scruggs' rights could be transferred elsewhere. The very next entry in the town records states that Master Scruggs was satisfied by Captain Trask[3] relinquishing to him a two-hundred-acre grant 'beyond Bass River,' in what later became the town of Beverly. Thereby the Plains Farm was set free for the use of the College, if and when it should be established. A somewhat obscure entry in the records of the General Court suggests that

1. *Essex Inst. Hist. Coll.*, IV. 14. Thomas Scruggs probably came with Endecott to Salem, which he represented in the General Court at the session when Harvard College was founded. For supporting Anne Hutchinson he was disarmed and was refused re-election. He built a house in Beverly after taking over Trask's grant, and died there in 1654.

2. *Records of Court of Assistants*, III. 1–4.

3. William Trask (*c.* 1587–1666) came to Salem with Governor Endecott in 1628, and later joined the 'Old Planters' at Beverly. A large landowner, he commanded a company in the Pequot war, and served as deputy to the General Court.

Hugh Peter, after being appointed Overseer of the College in 1637, purchased for it a house in Salem, which he intended as the temporary seat of the College until a building could be erected on the Plains Farm.[1]

The next reference in existing records to the College is the act of foundation.

GOVERNOR VANE AND THE GENERAL COURT

One of the most prominent emigrants of the year 1635 had been young Henry Vane, son and heir to Sir Henry Vane, privy councillor and treasurer of King Charles' household. Converted to the puritan point of view when an undergraduate at Magdalen Hall, Oxford, young Harry still remained of that persuasion after taking the grand tour and being attached to a foreign mission. He then 'forsook the honours and preferments of the court,' wrote Winthrop, 'to enjoy the ordinances of Christ in their purity here.' Although old Sir Henry was averse to the journey, King Charles not only consented but commanded the young man to depart, expecting perhaps that the communion with New England saints would cure him of all yearning toward men of that kidney. Friends and enemies alike have testified to the charm and courage of young Henry Vane; even the grave Winthrop, after a bitter political contest, could call him 'a man of a noble and generous mind'; and the freemen of the Bay were eager to secure him as a permanent resident. On the first Lord's Day of November, shortly after his arrival, the Boston church admitted him to their covenant; within two months he was given magisterial duties; and on May 25, 1636, the day before his twenty-third birthday, young Harry was elected Governor of Massachusetts Bay.

Accordingly it was Governor Vane who presided over the Great and General Court 'houlden at Boston September 8th 1636,' which adjourned to October 25. The members of this court, for having made the earliest recorded appropriation for

---

1. *Mass. Bay Recs.*, I. 263. Five days after the General Court had decided (November 15, 1637) in favor of the Newtown site for the College, the General Court appointed a committee to lay out 'Mr Humfrey's farm', and on March 12, 1637–38, they reported in favor of including the Plains Farm with Humfrey's previous grant across the Lynn line. *Id.*, I. 217, 226.

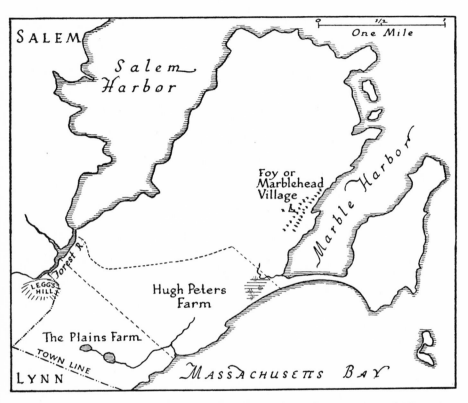

THE PROPOSED SALEM-MARBLEHEAD SITE OF THE COLLEGE

public education in New England, may well be held in grateful memory. These are their names, as we find them in the Court records:

The Governour	Mr John Winthrope, Juni: [4]
Deputie Governour [1]	Mr John Humfrey [4]
Mr Tho: Dudley [2]	Mr Willi: Coddington [5]
Mr John Haynes [3]	Mr Pinchon [6]
Mr Richard Bellingam [4]	Mr Richard Dummer [7]

1. John Winthrop.
2. Assistant; see below, Chapter XIV.
3. John Haynes, born *c.* 1594, was the son of John Haynes, Esq., of Old Holt, Essex,

 and lord of the manor of Copford Hall, Essex. Emigrated with Cotton and Hooker in 1633, resided in Cambridge, and in 1635 was chosen Governor of the Colony; Assistant in 1636. Removed to Connecticut in May, 1637, and became the first governor of that Colony under the Fundamental Orders of 1639; thenceforth Governor and usually Deputy-Governor in alternate years until his death at Hartford, in January 1653/54. Father of John (A.B. Harvard 1656) and Joseph Haynes (A.B. 1658), and of Roger, Joseph's classmate.

4. For these three Assistants, see Appendix B.
5. William Coddington, Assistant, was born in 1601 at Boston, Lincs, and came to Boston, New England, as an Assistant of the Massachusetts Bay Company in 1630. From 1634 to 1636 he was Treasurer of the Colony. A prominent supporter of Anne Hutchinson, he was defeated for reëlection in 1637 and 'withdrew' to Rhode Island; he then withdrew from Mrs. Hutchinson to found Newport. After an attempt to play the autocrat had failed, he became a Quaker, was thrice elected Governor of Rhode Island and Providence Plantations under the Charter of 1663, and died in 1678. *D. A. B.*

6. William Pynchon, Assistant, was born at Springfield, Essex, *c.* 1590; son of John Pynchon, Esq., a graduate of New College, Oxford (but not himself a university man).

 He was one of the founders of the Massachusetts Bay Company, and came over with the Winthrop fleet in 1630. He settled in Roxbury, and engaged in fur trading; from 1632 to 1634 he served as Treasurer of the Colony. In 1636 he removed to the Connecticut Valley and founded Springfield, which under his and his son John's energetic efforts became the principal fur-trading post in New England; but he was present at the General Court in October, 1636. Like others of the puritan gentry, Pynchon was an amateur theologian; and in consequence of a pamphlet on the Atonement which he published in London, and which the General Court declared to be heretical, he was deprived of his magistracy; in 1652 he returned to England, where he died in 1662. Grandfather of Joseph Pynchon, A.B. Harvard 1664. *D. A. B.*; S. E. Morison, in *Proc. M. H. S.,* LXIV. 64–107.

7. Richard Dummer, Assistant, was a merchant. Born *c.* 1598 at Bishopstoke, Hants, he came to New England in 1632 and first settled at Roxbury; in 1635 he removed to Newbury. In 1637 he was left out of the magistracy and disarmed, as a Hutchinsonian; after a year's sojourn in England he returned, and served for several years as deputy of Newbury and magistrate of the Essex County Court. The wealthiest man in Newbury, perhaps in the Colony; died 1678. Father of Shubael Dummer, A.B. 1656.

Mr Herlakenden [1]
Mr Bradstreete [2]
Increase Nowell [3]
Mr John Spencer [4]
Mr Woodman [5]
Mr Rich: Saltonstall [6]
Mr Boreman [7]
Captaine Traske [8]
Mr Bishop [8]

Mr Scruggs [8]
Leiftenant Howe [9]
Mr Tym: Tomlins [10]
Mr Beacher [11]
Goodm: Lynes [12]
Sargent Sprage [13]
Mr Cooke [14]
Mr Willi: Spensar [15]
Mr Danforth [16]

1. Roger Harlakenden, Assistant; see below, Chapter XIV.
2. Simon Bradstreet, Assistant; see Appendix B.
3. Increase Nowell, Assistant, was a nephew or grand-nephew of Alexander Nowell, Dean of St. Paul's, according to Thomas Prince's *Annals* (1736). His family belonged to the Lancashire gentry, but Increase modestly omits the 'Mr.' from his name when recording the above roll of the General Court. Nowell was one of the earliest members and Assistants of the Massachusetts Bay Company; he emigrated in the Winthrop fleet and settled in Charlestown; a neighbor of John Harvard. Secretary of the Colony, 1636–50; Assistant until his death in 1655. Father of Samuel (A.B. August 9, 1653) and Alexander Nowell (A.B. 1664).
4. John Spencer, who settled at Ipswich in 1634, later moved to Newbury, and after serving as deputy returned to England, and died there *c.* 1650.
5. Edward Woodman, a mercer of Melford, emigrated in 1635 and settled at Newbury; deputy, town officer, assistant to local magistrates, merchant, and licensed to sell wine and strong water.
6. Richard Saltonstall, Jr., Assistant; see Appendix B.
7. Thomas Boreman (1601–1673), deputy of Ipswich, came from Claydon, Oxon, and settled at Ipswich with John Winthrop, Jr.
8. For these deputies of Salem see above, pp. 162–63.
9. Daniel Howe, deputy of Lynn, commissioned by Governor Vane as lieutenant of the trained band; Commissioner of the Essex Quarterly Court. Removed to Southampton, Long Island, *c.* 1640.
10. Timothy Tomlins was a kinsman of Thomas Willis (see Appendix B). After a sojourn at Newtown, he removed to Lynn in 1638, where he was a leading planter and deputy, and was licensed to 'keep a house of entertainment.'
11. Captain Thomas Beecher, master of the *Talbot* of the Winthrop fleet, in which he had already made a voyage to Salem in 1629, settled in Charlestown, and served as deputy, town officer, and Captain of the Castle in Boston Harbor. Died in 1637, leaving a considerable estate.
12. Thomas Lynde, a yeoman of Dunstable, Bedfordshire, came *c.* 1634 to Charlestown, where he followed the trade of maltster, and served as deputy and town officer. Died in 1671.
13. Ralph Sprague, son of Edward Sprague of Upway, Dorset, came to Salem in 1628, and the next year built the 'great house' at Charlestown in preparation for Winthrop's company. Deputy and lieutenant of militia; later removed to Malden, and died in 1650.
14. George Cooke, deputy of Newtown; see Appendix B.
15. William Spencer settled at Newtown in 1632; town officer and deputy; a founder of the Ancient and Honourable Artillery, Company of Boston. Removed in 1639 to Hartford, where he served as town officer and deputy.
16. Nicholas Danforth, who according to Cotton Mather had been at some pains to avoid knighthood, came from Framlingham, Suffolk, with the Shepard party to

Mr Tho: Mayhewe [1]
Leiftenant Feaks [2]
Mr Howe [3]
Mr Willi: Hutchinson [4]
Mr Brenton [5]

Mr Coxall [6]
Isaack Heathe [7]
John Johnson [8]
Joseph Wells [9]
Mr Duncon [10]

Newtown in 1635. Deputy and town officer; died 1638. Father of Treasurer Thomas Danforth and of Samuel Danforth (A.B. 1643), fellow of the College.

1. Thomas Mayhew (1593–1682), a mercer of Southampton, came over before 1632 as factor for Matthew Cradock, the early governor of the Massachusetts Bay Company who did not emigrate. He operated Cradock's farm in Medford, which he represented in the General Court. In 1641 Mayhew purchased Martha's Vineyard, Nantucket, and the Elizabeth Islands, and a few years later settled on the Vineyard, which he governed, first as proprietor, and after 1671 as representative of the Duke of York.

2. Robert Feke, deputy of Watertown, came from a long line of London goldsmiths. Admitted freeman of the Bay Colony in 1631, he married that year Elizabeth (Fones), widow and cousin of Henry Winthrop, the Governor's son. Active in military affairs, and one of the organizers of Dedham in 1636, but accompanied Captain Daniel Patrick to Greenwich, Connecticut, in 1640, and after many other wanderings died at Watertown in 1663. Henry W. Foote, *Robert Feke.*

3. Edward Howe, deputy of Watertown, town officer, and ruling elder. Died in 1644.

4. William Hutchinson (1586–1642), deputy of Boston, son of Edward Hutchinson, mercer of Alford, Lincs, is known to fame as the husband of Anne, the Boston prophetess, whom he married in 1612. Mr. Hutchinson, described by Winthrop as 'a man of a very mild temper and weak parts, and wholly guided by his wife,' followed her fortunes until his death. Ancestor of Governor Thomas Hutchinson (A.B. 1727).

5. William Brenton, deputy of Boston, was a merchant from Hammersmith near London who came over *c.* 1633; one of the Boston church members who followed the Hutchinsons to Rhode Island. Established himself at Newport *c.* 1639, but retained a residence in Boston, and also acquired property in Taunton. Named Deputy-Governor in the Rhode Island charter of 1663, and thrice elected Governor (once declined). Died in 1674 at Newport, where his descendants were wealthy merchants until the Revolution, when they returned to England. Brenton's Reef is named after them. Grandfather of Ebenezer Brenton (A.B. Harvard 1707).

6. John Coggeshall, merchant, deputy of Boston. Exiled to Rhode Island with Mrs. Hutchinson, and with Coddington and Brenton withdrew to found Newport. Assistant of Rhode Island 1640–44, President of Colony 1647, died 27 Nov. 1647.

7. Isaac Heath, 'harms maker' (armorer), arrived at Roxbury in 1635. Town officer, deputy, and ruling elder; died in 1661.

8. John Johnson, constable and deputy of Roxbury and colonial surveyor of arms in 1630, was described by Winthrop as 'a very industrious and faithful man in his place.' Died in 1659.

9. Joseph Weld, brother of Master Thomas Weld of Roxbury (see Appendix B), where he settled *c.* 1635. Town officer, deputy, and captain of militia. Died in 1646, leaving £10 to the College and the yearly profit of a share in the ironworks 'to bring vp my son Thomas at Cambridg till he com to be mr of Art, and if my son daniell be capiable of larning, my desire is, that he allso after my son Thomas have the like benefit.' *N. E. H. G. R.*, VII. 33–34. Thomas died at the age of seventeen, but Daniel graduated A.B. 1661.

10. Nathaniel Duncan, deputy of Dorchester, came over in the *Mary and John* in

George Mynott [1]   Mr Waltam [4]
Rich: Collicott [2]   Joseph Andrewes [5]
Will: Smythe [3]

THE ACT OF FOUNDATION

The Court met according to adjournment on October 25, 1636. On the 28th, the fourth day of that session, the marshall's stipend was raised, and John Sanford was chosen cannoneer for Boston and surveyor of arms and munitions; George Munnings was 'graunted 5*l* in regard of the losse of his eye in the voyage to Block Iland'; Lovells Island was granted to Charlestown 'provided they imploy it for fishing'; the sale of lace for garments excepting 'binding or small edging laces' was forbidden; the towns were ordered to fix wages; Nicholas Simkins was summoned 'to give satisfaction for his misdemeanour'; the towns were ordered to pay their own deputies in order 'to ease the publike'; and finally, almost at the end of a heavy day's business, the Court passed the legislative act that founded Harvard College:

𝕿𝖍𝖊 𝕮𝖔𝖚𝖗𝖙 𝖆𝖌𝖗𝖊𝖊𝖉 𝖙𝖔 𝖌𝖎𝖇𝖊 400 𝖑 𝖙𝖔𝖜𝖆𝖗𝖉𝖘 𝖆 𝖘𝖈𝖍𝖔𝖆𝖑𝖊 𝖔𝖗 𝖈𝖔𝖑𝖑𝖊𝖉𝖌𝖊, 𝖜𝖍𝖊𝖆𝖗𝖔𝖋 200 𝖑 𝖙𝖔 𝖇𝖊𝖊 𝖕𝖆𝖎𝖉 𝖙𝖍𝖊 𝖓𝖊𝖝𝖙 𝖞𝖊𝖆𝖗𝖊, 𝖆𝖓𝖉 200 𝖑 𝖜𝖍𝖊𝖓 𝖙𝖍𝖊 𝖜𝖔𝖗𝖐𝖊 𝖎𝖘 𝖋𝖎𝖓𝖎𝖘𝖍𝖊𝖉, 𝖆𝖓𝖉 𝖙𝖍𝖊 𝖓𝖊𝖝𝖙 𝕮𝖔𝖚𝖗𝖙 𝖙𝖔 𝖆𝖕𝖕𝖔𝖎𝖓𝖙 𝖜𝖍𝖊𝖆𝖗𝖊 𝖆𝖓𝖉 𝖜𝖍𝖆𝖙 𝖇𝖚𝖎𝖑𝖉𝖎𝖓𝖌.[6]

1630, and removed to Boston in 1636. A merchant and accountant, 'learned in Latin and French'; Auditor General of the Colony, 1645–57. Died *c.* 1668.

1. George Minot, son of Thomas Minot of Saffron-Walden, came to Dorchester before 1634. Deputy, town officer, and ruling elder for thirty years; died in 1671. James Minot (A.B. 1675) was his grandson.

2. Richard Collicott (*c.* 1603–1686), a tailor, settled in Dorchester in 1633; deputy, town officer, sergeant in the Pequot war, Indian trader, and a large landowner.

3. William Smith, deputy from Weymouth, became a local magistrate in 1638.

4. Henry Waltham, from Weymouth, Dorset, settled as a merchant at Weymouth, Massachusetts, and organized the fishing trade.

5. Joseph Andrew (1597–1679), deputy, was one of the early proprietors of Hingham, the first town clerk, and constable.

6. *Mass. Bay Recs.*, I. 183. Up to a century ago, the date often assigned for the founding of Harvard College was 1638, the year it was opened to students. Thomas Hutchinson, in *Hist. of Mass. Bay* (2d ed., I. 90), states that 'Harvard College takes its date from the year 1638. Two years before, the general court gave four hundred pounds towards a public school at Newtown.' But William Hubbard (A.B. 1642), in his *General History of New England*, probably finished in 1680, enters the founding of the College under the year 1636 (1848 ed., p. 237). Joseph Browne (A.B. 1666), in the chronology in his Almanac for 1669, after mentioning John Harvard, writes '1642, Harvard Colledge Founded, and the Publick Library (given by Magistrates and Ministers) was translated thither.' By 'Harvard Colledge' he probably meant the first building, which was often so called; but later Harvard almanac-makers assumed that he meant the instruc-

GOVERNOR HENRY VANE

It is not known what member offered this motion, and no word of the discussion, if it was discussed, has come down to us. Governor Vane, as presiding officer, cannot have made the motion; but there is every reason to suppose that his attitude was favorable. Coming to New England on the same ship with Hugh Peter, Vane struck up a warm friendship with that experienced clergyman of thirty-seven. Superficially, they had much in common. Both were university men who had travelled far; both were full of enthusiasm and energy. But Vane had a speculative and dreamy temper, whilst Peter was a restless busy-body, always managing and interfering, throwing off a dozen new ideas a day and then forgetting them. Peter's hand is evident in the attempt to secure the College for Salem; and although as a clergyman he could not be a member of the General Court, he may well have coached the Salem deputies, or John Humfrey, so that the matter of founding the College came to a head at the autumn session.

This vote was the foundation of all subsequent proceedings that led to the establishment of Harvard College. The sum of £400 was a formidable one for so small a community as Massachusetts Bay: more than half the entire colony tax levy for 1635, and almost one-quarter the tax levy for 1636.[1] And although payment was made by instalments stretching over sev-

tion, for John Foster (A.B. 1667), in his Almanac for 1676, has '1642, Harvard Colledge founded'; Samuel Danforth (A.B. 1683) dates his Almanac for 1686 in the year 'since the Founding of Harv. Coll. 44,' and Henry Newman (A.B. 1687) dates his Almanac for 1691 in the 49th year of the 'Founding of Harvard Colledge' (Nichols Photostats of Early American Almanacs). James Savage was probably the first to print the vote of 1636, in his 1825 edition of Winthrop's *Journal*, II. 87, 88; and although Benjamin Peirce in the very title of his *History of Harvard University from its foundation in the year 1636* (Cambridge, 1833) proclaims the earlier date, he states in his text (p. 3), 'In the year 1638 the regular course of academic studies seems to have commenced. Historians fix on this period as the date of the foundation of the College.' When the celebration of the bicentenary was impending the Corporation appointed a committee consisting of President Quincy, Joseph Story, and James Walker to ascertain the exact date to be commemorated. They consulted Savage, who pointed out the resolve of October 28, 1636, but suggested no date for the celebration. Edward Everett, on being consulted, suggested that September 8, when the General Court which passed the resolve first met, was the proper date for the celebration; and this the committee settled on, after some attempt to juggle it by new style into the 'third Wednesday in September' (Quincy, II. 639-43). There has never since been any serious question that the event from which to date the founding of Harvard College is this vote on October 28, 1636. The colleges of the British Isles and Latin America date their foundation from the first charter, papal bull, or formal act authorizing the institution; for it is usually impossible to ascertain the date of breaking ground for the first building or that of first receiving scholars.

1. *Mass. Bay Recs.*, I. 460.

eral years, it is clear that subsequent General Courts regarded the promise of October 28, 1636, as the 'country's gift,' and a sacred obligation.[1]

A building was evidently contemplated; but the language of the resolve, 'a schoale or colledge,' is vague as to what sort of institution was to be established.   A 'school,' in contemporary usage, might mean any institution of learning, up to and including one of university grade;[2] a college did not necessarily mean one of university grade, but any self-governing corporation or society for educational or eleemosynary purposes.[3] Something of an educational nature had been authorized; but all depended on the execution of the vote, and the purpose read into it, whether the proposed 'schoale or colledge' should be a mere boys' boarding-school, a college of university standing, or something between the two.

1. See below, Chapter XXI.
2. *New English Dictionary*, 'school,' 7: 'An organized body of teachers and scholars in one of the higher branches of study cultivated in the Middle Ages.' An example is given from Fynes Moryson's *Itinerary* of *c.* 1620: 'The publike schoole at Strasburg was not reputed an universitie yet gave the degrees of Bachelors and Masters of Artes.'
3. *N. E. D.*, 'college,' 4.

XIII

DUX FEMINA FACTI
1636–1637

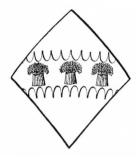 In October, 1636, John Winthrop wrote to his sister and his brother-in-law, Lucy and Emmanuel Downing, inviting them to New England. It is probable that he held out the projected college as an inducement, for their replies offer some interesting advice on the subject.

Mrs. Downing answered first, on March 4, 1636–37:

George and his father complye moste cordyally for new Eng: but poor boy, I fear the journie would not be so prosperous for him as I could wish, in respect you haue yet noe sosieties nor means in that kinde for the education of youths in learninge: and I bless God for it he is yet reasonable hopefull in that waye; and it would I thinke as wee saye greue me in my graue to know that his mynde should be withdrawne from his booke by other sports or imployments, for that weer but the way to make him good att nothinge. Its true the colledges hear are much corruptted, yet not so I hope, but good frinds maye yet finde a fittinge tutor for him: and if it maye be with any hopes of his well doeinge hear. Knowinge your preualency with my husband, and the hazard the boy is in by reson both of his fathers and his owne stronge inclination to the plantation sports, I am bould to present this sollisitous suit of myne, with all earnestnes to you and my nephew Winthrop, that you will not condecend to his goeinge ouer till he hath either attayned to perfection in the arts hear or that theer be sufficient means for to perfect him theerin with you, wich I should be moste glad to hear of: it would make me goe far nimbler to new Eng: if God should call me to it, then otherwise I should; and I beleeu a colledg would put noe small life into the plantation. . . .[1]

Emmanuel Downing wrote two days later:

The name of a Colledge in your plantation would much advantadge it considering the present distast against our vniversityes, you need

1. *5 Coll. M. H. S.*, 1. 19–20.

not stay till you haue Colledges to lodge schollars, for if you could but make a combination of some few able men, ministers or others to read certeyne lectures, and that it were knowne here amongst honest men, you would soone haue students hence, and Incouradgement to proceed further therein. What great burthen would it be to a Minister for the present (till you haue meanes and be better supplyed with schollars) once a week for a moneth in eurie quarter to reade a logick, greke or hebrew lecture or the like.[1]

It was an unconsciously humorous suggestion of Robert C. Winthrop that Harvard College was 'prompted or quickened' in order to keep out of mischief this poor boy George (better known as Sir George Downing, Bart.), easily the most eminent among early Harvard graduates, and certainly one of the most successful and accomplished scoundrels on her entire roster of alumni. Unfortunately for this seductive theory,[2] the College was already founded when the Downings wrote their letters; and by the time they arrived, Mr. Winthrop was too deeply involved in a political and religious conflict to further his sister's worthy ambition for that 'reasonable hopefull' lad.

Mistress Anne Hutchinson

In the vote of £400 for 'a schoale or colledge,' it was provided that the 'next Court . . . appoint wheare and what building.' The next General Court, which met at Boston on December 7, 1636, paid no attention whatever to this promise, for it had more serious and immediate problems to consider. The cause of learning marked time while the authorities wrestled with a clever woman who held them and learning in contempt; and one outcome of the contest was to fix the location of the College.

Dux foemina facti.[3] Mistress Anne Hutchinson, the consort to a Bostonian 'of a very mild temper and weak parts,' was a lady of forty-five years, already several times a mother. If still capable of stimulating that sexual excitement which generally lurks in religious revivals, she was never accused of it by her recorded critics, who, to be sure, were all men. 'This gentlewoman,' writes our first Harvard historian, 'was of a nimble wit, voluble

1. 4 *Coll. M. H. S.*, VI. 47.
2. 5 *Coll. M. H. S.*, I. xxxvii; cf. *The Landmark*, XIII. 692.
3. Quoted by Winthrop from *Aeneid*, i. 364, in his *Short Story of the Antinomians* (London, 1644), p. 157.

tongue, eminent knowledge in the Scriptures, of great charity, and notable helpfulness, especially in such occasions where those of that sex stand in need of the mutual help of each other.'[1] The daughter and sister of university men,[2] easily the first woman in Boston for natural parts, and superior in perception to most men, she was eagerly heard when the goodwives gathered to drink 'groaning beer' at the home of an expectant mother. Her remarks on religion, the great topic of the day, were considered so helpful that she began to hold evening sessions in her husband's house. At these she took the chair, delivered running comments on the Lord's Day sermons and the weekday lectures, invited questions, expounded 'dark places of Scripture,' and, when the spirit moved her, released a prophecy. At the height of her popularity, some sixty to eighty men and women crowded twice a week into her husband's house on the corner of what are now Washington and School Streets in order to hear the Boston prophetess hold forth.

For some time the ministers and magistrates supposed that these meetings were highly edifying; but by the autumn of 1636 they began to be apprehensive. The more enthusiastic followers of Anne were declaring that only two ministers in the colony, her brother-in-law John Wheelwright and John Cotton, teacher of the Boston Church, were genuine ministers of Christ, sealed in his spirit and sanctified with his grace. The rest, including John Wilson, pastor of the Boston Church, were scribes, Pharisees, false hirelings, wolves in sheep's clothing, and priests of Baal. John Wilson, the product of a Windsor deanery, of Eton, and of King's, was an unusually cultured man, a writer of good Latin poetry, and of English verse that is not contemptible. He had sacrificed one of the pleasantest posts in the University of Cambridge, renounced his certain opportunity of high ecclesiastical preferment, broken with his family, liquidated his property, and emigrated to New England, in order to live according to the way of truth; and he did not relish being called a false hireling and a priest of Baal. Nor did he like having half his congregation walk out when he began to preach, and a good part of the rest, well primed by Mrs. Hutchinson, remain to ask

1. William Hubbard, in 2 *Coll. M. H. S.*, v. 283.
2. She was the daughter of the Rev. Francis Marbury, formerly of Christ's College, Cambridge, and her three brothers were educated in Brasenose College, Oxford. F. L. Gay in *Proc. M. H. S.*, XLVIII. 280–81; W. K. Rugg, *Unafraid*, p. 36.

impudent and embarrassing questions after the close of the
sermon. Master Wilson complained to his colleagues that the
lady's followers were 'casting dung on the ministers' faces';
they felt that something should be done about it. For was one
clever woman to be allowed to dictate who should preach and
who should be silent in New England? [1]

This challenge to the ministers' prestige and authority was
enough to explain what followed; but in addition, Anne vented
an opinion which to the orthodox puritans seemed highly dangerous: namely, that 'sanctification was no evidence of justification.' It is now difficult to explain those matters of familiar
discourse in the puritan century without a glossary and a course
in theology; but it is worth trying. Anne Hutchinson and her
opponents agreed on the Calvinist dogma of predestination.
Orthodox puritans (and Anglicans too) believed that 'sanctification' — a proven ability on your part to be and to do good,
together with a calm, rational assurance of divine favor — was
evidence of 'justification' — of salvation. But Mistress Anne
denied that goodness, good works, or rational processes of the
intellect were any evidence whatsoever of salvation. According
to her, your only evidence of probable escape from hell-fire
was an emotional and rapturous illumination, revelation or
perception of the divine voice within you. It followed that the
person thus 'justified' could do no wrong in God's sight; he
might break every one of the ten commandments, yet be saved,
since he was so predestined — and the divine voice could not
easily be mistaken.

The doctrine thus outlined or suggested by Anne Hutchinson
(for she always denied the conclusion to her premise) was cer-

---

1. For Wilson see above, pp. 113–15; the end of Chapter XVI; Appendix B; and
K. B. Murdock, *Handkerchiefs from Paul* (1927). Wilson has not been a favorite with
historians of New England, on account of his harsh policy toward Baptists and Quakers
twenty years later. But there is no excuse for C. F. Adams' description of him as
'harsh in feature and thick of utterance,' and 'coarse of fibre, — hard, matter-of-fact,
unimaginative' (*Three Episodes*, p. 407; the Baptist and Quaker views of him are summarized on pp. 408–10). The remark on his diction is based on a misunderstanding of a
phrase in Johnson's doggerel poetry — 'By thy thick utterance' (*W. W. P.* 1910 ed.,
p. 67), in which Johnson used 'thick' in the contemporary sense of 'plentiful, abundant'
(cf. Milton's 'Thick as autumnal leaves...') Both Winthrop and Cotton Mather bear
abundant evidence to Wilson's fine qualities; and Mather tells the story that he was
once viewing a muster of militia when a bystander remarked, 'Here's a mighty body of
people, and there is not seven of them all, but what loves Master Wilson.' To which the
pastor replied, 'And there is not so much as one of them all, but Master Wilson loves
him.'

tainly more logical, to our way of thinking, than the greatly overrated logic of John Calvin. But it was instantly recognized by the learned as the antinomian heresy of John Agricola, which in Germany had produced licentious orgies by religious enthusiasts who considered themselves as 'justified,' incapable of sin and above the law. And whatever the consequences might be, it was a fact that Anne Hutchinson had already broken the unified religious front of New England puritanism, which needed unity above all things if the experiment in Christian living was to succeed. The colony was divided into two wrangling camps, and 'it began to be as common here,' wrote Winthrop, 'to distinguish between men being under a covenant of grace or a covenant of works,[1] as in other countries between Protestants and Papists.' It was indeed on a small scale a replica of the great Calvinist-Arminian controversy in Holland twenty years before, which had ended with the murder of John Olden Barneveldt. A large majority of the town and church of Boston, and young Governor Vane, were of the Hutchinson or 'covenant of grace' party. All Winthrop's authority was required to prevent John Wilson being driven from his pastoral office; and out-of-town visitors to the Hutchinson parlor meetings were spreading the fire in the other churches. The party was bitter and truculent, sowing distrust, suspicion, and hatred, and confident of success.

Morally and socially, the Hutchinsonian leaders were of the best in New England — and their triumph would have led to no antinomian orgies, as their subsequent conduct in Rhode Island proved. But their success would have divided New England into a multitude of little jangling sects (as later occurred in Rhode Island and old England), and inaugurated an era of frontier revivalism and hot-gospelling. It is highly probable that a defeat of orthodox puritanism at their hands would have meant a stillborn College. For if the Arts, the Tongues, and the Philosophies were no help to a preacher, if the Church Fathers

---

1. These phrases, both of Biblical origin, were used by Anne Hutchinson to distinguish those preachers whom she liked from those whom she disliked, the implied distinction being that the one class emphasized the divine grace as a free gift which might come to sinner as well as saint, while the other emphasized morality and good works as a means to, or evidence of, grace. As judged by their published sermons, there was no such distinction between the preaching of Cotton and of Shepard, whom Mrs. Hutchinson placed in the opposing camps; although there may have been between that of Cotton and Wilson.

and Protestant divines were beside the point, and if learned ministers could be silenced by the 'immediate revelations' of an untrained woman, what was the use of a college to train ministers? If the gift of prophecy was granted gratis by the Holy Ghost, why study four years for a degree? The inference was plain; and there is evidence that Anne Hutchinson's followers, like 'new lights' of all time, grasped it with enthusiasm. Captain Edward Johnson reports, 'shee and her consorts mightily rayling against learning, perswading all they could to take heed of being spoyled by it, and in the meane time, shee her selfe would dispute (forsooth) and to shew her skill in that way. "Here is a falacy," quoth she, "in this syllogisme."' And said one of them to Johnson, '"Come along with me . . . I'le bring you to a Woman that Preaches better Gospell then any of your black-coates that have been at the Ninneversity, a Woman of another kinde of spirit, who hath had many Revelations of things to come, and for my part," saith hee, "I had rather hear such a one that speakes from the meere motion of the spirit, without any study at all, then any of your learned Scollers, although they may be fuller of Scripture."' [1]

During the same General Court of October, 1636, in which £400 was voted for the College, magistrates and ministers tried to 'iron out' the schism 'in conference,' but only succeeded in widening their irreconcilable differences. Hugh Peter openly broke with Governor Vane, who 'went so far beyond the rest, as to maintain a personal union with the Holy Ghost.' [2] Anne told the assembled ministers to their faces that they were not only not preaching the Gospel, but incapable of doing it, as unconverted. John Wilson 'made a very sad speech of the condition of our churches' [3] before the General Court, and was bitterly arraigned for it in his own church, Governor Vane leading the attack. 'It was strange to see,' records Winthrop,[4] 'how the common people were led, by example, to condemn him in that, which (it was very probable) divers of them did not understand, nor the rule which he was supposed to have broken; and that

---

1. *W. W. P.*, pp. 127–28. Although Vane and Coddington were educated men, the strength of her support came from those whom Winthrop described as of 'meane condition, and weake parts' (*Antinomianism*, p. 157). In one of the Hutchinsonian petitions, seven out of twenty-four of the petitioners made their mark, a low proportion of literacy for a New England document of that time. 5 *Coll. M. H. S.*, I. 486.

2. Winthrop (1908 ed.), I. 201.

3. *Id.*, I. 204.   4. *Id.*, I. 205.

such as had known him so long, and what good he had done for that church, should fall upon him with such bitterness for justifying himself in a good cause; for he was a very holy, upright man, and for faith and love inferior to none in the country, and most dear to all men.' Although the orthodox puritans had a majority in the General Court, the other side had the Governor, and Boston almost to a man and woman. Both sides bided their time until election day, May 17, 1637. The majority made a clever political move in transferring the Court of Elections to Newtown, in order to prevent a full attendance of schismatic Bostonians. Yet many came, and hundreds of freemen gathered under an ancient oak on Cambridge Common, and overflowed into what, a year later, became the College Yard. 'There was great danger of a tumult that day; for those of that side grew into fierce speeches, and some laid hands on others.' On the other side, John Wilson 'in his zeal gat up upon the bough of a tree' and harangued the multitude.[1] When hands were counted it was found that Winthrop had been elected Governor, Dudley Deputy-Governor; Vane was not even an Assistant.

A few days later began the first serious Indian war in New England, against the Pequots, who had been harassing the new settlements on the Connecticut. Success was complete and overwhelming. The Lord delivered up the heathen as stubble to the sword of his chosen people and dunged the soil with their flesh. Woe to the contemners of his Saints!

THE CAMBRIDGE SYNOD OF 1637

In the August heats, as the soldiers returned to Boston bearing grisly trophies of the slaughter at Mystic fort, the ministers and fighting chaplains of the three puritan colonies converged on Newtown to hold the first church council or synod in New England. They found a formula to which Cotton, but not Wheelwright, would subscribe; they condemned some eighty 'erroneous opinions,' together with sundry 'unlawful practices' such as evening séances of female prophets, and contemptuous heckling of parsons.

The conclusions of the synod were of no force unless implemented by the civil arm; that was not done until the old Court

1. Hutchinson, *Mass. Bay* (2d ed.), 1. 61 n., quoting a manuscript life of Wilson, since lost.

had been dissolved and a new one elected in November, 1637. In the meantime Wheelwright continued his preaching and Mistress Hutchinson her prophesying, confident that the Lord was on their side, and defying man to do his worst.

The newly elected General Court assembled in the meeting-house at Newtown on November 2. A technicality was soon found in order to oust two of the Boston deputies, who were Hutchinsonian; and only William Coddington remained to represent that party. 'In regard of the great abuse in ordinaries,'[1] their keepers were forbidden to sell sack or strong water; but tobacco was 'set at liberty.' 'Mr. John Harvard' and four other recent immigrants appeared before the bar of the Court to be sworn in as freemen of the Colony; John would have been less than human if he had not tarried to see what followed. Sundry petty affairs were dealt with. The boundaries of certain towns were enlarged, and Winthrop and Dudley were each rewarded for their unpaid services by a thousand acres of land. Then the Court got down to real business. John Wheelwright and William Aspinwall were disfranchised and banished, John Coggeshall disfranchised and ordered to be silent. And then, toward the gloomy close of a November day, Mistress Anne Hutchinson was arraigned before the Great and General Court on the charge of having 'troubled the peace of the commonwealth and the churches.' It was on a small scale a state trial of the sort then common in England, where no legal forms or safeguards were observed; and the result was a foregone conclusion. Yet the clever and witty woman conducted her own case admirably. She admitted nothing and denied everything, John Cotton gallantly supporting her to the confusion of his over-eager colleagues. But just at the point when the ministers and magistrates were at their wits' ends what to do next, Anne's unruly member gave her away. She declared, even boasted, of her personal revelations from the Almighty; and that was to confess the worst. For in this the puritan agreed with historical Christianity, that divine revelation closed with the Book of Revelation. Convicted out of her own mouth, Anne Hutchinson was sentenced to banishment from Massachusetts Bay 'as being a woman not fit for our society.'

---

1. Eating houses, where meals were provided at fixed prices. It was perhaps not unconnected with the religious excitement that the General Court had to deal with an unusual number of sexual offenses and cases of drunkenness in 1637.

Indian enemies destroyed; internal enemies crushed; the Devil routed on both fronts — it was time to get on with the College.

At the next meeting of the Court on November 15, 1637, after a few more Hutchinsonians had been disfranchised and Indian fighters suitably rewarded, the assembled magistrates and deputies passed the following order:[1]

𝕿𝖍𝖊 𝖈𝖔𝖑𝖑𝖊𝖉𝖌 𝖎𝖘 𝖔𝖗𝖉𝖊𝖗𝖊𝖉 𝖙𝖔 𝖇𝖊𝖊 𝖆𝖙 𝕹𝖊𝖜𝖊𝖙𝖔𝖜𝖓𝖊.

The Court then took another recess of five days.

On November 20, following a flood of secular legislation, the building of the College is committed to six magistrates and six elders, the first Board of Overseers.[2] And at the Court of Elections on May 2, 1638, it is

𝕺𝖗𝖉𝖊𝖗𝖊𝖉, 𝖙𝖍𝖆𝖙 𝕹𝖊𝖜𝖊𝖙𝖔𝖜𝖓𝖊 𝖘𝖍𝖆𝖑𝖑 𝖍𝖊𝖓𝖈𝖊𝖋𝖔𝖗𝖜𝖆𝖗𝖉 𝖇𝖊 𝖈𝖆𝖑𝖑𝖊𝖉 𝕮𝖆𝖒𝖇𝖗𝖎𝖌𝖊.[3]

The suppression of Hutchinsonianism was the price that New England had to pay for a college. To many nineteenth-century historians, the price has seemed excessive. Such arbitrary proceedings against ideas, it has been asserted, cast a blight on Colony and College, and inaugurated a 'glacial age' of New England history. One must have slight knowledge of the seventeenth century to suppose these local proceedings to have been in any way exceptional, unless in the failure of the authorities to put anyone to death. One must be very ignorant of twentieth-century America, and the story of such women as Emma Goldman and Rosika Schwimmer, to suppose that we are more tolerant than John Winthrop of dissents that matter to us. Nor would any college or university be the home of free speech on subjects affecting the safety of the State until Thomas Jefferson had proved free speech to be the only safeguard of representative government. What good would the triumph of Anne Hutchinson have brought to New England? Not toleration, which found no place in her system of theology; light perhaps, of a lunar sort; but no love, or beauty, or civility. Even John Wheelwright said that 'whilst they pleaded for the Covenant of

1. *Mass. Bay Recs.*, I. 208.
2. *Id.*, I. 217.
3. *Id.*, I. 228.

Grace, they took away the Grace of the Covenant,' [1] and conspicuously struck north when the Hutchinson family headed south. On the other hand, for a colony but seven years old to have succumbed to the pretended revelations of illuminated fanatics would have undone most of the founders' painful efforts to maintain civilized standards of life, and would have postponed indefinitely 'A *Colledge*, the best Thing that ever *New-England* thought upon.' [2]

1. Quoted by John Cotton.   C. F. Adams, *Antinomianism*, p. 371.
2. *Magnalia*, book iv. 126.

XIV

'THE COLLEDG IS ORDERED TO BEE AT NEWETOWNE' [1]

Eight words moved by some member unknown to us on November 15, 1637; put to the vote by the worshipful John Winthrop, Esq.; carried, we hope, by a tumult of ayes; well and properly recorded by Mr. Secretary Nowell — these eight words established the college soon to be named Harvard, at Newtown, presently renamed Cambridge. There it has remained these three centuries, and expects to remain for all future time. The Holy See is not more fixed at Rome than Harvard College at Cambridge. Harvard too made a short sojourn elsewhere in troublous times; but in comparison with the migrations and secessions of her medieval ancestors, or youthful wanderlust of her daughter Yale, Harvard has clung to the place of her birth as the Holy Sepulchre to Jerusalem.

How then came she there? We have no evidence of any rivalry for the site other than that of Salem. That town, the oldest in the Bay Colony, and robbed of her expected preëminence by Winthrop's preference for the valley of the Charles, had put in a bid for the College early in 1636; and we may be sure that John Endecott and Hugh Peter left unused no resource of bullying and blarney, politics and prayer, to attain it. Why the General Court rejected the three-hundred-acre Plains Farm between Salem and Marblehead, we do not know. There was no lack of

1. Lucius R. Paige, *History of Cambridge* (Boston, 1877), is a thorough and painstaking work, rendered more available by a *Supplement and Index*, published by the Cambridge Historical Society, 1930. That society has printed 19 volumes of *Publications* containing numerous papers of value for the history of Cambridge, and of the College. Lewis M. Hastings, 'The Streets of Cambridge,' in these *Publications*, xiv, is well illustrated with maps. The early records of Cambridge have been fully published in three volumes: *The Records of the Town of Cambridge* (Cambridge, 1901); S. P. Sharples, *Records of the Church of Christ at Cambridge in New England* (Boston, 1906); and *The Proprietors' Records*, the full title of which is *The Register Book of the Lands and Houses in the "New Towne" Generally Called "The Proprietors' Records"* (Cambridge, 1896).

room anywhere in New England. Boston Common, William Blackstone's legacy to that town, would have served a college well enough for two centuries or more, but schismatic Boston presumably wanted no 'Ninniversity' in her midst; and if she had, her recent goings-on were an abomination to the godly. Charlestown had a beautiful hill-top where Tufts College now stands; Dorchester would doubtless have been proud to crown Meetinghouse Hill with a college; and Roxbury, still for the most part a rugged wilderness, was ministered to by a pair of enthusiasts for learning: Thomas Weld and the Apostle Eliot. Why were none of these preferred?

For one thing, our founders must have brought with them from Oxford and the ancient Cambridge a definite vision of a university site. It should be inland, sheltered from the rude winds and tempests of the Western Ocean. A river there must be, and a level place for building. The Salem site was but a rough clearing, a desolate wilderness at whose rocky verge the sea tumbled and roared. But the 'spacious plain' of the New Town, 'more like a bowling green then a Wilderness,' [1] and the placid Charles, with the salt marshes beyond and low hills on the horizon, could be envisaged as the seat of a university with gardens, lawns, and water-walks that might vie with *alma mater Cantabrigia* in beauty, if not in learning.

Apart from sentimental and aesthetic considerations, there was one emphatic reason why Newtown should have been preferred: it was under the pastorate of Thomas Shepard, a young graduate of Emmanuel who was a favorite with younger men, and the most powerful evangelical preacher in New England. Moreover, Thomas Shepard had kept Newtown clean of antinomian taint. Indeed, he admits this consideration in his autobiography, written within ten years of the event:

> Thus the Lord hauing deliuered the cuntry from war with Indians and Familists [2] (who arose and fell together) he was pleased to direct the harts of the magistrates (then keeping court ordinarily in our town because of ther stirs at Boston) to thinke of erecting a Schoole or Colledge, and that speedily to be a nursery of knowledge in these deserts and supply for posterity; *and because this town (then called Newtown) was thorow gods great care and goodnes kept spotles from the*

1. *W. W. P.*, p. 201.
2. 'Familists' was a theological nickname of opprobrious connotation like 'antinomians,' which Shepard always used for Anne Hutchinson's party.

contagion of the opinions therefore at the desire of some of our town . . . the court for that and sundry other reasons determined to erect the Colledge here.[1]

Edward Johnson, writing in 1651, two years after Shepard's death, is emphatic as to Shepard's influence on the choice:

For place they fix their eye upon *New-Town*, which, to tell their Posterity whence they came, is now named *Cambridg*, and withal to make the whole world understand, that spiritual learning was the thing they chiefly desired, to sanctifie the other, and make the whole lump holy, and that learning being set upon its right object, might not contend for error instead of truth; they chose this place, being then under the Orthodox, and soul-flourishing Ministery of Mr. *Thomas Shepheard*, of whom it may be said, without any wrong to others, the Lord by his Ministery hath saved many a hundred soul.[2]

Cotton Mather, writing about the year 1690, records what was already a tradition:

The Vigilancy of Mr. *Shepard* was blessed, not only for the Preservation of his own Congregation from the *Rot* of these Opinions. . . . And it was with a respect unto this Vigilancy, and the Enlightning and Powerful Ministry of Mr. *Shepard*, that when the Foundation of a *Colledge* was to be laid, *Cambridge* rather than any other place, was pitch'd upon to be the Seat of that happy Seminary. . . .[3]

What were the 'sundry other reasons,' alluded to by Shepard, which determined the Court 'to erect the Colledge here'? The nature of the site probably was one; and the previous history of Newtown was certainly another.

Founding and Early History of Newtown

Newtown was one of those descriptive names, like New College at Oxford and the New Lecture Hall at Harvard, which in course of time mean the second oldest. Still uninhabited after the emigrants of the Winthrop fleet had settled down in 1630, it was chosen by the government as a proper site for a fortified capital. From the beginning the founders of Massachusetts

1. *C. S. M.*, xxvii. 389. Italics mine. Shepard, however, reverses the order of events; there must have been much thought 'of erecting a Schoole or College' before the end of 1637, as the vote of 1636 proves; it is curious that he should have used the very words of the legislative act.

2. *W. W. P.*, 1654 ed., pt. ii. 164.

3. *Magnalia*, book iii. 87–88.

Bay feared an attack on their liberties from England far more than an assault on their persons by the Indians. As Johnson puts it in his 'Wonder-Working Providence':[1]

At this time those who were in place of civill Government . . . began to thinke of a place of more safety in the eyes of Man, then the two frontire Towns of *Charles* Towne, and *Boston* were for the habitation of such as the Lord had prepared to Governe this Pilgrim People. Wherefore they rather made choice to enter farther among the *Indians*, then hazard the fury of malignant adversaries, who in a rage might pursue them, and therefore chose a place scituate on *Charles* River, between *Charles* Towne and Water-Towne, where they erected a Towne called New-Towne, now named *Cambridge.*

That the founders considered Charlestown and Boston 'frontier' towns shows their imperfect adjustment to New World conditions. It was contrary to their experience to establish a capital city in a place so exposed to maritime attack as Boston. Most of the capitals of the Old World — Rome, Paris, London, Antwerp — were established on tidal or navigable rivers, well up into the country, for protection against pirates and foreign enemies. The founders of Virginia followed the same notion in the site they chose for Jamestown. According to all precedents, the proper site for the capital of New England was at the head of navigation of the Charles. But in the summer of 1630 the company led by George Phillips and Sir Richard Saltonstall had pitched their village of Watertown on the spot later known as Gerry's Landing, and preëmpted the land from that place up to the falls and for half a mile downstream. There was only one other place on the tidal Charles where dry upland approached the river near enough to make a convenient landing; and that was the place selected by the government, and for want of a better name called the New Town. On December 28, 1630, the Assistants agreed to

build houses at a place a mile east from Waterton, near Charles river, the next spring, and to winter there the next year; that so by our examples, and by removing the ordnance and munition thither, all who were able might be drawn thither, and such as shall come to us hereafter, to their advantage be compelled so to do; and so, if God would, a fortified town might there grow up. . . .[2]

1. 1654 ed., pt. i. 60.
2. Thomas Dudley's letter of March 12, 1630–31, to the Countess of Lincoln. A. Young, *Chronicles of Mass. Bay,* p. 320.

Few of the Assistants honored this agreement. In the spring of 1631 Dudley built a house (which Winthrop considered too luxurious) at the northwest corner of the present Dunster and South Streets; Bradstreet, his son-in-law, built another on the southeast corner of the present Massachusetts Avenue and Dunster Street; and a few migrants of lower rank built their dwellings nearby. Governor Winthrop put up a house at Newtown, but shortly after took it down and removed the frame to Boston, greatly to Dudley's indignation; and no other Assistant made even that gesture of carrying out the agreement.

Despite this neglect, Newtown was generally regarded as the colonial capital until it became the seat of the College. The first improvements and defences were paid for by the Colony. On June 14, 1631, the General Court employed John Masters to dredge a channel six feet deep and twelve feet wide in a salt creek that led from the Charles up to Thomas Dudley's house, in order to accommodate vessels. In February, 1631-32, the Court levied £60 on the other towns [1] 'towards the makeing of a pallysadoe aboute the newe town'; [2] and a part at least of this palisade was built. In the summer of 1632 a company of people from Braintree in Essex, who had first settled at Mount Wollaston, joined the eight or ten families already at Newtown. Village streets were laid out, lots apportioned, houses built, and local government begun. In September, 1633, arrived the great Thomas Hooker, who had agreed in England to follow the Braintree people and be their minister. With him were his inseparable companion Samuel Stone, and John Haynes, a landed gentleman of large estate from Essex. A church was promptly gathered, over which Hooker was ordained pastor and Stone teacher. The Braintree company evidently had a taste for security and symmetry, for they agreed to roof their houses with slate or shingle instead of the usual thatch of marsh-grass, and declared that all the houses should 'range eevn,' six feet back from the streets. William Wood, in his 'New Englands Prospect,' reported that in 1633 Newtown was already 'one of the neatest and best compacted Towns in *New England*, having many faire structures, with many handsome contrived streets.

1. *Mass. Bay Recs.*, I. 93-95.
2. It is said that as late as 1800 a part of the ditch could be traced. It began on the river near the foot of Ash Street, and formed the arc of a circle around the northwest side of the Common. I *Coll. M. H. S.*, VII. 9.

The inhabitants most of them are very rich, and well stored with Cattell of all sorts; having many hundred Acres of ground paled with one generall fence, which is about a mile and a halfe long, which secures all their weaker Cattle from the wilde beasts.' [1]

By the end of 1634, the town contained about sixty families. Thomas Dudley, the oldest resident, had been elected Governor of the Colony in May, and John Haynes succeeded him the next year. The General Court and Court of Assistants sat at Newtown from the date of Dudley's election to the spring of 1636, when they moved to Boston. In the spring of 1637 they returned to Newtown in order to be out of reach of Anne Hutchinson. Eighteen months later they went back to Boston, and there remained; but for four years Newtown was the capital.

At the first general tax levy, in 1634, Newtown was assessed the same amount as Boston and Dorchester; in 1636 it paid the largest tax of any town in the Colony.[2] But the people were not contented. In 1634 they 'desired leave of the Court to look out either for enlargement or removal,' and finding no eligible site on the Bay determined to remove to the rich meads of the Connecticut Valley. This decision was communicated to the General Court the same year. 'The principal reasons for their removal,' records Winthrop, 'were, 1. Their want of accommodation for their cattle, so as they were not able to maintain their ministers, nor could receive any more of their friends to help them; and here it was alleged by Mr. Hooker, as a fundamental error, that towns were set so near each to other.' [3]

Strange as it may seem to us, Master Hooker was right. New Englanders could not live by taking in each other's washing; their only means yet discovered to a comfortable livelihood was the raising of cattle; and cattle required an enormous amount of land when the country was still wooded. Newtown was pinched between Charlestown and Watertown. The Charlestown line, fixed in 1632–33, ran parallel to and a little southwest of the present Beacon Street, Somerville,[4] and a little more than half a

1. 1635 ed., pp. 33–34.

2. *Mass. Bay Recs.*, I. 129, 166. After that its relative wealth and population, judged by tax levies, fell off rapidly.

3. Winthrop, *Journal*, for September 4, 1634.

4. A large part of this line is still the boundary between Cambridge and Somerville, although some jags have been made in it in order to place the Norton (Sachs) and other estates wholly within Cambridge. For Cambridge boundaries, see Paige, chap. 1.

mile from Harvard Square. The village center of Watertown was not at its present place, but on the Elmwood estate; and when the line between Newtown and Watertown was established, in 1635, the site of Sparks Street, a little more than half a mile from Harvard Square, was made the boundary.[1] It is true that these boundaries spread out fanwise to the northwestward. When Master Hooker's flock complained of want of room the General Court endeavored to placate them by granting to Newtown the present area of Brighton and Newton on the south side of the Charles; and in 1635–36 the Court agreed that 'Newe Towne bounds shall run eight myles into the country from ther meeteing house,' which gave them all Arlington and most of Lexington.[2] But these annexations were too remote for any immediate purpose. It was inconvenient to keep cattle across the river, and living there or in the future Lexington was out of the question for people who valued neighborliness to each other and ready access to the meetinghouse. The ideal New England town was about six miles square, with the village on a stream near the center, and arable lands and pasture radiating on all sides; and if few towns came up to this ideal, Newtown, shaped 'like a list cut off from the Broad-cloath' of Charlestown and Watertown,[3] fell so far short of it as to disgust the people with the place. Besides, the arable land in and around the village of Newtown had a thin and gravelly soil unsuitable for wheat; that of the Connecticut Valley was a rich, deep mould. So there is no need to suppose the existence of religious, political, or personal antagonisms to explain the wholesale transfer in 1636 of the Church of Newtown, with its eminent pastor and teacher, to Hartford — especially as we find their successors being tempted to do the selfsame thing. John Haynes followed his friends in 1637; Dudley and Bradstreet removed to Ipswich in 1636; so that when Harvard College was established there were hardly eight of the hundred families of the Hooker period left on that site. But in the meantime, Newtown had been repopulated.

1. This remained the line between Cambridge and Watertown until 1754.
2. To this, Shawsheen (Bedford) and all the land between that plantation and Concord and the Merrimac, including parts of Lincoln, Billerica, and Lowell, were added in 1641–42; so that at its greatest extent Cambridge extended from the Charles opposite Dedham to the Merrimac, and in shape closely resembled the famous Gerrymander (Paige, p. 3).
3. *W. W. P.* (1910), p. 90.

In the summer of 1635, Thomas Shepard arrived at Boston with a company of neighbors and other friends who on shipboard had come to appreciate his sweet character and his strangely moving manner of preaching. Two days after landing, Shepard was a guest at the house of Samuel Stone, his classmate at Emmanuel; and with Stone and Hooker he soon arranged a treaty by which the newcomers purchased the houses and lands which were rapidly being vacated. On February 1, 1635–36, Shepard's company organized a new church at Newtown; in June of that year Hooker and the bulk of his congregation with their great herds of cattle began their two weeks' westward journey.

A year later Thomas Shepard married for second wife a daughter of Thomas Hooker, who at once began a campaign of cajolery in order to get his son-in-law's company to abandon Newtown for the Connecticut. Shepard's diary and the town records show that removal to the site of Middletown was being seriously considered as late as 1641.[1]

It seems clear enough, then, what were some of the 'sundry other reasons' which induced the General Court to fix the college at Cambridge. The site, more than any other in the Bay Colony, recalled Oxford and Cambridge. Something was owing to Newtown from the Colony. Intended as a favored capital, it had been abandoned first by the magistrates, then by its residents. It was more pinched for the obvious means of livelihood than any town in the jurisdiction. Depopulation had taken place once, and was threatened again. The College, promising much business for artisans and shopkeepers, a market for the farmers, and a cultivated society for the gentry, would be an inducement for Master Shepard's company to remain, and 'stop the leake' to Connecticut. And, as if to ratify this promise, the General Court on May 2, 1638,

𝔒𝔯𝔡𝔢𝔯𝔢𝔡, 𝔱𝔥𝔞𝔱 𝔑𝔢𝔴𝔢𝔱𝔬𝔴𝔫𝔢 𝔰𝔥𝔞𝔩𝔩 𝔥𝔢𝔫𝔠𝔢𝔣𝔬𝔯𝔴𝔞𝔯𝔡 𝔟𝔢 𝔠𝔞𝔩𝔩𝔢𝔡 𝔠𝔞𝔪𝔟𝔯𝔦𝔤𝔢.

---

1. Paige, pp. 51–53. The reasons given are the lack of room for expansion, which threatened a subdivision of estates to the point of beggary, and the fear that 'Mr. Vane will be upon our skirts.' Sir Henry Vane, as he had now become, was magnanimous, and proved a staunch friend to the Colony.

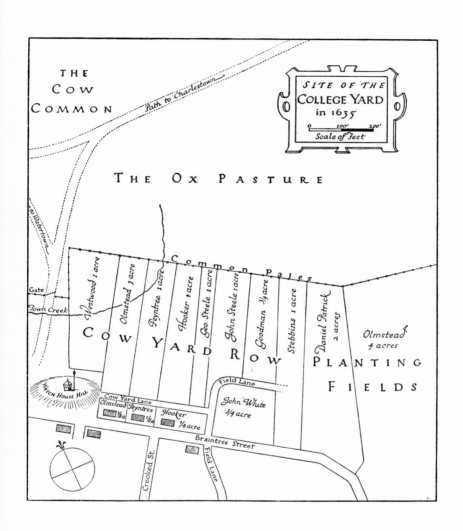

THE
COW
COMMON

Path to Charlestown

SITE OF THE
COLLEGE YARD
in 1635
0   100'   200'
Scale of Feet

THE OX PASTURE

to Watertown

Common Pales

Gate

Town Creek

Westwood 1 acre

Olmstead 1 acre

Peyntree 1 acre

Hooker 1 acre

Geo Steele 1 acre

John Steele 1 acre

Goodman ½ acre

Stebbins 1 acre

Daniel Patrick 2 acres

Olmstead 4 acres

COW YARD ROW PLANTING

Watch House Hill

FIELDS

Field Lane

Cow Yard Lane

Olmstead 1/8 a

Peyntree 1/8 a

Hooker ¼ acre

John White ¼ acre

Braintree Street

Crooked St.

Field Lane

Newtown in 1636–1638 [1]

It is not difficult to visualize pre-Harvardian Newtown. The forest came down from the north to the neighborhood of the University Museum and the Law School, where it parted around 'a spacious plain, more like a bowling green then a Wilderness.' [2] This plain narrowed down to a rounded and wooded [3] point on the edge of the salt marshes. The early settlers built their houses on this rounded tip of the plain, containing less than twenty-five acres, and smaller than the College Yard of to-day. It was bounded on the north by Braintree Street (Massachusetts Avenue), on the east by Crooked Lane (Holyoke Street), and on the south and west by what is now the curved line of Brattle Street, Brattle Square, Eliot Square, and Eliot Street. This westerly line was determined by a water course. A rill, or brook, arising from a spring or low spot within the College Yard or from the path to Charlestown (Kirkland Street) crossed Harvard Square, and emptied into the upper end of a salt creek at about the middle of the present Brattle Square. There the town provided a causeway and a footbridge in 1635. The salt creek followed the present line of Eliot Square and the northerly edge of Eliot Street, then flowed easterly, where one can still see a distinct contour, between the northern edge of Kirkland House and the buildings on the southern side of Marsh Lane (South Street). At the foot of Water (Dunster) Street was the town landing, where a 'sufficient bridge' led down to low water mark on the edge of the creek. Thanks to John Masters' £30 worth of dredging, vessels of ten-foot beam and six-foot draught could get up to this landing at low tide, or at high water even to Brattle Square, where there was a shipyard in the early days. The town landing was the terminus of a ferry to the south bank of the Charles, where a 'broad ladder' was set up 'for convenience of landing' in 1636. [4]

---

1. Consult the map by Doctors Norris and Raisz in this chapter.

2. *W. W. P.*, p. 201. Presumably this plain had been cleared for cornfields by the Indians, who had been killed off by a pestilence before the puritans arrived.

3. Joseph Cooke was paid 9*d* apiece for taking up the 'stubs' in the town streets and filling up the holes, in 1636. Paige, pp. 39–40.

4. The southerly part of the creek was not filled up until after Paige's *History of Cambridge* appeared, in 1877. It may be recognized as the westerly berth of the College Wharf, in nineteenth-century maps. Very little inroad was made on the marshes between South Street and the Charles until 1856, when a dike was built along the

East of the town creek, which limited the eligible building sites on the west, the salt marsh thrust another long finger through the site of the dining hall of Leverett House up to the northeast corner of Lowell House. This creek was fed by a brook which arose in a small pond, used for watering cattle, behind Holyoke House. The brook crossed Mount Auburn Street in front of Claverly.

In the little space that was left, the streets were laid out fairly straight and symmetrical — excepting Crooked Lane,[1] which had to avoid the brook. The first meetinghouse, where the General Court dealt with Anne Hutchinson, and where John Harvard received the franchise, was on the southwest corner of Spring (Mount Auburn) and Water (Dunster) Streets. For a marketplace, there was set aside a plot of ground which is still open: Winthrop Square and the lawn in front of the Pi Eta Club, whose house is the site of Governor Haynes' homestead.

As you walked in the year 1638 from the town creek up Creek Lane (Brattle Street) toward that now busy spot called Harvard Square, you observed a scene of thrifty pioneer economy. Facing you, at the southwest corner of the present College Yard, was a little eminence called Watch-house Hill, a convenient vantage point for the town watch to give warning of fires, or of a nocturnal disturbance by marauding animals in the cowyards. On your left, as you faced this hill, the cow common came down from the north between gradually narrowing fences, ending at a gate a few yards north of the present Square. To your right, Braintree Street, a lane just wide enough for two carts to pass, led off uncertainly toward the woods and the oyster bank. Along this street was the northernmost row of Newtown homesteads, where some of the most substantial citizens lived. On the south side, beginning at the corner of Wood Street, dwelt Herbert Pelham, grandson of Lord de la Warr; next him lived Nicholas Danforth, founder of a veritable dynasty; then Edward Goffe;[2] Goodman Bradish was on the site of Holyoke House, and Samuel Shepard, the minister's brother, had the lot from Crooked Lane to Field Lane. The three houses on the left (north) side of Braintree Street are of more immediate interest

river front and the marsh drained. Until then, students approached the boathouse near the College Wharf by a plank walk from the foot of Dunster Street, raised about three feet above the marsh. *The Harvard Book*, ii. 195.

1. Straightened in 1793 and later named Holyoke Street.
2. Goffe owned this house (no. 20 on map), but probably lived across the street.

to us, since the middle one, formerly Goodman Peyntree's, was in the spring of 1638 being fitted up for the new Harvard College. Next door to it on the west was the house built by Goodman Olmstead the town constable, later acquired by Harvard College from his assignee Edward Goffe. Next door on the east the house formerly the residence of Thomas Hooker, was in 1638 occupied by his successor Thomas Shepard; this minister's house-lot was a rood (one quarter acre) in area, twice that of the other two.

Behind these houses lay a series of long, narrow lots of from two roods to one acre in area, known as Cowyard Row.[1] Those behind the Goffe, Peyntree, and Shepard houses belonged to their respective homesteads, and changed hands with them; the others belonged to men who lived elsewhere in the village, the principal cattle owners of Newtown, and were used for protecting their cattle at night. Anyone who has seen stockyards can imagine what the Harvard Yard looked (and smelt) like before the College was founded.

The cowyards terminated on the north, at the 'common pales' or 'generall fence.'[2] This long line of paling began at the Charlestown boundary, near the present Inman Square, and ran due west (magnetic) to a point within the present College Yard, where it changed direction in order to parallel Braintree Street, and so serve as the northern boundary of Cowyard Row. East of the cowyards, planting fields (which the common pales protected from stray cattle) extended southerly to the Highway to the Oyster Bank. North of the common pales, and extending to the forest, was the common 'Ox Pasture,' through the middle of which ran the 'Charlestown Path' (Kirkland Street), the principal approach to Cambridge by land.

Cambridge Common is all that is now left of the original cow common or grazing land, which lay within the angle between Massachusetts Avenue and Garden Street. Here the herds of goats, swine, and neat cattle were driven forth to pasture under the care of their several herdsmen, and brought home at night to homestall or cowyard. Most of the cow common was wooded, although the trees were gradually thinned as the people cut

1. There was another Cowyard Row along the present Mount Auburn Street, near Bow.
2. William Wood, *New Englands Prospect* (1635 ed.), p. 34.

timber and the cattle destroyed young shoots. Travellers from Boston by the Charlestown path entered the cow common by a gate just north of Holworthy Hall. If bound for Watertown, they continued straight across the common to the present Mason Street; if to Newtown, they turned the corner by the site of Phillips Brooks House, and emerged from the common into the present Harvard Square by another gate.

Newtown was a seaport, to which goods were brought in hoys or lighters,[1] and passengers in row-barges or shallops. Large seagoing vessels could ascend the river, but not the town creek. Passengers who embarked on the west side of Boston with a fair wind and flood tide might reach the Newtown landing in a little more than an hour; but this route was closed by ice in winter, and was dangerous in an easterly blow, when the wind had the entire stretch of the original Back Bay to kick up a nasty chop. Foot-passengers and impatient horsemen commonly crossed by ferry from Boston to Charlestown, just north of the present railroad bridges, and then followed the path that we have already described. It was about four and three-quarters miles by this route from the Old State House in Boston to Harvard Square. From the ferry terminus on the south bank of the Charles there was a path or road to Muddy River (Brookline), Roxbury, and the towns in that direction. The first bridge across the Charles was built at tidal foot of Wood (Boylston) Street, on the site of the present Anderson Bridge, in 1662. It was eight miles to Boston by that route, as the old Paul Dudley milestone on the corner of the First Church burying ground still informs us.

1. The Cambridge Church in 1639 paid a 'hoyman' for bringing John Philip's household goods from Salem. *C. S. M.*, XVII. 212. The hoy was a sloop-rigged vessel for carrying freight.

KEY TO THE MAP OF CAMBRIDGE

By Dr. Albert P. Norris

College Lots

The roman numerals designate lots in or sections of the present Harvard Yard, in the order of their acquisition by the College. The boundaries on this map, however, are of 1638, not of the date when these properties were acquired by the College; and the names in the list below are the usual ones at the time of acquisition. The names on the map are those of 1638. The capital letters designate College property outside the present Yard.

    I. Peyntree house lot, and cowyard, acquired 1637 or early in 1638

    II. Town Grant out of old Ox Pasture to Eaton, 1638; later confirmed to the College

    III. Fellows' Orchard, given in 1645 and 1649

    IV. Goffe house, lot, and 'backside,' 1651

    V. Betts lot, 1661

    VI. Sweetman-Spencer lot, 1697

    VII. Appleton pasture, formerly part of Shepard estate, 1786

    VIII. Shepard-Mitchell-Leverett-Wigglesworth estate, 1794

    IX. Sewall lot (Bradish Garden with part of adjoining properties), 1805

    X. Meetinghouse and Parsonage lots, including the Champney cowyard, purchased from the Parish, 1833

    XI. Goffe-Dana property, acquired (as far east as Quincy Street) in 1835

    XII. Danforth-Bigelow lot, acquired with the same limitations in 1835

    A. Town Grant to 'the Professor,' 1638. Not secured by the College

    B. Bradish lot, c. 1651

Owners of House Lots

The first name following each arabic numeral is that of the owner in 1635, according to the Cambridge Proprietors' Records. Almost all these persons removed to Connecticut in 1636–37, and there is not another complete survey of the town in the Proprietors' Records until 1642. One cannot, therefore, be certain as to who the owners were in 1638, except when evidence is found of an earlier transfer; but, in general, it is safe to assume that the owner in 1642 was in possession four years before, since most of the purchases from Hooker's company were made in 1635–37.

Several of the second group of settlers, such as Pelham and Danforth, were extensive landowners, and it is not always possible to tell which of several houses owned by them was the homestead.

With few exceptions, house lots only are shown in this map. An exception is made of the cowyards and pasture lots in and north of the College Yard.

1. (Same as X) Watch House Hill; William Westwood; John Betts, 1638; Second Meetinghouse, 1651
2. (Same as IV) James Olmstead; Edward Goffe, 1638; 'Goffe College,' 1651
3. (Same as I) William Peyntree; Harvard College, 1638
4. Thomas Hooker; Thomas Shepard, 1636; Jonathan Mitchell, 1650; John Leverett, 1696
5. Francis Grizzel; Barnabas Lamson, before 1640
6. Herbert Pelham, 1638; John Phillips, 1639; Thomas Danforth, 1652
7. William Wadsworth; Richard Champney, 1637
8. The widow Sackett; Nicholas Danforth, before 1638
9. John Hopkins; William Lewis; Mark Pierce; Edward Collins, 1636; Daniel Gookin
10. Nicholas Danforth; Thomas Danforth, 1638
11. William Goodwin; Samuel Shepard, c. 1638; Edward Mitchelson, 1650
12. (Same as B) John Steele; Robert Bradish, 1638; Harvard College, c. 1651
13. William Wadsworth; Richard Champney, 1637
14. Hester Musse; widow Glover, c. 1638 (site of printing press); Henry Dunster, 1641; the Grammar School, 1649
15. Daniel Abbott; John Russell, c. 1639; Francis Moore, 1642
16. Daniel Abbott; John Russell, c. 1639
17. Thomas Heate; Thomas Marrett, 1639
18. Christopher Cane; William Towne, c. 1639
19. Nathaniel Hancock; Nathaniel Hancock, Jr., 1648
20. George Steele; Edward Goffe, c. 1637; William Bordman, c. 1656; Aaron Bordman, 1685
21. Edward Stebbins; Nicholas Danforth, 1636; Stephen Day, 1656; William Bordman, 1668; Aaron Bordman, 1685

22. Timothy Stanley; William French, c. 1638; William Barrett, 1656
23. Jonas Austin; Thomas Blodgett; Edmund Frost, c. 1638; Katherine Haddon, 1639
24. John Hopkins; Edmund Angier, c. 1637
25. Thomas Beale; Edward Mitchelson, before 1641
26. Samuel Stone; Nathaniel Sparhawk, 1636
27. Simon Bradstreet, to 1636; Herbert Pelham, c. 1638
28. Abraham Morrill; Thomas Skidmore, before 1642; Henry Dunster, 1646
29. Samuel Greenhill; William Turges, before 1642
30. John Pratt; Joseph Isaac, c. 1639
31. William Spencer; John Stedman, c. 1638
32. Thomas Spencer; Edward Angier, c. 1639; William Dickson, 1642; Town Jail, 1693
[33.] John Haynes; widow Glover, c. 1638; Henry Dunster, 1641
[34.] The Market Place
35. James Ensign; Edward Goffe, c. 1638
36. Samuel Stone's garden; Nathaniel Sparhawk, 1636
37. Simon Sackett; William Blomfield; Robert Stedman, c. 1638
38. Matthew Allen; Thomas Chesholme, c. 1637
[39.] Meetinghouse, 1632
40. Samuel Dudley; Robert Sanders, c. 1639
41. William Andrew; Hezekiah Usher, 1642
42. William Lewis; John Bridge, c. 1639

43. George Stocking; William Manning, c. 1639
44. Nicholas Olmstead; John French, c. 1638; Robert Browne, 1690
45. Joseph Reading; Joseph Cooke, c. 1638; Joseph Cooke, Jr., 1658
46. Stephen Hart; Joseph Cooke, c. 1638
47. Nathaniel Richard; Joseph Cooke, 1637
48. William Westwood; John Betts, c. 1638; John Shepard, 1662
49. Dolor Davis; Simon Willard, to 1636; Edward Mitchelson, 1639
50. John Bridge; William Andrew, 1637; Samuel Andrew, 1652
51. Thomas Fisher; Edward Shepard, c. 1639
52. John Benjamin; John Betts, 1642
53. John Benjamin; Edward Shepard's garden, 1642
54. John Benjamin; Moses Paine, 1642; Henry Adams, 1646
55. Thomas Dudley; Roger Harlakenden, c. 1635; Herbert Pelham, c. 1639
56. Matthew Allen; William Cutler, c. 1638; Richard Cutler, c. 1656
57. Humphrey Vincent; John Moore, c. 1637
58. Daniel Patrick; Joseph Cooke, 1636
59. Richard Lord; Herbert Pelham, 1642
60. Matthew Allen; Joseph Cooke, c. 1636
61. Edmund Gearner; Elizabeth Sherborn, c. 1639
62. John Arnold; Robert Fitt, 1638; Thomas Hosmer, 1642
63. William Kelsey; John Sill, c. 1639
64. Andrew Warner; George Cooke, 1636
65. Daniel Denison; John Knight; Roger Shaw, 1636

INDEX

AIR VIEW OF APPROXIMATELY THE SAME AREA AS THE MAP OF CAMBRIDGE IN 16

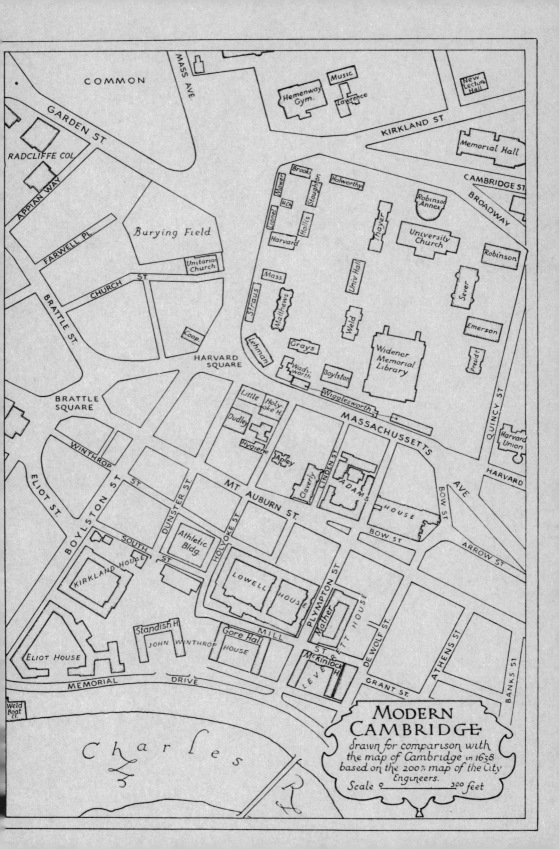

COMMON

MASS AVE.

GARDEN ST.

RADCLIFFE COL.

APPIAN WAY

FARWELL PL.

CHURCH ST.

BRATTLE ST.

Burying Field

Unitarian Church

Coop.

HARVARD SQUARE

BRATTLE SQUARE

Hemenway Gym.

Music

Lawrence

New Lecture Hall

KIRKLAND ST.

Memorial Hall

CAMBRIDGE ST.

BROADWAY

Brooks

Mower

Holworthy

Stoughton

H.CH.

Lionel

Hollis

Robinson Annex

University Church

Robinson

Harvard

Thayer

Mass

Matthews

Straus

Lehman

Grays

Wads-worth

Boylston

Univ Hall

Weld

Widener Memorial Library

Sever

Emerson

Pres.dt

Wigglesworth

MASSACHUSSETTS

QUINCY ST.

Harvard Union

HARVARD

Little

Holyoke H.

Dudley

Hygiene

Apley

Claverly

LINDEN ST.

ADAMS

HOUSE

BOW ST.

AVE.

ARROW ST.

WINTHROP

ST.

ELIOT ST.

BOYLSTON ST.

DUNSTER ST.

MT. AUBURN ST.

HOLYOKE ST.

BOW ST.

Athletic Bldg.

SOUTH

HOUSE

ST.

KIRKLAND HOUSE

LOWELL HOUSE

MILL ST.

PLYMPTON ST.

Mather

LEVERETT HOUSE

DE WOLF ST.

ATHENS ST.

BANKS ST.

Eliot House

Standish H.

JOHN WINTHROP HOUSE

Gore Hall

McKinlock H.

MEMORIAL DRIVE

GRANT ST.

Weld Boat Cl.

Charles

MODERN CAMBRIDGE

drawn for comparison with
the map of Cambridge in 1638
based on the 200% map of the City
Engineers.

Scale 0   300 feet

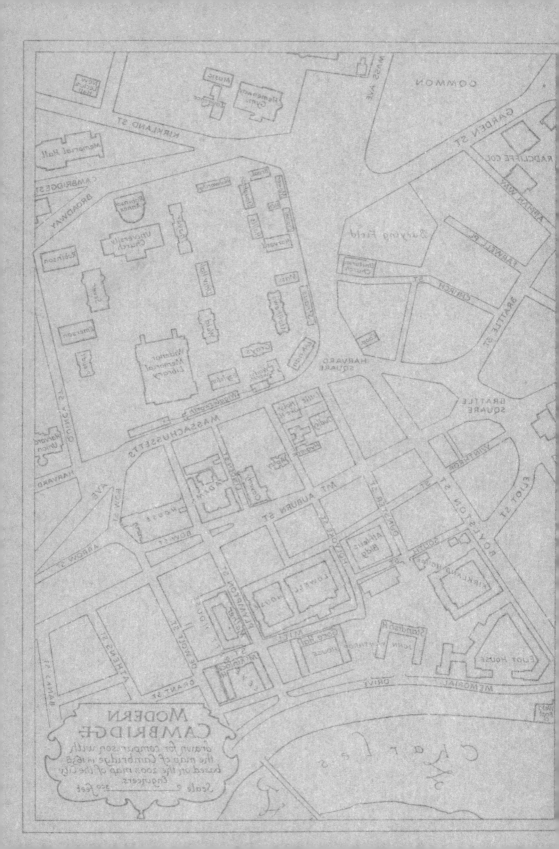

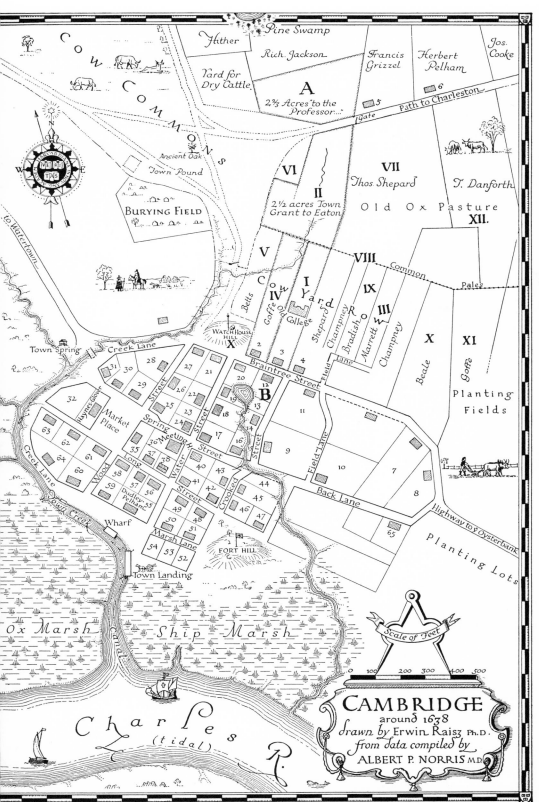

CAMBRIDGE
around 1638
drawn by Erwin Raisz Ph.D.
from data compiled by
ALBERT P. NORRIS M.D.

Prepared at the Institute of Geographical Exploration, Harvard University. 1934.

XV

THE COLLEGE OPENED
1637-1638 [1]

The days of miracles were past, and it was not sufficient for the General Court to pronounce *aedificetur* in order to see a college arise on the 'spacious plain' overlooking the Charles.

When Anne Hutchinson had been disposed of, and the College 'ordered to bee at Newetowne,' the next thing in order was to appoint a committee to bring the College into existence. On November 20, 1637, the next session of the Court after the 15th, action was taken of which the record (to which the marginal gloss is prefixed as title) is as follows:

Committee as to the colledg at New Towne

For the colledge, the Governour, Mr Winthrope, the Deputy, Mr Dudley, the Treasurer, Mr Bellingham, Mr Humfrey, Mr Herlakenden, Mr Staughton, Mr Cotton, Mr Wilson, Mr Damport, Mr Wells, Mr Sheopard, and Mr Peters, these, or the greater part of them, whereof Mr Winthrope, Mr Dudley, or Mr Bellingham, to bee alway one, to take order for a colledge at Newetowne.

This was the first Board of Overseers: [2] the governing body which established the College, appointed the first master and

1. With this chapter the old 'College Books' of records, printed in *C. S. M.*, xv–xvi, begin to be useful (see Appendix on the University Archives in *H. C. S. C.*). For sources of Cambridge history, see note to Chapter XIV. The best monograph on the early history of the Yard is by Andrew McFarland Davis, in *Proceedings Am. Antiq. Soc.*, n.s., v (1887–88). 469–86; also printed separately as *The Site of the First College Building at Cambridge* (1889). Davis' 'The College in Early Days,' *Harv. Grads. Mag.*, i. 363–77, is in part a digest of this. The Rev. Hosea Starr Ballou, 'The Harvard Yard before Dunster,' in the *N. E. Hist. Gen. Reg.*, lxxx. 131–38, is suggestive, but the author is rather too eager to drag Comfort Starr into the picture.

2. It is not so called in the vote of the General Court; but this committee was regarded as the first Board of Overseers in common speech, and called *Inspectores* on the dedication of the Commencement Theses in 1642 (see Appendix D). The preamble of

first president, and conducted the 'infant seminary' through her first Commencement in 1642. Reorganized and put on a permanent basis by act of the General Court on September 27, 1642, the Board of Overseers remained the sole governing body of the College until the charter of 1650 was granted; and from that day to this it has shared the governing power with the Corporation of President and Fellows.

Of this first Board of Overseers, six were magistrates and six clergymen; seven were alumni of Cambridge, one a graduate of Oxford, and the other four, brothers or fathers of Cambridge alumni. Taking them individually, we have already seen something of the university members (Governor Winthrop, John Humfrey, Thomas Weld, John Cotton, John Wilson, Thomas Shepard, John Davenport, and Hugh Peter) in their English colleges. Of the others:

Thomas Dudley, the Deputy-Governor, was the most important layman on the Board after Governor Winthrop, and the oldest. Baptized October 12, 1576, at Yardley Hastings near Northampton, the son of a Captain Roger Dudley who was 'slain in the wars,' his education was had partly in a grammar school, subsequently as page in the household of the Earl of Northampton, and finally as captain of English volunteers who went over to support Henry of Navarre. A well-read man, he gave to his daughter Anne, the poetess, a thorough grounding in English literature, and sent two sons through Emmanuel College. For many years he was steward to that Earl of Lincoln whose daughters married Isaac Johnson and John Humfrey; and for a short time he resided in John Cotton's parish of old Boston. One of the organizers of the migration in 1630, Dudley came over with Winthrop as Deputy-Governor, and served the Colony in that office, or as Governor, for seventeen annual terms. A stout, energetic man of sixty-one, autocratic by temperament and irascible in temper, he distrusted the gentler instincts of Winthrop, and deplored his patience with poor human nature. Stern men such as Dudley 'with empires in their brains' were doubtless needed in a new commonwealth, where

the Act of September 27, 1642, establishing the Board of Overseers as a permanent institution, shows that it was considered a reorganization of the Board of 1637. *Mass. Bay Recs.*, II. 30. Frederick L. Gay first made these points in *C. S. M.*, XVII. 124–25.

even puritans tended to become slack and lawless. But we love Winthrop the better for saying on his deathbed, when Dudley pressed him to sign an order banishing some dissenter, that 'he had done too much of that work already.' To heretics, Dudley was ever 'a whip and maul.' As Assistant in the General Court of 1636, as Overseer of Harvard College from 1637 to his death in 1653, and as signer of the charter of 1650, he was one of our principal founders; and from his lusty loins sprang the seed of many future graduates.[1] His services to the College — which included no gifts or benefactions — are commemorated by the Dudley Gate, on which is inscribed a part of his epitaph by his daughter Anne Bradstreet:

> One of thy founders, him New-England know,
> Who staid thy feeble sides when thou wast low,
> Who spent his state, his strength, and years with care
> That after comers in them might have share.

More characteristic of him was the epitaph written many years later by Governor Belcher:

> Here lies Thomas Dudley, that trusty old stud,
> A bargain's a bargain, and must be made good.[2]

Richard Bellingham, third of the members whose presence on the Board was necessary to make a quorum, undoubtedly owed that distinction to the fact that he was Treasurer of the Colony; and as magistrate he remained Overseer until his death in 1672. Richard and his brother William, alumnus of Christ's College, Cambridge were almost the last representatives of an ancient family who for generations had been lords of the manor of Manton in Lincolnshire. Trained to the law, Richard served for many years as Recorder of Boston, and as a member of the parliament of 1628; and it was probably his legal

1. Thomas Dudley (A.B. 1651) was his grandson; and Joseph Dudley (A.B. 1665) his seventh son, born when he was seventy years old.

2. Savage's notes to his 1853 edition of Winthrop's Journal, I. 61. In Chesholme's manuscript Steward's Book (*C. S. M.*, xxxi. 48) there is a characteristic entry under the accounts of his grandson Thomas: 'payd by Siluer and Indian, which was all the gouernore would owne tho more was demanded as appeareth on the debitors side: 4*l* 9*s* 4*d*.' There is a good sketch of Dudley by J. Truslow Adams, in the *D. A. B.*, and a rambling biography by Augustine Jones (1899); cf. Anson Phelps Stokes, *Stokes Records* (1910), I. 93.

acumen which secured the omission of the residence requirements in the colony charter of 1629, in which he was named
patentee and freeman. Either his temperament or his legal
training made Bellingham an opponent to the arbitrary methods
of Winthrop, Dudley, and Endecott, and a leader of the popular
opposition; but when first elected Governor, in 1641, he became
embroiled with the deputies. Although called 'melancholic' by
Winthrop, who did not like him, Bellingham played a practical
joke on his colleagues by performing his own marriage ceremony to his ward, the lovely young Penelope Pelham, and by
refusing to leave the magistrates' bench when they proposed to
discuss this doubtful manner of entering holy wedlock. Nevertheless Bellingham was annually elected Governor from 1665 to
his death. His greatest service to the Colony was on the committee which compiled the Body of Lawes and Liberties of
1648. He and his fellow-magistrate Richard Saltonstall, also of
the opposition, were the heaviest contributors to the collection
for the College in 1653–54; Bellingham also presented a score of
theological books to the College Library and inaugurated the
'drive' for a new building in 1672. His son Samuel was a graduate of the first Harvard class.[1]

Israel Stoughton was a brother of Dr. John Stoughton, the
rector of St. Mary Aldermanbury, in whose study the subscription paper for a New England Indian College was found.[2] At
that time Israel, too, was in trouble, but in Massachusetts Bay.
Admitted freeman of the Colony in 1633, he had been chosen
deputy to the General Court from Dorchester, where he had
established the first mill, and built a bridge over the Neponset
River. In protest against the magistrates' claim to a veto on all
decisions of the deputies, Stoughton drew up a brief, the circu-
lation of which caused him to be denounced by Winthrop as a
'troubler of Israel' and 'underminer of the state,' and to be disqualified for office. The disability was removed for his staunch
support of authority in the Hutchinson affair; in 1637 he was
chosen an Assistant, and led the Massachusetts forces in the
Pequot war. In 1642 he contributed £5 toward completing the
first college building. Stoughton's service as Overseer was
short, for in 1642 he returned to England, served as lieutenant-

1. R. P. Stearns, in *D. A. B.*; *C. S. M.*, xv. 156, 185, 220; S. E. Morison, *Builders of the Bay Colony*.
2. See Appendix C.

colonel in the New Model Army, fought at Naseby, and died at London in 1645. The College was remembered in his will.[1]

 Roger Harlakenden, the 'most deare friend' of Thomas Shepard and brother to Richard Harlakenden, Shepard's contemporary at Emmanuel College, was born October 1, 1611. His father, known as 'the Good Harlakenden,' was a puritan of ancient family.[2] Their seat, 'The Priory,' was the great house of Earls Colne in Essex, where Shepard became a lecturer shortly after commencing M.A. in 1627. The young preacher when sought by the bishop's pursuivants took refuge in the Priory. Doubtless as a result of his frequent visits, 'the lord wrought mightily' on Richard and Roger, who was then sixteen years old, and on their sister Mabel. The next year Roger entered a student of Gray's Inn, but apparently did not take to the law. In 1630, when Shepard was silenced by Bishop Laud, 'the house of the Harlakendens were so many fathers and mothers' to him, and later, when thwarted in his first effort to emigrate and deprived of his first-born child, he writes that Roger 'much refreshed me, and clave to me in my sorrows.' Richard, the eldest son, was an early proprietor of Newtown, probably by way of investment or to help his brother; Roger and Mabel accompanied Shepard to New England in the *Defense*, together with Roger's eighteen-year-old wife,[3] whom he had married but two months before. They purchased the great house of Thomas Dudley by the town landing in Newtown, and found living near by Governor John Haynes, their father's friend and neighbor.

Young men of blood and spirit like Henry Vane and Roger Harlakenden were appreciated in New England; and in Roger the people were not disappointed. When the trained bands were organized in regiments, he was commissioned lieutenant-

1. Quincy, I. 170–72; *Proc. M. H. S.*, LVIII. 446–58.
2. Richard Harlakenden, B.A. Cambridge (Magdalene) 1586–87, and member of Staples Inn. His wife was Margaret, sister of Sir Francis Hubert of the Court of Chancery. Lord Culpeper, aide-de-camp to Charles I and father to the Governor of Virginia, was a cousin. Colne Priory is still owned by a descendant, Geoffrey C. Probert, Esq., who has kindly furnished me with most of this information on the Harlakendens.
3. Elizabeth, daughter to Colonel Godfrey Bosville, M.P., of Yorkshire. Richard Harlakenden married Alice, daughter of Sir Henry Mildmay of Graces, Little Baddow, Essex, a cousin of Governor Winthrop.

colonel of militia. But this gallant and generous young man, who might have been a pillar to the College, died at Cambridge of smallpox on November 17, 1638, when just past his twenty-seventh birthday. He was buried with military honors — the first of our founders, perhaps, to be laid in the old Cambridge burying ground, where Dunster, Shepard, and Chauncy are interred. 'He was a very godly man, and of good use both in the commonwealth and the church,' recorded Winthrop. 'He died in great peace, and left a sweet memorial behind him of his piety and virtue.' Edward Johnson, an officer in Harlakenden's regiment, honored his departed leader with one of the best of his naïve epitaphs:

> Harlakenden,
> Among these men
> Of note Christ hath thee seated:
> In warlike way
> Christ thee array
> With zeal, and love well heated.
> As generall
> Belov'd of all,
> Christ's Souldiers honour thee:
> In thy young yeares,
> Courage appeares,
> And kinde benignity.[1]

Captain John Endecott's appearance among the Overseers at the first Harvard Commencement, in 1642, indicates that he had been coöpted to fill the vacancy caused by Harlakenden's death.[2] A man of Winthrop's age, born probably at Chagford, Devon, in 1589, he was one of the west-countrymen who obtained a patent to Massachusetts Bay before the royal charter was granted; and he governed the Company's plantation at Salem for two years before Winthrop arrived. Although Devonshire usually produced a more genial type of puritan than the praying colonels of East Anglia, Endecott was one of the bigoted and fanatical sort that made the very name of puritan odious to later generations. His defacing the cross on the English ensign alarmed the Colony, and caused him to be left out of the magistracy for a year; his administration as Governor is remem-

1. *W. W. P.*, p. 103. Harlakenden's widow married Herbert Pelham, the first treasurer of the College. His sister Mabel married Governor Haynes.
2. There is no record of his appointment by the General Court.

bered for the persecution of Quakers; in harshness to heretics he surpassed even Dudley. Endecott was a man of education, and retained enough French from youthful military service in the Low Countries to converse in 1650 with Father Druillettes in that language. He endeavored to have the town school at Salem made a free one, supported by taxation,[1] but seems to have taken little interest in the College after it was lost to Salem, the only mention of his name in the college records being at the head of a protest against the students 'wearing of long haire after the manner of Ruffians,' when he was Governor of the Colony.[2]

NATHANIEL EATON CHOSEN 'PROFESSOR'

'To take order for a colledge at Newetowne,' the assigned function of this first Board of Overseers, was a large order indeed. As yet the College existed only on paper — not even on the parchment of a charter or grant. It had no property, no officers, no students, and no funds. Nothing had yet been paid on account of the £400 voted by the General Court in 1636. But the Board went bravely ahead, and engaged a 'Professor' to open and conduct the College. As Thomas Danforth, Treasurer of the College, recorded in 'College Book III' at least fifteen years later:

Mr Nathaniel Eaton was chosen Professor of the sd Schoole in the yeare One thousand six hundred thirty seaven, to whose care the management of the Donations before mentioned were betrusted for the erecting of such Edifices as were meet and necessary for a Colledge: and for his own Lodgings.[3]

1. M. W. Jernegan, *Laboring and Dependent Classes*, p. 76.
2. *C. S. M.*, xv. 37. Until L. S. Mayo's promised Life of Endecott appears, the best sketch of the Captain is in the *D. A. B.*, by J. Truslow Adams. The first among the Governor's descendants in the male line to graduate from Harvard College was William Putnam Endicott (A.B. 1822). His son William Crowninshield Endicott (A.B. 1847) served as Overseer and Fellow of the College, and as Secretary of War under President Cleveland.
3. College Book No. 3, p. 2; *C. S. M.*, xv. 172; the date of the entry is subsequent to 1654. Danforth first wrote 'eight,' but substituted 'seaven.' Timothy Farrar, writing anonymously in *N. E. H. G. R.* (ix. 269–71), adduces an entry in the *Mass. Bay Recs.* (i. 210) for November 20, 1637, as proof that Eaton was appointed head of the College before the Board of Overseers was appointed. The entry reads, 'Mr Eaton is left out of this rate, leaveing it to his discretion what hee will freely give towards these charges.' Mr. Eaton, with no Christian name, obviously means Theophilus, the eldest

Nathaniel Eaton, 'the first head of Harvard College but not dignified with the title of President,'[1] was a younger son of Richard Eaton, a university graduate and vicar of Great Budworth, Cheshire. There Nathaniel was born, about 1610. His brother Theophilus, twenty years his senior, was a merchant of London, Deputy-Governor of the Eastland Company which traded to the Baltic, and one of those wealthy city puritans who organized the Massachusetts Bay Company and financed the great puritan migration.[2] Nathaniel attended Westminster School, whence he was elected a scholar to Trinity College, Cambridge, in 1630. There, so he declared in his confession to

brother (cf. 1. 305). Nathaniel Eaton's first name is always given when he is mentioned in the records (1. 262, 275, 277, 302, 374). The other interpretation is, at first glance, confirmed by an entry in Shepard's Autobiography in the middle of the passage quoted in Chapter XIV: 'And because this town (then called Newtown) was thorow gods great care and goodnes kept spotles from the contagion of the opinions therefore at the desire of some of our town [,] the Deputies of the court, hauing got mr Eaton to attend the Schoole, the court for that and sundry other reasons determined to erect the Colledge here' (C. S. M., XXVII. 389). This has sometimes been taken to mean that the two deputies of Cambridge at the General Court had made a tentative contract with Eaton, and on the strength of it induced the Court to fix the College in their town. But if we supply a comma after 'town' (which came at the end of a line, where Shepard seldom troubled to place punctuation), it seems clear that by 'Deputies of the court' Shepard meant men deputed by the Court, that is the Board of Overseers. If he had meant the deputies of Newtown he would have called them that, or 'deputies of this town.' Members of the General Court were never called 'Deputies of the court.' Shepard simply got the order of events wrong, as in the earlier part of the paragraph.

1. Savage, *Genealogical Dictionary*, II. 96. Frederick L. Gay, in a communication to the *Harvard Al. Bull.*, XVII. 612–13, made a gallant effort to have Eaton officially recognized as the first President of Harvard College. But there is no evidence that he was ever called by the title of President, or that any such office then existed. Danforth's record cited above, and the Cambridge town records for May 11, 1638 (p. 33), refer to him as 'the Professor.' Winthrop calls him 'a schoolmaster' (*Journal*, September 4, 1639). Neither Johnson nor *New Englands First Fruits* mentions him; Cotton Mather gives him no title; William Hubbard of the Class of 1642, writing about 1680, states that Eaton was 'the first man who was called to preside there,' *History of New England* (1848 ed.), p. 247; but presiding officers are not always presidents. Hutchinson, writing over a century after the event, says, 'The first master of the college was Nathaniel Eaton' (*Mass. Bay*, 1760 ed., 1. 91 n.). On the other hand, Dunster, according to Danforth's record, was 'invited to accept the place of President of the Colledge' in 1640 (C. S. M., XV. 173), and is frequently referred to as President in contemporary documents, even before he was so described in the charter of 1650. Nor is there any authority for the *D. N. B.*'s calling Eaton 'president designate.'

2. *D. N. B.* Theophilus Eaton married Ann Lloyd, daughter of George Lloyd (1560–1615), Bishop of Chester, and widow of Thomas Yale. Elihu Yale was her grandson. See C. S. M., XXV. 418, where common errors about these relationships are corrected by Mr. Matthews, who has also, in *Notes & Queries*, 11th ser., VIII. 70–71, corrected some erroneous statements about Nathaniel Eaton's children. There was a Boston man of the same name, with whom the Harvard Eaton is sometimes confused.

the church of Newtown,[1] he was a loose liver and a Sabbath-breaker. In 1632 he left the University, and after stopping a short time with his brother in London, crossed over to the Low Countries. There he studied theology under William Ames, during the last year of that eminent puritan's professoriat in the University of Franeker.

During his sojourn at Franeker, Eaton appears to have made sabbatarianism his special subject. The Dutch had wisely embraced Calvinism without the puritan Sabbath; their gaiety and drunkenness on the Lord's Day distressed exiled Englishmen, and even shocked so broad-minded a scholar as J. J. Scaliger. Dr. Ames, on being asked by Eaton for a 'thesis subject,' probably suggested that he collect from books and from living authorities the opinions of eminent theologians on the proper and scriptural observance of the Lord's Day. These, if published, might curb the sabbatarian licentiousness of the Dutch.

At any rate, that is what Nathaniel did; and the 'Investigation' no doubt gave him some interesting contacts with Dutch scholars. When the young man had completed his *Arbeit* Dr. Ames allowed him to present it in the form of a disquisition before a university audience; and the results appeared in a Latin booklet printed at Franeker in 1633, entitled 'Inquisitio in varientes Theologorum quorundam sententias, de Sabbato, & die Dominico, quam . . . proponit, sub Praesidio D.D. Guilielmi Amesii . . . Nathanael Eatonus, Anglus.'[2] This tract was considered sufficiently valuable to be reprinted by a Dutch theologian [3] twenty-five years later, and to be attributed to Ames.[4]

1. Thomas Shepard's Ms. 'Confessions of diuerse members' (Ms. in N. E. H. G. S.), p. 14.
2. Translation of the full title: 'Investigation into differing opinions of certain Theologians on the Sabbath and the Lord's Day, which Nathaniel Eaton, Englishman, made out of zeal for the truth, and defended by way of exercise, under the presidency of Dr. William Ames, Professor of Sacred Theology, on the [*blank*] day of March, at 1 p. m., in the accustomed place.' Ninety-two numbered pages and four unnumbered, containing a poem in Latin hexameters *de Die Dominico*, and one in Greek hexameters, *de Numero Septenario*, signed 'N. E.' The copy in the M. H. S. probably belonged to John Winthrop's library.
3. Christian S. Schotanus (1603–1671), professor of Greek and Theology at the University of Franeker.
4. *Guilielmi Amesi Sententia De Origine Sabbati & Die Dominico, Quam ex ipsius mente Concepit scripto & publice disputavit. Nathanael Eatonus, Angl.* Amstelodami, Apud Ioannem Ianssonium, 1658. Copy in H. C. L. The prefatory note by Schotanus to the reader may be translated: 'Appeareth once more a disputation of our Preceptor Master Ames concerning the controversies amongst us on the Sabbath and the Lord's Day, which, taken down from his very mind, a worthy youth many years past made the

According to Eaton's own statement,[1] it was the same master who converted him to the way of truth. Ames, as we have seen, left Franeker for Rotterdam shortly after Eaton's *Inquisitio* was presented, and died the same year. According to Governor Winthrop, Eaton now got himself 'initiated among the Jesuits, and, coming into England, his friends drew him from them'; [2] but this is probably a cock-and-bull story. The puritans were apt to attribute Jesuit antecedents to any 'troubler of Israel.' There is no reason to doubt Eaton's own statement to the Cambridge church that after Ames' death he returned to England and taught school at two different places, of which the second was 'prophane and bent on sinne and people haters of the truth.' Temptation was too strong for him: 'they inuited me, I must do the like for them and if I was familiar with any that were godly they would diswade.' Only in New England could he hope to escape these evil influences; the way became clear when his eldest brother organized an emigrating company.

Theophilus Eaton, although an early member of the Massachusetts Bay Company, had too many irons in the fire to emigrate in 1630. Seven years later the pressure on puritans had become so severe that he could endure England no longer. Accordingly, with John Davenport, his old schoolmate and former pastor,[3] and Edward Hopkins, a wealthy merchant whose benefaction still provides 'deturs' for Harvard scholars, he organized a group of emigrants, mostly Londoners. Their purpose was to find a place in New England where they could resume trading activities, and enjoy the ministry of their beloved pastor. Nathaniel, with his young wife, and probably John Harvard,[4] joined the company, which arrived at Boston on June 26, 1637. There they tarried while Theophilus looked

---

subject of a public disquisition.' Eaton's original preface comes next, and the text follows almost word for word that of the first edition. Eaton's *corollaria* and poetry are omitted. There is no reason to suppose that Eaton had anything to do with this edition, which unjustly makes him the mere reporter of Ames, rather than the author.

1. Shepard Ms. 'Confessions,' p. 15.

2. *Journal* (1908 ed.), I. 314–15. Repeated in Hubbard, *History of N. E.*, p. 247; Nathaniel Rogers calls Eaton *Jesuita versipellis* in his valedictory oration at Commencement, 1652. *C. S. M.*, xxxi.

3. Davenport had gone to the Netherlands in 1633, but had been forced to leave, like Hooker and Peter, owing to the combination of English diplomatic intervention and the pressure of the authorities to conform to Dutch ecclesiastical polity. R. P. Stearns in *N. E. Q.*, vi. 778–87.

4. See next chapter.

INQUISITIO

In variantes Theologorum quorun-
dam sententias,

DE

SABBATO,

& die Dominico,

QUAM

Ex veritatis studio instituit, & exercitii
gratia proponit,

SUB PRÆSIDIO

D. D. GUILIELMI AMESII,

SS. Theologiæ Professoris,

NATHANAEL EATONUS, Anglus;

Ad diem   Martij hora prima pomeridiana
loco consueto.

FRANEKERÆ,

Excudebat Fredricus Heynsius

Typogr. in Academiâ Franekeranâ,

ANNO M. DC. XXXIII.

EATON'S DISSERTATION ON THE SABBATH

over eligible sites for settlement; and while they were waiting, Davenport was appointed an Overseer, and Nathaniel Eaton 'Professor' or head of the College.

In view of his future performance, the appointment of this man of twenty-seven, who had no university degree,[1] to so important and responsible a post requires some explanation. The Overseers could not hope to obtain a settled minister of scholarly reputation and teaching experience, such as Cotton, Hooker, Parker, or Mather. New England churches had a vested interest in their ministers, and would not have considered for a moment releasing such men to the College. There were several young schoolmasters in the Colony with university degrees, and a number of young parsons like John Harvard who had not yet found parishes.[2] But Nathaniel Eaton had several qualifications that they lacked. A pupil of Doctor Ames, of famous memory, he had already 'published something,' an asset for ambitious teachers in those days as in ours; and when he distributed copies of his sabbatarian tract among the Overseers (we still have Winthrop's copy), they doubtless found it an edifying 'contribution to knowledge.' His 'teaching experience' in England was another good point. The Latin and Greek verses appended to the *Inquisitio* advertised him as a 'good classical scholar,' with at least a 'reading knowledge' of Hebrew. 'Home influences' and 'background' were of the best; and although not yet sealed and sanctified by the Cambridge brethren, he was practically speaking a church member. And it probably did not hurt Nathaniel that his Cambridge college was Trinity, for there were five old Trinity men on the Board of Overseers. Thomas Hooker, to be sure, who had known Eaton in the Netherlands, declared 'he did not approve of his spirit, and feared the issue of his being received here';[3] but Hooker was at Hartford, and an Emmanuel man. Hugh Peter must have known Eaton at Amsterdam, and doubtless answered for his character and competence. A small college, opening in a new

1. He certainly had no Cambridge degree; no Franeker degree is mentioned on his Franeker book; and on his English pamphlet only his Padua degrees of 1647 are mentioned. But he is referred to as Master of Arts in legal documents in New England. Lechford, *Note-Book*, pp. 248–49.

2. For example, Newman, Cobbett, and Wetherell; Cheever, who probably came on the same ship as Eaton; and Maude, then master of the Boston Latin School. See Appendix B.

3. Hutchinson, *Mass. Bay* (2d ed.), I. 91, apparently quoting a letter of Hooker subsequently lost.

country, was glad enough to find a man of Nathaniel's record for master.

Eaton, then, was appointed Professor or head of the College in late November or December, 1637; but it was some months before he took up his residence at Cambridge and opened the College. Probably he removed to Charlestown early in 1638, about the time that his brothers left the Bay; for the Charlestown records inform us that on April 6, 1638, 'Mr. Nathaniel Eaton and Mr. John Oliver were chosen to determine the Bounds bettwixt the Towne and Mr. Cradock Farme.' [1] For some reason unknown to us, it was probably more convenient for the Eatons to live in Charlestown while the first college building was being altered for their reception. On May 2, 1638, the General Court 'ordered, that Newetowne shall henceforward be called Cambrige' — a vote that needs no explanation.[2] At some time around that date, but not later than June 9, 1638, the Eatons installed themselves in the house that the Overseers had acquired for the College.

The College in Cowyard Row

It was a decidedly bovine atmosphere in which the College was set down — in the very midst of Cowyard Row,[3] where the ammoniacal steams emanating from yarded cattle mingled not inappropriately with odors from Mistress Eaton's cooking. But the pastoral considerations that caused this site to be selected were those connected with Thomas Shepard. His house, formerly Master Hooker's, was the one furthest along Braintree Street from Watch-house Hill, and hardly a stone's throw from the College. It stood long enough to be depicted; and the drawing of it, with its steep seventeenth-century roof (more suitable for thatch than shingle) and numerous jogs and ells, is a good indication of what the Peyntree house must have looked like in 1638, after it had been altered to receive the Eatons and their

1. Charlestown Archives, xx. 66 (Mss., Boston City Hall).
2. Lest the entry for September 8, 1636, in the *Mass. Bay Recs.*, I. 180 — 'Thomas Cheesholme is licensed to keepe a house of intertainment at Newe Towne, *now called Cambridge*' — prove a stumblingblock to others as it did to me, be it noted that the words in italics are in a different ink from the rest of the entry, and that in a manuscript copy of the General Court records made before 1650, and now in the Boston Public Library, these three words do not appear.
3. See Chapter XIV.

unfortunate scholars.[1] William Peyntree, the early inhabitant who owned this property in 1635, followed his parson and next-door neighbor to Connecticut, leaving no record of the transfer of his property. It must have been acquired by the Overseers, either from him or a third party,[2] before May 3, 1638, when Eaton received some additional grants from the Town of Cambridge for himself and the College.[3]

We may pause a moment to survey this property of an acre and an eighth, which was the nucleus of the College Yard and of the Harvard University estate. In 1635, when Peyntree owned it, the property is described in the records as 'one House with backside and garden about halfe a rood' (one-eighth of an acre), together with 'one Cowhouse with a backside aboute one acker' in 'Cowyard Rowe.'[4] The actual site of the Peyntree house is now included within Massachusetts Avenue (Braintree Street), several times widened at the expense of the College Yard. Early in 1910, when excavations were being made for the Cambridge subway, a cellar wall of this building that housed Master Eaton and the earliest Harvard students almost three centuries ago was uncovered by the pick and shovel.[5]

1. The Hooker-Shepard house, which has had as many distinguished occupants as any in Cambridge (Jonathan Mitchell, President Leverett, the two Edward Wigglesworths, professors of Divinity), stood until 1844. See *The Harvard Book* (1875), II. 22–25, and plan of Leverett's property reproduced in *H. C. S. C.*

2. Hosea Starr Ballou, in *N. E. H. G. R.*, LXXX. 133, claims that between Peyntree's departure and the establishment of the College, the Peyntree house was the residence of Comfort Starr, chirurgeon from Ashford in Kent, who came late to Newtown and departed early. The only evidence is the order of Starr's name in a list of heads of families, dated 8 February 1635–36 (*Cambridge Town Records*, p. 18). Mr. Ballou assumes that because Starr's name comes between Hooker's and Olmstead's (Goffe's predecessor), he lived between them. But the name of Harlakenden, who is known to have lived at the foot of Dunster Street, is on the other side of Hooker's; it seems that the gentry, not neighbors, were placed together on this list. In the *Cambridge Proprietors' Records* there are several instances (for example, p. 52) of purchases being made from Hooker's followers after they had settled at Hartford.

3. President Wadsworth in the eighteenth century (*C. S. M.*, xv. 265, lxxvii n. and ff.) confused the Peyntree lot (I) with one of the town grants of May 3, 1638; but Andrew McF. Davis, in *Proc. A. A. S.*, n.s., v (1887–88). 469–86, shows that this cannot be correct. Treasurer Eliot added to the confusion by putting the date 'Abt. 1640' on lot I on his map (*Sketch*, p. 190), which has unfortunabely been copied on the map in *C .S. M.*, xv. lxix. Obviously the lot must have been acquired before the Eatons moved into the house; and as early as September, 1638, we find evidence that ground had been broken for the building subsequently called the Old College.

4. *Proprietors' Records*, p. 16.

5. William C. Lane, in *Harv. Grads. Mag.*, XVIII. 451–52, with photographs, pp. 460–61.

No description of the Peyntree house has come down to us, and it was taken down before 1645, when the President's Lodging was built on the same site.[1] Presumably it was one of the wooden two-story-and-a-half, steep-roofed dwellings erected at that time, with a central chimney, two large rooms (the hall and parlor) on either side of the front door on Braintree Street, a kitchen in a lean-to on the north or yard side, and chambers overhead. It must have been fairly commodious, as in it the Eatons boarded, taught, and underfed the student body during the first academic year.

As the story of these early college lots is obscure and complicated, each section of the present College Yard has been numbered on the maps in the order of its acquisition by the College. The Peyntree lot is numbered I. Lots outside the present Yard are designated by letters.

On May 2, 1638, as we have seen, the General Court rechristened Newtown, Cambridge. Possibly in recognition of this notice, the Cambridge town meeting granted three lots to Master Eaton, and/or the College, on the following day.[2] The Town was dividing up the 'ould ox pasture,' which included all the region east of the cow common and north of the cowyards and the common pales, on both sides of Charlestown Path (Kirkland Street). 'On the south syde' of that way, the Town made what we have designated as grant II, two acres and two roods,[3] to 'Mr. Eaten.' This important section of the present Yard was situated just north of the Peyntree (I) and Goffe (IV) lots. A part of it, at least, abutted on the Common,[4] but it probably did not include the present northwest corner of the

1. No mention of the house is found after President Dunster vacated it in 1641. Mr. Matthews' conjecture that it was the 'old house' mentioned in an account of college rents in Chauncy's time (*C. S. M.*, xv. lxix, civ, 19) is incorrect; the 'old house' there is clearly the 'Old College.'

2. *Camb. Town Records*, p. 33. The lots were all granted to Eaton because the College had as yet no corporate existence.

3. That is, two and one-half acres. The tract measured two and one-quarter acres when surveyed by Wadsworth for Eliot's *Sketch*, but is less now, owing to the triangle taken off by Cambridge Street.

4. In the bounds given to the Betts lot (V) in 1642 (*Proprietors' Records*, p. 108), the 'land intended for the Colledge' is on the north; but in Betts' deed to the College in 1661, 'Thomas Swoetman' is on the north. This man, from whose assignee Spencer the College acquired lot VI in 1697, came to Cambridge about 1645 (Paige, p. 668). Probably he was allowed by the Town to locate on this corner; and probably Betts was allowed to extend his line north in order to compensate him for having no houselot on Braintree Street.

Yard. Lot II was granted to Eaton personally, and some years elapsed before the College acquired undisputed title to it. In the proprietors' survey of 1642 it is designated as land 're-served' or 'intended' for the College;[1] and Treasurer Danforth did not venture to include it in his inventory of college property at the end of Dunster's administration.[2]

A second grant made to Eaton the same day, which we may designate as A (since it was outside the present Yard), has caused much confusion among college historians.[3] It was on the north side of the Charlestown Path (Kirkland Street): two and two-thirds acres to 'the professor.' On the same page of the town records where this allotment is mentioned, there is a memorandum to this effect:

The 2 acres and 2/3 above mentioned to the Professor is to the Towns vse for euer for a publick scoole or Colledge And to the vse of mr Nath Eaten as long as he shall be Imployed in that work so that att his death or ceassing from that work he or his shall be allowed according to the Charges he hath bene att in buylding or fencing.[4]

This is the lot on which the Hemenway Gymnasium, Lawrence Hall, and the Paine Music Building are now located. In a list of about 1639 in the proprietors' records, Eaton is described as owning two parcels of land; the one, described as 'In the Old Oxe pasture two Acres for a houselott,' and bounded by Richard Jackson, the ox pasture, 'a towne lott,' and the cow common,[5] is evidently grant A. Apparently Eaton had intended here to erect his official residence. In the proprietors' survey of 1642,[6] lot A is described in the bounds of adjoining properties as 'Colledg land' or the 'Colledge Lootte'; but it is not mentioned in Danforth's inventory of 1654. In contrast to lot II, whose history to this point is the same, lot A got into the

1. *Proprietors' Records*, pp. 78, 84, 108.
2. *C. S. M.*, xv. 208. The 'about 3 acres' that he there lists in the present Yard is barely enough to cover the Peyntree (I) and Goffe (IV) properties and Fellows' Orchard (III).
3. President Wadsworth (*C. S. M.*, xv. 265) confused A with II; so did the Wadsworth map in Eliot, *Sketch*, p. 190. Paige (p. 42 n.) followed Wadsworth; and I made the same mistake in *Harv. Grads. Mag.*, xli. 313. The first approximately correct explanation of the three grants was by A. McF. Davis in 1888 (*loc. cit.*, pp. 473–78), but his map on p. 470 repeats the ancient error.
4. *Town Records*, p. 33.
5. *Proprietors' Records*, p. 54.
6. Pp. 83 and 65.

hands of private citizens, and the College had to buy it back in the nineteenth century.[1]

The third grant to Eaton on May 11, 1638, which we may designate as A′, is described simply as four acres to 'Mr. Eaten.' In a list of about 1639 in the proprietors' records, the second of the two lots designated as Eaton's is described as 'two Acres vpon the Oxe pasture,' bounded by John Champney, the Charlestown line, the highway, and the Swamp Field. Dr. Norris has identified this somewhat shrunken lot A′ as two acres fronting on Kirkland Street, between Holden Street and the Somerville line. It is not mentioned as Eaton's, or the College's, in any later survey, and was probably considered forfeited to the Town after Eaton fled to Virginia.

THE COLLEGE OPENED

Nathaniel Eaton with his wife and several small children moved over from Charlestown and settled themselves in the Peyntree house before June 9, 1638.[2] The College probably opened in July or August, certainly at some time between early June and September 7, for the last date is that of a letter from Edmund Browne at Boston to Sir Simonds d'Ewes, enclosing a report of which this extract is significant: 'Wee have a Cambridge heere, a College erecting, youth lectured, a library, and I suppose there will be a presse this winter.'[3] Another gossipy immigrant wrote home on September 27, 1638: 'Newtowne now is called Cambridge. There is a University house reared, I heare, and a prity library begun.'[4]

The 'College erecting' and 'University house reared' indicate

1. A lot of the same situation and dimensions as the one identified as A is found on several nineteenth-century maps of Cambridge designated as 'The Pound Lot.' The name probably came from its abutment on the 'Enclosure for dry cattle' (see map of Cambridge in 1638), which was responsible for the right angle of Holmes Place, and which later replaced as town pound the lot near Christ Church.

2. He was admitted freeman of the Colony on that date (*Mass. Bay Recs.*, I. 374); hence his admission to the Cambridge Church must have taken place before; and he could not have been admitted to the ch urch before taking up residence at Cambridge. He was never a member of the Charlestown Church.

3. The letter, dated September 7, and the enclosed report (Harleian Mss., British Museum) are printed in *C. S. M.*, VII. 74–80; cf. XV. lxx. No year is mentioned on the letter or the report, but, as Mr. Matthews shows, it cannot be other than 1638. Browne had landed at Salem or Boston June 27, and had been in or around Boston ever since (Thomas Lechford, *Note-Book*, pp. xiii, 1, 45; see Appendix B).

4. *Historical Mss. Comm. Reports, 14th Report*, Appendix, pt. IV. 56.

that the Overseers had already broken ground for the 'Old College,' if they had not also raised the frame. 'Youth lectured' can only mean that Professor Eaton had already gathered his first freshman class, and opened the College, before the seventh day of September, 1638.[1]

One week after, on September 14, Master John Harvard died at Charlestown; and dying, left immortal fame.

---

1. It may also be inferred from a statement in *New Englands First Fruits* (Appendix D) that the College opened in 1638, since the Class of 1642 had 'beene these foure yeeres trained up in University learning'; and William Hubbard, a member of that class, says that the 'College was erected in the year 1638' (*Hist. of N. E.*, 1848 ed., p. 247).

XVI

JOHN HARVARD [1]
1635–1638

John Harvard cannot rightly be called *the* founder of Harvard College, as sentiment and tradition would have him. Unlike Sir Walter Mildmay with respect to Emmanuel, or founders of American universities like Ezra Cornell and Leland Stanford, John Harvard did not initiate the foundation that bears his name, or obtain the charter that gave it corporate existence, or provide the funds to set it in motion. The College, as we have seen, was founded by the General Court of Massachusetts Bay in 1636, when John Harvard was still in England; and behind the College stood the puritan churches and the entire body of educated and religious people in New England. John Harvard

---

1. See pedigree on p. 104, above. Henry F. Waters' data on Harvard were first presented in *N. E. H. G. R.*, xxxix. 265–84 and xl. 362–79, and are reprinted in two pamphlets called *John Harvard and his Ancestry* (1885; 'Part Second,' 1886); but all these with additional data may be found in his *Genealogical Gleanings in England* (2 vols., 1901). Henry C. Shelley has woven these facts into a charming romance entitled *John Harvard and His Times* (Boston, 1907), where the hypothetical friendships with Shakspere, Milton, and others are described. Less interesting but more scholarly, although not altogether dependable, are James K. Hosmer, 'John Harvard in England,' *C. S. M.*, xi. 366–82, and Andrew McF. Davis, 'John Harvard's Life in America,' *C. S.* M., xii. 4–45. The Davis paper, which is also printed separately (Cambridge, 1908), is valuable as a description of the scene of Harvard's short American sojourn. Owing to the romantic interest attached to Harvard's name, many well-intentioned persons have delivered themselves of orations, articles, and booklets on John Harvard, which for historical purposes are worthless. Most of the Charlestown records, as described in Richard Frothingham's *History of Charlestown* (1845), pp. 1–4, are now gathering dust in the basement of the Boston City Hall, and few of them have been printed. The original records of Harvard's period have disappeared, but copies from them, made in 1664, are in the volumes now called Charlestown Archives, vols. xix and xx (subtitle 'Town Records,' vols. i and ii, 1629–61). These are badly arranged, with many of the pages unnumbered, and are not indexed. A careful copy of these two volumes was made, and arranged in chronological order under the direction of the late Henry H. Edes; this volume is accurately indexed. It is known as 'Charlestown Archives, vol. xx, copy made by Frederic Monroe,' and is also in charge of the Boston City Clerk. An old Book of Possessions (Charlestown Archives, vol. xxxiv), begun in 1638 and added to by subsequent town clerks, has been printed under the title *Charlestown Land Records* as the Third Report of the Boston Record Commissioners (1878). The *Records of the First Church in Charlestown, 1632–1789*, were printed in 1880 by James F. Hunnewell, in an edition limited to 62 copies, and also in the *N. E. H. G. R.*, vols. xxiii–xxxiii.

was not a member of the Board of Overseers which established the institution; nor did his legacy 'breathe life into' or 'make possible' the foundation, as so often has been said. The College was already in operation, and the new building had been begun, some weeks or months before his death. Nevertheless, as eponym and earliest benefactor, John Harvard personified that love of God and man which created and maintained a university, *hic in silvestribus et incultis locis.*[1]

HARVARD'S LIFE AFTER LEAVING EMMANUEL

Although more effort and ingenuity have been expended on searching for facts on John Harvard than on the entire early history of the College, John yet remains an elusive figure. Not a single letter of his, and but two signatures, have come down to us. Except for John Wilson's elegy, twenty-four words in Shepard's autobiography, and a doggerel verse in Johnson, no characterization of him by a contemporary has survived. We know naught of his joys and sorrows, hopes and fears. Only a bare outline of his life can be picked out from wills and other legal documents.[2]

We left John Harvard after he had taken his M.A. from Emmanuel in 1635, at the comparatively advanced age of twenty-seven. On April 19, 1636, he married a fellow-colle-

---

1. The tradition that John Harvard founded the College was started in 1643 by *New Englands First Fruits* (see Appendix D), and is still generally believed. John Wilson, in his elegy on John Harvard, makes him declare himself her founder. Thomas Shepard, too, in his Autobiography allows one to infer that nothing was done about the College until Harvard's legacy had been paid in. And Professor Edward Kennard Rand, pointing to these early ascriptions, declares: 'Our ancestors knew what they were about in calling John Harvard the Founder of the college that bears his name.' (*Harvard Graduates Magazine*, XLII. 44). The General Court described John Harvard as the 'principal founder' of the College in 1661 (Quincy, I. 39); but on January 5, 1747, the Corporation declared in a petition to the General Court, 'your Predecessors were the Founders of the College' (*C. S. M.*, XVI. 769). A commencement orator of *c.* 1670 calls him 'Dignissimus . . . 'Ευεργετάρχοs noster Harvardus' — 'Our most worthy Chief Benefactor' (see p. 221 n.). Cotton Mather puts the matter accurately as well as gracefully where he says that John Harvard's will 'laid the most significant *Stone* in the Foundation' (*Magnalia*, book iv. 126). Benjamin Peirce, in his *History of Harvard University* (1833), calls John Harvard our 'great benefactor.' Quincy (I. 10) inverts the order of events and rather begs the question in declaring that the General Court after Harvard's death 'immediately commenced the seminary, and conferred upon it the name of Harvard, thus acknowledging him as its founder.' Henry F. Waters judiciously calls Harvard 'our earliest benefactor' and 'godfather,' but not our founder. See also *C. S. M.* XXXI. 311 for an early 'founder' reference.

2. See above, pp. 103–06.

gian's sister, Ann Sadler. She was born in 1614, at Patcham, Sussex, where her father John Sadler was then vicar.[1] At the time of her marriage he was vicar of Ringmer, near Lewes; but the wedding took place at South Malling, another village near by. Romantic readers may imagine a runaway match; but South Malling may well have been chosen in a search for simplicity. The church there had just been rebuilt in the plainest fashion, with an interior arrangement resembling that of a New England meeting-house; and Esdras Coxall, the parson who united Ann to John, was presumably the 'honest preaching Minister' that the patron desired.[2]

John Harvard is described as 'clerk' in at least four legal documents of these years: his mother's will, his father-in-law's will,[3] a lease of real estate,[4] and a recognizance for debt.[5] The word 'clerk' used in that connection as good as proves that John had taken holy orders; [6] but no record of his ordination has been found, and he certainly enjoyed no church living.

Most of the Harvard patrimony in Southwark and in London proper became concentrated in the hands of John Harvard and his mother when the plague of 1625 carried off his father the butcher, and four of his five brothers and sisters. This process went on after his graduation. His mother, who had married twice since his father's death, died on July 9, 1635, leaving to her 'eldest sonne John Harvard Clarke' the Queen's Head in Southwark, half her leasehold in the parish of All Saints, Barking (near the Tower of London) and £250 in money. There were many small benefactions such as to 'my loveing frend Mr. Moreton our minister of St Saviours . . . in token of my love I

1. H. F. Waters, *John Harvard and His Ancestry*, p. 23 n.; *Genealogical Gleanings*, I. 133.

2. Henry W. Foote, 'The Church in Which John Harvard was Married,' *Harv. Al. Bull.*, XXXIV. 472–78 (1932). The owner of the impropriation, John Stansfield, was grandfather to John Evelyn, who mentions South Malling church in his memoirs. It is a rare example of an English parish church showing puritan principles in its architecture.

3. Waters, *John Harvard and His Ancestry*, pp. 15, 23; *Gen. Glean.*, I. 124, 133. The dates are July 2, 1635, and February 6, 1637–38.

4. Waters, *Gen. Glean.*, I. 267; *N. E. H. G. R.*, XLII. 109–10.

5. *C. S. M.*, XXVI. 231.

6. 'Clerke hath two significations; one as it is the title of him that belongeth to the holy Ministrie of the Church . . . The other . . . noteth such as . . . use their pen in any Court or otherwise, as namely the Clerke of the Rolles of the Parliament, Clerks of the Chancerie, and such like.' Rastell, *Les Termes de la Ley* (1636), p. 66. There is no possibility of Harvard's having been clerk of a court, and the use of the word to describe a student was obsolete.

THE QUEEN'S HEAD, SOUTHWARK

give three pounds and my paire of silver hafted knyves'; and to Mistress Morton 'I give my best gould wrought Coyfe which of my two best shee please.' [1] But the bulk of the estate went to John and to his brother Thomas, 'Citizen and Clothworker of London.'

It was the next year, 1636, that John married Ann Sadler, and brought her to live in one of his houses in the parish of St. Olave's, Southwark. Thomas Harvard, John's only surviving brother, died in the spring of 1637; his will, proved May 5, 1637, left to 'my said brother John Harvard my said moitie or half parte' of the Tower Hill property (subject to an annuity for his widow), 'the summe of one hundred poundes lawfull English mony, and my standinge bowle of silver guilt and my Chest with twoe lockes. . . . Together with my best whole suite of apparell and my best cloake.' There were numerous other legacies to Thomas' children, his cousins, his wife's relations, and the two parishes with which he was connected. As executors, Thomas appointed brother John and Nicholas Morton, Rector of St. Saviour's, who was left 'the some of Forty shillings in recompence of a Sermon which I desire he should preach at my funerall, for the better Comforte edifyinge and instruccion of such my freinds and neighboures and other people as there shalbe assembled.' [2]

In February, 1636–37, before his brother's death, we find John selling for £120 a messuage and three cottages in the parish of St. Olave, Southwark, presumably to raise money for his intended journey.[3] And Dr. J. Leslie Hotson, the Sherlock Holmes of the Public Record Office, has unearthed from a roll of recognizances for debt an entry showing that on May 26, 1637, one Francis Norton, citizen and haberdasher of London, appeared before Sir John Finch (of ship-money fame) and acknowledged 'that he owed to John Harvard, of the parish of St. Olave in Southwark, clerk, three hundred pounds, to be paid on Whitsunday next.' [4] As John could hardly have neglected to collect so formidable a sum as £300 on the eve of his departure for New England, he must have been in London on or shortly after the day of payment: Whitsunday, May 28, 1637.

1. Waters, *Ancestry*, pp. 15–16. Nicholas Morton was the father of Charles Morton, later Vice-President of Harvard College.
2. Waters, *Ancestry*, pp. 18–19.
3. Waters, *Gen. Glean.*, I, 132.   4. *C. S. M.*, XXVI. 231–32.

John Harvard, then, was a well-to-do member of London's great middle class: grocers and goldsmiths, clothiers and haberdashers, who lived well and heartily in their own houses, owned solid furniture, gay clothing, and silver plate, invested their surplus profits in real estate, maintained churches, and assisted the needy; yet rarely sent a boy to the university.[1] They neither bore arms nor ranked as gentlemen, but lived better and more comfortably than a great many of the gentry. It can have been no economic pressure that sent John Harvard and his wife on the quest for a new home in a new world. They had plenty to live on at home without labor,[2] and although a poor man might better his condition in New England, it was well understood that 'great men must look to be losers, unless they reckon that gain which, by the glorious means of life, comes down from heaven.'[3] There is no reason, then, to challenge the tradition that John Harvard crossed the ocean to enjoy 'Christ's ordinances' in their purity. In Edward Johnson's halting rhyme:

> If Harverd had with riches here been taken,
>   He need not then through troublous Seas have past,
> But Christs bright glory hath thine eyes so waken,
>   Nought can content, thy soule of Him must tast.

HARVARD'S LIFE AT CHARLESTOWN

We left John collecting his debt at London, on Whitsunday, May 28, or a day or two after. The next trace of him is at Charlestown in the Massachusetts Bay, where he was admitted an inhabitant on August 1, 1637. That narrows down the period of his passage to the space of two months, and challenges us to find a ship for him.

1. The Master of Emmanuel informs me that there has never been a Harvard at Emmanuel or in the University of Cambridge since John went down; and no Harvard ever appeared at Harvard University until 1911, when connections were established with a Harvard family in England which descends from John's second cousin Robert, and a young member of this branch, Lionel deJersey Harvard, entered Harvard College and graduated with the Class of 1915. M. A. DeW. Howe, *Memoirs of the Harvard Dead*, II. 351–60.

2. If his estate was worth £1800 at his death, it was probably worth much more before he emigrated; for we have abundant evidence from the lives of John Winthrop, Peter Bulkeley, and others that estates of wealthy men suffered from the expenses of emigration, and from the large amount necessary to put into the New England soil before you got anything out.

3. T. Hutchinson, *Hist. of Mass. Bay* (2d ed.), I. 484.

We may eliminate three ships which arrived at Boston on June 20, as having sailed too early. On June 26, the *Hector* and a consort arrived from London, bringing the Eaton company, John Davenport, 'and another minister,' records Governor Winthrop.[1] Was this other minister John Harvard? If he was on board, the ship could not have sailed before Whitmonday, May 29. Twenty-seven days was a fast passage from England to Boston, but a possible one in June, when with good luck a ship might have a run of easterly winds.[2] It is not probable that Winthrop would have called John Harvard a minister, since he had never had a parish; and at least eight ministers besides Davenport came to New England that summer.[3] But what other possibilities are there besides the *Hector* and her sister ship? Only, so far as our records go, the *Hercules*, with a passenger list of Kentish men.[4] She sailed not earlier than June 9, from Sandwich. John Harvard is not on the list; but the absence of his name is not so significant as the fact that one passenger on the *Hercules* was Edward Johnson, author of the 'Wonder-Working Providence of Sions Saviour in New England.' This unconsciously humorous chronicle includes a chapter on the foundation of the College, which Johnson regarded as one of the principal glories of New England, but only eight lines and a poem on John Harvard.[5] Considering Johnson's zest for biographical detail, it is unthinkable that he would have dismissed our benefactor thus, had they shared the promiscuous intimacy of an emigrant vessel. Sandwich, moreover, was an inconvenient port for Londoners; John would naturally have joined a London company. Hence, unless there were other ship arrivals that summer of which we know nothing, the Harvards must have crossed on the *Hector* or her consort from London; and there is every probability that they would have chosen the

1. *Journal* (1908 ed.), I. 222–23.

2. Winthrop mentions a passage of 23 days from Boston to Gravesend in the summer of 1639. *Journal* (1908 ed.), I. 331. Westerly passages were usually slower than easterly ones, on account of heavier lading and prevailing winds. If the *Hector* had made Boston in twenty-seven days from London, the fact would hardly have escaped Winthrop's record. It seems likely that she sailed earlier from London, and that Harvard caught her at one of the Channel ports, after collecting his debt.

3. Samuel Eaton, George Moxon, John Yonges, Ralph Wheelock, William Tompson, Peter Prudden, John Allin, and John Fiske. See Appendix B.

4. C. E. Banks, *Planters of the Commonwealth*, p. 188. Found in the corporation records of Sandwich, certified under date of June 9, 1637.

5. *W. W. P.*, pp. 187, 201.

same ship as the Eatons. Nathaniel Eaton was of John Harvard's age, and his contemporary at Cambridge.

One may note in passing that another Cambridge contemporary who ventured on the deep that summer was not so happy. It was on August 10 that Edward King perished from a shipwreck in the narrow seas. John Milton, in 'Lycidas,' provided King with a memorial imperishable as Harvard's.

Charlestown and Boston, shaped like two slender-wristed fists, approach each other from right angles, and between their knuckles the Charles River flows into Boston Harbor. In 1637, when the Harvards settled there, the village of Charlestown consisted of a hundred and fifty 'comly and faire' houses,[1] with their gardens and orchards nestling between the river and the southwest slope of these heights so bitterly contested in 1775. The boundaries of the town went far beyond the Neck into the country, where the inhabitants pastured their cattle. Zechariah Symmes and Thomas James, the ministers, were both Emmanuel men; Edward Mellowes, who had entered Emmanuel the same year as John Harvard, was also a resident. Other leading citizens were Captain Robert Sedgwick, later one of Cromwell's major-generals; Mr. George Bunker, who gave his name to the famous hill; Increase Nowell, Assistant and Secretary of the Colony; and Ralph Sprague, the first settler. The two last had been members of the General Court that founded the College. It would be idle to speculate why the Harvards settled here rather than in another of the thirty or so settlements available;[2] but whatever the reason of his choosing Charlestown, the records show that Harvard was considered a desirable member of that community. On August 1, 1637, 'Mr John Harvard is admitted a Townsman with promise of such accommodations as wee best Can.'[3] He built or purchased a house, which must have been one of the best in the village, since it was used as the parsonage sixty years later;[4] it was one of a

1. *Id.*, p. 68.

2. Several of Harvard's contemporaries at Emmanuel — Samuel Dudley, Daniel Denison, Giles Firmin, and Richard Saltonstall — were then living at Ipswich.

3. Charlestown Archives, xx. 16. The caveat in this vote means that a first division of planting lands and cow commons had already taken place.

4. Its location has been identified by the fact that Judge Sewall spent a night there in 1697, and stated in his *Diary* (1. 446–47) that it had been John Harvard's house. Frothingham in 1845 described it as 'on Gravel Lane, running from Main street, near

THE HARVARD CHAPEL, ST. SAVIOUR'S

circle of houses that surrounded the top of Town or Windmill Hill. Increase Nowell was his neighbor on the north, and near the foot of the hill to the southward, across an open field, was the 'Great House' originally built for Governor Winthrop, and since used as the town meetinghouse. Apparently the Harvard house was too near the road, for on November 27 'Mr. Harvard is yeelded 3½ foote for A Portall'[1] — one of those covered porches which the early settlers built to provide protection from cold. On November 2, 1637, 'Mr. John Harvard' appeared before the General Court and was 'made free, and tooke the oath of freedome';[2] and on November 6, 'John Harvard and Anna Harvard his wiffe' were admitted members of the Charlestown Church.[3]

John Harvard obtained generous shares in all divisions of land made subsequent to his arrival. When, 'in Consideracion of the straitnesse of the Common on this side Misticke River it was agreed, that all that ground from the Towne to Menotomies River, that is without the enclosures, should bee reserved in Common, for such Cattle neare home, as milch Cowes, working Cattle, goates, and Calves of the first yeare,' John received five and a half 'cow commons,' which was exceeded by only nine of the 120 grantees.[4] On April 23, 1638, when lots were laid out in Waterfield 'on Mistickeside and aboue the Ponds,' only Increase Nowell received more than Harvard's share of 120 acres.[5] The size of this grant proves that the Harvards brought over cattle,

its junction with the Square, to the Town Hill' (*Hist. of Charlestown*, p. 75, n. 4). Gravel Lane is now an unnamed alley running from Main Street to Harvard Square (the top of the hill), just east of Henly Street, which did not exist in 1638. The house on the site is marked by a tablet, and the other streets around Town Hill follow almost the exact direction of those in Harvard's day; but their names have all been changed. The best description and map of early Charlestown is in James F. Hunnewell, *A Century of Town Life* (1888), pp. 109–11.

1. Charlestown Archives, xx. 59.
2. *Mass. Bay Recs.*, i. 206.
3. James F. Hunnewell, *Records of First Church in Charlestown* (1880), p. 9. It was contrary to the law for an inhabitant to be admitted freeman before he was admitted to a church; but these dates have been verified in the Ms. records.
4. Charlestown Archives, xx. 60.
5. *Id.*, p. 66. This grant was situated at what are now Washington and Forest Streets, Winchester, and is marked by a tablet. *Historical Markers Erected by Mass. Bay Tercentenary Commission*, p. 37. He also received one or more wood lots in Misticke Field, and ten acres of arable. These grants may be traced in *Charlestown Land Records* (3d Report, Boston Record Commissioners). On December 30, 1638, after John's death, 'Mrs Ann Harvard' received 11½ acres (Charlestown Archives, xx. 77), and in 1641 there is a puzzling grant of 4 acres to 'Mr Harvard' — probably the recorder's error for 'Mrs.' *Ibid.*, p. 105; cf. *C. S. M.*, xii. 9–10.

and servants to care for them — a good provision, since cattle-raising was then the most profitable industry in New England.[1] I like to think that John had a good laugh over resuming the ancestral occupation. In a new country, his memories of the paternal butcher-shop were more immediately useful than his Cambridge degrees.

Not that his education went for naught. John Harvard, Increase Nowell, Zechariah Symmes, and three others were appointed a committee 'to consider of some things tending towards A body of Lawes, etc.'[2] The General Court had invited the freemen to assemble in their respective towns and draft 'such necessary and fundamentall lawes as may bee sutable to the times and places whear God by his providence hath cast us.' These drafts or heads of laws were handed to a committee of the General Court, including Nathaniel Ward, who eventually worked them up into the famous Body of Liberties.[3] Thus John had some part in making the government of Massachusetts Bay a government of laws.

When the Harvards arrived in Charlestown, the teaching eldership of the church had been vacant for over a year, Master James having shown such unamiable temper and jealous disposition that a council of ministers had brought about his separation from the sacred office. A single preacher was seldom capable of satisfying the early New Englanders' appetite for sermons; and Master Harvard had not been long in Charlestown before he was invited to assist Master Symmes in the ministry. We have no recorded impression of Harvard's preaching except in the lame epitaph by his fellow-townsman, Edward Johnson:

> Christ ravisht hath thy heart with heavenly joyes
> To preach and pray with teares affection strong.[4]

This is faint praise indeed from Johnson. Harvard probably performed the duties of teaching elder, but he was never formally ordained to that office.[5]

---

1. In the early years of the Colony, ownership of cattle was a determining factor in the size of land grants. John also brought a supply of gunpowder, since on September 8, 1642, during a war rumor, the General Court appointed a committee 'to take account of Mr Harvards ammunition supplied to the countrey.' *Mass. Bay Recs.*, II. 27.

2. *Charlestown Land Records*, p. iv.

3. S. E. Morison, *Builders of the Bay Colony*, p. 229.

4. *W. W. P.*, p. 188.

5. John Wilson, in his elegiac poem on Harvard, describes him as *e suggesto sacro Caroloensi ad coelos evectum*. If Harvard had been ordained, this careful ecclesiastical

Although proof is wanting, it is highly probable that John Harvard and Nathaniel Eaton were friends, and that before his death Harvard had visited the college that was to bear his name. The Eatons belonged to a higher social stratum than the Harvards; but John and Nathaniel were contemporaries at the University, though at different colleges. They were within two or three years of the same age, and it is a safe assumption that they crossed the ocean in the same ship. Eaton was living at Charlestown in the spring of 1638. The College, as we have seen, opened sometime between early June and the seventh of September, probably in July or August. What is more likely than that Master Harvard, before he became bedridden, rode over to Cambridge and dined with Master Eaton? May not an actual inspection of the infant college have moved his heart, and inspired his gift? As there is little good we can impute to Eaton, let us at least give him the benefit of this inference: that he had some part in attracting John Harvard's interest and stimulating his benevolence.

Harvard's Death, and Naming of the College

The summer of 1638 was one of signs and portents, which the fathers of this new Israel supposed that the Almighty sent for their special edification and warning. On the first of June 'between three and four in the afternoon, being clear, warm weather, the wind westerly, there was a great earthquake. It came with a noise like a continued thunder or rattling of coaches in London, but was presently gone. . . . It shook the ships, which rode in the harbor, and all the islands.' [1] 'The motion of the Earth was such,' writes Johnson, 'that it caused divers men (that had never knowne an Earthquake before) being at worke

poet would have written *officio* instead of *suggesto*. The original church records make no mention of officers. Jedediah Morse, in a record book begun in 1789 and probably compiled from some manuscript now lost, states that John Harvard 'was only a supply for a time' (J. F. Hunnewell, *Records of First Church*, p. 165). This view of Harvard's position is accepted by Frothingham (*Hist. of Charlestown*, p. 74) and Budington (*Hist. of First Church*, pp. 44–45). Edward Johnson calls Harvard 'a reverend Minister' (*W. W. P.*, p. 201), but not in connection with the Charlestown Church. Shepard does not even call him a minister. Cotton Mather (*Magnalia*, book iv. 126) calls him 'a Reverend, and Excellent Minister of the Gospel.' Thomas Danforth refers to him in his college records (written not before 1654) as 'sometimes Minister of Gods Word at [*blank*]' into which a later hand, probably that of Tutor Flynt, has written 'Charlstown.' *C. S. M.*, xv. 171.

1. Winthrop, *Journal* (1908 ed.), i. 270–71.

in the Fields, to cast downe their working-tooles, and run with gastly terrified lookes, to the next company they could meet withall.'[1] In the night of August 3, there arose from the south-west 'a very great tempest or hiracano . . . which drave a ship on ground at Charlestown, and brake down the windmill there,'[2] on the hill above the Harvard house.

John Harvard died 'at *Charlestown*, of a Consumption,'[3] on September 14, 1638.[4] He·had not yet reached his thirty-first birthday. How long he lay ill before 'lifted from the pulpit by the Charles to Heaven,' we do not know. But on some day not long before his decease, 'it pleased God to stir up the heart of one Mr. *Harvard* (a godly Gentleman and a lover of Learning, there living amongst us) to give the one half of his Estate (it being in all about 1700. l.) towards the erecting of a Colledge, and all his Library.'[5] No doubt he was already too weak to make a formal will. One may imagine a conference at his bed-side, Mistress Harvard and Pastor Symmes and Elder Nowell as witnesses, a whisper from the dying man: 'My books and half my estate to the College, the rest to my beloved wife'; and the deed was done.[6]

This was rightly thought to be a very remarkable benefaction. New Englanders had already begun to leave small legacies to their churches; but John Harvard, as a Commencement orator remarked some thirty years after his death, followed Maimon-

1. *W. W. P.*, p. 185.
2. Winthrop, *op. cit.*, I. 272.
3. *Magnalia*, book iv. 126.
4. '1638. 7 [Sept.] 14. John Harvard master of Arts, of Emmanuel Colledge in Cambridge, deceased: and by will gave the half of his estate (which amounted to about 700 pounds) for the erecting of the Colledge.' Chronological Table in *An Almanack for 1649*, compiled by Samuel Danforth (A.B. 1643). The only surviving copy, in the New York Public Library, is reproduced in the Charles L. Nichols Photostats of American Almanacs; this page is reproduced in Winthrop's *Journal* (1908 ed.), II. 340. Harvard's grave was marked by a stone which disappeared in the Revolution. In 1828 a sum was collected among Harvard graduates with which a small granite obelisk was erected, not on the site of the burial ground used in Harvard's day, but on the later Burial Hill, now the Old Burying Ground off Phipps Street. That spot was selected, according to George E. Ellis, 'because it commanded then a view of the site of the College' (5 *Coll. M. H. S.*, v. 447). The inscription gives the date of Harvard's death as September 26, as the committee in charge attempted to translate September 14 from old style into new, and added two days too many. Frothingham, *Charlestown*, p. 76.
5. *New Englands First Fruits*. See Appendix D.
6. The absence of any mention of a will so important for the College, whether in the college records, the colony records, or the registries in England, makes one as nearly certain as one can be with negative evidence that John Harvard's will was nuncupative.

ides in considering the school superior to and more sacred than the synagogue.[1]

On March 13, 1638–39, the Great and General Court met at Boston. Among its members were four Overseers of the College,[2] three fellow-townsmen of John Harvard,[3] and two of his Emmanuel College mates.[4] Before the first day's session of this court was over, it was

𝕺𝖗𝖉𝖊𝖗𝖊𝖉, 𝖙𝖍𝖆𝖙 𝖙𝖍𝖊 𝖈𝖔𝖑𝖑𝖊𝖉𝖌𝖊 𝖆𝖌𝖗𝖊𝖊𝖉 𝖚𝖕𝖔𝖓 𝖋𝖔𝖗𝖒𝖊𝖗𝖑𝖞 𝖙𝖔 𝖇𝖊𝖊 𝖇𝖚𝖎𝖑𝖙 𝖆𝖙 𝕮𝖆𝖒𝖇𝖗𝖎𝖉𝖌 𝖘𝖍𝖆𝖑𝖇𝖊𝖊 𝖈𝖆𝖑𝖑𝖊𝖉 𝕳𝖆𝖗𝖇𝖆𝖗𝖉 𝕮𝖔𝖑𝖑𝖊𝖉𝖌𝖊.[5]

THE BENEFACTION

Our knowledge of the gift that made the name of Harvard immortal is almost as perplexing as that of the man himself. Josiah Quincy went into the question carefully almost a century ago, and no additional facts have come out since.[6] As no inventory or administrative records of Harvard's estate have been found, either in Massachusetts or in England, the exact amount of his bequest is unknown. What the College received must have been largely realized from debts due to Harvard,[7] and from the

1. Oration of *c.* 1670 beginning 'Non Semel tantùm' in H. U. Archives, President Leverett Discourses. Professor Harry A. Wolfson kindly supplied the reference to Maimonides' *Mishneh Torah, Tefillah,* xi. 14, a copy of which (Venice, 1615) is noted in the H. C. L. Catalogue for 1723: 'It is allowed to convert a synagogue [*lit.* house of assembly] into a school [*lit.* house of study] but it is not allowed to convert a school into a synagogue, for the sanctity of a school is greater than that of a synagogue and we may promote a thing to a higher grade of sanctity, but we must not degrade.'

2. Winthrop, Dudley, Endecott, and Stoughton.

3. Nowell, Sedgwick, and Sprague.

4. Bradstreet and Saltonstall.

5. *Mass. Bay Recs.,* i. 253.

6. Quincy, i. 460–62.

7. In the Winthrop Mss. at the M. H. S., i. 123, is a torn, undated, unsigned document, addressed 'To our honored, and well beloved friends, Mr. Bellingham, Mr. Saltonstall, Mr. Winthrop junior, Mr. Stoughton, Mr. Dummer, Mr. Hubbert, Mr. Ting, Mr. John Hubbert; and others whom this may concerne. Whereas there is a debt of eightie Pounds, and upwards, due to Mr. Harvard, from the Owners of the Ship, called the Desire; and by the Accounts thereof, made up by Mr. Peirce, Master of the said Shipp, and [*torn*] Agent for Mr. Craddocke, one of the Owners; beeing al [*torn*] by Mr. Peters, another of the Owners, and that the . . . .' After a large tear, the document continues: 'wee doe presume to expresse what we conceive of your Pietie, and Prudence, viz. that you would (out of your desire of soe Publique a goode) rather freely contribute (as much as is herein charged up [*torn*]) towards the welfare, and prosperity of the Colledge here amongst us, then in the least measure hinder the same.' The conclusion is also torn. This appears to have been in some connection with an action entered in the Middlesex Court records October 1, 1650 (Pulsifer transcript, i. 13): 'The President of Harvard College against William Peirce and Richard Web in action of debt. Mr. No-

sale of his property in England. There is no evidence in the Charlestown records that his widow, who presumably received the other half of the estate (as they left no children), handed over any of her husband's lands to the College.[1] No doubt the Queen's Head at Southwark, a valuable tavern property, head-quarters for the carriers who plied between London and the Channel ports, and the place where the vestrymen of St. Saviour's held their annual dinners, was the most important part of the college legacy.[2]

Governor Winthrop, in a memorandum of uncertain date at the beginning of the second volume of his Journal, says, 'Mr. Harvard gave to the college about £800.'[3] A more precise and authoritative statement is that of Thomas Danforth, who records that the College 'Moiety' of the Harvard estate amounted to £779 17s 2d.[4] But how much of this did the College actually receive? Nathaniel Eaton acknowledged having received of Thomas Allen, who married the widow Harvard and acted as executor of John's estate, the sum of £200.[5] The Board of Overseers on December 27, 1643, 'ordered that, 1. The Accounts of Mr Harvards Gift are to be finished, and Mr Pelham, Mr Nowell, Mr Hibbons, Mr Symms, Mr Wilson are chosen to finish it, that an acquittance may be given Mr Allin.'[6] Evidently the Harvard estate was not yet settled. Within six months, Allen must have paid £175 3s, which was deposited in the Colony Treasury; for the Treasurer of Massachusetts Bay, William Tyng, acknowledged on May 16, 1644, 'The Country debtor to the Coll. for Mr Harvards estate lent to it: 175-03-0.'[7] This sum was afterwards handed over; and these two pay-

---

well testified that old Mr. Peirce deceased acknowledged a debt of about 21 *li* and upwards. Mr. Hodges testified the sam, debt due to Mr Harvard. The Jury find for the plaintiffe the debt 21 *li* 9s 2d and the interest due for ten years determining it after 8 *li* per cent and costs 1 *li* 15s 3d.' William Pierce was a master mariner who commanded the *Lyon* of the Winthrop fleet and later settled in Boston. (C. E. Banks, *The Winthrop Fleet*, p. 106.) Obviously these two records, whether or not they refer to the same case, are efforts to recover debts which the Captain owed to John Harvard, and which were assigned to the College as part of its half of the legacy.

1. On the contrary, she sold his 120 acres at Waterfields and his ten acres of tillage before the end of 1638. *Charlestown Land Records*, pp. 52, 148.

2. H. C. Shelley, *John Harvard and His Times*, pp. 203-04.

3. 1853 ed., II. 419.

4. *C. S. M.*, xv. 171. The record was made by Danforth after 1654, when Treasurer of the College. The same sum is mentioned in the Commencement oration of about 1670 cited on p. 221, above.

5. *C. S. M.*, xv. 172.   6. *Id.*, p. 16.   7. *Id.*, p. 21.

ments, amounting to £375 3s, are all that can be shown by the records to have been actually received by the College. The records make it fairly clear that the entire sum was used for buildings. What, then, became of the balance of £404 14s 2d?

Thomas Shepard points the finger of suspicion at Nathaniel Eaton. For 'no sooner was this giuen,' he writes of the Harvard legacy, 'but mr Eaton (professing eminently yet falsely and most deceiptfully the feare of god) did lauish out a great part of it. . . .' [1] We have Governor Winthrop's statement that Eaton left the country £1000 in debt. Accounts formerly existed, well known to Danforth, but have long since disappeared. It seems likely therefore that the unaccounted balance of over £400 represents (1) moneys advanced out of the estate by Thomas Allen to Eaton, and by him squandered,[2] and (2) the debt of £80 due to the estate from the owners of the *Desire*.

Be that as it may, we are most fortunate in having a contemporary catalogue of John Harvard's library, the whole of which came to the College.[3]

Elegies and Eulogies

Whoever has had the patience to read this chapter will know all the facts yet discovered on the life of John Harvard; and so few are they that anyone with imagination may weave them into almost any human pattern he may wish. My own conception of John Harvard is that of a quiet and studious but not especially learned or extraordinarily pious young man, with an unobtrusive personality which did not greatly impress his contemporaries. At the age of twenty-nine he sacrificed a life of comparative ease and security to do his part toward building a New England where men might lead the good life. And the one deed which has given glory to his name perhaps did more in its consequences to bring future generations within reach of the true and the good, than all the efforts of the more gifted and prominent founders of New England.

There are countless eulogies on John Harvard, from which we may choose three. The first, an ambitious Latin elegy, was com-

---

1. *C. S. M.*, xxvii. 389.
2. Quincy thinks this conclusion 'incredible' (1. 461); but it is easier to believe than the amount of Eaton's debts.
3. See Chapter XIX.

posed by the principal elegiac poet in New England, the Reverend John Wilson of Boston: [1]

In pientissimum, reverendissimumque virum,

JOHANNEM HAVARDUM,

e suggesto sacro Caroloensi ad coelos evectum,
Ad alumnos Cantabrienses literatos, poëma.

Johannes Harvardus.

Anagr.

Si non (ah!) surda aure.
En, mihi fert animus, Patroni nomine vestri
(*Si non*, (*ah!*) *surda* spernitur *aure*) loqui.

Sic ait.
Me Deus, immenso per Christum motus amore,
　　Ad cœlos servum jussit abire suum.
Parebam; monituque Dei praeeunte parabam
　　Quicquid ad optatum sufficiebat opus.
Me (licet indignum) selegit gratia Christi,
　　Fundarem Musis qui pia tecta piis.
(Non quod vel chara moriens uxore carerem,
　　Aut haeres alius quod mihi nullus erat:)
Haeredes vos ipse meos sed linquere suasit
　　Usque ad dimidium sortis opumque Deus.
Me commune bonum, praesertim gloria Christi,
　　Impulit, et charae posteritatis amor,
Sat ratus esse mihi sobolis, pietatis amore
　　Educet illustres si Schola nostra viros.
Haec mihi spes (vita morienti dulcior olim)
　　Me recreat, coeli dum requiete fruor.
At si degeneres liqueat vos esse (quod absit!),
　　Otia si studiis sint potiora bonis,
Si nec doctrina nec moribus estis honestis
　　Imbuti (fastu non leviore tamen),
Grata sit aut vobis si secta vel haeresis ulla,
　　Vos simul inficiens vos Dominique gregem,

---

1. First printed, so far as is known, in C. Mather, *Magnalia* (1702), book iv. 139; but there may well have been an earlier broadside edition. There is no record of the date; but on account of the monitory references to heresy it seems probable that Wilson composed it about 1654, the date of Dunster's defection to antipaedobaptism. Also printed in Benjamin Peirce, *History of Harvard University* (1833), Appendix, pp. 53–54, and K. B. Murdock, *Handkerchiefs from Paul*, pp. 79–80. Our text was established by Professor Edward Kennard Rand.

Haec mihi patrono quam sunt contraria vestro!
   Atque magis summo displicitura Deo!
Nec tamen ista meo sic nomine dicier opto,
   Mens quasi promittat non meliora mihi!
Gaudia cœlorum vix me satiare valerent,
   Si tanta orbatus speque fideque forem.
Ille Deus vobis vestrisque laboribus almam
   Et dedit et porro suppeditabit opem.
Ejus in obsequio, sic, O! sic, pergite cuncti,
   Ut fluat hinc major gloria lausque Deo.
At si quis recto male sit de tramite gressus
   (Quod David, et Solomon, et Petrus ipse queat),
Hic sibi ne placeat monitus neque ferre recuset,
   In rectam possint qui revocare viam.
Sic grati vos este Deo! vestrique labores,
   Quos olim in Christo suscipietis, erunt.
Utque *Vetus* meruit sibi *Cantabrigia* nomen,
   Sic nomen fiet dulce feraxque *Novae*.
                Johannes Wilsonus.

(Translation by Edward Kennard Rand)

In honor of the most pious and reverend man

JOHN HARVARD

Borne aloft from the sacred pulpit of the Charles to Heaven.
A poem addressed to the cultivated alumni of Cambridge.

Anagram of John Harvard

'If not, ah me! with deaf ear.'

My spirit moves me in your Patron's name —
If deaf ear spurns me not — to speak his fame.

John Harvard speaks

'The Heavenly Father, touched by Christ's deep love,
Bade me His servant be in courts above.
I came, but first what His decree began,
I made provision for a cherished plan.
Me, all unworthy, chose the Grace Divine
To found the Sacred Muses' sacred shrine.
Not that I, dying, lacked a dear wife's care,
Or for my goods there was none other heir —
'Twas God that did to you, my heirs, decree
The half of what His mercy granted me.

For Christ I did it and for hearth and home
And for the love of ages yet to come.
As children, let our School bring forth for me
True filial pupils known for piety.
This hope, more sweet than life in my last hours,
Still gives me joy amid the heavenly bowers.
But if you (Heaven forbid!) degenerate prove
And wanton leisure more than learning love,
If you no more for gentle studies care,
Though cultivating still a superb air,
If some new sect your ancient faith would rock
Staining yourselves and all God's holy flock,
Sad were your Patron woe like that to see
And sad the Heavenly Father's heart would be.
Yet let me utter not such thoughts unkind;
A better presage fills my hopeful mind.
Little of heavenly transport would be left,
Were I of my good hope and faith bereft.
God, who hath helped you in the toils of yore,
Will give you courage for those yet in store.
Forth in His mighty name obedient go
That greater glory unto Him may flow!
But if some sinner from the path should stray
(As David, Solomon, Peter, fell away),
At sound rebuke let him from pride refrain
And, chastened, seek the upward road again.
So may God's tender mercies prosper you
And the good works that for His Christ you do.
As the Old Cambridge won a glorious name,
So may the New have fair and fruitful fame.'

President Eliot, with his peculiar felicity, thus phrased the lesson of John Harvard's life when French's ideal statue of him was unveiled in 1884:

He will teach that one disinterested deed of hope and faith may crown a brief and broken life with deathless fame. He will teach that the good which men do lives after them, fructified and multiplied beyond all power of measurement or computation. He will teach that from the seed which he planted in loneliness, weakness, and sorrow, have sprung joy, strength, and energy ever fresh, blooming year after year in this garden of learning, and flourishing more and more, as time goes on, in all fields of human activity.[1]

1. *Memorial of John Harvard* (1884), pp. 17–18.

But to all the elegies, orations, and eulogies, I imagine that John Harvard would have preferred the puritan simplicity of Thomas Shepard's epitaph: [1]

𝕿𝖍𝖊 man was a 𝕾choller and pious in his life and enlarged toward the cuntry and the good of it in life and death.

1. Autobiography, *C. S. M.*, xxvii. 389.

XVII

A SCHOOL OF TYRANNUS [1]
1638–1639

Harvard College made a very bad beginning, as one who experienced it, William Hubbard of the Class of 1642, wrote some forty years later: [2]

It was matter of great encouragement to those who had laid out their estates, and hazarded their lives, to make a settled Plantation here, to see one of the Schools of the Prophets set up; that from thence they might be supplied with persons fit to manage the affairs both of church and state, at such a time when a supply was like to fail elsewhere. But herein they were very unhappy, that the first man who was called to preside there so much failed the expectation of those that reposed so much confidence in him; viz. Mr. Nathaniel Eaton, who proved a mere Orbilius,[3] and fitter to have been an officer in the inquisition, or master of an house of correction, than an instructer of Christian youth.

Cotton Mather, taking up this cue, proceeds:

And though his *Avarice* was notorious, enough to get the Name of a *Philargyrius* [4] fixed upon him, yet his *Cruelty* was more scandalous than his *Avarice*. He was a *Rare Scholar* himself, and he made many more such; but their Education truly was *In the School of Tyrannus* . . . [5]

What little we know of Eaton's régime is mostly a development of this theme; and certainly the College under him was inchoate. There was a break of one entire academic year (1639–40) between the passing of Eaton and the coming of

1. The best sketch of Nathaniel Eaton's life is by Gordon Goodwin in the *D. N. B.*; but see criticisms of it by Mr. Albert Matthews, with addenda, in *Notes and Queries*, 11th ser., VIII (1913). 70–71. For the question of his title see p. 200, above. The few surviving records of the Eaton régime are printed in *C. S. M.*, vol. xv.

2. *General History of New England* (1848 ed.), p. 247.

3. Orbilius *plagosus*, Horace's flogging schoolmaster. Nathaniel Rogers so called Eaton in his valedictory oration at Commencement, 1652. *C. S. M.*, vol. xxxi.

4. An early commentator on Virgil, introduced here doubtless for the pun on his name.

5. *Magnalia*, book iv. 126.

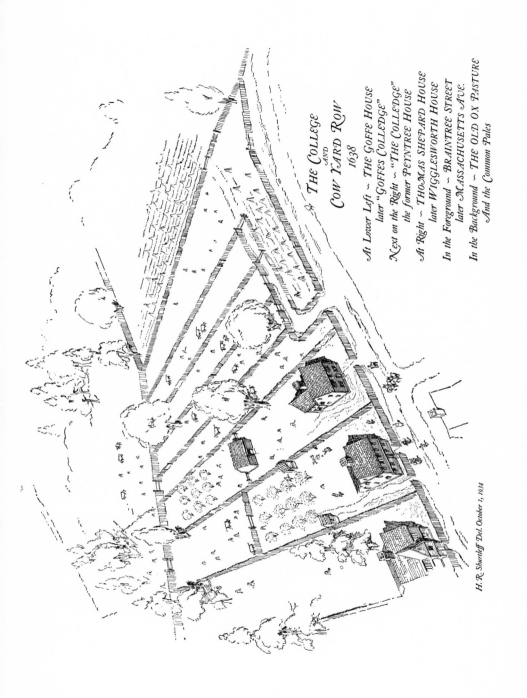

THE COLLEGE
AND
COW YARD ROW
1638

At Lower Left ~ THE GOFFE HOUSE
later "GOFFES COLLEDGE"
Next on the Right ~ "THE COLLEDGE"
the former PEYNTREE HOUSE
At Right ~ THOMAS SHEPARD HOUSE
later WIGGLESWORTH HOUSE
In the Foreground ~ BRAINTREE STREET
later MASSACHUSETTS AVE.
In the Background ~ THE OLD OX PASTURE
And the Common Pales

H. R. Shurtleff Del. October 1, 1934

Dunster, who began anew. Although some of Eaton's pupils returned to resume their studies under Dunster, it is improbable that they cared to restore any customs or traditions of the late 'School of Tyrannus.'

For one thing, however, we may credit Eaton. He named, fenced, and planted the College Yard, which is still the center of the University, and the focus of sentiment and affection for alumni of Harvard College. In 'Mr Nathaniel Eaton's Account under his own hand,' copied by Treasurer Danforth into the College Records, we find these items: [1]

Inprimis. The frame [of the new building] in the Colledge
    yard and digging the cellar, carriage and setting it up.   £120
Item. Fencing the yard with pale 6 foot and ½ high £30
It. For thirty Apple-Trees and setting them £6

Enclosing the Yard seems to have been the only policy common to the first Harvard administration, and the last. Presumably the wooden wall was to keep students in rather than cattle out; six-foot-and-a-half paling was excessive precaution against the most enterprising of bovine timber-toppers. This first Yard comprised no more than the Peyntree house-lot and cowyard (I), and only half an acre or less was planted with apple trees.[2] The lot (II) granted to Eaton personally, which extended through to the Charlestown Path, was not, as we have seen, considered college property until after 1654.

For the origin of the name 'yard' we need only remember that the bulk of the Peyntree lot had been one of the units of Cowyard Row. *Yard*, to be sure, was the common English word for an enclosure, especially in connection with buildings. There was (and is) a Senate-House Yard at Cambridge,[3] and a College Yard at St. Andrews.[4] But the Harvard Yard was doubtless suggested by Newtown cows and palings, rather than old-world quads and colleges. Beginning with this Peyntree acre and an eighth, the Yard expanded little by little until 1835, when it

1. *C. S. M.*, xv. 172.
2. Danforth, in the inventory of 1654, mentions half an acre 'planted with fruite Trees' (*C. S. M.*, xv. 208); but this, or part of it, may have been the Fellows' Orchard (III). Consult map of the Yard in Chapter XIV, and Chapter XV for a discussion of the earliest college lots.
3. Willis and Clark, *Arch. Hist. Univ. of Cambridge* (1886), III. 72.
4. 'Mr Knox wald sum tyme com in and repose him in our collage yeard, and call ws schollars vnto him and bless ws.' James Melvill, *Diary*, p. 21.

attained its maximum dimensions; for a yard cannot cross a street. Other colonial colleges, too, had their 'yards.' But in 1774, Princeton rejected the homely monosyllable for *campus*.[1] One by one every other American college has followed suit, until Harvard alone has kept her Yard. *Esto perpetua!*

In Eaton's administration, too, was begun the 'Old College,' which was completed by Dunster in 1642. But we shall hear so much about that ill-contrived building before long, that we may well be spared the painful details of its erection.

STUDENTS AND INSTRUCTION

Another phrase of William Hubbard, our first and worst historian, has given currency to the notion that Eaton's Harvard was a mere boys' boarding-school. Under Henry Dunster, says he, 'that which was before but, at the best, *Schola Illustris*, grew to the stature or perfection of a College.'[2] Master Hubbard was probably trying to convey, in his customarily obscure style, that the organization of Harvard under Eaton was simply that of master and pupils; whilst Dunster adopted a collegiate organization, in the English sense of the word. Cotton Mather admitted that Eaton was a 'Rare Scholar' who 'made many more such'; and he must have given instruction of freshman grade to at least some of the inmates, since the class which graduated in 1642 had 'beene these *foure yeeres* trained up in University Learning (for their ripening in the knowledge of the tongues and Arts).'[3] Their freshman year, consequently, was the academic year 1638-39.

Of the nine members of that class, we know positively that John Wilson was in college in 1638-39. George Downing, that 'reasonable hopefull' youth, arrived in New England with his doting mother in June, 1638, just in time to enter freshman under Eaton. In view of his parents' eagerness to send him to college, and place him under such discipline as would curb his 'stronge inclination to the plantation sports,'[4] there is every

---

1. Mr. Matthews has gone into the question of *yard* and *campus* with his customary thoroughness in *C.S. M.*, III. 431-37. *Campus* first appears at Princeton in 1774; Yale used *yard* exclusively until after 1871; and William and Mary until even later.
2. *Op. cit.* (1848 ed.), p. 247.
3. *New Englands First Fruits* (Appendix D).
4. See above, p. 171.

reason to suppose that the future Ambassador to the States General was one of the first freshmen on whom Professor Eaton tested his cane. Presumably the other members of the Class of 1642 were living under the Eaton rooftree in 1638–39, excepting Benjamin Woodbridge, who joined the class during senior sophister year.

At least two other Harvard students of the Eaton régime did not graduate. Samuel Hough, son and heir of Atherton Hough, former mayor of old Boston and Assistant of the Bay Colony, was entered by his father in July, 1639, 'a scholler to be taught by his late master Mr. Nathaniell Eaton at Cambridge in New England and to be boarded in house with him for the reward of sixteene pounds by the yeare unto the said Natha: Eaton to be payd quarterly.'[1] This is probably a sample of the financial arrangements made by the parents of all Eaton's scholars. Atherton Hough paid £10 down on July 31, and having had only four weeks' instruction for his son before Eaton was ousted by the Court, sued the Professor for a rebate. Sam Hough was about nineteen years old when he entered this 'School of Tyrannus,' and subsequently he became minister of Reading.[2] Hence it is a fair assumption that his studies were of university grade, and that if he had remained he would have graduated with the Class of 1643.

The other student whose name has been preserved was a mere schoolboy. Nathaniel Rowe, the black sheep of his family, was given a year's provision by his father and shipped to New England in charge of those who founded the Colony of New Haven, where he lost some of his provisions and sold the rest. 'Then Mr. [Theophilus] Eaton and Mr. Dauenport,' he writes,[3] 'haueing noe direct order what to doe, wished mee, and sent mee vnto Mr. [Nathaniel] Eaton, the marchants brother, to be instructed in the rudiments of the Lattine tongue (in which with practise, I shalbe prettie skilfull). I liued with him about a moneth, and uerily in that space he spake not one word to mee, *scilicet*, about my learninge, and after he went awaie, I liued an idle life, because I had noe instructour.'

---

1. Thomas Lechford, *Note-Book*, p. 361.
2. *W. W. P.* (1910 ed.), p. 226; Savage's note to Winthrop's *Journal* (1853 ed.), I. 374.
3. Rowe's letter to Governor Winthrop of *c*. March, 1641, in 5 *Coll. M. H. S.*, I. 319–21.

Probably there were several more Harvard students this first year, whose names are lost; for Winthrop says that Eaton 'had many scholars, the sons of gentlemen and others of best note in the country' ; and he employed two ushers or assistants.[1]

STARVATION AND SADISM

A dismal picture of living conditions in primitive Harvard, and of the loathsome catering by Mistress Eaton and her corps of sluttish servants, is afforded by her own confession:

For their breakfast, that it was not so well ordered, the flower not so fine as it might, nor so well boiled or stirred, at all times that it was so, it was my sin of neglect, and want of that care that ought to have been in one that the Lord had intrusted with such a work. Concerning their beef, that was allowed them, as they affirm, which, I confess, had been my duty to have seen they should have had it, and continued to have had it, because it was my husband's command; but truly I must confess, to my shame, I cannot remember that ever they had it, nor that ever it was taken from them. And that they had not so good or so much provision in my husband's absence as presence, I conceive it was, because he would call sometimes for butter or cheese, when I conceived there was no need of it; yet, forasmuch as the scholars did otherways apprehend, I desire to see the evil that was in the carriage of that as well as in the other, and to take shame to myself for it. And that they sent down for more, when they had not enough, and the maid should answer, if they had not, they should not, I must confess, that I have denied them cheese, when they have sent for it, and it have been in the house; for which I shall humbly beg pardon of them, and own the shame, and confess my sin. And for such provoking words, which my servants have given, I cannot own them, but am sorry any such should be given in my house. And for bad fish, that they had it brought to table, I am sorry there was that cause of offence given them. I acknowledge my sin in it. And for their mackerel, brought to them with their guts in them, and goat's dung in their hasty pudding, it's utterly unknown to me; but I am much ashamed it should be in the family, and not prevented by myself or servants, and I humbly acknowledge my negligence in it. And that they made their beds at any time, were my straits never so great, I am sorry they were ever put to it. For the Moor [2] his lying in Sam. Hough's sheet and pillow-bier, it hath a truth in it: he did so one time, and it gave Sam.

1. *Journal* (1908 ed.), I. 310.
2. Apparently a negro slave, the first in New England of whom we have any record.

Hough just cause of offence; and that it was not prevented by my care and watchfulness, I desire [to] take the shame and sorrow for it. And that they eat the Moor's crusts, and the swine and they had share and share alike, and the Moor to have beer, and they denied it, and if they had not enough, for my maid to answer, they should not, I am an utter stranger to these things, and know not the least footsteps for them so to charge me; and if my servants were guilty of such miscarriages, had the boarders complained of it unto myself, I should have thought it my sin, if I had not sharply reproved my servants, and endeavored reform. And for bread made of heated, sour meal, although I know of but once that it was so, since I kept house, yet John Wilson affirms it was twice; and I am truly sorry, that any of it was spent amongst them. For beer and bread, that it was denied them by me betwixt meals, truly I do not remember, that ever I did deny it unto them; and John Wilson will affirm, that, generally, the bread and beer was free for the boarders to go unto. And that money was demanded of them for washing the linen, it's true it was propounded to them, but never imposed upon them. And for their pudding being given the last day of the week without butter or suet, and that I said, it was miln of Manchester in Old England, it's true that I did say so, and am sorry, they had any cause of offence given them by having it so. And for their wanting beer, betwixt brewings, a week or half a week together, I am sorry that it was so at any time, and should tremble to have it so, were it in my hands to do again.[1]

Englishmen of the seventeenth century considered themselves starved without a full allowance of bread, beef, and beer. By Mistress Eaton's confession, the Harvard students had no beef, their bread was sometimes sour and always scant, and their beer gave out for as much as a week at a time. Yet this, and worse, went on for an entire academic year without being discovered by the Overseers, even by Thomas Shepard, who lived next door to the College. 'After more full information' of Eaton, writes Shepard, 'I saw his sin great and my ignorance and want of wisdom and watchfulnes ouer him very great for which I desire to mourne all my life.'[2] A strange overseer, forsooth!

Governor Winthrop, who fortunately for us had a taste for college scandal, tells in full detail the story of how the Eatons

---

1. Note to Savage's Winthrop (1853 ed.), I. 373–74. The document, which Savage borrowed from the State Archives, was probably destroyed in the fire in his office which consumed the second volume of Winthrop's Journal.

2. *C. S. M.*, XXVII. 389.

came to grief.[1] In the summer of 1639 [2] Eaton engaged as
'usher' or assistant master 'one Nathaniel Briscoe, a gentleman
born.' [3] Three days later they had a falling out, and Eaton discharged Briscoe, turning him outdoors after dark. The usher
talked back, and was pulled inside by the master. There was an
unseemly scuffle in the front entry, after which Briscoe went
upstairs to bed. Eaton then called for help from the Cambridge
constable, who answered that he ought to 'admonish' and 'reform' the assistant himself. Eaton proceeded to reform Briscoe
with a 'cudgel, which was a walnut tree plant, big enough to
have killed a horse, and a yard in length.' While the two
menservants held the wretched usher, Professor Eaton administered some two hundred blows about his head and shoulders
during the space of two hours (says Winthrop), when Thomas
Shepard and others, hearing the outcry, rushed in. The gullible
overseer was persuaded by Eaton that he was beating Briscoe
for pulling a knife on him (which he had done in self-defense) and
for swearing — the truth being that the poor man thought he
was about to be murdered, and cried out to God to save his
soul. Eaton then had the effrontery, and Shepard the folly, to
lay a complaint with the authorities against Briscoe, on these
counts. The magistrates wisely determined to hear Briscoe's
version; and at the General Court beginning September 4, 1639,
the whole disgusting story of the first year of Harvard College
was ventilated. Several students and others testified that they
had often been given twenty or thirty stripes at a time, until
they would confess what the master compelled them to. Eaton,
defiant, declared 'he had this rule, that he would not give over
correcting till he had subdued the party to his will. Being also
questioned about the ill and scant diet of his boarders (for,
though their friends gave large allowance, yet their diet was
ordinarily nothing but porridge and pudding, and that very
homely), he put it off to his wife.' Mistress Eaton was then
examined, and made the vivid confession of her housekeeping
and catering which we have already quoted.

1. *Journal* (1908 ed.), I. 310–15; (Savage ed., 1853) I. 370–76.
2. Eaton's case came up before the General Court of September 4. At the time of
the previous Court, on June 6, Eaton must have been still in good odor, for he was
granted 500 acres of land, 'if hee continew his imployment with vs for his life,' *Mass.
Bay Recs.* I. 262.
3. Son of Nathaniel Briscoe, a wealthy tanner and selectman of Watertown. The
'usher' afterwards emigrated to Milford, Connecticut, where he died in 1683, leaving
many descendants.

THOMAS SHEPARD'S HOUSE, NEXT TO THE COLLEGE

EATON DISMISSED AND THE COLLEGE CLOSED

By this time the news had spread about, and the court-room on September 9 was crowded with spectators. The Professor was attended by several ministers who said that he had 'freely and fully acknowledged his sin, and that with tears,' and prayed 'that he might be pardoned, and continued in his employment.' He then proceeded to make 'a very solid, wise, eloquent, and serious (seeming) confession, condemning himself in all the particulars.' The magistrates were impressed; but 'because of the scandal of religion, and offense which would be given to such as might intend to send their children hither,' decided to fine the unfaithful Professor and dismiss him from office. Their sentence stands thus in the records:

Mr Nathaniell Eaton, being accused for cruell and barbaros beating of Mr Naza: Briscoe, and for other neglecting and misvseing of his schollers, it was ordered, that Mr Eaton should bee discharged from keeping of schoale with vs without licence; and Mr Eaton is fined to the countrey 66*l* 13*s* 4*d*,[1] which fine is respited till the next Court, vnles hee remove the meane while. The Court agreed Mr Eaton should give Mr Naza: Briscoe 30*l* for satisfaction for the wrong done him, and to bee paid presently.[2]

After sentencing Eaton, the Court expected him to do the proper thing by acknowledging their 'justice and clemency' in an edifying and penitent speech. Instead, 'he turned away with a discontented look,' saying, 'If sentence be passed, then it is to no end to speak!' And that was that.

Left without master or mistress at the beginning of her second academic year, Harvard College closed her doors and dismissed those scholars who had not already escaped from the 'School of Tyrannus.'[3] Students who had parents in New England went

---

1. This sum represented 100 marks of 13*s* 4*d* each, marks being in legal use in England for stating a fine as late as 1770. Winthrop says, 'Yet the court remitted his fine to £20, and willed Briscoe to take but £20.'

2. *Mass. Bay Recs.*, I. 275.

3. On the assumption that the students remained in Cambridge, and that someone had charge of them, it has been a favorite sport of college antiquarians to discover an 'acting president' for 1639–40. Thomas Shepard is the favorite; but he says nothing in his autobiography about taking charge of any students. Elijah Corlett has been suggested, on the slender evidence that in 1659 he and another, petitioning for land, said they had been in the country twenty years and upward. John Philip, who removed from Salem to Cambridge in the summer of 1639, and in May, 1640, to Dedham, is a

home, and studied, if they did study, under the local minister
or schoolmaster. George Downing, for instance, was tutored by
John Fiske at Salem, where his parents lived; [1] and Nathaniel
Rowe, whose home was in England, was sent by Richard Bellingham's order 'vnto Mr. Willis of Linne, the schoole-maister.' [2]
It must have seemed doubtful to many whether the experiment
in higher education would be soon renewed. Did not events indicate that God frowned on the College, as an extravagance for
a poor plantation? Fortunately, John Harvard's legacy had not
been consumed, although Eaton made off with whatever funds
he could lay hands on.

FINANCIAL IRREGULARITIES

Besides what parents had paid for board and tuition, and the
£200 paid by Thomas Allen from the Harvard legacy, Eaton
handled considerable moneys. In 'New Englands First Fruits'
it is stated that after John Harvard had shown the way,
'another gave 300. *l.*'; but we are still ignorant of the name of
this generous donor, or what became of his gift. According to
Thomas Shepard there had been an unsuccessful attempt to
raise funds in England before John Harvard's death.[3] However,
we have records of several early English contributions. John
Humfrey, a successful money-raiser for the Colony, was ordered
by the General Court on June 6, 1639 'to send in the 100 *l* which
is in his hand to further the colledge.' [4] The same day the
Court appointed a committee of Salem men 'to dispose of the
house which Mr Peters bought as they can, and returne the
money for the colledge.' [5] If anything was received from these
sources before Eaton departed, he probably made off with it.

---

third. In my *Builders of the Bay Colony*, p. 192, I misinterpreted a clause in Dunster's
letter of December, 1653 (Appendix E), 'the students dispersed in the town and miserably distracted in their times of concourse,' to mean that he found them in that condition on taking office. A closer examination of the context shows that Dunster was
merely describing the students' condition before he got the 'Old College' ready for
them in 1642. There is no evidence or even likelihood that any students remained in
Cambridge, or that the Peyntree house even had a caretaker during the rest of the
academic year 1639–40.

1. *Magnalia*, book iii. 142.
2. 5 *Coll. M. H. S.*, I. 320.
3. *C. S. M.*, XXVII. 389.
4. *Mass. Bay Recs.*, I. 263.
5. *Ibid.*; cf. above, Chapter XII.

Thomas Adams and Christopher Coulson,[1] merchants of London, wrote to Theophilus Eaton on March 26, 1640:

Whereas we understood by your former letter that the monny which was appoynted heretofore for publique uses was not all yet disposed of, we therefore for our parts, desire that what is remayning, may be expended wholly about the building of the New Colledge at Cambridge, in N. England, which we understand is now erecting.[2]

This money appointed 'for publique uses' was probably a part of the 'common stock' subscribed by some of the original members of the Massachusetts Bay Company for charitable purposes in the Colony. Governor Eaton, as he acknowledged with his own hand in the College Records seven years later,[3] paid over this sum — apparently £50 — to his brother the Professor; and the Governor's later contribution of £40 'towards the building the edifices of the Colledge'[4] was probably a partial restitution. The considerable difference between the amount of John Harvard's legacy, as stated by Treasurer Danforth, and the sums shown by the records that the College received, could probably have been explained by Professor Eaton.

EATON'S SUBSEQUENT CAREER

Next on the docket for Nathaniel Eaton was to answer for his misdeeds before the Cambridge church brethren. No more than modern plunderers of the public was he inclined to 'take the rap.' Before the date set for the church trial, Eaton fled to the Piscataqua, and took passage on 'Neles barke'[5] about to sail

---

1. Thomas Adams was a woolen draper of London, one of the original grantees and adventurers, and afterwards Assistant, of the Massachusetts Bay Company. In 1647, when an alderman of London, he was sent to the Tower for treason. Christopher Coulson was a freeman and Assistant of the Company. Frances Rose-Troup, *The Massachusetts Bay Company and its Predecessors* (1930), pp. 60–62, 131, 138.

2. *C. S. M.*, xv. 16; cf. p. 171. Theophilus Eaton brought to New England £50 from this stock. Rose-Troup, *Mass. Bay Company*, p. 104.

3. *C. S. M.*, xv. 16, and facsimile of page of College Records showing design for the first seal.

4. *Id.*, p. 174. In Danforth's list of early benefactors, Theophilus Eaton's gift comes after one of £10 from Henry Poole, which was left by a will dated August 20, 1643. *N. E. H. G. R.*, xlvi. 244; *Trans. Hist. Soc. Lancs. and Cheshire*, n. s., xvi. 202–06.

5. 4 *Coll. M. H. S.*, vi. 136. The barque probably belonged to Captain James Neale of Maryland, whose daughter Henrietta Maria married Richard Bennett, Jr., of the Harvard Class of 1659.

for Virginia. Three constables sent after him by Governor Winthrop arrested him on shore. Eaton 'acknowledged his great sin in flying, etc., and promised (as he was a Christian man) he would return,' but begged leave to fetch his personal belongings from the vessel. The amiable emissaries escorted him aboard and ashore in the ship's boat. When the boat touched the beach, Eaton politely allowed two of his guardians to step ashore first, quickly ordered the boatmen to shove off, threw overboard the third constable, and scrambled aboard the ship, which promptly set sail for Virginia.[1]

'Being thus gone,' continues Winthrop, 'his creditors began to complain; and thereupon it was found, that he was run in debt about £1000,' most of which he had obtained by drawing bills on his brother's friends in London. The amount seems incredible; how could the most extravagant prodigal have spent £1000 at Charlestown and Cambridge in the years 1638–39? But we have definite record of his having induced a shipmaster and two Boston merchants to part with £500 in return for bills of exchange on well-known London merchants, who promptly protested them, one of the drawees being that same Thomas Adams whose contribution to the College was pocketed by Eaton.[2] John Cogan of Boston, who had advanced £100 on one of these bad bills, appointed an attorney to sue for it, in Virginia.[3] All that Cogan recovered was 'but one Cowe,' his dividend when commissioners appointed by the Massachusetts government liquidated the visible assets of the late Professor.[4]

Nathaniel Eaton still had two careers ahead of him, in Virginia and in old England. Captain Neale's barque landed him on the eastern shore of Virginia, where the people, if not puritans, were low-church conformists. They received him kindly, made him clerk of Hungar's parish, Northampton County, and assistant to the settled minister there. Eaton then sent for his wife and children, who had remained in Cambridge. All except

---

1. Winthrop's *Journal* (1908 ed.), I. 314.

2. 5 *Coll. M. H. S.*, I. 285, 295; Thomas Lechford, *Note-Book*, pp. 196–98, 248, 318.

3. Entry of the suit is found in the records of Northampton County, Virginia, in 1646–47. *N. E. H. G. R.*, XL. 294.

4. Thomas Lechford, *Note-Book*, pp. 248–49, 356, 410. John Endecott urged Governor Winthrop to demand Eaton's extradition from Governor Harvey of Virginia, but there is no evidence that the request was made. 4 *Coll. M. H. S.*, VI. 135–36. For the liquidating commissioners, see *Mass. Bay Recs.*, I. 277, 282, 302.

Benoni,[1] the eldest son, embarked, and were lost at sea. Nathaniel then married Anne, daughter of Thomas Graves.[2]

According to Winthrop, Eaton succumbed 'to extreme pride and sensuality' in Virginia, 'being usually drunken, as the custom is there.' As to that, the records of the county are silent; and it should be said that drunkenness was no more the 'custom of the country' in Virginia than anywhere else in the seventeenth century. In the records of Northampton County we find Eaton having a difference of opinion with his rector, John Rozier, who was ordered by a board of arbitrators to pay him 600 pounds of tobacco. The following year, the vestry paid him that sum as a salary. In January 1646–47, John Cogan finally brought suit against Eaton for the £100 that he had advanced to him in Cambridge; but Eaton had already fled the country, abandoning his second wife.

The next trace of our hero is his matriculation at the ancient University of Padua, a mecca for English medical students.[3] With a fellow-student named Richard Danby he struck up a partnership, according to a pleasant practice of the times, in obtaining degrees. Eaton supplied the brains and performed the exercises; Danby advanced the money. Before the year was out each took a Ph.D. and M.D., and Eaton's oration on that occasion was printed.[4]

Thereafter, according to Cotton Mather, Eaton 'lived privately' in England until the restoration,[5] when he conformed

---

1. Benoni was brought up by Deacon Thomas Chesholme, Steward of Harvard College, the Church finding his clothes. He became a maltster in Cambridge, married, and left numerous descendants. Paige, pp. 258, 539.

2. E. D. Neill, in *N. E. H. G. R.*, XL. 294–95. This brief note, based on the Northampton County Records, contains all that has yet appeared on Eaton in Virginia.

3. Andrich and Brugi, *de Natione Anglica et Scota Univ. Patavinae* (Patavii, 1892), p. 147. The date is September 11, 1647.

4. *Oratio habita a Nathaneele Eatono Anglo, pro laurea doctorali, sibi et per excellenti D. D. Richardo Danbæo Anglo. In Academia Patavina publice concessa. 7 Cal. Decembris anno 1647.* 3 pp., 4°. British Museum.

5. *Magnalia*, book iv. 127. In the meantime he published a book called Μηνο-Ετεολογια; *or a Treatise of Moneths and Years. Comprehending a Survey of the Solar and Lunar Moneths and Years. A description of the Moneths and Years heretofore in use among the Hebrews, Babylonians, Persians, Egyptians, Grecians, Arabians, and ancient Latines. An accommodation of all the said Moneths and Years to the present Julian and Gregorian. . . . To which is also adjoyned, An Abridgement of the History of the World, from the Creation unto Christ, and a continuation of the Brittish History from Christ to the present. . . . With many other Chronological and Mathematical Observations, no less useful than delightful. Composed by Nathanael Eaton, Doctor of Philosophy and Medicine.* 104 pp., London, 1657. Trinity College Library, Cambridge.

to the Church and was promptly rewarded with the vicarage of Bishops Castle, Shropshire.[1] In 1661 appeared his last work, *De Fastis Anglicis*,[2] a series of epigrammatic poems on church festivals, some of which were thought worthy to be included in a nineteenth-century anthology.[3]

Prosperous once more and apparently secure, Eaton married a third time, but resumed his old spendthrift habits. Arrested for debt in 1665 at the suit of Francis Buller, M.P., he attempted to free himself by perjury and bribing Buller's servant.[4] Notwithstanding this slip, within four years Eaton was presented by the Earl of Bath to one of the best livings in Devonshire, the rectory of Bideford,[5] where he became 'a bitter Persecutor' of dissenters.[6] But Eaton's extravagance still outran his income. Again arrested for debt in 1674, he was lodged in the King's Bench prison in Southwark; and there, within a stone's throw of the old home of John Harvard, the first head of Harvard College died in jail.[7]

1. Anthony Wood, *Athenae Oxonienses* (Bliss ed., 1817), III. 674.

2. *De Fastis Anglicis, sive Calendarium Sacrum. The Holy Calendar. Being a treble series of epigrams upon all the Feasts observed by the Church of England. . . . Composed by Nathanael Eaton Doctor of Philosophy and Medicine, and Vicar of Bishops-Castle in the County of Salop.* 80 pp., London, 1661. British Museum.

3. R. Cattermole, *Sacred Poetry of the Seventeenth Century* (1836), II. 353–57.

4. *D. N. B.*; but this is not clear in the document to which the writer of that article refers: Public Record Office, State Papers Domestic, Charles II, CXXXVIII. 70.

5. Public Record Office, E. 331, bundle 12, September 10, 1669. Cf. John Watkins, *History of Bideford* (1792 ed. reprinted in 1883), pp. 116–17.

6. *Magnalia*, book iv. 127.

7. *Id.*; Records of the Prerogative Court of Canterbury, Act Book, 1674 (issuance of commission of administration to Mary Eaton, widow, relict of Nathaniel Eaton late of Bideford, clerk). His successor in the Bideford rectory had been admitted October 29, 1674. P. R. O., E. 331, bundle 13.

ORATIO

HABITA

A

NATHANEELE
EATONO
ANGLO

Pro Laurea Doctorali, Sibi & Per Excellenti

D.D. RICHARDO
DANBÆO
ANGLO

In Academia Patavina publice concessa.

7. Cal. Decembris Anno 1647.

EATON'S PADUA ORATION

XVIII

DUNSTER TAKES HOLD [1]
1640–1642

For almost a year after the dismissal of Eaton, Harvard College was in a state of suspended animation. Building operations went on slowly, but the College had neither master nor scholars. If the Overseers endeavored at once to remedy this depressing state of affairs, no record of their activity has survived. What ministers or schoolmasters, if any, were 'approached' we do not know. Only this is certain, that on August 27, 1640, when there wanted but two weeks for the vacancy to have lasted a full year, a meeting of ten magistrates and sixteen ministers of the Bay Colony invited Henry Dunster 'to accept the place of President of the Colledge,' which he accordingly did. [2]

Of all events in the early history of Harvard College, this was the most vital. It was equivalent to a fresh foundation. Henry Dunster infused such life and energy into the inchoate and all but extinct College as to realize the high expectations of her founders, and to provide a sound core around which to build a great university.

1. There have been two attempts to write Dunster's biography since the unsatisfactory notice in Mather's *Magnalia*. Of these Jeremiah Chaplin, *Life of Henry Dunster* (1872), is the best; Samuel Dunster, *Henry Dunster and his Descendants* (1876), is mainly genealogical. The Dunster manuscripts in the Harvard University Archives were collected from several sources; they include an important autobiographical memorandum (printed below in Appendix E), the originals of the letters to Dunster that are printed in 4 *Coll. M. H. S.*, II. 190–98, and several papers in the Glover-Dunster cases, copies of originals in the Middlesex County Court files, East Cambridge. Some of these documents are printed by Chaplin, and very inaccurately in G. E. Littlefield, *The Early Massachusetts Press* (Club of Odd Volumes, 1907). Dunster's manuscript notebook, which contains his copies of several of his letters, is in the M. H. S., together with an enlarged photostat of Thomas Shepard's Book of Confessions of persons entering Cambridge Church (original in N. E. H. G. S.). Joseph G. Bartlett and Mr. G. Andrews Moriarty have straightened out Dunster's ancestry and provided new data on his life at Bury in *N. E. H. G. R.*, LXI. 186–89 and LXXX. 86–95.

2. Thomas Danforth's entry in College Book III (*C. S. M.*, XV. 173); but Dunster says that he was only called 'to undertake the instructing of the youth' (Appendix E). The '10 magistrates and 16 Elders' there mentioned by Dunster doubtless consisted of the Board of Overseers (composed of six of each), reinforced by others in order to give greater weight to the call.

We left Henry Dunster taking his Master's degree at Cambridge in July, 1634, with the low rank of 115 in an *ordo senioritatis* of 188. Then, if not earlier, he became schoolmaster in his native place, Bury,[1] a brisk little market town in the Lancashire woollen district. On the Baleholt farm near by his father was doing well,[2] and it was there that the young graduate probably lived. No record has been found of Dunster's ordination, but it must have taken place before or very shortly after his proceeding M.A., since in a document dated between 1634 and 1636 he is mentioned as the curate of St. Mary's, Bury; and in a will dated October 22, 1634, a legacy of 20*s* is left to 'Mr. Dunster that studious and painfull minister.'[3] Master Dunster may have been painful, but by his own account he was not yet puritan. 'As corruptions in the church came I began to suspect them, then to hate them. But here was my falsenes that I was loath to read such bookes as might make me see such truths, but the Lord helped me. . . .'[4] Many were his soul-strivings, and as he looked back upon them his last ten years in England seemed full of trouble, from which he sought the peace of God among 'his people' in New England.

In the summer of 1640, still unmarried, Henry Dunster emigrated with his younger brother Richard, and arrived in Boston on or about August 6. Three weeks later he was called to the presidency.

It would be interesting to know why Dunster was chosen — what evidence he had given of those remarkable qualities he was to show as a teacher and administrator, or what there was in his personality that appealed to the Overseers. Eaton had many more points to impress a college board, and Dunster possessed but one visible asset, a master's degree, which Eaton had not. He belonged to an obscure family of a county which sent few emigrants to New England; and he was proud of his native Lancashire. 'Ego enim Lancastrensis sum,' he writes defending to a learned correspondent [5] the North-Country accent, which

---

1. 'When I came from Vniversity to teache schoole, the Lord wounded my soule with temptations for 5 yeares together.' Thomas Shepard's Book of Confessions, p. 107 (Chaplin, p. 263).

2. Henry Dunster the elder died in 1646, leaving an estate valued at £165, of which the most valuable part consisted of horses and cattle. *N. E. H. G. R.*, LXXX. 89.

3. *N.E.H.G.R.*, LXI. 186–89; LXXX. 95. Dunster's failure to mention this cure in his confession suggests that the curate may have been a cousin of the same name.

4. Book of Confessions, p. 109 (Chaplin, p. 265).

5. Chaplin, p. 272.

sounds uncouth to southern and East Anglian ears. He had published nothing, and shone with no reflected glory from a master like Ames. Pugnacious Peter Hobart, who had been at Magdalene with Dunster, was already in Massachusetts; but Peter was never in good odor with the authorities. If anyone on the electoral board knew Dunster, it was Richard Mather, minister of Dorchester. His old home was not far from Dunster's, and in 1624 he had married Katherine Holt of Bury, whose brothers sat in the court-baron of Tottington, whence Dunster's father held his lands.[1] It seems likely that Mather knew the Dunster family and could vouch for Henry's antecedents. Perhaps he was the 'one in this cuntry' who 'spoke peacably'[2] to Dunster when beset by temptations; but Mather had left England in 1635.

Yet, after all, the magistrates and elders by the summer of 1640 may have felt so desperate a need of someone to revive the College as to draft any well-appearing university man who seemed likely to accept. It may well be that their experience with Eaton had made them a bit shy of highly-praised scholars; and like Thomas Fuller they believed that 'sometimes ordinary scholars make extraordinary good masters. Every one who can play well on Apollo's harp, cannot skilfully drive his chariot; there being a peculiar mystery of government. Yet, as a little alloy makes gold to work the better, so, perchance, some dulness in a man makes him fitter to manage secular affairs; and those who have climbed up Parnassus but half-way, better behold worldly business . . . than such as have climbed up to the top of the mount.'[3]

THE COMENIUS STORY

There is some reason to believe that, as President, Dunster was not expected to be the master of Harvard College. His title was uncommon for the head of an English college; the office of President in his own college of Magdalene (and also in St. John's) was inferior to that of Master, corresponding more or

---

1. 'Robert and William Holte, Esquires' appear as members of the hallmote which gave notice of the surrender of a certain 'messuage' from two copyholders to Henry Dunster, senior. *N. E. H. G. R.*, LXXX. 91.

2. Book of Confessions, p. 107 (Chaplin, p. 263).

3. *The Holy State and The Profane State* (1841 ed.), p. 93.

less to the Dean of the Faculty in an American college.[1] Dunster reminded the magistrates in 1653 that they had called him 'to undertake the instructing of the youth of riper years and literature after they came from grammer schools. . . . No further care or distraction was imposed on mee or expected from mee but to instruct.'[2] It seems that Dunster had expected to play the part of senior fellow, or President in the Cambridge sense, under a master who would be President in the later American sense.

This puts a new complexion on the story that Comenius (Komenský), the great Moravian educational reformer, author of the *Janua Linguarum* and other famous works, was invited to become head of Harvard College. Cotton Mather, who first told the story in print, states that on Dunster's resignation, in 1654, John Winthrop, Jr., 'in his Travels through the *Low Countries*' invited 'that brave old man *Johannes Amos Commenius*' to 'come over into *New-England*, and Illuminate this *Colledge* and *Country*, in the Quality of a *President*.'[3] Mather's version cannot be literally true, since the younger Winthrop was not in Europe in 1654, and the Overseers did not wait long after Dunster's resignation before they appointed Chauncy President. But Winthrop was in England for over a year from September, 1641; and Comenius arrived in England about the same time, for the purpose of founding a 'Universal Pansophic College.' An appropriation by the Long Parliament for that purpose seemed likely to go through when in November, 1641, news of war and massacre in Ireland shelved the grand design forever. Comenius was left in an embarrassing situation, having already resigned from his Polish post; and we know that during the next six months he was considering invitations from France and Sweden.[4] May he not also have received one from New

1. Mullinger, II. 68; *Docs. Univ. Camb.* (1852), III. 253, 348. Master was the usual title of the heads of Cambridge colleges; only the head of Queens' was called President. At Oxford the heads of Corpus Christi, Magdalen, Trinity, and St. John's were Presidents. I have not found the title in Ireland or Scotland.

2. Appendix E.

3. *Magnalia*, book iv. 128. The story is repeated, less circumstantially, in Mather's *Ratio Disciplinae Fratrum Nov-Anglorum* (1726), introd., pp. 5–6. Mr. Albert Matthews has gone thoroughly into this incident in *C. S. M.*, xxi. 146–90; and some important additional data are in Robert Fitzgibbon Young, *Comenius in England* (Oxford Univ. Press, 1932), and *Comenius and the Indians of New England* (School of Slavonic Studies, Univ. of London, 1929).

4. W. M. Keatinge, *The Great Didactic of John Amos Comenius* (1891), pp. 47–48.

IOHAN·AMOS COMENIVS, MORAVVS·A° ÆTAT 50° 1642

Exfump: M: S:

G. Glouer. fc:

Loe, here an Exile! who to serue his God,
Hath sharely tasted of proud Pashurs Rod;
Whose learning,Piety,& true worth, being knowne
To all the world, makes all the world his owne
                                        F. Q:

JOHANNES AMOS COMENIUS

England? Samuel Hartlib, his principal English patron, was a friend of the younger Winthrop. Comenius himself, greatly interested in converting the Indians, stated that he was asked to come to England in part for that purpose.[1] He belonged to the *Unitas Fratrum* or Moravian Brethren, a puritan sect; he was well known to the university alumni in New England by reputation, and as author of text-books which were used both at the College and in the Latin schools.[2]

It seems, then, very probable that the truth behind Cotton Mather's story was this. John Winthrop, Jr., was asked by the first Board of Overseers, when he went abroad in 1641, to invite some outstanding figure in education to be Master of Harvard College — someone whose name alone would advertise the College, and attract more students from England.[3] Winthrop sounded Comenius after the 'Pansophic College' had fallen flat; but Comenius wisely declined. The same martial events that made Comenius available, prevented any distinguished English puritan from accepting the proffered post; and if Winthrop continued his search for a master at the universities of the Netherlands, which he visited in the summer of 1642, nothing came of it.

We need not regret the failure of John Winthrop's mission. The great Moravian, or a progressive Leyden professor, would have been a complete misfit at Cambridge in New England, doomed to disappointment and frustration. In these early and critical years, Harvard College wanted at her head no productive scholar or educational reformer, but an energetic and resourceful young man, who might 'better behold worldly business' from a point on Parnassus below the clouds. Finding such a one in Henry Dunster, the College was fortunate; and if there had been any plan to put someone over him, it was soon forgotten as his talents became manifest. Whatever his original attributions, Dunster was indisputably both President and head of the College at the first Commencement in 1642,[4] and as such

1. 'Ego autem consilio piorum quorundam Theologorum et Episcoporum (de propagando ad gentes orbis evangelio occasione tum in Anglia Nova feliciter factae sementis, pie sollicitorum) vocatus anno 1641 comparui.' Comenius' dedicatory letter to his *Via Lucis* (1668), quoted in R. F. Young, *Comenius and the Indians of New England*, p. 6 n.
2. See index to *H. C. S. C.*, and to *C. S. M.*, vols. XXI and XXVIII.
3. Similarly, in 1679 the Governing Boards requested William Stoughton, then in England, 'to Provide a President for this Colledge.' *C. S. M.*, XV. 66, 238.
4. Dedication to Theses of 1642, in *New Englands First Fruits* (Appendix D).

he was officially recognized by the General Court a few days later.[1] His title of President was confirmed in the Charter of 1650; and from that day to this, the head of almost every college and university in the United States has been called the President.

THE COLLEGE REOPENED

Dunster found Harvard College deserted by students, devoid of buildings, wanting income or endowment, and unprovided with government or statutes. He left it a flourishing university college of the arts, provided with several buildings and a settled though insufficient income, governed under the Charter of 1650 by a body of fellows and officers whose duties were regulated by statute. The Harvard College created under his presidency and largely through his efforts endured in all essential features until the nineteenth century, and in some respects has persisted in the great university of today. It will be necessary, therefore, to make a careful study of the laws and customs, curriculum, buildings, and finances as they developed under his fostering care. Postponing this detailed examination to subsequent chapters and the next volume, let us here review the beginning of Dunster's administration, and the purposes that he was expected to carry out.

Michaelmas, the traditional English season for opening the academic year, was approaching when Dunster was elected President on August 27, 1640. No doubt he promptly established his residence in the Peyntree house, scene of Eaton's sadistic exploits, and took measures to attract Harvard's stray sheep within the fold.[2] The Class of 1642, or part of it, was lured back to the scene of its freshman floggings; a new freshman class was admitted, and a three-year course in the Arts established, so that there should be no break in the succession of graduating classes. The hours were so arranged that the President could personally instruct each of the three classes in

1. *Mass. Bay Recs.*, II. 30.
2. In several histories of Boston, the statement will be found that Dunster owned a house there and resided there. The house and lot in question, on the site of the Ames building, belonged to Mrs. Glover, who married Dunster in 1641 and died in 1643. Dunster, as one of the executors of her first husband's estate, joined in a deed of the property to Theodore Atkinson in 1645. Suffolk Deeds, Lib. I. 254; copy in Dunster Mss. I am indebted to Mr. Samuel C. Clough for this information.

the Arts and Philosophies and Oriental Languages, and moderate their disputations.[1] And work was pushed on the new college building as fast as money could be procured.[2]

PURPOSES AND STANDARDS

At this point we may well pause to inquire what were the purposes and objects of this Harvard College, now revived with fair prospects of success. No direct contemporary answer has survived; but we may fairly infer from documentary evidence what the founders intended and what the early governors hoped to accomplish.

The most important of these records, which amounts almost to an official statement of the founding fathers, is the famous opening paragraph of 'New Englands First Fruits' (1643): 'One of the next things we longed for, and looked after was to advance *Learning* and perpetuate it to Posterity; dreading to leave an illiterate Ministery to the Churches, when our present Ministers shall lie in the Dust.'[3] In other words, the advancement and perpetuation of learning were the broad and ultimate objects of the foundation; the education of ministers was the immediate purpose; the fear of an illiterate clergy was the dynamic motive.[4] Theological learning was to be included, but not to the exclusion of other branches of learning. This distinction between ultimate and immediate objects, between the 'tree of knowledge' and its most noble branch, was clear to everyone in the puritan century; nobody then thought of calling Harvard a 'theological seminary' or 'divinity school.' Harvard was, in fact, rather less ecclesiastical than Oxford or Cambridge; and a smaller proportion of her graduates than of theirs became clergymen.[5] The course was more deeply impregnated with

1. See *H. C. S. C.*, Chapter VIII.
2. See Chapter XX.
3. Appendix D. See Chapter XXI for the authorship of this pamphlet.
4. Cf. end of Chapter XI, above.
5. Fifty-two per cent of the seventeenth-century Harvard graduates, according to Mr. Matthews' calculation, became ministers; but if the total number of students, not merely of graduates, be taken, the proportion is little over forty per cent. Note what Dr. John Venn says in the introduction to his *Alumni Cantabrigienses*, I. xiv: 'Until recent years, the clerical career accounts for much the larger proportion of our students, especially of those who graduated. Indeed it would hardly be too much to say that, during the seventeenth century, the odds are almost ten to one that a man who proceeded to the M.A. degree either had taken, or eventually did take, holy orders.' This estimate

religion than that of any liberal college today, because the puritan way of life brought religion into every sphere; but it was a course in the Liberal Arts and Philosophy, not in Divinity.[1] No pledge expressed or implied that he would enter the ministry was required of any student entering Harvard; and it is obvious that many of the students never had the slightest intention of becoming ministers.

Other documents of the first generation point to the same conclusion: that Harvard was founded for the advancement and perpetuation of learning, in the broadest sense of that word. Thomas Shepard, who must often have discussed objects and purposes with his fellow-members of the first Board of Overseers, declared that the College was intended 'to be a nursery of knowledge in these deserts and supply for posterity.'[2] Israel Stoughton, a member of the same board, left the College a tract of land 'towards the advance of Learning.'[3] The New England Confederation, in 1644, recommended the several courts of the New England colonies to support scholarships 'for advance of learning.'[4] In the Charter of 1650, the training of ministers is not even mentioned. According to that basic document, the purposes of Harvard College are:

'The aduancement of all good literature, artes and Sciences.'

'The aduancement and education of youth in all manner of good literature Artes and Sciences.'

'All other necessary provisions that may conduce to the education of the English and Indian youth of this Country in knowledge: and godliness.'

'Good literature' as used here is a literal translation of the Ciceronian *bonae litterae*, which the humanists interpreted as 'polite letters,' the proper education of a gentleman.[5] 'Artes and

has been tested by looking up the subsequent careers of men who graduated in the same *grex* (Dunster, Chauncy, and others of that period), and has been found to be substantially correct.

1. See *H. C. S. C.*, Chapter VII, for analysis of the curriculum.

2. *C. S. M.*, xxvii. 389. Cf. *Mass. Bay Recs.*, iii. 279: 'A Declaration concerninge the advauncment of learninge in New England by the Generall Court. If it should be graunted that learninge, namely, skill in the tongues and liberall artes, is not absolutely necessary for the being of a common wealth and churches, yet we conceiue that the judgment of the godly wise, it is beyond all question, not only laudable, but necessary for the beinge of the same. . . .'

3. *C. S. M.*, xv. 22. The date is 1644.

4. *Plymouth Colony Records*, ii. 20. Cf. Chapter XXI.

5. Used in that sense in W. Dillingham, *Vita L. Chadertoni* (1700), p. 7. See Chapter IV, above.

Sciences' meant simply the usual subjects of university study, and had no reference to what we call science.[1] Both these phrases recur in sundry benefactions to Harvard College in the seventeenth century.[2]

More specific objects are indicated in the title and the contents of a document called 'Modell For the Maintaining of students and fellows of choise Abilities at the Colledge in Cambridge, Tending to advance Learning among us, and to supply the publike with fit Instruments, principally for the work of the Ministry,'[3] which was composed by Jonathan Mitchell (A.B. 1647), Senior Fellow of the College, and presented to the General Court in 1663. Herein emphasis is placed on the need of learned ministers. But Mitchell also insists on the necessity of providing masters for grammar schools, and educated gentlemen for the magistracy. 'It sufficeth not to Have supplyes for the ministry, for time will shew that unlesse we Have the Helps of Learning and education to accomplish persons for the magistracy and other civill offices, things will languish and goe to decay among us.' In his scheme of endowed fellowships, one is to be the 'Linguist,' a second the 'Historian and Antiquary,' a third the 'polemicall Divine,' and 'Another the Civilian well-studyed in the Law and especially in the Laws of the English nation'; while still others 'may be set apart for Choise and Able Schoolmasters in the severall townes, and for Teachers of the Mathematicks. some for physitians who may become able eminent and approved in that faculty.' Even earlier, President Dunster showed that he had the same high ambition for the College. In a petition of 1647 to the New England Confederation he asks for means to purchase suitable books, 'especially in law, phisicke, Philosophy and Mathematickes,' for the use of the scholars, 'whose various inclinations to all professions might thereby be incouraged and furthered.'[4]

---

1. See *N. E. D.*, 'science' 3. The first instance there given for the use of *science* in its modern sense is dated 1725.

2. For example, the will of Richard Russell of Charlestown (d. 1676; Sibley, ii. 284): 'To Harvard College in Cambridge I do give and bequeath one hundred pounds' to support 'Two poor Students, that may need the Same for their furtherance in good literature'; the Piscataqua Donation of 1669: £60 per annum 'for . . . the advancement of good litterature.' And see other examples in Chapter XXI and *H. C. S. C.*, Chapter XVIII.

3. *C. S. M.*, xxxi. 308–22.

4. *Plymouth Colony Records*, ix. 95.

From these several statements we may infer that the founders and early governors of Harvard College intended to provide a sound course in Philosophy and the Liberal Arts, which would be suitable either for a general education or as a basis for professional training in divinity, law, and medicine. Such specialized studies they hoped to offer as soon as circumstances permitted. And under the broad provisions of the charter, 'for the aduancement of all good literature artes and Sciences . . . and all other necessary prouisions that may conduce to the education of the English and Indian Youth of this Country in knowledge: and godlines,' it may be said that the entire development of Harvard University for three centuries and more was portended.

That there were broadly social purposes in the foundation, too, is probable; at least such purposes were assumed before the College was half a century old. An unknown Commencement orator, speaking at the time when the College was declining, and, probably, when news had reached Cambridge of Bacon's Rebellion in Virginia, turned to the assembled magistrates and said in Latin:[1] 'The ruling class would have been subjected to mechanics, cobblers, and tailors; the gentry would have been overwhelmed by lewd fellows of the baser sort, the sewage of Rome, the dregs of an illiterate plebs which judgeth much from emotion, little from truth; we should have seen . . . no flashing sparklets of honor; the Laws would not have been made by *senatus consulta*, nor would we have rights, honors, or magisterial ordinances worthy of preservation, but plebiscites, appeals to base passions, and revolutionary rumblings, if these our fathers had not founded the University.'

Yet we should miss the spirit of early Harvard if we supposed the founders' purpose to be secular. *In Christi Gloriam*, inscribed on the College Seal of 1650, expressed the fundamental object of their foundation. The English mind had barely conceived a lay system of higher education, and any such plan would have been abhorred by puritans. Like the medieval schoolmen, they believed that all knowledge without Christ was vain. *Veritas* to them, as to Dante, meant the divine truth, although, more humble than he, they never hoped to attain

---

1. Ms. Oratio Comitialis, *c.* 1670–80, in H. U. Archives, 'Pres. Leverett Discourses.'

QÆSTIONES IN PHILOSOPHIA

DISCUTIENDÆ SUB *HENR: DUNSTERO*
PRÆSIDE, COL: HARVARD: *CANTAB:*
N: ANGL: IN COMITIIS PER
INCEPTORES IN ARTIB:
NONO DIE SEXTILIS
M. DC. LIII.

I   A*N Materia & forma separatim existere possint?*
     Negat Respondens Joshua Hubberdus.

II   A*N anima patitur a corpore?*
     Negat Respondens Jeremiah Hubberdus.

III A*N Astrologia judicialis est licita?*
     Negat Respondens Samuel Philipsius.

IIII A*N Elementa sunt solæ causæ essentiales mistorum?*
     Negat Respondens Leonardus Hoaretius.

V   A*N Aliquid creatum annihilatur?*
     Negat Respondens Jonathan Inceus.

MASTER'S QUAESTIONES, 1653

it.[1] The first college laws declared that every student was to be plainly instructed that the 'maine end of his life and studies' was '*to know God and Iesus Christ* . . . and therefore to lay *Christ* in the bottome, as the only foundation of all sound knowledge and Learning.' Dunster, no less than Augustine and Aquinas, accounted pride of knowledge a deadly sin; as such he confessed his 'inordinate loue of humane learninge' when a youth. 'Take heed of this,' he warned his Harvard pupils, 'least Desiring to be as gods, we become as Deuills.' [2]

This ideal of learning through Christ, this purpose of attaining a more perfect knowledge of God by the discipline of the mind, dominated Harvard College at least until the American Revolution. Only a burning desire to serve God, and to provide posterity with means to a greater knowledge of God, could have inspired the devotion and sacrifice that went into this 'poor Colledg in a wildernes.' And John Harvard, in the words imputed to him by Wilson,[3] declared that ambition to serve the commonwealth, and loving-kindness toward future generations of youth, were inferior motives, in his mind, to enhancing the glory of his risen Lord.

A Collegiate Way of Living

As to the means and methods by which this high purpose was to be carried out, the founders were quite clear. Nothing mean, poor, or second-rate would satisfy them, or please God. No prudent considerations of economy must limit their ambition; they would aim high from the start. Emmanuel Downing, writing from England, thought that it would be enough at first to hire some minister to read a weekly lecture on 'logick, greke or hebrew,' and let the students shift for themselves — 'you need not stay till you haue Colledges to lodge schollars.' [4] There was ample precedent for this in the great universities of the

1.
> I see our mind unsated still with grace
> of *any* truth, till of *that truth* aware
> beyond which there exists *no* truth in space.
> We rest in it, like lion in his lair
> when we attain it, and we *can* attain;
> if not, all striving for it, frustrate were.
> — *Paradiso*, iv. 124–29.

2. Shepard's Book of Confessions (Chaplin, *Dunster*, p. 263).
3. 'Praesertim gloria Christi,' above, p. 224.
4. See above, pp. 171–72.

Netherlands. Neighboring ministers like Cotton, Wilson, Mather, Eliot, Symmes, and Knowles,[1] all university graduates and many with teaching experience, could easily have spared the time to lecture once or twice a week on the Arts and Sciences. But, as Cotton Mather observed, 'the Government of *New-England* was for having their Students brought up in a more *Collegiate* Way of Living.'[2] To the English mind, university learning apart from college life was not worth having; and the humblest resident tutor was accounted a more suitable teacher than the most eminent community lecturer. Book learning alone might be got by lectures and reading; but it was only by studying and disputing, eating and drinking, playing and praying as members of the same collegiate community, in close and constant association with each other and with their tutors, that the priceless gift of character could be imparted to young men. Hence President Dunster trained his own tutors, and devoted some of his best efforts to completing the college building which had been begun as soon as the College was established.

Dunster found this building, the future 'Old College,' which had been framed in Eaton's administration, in charge of a committee of the Overseers composed of Hugh Peter, Samuel Shepard, and Joseph Cooke, 'who prudently declined the troble and left it to the two first.'[3] By October, 1641, when both Peter and Shepard left for England, 'leaving the work in the Carpenters and masons hands without Guide or further director,' this building was framed, boarded, and roofed; but only the hall floor was laid, no partitions had been raised, nor furniture provided.[4] In the meantime the students, having overflowed the old Peyntree house, were 'dispersed in the town and miserably distracted in their times of concourse.' And also, in the meantime, New England had entered the most severe economic depression in her history, one which threatened to quench the very life of the Bay Colony.

1. See Appendix B. Knowles was later suggested as President of the College.
2. *Magnalia*, book iv. 126; and cf. *C. S. M.*, xi. 339–40.
3. Appendix E, below. Danforth, however, says that Shepard alone had charge (*C. S. M.*, xv. 173). Mr. Matthews believes that Danforth was right, and that Hugh Peter had nothing to do with the building. But it would be difficult to name any other New England pie in which Hugh Peter had no finger. Shepard's account is in *C. S. M.*, xv. 17; but it does not reveal whether any progress had been made in the building between Eaton's dismissal and Dunster's appointment.
4. Appendix E.

The Depression of 1641

Harvard College had been launched on a rising tide of prosperity. Owing largely to the great puritan migration, the white population of New England had risen in ten years from less than a thousand souls to something between seventeen and twenty-five thousand.[1] As very many of the immigrants were families of some means, who brought money and goods with them, those already in the country had merely to raise foodstuffs and cattle, which by 1640 had reached prices unheard of in England save in time of famine. Wages of common laborers and artisans rose in spite of the authorities' efforts to peg them. These high prices attracted 'great store of provisions' from England and Ireland in 1640, a year when there came 'but few passengers, (and those brought very little money,) . . . so as now all our money was draind from us, and cattle and all commodities grew very cheap,' wrote Winthrop.[2] During the summer when Dunster became President, the General Court found great difficulty in collecting taxes, and was forced to make grain and wampum legal tender at rates in excess of their falling market value.[3]

The reason why 'but few passengers' came was the beginning of civil turmoil in Britain, which gave the puritans hope of a new England at home. In the summer of 1640 an army of psalm-singing Scottish covenanters came over the border, routed the royal troops at Tyne water, and seized Newcastle. 'Then was England in a fright,' wrote President Dunster's father to his son; the trained bands were called out, the little town of Bury was swamped with raw militia, armed with clubs and eating up the country-side. The Scots were bought off, and the Long Parliament met in November. Representative government, suspended for eleven years, was promptly restored; Laud and Strafford and other high churchmen were committed to the Tower. In March, 1641, the elder Dunster wrote a letter so crammed with exciting news that he quite forgot to congratulate his son on attaining the Harvard presidency. High-flying bishops in jail and my Lord Keeper fled; nonconformists suffered to preach, surplices and prayerbooks torn up; altars pulled down, communion tables brought into the body of the

1. See Appendix B.
2. *Journal* (1908 ed.), II. 6; T. Hutchinson, *History of Mass. Bay,* 2d ed., I. 93, 96.
3. *Mass. Bay Recs.*, I. 294, 302–03.

church; Burton and Prynne make triumphal progress into London; my Lord Saye and my Lord Brooke on the Privy Council; monopolies overthrown 'so that euery man may buye and sell att theire pleasure'; a Thursday lecture set up at Bury; and we 'goe on very Joyffully god bee praysed for the same.' [1]

Things were not so joyful in New England. 'This caused all men to stay in England in expectation of a new world,' wrote Winthrop, 'So as few coming to us, all foreign commodities grew scarce, and our own of no price.' The bottom fell out of the stock market: a cow worth £20 in the spring of 1640 fetched but £8 in December, and £4 in June; [2] so that the bewildered General Court voted that cattle received for taxes be appraised not at their sale value, but by the 'benefit' they might bring — whatever that might mean.[3] It took a Harvard wit, Sam Danforth of the Class of 1643, to find consolation

> That since the mighty Cow her crown hath lost,
> In every place she's made to rule the roast.[4]

Corn paid to the Harvard building committee at 4*s* a bushel fetched only 2*s* 6*d*.[5] Naturally many of those who had come to New England as a refuge from persecution saw no reason why they should not now return; and many others, seeing no prospects in so depressed a country, talked of removing to a balmy climate and more fruitful soil. The puritan lords and gentlemen who were promoting the colonization of Old Providence in the Caribbean circulated flattering proposals, and succeeded in attracting John Humfrey by an offer of the governorship. This re-emigration was serious not so much for the numbers as for the quality of those who left New England never to return; out of the 114 university men who were in the country in 1640, 14 went back to England in 1641-42, and many more between that date and the restoration.[6] Sundry debtors decamped, following Nathaniel Eaton's example. Winthrop even recorded in his Journal that if he could have foreseen the faintheartedness of his followers he might never have left the old country.

Cambridge, it appears, was hard hit by the depression, and

1. 4 *Coll. M. H. S.*, II. 191–94.
2. Winthrop, *Journal* (1908), II. 19, 31; 4 *Coll. M. H. S.*, VI. 166.
3. *Mass. Bay Recs.*, I. 331.
4. K. B. Murdock, *Handkerchiefs from Paul*, p. 106.
5. *C. S. M.*, XV. 18.
6. See Appendix B.

for a time there was grave danger lest Thomas Shepard and his followers abandon the place, leaving Harvard College high and dry. Thomas Hooker, whose daughter married Master Shepard in 1637, had constantly endeavored to attract them to Connecticut. Late in 1640 he wrote a most persuasive letter offering the Cambridge congregation the excellent plantation of Mattabesett (later Middletown) if they would remove. All manner of godly and religious reasons, well buttressed with Biblical texts, were advanced for abandoning 'so forlorn and helpless' a place as Cambridge; and if that were not sufficient, a second letter, doubtless filled with even more edifying arguments, was enclosed for Shepard to show to the brethren. Hooker even insinuated a fear lest Sir Harry Vane become powerful in England and take vengeance on Massachusetts for his political humiliation in 1637. The Connecticut proposition was discussed in Cambridge church-meeting on February 14, 1640–41, and apparently turned down once and for all.[1]

Shepard became a tower of strength to Dunster and the College, by his saintly life, his influence over students, and his constant advocacy of the college interests. His removal with the major part of the inhabitants at this critical time might well have meant a second suspension of the College; and it is doubtful whether it could have recovered from another such blow.

Owing probably to the depression, not one student who subsequently graduated entered freshman in the autumn of 1641. Fortunately for Dunster, his personal financial problems were at least put in the way of solution by marrying the widow of Jose Glover,[2] a clergyman who provided the Cambridge printing

1. Paige, pp. 46–53.
2. See Appendix B. The historians of printing and of the Glover family have built up a myth to the effect that Mr. Glover first came over to Boston about 1634, and that he later returned to England to acquire a printing press and funds for the College, of which he was slated to be the president. See Isaiah Thomas, *History of Printing* (Am. Antiq. Soc. ed., 1874), I. 39–42; Anna Glover, *Glover Memorials* (1867), pp. 560–62; and G. E. Littlefield, *Early Massachusetts Press*, I. 19, 41–58. The only basis for this theory is the fact that Jose Glover was granted forty-nine acres at Rumney Marsh by the town of Boston on January 8, 1637–38 (*2d Report Boston Record Commissioners*, pp. 22, 29 of Boston Town Records; Littlefield, I. 48–49, antedates the grant one year), whilst the ship aboard which he died did not arrive in Boston until the summer of 1638. But it was the practice of Boston and other early New England towns to make grants in advance of their arrival to prominent persons who had given assurance of coming; and it is highly improbable that a person of Glover's wealth could have come to Boston earlier, wholly unnoticed by the contemporary chroniclers. Other parcels of real estate in Boston were later in possession of Mrs. Glover, but there is no evidence that her husband acquired

press, but died on his way over. Mistress Elizabeth Glover, undaunted by the loss of her reverend consort, had the printing press set up on what is now Holyoke Street, purchased the house of Governor Haynes, on the Market Place, and set up an expensive establishment, with five men-servants and four maids. Her furniture and plate were the talk of Cambridge for years. Former domestics remembered eleven feather beds, one with 'philop and Cheny curtaines in graine with a deep silke fring on the vallance, and a smaller on the Curtaines, and a Coverlett sutable to it, made of Red Kersie, and laced with a green lace, round the sides, and 2 downe the middle'; a blue bed-rug and an 'outlandish quilt'; a chest full of fine linen and damask; tapestry and green dornick hangings on the walls; a great store of brass, pewter, and latten ware; and as 'faire and full cubbard of plate there was as might ordinarily be seene in most Gentlemens houses in England.[1] Mistress Glover also had two stepchildren, Jose Glover's by a former marriage, and three of her own, together with sundry parcels of real estate in Boston, Cambridge, and Sudbury, and a large herd of cattle. The depression hit her hard; some of the plate and linen had to be sold, and £40 borrowed from a servant; and bills for stuff she had ordered in England kept coming in for years. One gathers that Mistress Glover needed a husband and manager of her property, quite as badly as Master Dunster needed a wife and property, and that only his prudent management saved her estate from liquidation during the depression. They were married on June 22, 1641, doubtless from Mrs. Glover's fine 'slate house' in the Market Square, and by one of the worshipful magistrates like Dudley or Nowell. Dunster, in the New England phrase, 'took right holt' of his wife's affairs, as he had of the College, discharged the idle servants, save a personal maid for the mistress, collected rent in arrears, and paid the debts.

A few weeks before Dunster's wedding the General Court authorized Hugh Peter, Thomas Weld, and William Hibbens to

---

them before her arrival. The 'Mr. Glover' mentioned by Bradford, who was engaged for the ministry at Plymouth, but died 'when he was prepared for the viage' (*Hist. of Plimmoth Plantation*, 1912 ed., II. 224–25), may or may not have been Jose; but there is no evidence or even probability that Jose acted as a sort of financial agent for the College in 1636–38, and came over expecting to be President.

1. Testimony of Sarah Bucknam and Joane Hassall, in case of Glover v. Dunster, 1656, Middlesex Court files; printed in *Old-Time New England*, xxv (1934). 31–32; and testimony of Stephen Day, April 2, 1656, Dunster Mss. One of the pieces of plate mentioned was the 'great salt' that Mrs. Dunster's brother gave to Harvard College.

go on a mission to England, in order to raise money for the Colony, the College, and the conversion of the Indians.[1] Samuel Shepard departed for England that summer, leaving President Dunster in sole charge of building operations. Money was obtained somehow: £40 from Governor Eaton of New Haven, £50 from 'A Gentleman not willing his name should be putt upon Record,' small sums from several merchants of Boston. In September, 1642, the college building — 'Harvard College' or the 'Old College' as it came to be called — was ready for occupation.

THE FIRST COMMENCEMENT

Quite imposingly 'Harvard College' rose above the apple trees which Master Eaton had planted in the yard: 'very faire and comely within and without,' an E-shaped clapboarded building with two wings and a square staircase-turret, two floors and a garret.[2] Within there were all things proper to a college: kitchen and butteries, chambers and studies, a library where John Harvard's and other books were shelved, and 'a spacious Hall' where Commencement was celebrated on September 23, 1642.[3]

Fortunately this first Harvard Commencement made such an impression that we can reconstruct the ceremony with sufficient completeness.[4] At an early hour in the morning Governor Winthrop, attended by his guard and a number of magistrates and gentlemen, crossed to Charlestown by the ferry and rode thence to Cambridge; or perhaps they were rowed in barges

1. *Mass. Bay Recs.*, I. 332. For this mission, see Chapter XXI.
2. See Chapter XX for detailed description.
3. Mr. Matthews, in *C. S. M.*, XVIII. 317-21, proves that Commencement must have been before Monday, September 26 (the date of the letter in *New Englands First Fruits* which mentions Commencement as 'lately' kept), and disposes of the various wild guesses at the date by previous writers. Winthrop mentions the Commencement in his *Journal* (1908 ed., II. 84) at the end of an entry of several pages headed [Thursday] September 22. His next entry, which describes the legislative act passed on September 27, and includes an incident at Commencement, is dated October 5. Commencement cannot then have been earlier than September 22. That being a fast day, and a prominent feature of the Commencement being a feast, it must have been held on Friday the 23rd; for Saturday the 24th would have impinged on the puritan Sabbath, and the 25th was the Lord's Day.
4. See *New Englands First Fruits*, Appendix D. Certain details are supplied from Cotton Mather's account of Commencement in his time, in *Magnalia*, book iv. 128, others from the College Records; and I plead guilty to supplying a few details from later Harvard and earlier Cambridge Commencements.

to the town landing at the foot of Dunster Street. By nine or ten o'clock in the morning an expectant audience consisting of the nine Commencers, four junior sophisters, and eight or ten freshmen,[1] together with 'great numbers' of gentlemen, ministers, and others, assembled in the newly finished college hall, sitting on forms and borrowed chairs. Thesis sheets on the Edinburgh model,[2] hot off Stephen Day's press, are distributed to members and guests. Enters a small but solemn procession, headed by Edward Mitchelson, Marshal-General of Massachusetts Bay. The four halberdiers of the Governor's guard precede proud Dunster, marching side by side with grave Winthrop. Next come six members of the Honorable and Reverend the Board of Overseers: Deputy-Governor Endecott, Assistants Bellingham and Dudley, Masters Wilson and Cotton of Boston Church, and Master Shepard of Cambridge.[3] Possibly some other magistrates and ministers bring up the rear. All take seats behind the high table on the dais — the President, as moderator of Commencement, in the center, Governor Winthrop on his right, and Deputy-Governor Endecott on his left. The halberdiers shamble off to the buttery to sample college beer. Marshal-General Mitchelson calls the assembly to order by striking the dais with the butt of his pikestaff,[4] and the 'Solemn Act' begins. Master Shepard offers a long extemporaneous prayer in Latin, praising the singular providence of God for bringing them thither through the dangers and difficulties of the sea, for preserving them in the wilderness from famine, heretics, and infidels, and for thus bringing so early to fruition in good letters and godly learning the first *classis* of this School of the Prophets. One of the ministers delivers a salutatory oration in Latin, 'wherein all *Persons* and *Orders* of any fashion then present, were Addressed with proper Comple-

1. There was no graduating class of 1644; but the Class of 1645 had in all probability already entered college.

2. See above, p. 136, and illustrations; also pp. 16–17 of *New Englands First Fruits*, Appendix D.

3. Of the other members of the 1637 Board of Overseers, which was not superseded until September 27, 1642, Peter, Weld, and Humfrey were in England, Stoughton was on his way thither, and Davenport would hardly have come up from New Haven for the occasion. All twelve are mentioned in the dedication of the theses as though they were present.

4. Since time immemorial this function has been performed by the Sheriff of Middlesex; but there was no county organization in 1642; the Marshal-General, who was a Cambridge man, would have been the logical person to open the meeting.

ments, and Reflections were made on the most Remarkable Occurrents of the praeceeding Year.' [1] The first scholar among the Commencers delivers an oration in Greek. One or possibly more offer a 'Hebrew Analysis Grammatical, Logicall and Rhetoricall of the Psalms,' based on William Ames' *Lectiones in Psalmos Davidis*.[2] The Commencers now having proved their proficiency in the three learned tongues, and the audience being suitably impressed and exceedingly fatigued, the assembly adjourns at eleven o'clock for dinner.[3] On most future occasions a feast was provided (*more Anglico*) at the expense of those taking degrees; but at this depression dinner the Overseers and guests 'dined at the college with the scholars' ordinary commons, which was done of purpose for the students' encouragement, etc., and it gave good content to all.' [4] Probably the students would have been better contented with a feast; but no doubt plenty of good substantial food was served on wooden trenchers, with college beer to wash it down.

Following dinner, the assembly may stretch themselves and take a breath of air in the Yard. While the tables are being cleared in the college hall, and the dogs snuff about in the straw and rushes for discarded morsels, the Board of Overseers holds a session in the library, or the Peyntree house. Master Dunster no doubt takes occasion to hint pretty broadly that even a 'School of the Prophets' cannot be maintained without funds; and the Overseers reply that until prosperity returns to New England the College must get along as best it can. The President may also point out that he has had difficulty assembling so scattered and dwindling a governing body as the Board of Overseers for necessary college business, and may express the hope that the General Court will see fit shortly to make some more suitable and permanent arrangement for college government. But one thing that we can be certain came up at this Overseers' meeting, since Governor Winthrop recorded it, was this: 'Complaint was made to the governors of two young men, of good quality, lately come out of England, for foul

---

1. *Magnalia*, book iv. 128. An example of one of these early salutatory orations is reprinted in *C. S. M.*, vol. xxviii.

2. See *H. C. S. C.*, Chapter XIII.

3. *New Englands First Fruits* mentions 'two solemne Acts,' hence the Commencement feast must have come between, as in the years after 1645 when the bachelors performed in the morning and the masters in the afternoon.

4. Winthrop, *Journal* (1908 ed.), II. 84.

misbehavior, in swearing and ribaldry speeches, etc.' The President asked authority to administer a flogging, which was readily granted; and after the festivities were over the two errant freshmen, 'though they were adulti' (eighteen years or over), 'were corrected in the college, and sequestered, etc., for a time.'[1]

At one or two o'clock, when the Board of Overseers has concluded its deliberations, President Dunster again takes the chair and the second Solemn Act of the day begins. This is in the form of a Latin disputation between Commencers, in syllogistic style, on some — certainly not all — of the twenty-five *Theses Philologicae* (*Grammaticae, Rhetoricae, Logicae*) and the thirty *Theses Philosophicae* (*Ethicae, Physicae, Metaphysicae*) on the printed thesis sheet. Most of these, such as 'Universalia non sunt extra intellectum' and 'Voluntas est formaliter libera,' are propositions from Aristotle, Aquinas, and Duns Scotus which had done duty at university commencements since the thirteenth century, and would never be entirely superseded as whetstones for young scholars' brains.[2] Others, such as 'Haebraea est Linguarum Mater' and 'Lingua Graeca est ad accentus pronuntianda,' smacked of the revival of learning; and still others, such as 'Oratoris est celare Artem,' 'In Elocutione perspecuitati cedit ornatus, ornatui copia,' gave opportunity for a play of classical wit. Possibly some of the Oxford and Cambridge men present, fired by memories of their own university days, caught the moderator's eye, and informally entered this battle of the Arts.[3] At least that is what the dedication of the theses invited them to do.

After disputations have been going on for a couple of hours, and the nine Commencers have 'performed their acts, so as gave good proof of their proficiency in the tongues and arts,'[4] comes the solemn moment for the conferring of degrees. The

---

1. Winthrop, *Journal* (1908 ed.), II. 84–85.

2. Similar theses are still used in disputations in Jesuit colleges. Dr. James J. Walsh, in *N. E. Q.*, v. 483–532.

3. This was the medieval practice, current in 1642 at the University of Edinburgh, and still current in American Catholic universities; but it was not the English practice, and I doubt that it was often done at Harvard. Samuel Sewall notes in his *Diary* (II. 111) that at Commencement, 1704, Jeremiah Dummer (A.B. 1699) made an opposition in excellent Latin, after obtaining the moderator's permission; but Dummer had just returned from the Continent. His action was probably exceptional.

4. Winthrop, *Journal* (1908 ed.), II. 84.

nine Commencers approach the platform, and stand in line.[1]
President Dunster addresses the Overseers:

Honorandi viri, vosque Reverendi Presbyteri, praesento vobis
hosce Juvenes, quos scio tam Doctrina quam moribus idoneos esse ad
primum in Artibus gradum suscipiendum, pro more Academiarum in
Anglia.[2]

Upon the approbation of the Overseers, doubtless delivered
by the time-honored word *placet*,[3] President Dunster confers the
degrees individually, presenting each bachelor as he does so
with 'a Booke of Arts.' [4]

Admitto te ad primum gradum in Artibus, scilicet, ad Respondendum Quaestioni pro more Academiarum in Anglia.
Tibique trado hunc librum una cum potestate publice praelegendi
(in aliqua Artium quam profiteris) quotiescunque ad hoc munus
evocatus fueris.[5]

The nine 'young men of good hope' [6] thus admitted to their
first degree in Arts were *Benjamin Woodbrigius*, aged twenty, a
recent acquisition from Magdalen Hall, Oxford, whither he re-

1. In England they would have knelt. I assume that owing to the puritans' hatred
of 'idolatry' they would have stood at Harvard. They certainly did in 1727 — see
President Wadsworth's diary (*C. S. M.*, xxxi).

2. 'Honourable Gentlemen and Reverend Ministers I present to you these youths,
whom I know to be sufficient in knowledge as in manners to be raised to the First Degree
in Arts, according to the custom of the Universities in England.' *C. S. M.*, xv. 35.

3. President Wadsworth's diary for Commencement 1729 (*C. S. M.*, vol. xxxi) informs us that the Overseers' *placets* were delivered by the Governor, as president of
the board.

4. It is not to be assumed that this book became the permanent possession of the
bachelor. Doubtless, as at Cambridge, it was immediately recovered by the College.
Degree diplomas were not presented at Harvard Commencements until 1813. *Harv.
Al. Bull.*, xxxv (1933). 810.

5. 'I admit thee to the First Degree in Arts, namely to reply to the Question, according to the custom of the Universities in England. And I hand thee this book, together
with the power to lecture publicly in any one of the arts which thou hast studied, when-
soever thou shalt have been called to that office,' *C. S. M.*, xv. 35; *Magnalia*, book iv.
128. Compare the Cambridge formulas above, pp. 72–74. It will be noticed that the
Harvard authorities recognized that the 'admission to the Question' was the essential
rite of becoming a Bachelor of Arts. They omitted the actual replying to the question,
and the subsequent determinations. These same omissions were made at Old Cambridge
in the nineteenth century, and until recently students were there admitted B.A. by
the 'ad respondendum' formula.

6. Winthrop, *Journal* (1908 ed.), ii. 84. Biographies in Sibley, vol. i (1873), and in
John Farmer's incompleted work, 'Memorials of the Graduates of Harvard University,'
Collections New Hampshire Historical Society, iv (1834), reprinted as *Old South Leaflet*
no. 160; Downing, Hubbard, and Woodbridge are in the *D. N. B.*

turned to take his master's degree, and to become, as minister of Newbury in Berkshire, 'the lasting Glory as well as the first Fruits' of Harvard;[1] *Georgius Downingus*, aged nineteen, destined to a Harvard tutorship, a New Model Army chaplaincy, a seat in the House of Commons, an embassy, and a baronetcy; *Gulielmus Hubbardus*, aged twenty-one, future historian and minister of Ipswich; *Henricus Saltonstall*, son of Sir Richard, who proceeded to Padua for his M.D. and to New College in Oxford for a fellowship; *Johannes Bulkleius*, not quite twenty-three, son of the minister of Concord, future minister and physician in England, and donor of an important part of the College Yard; *Johannes Wilsonus*, aged twenty-one, son of the minister of Boston, himself a minister, physician, and schoolmaster at Medfield for more than forty years; *Nathaniel Brusterus*, aged twenty-two, son of Francis Brewster of New Haven, a friend of Oliver Cromwell who served under his brother the Lord Deputy of Ireland, and subsequently lived for twenty-five years as minister on Long Island; *Samuel Bellingham*, son of the magistrate, later a student at Leyden and physician in London; and *Tobias Bernardus*, of whom nothing is known. Each was mentioned, with a few complimentary remarks, in a valedictory oration delivered by one of the ministers, who closed by invoking the congratulations — not the blessing — of God.[2]

The first Harvard Commencement was over.

1. I give the names as Latinized (after the Edinburgh model) on the theses, as printed in *New Englands First Fruits*. Woodbridge, apparently unsatisfied with official Harvard Latinity, appears as *Filodexter Transilvanus* on the title-page of his *Church-Members set in Joynt* (London, 1648), the first work by a Harvard graduate to appear in print. George Downing followed, in 1651, with *A True Relation of the Progress of the Parlaments Forces in Scotland*, written when he was Scoutmaster-General to that army; but William Ames' *The Saints Security* (1652) is not by the Harvard Ames. *C. S. M.*, xvii. 128–30, with facsimiles; *Notes and Queries* (1916), 12th ser., i. 508.

2. The Reverend Nathaniel Rogers, in his valedictory oration of 1652, states that it is a long established custom 'ut Presbyterorum aliquis (non dicam Benedictionem, sed) Gratulationem. Comitiis hisce literariis, tanquam Coronidem imponat.' *C. S. M.* vol. xxxi.

XIX

'A PRITY LIBRARY BEGUNE'
1638–1650

The Harvard College Library is at least as old as Harvard College.[1] Edmund Browne mentions it in his letter of September 7, 1638;[2] and three weeks later John Wiswall writes from Dorchester to a friend in England, 'Newtowne now is called Cambridge. There, is a University house reared, I heare, and a prity library begune.'[3]

This was a few days after John Harvard's death; but Harvard's books were not the first or only ones in the College Library. A general collection was taken up among the educated people in the Colony; at least so we infer from Treasurer Danforth's statement that 'the Honoured Magistrates and Reverend Elders gave . . . out of their own libraryes' books to the value of £200.[4] And Joseph Browne (A.B. 1666) recorded in his 'Almanack of Coelestial Motions for 1669': '[16]42 Harvard College Founded, and the Publick Library (given by Magistrates and Ministers) was translated thither.'

Presumably the 'Harvard College' in Browne's mind was the 'Old College' first occupied in 1642, and the 'translation' took place from the Peyntree house, or some place of temporary storage, to the library room in the new building. This room, as we shall see, was in the southeast corner of the 'middle' floor, between the long and the east middle chambers.[5] According to

1. The only older English colonial library which has retained some measure of identity is that of John Winthrop, Jr., which he brought out with him in 1631. The remnant is now part of the Society Library in New York. See *Catalogue of the New York Society Library* (1850), pp. 491–505; C. A. Browne, 'Scientific Notes from the Books and Letters of John Winthrop, Jr.,' *Isis*, XI. 325–42.

2. *C. S. M.*, XV. lxx.

3. *Historical Mss. Commission, 14th Report, Appendix*, pt. iv. 56.

4. *C. S. M.*, XV. 174.

5. Chapter XX.

an architectural canon handed down from Vitruvius, libraries should run north and south, in order to get the early morning light.[1] For so small a collection as ours no room of that description could be spared; but this library in the Old College, facing east and south, had the light from early morning until late afternoon. We have not the slightest hint as to the arrangement of books, whether in cases against the walls, or on presses at right angles to them; we only know that the books were not chained.[2] There the Library remained until the summer of 1676, when it was removed to Old Harvard Hall.

Edward Johnson, writing in 1651, describes the collection as 'a good Library, given by the liberal hand of some Magistrates and Ministers, with others'; [3] and the college inventory of 1654, taken shortly after President Dunster's resignation, mentions 'A library and Books therein, vallued at 400 *li*.' [4]

JOHN HARVARD'S LIBRARY

At an early date an unknown hand copied into the College Records [5] a brief list of the titles that came from John Harvard's library; and most of them have been identified by Mr. Alfred C. Potter.[6] There were 329 titles, and over 400 volumes. Nearly three-quarters of the collection consists of theological works, mainly in Latin, but by no means all of a Calvinistic or even a Protestant cast. Although Chrysostom and Augustine are the

1. Mullinger, III. 584. A common location of college libraries at Oxford and Cambridge was over the kitchen, in order to keep out damp. Willis and Clark, *Arch. Hist. Univ. Cambridge*, III. 416–17.

2. Jonathan Mitchell so states in his 'Modell' of 1663 (*C. S. M.*, XXXI. 319). In almost all European public libraries in the seventeenth century the larger and more valuable books were chained. The executors of John Selden proposed that his books which they gave to the Bodleian about 1660 'bee within the space of Twelve months next ensueing placed and chayned' (Anthony Wood, *Athenae* (1813 ed.), I. xxxviii). Chains were not removed from the Bodleian books until 1757, nor from some of the Oxford college libraries until even later. See Burnett H. Streeter, *The Chained Library* (1931), where the different systems of shelving books in the seventeenth century are described on pp. 64–76.

3. *W. W. P.* (1910 ed.), p. 201.

4. *C. S. M.*, xv. 208. As Danforth had already noted £150 worth sent from England by Weld and Peter (*id.* 175), his £200 estimate of the books given by 'the Honoured Magistrates and Reverend Elders . . . out of their own libraryes' must have included John Harvard's collection.

5. *C. S. M.*, xv. 158–66. Probably done by one of the scholars after 1667, when the new library laws called for a catalogue. It is full of mistakes, but not those due to ignorance of Latin.

6. *C. S. M.*, xxi. 190–230, and printed separately.

only Church Fathers represented, Aquinas is there, in the fine seventeen-volume edition printed at Venice in 1593, as well as the works of Luther, Calvin, Melanchthon, and Beza. Four volumes of Robert Bellarmine's works are answered by William Ames' *Bellarminus enervatus*; and seven commentaries by another Jesuit theologian, Cornelius à Lapide, balance reformed divines such as Ainsworth, Zanchius, Davenant, Pareus, and Lambert Daneau. Indeed, some of the omissions on the Protestant and puritan side are surprising. We miss not only 'Painful' Perkins, but

Whites ambo, Whitehead, Whitgift, Whitakerus uterque.

John Harvard evidently cared little for the polemical divinity that bulked so large in the Cambridge of his day.

There are ancient classics in the original tongues, including some rather unexpected works such as the Satires of Persius and of Juvenal; and famous translations such as North's Plutarch, Holland's Pliny, and Chapman's Homer. There are a number of grammars and dictionaries — Latin, Greek, and Hebrew; and compendia by Alsted and Keckermann. Bacon's Natural History and Advancement of Learning show that Harvard was not ignorant of the new philosophy, although he also possessed obsolete scientific works such as Pliny's Natural History and Duns Scotus on Aristotle's Physics. We should not look for Descartes' *Discours sur la Méthode*, which had only appeared in 1637. Polite learning is represented by La Primaudaye's French Academie, Lorenzo Valla *de Elegentia*, Poliziano's Letters, Erasmus' Colloquies, Bacon's Essays, Peacham's Garden of Eloquence, and Roger Ascham's Familiar Epistles. There are a number of text-books and anthologies that John probably used at Emmanuel, or even at grammar school, such as Aesop's Fables, Christopher Ocland's *Anglorum Praelia*, Grynaeus' *Adagia*, Eilhard Lubin's *Clavis Graecae Linguae*, Golius' epitome of Aristotle's Ethics, the commentary on Aristotle's *de Generatione et Corruptione* by Domingo Bañez, Thomas Draxe's *Calliepeia*, the *Apophthegmata* of Lycosthenes, the *Physiologia* of Magirus, Francesco Pavone's *Summa Ethicae*, Ramus' Greek Grammar, Latin Grammar, and Logic, John Seton's Logic, and Omer Talon's Rhetoric. English poetry is represented only by Wither, Quarles, and Niccols; but we find the comedies of Plautus and Terence, and William Alabaster's tragedy Roxana, which was acted at Trinity College when John was an under-graduate.

Among the miscellaneous works may be mentioned King James' Βασιλικὸν δῶρον, Andrea Alciati's *Emblemata*, Francesco Piccolomini's *Universa Philosophia de Moribus*, and John Light-foot's *Erubhin*, nucleus of the excellent collection of rabbinical works that came to the College later in the century, in part from Dr. Lightfoot's own library. There are even three medical books: Sir William Vaughan's 'Directions for Health,' Lemnius *de Habitu et Constitutione Corporis*, and Andreas Laurentius, *Opera Omnia*. Only one of all these books certainly, and another probably, survived the fire of 1764: John Downame's 'Christian Warfare Against the Deuill, World and Flesh,' and the 'Statutes at Large,' edition of 1587.

The collection does credit to John Harvard's catholic learning and good taste. It would have been no contemptible library for an educated English gentleman of the day, remembering that theology was one of the great intellectual preoccupations of the age. And it was distinctly a modern library: over one quarter of the books were printed after 1630. That such a collection could be brought out to a country only seven years settled is striking evidence of the puritan purpose to maintain intellectual standards in the New World.

Other Early Donations

Who were the other 'diverse of our friends,'[1] magistrates and ministers, who bestowed on the College these essential tools of learning? Very few of their names have been preserved. Governor Bellingham at some date unknown gave twenty works, all theological except Grotius *de Jure Belli ac Pacis*. Peter Bulkeley, pastor of the church in Concord, gave thirty-five works, all theological but Camden's *Britannia*, Münster's 'Cosmography,' and perhaps one or two others. Governor Winthrop made his only recorded gift to the College in the shape of about forty works, mainly theological, but including a Livy, a Polydore Vergil, a Graeco-Latin Lexicon, and such curiosities as a Book of Hours of the Blessed Virgin, Francesco Piccolomini *de Arte Definiendi et Eleganter Discurrendi*, and Bartholomaeus de Glanville

---

1. *New Englands First Fruits*, p. 13.

de Proprietatibus Rerum (1535).[1] And 'Mr Thomas Graves gave some Mathematicall Books towards the furnishing of the Library.'[2] Ezekiel Rogers of Rowley bequeathed to the College in 1660 most of his English books, valued at £26 3*s*, and all his Latin books (save an Aquinas *Summa* of which the Library already had a copy), valued at £47 10*s* 8*d*.[3]

The first Harvard graduate on record to leave books to alma mater was the same Joseph Browne (A.B. 1666) who noted the translation of the Library in his almanac chronology. At his death in 1678, he left £100 in books to his father, £30 in books to one brother, several specified books to individuals, and 'unto Harvard College in Cambridge one hundred pound and to the Library . . . fifty pound in Bookes.'[4] The money bequest was never secured from his executors; the records are silent as to whether or not the books were received.

Other early donations to the Library came from England. Daniel Neal's statement in 1720[5] that the 'first Furniture' of the Harvard College Library 'was the Books of Dr. William Ames, the famous Professor of Divinity at Franequer,' is undoubtedly untrue;[6] but an effort was made to obtain a still more important collection. Thomas Shepard wrote to Hugh Peter in 1645:

You should do very well to helpe our Colledge with a more compleat Library, we have very good wits among us and they grow up mightily, but we want bookes; be intreated earnestly to helpe us herein speedily, God will certainly recompence that part of your care,

1. *C. S. M.*, xv. 156–68; on p. 200, Digby's collection is valued at £60 and Winthrop's at £20. Most of the short titles can be identified by referring to the H. C. L. Catalogue of 1723.

2. *C. S. M.*, xv. 200. This was probably the engineer and early settler of Charlestown, a neighbor of John Harvard and father of Thomas Graves (A.B. 1656).

3. *Essex Probate Records*, i. 333, 335.

4. Sibley, ii. 208–09.

5. *History of New England* (1720 ed.), i. 183; 1747 ed., i. 202.

6. The question is discussed by Mr. Julius H. Tuttle in *C. S. M.*, xiv. 63–66. The absence of mention in records and contemporary writers of any such important donation seems to me conclusive; and the fact that a catalogue of Ames' library was printed at Amsterdam in 1634, the year after his death, an event which left his family in financial straits, points to the probability that the books were sold in the Netherlands before Ames' widow emigrated. Cotton Mather states that she brought out the Doctor's library, but not that she gave it to the College.

into your bosom: we want schoolmen especially; helpe herein, devise some way to furnish us, we were thinking to desire the ArchBishop's Library. . . . [1]

Archbishop Laud's library, with its rich collection of Catholic and Protestant theology, would have been appreciated nowhere more than at Harvard; but even Hugh Peter was unable to land such big game. Plenty of 'schoolmen' did come in time — the Catalogue of 1723 fairly bristles with commentaries on Aquinas. Peter and Weld, moreover, procured 'from diverse Gentellmen and merchants in England towards the furnishing of the Library with book to the value of an hundred and fifty pound.' [2] From Weld's accounts we know that one of these English benefactors was Chief Justice Oliver St. John, and that out of money given by others he laid out £13 7s for books wanted by the College Library.[3] 'That noble and absolutely compleat Gentleman Sir *Kenhelme Digby* Knight,' [4] friend of the younger John Winthrop, sent over seventeen valuable and curious works, including several Church Fathers, the *Bibliotheca de Ratione Studiorum* (1607) of Antonio Possevino, S.J., the Works of Jacobus Alvarez, S.J., an Epitome of the *Annales Ecclesiastici* of Cardinal Baronius (Cologne, 1603), Harphius' *Theologia Mystica* (1611), and the Rosselus edition (Cologne, 1630) of the *Poemander* of Hermes Trismegistus.[5] And before 1650 the College possessed an Antwerp Polyglot Bible.[6]

COMPARISON WITH LIBRARIES ABROAD

In size, character, and content the Harvard College Library in the seventeenth century was similar to the smaller college libraries in the British Isles. John Harvard's bequest accounts for about four hundred volumes. By a rough estimate the total had risen by 1655 to about 800 works and possibly 900 volumes.[7]

1. *American Historical Review*, iv. 106.
2. *C. S. M.*, xv. 175. For the Weld-Peter mission see Chapter XXI.
3. 'In bookes sent over by request to the Coll Library,' £13 7s. 'For transporting bookes given by my Lord Judge St John and Mr Sansom,' £5 12s. Weld's account, in *N. E. H. G. R.*, xxxvi. 69.
4. Henry Peacham, *The Compleat Gentleman* (1634 ed.), p. 108.
5. *C. S. M.*, xv. 166–67, 200; titles identified from H. C. L. Catalogue of 1723.
6. Chaplin, *Life of Dunster*, p. 275.
7. Based on the valuation of £400 for the whole library in December, 1654, and the valuation of £20 to John Winthrop's forty titles, which were books of average worth.

SIR KENELM DIGBY

Emmanuel College Library had 503 books in 1610, and about 600 in 1637.[1] The Harvard Library was acquired by gift, like the English college libraries, not by purchase;[2] and, again like them, it was largely a professional library for students of theology. John Harvard's bequest, being the complete library of an educated gentleman, was not so predominantly theological as later acquisitions in this century. President Dunster himself was disturbed at the poverty of the library in most branches of learning. He petitioned the New England Confederation in 1647: 'seinge the publicke library in the Colledg is yet defectiue in all manner of bookes, especially in law, phisicke, Philosophy and Mathematickes, the furnishinge whereof would be both honourable and proffitable to the Country in generall and in speciall to the schollars, whose various inclinations to all professions might thereby be incouraged and furthered, we therfore humbly entreate you to vse such meanes as your wisdomes shall thincke meete for supply of the same.'[3] But their wisdoms thought meet to do nothing; and the Library had to wait a century or more for a respectable supply of books in other branches than theology.

Dunster, it will be observed, asked for no current literature. It is a rather favorite device of superficial historians to mention what was *not* in the Harvard College Library at this or that colonial epoch, and then bewail the cultural poverty from which New England in general, and Harvard in particular, suffered. But, as we shall see in our examination of one student's light reading,[4] it is unsafe to infer from the absence of a book in the fragmentary records of early donations, or in the first Library Catalogue (1723), that it was not to be had in Cambridge before 1700.[5] Not even the university libraries in England attempted to

1. 'Memorandum anno domini 1610 there were in the Library October 4th 503 books' — of which thirty were missing. Book of Expenses, Emmanuel College muniments; rough estimate from 'A Catalogue of all the Library Bookes' April 27, 1637, ms. *ibid*. Trinity College, Dublin, had only 40 volumes in 1600, but several thousand ten years later. J. P. Mahaffy, *An Epoch in Irish History*, pp. 143–44.

2. In all the English college muniments that I have examined for the period 1595–1640, I did not find a single instance of the college spending money for books, or receiving money for books.

3. Mass. Archives, LVIII. 8; printed in *Plymouth Col. Recs.*, IX. 95.

4. *H. C. S. C.*, Chapter VI.

5. Because no earlier edition of Milton's poems than that of 1720 is in the 1723 Catalogue, historians have jumped to the conclusion that the H. C. L. knew not Milton's poems before that date. Actually the edition of 1720 was given in 1722 by Ben-

keep abreast of general literature, or to provide books for undergraduate consumption. They were established to serve scholars, especially theologians;[1] and for such men the Harvard Library was well equipped. Undergraduates seldom had access to college libraries in the seventeenth century; they were expected to buy or borrow the required text-books, or to take notes on books read aloud in lectures. In the early years, nobody under a Bachelor of Arts had 'a liberty of studying in the Library' at Harvard.[2] There was some relaxation in respect of borrowing from it, by the time the library rules of 1667 were adopted;[3] but the notion that a college library should supply undergraduates with most of their reading grew up in America only in the nineteenth century.

jamin Colman in exchange for ' what of Milton's Poetical Works heretofore belonged to the Library . . . to be disposed of as he sees meet.' Here is proof positive that at least some of Milton's poems were in the library before 1722. *C. S. M.*, xvi. 466–67.

1. An analysis of the Emmanuel Library Catalogue of 1637, by 'sections,' each 'section' holding from twenty to sixty books, shows eleven sections of theology, two of ancient classics, one of Aristotle and Plato, three of law, history, geography, and cosmography, one of Cicero and manuscripts, and one of mathematics and miscellaneous works. The first printed Bodleian Library Catalogue (1605) devotes 241 pages to titles of theological works, 53 to medical, 112 to law books, 95 to 'arts,' and 9 to interpretations of Aristotle. On the Continent, university libraries were more general. The Library Catalogue of the University of Franeker in 1644 (copy in Bodleian) is arranged by *facies* (sides of a *pluteus*, or book-press), and shows that 18 *facies* were devoted to theology, 11 to law, 7 to history and geography, 4 to medicine, 4 to ancient classics and dictionaries, 3 to Aristotle and Plato, 3 to mathematics, physics, and agriculture, 2 to political theory, miscellaneous works, and books of reference.

2. *New Englands First Fruits*, p. 17 (Appendix D). At the Bodleian, Bachelors of Arts were allowed only in the Arts end. G. W. Wheeler, *Earliest Catalogues of the Bodleian* (1928), p. 43.

3. See *H. C. S. C.*, Chapter XIV.

THE OLD COLLEGE FROM THE YARD

Drawn by H. R. Shurtleff

XX

THE 'OLD COLLEGE'[1]

The college grounds as Dunster found them on assuming office in 1640 included only the original Yard and the Peyntree house-lot (I), with a somewhat doubtful claim to Eaton's town grant (II) adjoining it on the north, and his second town grant (A) on the other side of Kirkland Street. The only completed building on the grounds, so far as we know, was the Peyntree house with its outbuildings, where Eaton had held his 'School of Tyrannus.' This was at once occupied by President Dunster, and there the College was reopened in August or September, 1640. Presumably some of the students lodged in the Peyntree house until Commencement, 1642, and the rest, as he wrote, were 'dispersed in the town and miserably distracted in their times of concourse'[2] during the first two years of his administration, while the 'Old College' was being built.

This building, the first to be constructed especially for the College, never had any formal name; as in the case of English collegiate foundations that had but a single building, the name of the institution was applied.[3] Our building was originally known as 'Harvard College' or simply 'The College'; but its usual name after the Goffe house had been acquired in 1652 was 'The Old College,' and so we may conveniently term it here.[4]

1. In preparing this chapter I owe a special debt of gratitude to Mr. T. Mott Shaw, Mr. Harold R. Shurtleff, Mr. Singleton P. Moorehead, and Mr. Robert C. Dean, of the firm of Perry, Shaw, and Hepburn, architects (the restorers of Williamsburg, Virginia), who collaborated with me in interpreting the data on the Old College, and in drawing the plans and alterations. A more detailed article by us, 'A Conjectural Restoration of the "Old College" at Harvard,' will be found in *Old-Time New England*, XXIII (1933). 131-58. The materials are largely in College Book I (*C. S. M.*, vol. xv), and the introduction to that volume by Mr. Albert Matthews.

2. Appendix E.

3. *N. E. D.*, 'College,' 5, with examples from Chaucer down. If our founders searched their King James Bible for a precedent, they may have noted with some apprehension that Huldah the Prophetess 'dwelt in Jerusalem in the College' (2 Kings, xxii. 14).

4. Mr. Matthews refers to it as 'First Harvard College (1642–1679),' *C. S. M.*, vol. xv. I have preferred to use the colloquial 'Old College,' which has the sanction of contemporary usage, and was applied to this building in the Records as late as 1715 (*id.*, xvi. 430), although after Stoughton was built, Old Harvard Hall was sometimes called 'the Old College' (*id.*, xvi. 898).

Completed about 1644,[1] and in use only thirty-four years, it passed unregretted and unsung. No picture or plan of it has been discovered — indeed none is known ever to have existed; the tradition of it waned until even the site was forgotten; and only after the most careful collation of ancient records can we now determine that it was on or very near the place where Grays Hall now stands.[2] Yet the plan and construction of this first college building in the English Colonies, architectural ancestor of the hundreds of such buildings that have sprung up wherever the New England stock has settled, cannot fail to be of interest. Without some notion of how this building appeared, and what its arrangements were, we can have no solid, three-dimensional view of Dunster's and Chauncy's Harvard, nor can we understand what the founders meant by that 'collegiate way of living' which they thought no less essential than teachers, lectures, and books.

Building Operations, 1638–1642

Ground had been broken for the Old College and considerable work done on it by the summer of 1638.[3] Nathaniel Eaton had charge of the construction, and his accounts have been preserved. They include £120 for 'The frame in the Colledge yard and digging the cellar, carriage and setting it up'; £6 'To the Mason Thomas King for Chimneys'; £2 to 'the Smith' for iron casements; £4 for 'Felling, Squaring, Leading [hauling] timber to be added'; £1 10s for 'Leading Stone and clay for underpinning'; £3 10s for 'Bricks provided and layd in place'; £108 'Payd by me to the Carpenter for additions to be made to the frame already raised'; £1 in part payment for 'lime to be burnt for the Colledge'; £3 10s for 'unloading the Timber prepared for the Addition'; and £10 10s 'for 250 [foot of] Cedar boards with the Carriage of them.' The total charge, including the Yard

---

1. Dunster wrote on September 18, 1643, 'Seeing that now that work in this house will draw to a period (though haply 30*li* will not fully finish it yet) . . .'; and the study accounts (*C. S. M.*, xv. 4–13) indicate that certain studies were not completed before 1644 or 1645.

2. See Map of Cambridge in Chapter XIV, and Mr. Matthews' long note to *C. S. M.*, xv. lxxvi–lxxxii. It is certain that the Old College was on the Peyntree house backside (I), the original College Yard, which means that it must have been on the same north-and-south axis as Grays. It could not have been much closer to the street, for the Peyntree house was there; nor very far back, for convenience sake.

3. See above, pp. 208–09.

fence and thirty apple trees, was £301, of which £200 was paid by John Harvard's executor on account of the Harvard legacy,[1] and £20 by the Court as a first instalment on the £400 voted at the founding of the College.[2]

For two years after Eaton's expulsion the Old College was in charge of Samuel Shepard,[3] who accounted for donations in money,[4] materials, and labor, and town rates assigned by the General Court, to the amount of £251 15s 8d. The master builder whom he employed was John Friend of Ipswich, who had earlier constructed the fort at Saybrook, which was probably the largest building hitherto erected in New England.[5] John Friend should be enrolled among our early benefactors since he not only made the very moderate charge of £20 8s, almost half of which was 'discounted,' but gave his labor to the value of £7 2s 8d.[6]

Samuel Shepard's accounts show disbursements for wages to carpenters, brickmakers, bricklayers, 'Thomas the smith,' and 'Rich Harrington a Plaisterer'; for lime, hair, and other materials; for 'Meat to the workmen'; and £2 2s 6d 'To Mr Eldred for shooes.' According to our best calculations the Old College had cost £577 6s 4d by October 3, 1641, when Samuel Shepard handed over the building to President Dunster. The college hall was then finished, 'yet without skreen table form or bench,' but only the hall floor and the one above was laid, 'no inside separating wall made nor any one study erected throughout the house. Thus fell the work upon mee,' wrote Dunster.[7]

The General Court turned over to him £62 12s 6d in rates, on account of the Country's Gift, and paid a small lumber bill; Governor Eaton and several other well-wishers in England and

1. *C. S. M.*, xv. 172, lxxi–lxxii, and notes.
2. See Chapter XXI.
3. *C. S. M.*, xv. lxxii and note. Mr. Matthews argues plausibly that Shepard alone, not a committee as Dunster later stated, had charge.
4. *Id.*, p. 17. The gifts were from Hugh Peter, John Norton, Thomas Weld, Deacon Nathaniel Sparhawk of Cambridge, Francis Willoughby (merchant of Boston, afterwards M.P. in England and Assistant of Massachusetts Bay), and 'Mr Gourdon' (reading doubtful — probably Brampton Gurdon, M.P., a cousin and correspondent of Governor Winthrop).
5. For notes on John Friend, I am indebted to his descendant, Mrs. Ella Friend Mielziner.
6. *C. S. M.*, xv. 17–18.
7. Appendix E.

New England made generous gifts in money; [1] and immediately after the first Commencement on September 23, 1642, Dunster had the great satisfaction of moving all the 'students dispersed in the town' into the new building. It was still incomplete on September 18, 1643 when Dunster wrote, 'haply 30 *li* will not fully furnish it yet';[2] and not until 1644 or later were all the chambers and studies fitted up, at the cost of their first occupants.[3] So we may say that the Old College was eight years a-building, and cost between nine hundred and a thousand pounds.

The Old College, so an English observer reported, was built 'of timber covered with shingles of cedar,'[4] and framed, fastened, sheathed, and boarded with wood, the cheapest material available. Iron was used only for the frames and hinges of casement windows, for fastening the sheathing to the frame, and for nails, locks, and hinges in the studies. Inside walls were plastered, and the chimneys were of brick, probably laid in clay below the roof and in oyster-shell lime mortar above it. We also infer that the cellar was dug under a part of the building only, and that the timber sills were laid on rock-filled trenches, a common method both in England and the colonies.

PLAN, ETON PROTOTYPE, AND JOHN WILSON

 Contemporary descriptions of the Old College and comments on it, are few but precious. 'New Englands First Fruits' describes it as an edifice 'very faire and comely within and without, having in it a spacious Hall; (where they daily meet at Common Lectures) Exercises, and a large Library with some Bookes to it . . . their Chambers and studies also

1. *C. S. M.*, xv. 21, 174–75. Assuming that all gifts received before 1644, if not otherwise specified, were used for building, we have £272 12s. received by Dunster from these sources.

2. Letter quoted in Chapter XXI.

3. Adding the actual cost of fitting up chambers and studies, the accounts of which have been preserved, to the 'income' of these studies, whose actual cost we do not know (*C. S. M.*, xv. 5–14), one arrives at the estimate of £85 for this part of the building expenses.

4. Edward Randolph, in *Calendar of State Papers, Colonial, 1675–76*, p. 467; Thomas Hutchinson, *Collection of Papers* (1769), p. 501. By 'covered' he means 'roofed,' for the walls were sheathed with clapboard, not shingles.

fitted for, and possessed by the Students . . . and convenient.'[1] Edward Johnson wrote about 1651, 'the building thought by some to be too gorgeous for a Wilderness, and yet too mean in others apprehensions for a Colledg . . . hath the conveniencies of a fair Hall, comfortable Studies, and a good Library.'[2] It seems a fair inference from Johnson that the more narrow-minded puritans resented the Old College as a luxurious 'vanity'; whilst university men regarded it as a poor makeshift for the English colleges toward which they turned with aching affection when weary of wilderness life.

Fortunately we have evidence in the university archives which, seen in the light of English college architecture, enables us to reconstruct a plan and elevations of this Ark of American college buildings. In the first place, from the inventory of 1654 and study list,[3] we can name these rooms that the Old College contained:

'Low,' ground, or first story: porch, hall, kitchen, larder or pantry, buttery with adjacent study, passage, corn room, a small chamber, a large east chamber furnished with four studies.

'Middle' or second story: a 'Long' or 'Great' chamber, with six studies and two 'cabins'; the library; an east chamber with four studies, a west chamber 'over the Kitchen' with four studies; and two small chambers each with one study.

'Highest' or third story: an east and a west chamber, each with three studies.

A turret with four stories, containing the stairway, five studies, and a bell.

The studies as described in the schedule can be placed fairly accurately in the chambers to which they belong; for they are designated by points of the compass. It was essential that each study have a window; otherwise, in the seventeenth century, it could not have been used for study. And this means that the only possible shape of the Old College was the so-called open quadrangle, a main building with two wings, shaped roughly like a thick, square letter E lying on its back; the straight south façade, broken only by a porch, facing Braintree Street, the wings and turret looking north into the Yard.

1. Appendix D.
2. *W. W. P.* (1910 ed.), p. 201.
3. *C. S. M.*, xv. 208; the study list is printed on page 283, below.

The founders of Harvard were no strangers to the open quadrangle, then the fashionable plan for college buildings at the University of Cambridge. Oxford never abandoned the closed quadrangle of the middle ages; but Dr. Caius of Cambridge built a new court to his college in 1565, in which one whole side was left open to admit sun and air. His example was followed by Sir Walter Mildmay when Emmanuel was built in 1584, at Sidney-Sussex College in 1595, in Neville's court at Trinity in 1612, at Pembroke College in 1610, and at Jesus College in 1638. Moreover, this was the cheapest way to build Harvard College and get all the required rooms under one roof. A fourth side to the quadrangle would have been superfluous as well as old-fashioned; and if the whole had been made in a single range, the width of the narrow Yard would not have sufficed; and two more staircases would have been necessary.

For the arrangement in the central part of the Harvard building, there is a prototype at Eton College: the 'Long Chamber' range of the Old School quadrangle, built between 1443 and 1507.[1] Superficially and externally this building, with its crenellated brick walls and late perpendicular windows, bears little resemblance to the Old College at Harvard; but in plan the two have so much in common as to suggest a direct influence. In the Eton building the ground floor is divided, by a passage, into two large rooms, one of them the lower school, corresponding to the Harvard 'Hall or Schoole.' The passage emerges on the other side under a square turret, in which there is a staircase leading directly into the 'Long Chamber,' which before being subdivided in the last century, was 166 feet long, serving as dormitory for the entire College.[2] The turret not only connects these two floors, but continues upward for two stories and a half more, containing rooms which until recently were used for masters' and boys' studies, like the upper rooms in the Harvard turret.[3]

---

1. Willis and Clark, *Architectural History of the University of Cambridge*, 1. 430.

2. *Id.*, 1. 461–62.

3. Square turrets were a favorite device of English builders to solve the staircase problem, that bane of amateur architects. They gave more room in the main building, and made it easier to frame. A small brick building added to Caius College, Cambridge, in 1635, had just such a turret, and so has a famous old Virginia mansion, 'Bacon's Castle' in Surry County, built in 1676. Willis and Clark, 1. 172–73, 187; illustration from Loggan in *Old-Time New England*, XXIII. 145; measured drawings of Bacon's Castle in Fiske Kimball, *Domestic Architecture of the American Colonies* (1927),

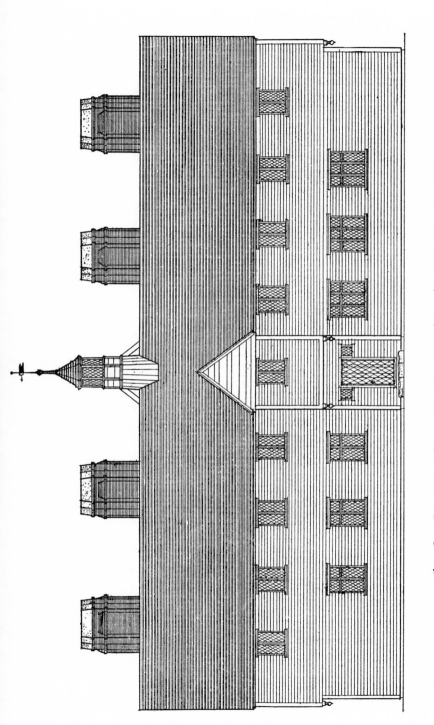

SOUTH ELEVATION

SOUTH ELEVATION OF THE OLD COLLEGE

Drawn by Singleton P. Moorehead.

1 5 10 20 FT

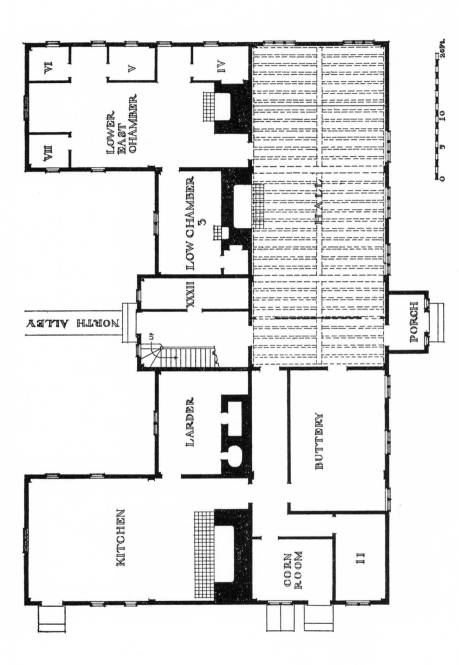

FIRST FLOOR PLAN

GROUND OR FIRST FLOOR PLAN OF THE OLD COLLEGE

Drawn by H. R. Shurtleff.

This striking resemblance is not surprising, when we find that there was a strong personal bond between early Harvard and Eton College. Master John Wilson[1] of Boston, a member of that Harvard Board of Overseers under whose direction the Old College was planned and begun, had passed several of his most impressionable years as scholar of Eton, studying in the lower school, sleeping in the long chamber, and running up and down the turret staircase. For many years thereafter his father, as a canon of Windsor, resided near by; and at least two of his brothers attended Eton College. Anyone who has been to boarding school will testify how indelible are the impressions of early school surroundings. It takes no stretch of the imagination to suppose that when the old Cantabrigians on the first Harvard Board of Overseers were casting about for some plan that would look collegiate and yet not ruin the Colony by the expense of building, Master Wilson produced from his memories of Eton a rough sketch which became the basis of the Old College plan.[2]

PUBLIC ROOMS

Let us examine first the rooms on the ground floor. Approaching the building by a short path from Braintree Street, leading past the President's Lodge, we enter through a small porch, which, with its 'porch chamber' overhead, was a common feature of New England dwelling houses to protect the interior from drafts. We then find ourselves in a passage, which emerges into the Yard under the turret. This passage was the main artery of college life. Everyone who entered or left the College went through it: the President on his way to hall for prayer or lectures; worshipful magistrates and reverend ministers inspecting the College; students many times a day; servants on their several occasions; and curious visitors from the country. On the right of this passage is the 'skreen' which President Dunster found lacking when he took over the building, a partition,

---

p. 40. This is the only example of an external staircase turret still standing in the United States.

1. See above Chapter VII, and Appendix B.

2. As an additional, though not very strong, bit of evidence connecting John Wilson with the Old College, we may note that when a contribution was taken up for repairs to that building, in 1654–55, Wilson, alone of the many clergymen who were or had been Overseers (excepting John Allin, who had just been appointed), contributed; and his gift, although paid by instalments, was the third largest received. *C. S. M.*, xv. 185.

probably of cedar wainscoting, which separated the hall from the passage.[1] A single door [2] opened into the 'fair'and 'spacious' hall, which as in the English colleges and the medieval manors was the principal room of the building, used for prayers, meals, and all college exercises. In one of our early accounts it is called the 'Hall and Schoole,' because it was used, like the public schools of medieval universities, for lectures and disputations.[3] It was probably plastered on three sides, certainly glazed with 112 square feet of glass, and provided with long refectory tables and backless forms and, in all probability, a dais at the east or further end for a 'high table' where the fellows and fellow-commoners dined. At about the center of the north side was the fireplace. The dimensions of the hall, about 20 by 50 feet, were sufficient to seat the entire College at its highest point of enrolment (about fifty) in the seventeenth century, and were about the same as those of the smaller college halls in England.[4] But unlike these it was ceiled, instead of having a timber roof; for economy required the space overhead for the 'long chamber.'

Returning to the passage, we face the cook's 'Hatch door' opening to the passage to the kitchen, and the 'Buttery hatch' [5] opening to the buttery. These were what are now called Dutch doors, the upper half opening without the lower, on which was a shelf to act as counter for the dispensing of food and drink. Buttery hatches are still a familiar feature of English colleges, and in this exact location. The buttery must have been a pleasant room, with its rows of country cheeses, firkins of butter, loaves of bread, and a fresh barrel of college beer from the college 'brew-hoose.' [6] Either on its walls or on that of the passage outside hung the 'buttery tables,' tablets on which were displayed, in order of seniority, the names of all members of the House. Twice a day, at morning and evening bever,[7] the buttery was a scene of great activity. It also seems to have been a

---

1. In the older English colleges and manor houses one entered the hall directly from the outer door; the screen was a refinement of the renaissance to keep out drafts. Cambridge college halls were not all provided with screens when our Old College was built. Willis and Clark, *op. cit.*, III. 357–60.

2. Sibley, II. 399.

3. *C. S. M.*, xv. 4.

4. Willis and Clark, *op. cit.*, I. 196.

5. So called in the regulations of 1650, 1667, and 1686 for the cook and butler. *C. S. M.*, xv. 34, 46–47, 203, 261.

6. *Id.*, p. 62.

7. See next chapter.

lounging place for masters of arts, fellows, the privileged fellow-commoners, and town friends of the butler; one bit of buttery gossip led to a libel suit—'Sir Phillips' (A.B. 1650), as he quaffed his beer at the hatch, informed the assembled cronies that in a certain frontier settlement 'all things are common, mens wives alsoe.'[1]

A passage from the cook's hatch door led to a corn room for storing grain, to a desirable corner study, and to the kitchen. This highly important room occupied the ground floor of the west wing, a common arrangement in English colleges such as Emmanuel.

In the days when food was none too plentiful for poor scholars, and heat a rare commodity for all, the warmth, appetizing smells, and cheerful bustle of a college kitchen were an irresistible attraction to undergraduates. Again and again the English colleges legislated against students entering the kitchen; and in the first Harvard regulations the cook is forbidden to 'suffer any Schollar or Schollars whatever, except the Fellows, masters of Art, and Fellow-Commoners, or Officers of the house, to come into the Buttery or Kitchen save with their parents, or Guardians, or with some grave and sober strangers; and if any shall presume to thrust in, he shall be punished 3*d*, but if presumptuously and continually, they shall so dare to offend, they shall be lyable to an Admonition, and to other proceeding of the Colledge discipline, as the Corporation shall determine.'[2] The reference to parents and 'sober strangers' suggests that the college kitchen was one of the sights of Cambridge. It was not well glazed at first; possibly most of the window openings were covered with oiled paper until better times. One side was almost taken up by the fireplace, where the cooking was done over an oak and hickory wood fire, except that there must have been a brick oven for baking cut into the chimney stack. According to an inventory of 1674, the kitchen seems to have been well furnished. The fireplace is provided with a proper equipment of tongs, dogs, bars, trammels, racks, pot-hooks, and no less than five spits, with a 'small Jack to turn spitts.' There are iron pots great and small, a 'prettie big kettle' and a 'Little kettle,' a 'Great grid-Iron,' skillets, frying pans, and an 'Iron peale' or shovel for the brick oven. The chopping-blocks and

1. *C. S. M.*, xxvii. 216–17.
2. *C. S. M.*, xv. 203; cf. p. 34.

perhaps the table-tops would have been made from sawn cross-sections of large trees, such as we see in the Christ Church kitchen at Oxford. There are sundry dripping-pans, ladles, cleavers, scales, rolling pins, kneading troughs, pestle and mortar, a 'Beafe fork' to spear junks of salt beef in barrels; besides '3 Drie Barrels' for flour and meal, '4 wooden pastie-plates,' and no less than fifty-two pewter platters — but not one piece of china or stoneware.[1] Opening from the kitchen was the larder for the storage of meats and other provisions, appropriately placed on the north side of the building.

Returning down the cook's 'way' and through the hall, we enter the 'Lower East Chamber' in the east wing, with studies arranged as we shall presently describe. 'Betwixt' this chamber and the turret is the 'Low Chamber,' a single bedroom-study fitted up by Richard Harris, a brother of the first Mrs. Dunster who early took up residence in the College as a fellow-commoner. Mr. Harris had this 'low' (ground-floor) chamber 'Sieled with Cedar round about,' provided it with glass and casements, a table and form, and a lock and key, and shared the cost of the chimney with the man overhead, at a total cost of £5 19s 11d.[2]

Having completed our survey of the ground floor, we may, before climbing the turret stairs, take a look into the Yard through the north door, whence leads a 'North Alley unto the walk,'[3] probably a flag-stoned path. If so inclined, we may inspect the 'outhouse'[4] of Master Eaton's accounts, which in later college records is more elegantly named the 'House of office.'[5]

CHAMBERS, STUDIES, AND CABINS

Having ascended to the second or 'middle' floor, let us pause to consider the question of chambers and studies. Both words in the Harvard records are to be understood in their medieval sense. A chamber (*cubiculum*) was a large rectangular room which was used as a dormitory for three or more students; a study (*studium, musaeum, musaeolum*) was a small closet-like apartment, structurally comprised within the chamber, where a student kept his books and other personal belongings, and did

1. *C. S. M.*, xv. 61–62. 2. *Id.*, p. 7.
3. *Id.*, p. 34. 4. *Id.*, p. 172.
5. *C. S. M.*, xvi. 522.

CHAMBERS AND STUDIES IN PERSE AND LEGGE BUILDINGS,
GONVILLE AND CAIUS COLLEGE, 1618–19
Floor plan, and sketch of interior of a chamber, showing study.
Letters indicate chambers; numerals, studies

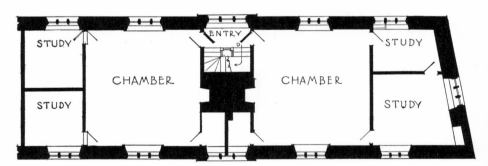

TWO CHAMBERS WITH THEIR STUDIES

EMMANUEL COLLEGE
MIDDLE FLOOR OF BRICK BUILDING, 1633

BRICK BUILDING, EMMANUEL COLLEGE, AND PLAN OF CHAMBERS
AND STUDIES (THE 'HARVARD SET'), ON MIDDLE FLOOR

his reading and writing.[1] This arrangement, monastic in origin, is found in Merton, the earliest English college. The purpose was to afford privacy of study in community of living. Three or more members of the College roomed in each chamber, usually two-a-bed, with trundle-beds for the juniors that could be pushed under the four-posters by day. One of the *camerarii* or chamber-fellows — a term shortened in collegiate slang to 'chum' in the seventeenth century — was always a fellow or other senior student, 'to assist . . . in the maintenance of discipline, and especially to enforce the rule of Latin-speaking.' [2] The studies were contrived in the corners of the chamber so that each had a small window, which explains the irregular fenestration of medieval college buildings. The college builders of the renaissance had to fit in this scheme with regular fenestration; for although they tolerated certain irregularities like turrets, the Palladian ideal of symmetry was beginning to have some influence on window spacing. In the Perse and Legge Buildings constructed at Caius College in 1618-19, the problem was fairly well solved, as appears from the appended picture and plan of the ground floor. These cell-like studies were only about four feet wide and from five to six feet long. The partitions of a study could be taken down and the space thrown into the chamber if by a decrease of enrolment the whole number were not needed; but even with three to a chamber there was ample room for bed space, and for the simple furniture of the day.

A more symmetrical system of fitting studies into chambers may be seen in certain buildings put up at Oxford and Cambridge after 1610. Regular and uniform fenestration was achieved in the Brick Building, Emmanuel, a range of chambers and studies completed in 1634.[3] The sketch of these and adjoining rooms, based on measured drawings, indicates the system: two studies about ten feet square for an interior chamber, two larger corner studies for an end chamber, and a closet between the chimney stack and the outer wall. Other features in the Harvard system are explained by a similar arrangement in Wadham College, Oxford, built in 1610-13, which remains

1. Willis and Clark, *op. cit.*, III. 297-327.
2. Rashdall, II. 484.
3. As the academic year that followed was John Harvard's last, he may well have lived here. On that hypothesis, one of the pleasantest 'sets' (as the chamber and its appurtenances are now called at Cambridge), has been set aside for the Lionel de Jersey Harvard scholar.

substantially unaltered to this day. The buildings, as frequently happens, cost more than the founders expected; and they left the college with a very rough interior. In order to make the chambers and studies habitable, the Warden and Fellows adopted a method that was found equally useful by the President and Fellows of Harvard College. The first occupant of a chamber and study was encouraged to complete and furnish it at his own expense, with the hope of recovering most of the cost from his successor in the form of 'income.' This word, which has frequently puzzled searchers in the early records of Harvard College, has nothing to do with rent; it meant an entrance-fee, a sum paid at coming in. From the manuscript Chamber Book of Wadham College,[1] it seems that the chambers and studies were not all completed until twenty years after they were built. The first occupant of a study paid the expense of fitting up — always including the lock and in some instances the door — and collected the 'income' from his successor, subject to a regular scale of depreciation.[2]

We are now prepared to interpret the list of chambers and studies in the Harvard College records which was drawn up in or about the year 1645. In this list the arabic numerals, mostly representing chambers, are found in the original. I have added a small roman numeral for each study, in order to have a symbol of ready reference between this list and the plan.

Beside this table of chambers and studies we have detailed accounts of the cost of fitting up seventeen studies and three chambers,[3] which prove that 'income' was based roughly on the

1. Placed at my disposal through the kindness of the Warden and Fellows. Extracts from it, including a list of chambers and studies with furnishings, strikingly similar to those of Harvard, may be found in R. B. Gardiner, *Registers of Wadham College,* i. 471 ff.

2. In the Emmanuel College Order Book (ms.) under the date April 8, 1605, and rubric 'Fellowes incomes,' it is provided that 'income' can be paid on the instalment plan if the outgoing fellow agrees. In the Trinity College, Cambridge, Conclusions Book (ms.), p. 75, November 6, 1618, 'It is agreed by the Master and Seniores that upon any fellow leaveth his chamber . . . he which is to succeed by senioritie thereunto, shall either within one week pay the due Income for the same to his predecessor,' or give him security. In the manuscript Register of Magdalene College, Cambridge, 4 May 1641, it is required that the Registrar keep a book wherein 'the Income of all studies and chambers as well of fellowes as schollars shallbe entered before they take possession, and only that summe shalbe accounted repayable Income which shalbe found in his booke . . . and when by abatements the Income shalbe reduced to nothing, no new Income shalbe imposed above the rate of ten shillings.' Cf. Willis and Clark, *op. cit.,* ii. 247 (St. John's College, 1637).

3. *Id.,* pp. 5–14.

The Studdies in Harvard College with their Incomms
and quarterly Rents [1]

			Incomme			Quarters rent	
			li	s	d	s	d
1		Imprimis The Senior Fellow's study in the great chamber	5	0	0	2	6
	ii	in the corner west off the buttery	4	0	0	2	0
	iii	His sizers studdy over the porch off that Chamber	1	10	0	0	9
2	iv	In The lower East chamber the studdy by the Hall ...	3	0	0	1	6
	v	The middle studdy next therto	3	0	0	1	6
	vi	The norther-most studdy in the same row	3	0	0	1	6
	vii	The corner studdy over against it	3	0	0	1	6
3		The low Chamber westward off this betwixt it and the Turret	3	10	0	1	9
4		The studdy with the fire in it over this little chamber ..	3	4	8	1	8
	viii	The little studdy next to it East-ward	1	0	0	0	6
5	ix	In the East middle-chamber the Souther-most studdy .	2	17	6	1	6
	x	The middle studdy	2	12	5	1	4
	xi	The Norther-most study in the same row	3	0	10	1	6
	xii	The corner study over aginst it	2	13	4	1	4
6	xiii	In the highest East Chamber, the Southermost study ..	3	0	0	1	6
	xiv	The middlemost study	2	10	0	1	3
	xv	The norther-most study	2	10	0	1	3
7	xvi	In the turret, the South-East study	2	0	0	1	0
	xvii	The North-East studdy	2	0	0	1	0
	xviii	The North-west study	2	0	0	1	0
	xix	The South-west study	2	0	0	1	0
8		In the Great Chamber next the library, the					
	xx	East study next the Library	2	10	0	1	3
	xxi	The west study in the Corner	3	8	0	1	9
	xxii	The west study with the fire	3	6	5	1	8
	xxiii	The middle west study	2	13	9	1	4
9		In the middle [W.] chamber over the kitchins					
	xxiv	The Souther-most study	2	10	0	1	3
	xxv	The middle study	3	8	5	1	9
	xxvi	The norther-most study	2	10	0	1	3
	xxvii	The corner study over agst it	2	10	0	1	3
10	xxviii	The study in the chamber East off this over the Larder	2	10	0	1	3
11	xxix	In the highest [W.] Chamber over the kitchin the study with the fire	3	5	1	1	3
	xxx	The middlemost study	3	1	3	1	6
	xxxi	The corner study next to it	2	10	0	1	3
	xxxii	The lowest study in the turret	3	0	0	1	6

---

1. *C. S. M.*, xv. 14–15.

first cost; and an additional account of glass furnished by Christopher Grant of Watertown. The number of feet of boards in the study accounts helped us to determine their dimensions. For instance, Sir Downing used 272 feet in his study (xi). Assuming an eight-foot stud, we have made this study 7 feet 9 inches by 5 feet 6 inches. In every case it is clear that the partitions went up to the ceiling, and that the studies, although made after the rest of the building, were well and solidly constructed. They were no mere booths to be knocked down and moved about at will.

The compass directions in this list enable us to place the studies fairly accurately in their several chambers; the detailed accounts indicate their size and fenestration; [1] and from Steward Chesholme's accounts, which show what quarterly rents each student paid, as well as the 'income' debited on acquiring a study and credited on his giving it up,[2] one can even draw up a list of the occupants of each study in the Old College from 1644 to 1655. The usual charges for fitting up a study were for boards, at about three farthings[3] a foot; glass at 10*d* a foot; carpenter's labor at 22*d* a day, 'seeling,' 'calking,' 'gimmels' or 'jimmews' (hinges), locks, sixpenny nails, 'dawbing the walles,' hangings of 'greene say'; and, in the few studies that had a fireplace, bricks, clay, mason's work at 2*s* a day, and 'mentletree.' In most cases the cost of a study on which 'income' was based included that of fitting up a share of the chamber where the owner had a bed.

The appearance of corner studies, especially those under the eaves, must have been very like that in the Legge Building (Caius) as sketched by Professor Willis; but it is possible that more of them were contiguous than we have indicated on the plan, and that they were so fitted in as to appear organic parts of the building, like the studies in Emmanuel and Wadham. Of their furnishings we have no hint; but there must at least have been a folding leaf for writing table, a joint stool, and a shelf for books. Every study had to be lighted from without, for scholars

---

1. *Ibid.*; the amounts of glass and boards used for each study and some chambers are conveniently assembled in *Old-Time New England*, xxiii. 152.

2. At Harvard, unlike Wadham, 'income' was not subject to a scale of depreciation, although there are a few reductions evident in Chesholme's accounts, probably due to dilapidation.

3. Represented in the account by 'ob. q' — halfpenny farthing; cf. Falstaff's tavern bill in Henry IV, act ii. l. 538.

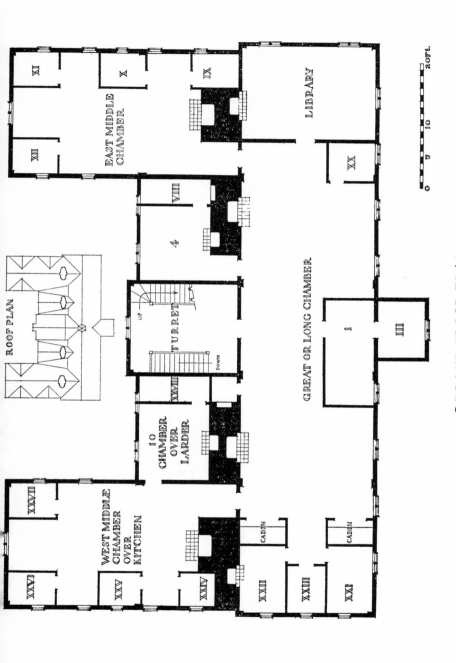

SECOND FLOOR PLAN

MIDDLE OR SECOND FLOOR PLAN OF THE OLD COLLEGE

Drawn by H. R. Shurtleff.

in those days had no midnight oil to burn; and few studies could be placed against a chimney stack so that a fireplace was practicable. One would suppose that the average study, shut off from such warmth as the chamber fireplace might project, would have been unbearably cold in winter. But in those days people expected to be cold in winter, and dressed accordingly. We may suppose that when lectures were going on and no particular occasion called the students to their studies, they sat about a chamber fire talking and smoking, as two visiting Dutchmen found them doing in 1680.

Of chamber furniture we have few hints. No doubt it was very simple: stools rather than chairs, clothes and other effects kept in chests, and fewer beds than students. It was still the fashion at Old Cambridge for students to sleep two in a bed;[1] and from Samuel Sewall's diary we know that he had a 'bed-fellow' as well as 'chamber-fellow' or chum when he lived in the Old College.

Equipped with this information, we may confidently mount the turret stairs and enter the long or great chamber.[2] Except for the space occupied by the library, this room extended the entire length of the building. There must have been enough bed space for twelve or fifteen students; and in addition there was a row of three studies along the west end, one of them with a fireplace. Another lighted corner was occupied by the 'East study next the library.' Where then was the senior fellow's study? Now, the second line in the study list of 1645 was later interpolated by the college scribe; hence the possessive in 'His sizers studdy' refers to the senior fellow in the first line.[3] In order to have his sizar at beck and call, the senior fellow would have had his study adjoining; and as the sizar's study is expressly described as 'over the porch,' his master's study must have been in or near the place indicated on our plan. Such a position, overlooking the main entrance, was the traditional one in the older English colleges for the Master's Lodging, in order that he might observe whosoever passed in and out.[4] But this

1. David Masson, *John Milton* (1859), I. 108.
2. 'Great' in the list just quoted; 'Long' in the list made early in Chauncy's administration (*C. S. M.*, xv. 19) and in Chesholme's S.B. (*C. S. M.*, xxxi. 83, 162.)
3. Cf. manuscript Order Book, Sidney Sussex College: 'Every fellow shall have one study for his syser, which they shall have without any annual rent.' Also *The Eagle*, xxiv. 13, for the same custom at St. John's in 1605.
4. T. G. Jackson, *Wadham College*, p. 143.

study was not popular with senior fellows. After John Bulkeley (A.B. 1642) had finished with it, William Ames (1645) took it on; Samuel Eaton, senior fellow, moved into it in 1651; and after he left Cambridge for New Haven it was occupied successively by Samuel Megapolensis, sophomore son of the Dutch minister at New Amsterdam, and by 'Mr. Bennett,' fellow-commoner, son of the Cromwellian Governor of Virginia.

In the detailed accounts of fitting up the studies, we find two 'cambins' or 'cabins' in the long chamber.[1] One is shared by the two men who fitted up studies xxii and xxiii; the other by Bradford and John Brock, who fitted up two turret studies. 'Cabin,' in the seventeenth century, meant a small room or bedroom, on land as well as at sea; and in that century, fresh air was distinctly not wanted when you slept. Hence we infer that these 'cabins' in the long chamber were sleeping closets, like the Breton *lits-clos*, with two bunks each.[2] Such a sleeping place would have been a boon on winter nights, when snow and biting cold seeped in through the widening cracks in the Old College.

The 'East study next the library,' in the long chamber, fixes the position of the library between the long or great chamber and the east middle chamber. Beyond this fact we have no knowledge of the library's size or arrangements.

The three east chambers offer no difficulty, for the compass directions to the studies in our 1645 list allow no alternative to placing them as they are in our conjectural plan, except that the outer row may have been contiguous, at the expense of air and light to the chambers. In the glass accounts the lowest chamber is called 'Dominus Saltonstalls' and the highest 'Dominus Bellinghams,' indicating that Henry Saltonstall and Samuel Bellingham of the Class of 1642 had charge of them when studying for their master's degrees. By elimination, 'Sir Downing' must have been the senior student in the middle east chamber.

1. *C. S. M.*, xv. 9, 12.

2. In a plan of a fort in Governor Winthrop's Journal (reproduced in *Winthrop Papers*, II. 276–77) there is a 'Seruants Chambre,' with six 'cabbins' to a side, arranged like alcoves in a boys' dormitory. In the old quadrangle at Corpus Christi College, Cambridge (completed 1515), there has recently been discovered a recess in one of the bedrooms that has two bed-places, stepped like a small yacht's bunk under the deck with the transom below. Other chambers in this same quad have closets 6 to 7 feet long and 3 feet deep on each side of the chimney breast, which, for want of light, could not have been studies, and which college tradition very plausibly asserts to have been sleeping closets.

The position of chamber [1] no. 4 'with the fire in it' and 'the little studdy next to it Eastward' (viii) is fixed by their description as over the low chamber. They were fitted up by Thomas Parris, another elderly fellow-commoner, who shared the cost of the chimney with Richard Harris, in the chamber below.

The middle or west chamber 'over the kitchen' seems to have been presided over by the senior tutor, 'Dominus Bulkeley,' [2] who was probably too dignified to sleep among the freshmen in the long chamber. Over the larder was another set of rooms, chamber no. 10 and study no. xxvii, which in the detailed accounts are described as 'Sir Alcocks Bed roome which was to him alone,' and 'Sir Alcocks Study.' 'For the whiteing, lathing, Doore-boards and workmanship of the chamber three bushels of Mault to Richard the mason' were paid by Sir Alcock; one John Tailour did thirteen days' work on the two rooms at 1s 10d a day; nine pair of hinges cost him 3s, 'window-hookes' 4d, glass 3s, and 'plaistring the Study' 1s. In all it cost Sir Alcock £3 1s 3d to finish this private suite; [3] but he could well afford it, for his father, an Oxford alumnus, [4] had died several years before, leaving half the revenue of his farm 'to eaducate my sone John in learninge, together with the wisest improvement of his £40.'

The third or 'highest' floor had but two chambers, in the wings; that over the kitchen had a 'fire study' which was fitted up by John Weld, perhaps on Lady Mowlson's bounty. [5] There remained a great unfinished attic on the south front. Probably it was intended to fit this up when needed as a second long chamber; the addition of Goffe's College in 1652 left it untenanted.

Finally, on the fourth floor of the turret were four small studies which rented for but a shilling a quarter. These were fitted up by Bradford and Prince, the two students from Plymouth Colony, by Comfort Starr, who later became a fellow, and by a son of Master John Cotton. One would suppose that these studies would have been intolerably cold in winter and hot in summer; but they seem always to have been occupied until 1653.

---

1. Called 'study' in the list — evidently a mistake.
2. *C. S. M.*, xv. 4.
3. *Id.*, pp. 10–11.
4. See Appendix B.
5. See Chapter XXI.

From what we know about the arrangement of rooms in the Old College, and about the framing, boarding, and roofing of New England dwelling houses, it has been possible to reconstruct elevations and perspectives of the Old College, which cannot differ very much from its actual appearance. The overhanging stories, steep-pitched roof, and fourteen gables, with their intersecting planes of light and shadow, and the four massive chimney stacks, that pulled the whole composition together, must have presented a very picturesque and pleasing appearance; although the 'refined' taste of the eighteenth century would have considered the building ill-proportioned, fussy, and 'gothick,' and would doubtless have pulled it down had it survived so long. What beauty the Old College possessed, came from its sincere adaptation to the use expected of it. Like all medieval buildings, it was dynamic rather than symmetrical; the builders decided what rooms they wanted, and enclosed them in the simplest possible way. There was no ornament save, possibly, drops from the corners and the glazed 'Lanthorne' mentioned in the early glass accounts. This was a survival of the structures anciently built over the smoke-holes in the roofs of college halls; the Harvard builders paid this tribute to their traditional feeling of what a college should look like,[1] as our imitators of 'colonial' architecture do today. On the turret, probably from a short projecting beam, there hung a bell as early as 1643; this was replaced within fifteen years by another given by Mr. John Willet,[2] and that was exchanged before 1663 for a third bell, the College paying £6 2s 6d to boot.[3] A college clock is mentioned as early as 1660, but whether it was inside or outside is unknown.[4]

Imposing as the Old College was in a 'wilderness,' its 'euill contrivall,' as Dunster complained in 1647, made it subject that early to 'yearely decayes of the rooff, walls, and foundation.'[5] Eaton may have allowed unsound timber to go into the frame, and the master builder may have been careless in other

1. See the plates in Loggan's *Cantabrigia Illustrata*, especially that of Magdalene College; and cf. *N. E. D.*, 'Lantern,' sb. 4, with quotation of 1634–35, 'a tower-like building, almost like your lanthorns in college halls.'

2. *C. S. M.*, xv. 200.

3. *New Englands First Fruits* (Appendix D); *C. S. M.*, xv. 48, 202, 212, and pp. lxxv–lxxvi; cf. A. H. Nichols, 'Bells of Harvard College,' *N. E. H. G. R.*, lxv. 275–84, and printed separately. Since the lanthorn was glazed, the bell could not have been hung there.

4. *C. S. M.*, xv. lxxxvi.   5. *Plymouth Colony Records*, ix. 95.

respects; but the real trouble was that the Old College was built before English housewrights had learned to adapt their craft to the New England climate. Complicated gabling made numerous snow pockets to decay the roof; rock-filled trenches as underpinning, instead of stone cellar walls, made the foundations rot prematurely, and the whole building settle and sag. Hence, the Old College was a constant source of worry and expense to the President and Fellows, and of discomfort to the students. As early as 1651 the Corporation declared the building to be 'in a decaying condition,' requiring 'a considerable charge ere long for a due Repaire.' [1] The next year Dunster describes it as 'ruinous'; [2] but in spite of being 'new groundsilled' at a cost of £127 15s 6d in 1654, 'it remains in other respects, in a very ruinous condition' (complains Chauncy in 1655), so that without a new roof 'some time this Summer both the whole Building will decay . . . and the Scholars will be forced to depart.' [3] In 1663 the roof was reshingled.[4] Indeed, for twenty years after it had been described as 'ruinous' the Old College had to serve; probably only the less leaky chambers and studies, besides the public rooms, remained in use. In 1676–77, library, kitchen, and commons were transferred to Old Harvard Hall. By the next year the 'old Colledge is part of it (besides the turret) fallen down.' [5] The remains apparently were not worth taking down; for Cotton Mather about the year 1695 wrote that the Old College 'is now so mouldred away, that *jam Seges est ubi Troja fuit.*' [6]

FELLOWS' ORCHARD

The first enlargement of the college grounds beyond the Peyntree lot (I) and Eaton's town grant (II) was a lot intended as a garden or orchard where the fellows of the House, like their

1. *Id.*, p. 216.
2. *Mass. Bay Recs.*, IV. pt. I. 91.
3. *C. S. M.*, xv. 213, 184–85; *H. C. S. C.*, Appendix A, doc. 6.
4. *Cambridge Town Records*, p. 148.
5. *Proc. M. H. S.*, IX. 101. 'Repairs of the Edifices' (including fences and the President's Lodge as well as the Old College) cost £337 11s 1d in 1654–63, and £139 10d in 1663–68. *C. S. M.*, xv. 212–14.
6. *Magnalia* (1702), book IV. 129. Mr. C. N. Greenough, in *C. S. M.*, XXVI. 297, shows that the *Magnalia* was being written in 1695, and was approaching completion in 1697. Book IV on the College, excepting the Catalogue of Graduates, must have been completed before July 12, 1696, when news of the disallowance of the Charter of 1692 arrived in Boston; for on p. 131 Mather describes the College as still being governed under that Charter.

precursors at Emmanuel or Trinity, might enjoy all licit recreations.

East of the college lot (I), as we have seen, was Thomas Shepard's property, which, after passing through the hands of Jonathan Mitchell, President Leverett, and the Wigglesworths, finally came to the University in 1794 (VIII), together with the next unit of Cowyard Row, which in 1642 belonged to Richard Champney, ruling elder of Cambridge Church.[1] The cowyard next to the eastward of Champney's belonged in 1642 to Robert Bradish, who lived on the site of Holyoke House. His wife conducted a home brewery whose product was highly appreciated by Harvard students and at least one Harvard president.[2] Their Yard lot was called Bradish's Orchard, indicating that the goodman followed Eaton's example and set out apple trees; after changing owners several times it came to the College in 1805 as part of the Sewall lot (IX).[3]

Just east of Thomas Shepard's houselot, Field Lane [4] crossed Braintree Street, and when reaching a point near the rear of the Shepard house made a right-hand turn, giving access to the Champney Cowyard, to Bradish's Orchard, and to the next three-quarter-acre cowyard, which especially interests us. In 1642 it was owned by Thomas Marrett, shoemaker.[5] Shortly after, this lot provided the first example of Harvard alumni clubbing together to purchase land for alma mater. John Bulkeley and George Downing of the Class of 1642, the first tutors (or, as they were often called, fellows) of Harvard College, together with Samuel Winthrop and John Alcock of the Class of 1646,

1. *Cambridge Proprietors' Records*, p. 78; cf. p. 22. Shepard probably acquired this before his death.

2. See *H. C. S. C.*, Chapter V, or S. E. Morison, *Builders of the Bay Colony*, pp. 203–04.

3. In 1700 the executors of Thomas Danforth sold 'Bradishes Orchard Sometimes Called Mr Rawsons Orchard of late called . . . Mr Danforths Orchard,' measuring ¾ acre, to Aaron Bordman (1649–1703), college cook and Steward (Middlesex Deeds, East Cambridge Registry of Deeds, XIII. 324). Aaron's son Andrew sold it in 1727 to Edward Wigglesworth (A.B. 1710), the first Hollis Professor of Divinity (*id.* XXVII. 205–07), whose daughter Rebecca married Stephen Sewall (A.B. 1761), Hancock Professor of Hebrew, whose nephew sold it to Harvard College as the 'Sewall lot' in 1805 (*id.*, LXV. 73–74, CXVIII. 260–61, CLX. 277; Middlesex Probate Records, XCV. 365). The house on it, probably built by the Sewalls, stood until about 1854.

4. The original Linden Street, but not reaching Braintree Street (Massachusetts Avenue) at the same point.

5. *Cambridge Proprietors' Records*, p. 87; Paige, p. 603; for earlier owners, see pp. 52 (Stebbins) and 24 (Goodman) of the *Records*.

purchased from 'Patre-familias Marrit' his lot, which they proceeded to plant with apple trees, and to name *Pomarium Sociorum*, or the Fellows' Orchard. It was doubtless intended, like the fellows' gardens in English colleges, as a place of recreation for the teaching staff.[1] On December 20, 1645, as he was going to England, 'Johannes Bulkleius, nuper studens Collegii Harvardini,' set a good example in generosity, though not in Latin, by this deed of gift: 'Dono Henricum Dunsterum dicti Collegii Harvardini Presidem, . . . mea parte Illius Jugeris, quod Ipse cum Domino Downingo,[2] Samuele Winthropo et Johane Alcocke eminus a Patre-familias Marrit; viz. Quarta parte pomarii dudum a nobis plantati, et dimidium reliqui manentis adhuc agrestis' — in other words, a quarter share of the orchard, and half the rest, still remaining uncultivated.[3] And if the said President shall die or resign, 'ut Collegium tanquam λεπτὸν Tenue, ab alumno maxime benevolo sibi in perpetuum appropriaret.'[4] In order (as I imagine) to discharge debts for commons and sizings, the other three owners must have deeded their shares in the orchard to Matthew Day, the college Steward; for it was he who, as he lay dying in 1649, declared, 'I doe give with all my heart all that part I have in the Garden unto the fellowes of Harvard Colledge for ever.'[5] After providing a shady refuge and (if the Cambridge urchins permitted) a certain amount of fruit for colonial fellows and tutors, this *pomarium sociorum* was chosen as the site of Gore Hall in 1841; and what part of it still remains uncovered by the Widener Library and Wigglesworth Hall is now used for a professors' parking space — the twentieth-century equivalent of a fellows' garden.

1. The Diary of Samuel Ward, in M. M. Knappen, *Two Elizabethan Puritan Diaries*, tells of bowling, eating fruit, and strolling in the Fellows' Garden at Emmanuel.

2. The *Dominus* (Latin for the baccalaureate 'Sir') establishes the date of the purchase as before Commencement, 1645, when Downing became *Magister*, and after December, 1643, when he and Bulkeley were appointed tutors. Winthrop did not graduate, but appears in the early study list.

3. This indicates that they had also purchased that part of Champney's property across Field Lane from Marrett's lot, and between it and Braintree Street; for the Fellows' Orchard at the time it came to Harvard measured 1¼ acres (*C. S. M.*, xv. 200–01), and in Marrett's hands in 1642 only ¾ acre.

4. *C. S. M.*, xv. 205–06.

5. *C. S. M.*, xv. cxxxiii n. A copy of the nuncupative will is in the Dunster Mss., H. U. Archives; printed in Samuel A. Green, *Ten Fac-simile Reproductions Relating to New England* (1902), pp. 9–10. Cf. Thomas Danforth's record of gifts, in *C. S. M.*, xv. 200–01.

XXI

THE QUEST FOR REVENUE [1]
1640–1650

University colleges of the Old World had been provided at their foundation with suitable buildings and a sufficient endowment; but when Dunster became President of Harvard College (August 27, 1640), the first building was still 'erecting,' and there was not a penny of revenue on which he could count to meet expenses. The sum of £400 voted in 1636 was simply a credit, against which specific appropriations made to the College were charged off; not the nucleus of an endowment. Everything hitherto received from John Harvard's legacy, or from other donors, had been spent on building — or carried off by Eaton. Harvard College had no landed estate, rents, annuities, funds, or income-yielding property of any sort. A good beginning was made by the General Court in assigning the Charlestown ferry rents to the College; but the financial prospect, forlorn at best, became so desperate when the economic depression of 1641 set in [2] as to daunt anyone without the faith, courage, and youth of Henry Dunster.

Happily his personal wants were relieved by marrying the widow Glover in 1641; and although she lived but two years, he

1. Samuel A. Eliot, Treasurer of Harvard College from 1842 to 1853, compiled a 'Catalogue of Donations' which is now in the H. U. Archives. A digest of it is incorporated in Eliot's *Sketch of the History of Harvard College*. Inaccurate and incomplete in many instances, this catalogue is largely superseded by the publication of the Harvard College Records (*C. S. M.*, xv, xvi). The later history of such properties as were still retained by the College after 1750 can be traced in the 'Lands' series of volumes, and the College Treasurers' MS. Journals in the H. U. Archives, the Treasurers' printed *Reports* and *Statements*, in numerous town histories and records. In this chapter, I have not attempted to describe all donations to the College; for college silver, see *H. C. S. C.*, Chapter V; for books, see above, Chapter XIX, and *H. C. S. C.*, Chapter XIV. Mr. G. Philip Bauer (A.M. 1929) has done most of the research for this chapter, at the expense of Mr. Allston Burr (A.B. 1889).

2. See above, pp. 253–55.

had the management of her property after her death. Apparently the General Court felt that this windfall absolved them from the obligation to provide the President with an honorable and regular emolument, such as heads of English colleges enjoyed. The salary promised him when elected President, 'yea with suitable advance of the stipend in case' he 'should marry,' was paid to Dunster for but one year, after which he got what he could from the Charlestown ferry rent, students' tuition fees, Commencement fees, and an occasional special grant.[1] The Committee to Investigate the College reported in 1654 that his average annual receipts from these sources for fourteen years had been £55 13s 10d, and recommended that he be paid the difference between that sum and what he had been promised, which was not done.[2] Even according to seventeenth-century standards, that was a miserably inadequate stipend; and the College certainly owes a debt of gratitude to the widow Glover, whose love cheered the first president in his well-nigh impossible undertaking, and whose property enabled him and the College to carry on.

THE COUNTRY'S GIFT

Yet, after all, it was the New England community, and more particularly the Bay jurisdiction, that shouldered the main financial burden. Harvard College was founded with the £400 voted by the General Court in 1636. Let us first see what became of the 'Countrys Gifte,' as this donation was called in the college records. Although half this sum had been promised for 1637, and the balance when the Old College was finished, no payment was made before 1639; and by May 16, 1644, when the Colony Treasurer had an accounting with the College, his total disbursements on account of the Country's Gift amounted to but £227 12s.[3] Since nothing had been paid after 1642, and most of the sums received also figure in Samuel Shepard's build-

---

1. Dunster's Memorandum, in Appendix E; cf. his letter of September 18, 1643, a few pages below. In 1647 the General Court voted him £56 as compensation for short salary the previous years.

2. *Mass. Bay Recs.*, II. 200. It is not clear what he had been promised in 1640 — probably £100, since the Committee recommended £80 as the President's salary in future, and remarked that the use of a house kept in repair by the College and 'landes adiacent' would 'make his maentenance as good as 100 *li* per anum.' *H. C. S. C.*, Appendix A, doc. 2.

3. *C. S. M.*, xv. 21.

ing accounts, it seems certain that the entire sum had gone toward building the Old College.

We may easily guess the explanation of this tardy paying by instalments. The Colony had no treasury in the modern sense. Taxes, especially during the depression, were paid in perishable commodities. Probably the Board of Overseers preferred to use up first the portion in hand of John Harvard's legacy, which they had no means of investing, and to let the Colony's £400 remain on the books as a credit, drawing upon it by instalments. When the Overseers asked for something on account, the Colony Treasurer turned over to the College a 'rate' of this or that town.[1] Thus, between 1639 and 1642 the College received four Cambridge rates, amounting to £122 12s 6d, and one Watertown rate of £30 12s. This was a sensible arrangement which avoided the unnecessary transport of corn from those towns to Boston, and then back to Cambridge; the town constable was simply authorized to pay over his local collections to Shepard of the building committee, or to President Dunster, instead of to the Colony Treasurer. These rates were, of course, paid in kind; and thrifty or impoverished planters naturally tried to work off their mouldy corn and spoiled provisions on the College; hence Shepard claimed £11 8s 9d abatement 'for insufficient pay,' and the Colony Treasurer added that amount to the college credit.[2]

In addition to these instalments met out of the rates, the Colony in 1642 paid a college lumber bill of £10, advanced £8 7s 6d to the President, and handed over to the College £56 from the English contributions secured by the Weld-Peter begging mission (of which more anon). This last sum, as the accounting of 1647 proves, was not debited to the Country's Gift.

A few months before Treasurer Tyng made his accounting of May 16, 1644, another (and, as it proved, the final) instalment of John Harvard's legacy, £175 3s, was deposited in the Bay treasury by Harvard's executor. This sum, added to the Country's Gift, and the abatement 'for insufficiency of pay,' made a total credit of £586 11s 9d. Deducting payments made to or on behalf of the College, there was a balance due of £470 19s 9d.

---

1. 'Rate' was used in Massachusetts Bay before 1646 in the contemporary English sense of a tax levy. The Cambridge rate meant that town's proportion of the total colony levy.

2. C. S. M., xv. 21.

President Dunster immediately requested payment of this sum, but was put off 'till the next session.' [1]

During that session the whole balance was not discharged, but on November 14, 1644, the Court appropriated £150 'to be gathered by the Treasurer for the colledge out of the mony due for the children sent out of England, to be expended for a house to be built for the said president, in part of the 400*l* promised unto him for his use, to belong to the colledge'; [2] and on November 4, 1646, another £100 was voted to Dunster 'to be paid him out of the next country rate in part of his debt.' [3]

The following year Dunster asked for an accounting; the Court consented, and on October 27, 1647, voted: [4]

First, we find due from the country to the colledge, out of that which was given by severall donors in England, 133 *l*, ... £133 00 0

2ly, there is supposed to be due to the colledge upon the countrys gifte, ...   190 16 0

3ly, we find due to the colledge, in relation to the president having falen short so much of that which he should have received annually from the country, ...   056 00 0

The first item was a not very accurate statement of the Lady Mowlson scholarship and other English donations, which we shall come to shortly; the last was in the nature of a salary grant; the second represented what the General Court believed to be still due from the £400 voted in 1636, and the balance of the Harvard legacy. Exactly how they computed this sum of £190 16*s* we have no data to determine; but we may make a near guess. The total college credit, as we have seen, consisting of the Country's Gift, the balance of John Harvard's legacy, and the 'insufficient pay' allowance, was £586 11*s* 9*d*. Before the accounting of 1644, £171 12*s* had been advanced, and since that time £250 had been paid to President Dunster. These payments would leave a balance of about £165 in the Colony Treasurer's hands, instead of the £190 16*s* that the General Court admitted. The difference of about £25 probably repre-

1. *Mass. Bay Recs.*, II. 70.
2. *Id.*, p. 84. For the children's money, see below, p. 312.
3. *Id.*, p. 176. By 'his debt' the Court doubtless meant its own debt to the College, which, we should remember, was not incorporated until 1650.
4. *Id.*, p. 200.

sented an unrecorded gift which the Treasurer had taken in charge.

Immediately following this accounting of October 27, 1647, the Court declared: 'we conceive it reasonable that there should be 50*l* taken out of the 190*l* 16*s*, and paid to Mr Davison, according as the president doth desire'; and that the balance of £140 16*s* 'be forthwith paid to the colledge, or otherwise to allow not exceeding 8 per cento to the colledge so long as it lyes in the handes of the country.' [1]

Obviously it was not then convenient for the General Court to discharge the balance due. But on October 15, 1650, after Dunster had twice petitioned for it, the Treasurer was 'ordred to pay the president of the colledge the sume of one hundred pounds, with two yeares forbearance for what is past, as also for the time to come vntill it be payd, which shalbe out of the next leuy. . . .' [2]

Assuming that all these specified appropriations were actually paid to Dunster — and there is no reason to suppose that they were not [3] — the College had, by October, 1650, consumed all but £40 of the Country's Gift, together with the balance received on

1. *Mass. Bay Recs.*, II. 200. Nicholas Davison is again mentioned on p. 205, in connection with Mrs. Glover.

2. Mass. Archives, LVIII. 19; also *Mass. Bay Recs.*, III. 214. The Court had already promised in June, 1650, to pay the £100 in reply to another petition of Dunster. *Id.*, III. 208.

3. Quincy (*History*, I. 473) and Mr. Matthews (*C. S. M.*, XV. cv) too readily concluded that Dunster never received the £150 appropriated in 1644, and failed to notice the appropriations of 1646 and 1650. Dunster, in his several communications to the General Court that have been preserved, never stated that these moneys were not paid, nor did he state that he had built the Lodge at his own expense; he merely asserted in his petition of November 10, 1654 (quoted *ibid.*), that 'its the place which upon very damagefull cond[ici]ons to myself, out of loue to the College I haue builded viz by taking contry pay in lieu of bils payd in England or the sayd house had not been built. . . .' The obvious meaning of these words is not that Dunster built the Lodge at his own expense, which would make the clause about taking country pay meaningless, but that he lost by accepting corn, etc., instead of insisting on bills of exchange, which would have yielded the full amount; consequently he had to make up the difference out of his own pocket. (Incidentally, see Dunster's letter of September 18, 1643, printed two pages below, showing him asking for payment 'in kinde' rather than assignment of rates.) Dunster goes on to say that 'a very considerable part' of the Lodge 'was given me at my request out of respect to myself albeit for the College.' This I take to mean that the Lodge cost more than was expected, when some of the President's friends paid the balance. In another petition of November 4, 1654 (*C. S. M.*, XV. cv), Dunster alludes to the 'singular industry thorow great difficultyes' with which he 'erected' the Lodge, but does not assert that he paid for it. It must be remembered that Dunster, writing under a strong sense of injustice, and clinging to his home, was emphasizing his own share, and not making a judicial apportionment of cost.

account of £175 3s of John Harvard's legacy. And already, on September 14, the General Court had ordered all accounts to be squared:

The Court, being informed that the present condition of the colledge at Cambridge calls for supply, doe order, that Cambridge rate for this yeare, now to be collected, be payd in to the steward of the colledge, for the discharge of any debt due from the country to the said colledge, and if there be any ouerplus, to be and remayne as the colledge stocke . . . [1]

Although no record can be found of what the Cambridge rate of 1650 brought in, there is no doubt that it satisfied the College Corporation; for no further claim was made on the General Court in respect of Harvard's legacy or the Country's Gift.[2] It is certain, then, that President Quincy's strictures on the General Court[3] were unfounded, and that the Governor and Company of the Massachusetts Bay not only discharged *in full* their promise made in 1636, but acted as faithful trustees for such part of John Harvard's legacy as his executor left in their hands.

Although the College received her just dues, it was exasperating to be assigned rates of this or that town. Local constables were supposed to collect the specified sums, and hand them over to the College; but they were sometimes delinquent in collecting, as the people were in paying. Collections were mostly in kind, and in the worst kind that would pass the constable's inspection; some of the more powerful and avaricious paid only at their convenience, and the less fortunate made heartrending

1. *Mass. Bay Recs.*, III. 331.

2. It is only on the assumption that the General Court had paid up in full that we can explain the absence of any claim to the contrary, among the 'debts due to the Colledge' or the 'sums in the hands of the Country Treasurer,' in Treasurer Danforth's reports for 1654 and the years that follow (*C. S. M.*, xv. 209, 215–16, 54–56, 225), although the Mowlson scholarship fund held for the College by the Colony is repeatedly mentioned. The rather obscure reference to £400 in the Committee Report of May 3, 1654 (*H. C. S. C.*, Appendix A, doc. 2), does not, I take it, refer to the Country's Gift, but to a possible appropriation from the town contributions of that time.

3. Quincy, I. 41, 474. Contemporary conditions doubtless had something to do with his conclusion. Quincy was constantly meeting the contention that the College had been nourished by the Colony, and was now playing traitor to the puritan fathers by going Unitarian and liberal; hence he was eager to prove that State aid had been a negligible part of the college income, even in its infancy. Treasurer Samuel A. Eliot, in his *Sketch* of 1848, illustrates the argument by comparative statistics (pp. 153–87), which are not complete, although he did not go so far as Quincy in asserting that the £400 had never been paid.

appeals to Dunster to let them off completely. A letter from the President to the Colony Treasurer, dated September 18, 1643, throws a vivid light on his difficulties in keeping the College alive under such circumstances, and emphasizes the President's complete identification of his own interests with those of Harvard: [1]

Worthy sir

Being informed that there is a part of the goods that bee com over in the late ships that belong to the colledge: therefore being unwilling to troble the whole court with the busines I thought it sufficient to acquaint you with my mynd so much rather because you haue received in my accounts for the last yeer: [2] and may when you please (on two dayes warning) for this year since the beginning of October 1642 to the same 1643. Now two things doe I desyre — : one fir[st] that which is coming to the Colledge may bee payd mee in kinde: for the last years rate which was given mee, [3] besydes all the delays and over pervailing intreaties of some poore neighbours that thought themselves overcharged and so haue got partly some releases, and many whole forbearance even to this day: this disconvenience hath been distractive that I was to receive it at so many mens hands: and albeit the constables should haue saved mee this labour: yet our neighbours knowing I should receive it inevitably appealed from them to myself. yea also that gross sum of 40 *li* that was to be payd from one man hath not; nor indeed could it bee payd without distraction to myself in accounts, and turnings over: and unwillingness in some to receive there, with som words of complaint as if their expectation were not answered in that which they received. where in they in a sort both blamed myselfe because they received not satisfaction at my hands immediately: and him from whom they had it, though [both] of us causlesly. Therefore my first desyre is that the colledge may have its due in kynde if this may bee no offence: els I submit.

The second thing is this. That you would bee pleased to informe those whom It may concerne that hitherto with all conscionable and diligent providence that I could: haue I disburst and expended what ever hath Come to hand in mere buildings for the house. and seeing that now that work in this house will draw to a period (though haply 30 *li* will not fully finish it yet) I desyre to know whether the country will allow mee any personall interest in any of the sayd goods; [4] for

1. *Mass. Archives*, ccxl. 58.
2. These accounts have not been preserved.
3. The Cambridge rate of 1642, listed in *C. S. M.*, xv. 21.
4. The goods sent over by Weld and Peter. Evidently this suggestion appealed to the General Court, for the grant of £150 for the President's Lodge on November 14,

and in consideration of the abatements that I haue suffered from sixty to fifty, from fifty to 45*li*, from 45*li* to thirty, which is now in rent from the ferry,[1] and you know in what manner in my family charged and by my tenants discharged. I was and am willing Considering the poverty of the country to descend to the Lowest step; if there can bee nothing comfortably allowd mee: I still sit down appeased. Desyring no more but what may supply mee and myne with food and rayment; (and to giue every one their own) to the furtherance of the success of our labours for the good of the Church and commonwealth, without distraction in the work wherunto I am called; and by Gods greate mercy and goodness chearfully therin abyde; desyring your prayers, for a continuance: and that prayses to God for the sanctiffying off all the passages of his fatherly providence towards

Your loving and much bounden

HENRIE DUNSTER

Cambr. Septembris. 18th. 1643.

THE CHARLESTOWN FERRY

The Charlestown ferry rent, to which Dunster here alludes, was the most substantial and lasting financial contribution that the College received from the Colony, and for a time the only certain income. For some centuries past, a common practice of English monarchs for rewarding faithful services, or aiding some worthy cause, was to earmark specific revenues, or a fractional part of them, for the beneficiary. On October 7, 1640, the General Court of Massachusetts Bay followed this ancient precedent in granting to Harvard College the revenues of the Boston-Charlestown ferry.[2] A glance at the map will show the importance of this ferry across the mouth of the Charles. It offered much the shortest route from Boston to Charlestown, Cambridge, Watertown, Medford, and all the 'plantations' in Middlesex County; and at Charlestown began the way to Connecticut. The ferry had been authorized as early as 1630, and let out to one Edward Converse the next year, he undertaking to pay the Colony a certain sum for the privilege of charging twopence

---

1644, was 'to be gathered by the Treasurer for the Colledge out of the mony due for the children sent out of England,' *Mass. Bay Recs.*, II. 84.

1. See next section of this chapter.

2. *Mass. Bay Recs.*, I. 304. Similarly, a large proportion of the income of William and Mary College, chartered in 1693, came from crown revenues in Virginia specifically assigned to the College.

per person, or a penny a head if there were two or more. In 1637, the Governor and Treasurer had been instructed to sign a new lease at £40 per annum. Converse, who again obtained the privilege, proved neglectful, and was the cause of drowning three passengers by using a 'canooe' instead of a skiff. The Court was still looking for a competent ferryman when Dunster became President.[1] Someone then conceived the plan of granting the ferry privilege to the College, she undertaking to keep the ferry running at the usual rates, and to get what she could out of the ferryman, so long as he kept within the statutory toll.

This Charlestown ferry was the cause of much vexation to Court and College. Ferrymen were rude fellows — perhaps of necessity, for they had tough customers. In 1646 the lessees, James Hayden and Francis Hudson, claimed that the College had driven too hard a bargain, and begged the Court either to cancel the free list of magistrates and deputies, or make a grant for such public service; the Court declared that public officials must pay toll, for which the Colony treasury would reimburse them.[2] In 1648 the lessees again petitioned:

That notwithstanding all Former orders for the regulating off the said Ferry, yet many times passengers will not only disorderly press into our boats, but sundry escape out of them and will not pay their fare at all; some on pretences they haue nothing to pay; some pretending they are on the countryes service; whereby it comes to pass, that albeit as many are transported as ever, yet the ferry was never less able to be sufficiently maintained, and attended. . . . And as for the payment which generally is made, it is usually in such refuse, unwrought, broken, unstringed, and unmerchantable peag, at 6 a penny, that wee neither can ourselves make use thereoff, without evident loss of 2d at the shilling . . . nor can wee with comfort or good conscience pay our rents to the president, who hath sundry times witnessed the loss he is forced to suffer by the said peag. . . .[3]

This matter of peag was another cross for President Dunster. Although the Court had thoughtfully provided that licensed fur traders must buy not more than £25 worth of wampum annually from the College, if offered, at the current price,[4]

1. *Id.*, I. 81, 88, 208, 246, 290, 292.
2. *Mass. Archives*, cxxi. 7–8. The decision is in Governor Winthrop's handwriting.
3. *Id.*, p. 15. 'Peag' is wampum, Indian shell money, which was legal tender in the New England colonies for small sums.
4. *Mass. Bay Recs.*, I. 323 (1641).

this was not easy to enforce. Dunster complained in 1648 that all the 'badd and unfinished peague' that the Indians worked off on their customers returned to the College as ferry toll, and was then refused when tendered to fur traders. He proposed that the New England Confederation regulate this fractional currency, and that all imitation wampum (made of stone or of white shells dyed black) tendered by the Indians be treated as counterfeit coin, and destroyed forthwith.[1]

In return, the ferrymen were complained of for 'miscarriage' or insolence by the Deputies. Yet during Dunster's administration the Charlestown ferry provided the largest certain revenue from outside sources. At the beginning, it would seem, the College farmed it out for the annual rent of £30.[2] It was certainly let for £40 in 1654;[3] and in Treasurer Danforth's 'abbreviate of the Colledge accounts' from October, 1654, to December, 1663, he notes that £328 10s was received 'by rent of Charlestown ferry in Peage at 8 a penny,'[4] an average of less than £37 per annum.

By that time there were two fresh sources of woe for the ferrymen. First, 'the wante of small money for Cheange: by such persons that doe pass ouer the said ferry: So as that many times we are forced to trust those whom we cary ouer: And many times neuer haue our pay but doe our Labour for noe thing: which is more then we cane beare.'[5] As a remedy to this currency shortage, they hoped that the Court might shortly supplement the pine-tree coinage with twopenny bits and groats. The second, and more serious, evil was the completion in 1662 of the 'Great Bridge' over the Charles between Cambridge and Brighton.[6] 'Many persons,' allege the petitioners, 'which formerly did pass ouer: Come not to us now; but pass

1. Mass. Archives, II. 326; *Mass. Bay Recs.*, II. 200–01; *id.* III. 207–08, 214, 432. Also in *Plym. Col. Recs.*, IX. 136–37.

2. Dunster's letter, p. 299 above; but Samuel Shepard's building account (*C. S. M.*, xv. 17) for 1639 includes under receipts 'of the ferry £50.' Probably he was mistaken in the date, and £50 represents the sum realized the first year, or two years.

3. *H. C. S. C.*, Appendix A, doc. 2; *C. S. M.*, xv. xxi.

4. *Id.*, p. 213. On the debit side, he notes 'to loss in peage received at 8 a penny,' £55 6s 11d; not all of this was necessarily from the ferry rent, since Chesholme's steward's accounts note occasional receipts of wampum for college dues.

5. Petition of Francis Hudson and John Burrage, May 8, 1662, *Mass. Archives*, cxxi. 34.

6. This bridge, very near the site of the Anderson Bridge, was the only one over the Charles below Watertown until 1785, when the Charles River Bridge was opened at the site of the old Charlestown ferry.

ouer Cambridge Bridge: many horsis also which did formarly Add to our benifett by passing ouer the said ferry doe now pase ouer the said Bridge: so that since it hath been built: we are de-priued of a great part of our profitt.' 'Fortie pounds by the yeare,' they conclude, 'is to great a Summe for us to pay.' In answer, the Deputies proposed to scale down the rent to £30; but the ferrymen's petition is endorsed, 'The magist[rate]s Consent not.' [1] Nevertheless, the College obtained but £27 from ferry rent in 1668, 'besides the ferrage of the Corporation,' who crossed free.[2] Goodman Hudson doubtless felt better in 1670, when the town of Cambridge was authorized to levy tolls on the Great Bridge in order to keep it in repair;[3] and by 1674 Charlestown ferry traffic had picked up so that he agreed to pay the Corporation £40 per annum again for seven years, after which the rent was raised £10.[4] The General Court of the Prov-ince confirmed the original grant in 1693,[5] and by 1696 the College was farming it out for £60 per annum.[6] Throughout the first half of the eighteenth century the rent continued to in-crease, and as late as 1747 the Corporation claimed that this was 'a considerable Part of the Support of the College.' [7]

If New England had been old England, Harvard College would still be deriving an immense revenue from all passengers crossing the Charles by its several bridges. As it was, the Col-lege was 'devested of its right' in 1785, as President Quincy wrote, when the Charles River Bridge was built from Boston to Charlestown. The bridge corporation was required to pay to the College £200 or $666.66 per annum for forty years, when the bridge was to become State property, 'saving to the said College a reasonable and annual compensation for the annual income of the ferry, which they might have received, had not said bridge been erected.' [8] When this corporation was made bankrupt by the State's building a free bridge next to its property, in 1828, the annuity came to an end; and the only compensation made to the College for the loss of this ancient source of income was a State grant of $3,333.30 in lieu of five years' income, in 1846.[9]

1. *Mass. Archives*, cxxi. 34.
2. *C. S. M.*, xv. 216.   3. Paige, pp. 195–96.
4. Treasurer Richards' ms. accounts, 1669–93, H. U. Archives, p. 12.
5. *Acts and Resolves of the Providence of Mass. Bay*, vii. 452.
6. *C. S. M.*, xvi. 413.   7. *Id.*, p. 766.
8. Quincy, ii. 271–72.
9. *Id.*, pp. 403–04, 594–95; College Treasurer's *Report* for 1846–47, p. 3.

The Weld-Peter Mission and the Lady Mowlson Scholarship

The Weld-Peter begging mission, which one may call, in modern terms, the first concerted 'drive' to obtain income and endowment for the College, began early. On June 2, 1641, the General Court entreated their respective churches to release Hugh Peter of Salem, Thomas Weld of Roxbury, and William Hibbens of Boston 'to go for England upon some weighty occasions for the good of the countrey, as is conceived.'[1] Governor Winthrop explained, putting the best 'occasions' first and the real reasons last, that the objects were 'to congratulate the happy success there' of the puritan party, to explain the New England depression 'to satisfy our creditors,' to distribute information on Congregational polity, and 'to make use of any opportunity God should offer for the good of the country here.' This last meant, in plain words, to raise money, although Winthrop made it clear that these ministers of good will and advice 'should not seek supply of our wants in any dishonorable way, as by begging or the like, for we were resolved to wait upon the Lord in the use of all means which were lawful and honorable.'[2] Since begging becomes 'solicitation' when done by a college or institution, there was sure to be no trouble about that; although the caution to 'wait upon the Lord' in a dignified manner was certainly not supererogatory when applied to Hugh Peter.

It brings home to us the isolation of New England to find that the three agents, although eager to get across and to work, could find no direct passage for England. They were forced to take ship to Newfoundland, where Hugh Peter had a pleasant time preaching to the fishermen. 'We were 14 dies from New-England thither,' wrote John Winthrop, Jr. (who had joined the party unofficially). 'We staied there thre weekes before we found a ship ready to sett saile for England. From thence we were 20 daies before we arrived in England; having very foule weather, continuall stormes betweene Newfoundland and Eng-

---

1. *Mass. Bay Recs.*, I. 332.
2. Winthrop, *Journal* (1908 ed.), II. 31.

land, and our ship very small, about 60 tunnes. But it pleased God to deliver vs out of all those many dangers we were almost every day in, so as we are now at Bristoll in safety (praised be His name).'[1]

It was now the end of September, 1641, and a strange England met the eyes of our three agents — a newer England, in some respects, than the one they had left. Irish massacre; Grand Remonstrance; Bishops committed to the Tower; impeachment of the Five Members; Nineteen Propositions; Committee of Public Safety; and, in August, 1642, civil war. Nevertheless, the faithful were generous to New England, and Mr. Hibbens returned before the year was out, bearing some £500 in contributions for the Colony.

This was encouraging, but only a beginning. In order to secure really big contributions, the agents wanted 'literature' to play up the best 'selling points' of New England. It may be assumed that Weld and Peter sent an urgent requisition for a moving description of the benighted state of the Indians, and their desire to hear the Gospel; a first-hand, convincing account of Harvard College; and a smart write-up of natural resources and wonder-working providences, to attract the right sort of emigrants. Hence the famous tract of twenty-six pages, 'New Englands First Fruits' (London, 1643),[2] to which we owe so much for our knowledge of early Harvard.

'New Englands First Fruits' was a promotion pamphlet; one half-expects to find in it a return postcard, on receipt of which 'our representative will call.' It is probable that President Dunster supplied the material for the Indian section, since he was a pioneer in work among the New England redskins;[3] and almost certain that he had the leading hand in compiling part two, 'In respect of the Colledge, and the proceedings of *Learning* therein'; although the encomiums on 'master *Dunster*,' that 'learned conscionable and industrious man,' prove that he did

1. 5 *Coll. M. H. S.*, VIII. 35.
2. Printed in full in Appendix D.
3. Thomas Lechford, in 1641, praised Dunster above all others in that respect; 'he hath the plat-forme and way of conversion of the Natives indifferent right, and much studies the same. . . . He will make it good, that the way to instruct the Indians must be in their owne language, not English; and that their language may be perfected.' *Plaine Dealing* (1642), p. 53. It will be observed that this is the very line that John Eliot followed five years later, and to a fairly successful conclusion; Eliot does not seem to have been interested in Indians so early.

MASTER HUGH PETER

not actually write it. This account of the College concludes with 'a Letter sent over from the Governour, and diverse of the Ministers' on 'The manner of the late Commencement,' dated at Boston three days later, on September 26, 1642. In it was enclosed a copy of the printed theses, which in 'First Fruits' are reprinted verbatim — fortunately for us, since no copy of the original broadside has survived. This was just the stuff to prove that Harvard College was a going concern, and not a college on paper, like the Virginian institution for which so much money had been collected twenty-five years before.

The concluding part of the pamphlet, concerning the religion, climate, and products of New England, together with sure evidence that the Lord had not withdrawn his guiding hand from the Colony, was in the nature of counter-propaganda to Lord Warwick and his friends, who were promoting tropical plantations in the West Indies.[1]

From Hugh Peter, it is not likely that the cause received any further assistance. Six months in Ireland as chaplain to the parliamentary army had renewed his taste for a life of action; and when, early in 1643, Parliament issued a call for contributions to the Protestant sufferers in Ireland, Hugh undertook to handle this 'drive' in the Low Countries, where he knew the ropes. He is credited with having raised some £30,000 through his eloquent and heartrending orations on the sufferings of Irish Protestants.[2] After a striking success of this kind, the business of wheedling shillings out of pious old women for the heathen in New England was beneath Master Peter's attention.

1. Mr. Worthington C. Ford, in *Proc. M. H. S.*, XLII, 259–66, points out the intimate personal knowledge of the writer with events in New England before 1641, his strong bias against the Hutchinsonians (the ghost of religious freedom was continually rising up to plague New Englanders in England at that time), a striking parallel between passages in the *First Fruits* and Weld's *Innocency Cleared*, and indications that this part was composed in England. Mr. Ford thinks that Hugh Peter also had a hand in it. Mr. Raymond P. Stearns, who is writing the life of Hugh Peter, makes the following points for Peter's share in the authorship: the preoccupation with material resources, characteristic of him and of his interests when in New England; the mention of Holland, with which Peter was well acquainted, in answer to objection 5; the statement on the absence of beggars on p. 23, parallel to his autobiographical fragment in *The Case of Mr. Hugh Peters Impartially Communicated* (London, 1660), p. 3: 'among thousands there dwelling, I never saw any drunk, nor heard an Oath, nor any begging, nor Sabbath broken'; and the reference to Peter's particular hobby, the transporting of poor children. But Mr. Stearns admits that the style is not Peter's, and agrees with Mr. Ford that Weld had the major part in the actual composition of *First Fruits*.

2. But he had numerous helpers. *Memoirs of Edmund Ludlow* (C. H. Firth ed., 1894), II. 312.

So Master Weld was left to carry on the good work alone. His efforts bore substantial fruit for the College, if far less than President Dunster had hoped.[1] To quote, first, his own summary:

Others gave to the Colledge and advance of learning which was paid (some little towarde the building of the Colledge per Bill, some to the President for his greate laboure taken upon request of the Feoffees of the Colledge some laid out for Utensills for the Colledge by theire desires as pewter, brass, Ironware, lynnen, some laid out in Bookes to supply theire Library) and for erecting a schoole att Roxbury, besides twoe Schollarshipps of 5£ per annum, apiece settled for ever on the Colledge.[2]

Most of these gifts can be identified from the records. There were £22 from 'Master Holbrouck schoolemaster,' £7 from Master William Greenhill, 'minister of God's word at Stepney,' and £50 from a 'Godly freind' of Weld 'who will haue his name Concealed.'[3] Probably the £56 paid to Dunster in 1642 by Treasurer Tyng[4] came out of these, and the balance went toward completing the Old College. Mr. Greenhill joined with a Mr. Glover and Mr. Francis Bridges, 'a man very eminent for Pietie' who dwelt in Clapham,[5] in contributing £20 which was laid out in pewter, 'table cloathes,' and the like. In addition, the three agents 'procured from diverse Gentellmen and merchants in England towards the furnishing of the library' books to the value of £150. Fourteen guineas was collected for the

1. Our main sources for the gifts procured by Thomas Weld are: (1) his 'True Account,' dated April 10, 1647, sent to the General Court of Massachusetts and by them accepted and allowed October 25, 1651. The original is in Massachusetts Archives, LVIII. 3–6; printed by Mr. Tuttle in *C. S. M.*, XIV. 123–26. (2) His other copy of the same account, sent to the Society for Propagation of the Gospel to be audited, original in Rawlinson Mss., C. 935, fols. 5, 19, 26 ff., Bodleian Library; printed in *N. E. H. G. R.*, XXXIX. 179–82. (3) His letter of January 2, 1649[-50], together with a manuscript tract 'Innocency Cleared, Containing a just defence of Mr Weld and Mr Peters,' Rawlinson Mss., C. 934; printed in *N. E. H. G. R.*, XXXVI. 62–70. (4) The college accounts, printed in *C. S. M.*, vol. xv.

2. *N. E. H. G. R.*, XXXVI. 63.

3. *C. S. M.*, XIV. 124; cf. xv. 175, and *N. E. G. H. R.*, XXXIX. 180. Treasurer Danforth calls the first donor 'Hobart.' William Greenhill, M.A. Oxford 1612, sometime vicar of New Shoreham, was a well-known puritan divine, a member of the Westminster Assembly, joint author of the Savoy Declaration, and first pastor of the Stepney Congregational Church. *D. N. B.* and *Calamy Revised*.

4. See p. 294.

5. *N. E. H. G. R.*, XXXVI. 68 (last line), 69; *C. S. M.*, xv. 175. Bridges was a citizen and salter of London, and lord of a manor in Essex. He was a cousin of the second wife of Samuel Aldersey, and both were original adventurers in the Massachusetts Bay Company.

Roxbury Latin School, and the two sons of Dr. William Ames, then at Harvard, received £10 'by request.' [1]

Mr. Bridges, the pious Claphamite, at his death in 1642 left the College £50 — its first legacy since John Harvard's — which the agents promptly obtained from his executor, in woollen cloth of that value. Deacon Sparhawk of Cambridge advanced the £50 to the Colony Treasurer, and Weld, by order of the Overseers, turned over the suitings to Thomas Adams, merchant and woollen draper of London, to whom presumably Sparhawk owed money — a neat operation in international exchange.[2]

The future history of the Bridges legacy [3] is bound up with Weld's big shot, the famous Lady Mowlson gift of £100. This was the first scholarship fund received by Harvard, and one which after two centuries and a half made the donor the patroness and eponym of Radcliffe College.

Lady Mowlson [4] was Anne, daughter of Anthony Radcliffe, sometime alderman and sheriff of London, and Master of the Gild of Merchant Taylors. This gild was concerned in many educational activities, including the grammar school that still bears its name, and the support of five poor scholars at St. John's College, Oxford. Alderman Radcliffe, with Sir Francis Walsingham and other prominent people, attempted without success to establish a new College of Liberal Arts at Ripon, in 1604.[5] Through the marriages of her nieces and nephews, Anne

1. Same sources; and see Chapter XIX for donations to the College Library.
2. *Id.*, and C. H. Pope, *Pioneers of Mass.*, p. 427. The pertinent extract from Bridges' will is printed in H. F. Waters, *Gen. Gleanings*, I. 508: 'Item I give and bequeath unto Mr. Wells, Mr. Hooker, Mr. Peters and Mr. Syms (Ministers of New England) the somme of Fiftie poundes towards the enlargement of a colledge in New England for students there. Alsoe I give unto the said Fower New England Ministers Twenty Poundes to bee disposed towardes the clothinge of the poore in New England according as they in their discretions shall thinke fitt.'
3. *C. S. M.*, xv. 54, 172–75; and see index to xvi.
4. These facts about Anne Radcliffe and Thomas Mowlson are the results of a research into their lives by Miss Florence Berlin (A.B. Radcliffe 1926). The best articles on them now in print are Andrew McFarland Davis, in *C. S. M.*, I. 158–62, 351–54, III. 90–94; *Proc. A. A. S.*, n.s. v. 129–39, VIII. 274–80; and *New England Magazine*, n.s. IX. 773–82; all but the first by Andrew McF. Davis. Their wills are printed in H. F. Waters, *Gen. Gleanings*, I. 658–60, arms *id.*, II. 1001. The date of Anne's birth is not known — probably not far from 1582, since she was married in 1600. She was buried on November 1, 1661.
5. Francis Peck, *Desiderata Curiosa* (1735), II. lib. vii. 56–68. Anne's elder brother Edward Radcliffe was of Gray's Inn; his son and grandson, both named Anthony, were university men — the latter a Student of Christ Church during the puritan régime.

Radcliffe was connected with the Gurdons, Saltonstalls, Barringtons, and Mildmays; and, through the last two, with the Cromwells and Winthrops. It is not improbable that Governor Winthrop suggested her as a likely 'prospect' to Thomas Weld.

In 1600 Anne Radcliffe married Thomas Mowlson, formerly of Hargrave-Stubbs, Cheshire, member and later Warden of the Company of Grocers, Governor of the Company of Merchant Adventurers, President of Christ's Hospital, Alderman and Lord Mayor of London, and Member of Parliament. In his lifetime Sir Thomas endowed a school, a chapel, and a charitable fund. Dying childless in 1639, he left half his comfortable estate to 'Dame Anne' his 'loving wife,' and appointed her executrix. Many years later, it was testified in court that 'Lady Molson, though old and infirm, was of clear understanding, and generally managed her business by her own directions. She kept her own cash, bonds, &c. herself.'[1] That she understood currency depreciation clearly enough, we may read in the East India Company's records for 1640: 'upon a rumour of the King's intention to coin copper money, Lady Moulson, who has lent the Company upon bills a round sum which is now due, requires to be repaid unless assurance is given that the debt shall be paid either in gold or silver coin at its present value.'[2]

By the time Thomas Weld visited her on behalf of the College, Dame Mowlson was of an age when childless and wealthy widows are apt to turn their thoughts to good works. She was the largest contributor in her parish toward hiring a puritan lecturer to preach sermons;[3] and in 1644 she lent £600 'towards the 20,000 *l* to be sent to the Scottish army in the North.'[4] With a keen eye to the future, Dame Mowlson determined to provide, so far as law could do it, against her donation to the college being misapplied. She insisted on Weld's signing a bond to that effect; and the original covenant, engrossed on parchment and dated May 9, 1643, is still in the College Archives:[5]

1. *Eighth Report of Historical Mss. Commission*, Appendix, pp. 140–41.

2. *Court Minutes of the East India Company*, II. 64.

3. *Accomptes of the Churchwardens of The Paryshe of St. Christofer's in London* (E. Freshfield ed., 1885), p. 94.

4. *Committee for Compounding, 1643–60*, Gen. Proc., I. 780. Her nephew Sir Gilbert Gerrard, and one of the Gurdons, were on the Commons committee 'for raising money for the Scots.'

5. H. U. Archives, 'Wills, Gifts, and Grants Miscellaneous,' p. 2. Facsimile in *C. S. M.*, I. frontispiece, and in *N. E. Magazine*, n.s. IX. 778. Weld probably signed another copy of the bond, which the donor retained.

ARMS OF SIR THOMAS MOWLSON, IN ST. PETER'S CHURCH,
HARGRAVE, CHESHIRE

LADY MOULSONS GIFT OF AN 100£ FOR A SCHOLLAR SHIP

Know all men by these presents That I Thomas Wells alls Weld Pastor of Roxbury in the plantacion of New England doe by these presents acknowledge that I haue receiued of the Lady Ann Mowlson of London widdow the full and intire somme of [one] hundred pownds current English mony the which she hath freely giuen to Harvards Colledge in New England to be imp[roved] by the feofees of the said colledge for the time being to the best yearly revenew that may be thought fitt in theire wisdomes, which yearly revenew according to her good and pious intention is to be and remaine as a perpetuall stipend for and towards the yea[rly] maintenance of some poor scholler which shalbe admitted into the said colledge by the said feofees or the major part of them the which poore scholler is to injoy the said yearly stipend only till such time as such poore scholler doth attaine to the degree of a Master of Arts and no longer, and then the said yearly stipend shall by the said feofees be bestowed upon another poore scholler of the said colledge whom the said feofees shall think most deserueing, and soe the said stipend to goe in succession from [one] poor scholler to another therfor and towards theire yearly maintenance in perpetuum in manner and forme as afforesaid. And in case it shall fall out at such time as the said yearly stipend shalbe appointed by the said feofees to be bestowed upon another poore scholler there, then if there shalbe any poore scholler admitted into the said colledge that shalbe a kinsman of the said Lady Mowlson, and shalbe deemed by the said feofees or the major part of them to be of a good and pious conversation and to be well deserueing the said yearly stipend as afforesaid that then [it is] the reall intention and desire of the said Lady Mowlson that such a poore scholler there being her kinsman shalbe first preferred and appointed by the said feofees to haue and injoy the said yearly stipend in manner and forme as afforesaid before any other scholler of the said Colledge whatsoeuer that is not her kinsman. And for the present the said Lady Mowlsons desire is that John Weld now a scholler in the said colledge shall haue the said stipend till he attaine the degree of a Master of Arts. To the dew and true performance of which good and pious intent and desire of the said Lady Mowlson I the said Thomas Weld for my selfe my executours and administratours doe couenant and promise to and with the said Lady Mowlson her executours and administratours in and by these presents that the said somme of [one] hundred pownds and the yearly revenew thereof shalbe dissposed of and imployed to the only intent and purpose in the s[ame] manner and forme as is herein before mentioned and not otherwise In Wittnes whereof I the said Thomas

Weld [have?] herunto sett my hand and seale this Ninth day of May in the Nineteenth yeare of the Raigne of our Soueraigne Lord King Charles etc. 1643

Memorandum that it is likewise the intent and desire of the said Lady Mowlson that such her kinsman as shalbe admitted into the said colledge shall imediatly from the time of his admittance haue the yearly revenew of the hundred pownds aboue menciond till he attaine the degree of a Master of Arts notwithstanding that it should be otherwise dissposed of foremerly to another poore scholler by the aboue said feofees.

ANN MOWLSON

Subscribed by the said Lady
Ann Mowlson in the presents of
ARTHER BARNARDISTON [1] THO: GOODYEARE

Master Weld remitted the gift promptly, since he had a son ready to use it; but unfortunately for this plan, son John was caught burglarizing the house of his uncle in Cambridge, and expelled after being well whipped by President Dunster. There being no Harvard treasurer to receive gifts, Weld sent the £100 to the General Court,[2] which combined it with Francis Bridges' legacy of £50, and 'other small Gifts, amounting to twelve pound Sixteen and a groate,'[3] in a 'stock' or fund, amounting to £162 6s 4d,[4] on which the Colony paid to the College £15 interest per annum (about 4.6 per cent) from 1648 to 1684.[5] Except for the unusually low interest rate, this arrangement was fair enough. Harvard soon acquired a treasurer, but no treasury, nor means of profitable investment; and the plan of ac-

1. Son of Sir Thomas Barnardiston of Witham, Essex. He was the second husband of Anne Harvey, Lady Mowlson's niece and namesake. Arthur was brother to Sir Nathaniel Barnardiston, a prominent parliamentarian (see *D. N. B.*), friend of Governor Winthrop, and supporter of the Massachusetts emigration (*Winthrop Papers*, II. 230, 306, etc.), who left by will £30 for scholarships 'in the College of New England' (H. F. Waters, *Gen. Gleanings*, II. 887); but there is no trace of this benefaction's ever being received.

2. It was in the 'Country Treasury' by December 10, 1643 (*C. S. M.*, xv. 17).

3. Possibly these small gifts included that of Andrew Latham, Dunster's successor as Curate of Bury, an Oxford graduate who 'gave to the Colledge Five pounds'; or that of 'Mr Stranguish' (Strangeways?) of London, who 'gave the Colledge ten pound.' *C. S. M.*, xv. 200.

4. *C. S. M.*, xv. 172. On November 14, 1644, the General Court appointed a committee to draft letters of thanks to 'the two ladies, and every such other person as hath bene benefactours to us.' *Mass. Bay Recs.*, II. 86. Winthrop notes this later in his *Journal* (1908 ed.), II. 222. Mary Armine was the other lady.

5. *C. S. M.*, xv. 54–56, 209, *et seq.*

cumulating an 'estate'[1] in the hands of the Colony was perhaps as sound an endowment policy as could have been adopted. But it was disturbing that the Colony Treasurer soon paid out the principal on objects for which the General Court had made appropriations without providing supply; hence he was never in a position to pay over the College estate on demand. A new and special tax would have to be levied by the General Court, or local rates assigned, as with the Country's Gift. That situation put rather a strain on the financial honor of the General Court, and by 1672 the College Corporation, apprehensive as to whether the £15 interest would be regularly paid, expressed a keen desire to secure the principal.[2] To this the General Court never found it convenient to consent; and the worst fears of the College were realized in 1686, when the Dominion of New England defaulted both principal and interest. Persistent efforts at recovery were rewarded in 1713, when the General Court paid to the College Treasurer £426 10s 4d, of which £263 14s represented accumulated interest at six per cent.[3]

It was then Harvard's turn to neglect the obligation to Lady Mowlson. The sum received was simply combined with the capital funds of the College; and although the income was presumably used for exhibitions and scholarships, only two specific appropriations for that purpose have been found.[4] Finally, on January 30, 1893, after Harvard antiquarians had succeeded in finding out who the Lady Mowlson was, and when the movement to call the 'Harvard Annex' after her maiden name was under way, the Corporation took $5,000 from its capital stock and established the Lady Mowlson scholarship with an income of $200, which has since been increased from other sources to $500.[5]

1. The word is used by Dunster in 1653 (Appendix E).
2. *C. S. M.*, xv. 225; Quincy, i. 183. The Deputies attempted in 1655 to appropriate £150 from the college estate 'for the repairing of the College,' but the magistrates defeated this. Davis misrepresented the incident in *N. E. Magazine*, n.s. ix. 775, stating that Dunster 'attempted to secure the money for repairs.' Several misappropriations by the General Court of moneys collected for the children and the Indians are noted by Dr. Raymond P. Stearns in his ms. dissertation on Hugh Peter (H. C. L.), i. 402–03.
3. *Proc. A. A. S.*, n.s. v. 136–38.   4. *Id.*, p. 138.
5. The *Harv. Univ. Catalogue* for 1893–94, p. 225, first lists the 'Lady Mowlson Scholarship,' with a short explanation. In the haste to do tardy justice to the memory of our first benefactress, it was forgotten that almost one third of the fund had been given by Francis Bridges, the 'man very eminent for Pietie' who dwelt in Clapham. The principal of the fund is stated as $7,876.71 in the *Statement of the Treasurer* for 1932–33, p. 238.

Even this stipend, exceeding the lady's entire gift, will not purchase for the 'poore scholler' of today as much tuition, board, and lodging as did the income of the original gift for his predecessors in the seventeenth century.

It would be interesting, but outside our story, to describe all the activities of the Weld-Peter mission. Some five hundred pounds in money and supplies for the Colony were brought home by William Hibbens in 1642; [1] and more followed. 'Some appropriated their Gifts to the Godly poore in New England, which was sent accordingly, some to Mr. Hooker's disposing.' The largest and most widely spread contributions, amounting to £874 9s 2d, were for a favorite scheme of Hugh Peter, the transporting of poor children, especially Irish refugees, to New England. Collecting alms in the London churches for this purpose was authorized by Parliament, country parishes with New England affiliations sent their share, and individuals gave the rest. It was a worthy project, but wretchedly mismanaged, by Weld's own confession. Most of the money was laid out on chartering and provisioning three vessels, owned by Emmanuel Downing of Salem, the father of Sir George; and after that was spent, there was little left for the poor children. Hugh Peter collected these unfortunates at a place called the Six Windmills in Essex; but the ships were not ready, disease broke out in the children's camp, many died, and others ran away or were recovered by their parents. Peter and Weld had promised to sail with the survivors, but either they could not bear to leave a country where so much was going on or, as is more likely, they feared catching ship-fever from the poor little wretches. So, as Weld apologized, 'providence appeared clearly to our consciences to stop us,' and the children came over with nobody but the seamen to care for them. How many actually arrived in New England or what became of them there, is not known.[2] We know only too well what became of the small balance from the collection that Weld and Peter sent to the General Court for the children's care when they arrived. The Court voted £150 of the money toward building the President's Lodge; and

---

1. *N. E. H. G. R.*, xxxvi. 63 (§1).

2. General Court's committee report on Weld's accounts, *C. S. M.*, xiv. 124–25; cf. *N. E. H. G. R.*, xxxvi. 64–67. Winthrop mentions twenty children arriving in June, 1643 (*Journal*, 1908 ed., ii. 96); Dr. Stearns, who has given me his notes on this episode, has found traces of others.

then, if we have drawn the correct inferences from the accounts, charged the same sum off against the Country's Gift.[1]

Finally, there were contributions for the Indians. For them Weld found another benefactress — the wife of Sir William Armine, M.P. for Lincolnshire. Wealthy in her own right, and childless, Lady Mary Armine lived 'close to the heart of the puritan party,' and 'for the next twenty-five years she was the cherished acquaintance of everyone who was concerned with the promotion of good works.'[2] She 'gaue out of pious zeal 20£ per annum for ever for the preacher to the poor Indians.'[3] John Eliot, Weld's former colleague at Roxbury, was fortunately chosen for this work; and for several years, until the Society for the Propagation of the Gospel in New England was formed to support him, the Lady Armine was the Indian apostle's mainstay. Eventually, Harvard profited from this movement in the erection of the Indian College; but the first effect was most embarrassing for President Dunster. Being taken at his word that what the Indians wanted was a Harvard education, a pair of 'hopeful young plants' were rounded up by John Eliot and dumped on the hard-worked President to be prepared for college. His expense account for them from August, 1645, to October 8, 1646, with some discouraging comments, still exists:[4]

For the Diet and washing of the two Indians since the 3d of the 8th month hitherto, considering the attendance of the younger, beeing a very childe, what you think meet	£16 0 0
Item for Physick for James During his sickness for 5 or 6 weekes	19 0
Item for Physick for Jonathan in that time of his sicknes	4 0
Item for making them 12 bands and 8 shirts and often mending their apparel	3 8
Item for buttons thred and other materials bought of Mr Russel for them	2 6
Item for half a years schooling for James	6 0

1. *Mass. Bay Recs.*, II. 84, and above, pp. 295–97. In the General Court's account of the disposing of the money that Weld sent over is 'to the Colledge £291 3s 10d' (*C. S. M.*, XIV. 125). Of this, £231 is accounted for by the Mowlson and other gifts earmarked for Harvard; but when and how the balance of over £60 was paid to the College, I cannot explain.

2. G. P. Winship, introduction to *The New England Company of 1649 and John Eliot* (Prince Society, 1920), p. vi; and see *D. N. B.* for Sir William.

3. *N. E. H. G. R.*, XXXVI. 68.   4. *Mass. Archives*, XXX. 9.

I pray you to appoint mee part of my pay as far as it will reach in the hands of Henrie Shrimpton both because I am ingaged to him and hee hath promissed to accept that pay. And if that the Indians require pay back at his hands I shall bee ready to repay him such as they shal accept.

Further wheras the Indians with mee bee so small as that they uncapable of the benefit of such learning as was my desire to inpart to them, and therefore they being an hindrance to mee and I no furtherance to them, I desire they may be somewhere else disposed of with all convenient speed. So I rest in what I can

Yours

HENRIE DUNSTER.

Following some undecipherable comments by John Winthrop, the two houses note on this paper:

Wee thincke meete mr Dunster should be paid 22*l* 16*s* 2*d*
The magistrates consent to this through the said Committee
    Jo: WINTHROP Govr.
Consented to by the Deputies
    EDWARD RAWSON

By this time Master Weld was busier trying to explain to irate English benefactors what had become of their contributions than in obtaining more; and on October 1, 1645, the General Court voted that he and Master Peter speedily return. This they declined to do. Hugh Peter continued his turbulent career, which ended on the scaffold; and Thomas Weld obtained a rectory in the County of Durham, where he spent the remainder of his days in preaching and contention.

THE COLLEGE CORN

 The Weld-Peter mission having labored for the College, and brought forth gifts indeed, but little revenue, and all appeals to the General Court having failed to secure the College any settled income besides Charlestown ferry rent, President Dunster turned to the New England Confederation. That 'perpetuall league of Frendship and amytie for offense and defence, mutuall advice and succour vpon all just occasions both for preserueing and propagateing the truth and liberties of the Gospell and for their owne mutuall safety and welfare,'[1] had been formed by the colonies of the Bay, the River, New Haven, and New Plymouth, in 1643. As a step toward placing the College squarely under united New England patronage, the bachelors' theses of 1643 were dedicated not only to Governor Winthrop, but 'caeterisque unitarum Nov-Angliae Coloniarum Gubernatoribus, & Magistratibus Dignissimis.'[2]

At their meeting at Hartford in September, 1644, the Commissioners of the United Colonies were presented by Thomas Shepard with a petition to take into their consideration 'some way of comfortable mayntenance for that Schoole of the Prophets that now is,' such as requesting every family in New England 'which is able and willing . . . to giue yearely but the fourth part of a bushell of Corne,[3] or somethinge equivolent therevnto.' That 'would be a blessed meanes of comfortable prouision for the dyett of diuers such students as may stand in neede of some support.' As the Commissioners' records state,

This ensuing proposicion of A generall Contribucion for the mayntenance of poore Schollers at the Colledg at Cambridge being presented to the Commissioners by Mr Shepard pastor to the Church at Cambridg was read and fully approoued by them and agreed to be comended to the seuerall generall Courts as a matter worthy of due consideracion and entertainement for advance of learneing and which we hope wilbe chearfully embraced.[4]

Three of the four United Colonies did 'chearfully embrace' this scheme. Massachusetts Bay 'ordered, that the deputies shall commend it to the severall towns, . . . with declaration of the course which was propounded by the said commissioners, . . . viz: of every family allowing one peck of corne, or 12d in mony or other commodity, to be sent in to the Treasurer, for the colledge at Cambridge. . . .'[5] The General Court of Connecticut on October 24 confirmed 'the propositions conserning the mayntenance of scollers at Cambridge, made by the said Com-

1. Articles of Confederation, in *Plymouth Colony Records*, ix. 3-4, a volume which contains the fullest contemporary records of the Confederation.
2. Note also the dedications of the theses of August 9 and 10, 1653, of 1670, and of 1678 (*H. C. S. C.*, Appendix B).
3. 'Corn' as used in the records of these contributions, means English corn — wheat. Maize is always called Indian corn, or merely 'Indian,' in contemporary records.
4. *Plym. Col. Recs.*, ix. 20-21.
5. *Mass. Bay Recs.*, ii. 86.

missioners,' and 'Ordered that 2 men shalbe appoynted' in each of the six towns of the jurisdiction, including Southampton, Long Island, 'who shall demaund what euery family will giue, and the same to be gathered and brought into some roome, in March; and this to continue yearely.' [1] New Haven Colony, at a General Court session on November 4, 1644, 'fully approved off' this plan 'for the releife of poore schollars att the colledge att Cambridg,' and appointed Joshua Atwater and William Davis to 'receive of every one in this plantation whose hart is willing to contribute thereunto, a peck of wheat or the vallue of itt.' [2] In March, 1645–46, the New Haven Treasurer 'informed the court that he had sent from Connecticott fortie bushells of wheat for the colledge by Goodman Codman for the last yeares gift of New-haven, although he had not received soe much.' New collectors were appointed 'for this present yeare for the gift of corne to the colledge, and wompom was allowed to be paid by those that had not corne to pay in, each pecke of corne being vallued 12*d* and 2 or 3 monthes time was allowed for men to bring it to the collectors in.' On May 17, 1647, Governor Theophilus Eaton (who evidently had the College on his conscience) 'propownded that the colledge corne might be fortwith paid, and that considering the worke is a service to Christ, to bring vp yonge plants for his service, and besides, it wilbe a reproach that it shalbe said Newhaven is falne off from this service.' [3] New Plymouth, alone of the United Colonies, took no official action, although the town of Plymouth contributed.

Some £50 a year was at first obtained by this means, as Dunster reported in 1647; thereafter the annual contributions declined so that six years later he wrote, 'Mr Shepheards motion of beneficence fell to grownd.' [4]

---

1. *Conn. Col. Recs.*, I. 112. On April 9, 1646 (*id.*, p. 139), the General Court touched up the towns in this matter.

2. *New Haven Col. Recs.*, I. 149, 210. Davis' son John graduated from Harvard in 1651.

3. *Id.*, pp. 225–26, 311–12. We find the Governor again trying to speed up collections in 1647–48 (*id.*, pp. 318, 354, 357–58). Collections continued through 1652 (*id.*, p. 382, and *New Haven Town Records*, I. 20, 72, 131).

4. *Plym. Col. Recs.*, IX. 94 (§ 5); Appendix E; Chesholme's Steward's Book, p. 403 (*C. S. M.*, XXXI. 275–76), showing receipts of 'Cuntrey Stocke' amounting to £41 4s 1d in 1651, and £32 16s 2½d between January, 1652, and May, 1653, when the last contribution is recorded. Some of these may be private contributions not made through the towns.

Fortunately we can present a more cheerful view of Master Shepard's motion. The College Records preserve, in Treasurer Danforth's hand, this 'particular Accompt of the contributions made by the severall colonies' during the years 1645–53 inclusive.[1]

MASSACHUSETTS	£	s	d
Boston	84	18	7½
Brantrey	5	4	3
Cambridge	2	15	3½
Charlstown	37	16	2
Concord	8	17	4
Dedham	4	6	6
Dorchester	4	6	0
Glocester		12	0
Ipswich	5	0	0
Lyn	1	0	0
Mauldon		12	6
Newbury	1	10	0
Rowley	7	8	7½
Roxbury	16	18	3
Springfield	3	0	0
Sudbury	1	4	3
[W]oburne	5	13	7½

HARTFORD	£	s	d
Hartford	30	17	0
Saybrook	2	9	0
Windsor	5	15	0

NEW HAVEN	£	s	d
New haven	17	11	9
Millford	10	15	6
Stratford	6	14	0

PLIMOUTH	£	s	d
Plymouth Town	4	13	0

As to methods of collecting college corn, it is instructive to compare the town records of Charlestown, which was second only to Boston in generosity, with those of Salem, which gave nothing. Charlestown, at a meeting on January 27, 1644–45, 'agreed that one Peck of wheat or 12d in mony shalbe paid by every Family towards the maintainance of the Colledge at Cambridg it is to bee brought in to Serieant Spragues and Jno. Pentecost by the 21: of the xij month nex ensueing.'[2] At a corresponding meeting in January, 1646–47, the inhabitants 'agreed and voted to continue to bring in unto Ensigne Sprague and John Pentecost a Peck of Corne upon a house for the Colledge as in former yeares.'[3] The college contribution, when

1. *C. S. M.*, xv. 179–80, order of items rearranged, and names of towns that gave nothing omitted. On p. 175 Danforth, referring to this 'particular account,' states that it covers the 'Space of Eight years.' A comparison of the 'distribution made of the moneys' that immediately follows it in the records, and Chesholme's accounts (*C. S. M.*, xxxi, 275–76), proves that the years were 1645–53; there being only two contributions, however, in 1653.

2. Charlestown Archives, Boston City Hall, xx (Town Records, 11). 120. Frothingham, *History of Charlestown*, p. 115, gives the date incorrectly as August 27, 1644.

3. Charlestown Archives, xx. 128. Also in 1647–48, *id.*, 1. 43.

thus formally adopted by a town meeting, became in the eyes of the inhabitants an obligation at least equal to that of paying one's taxes. And at Charlestown it was doubtless enforced by a vigorous public opinion, and by memories of the choice young man whose name the College bore.

A Salem town meeting, on February 3, 1644–45, put the matter on a very different basis. The voters 'Ordered and Agreed that all such as God stirres vp their hearts to contribute to the advancement of learning For the maintayninge of poore skollers at the Colledge at Cambridge, that they bringe in to Mr Price within one moneth what they please to giue and to enter their names with mr Fogge and what they giue or contribute.' [1] Mr. Price was not embarrassed by this function, for the hearts of Salemites did not stir to the amount of a single penny. And other inequalities, no less flagrant, will be found in the list of town donations. The frontier trading post of Springfield, where the liberal and generous William Pynchon held sway, gave more than Cambridge; hard-scrabble Roxbury exceeded fertile Dorchester four-fold; distant Hartford and New Haven gave more than any town in Massachusetts save Boston and Charlestown. Indeed, the two Connecticut colonies were more generous, in proportion to their wealth and population, than Harvard's own foster-mother, the Bay.

It is astonishing how far the corn went toward supporting the College. These little gifts maintained for at least seven years, however meagrely, two or three teaching fellows, eight or ten scholars and exhibitioners, and two undergraduate stewards. In other words, the farmers of New England, with voluntary contributions amounting to 6,000 pecks of wheat, or their equivalent at a shilling a peck, supported the entire teaching staff of Harvard College, excepting the President, for a space of eight years; as well as assisting ten or twelve poor scholars. [2] Such testimony of a poor people's devotion to learning is not often found in history.

1. *Essex Inst. Hist. Coll.*, IX. 135.
2. Danforth's account of 'distribution made of the moneys given by the several colonyes' in *C. S. M.*, XV. 180, compared with Chesholme's S.B., with which it checks up fairly closely. Danforth's account includes payments for one 'James by order from N. Haven' (possibly Dunster's little Indian); to 'Mr Jenners Sons,' who do not appear in any other Harvard records; to '6 Students for writing for the Churches'; and to Elijah Corlett, the Cambridge schoolmaster. The outlay, to be sure, exceeds the income by £28 5s 6d; but these last four items amount to £25 7s 1½d.

A good excuse, if not the real reason, for the contributions' falling off after 1647 was the rather notorious propensity of Harvard graduates to go abroad. It was natural that young and ambitious puritans should return to England, where most of them had been born, where the Civil War had opened a career to talents, and where, as Nathaniel Mather wrote, ' to have been a New-English man, 'tis enough to gayne a man very much respect, yea almost any preferment.' [1] And these youths may well have observed of the Oxford and Cambridge men in New England pulpits, as Jefferson did of the office-holders, that few died, and none resigned. Of the twenty-four graduates of the Classes 1642–46, fourteen went to England or Ireland, one to the West Indies, and but nine stayed in New England. Accordingly, the Commissioners of the United Colonies

thought fitt that some course be taken with the parentes and with such schollers themselues (as the case may require) that when they are furnished with learning, in some competent measure, they remoue not into other Countries, but improue their partes and abillities for the service of the Colonies.[2]

Whatever course may have been taken, it was unavailing. From the next three graduating classes (1647–49–50), twelve or thirteen went abroad, and only eight 'improued their partes' in New England. Not all the exiles were permanently lost to New England: Hoar, for instance, returned to be President; Stoughton to hang witches and endow the College; others, like Downing, could well be spared; but whatever way one looked at it, the drain of youthful intellect and energy was most discouraging. And why should New England farmers send in pecks of corn to provide England with parsons and Cromwell with chaplains?

It rather looked as though the College were falling into a vicious circle: scholars went abroad because they found no encouragement at home, and the public withheld support because the scholars went abroad. There were no graduates in 1648, and but five in 1649.

1. Sibley, 1. 158.
2. *Plym. Col. Recs.*, IX. 82. September 24, 1646. This vote was quoted in the New Haven General Court as a special inducement to speed up the corn collections. *New Haven Col. Recs.*, I. 318.

Dunster's Appeal and the Parliamentary Bill of 1647

Dunster approached the Confederation again in 1647 with a series of leading questions, one general and nine special, some of which doubtless reflected criticism that had reached the presidential ear.[1]

The general question was this: will you uphold us in punishing students, and not retaliate by withholding support? To which the Commissioners 'conceiue that all who send any youthes to the Colledg doe, *eo facto*, submit and leaue them to the Colledg discipline, as is vsuall in such cases in all places in Europe.'

The special questions and answers follow.

1. Do you wish students from towns and colonies that send no college corn, or students from 'old England, Virginia and the like,' to share in exhibitions [2] founded by the contributions of others? The Commissioners desire deserving youths from contributing communities to have first consideration, but other worthy students not to be overlooked.

2. May these supplies, if sufficient, be diverted from Harvard 'for the maintenance of schoole schollars'? They may not.

3 (*a*). May Harvard College use these funds for general purposes, or only for scholarships to 'poore pious and learned' youths; and (*b*) will these forfeit their privileges if absent over a month? (*a*) 'Onely if no such youthes be present,' and (*b*) only if 'absent in a disorderly way.'

4. Must scholars be bound to stay in the country? Yes, if they are tendered suitable employment; if such offers be refused, and they depart, they should reimburse the College for their scholarships.

Dunster had now worked up by easy degrees to the acme of his proposals:

5. Will not the Confederation authorize a voluntary tax of a shilling per family, to be collected by constables, and allotted by the College at the rate of £8 per annum for scholar-

---

1. *Plym. Col. Recs.*, IX. 93–96. The original petition is in the *Mass. Archives*, LVIII. 8. Dunster alludes to this petition in his Memorandum of 1653 (Appendix E).

2. Dunster uses throughout this old English term for the scholarships founded on the college corn. It meant, in general, a small scholarship that did not provide complete maintenance.

ships and £16 for fellowships? The Commissioners reply that they have no taxing power, but recommend it 'to the wisedome and piety of the generall Corte for this Collony' (Massachusetts Bay).

There follow more questions to which the Commissioners did not reply, evidently fearing lest too much advice commit them a little more than might be convenient:

6. If 'pious, dilligent and learned graduates should be elected fellowes,' and no other source of salary appear, shall they 'haue for their encouragement' their pupils' tuition fees, 'which for the present is a considerable parte of the Presidents maintenance? therefore we humbly entreate you to state, what you thincke to be a meete allowance for the President and whence it shall arise.'

7. 'Seing from the first euill contrivall of the Colledg buildinge there now ensues yearely decayes of the rooff, walls and foundation,' will you 'propounde some way' to have it repaired? [1]

It is probable that the Confederation evaded the financial responsibilities which Dunster wished them to assume, because of renewed hopes for support from England. In the same year (1647) that Dunster made his appeal, a movement of great interest to him and to New England was being launched in the Old Country. In its first form, this was a Commons bill 'for the promoting piety and learning in that plantation'; [2] but it emerged from the legislative mill in 1649 as an act incorporating 'the President and Society for Propagation of the Gospel in New England.' Although the principal purpose was to provide support for the missionary work of John Eliot, Mr. Gurdon, M.P. for Suffolk,[3] attempted to place within the scope of the Society's benevolence whatever 'shall conduce for the maintaining of the universities at Cambridge in New England and other schools and nurseries of learning there.' [4] But on second reading this clause was struck out, and it could not fairly be

1. The 8th and 9th questions, also unanswered, referred to supplying the College Library with books, and to *ad eundem* degrees in England, and are noticed in Chapters XIX and XXII.

2. L. F. Stock, *Proceedings and Debates of the British Parliament respecting North America*, I. 203–06; *Commons Journals*, V. and VI, *passim*.

3. Either John Gurdon or his brother Brampton Gurdon, Jr., both M.P.'s and brothers-in-law of Richard Saltonstall.

4. Stock, *op. cit.*, I. 209; *Commons Journals*, VI. 264.

said that any proper interpretation of the act [1] would allow the new Society to do anything for the education of English youths, unless perhaps to prepare them to be Indian missionaries. Yet while hope remained of tapping this fount of benevolence, Dunster could get nothing done at home to strengthen or replace the diminishing flow of wheat and wampum from the country villages.[2]

COLLEGE LANDS AND ANNUITIES

John Harvard's legacy, the anonymous donation, and most of the early gifts to the College from individuals produced no revenue, because they were used for immediate and pressing needs. But the College received during her first two centuries, both by testament and deed of gift, many parcels of real estate that were expected to provide an income. It was only natural that well-wishers to the College should wish to see her richly endowed with landed property, for Englishmen still regarded wealth largely in terms of land, and English colleges obtained the bulk of their revenue from real estate. Moreover, few New Englanders had anything else to give.

This form of generosity was not altogether fortunate for the revenues; much of the College's landed property produced more vexation than income. There was a world of difference between England, where almost any land was a good investment, and New England, with a boundless supply of land for a sparse population. From the earliest planting of English colonies, almost to our own day, the chief ambition of newcomers to America has been to own a farm, and all the better class of farmers were landowners; hence the College always had difficulty in finding suitable tenants for her real estate, unless it was in some center of trade. And college treasurers were seldom able to collect rent, or keep off squatters, from distant farms. Occasionally an energetic official would comb the records and compile a sort of Domesday Book of college property, discovering that sundry landed benefactions had never been re-

---

1. Firth and Rait, *Acts and Ordinances of the Interregnum*, II. 197–200. Channing notes this incident in his *United States*, I. 493–94; but his statement that 'as the debate progresses, some jealousy appears to have developed against Harvard College' is merely his private inference.

2. For a continuation of these efforts to obtain something for Harvard from the English Society, see *H. C. S. C.*, the next volume in this series.

ceived, and that others had simply slipped out of the Corporation's possession through fraud, indifference, or neglect.

Completely useless to the College were claims on the Colony for land assigned to the College by will or deed of gift. Israel Stoughton,[1] of the first Board of Overseers, after he had been commissioned colonel in the New Model Army, left the first legacy of this description in 1646: two hundred acres of land in Dorchester 'about Mother Brookes' and one hundred acres more 'on the Blew Hill side.' These lots had simply been promised to the testator, but never laid out, and the College never received them. But the Colonel's son William (A.B. 1650) more than filled the empty bag.

It was also in 1646 that Nathaniel Ward (the 'simple cobler of Aggawam') assigned a grant of 600 acres 'lying near Andover by Merrimack,' to discharge a debt of £20 that he owed to the College 'for his son's expences there.' 'Through the negligence of former times,' wrote President Wadsworth,[2] this grant was never laid out — and the same is true of a grant of 800 acres from the Government to Captain Robert Cook of Charlestown, which he assigned to the College.[3]

The College was much more fortunate with land received from the Proprietors of Cambridge than with grants derived from the Colony, since the former were near at hand, where the Treasurer could keep an eye on them. In 1649, when Cambridge began to apportion her newly acquired plantation of Shawsheen (Billerica), President Dunster was granted 500 acres, 'whereof four hundred . . . to his own person . . . and the other 100 acres for the use of Harvard College.' Dunster promptly gave the College that quarter of his lot adjoining theirs; and these 200 acres were leased at an annual rent of 10s, which was doubled in 1654 — not bad, considering that the land was wild and unimproved. The College built a house and barn there in 1730.[4] Four years later, on representation of the Presi-

1. *C. S. M.*, xv. 22, 176, 209. The General Court took steps to have the land surveyed and laid out in 1650, but nothing was accomplished. *Mass. Bay Recs.*, iii. 208.
2. *C. S. M.*, xv. 283–84. But the General Court ordered the Ward grant laid out in 1664. *Mass. Bay Recs.*, iv. pt. ii. 113.
3. *C. S. M.*, xv. 208, 284.
4. *C. S. M.*, xv. 184, 269, 208, 214, 216, 240 (plan), 299, and see xvi, index; *H. U. Archives*, 'College Lands, Billerica to Narragansett.' It is the farm numbered XI in the map in H. A. Hazen, *Hist. of Billerica*, pp. 11–17; but on p. 41 Hazen incorrectly states that it was sold in 1750.

dent and Fellows that they had never been able to let this Billerica farm 'at any other than a very low Rent in Proportion to its Value,' the General Court granted them permission to sell it; [1] and in 1775 the entire Billerica estate, measuring 230 acres by a recent survey, was sold for £606 13s 4d lawful money of New England.[2]

In addition to special grants of this sort, the College was regarded as one of the Proprietors of Cambridge, and as such given a planting lot of two acres on Cambridge Neck,[3] a smaller meadow lot on Fresh Pond,[4] and a share in the several 'squadrants' or divisions of land made between 1662 and 1707. These were lots varying in size from 2 to 30 acres, scattered through the extensive Cambridge territory from Newton Lower Falls well into Lexington. They seem neither to have been improved by the College, nor to have produced revenue, but were held until the increase of population in the eighteenth century made sales at prices varying from £20 to £50.[5]

1. *Mass. Archives*, LVIII. 406, 408. June 6, 1754.

2. Middlesex Registry of Deeds, East Cambridge, LXXVII. 263. The grantees were Solomon Pollard, tanner; Jonathan Stickney, yeoman; Samuel Kidder, yeoman; and Solomon Kidder, gentleman.

3. Exchanged in 1653 for 'a long slip of Land in Cambridge Neck,' a part of the cornfields. This was let out to several respectable Cantabrigians, but, so far as the College Records show, brought in no rent. *C. S. M.*, xv. 266, and xvi, index under Cambridge Neck.

4. *Id.*, index under Cambridge West Fields.

5. *Cambridge Proprietors' Records*, pp. 143, 146, 165, 171, 190, 246, etc. The Ms. Catalogue of Donations, H. U. Archives, pp. 41, 60, 82, records the sale of some of these lots, but does not account for most of them. Cf. *C. S. M.*, xv. 217, 253, 265–68, and index to xvi under Cambridge Farms, Cambridge Rocks, Cambridge Village, Lexington, Newton.

XXII

GOVERNMENT BY PRESIDENT AND OVERSEERS
1642–1650

 President Dunster and his nine Commencers must have made a good show of the first Commencement. Governor Winthrop recorded that 'it gave good content to all'; and only four days later the General Court passed an act which placed the Board of Overseers on a permanent basis, and endowed it with quasi-corporate powers. One of the Commencers, William Hubbard, later wrote: 'the College at Cambridge was brought to some perfection, and feoffees were this year appointed, viz. all the magistrates of the Colony, and the elders of the six next adjoining churches; a needful provision for the taking care of the sons of the prophets, over whom we know of old they were set that were able, both as prophets to teach, and judges to rule and govern.'[1]

A new legislative grant was necessary because that of November 20, 1637, merely named certain persons to act as Overseers for an indefinite period, making no provision for filling vacancies, and because the only power granted to them under that act was 'to take order for a colledge at Newetowne.' The College was now a going concern; some form of government must be established.

The text of this act of September 27, 1642 (sometimes erroneously called the First Charter), follows:

Whereas, by order of Court in the 7th mo, 1636,[2] there was appointed and named six magistrats and six elders to order the colledge at Cambridge, of which twelue some are removed out of this iurisdiction, —

---

1. *History of New England* (1848 ed.), pp. 372–73. For 'sons of the prophets' see Chapter I.
2. A mistake for 9th month (November), 1637. The order of 7th month 1636 was the act of foundation, appropriating £400.

It is therefore ordered, that the Governour and Deputy for the time being, and all the magistrats of this iurisdiction, together with the teaching elders of the sixe next adioyning townes, that is, Cambridge, Watertowne, Charlestowne, Boston, Roxberry, and Dorchester, and the president of the colledge for the time being, shall have from time to time full power and authority to make and establish all such orders, statutes, and constitutions as they shall see necessary for the instituting, guiding, and furthering of the said colledge and the severall members thereof from time to time in piety, morality, and learning; as also that they shall have full power to dispose, order, and manage, to the use and behoofe of the said colledge and members thereof, all gifts, legacies, bequeathalls, revenues, lands, and donations, as either have bene, are, or shalbee conferred, bestowed, or any wayes shall fall to the said colledge; and whereas it may come to passe that many of the said magistrats and elders may bee absent, or otherwise implied in weighty affaires, when the said colledge neede their present helpe, councell, and authority, therefore it is ordered, that the greater number of the said magistrates, elders, and president shall have the power of the whole; provided, also, that if any constitution, order, or orders shalbee made that is found hurtfull to the said colledge, or the members thereof, or to the weale publike, that then, upon the appeale of the partie or parties aggrieved to the said overseers, that they shall repeale the said order or orders at their next meeting, or stand accountable thereof to the next Generall Court.[1]

Thus the General Court made an institution of the Board of Overseers, and of the College placed under their charge. The Board was granted quasi-corporate powers to govern the College, both directly and through by-laws, and to receive, hold, and dispose of property; appeals were allowed from the Board to the General Court, as the supreme authority in the Colony under the King. By virtue of this act the Overseers became in effect Feoffees (as Hubbard called them in the language of the day); a committee of twelve magistrates and ministers was transformed into a board of *ex officiis* trustees representing both Church and State, with the President of the College added to represent the teaching faculty. By 'magistrates' the act meant

---

1. *Mass. Bay Recs.*, 11. 30. The text in our first revised statutes, the *Book of the General Lawes and Libertyes* (1648), has a different preamble: 'Wheras through the good hand of God upon us there is a Colledge founded in Cambridge in the County of Midlesex called *Harvard Colledge*, for incouragement wherof this Court hath given the summe of four hundred pounds and also the revenue of the Ferrie betwixt Charlstown and Boston and that the well ordering and mannaging of the said Colledge is of great concernment. . . .'

the Assistants of the Bay Colony, who under the royal charter of 1629 were annually elected by the freemen on the day before Ascension.[1] By 'teaching elders' it meant the ordained ministers (both 'pastors' and 'teachers') of the churches named. As the freemen of the Bay Colony customarily reëlected their magistrates until they died or would serve no longer,[2] and as ministers generally served their respective churches for life, there was a strong element of continuity on the Board. Except that the General Court in 1654, alleging a shortage of elders, added four ministers not otherwise qualified,[3] the organization of the Board of Overseers remained unaltered until 1708; nor was it substantially changed until 1851, when reorganized as the elected representative of Harvard graduates.[4] Until that time the Governor of Massachusetts presided over meetings of the Board.

Although the Board lost its exclusive power in the charter of 1650, American college government has in general followed this earlier form at Harvard, rather than the typical English form of the charter. Even the Harvard government has tended to revert to the earlier form: the Fellows of today are in reality external trustees like the Overseers of 1642–50; but the President's position has become much stronger in relation to his associates.

The first Board of Overseers under the Act of 1642 had the following members:

John Winthrop, Esq., *Governor*
John Endecott, Esq., *Deputy-Governor*
Mr. Henry Dunster, *President*

MAGISTRATES	MINISTERS	
Thomas Dudley, Esq.	Mr. Thomas Shepard	*Cambridge*
Increase Nowell, Esq.	Mr. George Phillips	*Watertown*
Simon Bradstreet, Esq.	Mr. John Knowles	*Watertown*

1. *C. S. M.*, xviii. 56.

2. In forty-one years, 1643–83, only thirty-nine new names were added to the House of Assistants, although from seven to eighteen members were elected annually. W. H. Whitmore, *Mass. Civil List*, pp. 22–26.

3. John Allin of Dedham, Samuel Whiting and Thomas Cobbett of Lynn, and John Norton, then of Boston but not yet formally installed over the First Church. *Mass. Bay Recs.*, iv. pt. i. 204.

4. The successive acts altering the composition of the Board of Overseers are printed in the introduction to the annual Harvard University Catalogues; they will be discussed as they come up, in this and subsequent volumes. From July 23, 1686, to 1708 the Board of Overseers was in abeyance, except that one meeting was held on June 12, 1690. *C. S. M.*, xv. xxxiv–xxxv.

MAGISTRATES	MINISTERS	
John Winthrop, Esq.[1]	Mr. Zechariah Symmes	*Charlestown*
Richard Bellingham, Esq.	Mr. Thomas Allen	*Charlestown*
Israel Stoughton, Esq.[1]	Mr. John Wilson	*Boston*
Richard Saltonstall, Esq.	Mr. John Cotton	*Boston*
Thomas Flint, Esq.	Mr. John Eliot	*Roxbury*
William Pynchon, Esq.	Mr. Richard Mather	*Dorchester*

We have the record of but one meeting of the Board of Over-seers before the Charter of 1650 was adopted; fortunately it was an important one. The 'Governours of Harvard Colledge,' as the Overseers here called themselves, meeting in the 'Colledge Hall' on December 27, 1643,[2] order the accounts of Mr. Harvard's gift to be finished, appoint Mr. Herbert Pelham [3] Treasurer of the College, and order 'that there shall be a Colledge seale in forme following.' The rough sketch, here reproduced in facsimile, shows a shield of medieval shape, bearing three open books with clasps, the lower one face-down. On the open pages of the first two books and the covers and back of the third, is inscribed the word *Veritas*.

1. John Winthrop, Jr., was absent in England and Stoughton was on the high seas at the time the act was passed, and Stoughton never returned. Including these, the Board consisted of thirteen Cambridge alumni, one of Oxford, one of Dublin, and six non-university men.

2. The membership was the same as in 1642, with the addition of William Hibbens and Samuel Symonds to the magistrates. John Winthrop, Jr., had returned, but John Knowles had left for Virginia. It is impossible to determine who was actually present at the meeting of December 27, 1643. At the next meeting of the magistrates as Court of Assistants at Boston on January 25, 1643–44, only the Governor, Dudley, Hibbens, Flint, and Nowell were present. *Records of Court of Assistants*, II. 137.

3. Herbert Pelham (1600–73) was one of fourteen or sixteen children of Herbert Pelham, Esq., of Hastings, Sussex, and Boston, Lincs. His mother, Penelope West, was daughter to Thomas West, second Baron de la Warr, and sister to the third baron, commonly known as Lord Delaware, Governor of Virginia. His uncle, Thomas Pelham, had been a prominent member of the Virginia Company. Herbert Pelham was not an Oxford alumnus, as has often been stated, but his brother William (see Appendix B), with whom he emigrated to New England in 1638, had been a fellow-commoner at Emmanuel College, Cambridge. After the death of his first wife (Jemima Waldegrave), Herbert Pelham married the widow of Roger Harlakenden, and lived in the Harlakenden house at the corner of Dunster and South Streets, Cambridge, hard by the town landing. He was elected Assistant of Massachusetts Bay, 1645–49, and Commissioner of the United Colonies, 1645–46. He returned to England in 1647, lived quietly at Bures, Suffolk, and never revisited America, but continued to correspond with his Winthrop 'cousins' and to perform good offices for the country and the College. Nathaniel Pelham (A.B. 1651) was his son by his first wife, and Edward Pelham (A.B. 1673) by the second; his daughter Penelope married Josiah Winslow, a student at Harvard about 1643 and subsequently Governor of the Plymouth Colony. As College Treasurer, Herbert Pelham was a mere figurehead. President Dunster retained in his own hands the management of the college property. *D. N. B.*; 4 *Coll. M. H. S.*, VII. 138–45.

At the meeting of the Governors of Harvard Colledge, held in the Colledge Hall the 27 of 10 — 1643.

It is ordered that,

1. The Accounts of Mr Harbards Gift are to be finished, & Mr Pelhā, Mr Nowell, Mr Hibbons, Mr Syms, Mr Wilson are chosen to finish it, & an acquittance may be given Mr Allin. And it is agred of, if they find things cleare in the fulfilling ye will of ye dead they are to desire ye Governour of ye Colledge his hand to it as a full determinahon & acquittance.

2. Mr Pelhā is elected Treasurer of ye Colledge by the joynt vote of the Governours of ye Colledge.

3. It is ordered that there shall be a Colledge seale in forme following

4. A coppy of Mr Adams & Mr Coaltons letter to Mr Eaton.

Mr Eaton,
After oū love remembred to you, whereas we understood by your farmer letter that the mony wch was appoynted heretofore for publique use, was not all spent & bestowed of, we professe for our parts, desire that wt is yet remayning, may be expended wholly about the building of ye New Colledge at Cambridge, in N. England, wch we understand is now erecting. So we Rest your loveing friends

Thomas Adams
Christopher Coalton

26 March 1640.

This mony was wholly put into the hands of my brother Nath: Eaton, wch Theoph: Eaton

DESIGN FOR THE FIRST COLLEGE ARMS

SEAL OF THE PRESIDENT AND OVERSEERS, 1643
Enlarged one-half

VERITAS, AND OTHER HARVARD MOTTOES, ARMS AND SEALS

Although no word or phrase, excepting possibly 'Fair Harvard,' is now more sentimentally connected with the College than this, it is a curious fact that no record can be found of the *Veritas* device being actually used on a Harvard seal or arms for two centuries. *Veritas* first emerged from the college archives into the light of day at the same bicentennial celebration for which 'Fair Harvard' was composed; and it was not called to general public attention until 1840, when a design from the original sketch was printed in President Quincy's History.[1]

Thomas Danforth, named Treasurer of the College in the Charter of 1650, copied some of the older records into College Book III.[2] Summarizing the Overseers' meeting of December 27, 1643, he writes, 'A Common Seale for the Colledge was then also appoynted in forme following.'[3] In the space underneath this entry is attached an excellent impression of a seal. The arms contain three open books, very crudely cut, set askew, and devoid of *Veritas* or other lettering. The two upper books are separated from the third by a chevron, one limb of which is longer than the other. In the border is inscribed

SIGILLVM · COLL[EG·] HARVARDIN · CANTAB · NOVANG:

This is the only extant impression of the first college seal, cut by virtue of the vote of December 27, 1643.[4] Why the die-

1. 'On the morning of the 8th of September, 1836, a white banner, on which the device of the first seal of the University was emblazoned, was raised on the summit of the pavilion.' Quincy, II. 646. A footnote adds, 'Three open volumes, with the motto "Veritas."' The facsimile faces p. 48 of vol. I. Robert C. Winthrop alluded to President Quincy's discovery of *Veritas* in his bicentennial oration (*ibid.*, II. 702–03). Cotton Mather says nothing of any motto, seal, or arms in his history of the College in the *Magnalia* (1702), and Benjamin Peirce, in his *History of Harvard University* (1833), p. 8, mentions only *Christo et Ecclesiae*.

2. At what date Danforth began to compile College Book III is not known; probably not long after he actively assumed the duties of his office, late in 1654.

3. *C. S. M.*, xv, facing 176. See facsimile. The impression is made on a square of paper cut from a blank book, with the red ruling still on it, over sealing-wax. No part of the impression is colored, but the portions in higher relief come out darker in the photograph. The handwriting of 'The College Seal' is not Danforth's (as is the line above), but that of one of the numerous persons who perused the college records during the next two centuries, and added comments of their own.

4. The page, examined in a strong light, shows no pen-and-ink design under the seal; and there seems no reason to doubt that Danforth made the impression himself, at the time of making the record. Cf. the last note but one.

cutter did not follow his specifications we can only conjecture. It may be that his art was unequal to the task of placing *Veritas* on the books, and that he supposed the chevron would help the composition, as it certainly does.

A second motto, *In Christi Gloriam*, appears on a seal made for the college Corporation created by the Charter of 1650; and a third, *Christo et Ecclesiae*, on a seal made for the Corporation created by the Charter of 1692.[1]

What were the Overseers and Fellows attempting to symbolize in the three seventeenth-century seals? The arms of most Oxford and Cambridge colleges were based on those of their founders or earliest patrons and benefactors; but the Harvard family bore no arms. Hence our governing boards followed the universities of Oxford, Cambridge, St. Andrews, Glasgow, King's of Aberdeen, Edinburgh, and San Marcos de Lima, as well as Trinity College of Cambridge, Trinity College of Dublin, and the College of the Sorbonne of Paris, in using one or more books in their device; in particular they followed Oxford and Cambridge by inscribing a motto on the books.

For such simple and appropriate mottoes as *Veritas*, *In Christi Gloriam*, and *Christo et Ecclesiae* it is perhaps far-fetched to assume any specific source. It may be only a coincidence that *Veritas*, *Christo et Ecclesiae*, and the Yale motto *Urim & Thummim* (Light and Truth) are found in two volumes by William Ames; but when we consider that these volumes appeared early enough, and were used at Harvard and Yale late enough, to have inspired all three, one of them also inspiring the *theses technologicae* which were argued at Harvard Commencements; and when we further consider that Ames was the spiritual father of the New England churches, that his portrait was owned by Harvard College, that his family came to New England after his death and two of his sons were students at Harvard in 1643, that his works on logic, divinity, and physics were used as text-books at Harvard and Yale,[2] there would seem to be something more than a coincidence in finding the first Harvard motto in Williams Ames' *Philosophemata*, and the Yale motto, together with *Christo et Ecclesiae*, in Ames' *Disceptatio Scholastica*.

1. For details on these and later Harvard seals see S. E. Morison, 'Harvard Seals and Arms,' *Harv. Grads. Mag.*, XLII (1933). 1–15; and for reproductions, *H. C. S. C.*
2. See *H. C. S. C.*, Chapter VII, and William Ames in index.

The *Philosophemata* was a collection of six treatises or disputations by Ames on Theology and the Arts, printed posthumously in 1643, and reprinted in 1646 and 1651.[1] On the title-page or sub-title of every edition of this work is printed the sentiment attributed to Aristotle:

Amicus Plato, Amicus Aristoteles, sed Magis Amica VERITAS [2]
(Let Plato be your friend, and Aristotle, but more let your friend be Truth.)

This motto was paraphrased by Increase Mather in a presidential address.[3] To be sure, it was a well-known quotation, which might have occurred to any classical scholar without Ames' prompting; and of course there are many other quotations and even mottoes that include *Veritas*.[4]

Christo et Ecclesiae, the motto of the University of Franeker, was the text of Dr. Ames' inaugural address as Rector of that university in 1626. In this discourse,[5] Ames reminds his hearers

1. The British Museum and Bibliothèque Nationale have the first edition (Leyden, 1643), in which one finds 'Aristoteles' in the motto. A copy of the second edition (Cambridge, 1646), which belonged to Cotton Mather, is in the A. A. S.; another copy is in the Prince Collection at the B. P. L. The *Philosophemata* is also printed in volume v of Ames' collected works (Amsterdam, 1658). It may be objected that the first edition could not have been known at Harvard before November 27, 1643. But there is nothing unlikely in a book by an author revered at Harvard (and whose two sons were then at Harvard) being sent there hot off the press.

2. This sentiment, sometimes without the second clause, is generally attributed to Aristotle in classical dictionaries and the like. It is a paraphrase of the famous passage in the Nicomachean Ethics, ending ὅσιον προτιμᾶν τὴν ἀλήθειαν; which is translated by W. D. Ross, in his edition of the *Works of Aristotle* (Oxford, 1925), ix. 1096ᵃ : 'Yet it would perhaps be thought to be better, indeed to be our duty, for the sake of maintaining the truth even to destroy what touches us closely, especially as we are philosophers or lovers of wisdom; for, while both are dear, piety requires us to honour truth above our friends.'

3. '. . . Unicum *Aristotelis* Dictum verè Aureum, memoriâ teneatis, *Amicus* Plato, *Amicus* Socrates (addo ego *Amicus* Aristoteles) *sed magis Amica Veritas.*' *Magnalia,* book iv. 132; cf. *H. C. S. C.*, Chapter XVII. As to what the Mathers and their contemporaries meant by *Veritas*, Cotton Mather places a significant quotation at the foot of the page where Wilson's Elegy on John Harvard is printed (*Magnalia,* book iv. 139). It is from the *Orationes anti-Weigelianæ* of Dr. John Arrowsmith, sometime Vice-Chancellor of the University of Cambridge, and may be translated 'Let Almighty God make this University so tenacious of the Truth, that henceforth a wolf may more readily be found in England, or a toad in Ireland, than a Socinian or Arminian in Cambridge.'

4. For instance, one of the four different mottoes used by the University of Oxford in the early seventeenth century was *Bonitas regnabit, Veritas liberabit.* C. E. Mallet, *Hist. Univ. Oxford,* II. 214 n. 3; cf. title-page of Laudian Code of Statutes, printed 1636.

5. It is printed in Ames' *Disceptatio Scholastica* (Leyden, 1633; Amsterdam, 1644 and 1658). See Mr. C. B. Clapp's article in *C. S. M.*, xxv. 59–83, for location of copies,

again and again that their university was dedicated *Christo et Ecclesiae*, as distinct from *Baccho et Bacchantibus*, to which many of the students and some of the professors had lately been pouring libations. And in the same volume is Dr. Ames' inaugural lecture as Professor of Theology at Franeker in 1622, the text of which, *Urim & Thummim* [1] (Exod. xxviii. 30; Lev. viii. 8; *doctrina et veritas* in the Vulgate), was adopted in the next century as the Yale motto. And of course the same text may have prompted the Harvard *Veritas*.

The second Harvard motto, *In Christi Gloriam*, may well have been suggested by the words placed in John Harvard's mouth by John Wilson: [2]

> Me commune bonum, praesertim gloria Christi,
> Impulit, et charae posteritatis amor.

Having, as they supposed, fixed the design of the college seal, the Overseers at this same meeting of November 27, 1643, recorded a letter from two English friends of the College to Nathaniel Eaton about their donation, with which the errant Master had made away. President Dunster then proposed that an annual appropriation of £10 be made from the £100 gift of Lady Mowlson (Anne Radcliffe), but the Overseers declared the matter 'deferred for 2 Reasons. first because we have not the monny. And 2dly we cannot give any thing out of Country Treasury, till a Generall Court. had we the monny in hand we would presently effect it.' [3]

The Overseers then appointed 'Sir Bulkly' and 'Sir Downing,' of the Class lately graduated, 'for the present helpe of the president, to read to the Junior pupills as the president shall see fitt, and be allowed out of the Colleadge Treasury 4 *l* per Annum to each of them for their paines.' These were the first Harvard tutors.

Appointment of treasurer and tutors, audit of accounts, and college seal; a good day's work by the Overseers.

---

and facsimile. Harvard has a copy of the 1658 edition, bound up with the *Philosophemata*.

1. These are the Hebrew words on the Yale seal, which was used at least as early as 1740, though not officially adopted until September 11, 1745. Yale officially translates them *lux et veritas*; Ames, after a learned discussion, concludes that *Urim* means '*inflammationes & illuminationes*,' and *Thummim* '*sinceritates, id est, perfectiones & simplicitates*.'

2. See end of Chapter XVI.

3. *C. S. M.*, xv. 17. For the story of this donation see Chapter XXI.

COLLEGE LAWS OF 1642–1650

For the proper ordering of an Oxford or Cambridge college, the first thing necessary after the foundation charter was a set of college statutes. These often ran to hundreds of chapters and scores of pages. The Harvard Overseers began to pass by-laws even before the first Commencement; these 'Rules and Precepts'[1] were enlarged by supplementary legislation, codified about the year 1646, and 'published to the scholars' by being read aloud in the college hall. This first code of college statutes is recorded in College Book I both in Latin and in English. The former is, in a few instances, the more detailed; but as both versions were equally official and valid, I have here reprinted the vernacular:[2]

> the Lawes Liberties and orders of Harvard Colledge con-
> firmed by the Overseers and president of the Col-
> ledge in the Yeares 1642, 1643, 1644, 1645,
> and 1646. and published to the Scholars
> for the perpetuall preservation of
> their welfare and governement

1. When any Schollar is able to Read Tully or such like classicall Latine Authour ex tempore, and make and speake true Latin in verse and prose *suo (ut aiunt) Marte*, and decline perfectly the paradigmes of Nounes and verbes in the Greeke toungue, then may hee bee admitted into the Colledge, nor shall any claime admission before such qualifications.

2. Every one shall consider the mayne End of his life and studyes, to know God and Jesus Christ which is Eternall life. Joh. 17. 3.

3. Seeing the Lord giveth wisdome, every one shall seriously by prayer in secret, seeke wisdome of him. prov. 2. 2, 3 etc.[3]

4. Every one shall so exercise himselfe in reading the Scriptures twice a day that they bee ready to give an account of their proficiency theerein, both in theoreticall observations of Language and Logicke, and in practicall and spirituall truthes as their tutour shall require according to their severall abilities respectively, seeing the Entrance of the word giveth light etc. psal. 119. 130.

1. See *New Englands First Fruits*, in Appendix D.
2. *C. S. M.*, xv. 24–27, which consult for the diplomatics of this code; the Latin is on pp. 29–31. Thomas Danforth's copy of the English is *ibid.*, pp. 187–90.
3. Cf. Cambridge Elizabethan Statutes, cap. L, where masters of colleges are required to exhort the scholars 'ut se studiis literarum et pietati dedant et a Deo, fonte atque authore omnis pietatis cognitionis et scientiæ atque adeo bonarum rerum omnium, auxilium et suppetias ad suos labores impetrent.' *Docs. Univ. Camb.*, I. 490.

5. In the publike Church assembly they shall carefully shunne all gestures that shew any contempt or neglect of Gods ordinances [1] and bee ready to give an account to their tutours of their profiting and to use the helpes of Storing themselves with knowledge, as their tutours shall direct them. and all Sophisters and Bachellors (until themselves make common place shall publiquely repeate Sermons in the Hall whenever they are called forth [2]

6. they shall eschew all prophanation of Gods holy name, attributes, word, ordinances, and times of worship, and study with Reverence and love carefully to reteine God and his truth in their minds.[3]

7. they shall honour as their parents, Magistrates, Elders, tutours and aged persons,[4] by beeing silent in their presence (except they bee called on to answer) not gainesaying shewing all those laudable expressions of honour and Reverence in their presence, that are in use as bowing before them standing uncovered or the like.[5]

8. they shall bee slow to speake, and eschew not onely oathes, Lies, and uncertaine Rumours, but likewise all Idle, foolish, bitter scoffing, frothy wanton words and offensive gestures.[6]

1. Cf. Camb. Eliz. Statutes, cap. XLVII: 'Modestiam suo ordini convenientem omnes omnibus in locis colant, præsertim in concionibus et congressibus publicis.' *Docs. Univ. Camb.*, I. 483. See also Statutes of Emmanuel College: 'Scholares praedictos tam domi quam foris modestè et honestè se gerere volumus; contentionibus et rixis abstinere; in concionibus publicis audiendis frequentes esse; modestiam omnium vultu, gestu corporis et vestitus genere et formâ præferre.' *Id.*, III. 514–15.

2. This sentence is not found in the Latin version. See index, 'commonplacing.'

3. Cf. preamble of Camb. Eliz. Statutes: 'Deum timeto: regem honorato: virtutem colito: disciplinis bonis operam dato.' *Id.*, I. 455.

4. The Latin version here has 'tutores suosque omnes seniores prout Ratio postulat,' which in English university Latin would have meant something different from 'aged persons,' viz. the students' seniors in the order of seniority. For instance, the Laudian statutes of Oxford (Griffiths ed., p. 146) require 'quod Iuniores Senioribus, id est, nondum Graduati Baccalaureis, Baccalaurei Artium Magistris, Magistri itidem Doctoribus, debitam et congruam Reverentiam, tum in privato, tum in publico, exhibeant; scilicet, ubi convenerint, locum potiorem cedendo; ubi obvii venerint, de via decedendo, et ad iustum intervallum caput aperiendo; atque etiam reverenter salutando et compellando.' Cf. the Trinity College (Dublin) statute *De Modestia*, in J. P. Maaffy, *An Epoch in Irish History*, p. 343. For seniority at Harvard, see *H. C. S. C.*, Chapter IV.

5. Cf. Camb. Eliz. Statutes, cap. XLVII: 'Inferiores ordines superioribus loco cedant et debita reverentia prosequentur.'

6. The 1628 statutes of Trinity College, Dublin, are severe on 'Seditionis domesticae, detractionis, dissentionis, rixæ authores.' Mahaffy, *op. cit.*, p. 344. Cf. in Rashdall, II. 769, 771, the statutes of the Oxford Halls, 1483–89: 'Eciam Statutum est . . . quod nullus fabulaciones iniquas aut garulaciones inhonestas verbave turpia aut scurrilia bonos mores corrumpencia proferat.' 'Ac eciam statutum est quod nullus aularis palam, publice vel occulte verbo signo vel facto, . . . occasionem litis, discordie, brige, vel discensionis generet, suscitet, moueat aut procuret, seu comparaciones odiosas . . . quomodolibet faciat aut alleget.' The Laudian statutes of Oxford (Griffiths ed., p. 151) have a paragraph against reciting or publishing libels.

9. None shall pragmatically intrude or intermeddle in other mens affaires.

10. During their Residence, they shall studiously redeeme their time, observe the generall houres appointed for all the Scholars, and the speciall hour for their owne Lecture, and then diligently attend the Lectures without any disturbance by word or gesture: [1] And if of any thing they doubt they shall inquire as of their fellowes so in case of non-resolution modestly of their tutours.[2]

11. None shall under any pretence whatsoever frequent the company and society of such men as lead an ungirt and dissolute life.[3]

Neither shall any without licence of the overseers of the Colledge bee of the Artillery or traine-Band.[4]

Nor shall any without the Licence of the Overseers of the Colledge, his tutours leave, or in his absence the call of parents or Guardians goe out to another towne.[5]

1. Cf. Camb. Eliz. Statutes, cap. v: 'Nullus scholaris . . . ullam publicam lectionem ejus professionis cui destinatus est omittat, sed a principio usque ad finem quiete et attente eam audiat.' *Docs. Univ. Camb.*, I. 457–58.

2. The Latin version of this last clause is 'Siquid dubitent sodales suos, aut (nondum exempto scrupulo) tutores modeste consulunto.' Apparently the object was to discourage students from asking embarrassing questions of lecturers.

3. Cf. statutes of Queen's College, Oxford, 1341: 'Abstineant etiam se scolares predicti a tabernis et locis inhonestis, ac comitivis suspectis, ne ex eorum comitatione suspecta scandalum oriatur.' Magrath, *Hist. of Queen's College*, I. 57 n.

4. *Latine*, 'bellicis lustrationibus interesse.' The 'Artillery' meant the Artillery Companies of Boston and Watertown, both gentlemen's corps; the 'traine-band' meant the local militia company, from service in which all members of the College were exempt. The statutes of the English colleges and medieval universities repeatedly forbade scholars to bear arms or take part in warlike exercises, as unsuitable for clerks, and a misspending of time. Charles the First's charter to the University of Oxford empowers the Vice-Chancellor to exclude from Oxford or its suburbs ' Jousts, Spear-playing, Spear-throwings, Feats of Arms, Tourneys, Adventures, and all manner of idle, vain or contentious spectacles, whereby Scholars may be drawn away from their studies.' *Bodleian Quarterly Record*, VII. 87–88. The *Laudian Code of Statutes* (Griffiths ed., p. 153) forbade any student to bear offensive or defensive arms, day or night, 'Exceptis, qui honestae recreationis causa arcus cum sagittis portaverint'— the favorite sport in Laud's own college! Similar stipulations may be found in the statutes of most medieval universities; and the University of San Marcos de Lima forbade its students 'meter armas ningunas, ofensivas ni defencivas en las Escuelas' (Alonso Eduardo Salazar y Zevallos, *Constituciones, y Ordenanzas Antiguas de la Real Vniversidad de San Marcos*, Lima, 1735, p. 48); and visitors to Lima are still shown the antechamber where scholars were required to deposit their lethal weapons before entering *las escuelas*.

5. The Latin of this law is more detailed: 'Nemo in pupillari statu degens nisi concessâ priùs à tutore veniâ ex oppido exeat; nec quisquam cujuscunque gradus aut ordinis fuerit forum frequentet, vel diutius in aliquâ oppidi plateâ moretur aut tabernas cauponas vel diversoria ad comessandum aut bibendum accedat, nisi ad parentes, curatores, nutricios vel hujusmodi accersitus fuerit.' Cf. Camb. Eliz. Statutes, cap. XLVII, §§ 5, 6: 'Nemo in pupillari statu degens nisi . . . concessaque prius a tutore vel decano vel collegii praefecto venia in oppidum exeat. . . . Statuimus etiam ut nemo cujuscunque gradus aut ordinis fuerit . . . forum frequentet vel diutius in aliqua oppidi platea

12. No Scholar shall buy sell or exchange any thing to the value of sixe-pence without the allowance of his parents, guardians, or tutours. And whosoever is found to have sold or bought any such thing without acquainting their tutour or parents, shall forfeit the value of the Commodity, or the Restoring of it, according to the discretion of the president [1]

13. the Scholars shall never use their Mother-toungue [2] except that in publike Exercises of oratory or such like, they bee called to make them in English

14. If any Scholar beeing in health shall bee absent from prayer or Lectures, except in case of urgent necessity or by the Leave of his tutour, hee shall bee liable to admonition (or such punishment as the president shall thinke meet) if hee offend above once a weeke.[3]

15. Every Scholar shall bee called by his Sirname onely till hee bee invested with his first degree; [4] except hee bee fellow-commoner or a Knights Eldest Sonne or of superiour Nobility.[5]

16. No Scholars shall under any pretence of recreation or other cause what-ever (unlesse foreshewed and allowed by the president or his tutour) bee absent from his studyes or appointed exercises above an houre at Morning-Bever, halfe an houre at afternoone-Bever; [6] an houre and an halfe at Dinner and so long at Supper.

17. If any Scholar shall transgresse any of the Lawes of God or the House [7] out of perversnesse or apparant negligence, after twice admonition hee shall bee liable if not adultus to correction,[8] if Adultus

---

moretur. . . . Inhibemus ne eorum quispiam, qui in oppido tabernas aut cauponas aperiunt vel cibaria vendunt, aliquem scholarem ad mensam, comessationes, compotationes, . . . recipiant . . . Baccalaurei tamen legum . . . pupilli etiam tutores comitantes vel ad parentes et amicos in oppidum tanquam hospites adventantes, accersiti solummodo, ad prandium et coenam impune recipi possunt.' *Docs. Univ. Camb.*, 1. 484–85.

1. 'Give and sell nothing, exchange nothing.' William Lyly's *Short Introduction of Grammar* (London, 1765), p. 62. Cf. Camb. Eliz. Statutes, cap. XLVII, § 6: 'Statuimus etiam ne quisquam . . . ne emat vilius quæ mox carius vendat, nisi per cancellarium admissus (quam paucissimos autem admittat) et interventu fidejussorum obligatus sub pœna carceris et decem librarum in usum academiæ convertendarum.' *Docs. Univ. Camb.*, 1. 485.

2. The Latin version here adds 'intra Collegij limites.'

3. The Camb. Eliz. Statutes, cap. L, require colleges to fine their members for absence from prayers, lectures, or other stated exercises. *Docs. Univ. Camb.*, 1. 490–91.

4. This was the universal custom in English and Continental universities; and Josiah Quincy was the first Harvard president who addressed undergraduates as 'Mr.' See index, 'Sir.'

5. 'Aut Nobilis alicujus filius' in the Latin version.

6. *Jentaculum* and *merenda* in the Latin. See *H. C. S. C.*, Chapter V, for 'bevers.'

7. The Latin is *hujus Collegij*. Harvard College was often called 'the House' in the seventeenth and eighteenth centuries (*C. S. M.*, xv. lxxxix, n. 3), as all Oxford and Cambridge colleges were then, and as Christ Church still is.

8. The Latin is more explicit: 'postquam fuerit bis admonitus si non adultus virgis

his name shall bee given up to the Overseers of the Colledge that he may be publikely dealt with after the desert of his fault but in grosser offences such graduall proceeding shall not bee expected.

18. Every Scholar that on proofe is found able to read the originall of the old and New testament into the Latin toungue, and to Resolve them Logically [1] withall beeing of honest life and conversation and at any publike act hath the approbation of the overseers, and Master [2] of the Colledge may bee invested with his first degree.

19. Every Scholar that giveth up in writing a Synopsis or summa [3] of Logicke, Naturall and morall Philosophy, Arithmeticke, Geometry; and Astronomy, and is ready to defend his theses or positions, withall Skilled in the originals as aforesaid and still continues honest and studious, at any publike act after triall hee shall bee capable of the second degree of Master of Arts.

This first code of Harvard College statutes appears to have been drawn from the Elizabethan statutes of the University of Cambridge, a printed copy of which was owned by President Dunster,[4] and from memories of certain college statutes. A puritan note appears only in the requirement to read the Bible twice daily, and to repeat sermons — unless we regard as puritan the brevity, simplicity, and common-sense character of the whole. The Overseers followed the principle of Governor Winthrop in secular legislation; [5] they believed that it was better to let college customs crystallize into laws, and to leave penalties and punishments to the discretion of college officers, than to indulge in the vanity of English collegiate founders, who endeavored to anticipate every possible exigency, to regulate in

coerceatur.' Cf. Camb. Eliz. Statutes on violations of the statute *De modestia* (cap. xlvii): 'Hujus rei violatores, si non fuerint adulti, virga a suis coerceantur: sin adulti, primo aspere verbis castigentur, secundo hebdomadæ commeatu, tertio menstruo commeatu, quarto e collegio ejiciantur.' *Docs. Univ. Camb.*, I. 483–84. Cf. also statutes of Trinity College, Dublin: 'Qui semel fecerit, si ætate adultus fuerit, commeatu trimestri privetur; si ætate puer, virgis castigetur: qui autem bis, Collegio amoveatur.' Mahaffy, *op. cit.*, p. 344. See also index, 'whipping.' *Adultus* meant eighteen years of age and upward.

1. The Latin statute here adds 'fueritque naturalis et moralis philosophiæ principijs imbutus' (instructed in the principles of Physics and Ethics). For 'logical analysis' see *H. C. S. C.*, Chapter XIII.

2. *Praeses* in the Latin version.

3. For synopses, see *H. C. S. C.*, Chapter VII.

4. 'Quorum Exemplar impressum habeo.' Dunster's *Quadriennium* Memoir, *C. S. M.*, xxxi. 293.

5. See Winthrop's *Journal* for 1639 and 1641 (1908 ed., I. 324, II. 49–52), where he argues for laws arising 'pro re nata upon occasions' as 'the laws of England and other states grew,' and argues that punishments be left 'to the wisdom of the judges.'

a minute degree the daily life of their foundations, and to pre-
scribe exact punishments for every imaginable crime and offense. But we must not suppose that because certain practices
were not forbidden in the Harvard College laws, they were
allowed. For instance, we miss the customary prohibition of
English college statutes against throwing dice, playing cards,
and frequenting *infames mulieres vel meretricas*; this does not
mean that such distractions were permitted, but that colony
laws and want of opportunity in the village of Cambridge rendered prohibition superfluous. When such abuses appeared
they were legislated against, as in the college laws of 1655.[1]
Far from thinking up all offenses that scholars had committed
in England, and might commit here, the Overseers followed the
good advice that Thomas Shepard gave Governor Winthrop:
'the consequences will be very sad . . . to make more sins then
(as yet is seene) God himselfe hath made.'[2]

A good instance of this principle of not anticipating evils in
the early Harvard statutes is the matter of frequenting public
assemblies. The Elizabethan statutes of Cambridge forbade
scholars to attend judicial sessions, or Sturbridge fair; there was
a similar prohibition in the Laudian statutes of Oxford.[3] Nothing was said about this in the first Harvard code. By 1650, presumably, Harvard students had begun to cut lectures in order
to attend the quarterly courts at Cambridge, the June fair at
Watertown, and the spring election in Boston — the nearest
equivalent to holidays that the Bay Colony afforded. And in
the meantime a local artillery company had been organized,
drilling alternately at Cambridge and Watertown. Probably
there were complaints of the prohibition to 'bee of the Artillery
or traine-Band' as unsuitable in a frontier community that
needed trained officers. At least, so I should explain an order
'agreed upon by the Overseers at a meeting in Harvard Colledge, May: 6th: 1650':

1. *C. S. M.*, xxxi. 330–31, 338. If anyone deem the prohibitions of these first
Harvard laws 'puritanical,' he is invited to read the chapter *de Ludis prohibitis* in the
Laudian Code of Statutes of Oxford, p. 150, in which undergraduates, under pain of
whipping, are required to abstain from the use of dice and playing-cards; from the
ludum pilæ pedalis (football), the *lusus Globorum* (tennis?), cudgel-play, and other
'vain sports' of this kind; from hunting and keeping hounds, hawks, ferrets, gins, and
nets; from discharging guns or cross-bows; and from attending exhibitions of strolling
players, rope-dancers, and prize-fighters.

2. 4 *Coll. M. H. S.*, vii. 270.

3. *Docs. Univ. Camb.*, i. 484–85; *Laudian Statutes* (1888 ed.), pp. 147–48.

No Schollar whatever without the fore acquaintance and leave of the President and his Tutor, or in the absence of either of them two of the Fellowes shal bee present at or in any of the Publike Civil meetings or Concourse of people as Courts of justice, elections, fayres, or at military exercise in the time or howers of the Colledge exercise Publike or private neither shal any schollar exercise himself in any Military band, unlesse of knowne gravity and of approoved, sober and vertuous conversation and that with leave of the President and his Tutor.[1]

Tobacco-taking was frowned upon by the Bay authorities, partly as a fire hazard, and partly as a 'waste of precious time.' Accordingly, at this same session of 1650, the Overseers ordered that

No scholar shall take Tobacco unlesse permitted by the President with the Consent of their parents or guardians, and on good reason first given by a Physitian and then in a sober and private manner.[2]

Many scholars, it would appear, secured the desired permission; for the Steward was dealing in the noxious herb before the end of President Dunster's administration.

Like the Elizabethan statutes of Cambridge, the Harvard code is purposely vague on the subject of studies, it being desired to leave President and tutors free, by trial and error, to work out a suitable curriculum. Historians wish that they had been more explicit, and so doubtless did President Dunster when, a few years later, he found great difficulty in extending the course for the B.A. from the *triennium*, with which he had perforce begun, to the *quadriennium* required by English university standards.

In another and very important respect the foundation statutes of Harvard departed from English precedent. Neither in the act of 1642, nor in the Charter of 1650, nor in the laws and statutes passed by Overseers and Fellows was any religious test or oath imposed. This omission is most remarkable; for there was probably no university in the Christian world in 1640 where the governors, professors, or graduates were not required to take some such religious test as attending Mass, or subscribing to some set of religious principles.[3] By what process of reason-

---

1. *C. S. M.*, xv. 27. 2. *Id.*, p. 28.

3. This was even true in the Dutch universities. See *Statuta et Leges Acad. Lugd. Bat.* (1654), art. 19, and *Statuta et Leges Fundamentales Academiae Franequerae*, 1547 (*sic*, 1647), in which the Professors are required to subscribe to the Heidelberg Confession.

ing did our puritan founders and governors deliberately omit such a common engine of orthodoxy?

This problem has puzzled all historians of Harvard. Josiah Quincy, who as President frequently had to defend the College against the charge of betraying her founders' principles, was wont to adduce this absence of sectarian tests as proof of a 'liberal spirit' in the early clergy and magistracy.[1] From what we know of the New England puritans, the mere thought of such conscious liberalism is ludicrous. President Lowell suggests that the omission of religious tests in the College was due to the fact that the whole community professed a single form of religious faith and discipline, organized dissent not being tolerated, so that no need was felt of subjecting every boy to a test of conformity. Yet the College was established when the Hutchinson affair was still fresh in memory, and for half a century both Church and State were frequently engaged in heresy-hunts.[2] It has also been argued that the puritans were opposed to taking oaths of allegiance. But the only puritans so opposed were the followers of Roger Williams, who was banished from the Bay Colony, partly for that very reason.

Need we exclude common sense as the reason for omitting oaths and religious tests? Our founders knew from their English experience that oaths were powerless to bind conscience, just as irrepealable statutes become unenforceable when conditions change. Every puritan graduate of Cambridge University before admission to a degree had sworn and subscribed obedience to the Three Articles, which he had no intention of obeying; and most of them had again committed constructive perjury when taking holy orders at the hands of a bishop. To have provided Harvard College at her birth with all this statutory and juramental apparatus would have been equivalent to launching a ship with all sails set, and the sheets and halyards padlocked. Accordingly this academic vessel was provided with

1. Quincy, I. 44–47; the same argument may be found in numerous presidential reports and controversial documents of the nineteenth century; President Eliot more than once made effective use of it.

2. And there were test oaths in the universities of Latin South America, from which heresy was more vigorously and successfully excluded than from New England. The *profesion de fé* required before the doctor's degree at Córdoba, beginning with the Nicene Creed and ending with a promise to maintain the Catholic faith 'whole and immaculate' until death, occupies two and a half pages (72–74) of Juan M. Garro, *Bosquejo Histórico de la Universidad de Córdoba* (Buenos Aires, 1882).

the barest possible code of statutes, and her master and crew, unhampered by oaths and religious tests, were left to exercise their best judgment, as God gave it them.

COLONY AND COLLEGE

In the meantime New England was pulling out of her economic depression, largely by establishing trading relations with the West Indies. All danger of these colonies being depopulated or removed to another and more favorable location was at an end. The return movement of educated New Englanders to the old country slackened, for civil war was raging in old England, and in comparison the colonies seemed comfortable and secure. In Massachusetts Bay the political strife between freemen and magistrates simmered down, and a bicameral system was adopted. The Bay Colony worked out a mercantile system of its own, taxing imports and restricting exports with a view to making Massachusetts a self-contained commonwealth. In 1643, the Bible Commonwealths of New England formed a confederacy, which was soon appealed to by President Dunster to assume financial responsibility for the College.[1]

In the same year, Cambridge, by reason of the accommodation in the College, became the 'convention city' of New England. 'There was a great assembly at Cambridge of all the elders in the country, about 50 in all,' records Governor Winthrop in September.[2] 'They sat in the college, and had their diet there after the manners of scholars' commons, but somewhat better, yet so ordered as it came not to above six pence the meal for a person.' We may be sure that President Dunster took occasion to point out the financial needs of the College, and that he did the honors acceptably; for the great synod of 1646–48, which produced the New England Platform of Church Discipline, held its three summer sessions at Cambridge.[3] Before the meeting of June 9, 1647, John Eliot, who had a sound showman's instinct, let it be known among the Indians that if they attended in sufficient numbers he would preach to them. He was rewarded by 'a great confluence of *Indians* [from] all parts.'[4]

1. See Chapter XXI, above.
2. *Journal* (1908 ed.), II. 138–39. By 'Elders' he meant ministers.
3. *Id.*, pp. 280, 324, 347.
4. Thomas Shepard, *The Clear Sun-shine of the Gospel Breaking Forth Upon The Indians in New-England* (London, 1648), pp. 11–12; 3 *Coll. M. H. S.*, IV. 45.

And in all the long history of the College Yard there has been no more picturesque scene than on that June afternoon. The reverend elders in their black doublets and white bands, the worshipful magistrates in their impressive cloaks, sundry townspeople, and such students as had not been turned out to make room for delegates, in their brighter and more varied costumes, were grouped about the steps of the Old College. John Eliot takes his place in the centre; and about him, eagerly drinking in his words, squat the 'heathen' in all their unspoiled dirt and color. The sermon over, Indians propound questions, such as

What Countrey man Christ was, and where he was borne?
How farre off that place was from us here?
Where Christ now was?
How they might lay hold on him, and where, being now absent from them?

And when these are answered, and the Indians have professed themselves satisfied by their accustomed grunts, John Eliot tries out his catechism on 'divers poore naked children,' who shrill out the answers in unison. All of which 'did marvellously affect all the wise and godly Ministers, Magistrates, and people, and did raise their hearts up to great thankfulnesse to God . . . for joy to see such a blessed day, and the Lord Jesus so much known and spoken of among such as never heard him before.'

'God's people' were in the saddle, both in Old England and New; it were strange if the School of the Prophets did not prosper.

Increase in numbers it did. At Commencement, 1650, there were over forty students in the College; fifty-five bachelors' and eighteen masters' degrees were granted in the first decade (1642–51). But financially the College was receiving a precarious and far from ample support from the Charlestown ferry, a few rents, and the 'Colledge Corne.'[1]

The Dunster Family, the new Lodging, and the Printing Press

President Dunster still had plenty to worry about. With the widow Glover he had acquired responsibility for considerable property, and for five stepchildren. Roger Glover, the eldest,

1. See Chapter XXI, above.

soon returned to England to seek his fortune in the war, and was slain in Cromwell's assault on Edinburgh Castle in 1650.[1] Unfortunately Mrs. Dunster died in August, 1643, before any of the younger children had grown up. The President took for second wife, in 1644, a seventeen- or eighteen-year-old girl named Elizabeth Atkinson;[2] and it was doubtless in this connection that, the same year, the General Court voted £150 for a new President's Lodging. The sum would seem to have been sufficient for a capacious mansion, since houses and lots were selling for £40 and £50 in Cambridge at that time. But Dunster received it in 'country pay' — corn and the like — which did not go so far as money; and his Lodging was not completed without 'great difficultyes' and contributions by his friends.[3]

This President's Lodging, which was the residence of Dunster, Chauncy, and Hoar, was in the original Yard (I), between the Old College and the street [4] — the best location to observe everything that was going on. Exactly when the presidential couple moved in we do not know; probably not until after their first child, David, was born, in May, 1645. Four more children, of whom two died young, followed;[5] and under the same roof lived the younger Glovers, whose education was taken in hand by their stepfather. As if that was not enough responsibility, two wretched little Indians were added to the President's household, to be prepared by him for college.[6] The Lodge on Braintree Street became a veritable Harvard Annex for the education of Indians and Glovers.

To support this establishment, Dunster had a salary of about £55, including the students' tuition fees, and an inconsider-

1. Dunster's petition of October 20, 1652, to the General Court. Dunster Mss.
2. The identification of the second Mrs. Dunster made by Mr. Moriarty in *N. E. H. G. R.*, LXXX. 94, may be considered proved by the President's reference to her sister Helen, wife of Joseph Hills of Malden, as 'my sister Mrs. Hills' in his will.
3. See Chapter XXI for data on the payment for the Lodging.
4. Littlefield, *Early Mass. Press*, I. 75–77, 80, states that it was on the site of Massachusetts Hall; Mr. Matthews and (*mea culpa*) the *D. A. B.*, v. 163, gave it their approval. But that site was not acquired by the College until 1661! Mr. Matthews has now made full amends for this untimely translation by pointing out that (1) the inventory of December 10, 1654 (*C. S. M.*, xv. 208–09), proves that the Lodging was on College land, and that (2) a vote of the Corporation in 1670, requiring the Treasurer 'to rebuild the Presidents fences against the high way with a stone wall' (*id.*, p. 225), proves that the Lodging was on or very close to the site of the Peyntree house, since the college grounds then abutted on no other highway than Braintree Street.
5. *N. E. H. G. R.*, LXXX. 95.
6. See his accounts for them, in Chapter XXI.

able revenue from the Glover estate. Fortunately, as each of the three Glover girls had been left £400 by their father's will on their marriage or majority, several ambitious young colonials showed a readiness to take them off stepfather's hands. The Winthrop family, as usual, showed a superior enterprise in this matter. Adam Winthrop, son of the Governor, married Elizabeth Glover in 1644; her younger sister Sarah was carried off by Adam's brother Deane, about four years later. Priscilla, to whom the President gave a 'liberal education' that he valued at £120, was the chosen bride of John Appleton of Ipswich in 1651. By that time John Glover had graduated from Harvard College and gone to Scotland to study medicine. Mr. and Mrs. Dunster were left comparatively lonely, with only their first-born, David (who turned out a prodigal), and little Henry, who did not long survive.

The first printing press [1] in the English colonies also became part of Dunster's responsibility through his marriage. Treasurer Danforth recorded in College Book III, some time after 1654, 'Mr Joss: Glover gave to the Colledge a Font of printing Letters,' and 'Some Gentlemen of Amsterdam gave towards the furnishing of a Printing-Press with Letters . . . fourty-nine pound and somthing more.' [2] But he omits to say that the press was operated for sixteen years after Glover's death as a private

---

1. Fortunately the Dunster Mss. in the H. U. Archives supply many facts about this press, which are used with good judgment in Samuel A. Green, *Ten Fac-simile Reproductions Relating to New England* (1902), of which the chapter on Stephen Day is printed separately. A. McF. Davis in *Proc. A. A. S.*, n.s. v. 295–302, printed one important document that Green did not. The other secondary literature on the press is undependable, as are the bibliographies (cf. George Parker Winship, *The Literature of the History of Printing in the U. S.*, 1923). Isaiah Thomas started a myth-making process in his *History of Printing in America*. Robert F. Roden, *The Cambridge Press, 1638–1692* (1905), is a chatty work for bibliophiles; the 'Bibliographical List' at the back, written before the discovery of several items, ignores all the Harvard *Quaestiones* and many of the *Theses*, and makes several bad errors. Charles Evans' *American Bibliography* is more nearly accurate, but includes a few items now known to have been printed in England. George E. Littlefield, *The Early Massachusetts Press, 1638–1711* (2 vols., Club of Odd Volumes, 1907), is one of the most exasperatingly inaccurate books I have ever used. From sad experience I have learned never to rely on it for a fact or a quotation. It is claimed that an old printing press now in the possession of the Vermont Historical Society is the actual one sent over by Glover and set up by Stephen Day, but the 'chain of evidence' which is presented by Rush C. Hawkins in *The Literary Collector*, VII. (1903–04) 33–39, 136–39, and summarized in Roden, *op. cit.*, pp. 45–48, has several very weak links. Day's press must have been too battered by 1700 to be of use to anyone but a junk dealer.

2. *C. S. M.*, xv. 174–75.

venture, before it came into possession of the College. It was President Dunster, if anyone, who made the gift.

There is no reason to suppose that Jose Glover purchased the press for the College, which was hardly in a condition at the time he sailed — in the summer of 1638 — to assume such a responsibility. Both Winthrop and Johnson, the chroniclers who mention the arrival of the press, imply that it was a public-spirited venture for which Glover assumed the charge.[1] Stephen Day and his two sons, his Bordman stepson, and three menservants, for all of whom passage money was advanced by Glover, were obligated to work for him (not for the College) 'at such rates and prizes as is vsually paid and allowed for the like worke in the Country there.'[2] And the reference to the 'Gentlemen of Amsterdam' is most significant. Hitherto the presses of the Netherlands (some of them, like Elder Brewster's at Leyden, operated by English exiles) had been the principal means by which puritans defeated the strict censorship in England. As part of Archbishop Laud's conformity campaign, the English puritan churches in the Netherlands were being disrupted in the sixteen-thirties, and the Dutch authorities were becoming unpleasantly interested in the English tracts that were being issued from Dutch printing houses.[3] Glover's press was a small one, costing but £20, but quite equal to printing the Bay Psalm Book, and the owner brought over a considerable quantity of book paper.[4] It might well become the nucleus of a large printing establishment, producing for the English market prohibited books, the smuggling of which into England would be a profit-

---

1. Winthrop's *Journal* (1853 ed.), I. 348; *W.W.P.*, p. 183, says that Glover 'provided, for further compleating the Colonies in Church and Common-wealth-work, a Printer.'

2. The indenture is in the Dunster Mss., and is printed in Samuel A. Green, *op. cit.*, pp. 1–3. For the myth about Glover's previous visit to Massachusetts, 'Presidency Elect,' etc., see end of Chapter XVIII.

3. This was a part of the pressure brought by the English government on the States General, which forced Davenport, Peter, and Hooker to emigrate to New England. R. P. Stearns, in *N. E. Q.*, VI. 747–92; and Mr. Stearns has given me notes on the Boswell Papers in Additional Mss. 6394, British Museum, which show the keen interest of that zealous ambassador of Charles I to the Netherlands in ferreting out English puritan tracts. Cf. *Calendar State Papers, Domestic, 1633–34*, pp. 279–80. That, doubtless, is why the 'Gentlemen of Amsterdam' gave one of the first fonts of type (*C. S. M.*, xv. 175). This entry conflicts with one made by President Hoar in 1674 (*id.*, pp. 20–21), crediting the first font to seven benefactors, mostly New Englanders — one of them, John Freake, not known to have been in the country before 1660.

4. Stephen Day's testimony, April 2, 1656; Dunster Mss. and *Proc. A. A. S.*, n.s. v. 296 n.

able and exciting occupation for New England shipmasters and supercargoes. Enterprising Hugh Peter even attempted to drum up trade for the Cambridge press in Bermuda. 'Wee haue a printery here,' he wrote to Patrick Copland on December 10, 1638, 'and thinke to goe to worke with some *speciall* things, and if you have any thing you may send it *safely* by these.' [1] But the outbreak of civil war in England opened English presses to all manner of religious and political heresies, leaving only local business for the Cambridge press.

The press seems to have been set up in Cambridge for no better reason than that Mrs. Glover settled there. Having both the press and the Day family on her hands, she bought them a house and lot on Crooked Lane, and there, presumably,[2] Stephen Day set up the 'printery' toward the end of 1638. Within four years he had printed the Freeman's Oath, the 1639 almanac, the famous Bay Psalm Book, the first Harvard Commencement theses, and 'The Capitall Lawes of New England.' For the last item, President Dunster was paid 12s 6d by the Colony in 1642.[3]

The President and his second wife, as we have seen, moved into the new Lodging on the site of the Peyntree house in 1645 or 1646; there the press was installed after a convenient interval.[4] Presumably it occupied the ground floor of a lean-to or addition on the north side of this first presidential mansion, facing the Old College.[5]

The fact that Sam Nowell of the Class of August 9, 1653, had

1. 4 *Coll. M. H. S.*, VI. 99; italics mine. Copland of course knew well what 'speciall' things meant — puritan tracts. 'These' meant the bearers, one of whom was Capt. William Pierce, 'an honest godly man of our church.'

2. No. 14 on Dr. Norris' map of Cambridge in 1638, at the end of Chapter XIV, above. No. 21 was Day's home after he ceased to be printer.

3. *C. S. M.*, xv. 21. Frederick L. Gay corrected the mistakes about the *Capitall Lawes*, and reproduced the English reprint of it, in *C. S. M.*, xvII. 116–18; cf. xxvII. 112–15. The fact that the 12s 6d was itemized separately from Dunster's receipts for the College, proves that his wife still owned the press.

4. A record in *Cambridge Proprietors' Records*, p. 133, shows that Dunster had sold the Day house to John Fownall before March, 1647–48, when he bought it back.

5. The President's Lodging had '2 leantoes' in 1654 (*C. S. M.*, xv. 208). Samuel Nowell (A.B. August 9, 1653) returned just before his Commencement his 'study in the printing roome,' which he apparently had had since 1649 (*C. S. M.*, xxxI. 69); Joshua Long (A.B. August 10, 1653) paid £3 Income in June, 1651, for 'the study that was sir Eatones in the chamber over the printing roome' (*id.*, p. 91), and which Eaton had hired a few months earlier (*id.*, p. 25); there was a third study 'In the Chamber aboue the prentinge roome' which Nathaniel Pelham (A.B. 1651) occupied, and which Mordecai Matthews (A.B. 1655) obtained in March, 1651–52. *C. S. M.*, xxxI. 138.

his 'study in the printing roome' indicates that the press had very little business; which Stephen Day's accounts show to be the case.[1] New England ministers eager to burst into print naturally preferred to play for the English market, and sent their manuscripts to London. In the years 1645-48 there were printed only a propaganda pamphlet on Indian relations, a catechism by Edward Norris, a second edition of the Bay Psalm Book, the annual almanacs, and the Book of the General Lawes and Liberties. This last was a creditable piece of presswork,[2] and the almanacs, besides their indispensable service to New England farmers and mariners, in some measure provided a poetry and scientific annual for Harvard graduate students.[3]

Although Stephen Day received a land grant from the General Court in 1641 as 'the first that set upon printing,'[4] he was much more interested in prospecting for minerals and in land speculation than in running the press. He was committed to jail in 1643 'for his defrauding several men,' and though released two days later by the General Court, the incident would hardly have recommended him to the President's continued favor. It is clear from Day's suit against Dunster in 1656,[5] and his malicious testimony in the Glover case — accusing the President, among other things, of appropriating Glover silver and a clock worth £4 10s — that the printer had an old grudge to pay off.[6] It seems probable that, after his first wife's death, Dunster discharged Stephen Day and put the press in charge of his young son Matthew, whose name appears as printer on the title-page of the almanac for 1647. Matthew Day, who also served as Steward, died on May 10, 1649, dictating on his

1. A. McF. Davis, in *Proc. A. A. S.*, n.s. v. 302, prints the list of imprints from the Dunster Mss.

2. No copy of this book was known when Roden's bibliography came out, but shortly after a copy turned up in England. It is now in the Henry E. Huntington Library, which generously issued a line-for-line and word-for-word reprint: *The Laws and Liberties of Massachusetts, reprinted from the copy of the 1648 edition in the Henry E. Huntington Library*. With an Introduction by Max Farrand (Harvard University Press, 1929).

3. See *H. C. S. C.*, Chapters VI and X.

4. *Mass. Bay Recs.*, I. 344; see sketch of Day in *D. A. B.*

5. April 1, 1656, 'for Labour and Expences about the printing presse and the utensils and appurtenances thereof, and the mannaging the said worke.' Dunster won the suit, and Day had to pay costs. Middlesex Court Records, Pulsifer transcript, I. 94.

6. S. A. Green, *op. cit.*, p. 11. Dunster, replying to this charge, said that he had never seen such a clock, and 'he spake seriously and truly. for mr Dayes soules good.' Acknowledgement in court, April 1, 1656, Dunster Mss.

deathbed a nuncupative will that testifies to his sweet nature: most of his chattels and money to his mother; a small fund to send a neighbor's child to school; one silver spoon each to little David and Dorothy Dunster and Sam Shepard; 'to Sir Brock (my ould and dear friend) all the books I have which he thinks may be useful to him'; and 'with all my heart all that part I have in the Garden unto the fellowes of Harvard Colledge for ever.'[1]

Dunster's choice of a successor to Matthew Day is a tribute to his eye for men. Samuel Green[2] of Cambridge was one of those popular, versatile, faithful, and energetic characters necessary to the good conduct of any college town. He had come over as a lad of eighteen with his parents in Hooker's company. 'Sergeant Green,' as he is generally called in the college accounts, became prominent in the militia; and when the House of Deputies first achieved the dignity of a separate room he was appointed their doorkeeper.[3] Later he became clerk of the writs, and the Steward's book shows that he acted as college barber and stationer. Green was thirty-four years old at the death of Matthew Day; he had had no experience of printing,[4] and accepted the position with some reluctance; but he was quick to learn, and the books that issued from the press during his forty-three years as college and independent printer showed constant improvement, up to a certain point. The first book that he printed was the Platform of Church Discipline, largely by Richard Mather, which had been adopted by the late Cambridge Synod. The next year he brought out Urian Oakes' Almanac, a Catechism by Samuel Danforth of Roxbury, and a supplement to the Laws of 1648. And in 1651 he issued the only printed work of which President Dunster is known to have been part author.

This was 'The Psalmes Hymns And Spiritual Songs Of the Old and New Testament, faithfully translated into English metre, For the use, edification, and comfort, of the Saints, in publick, and private, especially in New-England.' It was, in effect, a revised Bay Psalm Book, intended to replace the rude

1. S. A. Green, *op. cit.*, pp. 5, 9–10. Sir Brock was John Brock, A.B. 1646; for the 'Garden' or Fellows' Orchard, see Chapter XX.

2. Paige, pp. 567–68; *D. A. B.* His house was the one numbered 16 on our Map of Cambridge at the end of Chapter XIV.

3. *Mass. Bay Recs.*, III. 2.

4. See his autobiographical letter of 1675, in 5 *Coll. M. H. S.*, I. 422–24.

THE
PSALMS
HYMNS And SPIRITUAL
SONGS

Of the Old and New Test-
ament, *faithfully* tranflated
into *ENGLISH* metre,

For the ufe, edification, *and* comfort,
of the *Saints*, in publick, & private,
efpecially in New-England.

---

2 *Tim*: 3. 16, 17.

Col 3. 16. *Let the word of God dwell in
you richly in all wifdom, teaching & ad-
monifhing one another in Pfalms, Hymns,
and fpirituall Songs, finging to the* Lord
with grace in your hearts.
Ephe : 5. 18,19. *Bee filled with &c:*

James 5. 13.

Printed by *Samuel Green* at *Cambridg*
in *New-England.* 1 6 5 1.

TITLE-PAGE IN THE DUNSTER-LYON PSALM BOOK, 1651

Luke chaq: 1.

The labour of the Olive fail ,
And though ỹ fields no meat should bear ?

Though flocks shall be cut off from fold,
In stall no herd, should have abode.
18 Yet in the LORD rejoyce I would,
I'le joy in my salvations God :
The LORD God is my strength, and hee
Doth make my feet like Hinds also ,
And he it is that causeth mee
Upon my places high to go.

The Song of the blessed virgine
M A R Y.

Luke 1. *verse* 46,
MY soul doth Magnifie the LORD,
47   My spirit is glad also
In God my Saviour. Who beheld
his handmaids state so low :
For lo, henceforth all ages shall
mee ever blessed name.
49 For mee the strong, great things hath
and Holy is his Name.   (doue,

50 Such also as him reverence ,
his mercy is upon :
And that from generation ,
to generation,
Z   51

staves of that New England incunabulum at which even the elders poked fun. 'It was thought,' says Cotton Mather,[1] 'that a little more of Art was to be employ'd upon them: And for that Cause, they were committed unto Mr. *Dunster*, who Revised and Refined this Translation; and (with some Assistance from Mr. *Richard Lyon*, who being sent over by Sir *Henry Mildmay*, as an Attendant unto his Son, then a Student in *Harvard Colledge*, now resided in Mr. *Dunster's* House:) he brought it into the Condition wherein our Churches ever since have used it.' The Dunster-Lyon psalm book even outlasted Cotton Mather's day; it was frequently reprinted for the New England churches' use until 1758, when Thomas Prince (A.B. 1707) produced a new metrical translation. Dunster and Lyon, by paying due attention (as their preface promised) 'both to the gravity of the phrase' and to the 'sweetnes of the verse,' gave their version a life of over a century. In this matter, too, as the *Magnalia* reminds us, 'Mr. *Dunster* is to be acknowledged. And if unto the Christian, while singing of *Psalms* on Earth, *Chrysostom* could well say, Μετ' Ἀγγέλων ᾄδεις, μετ' Ἀγγέλων ὑμνεῖς, *Thou art in a Consort with Angels!* How much more may that *Now* be said of our *Dunster*?'

Harvard's first President seems to have had as much to do, and to have done as much, as any of his successors. In ten years' time he had obtained fellowships and scholarships, and established the forms, functions, even some of the amenities, of English colleges. The University of Oxford, by admitting a Harvard graduate *ad eundem gradum*,[2] had recognized that Harvard College was of university status, a member of the republic of letters. Her course for the first degree,[3] modelled on that of the University of Cambridge, fairly entitled Harvard to this privilege; although her young scholars, remote from the springs of learning in Europe, and deprived by their situation of the

1. *Magnalia*, book iii. 100. The only known copy of the first edition of the Dunster-Lyon *Psalms Hymns and Spiritual Songs*, in the New York Public Library, is described in Roden, *op. cit.*, pp. 59–62.

2. James Ward, A.B. 1645; incorporated B.A. in the University of Oxford, and admitted M.A. after examination, on October 10, 1648. Oxford Univ. Archives, Qu. 17, fol. 158; facsimile in *Harv. Alumni Bulletin*, xxxv. 805–06. A complete list of Oxford and Cambridge incorporations from Harvard (*ad eundem* degrees) will be printed in *H. C. S. C.*, Chapter XV.

3. A brief outline of it will be found on pp. 435–36, below, and the course will be described in detail in *H. C. S. C.*, Chapters VII–XIII.

competitive stimulus that comes from rival foundations, still wanted most of the advantages that a great and ancient university affords by reason of large numbers and sound traditions.

Looking back at these heroic days of small beginnings, it seems marvellous that so much had been attempted in the early years of the College, and that so considerable a part of the founders' generous hopes had been realized. But President Dunster was not the sort to rest on his oars or indulge in pride over victories won. As he looked into the future on New Year's Day, 1650, he doubtless felt more apprehension over what had not been done than satisfaction with what had been accomplished. As he saw it, two things, in the main, were wanting to place Harvard College on a firm foundation: adequate financial support, and corporate independence. The one was not to come for over a century; the other was provided before that year's end, through a Charter that is still in force.

Far more important than these things, in the long run, was the brave religious faith, serenely overriding all prudent objections and practical difficulties, that carried the puritan fathers, through poverty and struggle, into so ambitious and so excellent an enterprise. 'To advance *Learning* and perpetuate it to Posterity,' was their high purpose; posterity dared not fail to achieve the design so confidently pricked out on their white shield of expectation.

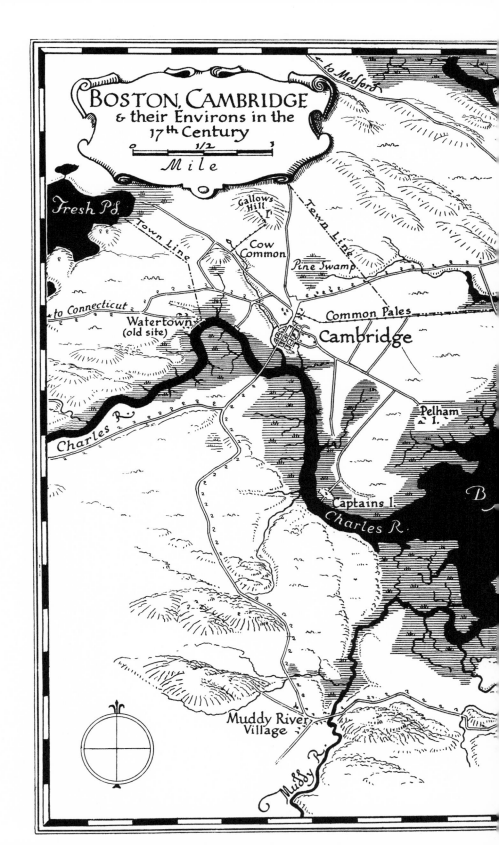

APPENDICES

APPENDIX A

THE STUDENT UNIVERSITIES OF BOLOGNA, SPAIN, AND SPANISH AMERICA

 Although Paris was the institutional ancestor of Oxford, Cambridge, and Harvard, we can hardly proceed without a brief note on the University of Bologna, in a somewhat remote sense the ancestor of the Harvard Law School, and in a very direct sense the ancestor of our sister universities of Latin America. In Italy 'the same spiritual force which manifested itself north of the Alps in the teaching of Roscellinus and Abélard'[1] took on the aspect of a revival of Roman law; for in Italy there had never been a complete breach of the Roman tradition of secular education. Within the walled towns of Lombardy 'at least the forms and the names of the Roman legal system maintained an unbroken continuity.' Naturally the Church gained less control over education in places where these secular vestiges survived than she did north of the Alps, where the barbarians obliterated all the intellectual glory of Rome that the Church did not save. Indeed, as many a pious pilgrim has had reason to observe, the nearer one got to Rome the less one saw of the Church; and the puritan movement which mothered Harvard was an attempt to liberate the Church from the Roman conquest.

In these regions where Roman law survived, the growth of commerce and of communal life in the twelfth century created a demand for trained lawyers, not only in the courts of justice but in the municipalities and notarial offices. At the same time the Church was developing a law of her own, through the successive decretals issued by popes and councils, and this discordant body of canon law was sadly in need of straightening out. Irnerius and Gratian, who flourished at Bologna during the first half of the twelfth century, bear the same relation to this legal and Italian aspect of the twelfth-century renaissance as Abélard to that of northern Europe; and in the work of Gratian at least, the method inaugurated by Abélard had a deep influence. Gratian's *Concordantia discordantium Canonum*, better known as the Decretal, was 'one of those great text-books which ap-

1. Rashdall, I. 91.

pearing just at the right time and in the right place, take the world by storm.'[1] Both Irnerius and Gratian are somewhat shadowy figures. Traditionally, it was due to the teaching of the one and the text-book of the other that *docta Bononia* became a Mecca for students of both laws; and eventually of arts and medicine as well.

At some time in the latter half of the twelfth century the teachers of civil and canon law at Bologna organized themselves into a *universitas* or gild. But Bologna's contribution to university organization was student sovereignty. The law students who flocked thither were older and of a higher social class than the arts students who converged on Paris and Oxford. Yet in Bologna, as in other Italian city republics, these mature students were aliens without rights; to rob or kill them was no crime in Bolognese law. Hence at an early period the students, for self-government and self-protection, organized 'nations' or gilds of their own. Their large contribution to Bolognese prosperity, and their frequent threat to remove elsewhere, enabled these student nations to wrest concessions from the municipality, including the right of jurisdiction under their own elected officers. The earliest Bolognese professors, as local citizens, were excluded from the students' gilds, and the same threat of secession soon brought them to a proper sense of dependence. Students of Bologna not only elected their professors and made their salary contracts, but regulated the length, methods, and scope of their lectures. Indeed the only statutory right which the professors retained was that of examining candidates and admitting them to degrees; but even here they were forced to submit to student regulations respecting the nature and conduct of the examination. In the middle ages, when students were more eager to learn than teachers were to teach, and in subjects of direct professional consequence such as medicine and law, this proved an excellent system for keeping the professors up to the mark; at a later age, and in the arts course, its advantages became less obvious.

Whatever influence Bologna may have had on the universities of the United States passed through so many institutions on the way as to be untraceable.[2] Nevertheless, Bologna ultimately had as pervasive an influence on the education of the New World as Paris, for the universities of Latin America are her direct descendants. Lérida, the first Spanish university, was deliberately founded on the Bolo-

1. Rashdall, 1. 129.
2. Rashdall believes that the degree ceremonies at Oxford and Cambridge were in part derived from the student universities, which were famous for the elaborateness and costliness of their commencements. On the other hand, the 'nations' and their Rectors came no nearer to the United States than Scotland and the Netherlands (see Chapters IX and X). The title Rector was used for the titular head of at least three colonial colleges — Yale, Philadelphia, and for a time Harvard; but it had none of the Bolognese or Scottish connotation of an officer elected by the masters or students to represent their interests in university government.

gnese model in the year 1300. 'It had come to be accepted as an ordinance of nature that law students should form a self-governing body,' [1] and what was granted to canonists and civilians could not be denied to artists. The same student government was extended to other universities of the Iberian peninsula, including the older foundation of Salamanca; with this important modification that the professors, although elected to office by their students, obtained independent support from the municipality or the Crown. By the time that America was discovered Salamanca had become one of the largest and most famous universities in Europe, numbering students by the thousands; and there were important universities at Alcalá de Henares, Santiago de Compostela, and Saragossa.

 The Royal University of Mexico, first in the New World,[2] was founded in 1551 and established in 1553 deliberately on the model of Salamanca. The statutes of Salamanca, modified as the Crown thought proper, served as the statutes of the University of Mexico until 1645. Serving the richest country in the world, the University of Mexico was born to full university stature, with professors of law, medicine, and theology, as well as arts, with a Chancellor, a Rector whose negro lackeys carried swords (a privilege denied even to the viceroy's servants), with imposing bedels and gorgeous ceremonies — all in marked contrast to little Harvard struggling to maintain an arts course in hard-scrabble New England. The democratic Bolognese influence appears not only in the *claustro pleno* or Congregation of Masters and Doctors, which gave every graduate *licenciado* within the Valley of Mexico a voice and vote in all university matters, but also in the popular election to professorial chairs. These chairs were of two sorts, 'proprietary,' which were held for life, and 'temporary,' which were restricted to four-year terms. Professors were elected by the method called *oposición*, a public oratorical contest of *opositores* (candidates) on some topic related to the subject of the chair, held before the assembled students and professors. When all the candidates had had their say, the students elected the professor by popular vote. This system was so destructive of university discipline that it was done away with about 1780.

A medieval curriculum and scholastic methods lasted in the University of Mexico until the close of the eighteenth century. As in most Continental universities during the fifteenth and sixteenth centuries, the B.A. course was depressed to the level of a public grammar school

1. Rashdall, II. 88.
2. The claim that the Dominican college at Santo Domingo was raised to university rank in 1538 does not appear to be well established.

in England and America; and the Arts course proper was rewarded by the degree of *licenciado* or M.A.; in the seventeenth century it was not uncommon for boys to take their B.A. at the age of twelve or fourteen, and at the age of fifteen some were already competing for professorial chairs. By 1775 the University had granted 1162 Doctorates and M.A.'s and 29,882 B.A.'s. It is evident that, except for the few law and medical students, the University of Mexico in the seventeenth and eighteenth centuries was, in Anglo-American terms, serving mainly as a preparatory school for the Jesuit colleges, which provided board and lodging and excellent discipline, and profited by the amazing educational efficiency of that order.[1]

 The University of San Marcos of Lima, oldest in the New World,[2] was also a university of masters and scholars on the Salamanca model. On the initiative of the Dominican father Thomas de San Martin, it was founded by a *cédula real* of Charles V dated May 12, 1551, and created a Studium Generale 'with the privileges, franchises and liberties which hath the Studium and University of Salamanca.'[3] Two years later it was actually established. These privileges were confirmed by Philip II and by a bull of Pius V in 1571; three years later the University moved out of a Dominican convent into buildings of its own which it still occupies; and in 1578 the right of incorporation *ad eundem gradum* was accorded to its doctors. [4] As early as 1576 the University had four chairs of theology and sacred scriptures, three of canon and civil law, and two of arts. Two chairs of medicine were added in 1634, one of anatomy in 1660, and one of mathematics in 1678; [5] by the end of the century

---

1. Herbert I. Priestley, 'The Old University of Mexico,' *University of California Chronicle*, XXI. 369–85 (1919); Joaquín García Icazbalceta, *México en 1554. Tres Diálogos Latinos que Francisco Cervántes Salazar escribió é imprimió en Mexico en dicho año.* Spanish translation with extensive notes by the editor (Mexico, 1875); Juan José de Eguiara y Eguren, *Bibliotheca Mexicana* (Mexico, 1755); Irving A. Leonard, *Don Carlos de Sigüenza y Góngora* (Berkeley, 1929); M. M. P. Myers, manuscript master's thesis on *Origin and Beginning of the University of Mexico* (1929), University of Texas Library. The manuscript chronicle of the Royal and Pontifical University of Mexico by Cristóbal Bernardo de la Plaza y Jaen, edited by Nicolas Rangel, was printed in 1931 by the Mexican Government.

2. Since the present National University of Mexico is a new foundation of the year 1910, not the colonial university, which came to an end about 1850.

3. Alonso Eduardo de Salazar y Zevallos, *Constituciones y Ordenanzas de la Real Universidad y Estudio General de San Marcos de la Ciudad de los Reyes del Peru* (Lima, 1735).

4. José Dávila Condemarín, *Bosquejo Histórico ... de la insigne Universidad Mayor de San Marcos de Lima* (1854), p. 13.

5. Luis Antonio Eguiguren, *Catálogo Histórico del Claustro de la Universidad de San Marcos* (Lima, 1912).

there were at least twenty-two professors, who were chosen by *oposiciones* as in the University of Mexico. Degrees of bachelor, *licenciado*, and doctor were granted in the faculties of theology, law, and medicine, and of bachelor and *licenciado* in the Arts faculty. The *claustro*, or governing body of the University, consisted of all resident doctors, and M.A.'s at least twenty-five years old. The University of San Marcos suffered various vicissitudes, due partly to financial troubles, especially in 1613, and partly to competition on the part of the monastic colleges and of the Jesuits. In 1636 the University, whose lecture-rooms were almost empty, opened its halls to professors holding chairs founded by the various religious orders. Thereafter, theology tended to overshadow all other kinds of study. A medical college was founded in 1792. During the colonial period the expenses incident to taking a degree were so high — five thousand pesos or more for the doctorate — that in general only members of the Peruvian aristocracy could graduate. Yet this close integration with the governing class of the Viceroyalty made the University of San Marcos the center of such intellectual life as there was in the seventeenth and eighteenth centuries. During the latter century, university life suffered not only from financial disorders but also from an academic snobbery which encouraged the giving of high degrees to the holders of high office, usually to the accompaniment of extremely bad versifying. Nevertheless, many illustrious men such as León Pinelo, historiographer of the Indies, and Pedro de Peralta Barnuevo, epic poet and universal genius, are found on its roll of graduates.[1] Nor was San Marcos the only university in Peru: Cuzco has had a seat of higher learning since 1598. That ancient capital of the Incas had contained remarkable schools for the education of the Incaic élite during the pre-Spanish period.[2]

During the last century the University of San Marcos has undergone many vicissitudes, owing in great part to the close connection of student life with national politics. Since 1919 there have been prolonged student strikes and frequent reorganizations, too complicated to relate here; at the moment of writing (1934) the doors of the University have been closed by the Government for over a year.[3]

1. Felipe Barreda y Laos, *Vida intelectual de la Colonia* (Lima, 1909); Manuel Vicente Villarán, *Estudios sobre Educación Nacional* (Lima, 1925); P. A. Means, *Fall of the Inca Empire and the Spanish Rule in Peru* (New York, 1932), pp. 269–70.

2. Louis Baudin, 'La formation de l'élite et l'enseignement de l'Histoire dans l'Empire des Inka,' *Revue des Études Historiques* (1927), pp. 107–14, and *L'Empire socialiste des Inka* (Paris, 1928); P. A. Means, *Ancient Civilizations of the Andes* (New York, 1931), pp. 240, 262, 306.

3. Carlos Wiesse, *Breve Noticia de la Fundación y Transformaciones de la Facultad de Filosofía y Letras* (Lima, 1918); Julio C. Tello (A.M. Harvard 1911), *Reforma Universitaria* (Lima, 1928; the first chapter is a comparison of San Marcos and Harvard); Tomás Escajadillo, *La Revolución Universitaria de 1930* (Lima, 1931); historical dis-

Another university on the Salamanca model was founded at Córdoba in the Viceroyalty of La Plata before Harvard was established; and many others have been founded since. After a period of centralization and state control, the traditions of the medieval student universities have been revived in Latin America. At Mexico, delegates of a student council sit on the *claustro* which makes appointments and promotions in the professoriat; and at Lima, as well as at Córdoba, it is impossible for an unpopular professor to retain his chair. It is, then, no wonder that the universities of the United States and Canada find it difficult to make satisfactory contacts and exchanges with the universities in other parts of America; for they have no common ancestor. The one group is descended from twelfth-century Paris, the other from twelfth-century Bologna, *Docta Bononia Mater Studiorum.*

course by Jorge Guillermo Leguía, Secretary of the University, in *Boletín Universitario*, año I. no. 6 (Lima, 1931). Dr. Jorge Basadre, professor of history and librarian in the University of San Marcos, and Mr. Philip Ainsworth Means (A.B. 1915), have kindly supplied me with indispensable facts and references.

APPENDIX B

ENGLISH UNIVERSITY MEN WHO EMIGRATED TO NEW ENGLAND BEFORE 1646

PROFESSOR FRANKLIN B. DEXTER of Yale was the first to point out the extraordinarily high proportion of English university men in early New England, and the significance of this emigration. In 1880, Mr. Dexter published a list of 72 Cantabrigians and 22 Oxonians who came to New England before 1650.[1] Mr. J. Gardner Bartlett in 1924 extended the numbers to 104 for Cambridge and 29 for Oxford.[2] The following list includes 130 names, of which 100 are Cantabrigians and 32 Oxonians — three being connected with both universities. It differs from Mr. Bartlett's, partly by way of correction, partly because my purpose is to include only those men who could have formed a part of the university-educated public opinion which founded and supported early Harvard.[3] None are included who came to New England after 1645; but extension to a later date would have made no appreciable addition to the number.[4]

1. 'The Influence of the English Universities in the Development of New England,' *Proceedings Massachusetts Historical Society*, XVII. 340–352, reprinted separately and in Dexter's *Historical Papers* (1918), pp. 102–115. Mr. Dexter left many gaps and made numerous errors, the most glaring being his statement that no member of Laud's College (St. John's, Oxford) came to New England. Actually four St. John's men emigrated, and only one Oxford college sent more.

2. *Publications Colonial Society Massachusetts*, XXV. 14–23. Mr. Bartlett's death unfortunately prevented his extending this list, which is defective as it stands, into a volume of biographies; but he provided most of the material for the New Englanders in Venn's *Alumni Cantabrigienses*.

3. I have omitted John Lyford, Francis Bright, and William Morrell, who came too early and left too soon to have had any influence; Richard Gibson, Robert Jordan, and William Josselyn, who sojourned or resided in Maine; and Thomas Harrison, who belongs to Virginia rather than New England. But I have retained several men who died or left New England before Harvard was founded — e.g., Francis Higginson, Isaac Johnson, and Sir Richard Saltonstall, because they were founders of the Commonwealth, and left families and friends here to carry on their tradition. William Pynchon is omitted, as I find no evidence of his being a university man; but Jose Glover, Henry Vane, Roger Ludlow, and John Woodbridge are admitted, on what seems to me sufficient evidence of their university education.

4. Some of those who came later are JAMES ALLEN (B.A. Oxford 1652), fellow of New College, emigrated in 1662 when ejected from his fellowship, and became teacher of the First Church in Boston, Overseer and Fellow of Harvard; JOHN OXENBRIDGE, admitted pensioner to Emmanuel College 1625 and B.A. from Magdalen Hall, Oxford, 1628, came to Boston in 1669, and became minister of the First Church; CHARLES MORTON, pensioner at Queens' College, Cambridge, 1646, Scholar and Fellow of Wadham College, Oxford (B.A. 1649; M.A. 1652), emigrated in 1686; minister of Charlestown; Fellow and Vice-President of Harvard (see *H. C. S. C.*, Chapter XI).

These 130 men may be analyzed as follows:

NUMBER ATTENDING EACH UNIVERSITY [1]

Cambridge 100
Oxford . . . . 32 [2]
Padua . . . . 1 (Child [3])

Dublin, 3 (Burdett,[3] Parker,[4] Winthrop Jr.)
Leyden, 2 (Child [3] and Parker [4])
Franeker, 2 (N. Eaton [3] and Parker [4])

DEGREES TAKEN BEFORE EMIGRATING [1]

B.A. 87
M.A. 63

B.D. 3
M.D. 1

COLLEGIATE STATUS [5]

Fellow- or Gentlemen-Commoners 5
Fellows 7
Scholars 14

Pensioners or Commoners 34
Sizars or Battelers 52

DATES OF EMIGRATION [6]

1620–29 5	1635 23	1639 12
1630 14	1636 10	1640 5
1631–32 6	1637 16	1641–45 5
1633–34 14	1638 18	

Of these 130 emigrants, 43 returned to England and died there: 3 in the years 1631–40, 14 in the years 1641–42; 11 in the years 1643–48; and 15 in the years 1650–59.

OCCUPATIONS IN NEW ENGLAND [7]

Ministers 98
Schoolmasters 15
Magistrates, deputies, and law-
makers 27

Physicians 3
Merchants, traders, and industrial
promoters 5

DISTRIBUTION AND PROPORTION

In 1639 or 1640 the proportion of university men to the total population was probably largest; for the great emigration came to an end in 1640, and a return movement began in 1641. The following estimates of population are taken from *A Century of Population Growth*

1. Incorporations *ad eundem gradum* are not included.

2. Including Corlet, Lothrop, and Streete, who also attended Cambridge.

3. Also attended Cambridge. Eaton also took degrees at Padua after leaving America.

4. Also attended Oxford.

5. Seven sizars rose to scholars, 4 pensioners rose to scholars, and 1 sizar rose to pensioner. These are counted under both classes. The terms 'commoner's son,' 'gentleman's son,' etc., as applied to the Oxonians do not indicate undergraduate status, and are not reliable indications of the student's family rank, as many gentlemen matriculated as commoners in order to benefit by the lower fees.

6. Many of these are approximate.

7. Those who had more than one occupation are counted more than once, and almost all these men did more or less farming.

(Census Bureau, 1909). These figures must not be taken too seriously, for they are little better than guesses, based on the careful but by no means scientific estimates of Franklin B. Dexter.[1]

	Population 1640	University men resident 1640	Proportion
Massachusetts Bay	11,600	74	.0064
Plymouth	2,400	16	.0067
Connecticut } New Haven } · · · · · · · · · · ·	2,500 [2]	18	.0072
New Hampshire	800	5	.0062
Rhode Island	300	2	.0066
	17,600	115	.0065

Conservatively estimating an average of five persons, including servants, to a family, there were (if these figures are approximately correct) about 3,680 families in New England in 1640, and on the average one university man to every thirty-two families. Even if we consider Dexter's estimates too low, and push up the total population of New England to 25,000, the proportion of university men to families would not fall below one to forty-four.[3]

This list is admittedly incomplete; and it does not pretend to include the numerous New Englanders such as Thomas Dudley, Roger Harlakenden, John Haynes, Israel Stoughton, Antony Thacher, William Pynchon and Herbert Pelham, who were sons, brothers, or fathers of Oxford or Cambridge alumni. Nor do the following sketches pretend to be complete biographies. I have merely attempted to give all available data respecting each man's education, and to indicate what part he took in the life of New England, especially in relation to Harvard College. Only a few of the available authorities have been cited:[4]

1. *Estimates of Population in the American Colonies* (Worcester, 1887), reprinted in *Historical Papers* (1918). Mr. Dexter's calculation of the population of Massachusetts Bay in 1643 is based on the following reasoning: — (1) The New England Confederacy fixed the quota of Massachusetts as five-fold that of Plymouth; (2) Plymouth by contemporary count had 627 males of military age in 1643; (3) Population is 'usually computed' as from 4.5 to 5.5 times the number of militia. 'This yields as a probable total in 1643 for Massachusetts including Plymouth . . . from 16,000 to 17,000 souls.' This estimate by Dexter for 1643 is reduced to 14,000 for 1640 by the editor of *A Century of Population Growth* (Census Bureau, 1909). It seems to me that one might equally well have started from the statement of Edward Johnson, writing about 1650, that in the fifteen years 1628–1642, 198 ships brought 21,200 passengers to New England (*Wonder-Working Providence*, Jameson ed., pp. 58, 61). Allowing for natural increase, this would make the total population around 25,000 in 1640.

2. I have added 500 to The *Century of Population Growth* estimates in order to include the English settlements on Long Island, which was a part of New England until 1664.

3. Channing estimates one to forty in his *United States*, I. 335.

4. The principal authorities consulted are Venn's *Alumni Cantabrigienses*; Foster's
(*Note continued on page 363.*)

INDEX BY COLLEGES

UNIVERSITY OF CAMBRIDGE

UNIVERSITY OF OXFORD

All Souls
Lenthall
Matthews

Balliol
Ludlow
Norris

Brasenose
Mather
Noyes
T. Peter
Tompson

Christ Church
Blakeman
Lothrop

Exeter
Maverick

Lincoln
Corlet

Magdalen College
Newman
Parker (?)

Magdalen Hall
Davenport
Mayo
Norris
Vane
B. Woodbridge
J. Woodbridge (?)

Merton
Davenport

New College
Whitefield

New Inn Hall
Blinman

Oriel
Lenthall
Pole

Pembroke
Streete

Queen's
Avery

St. Edmund Hall
Avery
Newman

St. John's
Alcock
Bacheller
Glover
Willis

St. Mary's Hall
Hull
Warham

Trinity
Cobbett
Hooke

GEORGE ALCOCK, probably one of the Alcocks of Sibert, Northamptonshire, matriculated in the University of Oxford sizar from St. John's College, Michaelmas term 1622. He married a sister of Thomas Hooker, emigrated with her in the Winthrop fleet, 1630, and became freeman of the Colony 18 May 1631. Resided in Roxbury. Physician, deputy to the General Court, and deacon of the church. At his death, *c.* 30 December 1640, 'Mr. Alcock,' as he is referred to in the colonial records, 'left a good savor behind him, the pore of the church much bewailing his losse.' Father of John Alcock (Harvard A.B. 1646); and, by a second wife, of Samuel Alcock (A.B. 1659).

JOHN ALLEN, or ALLIN, son of Reginald Allen, gentleman, of Colby, Norfolk, was admitted pensioner at Caius College, Cambridge, 27 April 1612, 'aged 16,' from the grammar school at North Walsham.

Alumni Oxonienses; Anthony Wood's *Athenae Oxonienses* (Bliss ed.); Andrew Clark's *Register of the Univ. of Oxford to 1622* (Oxford Historical Society); Edmund Calamy's *Abridgment* (1702); A. G. Matthews, *Calamy Revised* (1934); Savage's *Genealogical Dictionary of New England;* C. H. Pope's *Pioneers of Mass.;* H. F. Waters' *Genealogical Gleanings in England* ('*G.G.E.*'); Winthrop's *Journal;* Cotton Mather's *Magnalia* (1702 ed.); Edward Johnson's *Wonder-Working Providence* ('*W.W.P.*'); *Dictionary of American Biography* ('*D.A.B.*'); *Dictionary of National Biography* ('*D.N.B.*'); histories and records of towns in which the emigrants settled; the *New England Historical and Genealogical Register* ('*N.E.H.G.R.*'); the *Proceedings* and *Collections* of the Massachusetts Historical Society ('*M.H.S.*'); and the *Publications* of the Colonial Society of Massachusetts ('*C.S.M.*').

Scholar 1612–19; B.A. 1615–16; ordained 21 September, 1618; M.A. 1619. Curate successively at Denton and Wrentham, near Ipswich; forced to resign by Bishop Wren. Emigrated 1637 and settled at Dedham in July; took a leading part, with Ralph Wheelock, in gathering of the Church of Dedham in 1638, and was ordained their pastor, 24 April 1639. Assisted John Eliot in missionary work among the Indians. He was an Overseer of Harvard College from 1654 to his death, 26 August 1671. Co-author with Thomas Shepard of a tract defending the New England Way from the criticism of John Ball; and sole author of *Animadversions upon the Antisynodalia Americana*, a treatise in defence of the synod held at Boston in 1662. Drafted a reply to Dr. Robert Child and the Remonstrants of 1646. Married (1) at Wrentham in 1622, Margaret Morse; John Allin (A.B. Harvard 1643) was their son. Married (2) in 1653, Katherine, widow of Samuel Hegborne and of Governor Thomas Dudley; Daniel Allin (A.B. 1675) was their son. Not to be confused with a John Allen of Christ's College who was curate of St. Mary at Quay. *D.N.B.;* Venn, *Biog. Hist. Gonville & Caius*, I. 216; D. G. Hill (ed.), *Dedham Records*, II.

THOMAS ALLEN, or ALLIN, son of John Allen, dyer of Norwich, was admitted sizar at Caius College, Cambridge, 6 July 1624, 'aged 15.' Scholar 1625–29; B.A. 1627–28; M.A. 1631; ordained 2 March 1633–34. Minister of St. Edmund's, Norwich; silenced by Bishop Wren in 1638 for refusing to read the Book of Sports. Emigrated in 1638, settled in Watertown and after John Harvard's death became teacher of the church at Charlestown, married the widow Harvard and acted as John's executor. Overseer of the College and 'pious and painful minister' (*Magnalia*). Returned to England, 1651, became rector of St. George's, Tombland, 1651, and in 1657, also pastor of the congregational church at Norwich. Ejected 1662, and died 21 September 1673. His *Chain of Scripture Chronology* (London, 1659), is the best known of his works, which were not controversial; he is said to have remarked that others might dispute if they would leave him to compute. *D.N.B.; Magnalia;* Calamy; Venn, *Biog. Hist. Gonville & Caius*, I. 268; Budington, *Hist. First Church Charlestown*.

JOSEPH AVERY of Berkshire matriculated in the University of Oxford as a commoner's son from Queen's College, 28 April 1615, aged 15; B.A. from St. Edmund Hall 1618; M.A. 1621. Vicar of Romsey, Hampshire, 1626. Emigrated on the *James* in 1635 with his cousin Antony Thacher, with whom he had a 'league of perpetual friendship.' Drowned off Thacher's Island, Cape Ann, 15 August 1635, when on his way to minister to the fisherfolk of Marblehead. 'Avery's Woe,' the rock whence Joseph slipped to his death, is now called 'The Londoner,' but Avery's name has been transferred to a ledge off Straitsmouth Island. In the *Magnalia* Joseph is erroneously called John; but the meagre inventory of his estate — a sow and pigs and ten bushels of corn — *Mass. Bay Records*, I. 154, gives the name correctly. Antony Thacher's 'Narrative of Shipwreck' in Increase Mather's *Illustrious Providences* and Alexander Young's *Chronicles of Mass. Bay*.

STEPHEN BACHILER, born about 1561, matriculated in the University of Oxford from St. John's College about 1581; B.A. 1585–86. Vicar of Wherwell, Hants, on presentation of Lord de la Warr, 1587. Ejected 1605. In 1613 Bachiler and his son Stephen, who is described as having been 'expulsed out of Magdalen College in Oxford,' were sued for libel by a neighboring clergyman for having composed some scandalous verses about him, and singing them in divers places, including the house of George Wither the poet (*Proc. M.H.S.*, LX. 132–41). In 1622, Bachiler was living on his own property at Newton Stacy, Hampshire; in 1631 he visited Holland (Waters, *G.G.E.*, I. 520). The following years, in company with his second wife Helen, whom Winthrop refers to as 'a lusty, comely woman,' Bachiler emigrated to New England at the age of 71, in the *William and Francis*, as pastor for the Plough Company's colony of Lygonia. Settled in Lynn; ordered by the General Court in October to 'forbear exercising his gifts as pastor'; prohibition removed in 1633; moved to Ipswich, then to Newbury; attempted unsuccessfully in 1638 to found a settlement at Yarmouth on Cape Cod, walking 'thither on foot in a very hard season' (Winthrop); and in 1638–39, began the settlement of Hampton, N. H. Excommunicated as result of charge of immorality brought by his assistant, Timothy Dalton (*q.v.*). Excommunication withdrawn. Settled at Portsmouth, N. H., and at the age of 86 made a third marriage with a much younger woman, who deceived him. Returned to England *c.* 1653 and probably died at Hackney in 1660, in the hundredth year of his age. V. C. Sanborn, in *The Genealogist* (Exeter, England), XIX.

NICHOLAS BAKER, born *c.* 1610, matriculated in the University of Cambridge, pensioner from St. John's, Easter term 1628; B.A. 1631–32; M.A. 1635. Emigrated 1635; one of the first settlers of Hingham, which he represented in the General Court, 1636 and 1638; and a large landowner in Hull, whither he removed *c.* 1644. Invited to preach at Scituate after the death of President Dunster, and was ordained minister of the first church there in 1660; succeeded in effecting a reconciliation with the second church. 'Honest Nicholas

Baker,' as Mather calls him, died in office, 22 August 1678. Deane, *History of Scituate*, pp. 181–82; *History of Hingham* (1893), II. 17–18.

 WILLIAM BELLINGHAM, born about 1600, son of William Bellingham of Manton and Bromby, Lincolnshire, was brother to Richard Bellingham, Governor of Massachusetts Bay. They were the last male representatives of an ancient family (A. R. Maddison, *Lincolnshire Wills*, p. xliv) who were lords of the manor of Manton. William matriculated in the University of Cambridge pensioner from Christ's, Michaelmas term 1618. Emigrated not later than 1638 (Thomas Lechford, *Note-Book*, p. 3); admitted freeman of the Bay Colony, 12 October 1640; settled as a merchant at Rowley, and died unmarried in 1650, bequeathing his entire estate to his nephew Samuel Bellingham, of the first Harvard class. William's sister Susanna married Philemon Pormort, the first Boston schoolmaster. *Lincolnshire Notes & Queries*, XXI. 7.

WILLIAM BLACKSTONE or BLAXTON, b. 1595, probably at or near Salisbury, was admitted sizar at Emmanuel College, Cambridge, 16 May 1614; B.A. 1617–18; M.A. 1621; ordained 1619. Probably came to New England with Robert Gorges' colony in 1623, and established himself as a fur-trader on Beacon Hill, Boston, where the puritans found him in 1630, and whither he probably invited his Emmanuel classmate Isaac Johnson. Admitted freeman 18 May 1631. Blackstone, says Mather, was of a 'particular humor'; finding the 'lords brethren' as disagreeable as he had the 'lords bishops' in England, he removed with his library in 1635 to a ford on the Pawtucket river, in what is now Lonsdale, R. I.; 'neere Master Williams,' as Lechford wrote, but 'far from his opinions.' Befriended the Indians, and occasionally preached at Providence. Visited Boston in 1659 and married the widow Sarah Stevenson who returned with him to 'Study Hill,' as he called his place, and bore him a son. Died 26 May 1675. C. K. Bolton, *Real Founders of New England*.

CHRISTOPHER BLACKWOOD of Yorkshire, son of William Blackwood, matriculated in the University of Cambridge sizar from Pembroke College in Easter term, 1621, 'aged 13'; B.A. 1624–25; ordained 8 June 1628, 'aged 24.' In 1631 he was vicar of Stockbury, Kent. Emigrating in 1640, he purchased in Scituate the farm of John Lothrop, whom he was probably invited to succeed as pastor. Preached there for a short time; but in 1642 sold his farm to Charles Chauncy, and returned to England. The will of a Christopher Blackwood was proved at Dublin in 1670.

ADAM BLAKEMAN or BLACKMAN of Staffordshire matriculated in the University of Oxford as a commoner's son from Christ Church 23 May 1617, aged 19; B.A. 1617–18. Preached in Derbyshire and Leicestershire; emigrated 1638, 'attended with a desireable Company of the Faithful,' says Cotton Mather, who adds that 'notwithstanding his name,' Blackman was 'A Nazarite purer than Snow, whiter than Milk.' Settled at Stratford, Connecticut, by 1640, and became the first minister there. The great Thomas Hooker said that he preferred Blakeman above all other New England ministers to live under, for the 'sacred and solemn simplicity' of his discourse. Became disabled by age *c.* 1663 and died 7 September 1665. Father of Benjamin Blackman (A.B. 1663), who inherited his Latin books. *New Haven Col. Records, 1638–49*, pp. 347–349; S. Orcutt, *Hist. of Stratford*, pp. 97–99.

RICHARD BLINMAN, son of William Blinman of Chepstowe, Monmouth, matriculated in the University of Oxford as a commoner's son from New Inn Hall 24 April 1635, aged 20; B.A. 1635–36. 'A minister in Wales, a godly and able man' (Winthrop), he migrated *c.* 1640 with many followers from the borders of Wales and Gloucestershire. By invitation of Edward Winslow, the Pilgrim father, they 'set down' at Green Harbor (Marshfield). Dissension arose; John Wilson (*q. v.*) in vain endeavored 'to apease a broyle betwen one master Thomas . . . and master Blindman,' who 'went by the worst.' With his *fidelissimi* Blinman removed across the Bay to Cape Ann, there gathered a church, became its first ordained minister, and acquired recognition for the settlement from the General Court as the town of Gloucester. The fishermen already there made Blinman's ministry a turbulent one. As a result of frequent disturbances he removed in 1650 with a number of his flock to New London, where he preached to both English and Indians until 1658. Trouble arose over support and Blinman removed to New Haven; shortly after he sold some of his library to Harvard College and returned to England in 1659 via Newfoundland, where he declined an invitation to settle. Was residing at Bristol in 1670. J. J. Babson, *Gloucester;* Lechford, *Plain Dealing; Conn. Col. Records*, I. 299–300.

SIMON BRADSTREET, Governor of Massachusetts Bay, was the second son of Simon Bradstreet, vicar of Horbling, Lincolnshire, where he was baptized 18 March 1603–04. His father, an alumnus of Christ's College, had been one of the early fellows of Emmanuel. Bartlett, Waters, Venn, and indeed most writers have identified the future Governor with a Simon Bradstreet who matriculated in the University of Cambridge from Emmanuel College in 1618; B.A. 1620–21; M.A. 1624. But this was undoubtedly another man, Simon being a common name in the Bradstreet family (the will of one Symon Bradstreete, citizen and grocer of London, is given in Waters, *G.G.E.*, I. 47). Cotton Mather states that our Simon remained in grammar school until the age of 14; and 'within two or three years' was taken into the family of the Earl of Lincoln, 'where he spent about eight years.' Dr. Preston, Master of Emmanuel, then persuaded the Earl to let Bradstreet come up as tutor to Warwick's son, Lord Rich; to Emmanuel he went in advance of his pupil, but 'my Lord Rich not coming to the University,' returned to the Earl of Lincoln's 'after a year.' Bradstreet, therefore, must have resided at Emmanuel about the year 1628–29, without being formally a member of the college or university. In 1630 he emigrated in the Winthrop fleet. Assistant, Deputy-Governor, and Governor of the Bay Colony, Councillor of the Dominion of New England and of the Province of Massachusetts Bay. Overseer of Harvard College for over forty years from 1642. Died 27 March 1697. Anne Bradstreet the poetess, daughter of Governor Thomas Dudley, was his first wife; Samuel Bradstreet (A.B. Harvard 1653) and Simon Bradstreet (A.B. 1660) were their sons.

WILLIAM BREWSTER, senior of the university men who came to New England, and the only one who crossed on the *Mayflower*, was born in 1566–67. His father, also named William, was bailiff of the manor of Scrooby and postmaster on the Great North Road. Brewster matriculated in the University of Cambridge pensioner from Peterhouse, 3 December 1580. In 1583 he entered the service of William Davison, secretary to Queen Elizabeth; and accompanied him on missions to the Netherlands. Succeeded to his father's posts in 1590. One of the original members of the separatist congregation at Scrooby which became the nucleus of the Pilgrim church, he emigrated with them to Holland in 1608, and became elder and teacher of their church at Leyden. Conducted a printing press there, 1617–19 (A. Harris and S. K. Jones, *The Pilgrim Press*, 1922; and check-list of imprints in *Mayflower Descendant*, XXIII. 97–105). Returned to England in 1619, and embarked in the *Mayflower* in 1620. Elder of the church at Plymouth and a pillar of the Colony until his death, 10 April 1644, leaving a private library of 300 volumes. *D.N.B.; D.A.B.;* Bradford; *Proc. M.H.S.*, v. 37–85.

EDMUND BROWNE, son of Edmund Browne of Lavenham, Suffolk; baptized there 28 October 1606; matriculated in the University of Cambridge a sizar from Emmanuel in Easter term 1624. In 1638 he emigrated in the same ship with the Downings and Thomas Lechford, arriving June 27. His report on the state of the Colony, enclosed in his letter of 7 September 1638 to Sir Simonds d'Ewes, gives an important clue to early Harvard history. After a sojourn at Plymouth and Watertown he became in 1640 pastor of the church in the new settlement of Sudbury, and there remained until his death, except for occasional service in church councils, with a salary of £40, one-half payable in commodities. When King Philip's War broke, in 1675, the septuagenarian minister stood his ground, made the parsonage a garrison house, fortified with loopholes and flankers, and requested help from the government, in a letter beginning 'our woods are pestered with Indians.' During Sudbury fight his house was the refuge of women and children. Died in office 22 June 1678. He was a famous fisherman and hunter, and a noted musician, leaving a 'base vyol' and musical books in his will, a library of 180 volumes, £50 for a grammar school, which the town converted to other uses, and bequeathed £100 to Harvard College, which never managed to obtain it from his executors. *W.W.P.; C.S.M.* xv, xvi; A. S. Hudson, *Hist. of Sudbury*, pp. 98–99, 201, 212, 226, 260–62.

EDWARD BULKELEY, son of Peter Bulkeley (*q.v.*) and Jane Allen, baptized at Odell 17 June 1614, matriculated in the University of Cambridge pensioner from St. Catharine's in Easter term 1629. He accompanied his father to New England in 1635, and succeeded Richard Blinman as minister of Marshfield in 1642. In 1659 he succeeded his father as minister of Concord; and remained in that office until shortly before his death, 2 January 1695–96. Peter Bulkeley (A.B. Harvard 1660) was his son, and should not be confused with Peter Bulkeley, (class of 1662) his half-brother.

 PETER BULKELEY, born at Odell, Bedfordshire, 31 January 1582–83, son of Edward Bulkeley, D.D., sometime fellow of St. John's and a member of an ancient landed family. Peter took his B.A. from St. John's College, Cambridge, in 1603–04, being placed eleventh in the *ordo senioritatis* of that year, and became Fellow of the College in 1605. Took his M.A. 1608, ordained the same year, and in 1610 was incorporated *ad eundem gradum* at Oxford. Canon of Lichfield 1609, and university preacher at Cambridge 1610. At the death of his father in 1620 he inherited a considerable fortune, and succeeded to his father's rectory at Odell. Emigrated with his wife and family in 1635 on the *Susan and Ellen*. That autumn he was one of the grantees of Concord, began the settlement of it the same year, and served as pastor of the church there until his death on 9 March 1658–59. In his lifetime he presented

many books to Harvard College, and at his death his library was valued at £123; but most of his large estate was wasted by emigration. Moderator of the Cambridge Synod of 1637; author of *The Gospel Covenant* and other works. By his first wife (Jane, d. of Thomas Allen, gent.) he was the father of Edward Bulkeley (*q.v.*) and John Bulkeley of the first Harvard class; by his second wife (Grace, d. of Sir Richard Chetwode), father of Gershom (A.B. 1655), Eleazar (class of 1658), and Peter (class of 1662). Uncle of Chief-Justice Oliver St. John. *D.A.B.; D.N.B.;* Lemuel Shattuck, *Concord.*

GEORGE BURDETT, scholar of Trinity College, Dublin, 24 April 1619; B.A. Dublin; admitted to Sidney Sussex College, Cambridge, 1623–24. Curate of Saffron Walden; lecturer at Norwich, 1632. Suspended in 1635 for ridiculing in his lectures the sermons of the regular parson, and emigrated to New England, where he was admitted freeman of the Bay Colony and became a member of the church at Salem. Shortly after he moved to Dover, N. H., where he became both minister and civil ruler. Governor Winthrop having complained to him of harboring various undesirables from the Bay, Burdett 'returned a scornful answer,' and also entered into correspondence with Archbishop Laud, accusing the Massachusetts people of aiming at sovereignty. In 1639 Burdett removed to York, Maine; the next year he was tried before the Proprietor's court for incontinency, adultery, and breaking the peace, and fined £45. After one of the outraged husbands had threatened to shoot him, Burdett fled to the island of Monhegan, where he safely passed the winter 'carousing and singing of ribald songs.' In 1641 he returned to England, and took the royalist side in the Civil War. After the Restoration this reverend gentleman was made Chancellor and Dean of the diocese of Leighlin, Ireland; and after founding a much respected county family, died in 1671. Winthrop; Libby, *Province and Court Records of Maine.*

JONATHAN BURR, son of John Burr, yeoman of Suffolk, baptized at Redgrave 12 April 1604, matriculated in the University of Cambridge sizar from Corpus Christi in Easter term 1620; B.A. 1623–24; M.A. 1627. Rector of Rickinghall Superior, Suffolk, from 1630 until silenced by Archbishop Laud in 1639. Emigrated to New England that year, and after a stiff examination into his alleged 'erroneous opinions' by the magistrates and elders, and a humble recantation, was allowed to become teacher of the church of Dorchester, as colleague to Richard Mather, but died 9 August 1641, apparently before being ordained.

THOMAS CARTER, son of James Carter, yeoman, was baptized at Hinderclay, Suffolk, 3 July 1608. Matriculated in the University of Cambridge sizar from St. John's in Easter term 1626; B.A. 1629-30; M.A. 1633. Emigrated in the *Planter* in 1635; settled first at Dedham, removed to Watertown and admitted freeman of the Colony 21 May 1638. Ordained pastor of the new church at Woburn 22 November 1642, and there remained until his death 5 September 1684. Father of Samuel Carter (A.B. 1660). *W.W.P.*

 CHARLES CHAUNCY, son of George Chauncy of Yardley-Bury, Herts, member of an ancient landed family of that county, was baptized at Yardley-Bury 5 November 1592. Came up to Cambridge as a Westminster Scholar and matriculated pensioner from Trinity in Easter term 1610; scholar shortly after (Trinity Coll. muniments); B.A. 1613-14 (second in *ordo senioritatis*); fellow of Trinity 1614-26; M.A. 1617 (fourth in *ordo*); B.D. 1624; incorporated M.A. at Oxford 1619. Greek Lecturer at Trinity College, 1624-26. Vicar of St. Michael's, Cambridge, 1626; of Ware, Herts, 1627-33; and of Marston St. Laurence, 1633-37. Suspended and imprisoned for non-conformity, emigrated with his wife Catherine, d. of Robert Eyre, Esq., in 1638; colleague to John Rayner in the Plymouth church; minister at Scituate, 1641-54, when he was elected President of Harvard College, where he remained until his death, 19 February 1671-72. No less than six of his sons graduated from Harvard. See Index to this volume, and to *H. C. S. C.*

EZEKIEL CHEEVER, son of William Cheever of London, spinner, was born 25 January 1615-16. Admitted sizar at Emmanuel College, Cambridge, 12 January 1632-33, a 'Grecian' from Christ's Hospital; emigrated 1637 to New England, settled at New Haven in 1638 and became master of the grammar school. Refusing to 'make shipwreck of a good conscience' when censured by the authorities, he removed to the Bay Colony and became successively master of the grammar schools at Ipswich, 1650-61; Charlestown, 1661-70; and Boston (the Boston Latin School), from 1670 to his death on 21 August 1708. As Cotton Mather writes, 'he held the rod for 70 years,' and was the most famous schoolmaster in New England. Author of religious tracts, and of a Latin Accidence which was used in New England schools for two centuries. *D.A.B.;* Mather, *Corderius Americanus;* biography by E. P. Gould (1904).

ROBERT CHILD of Northfleet, Kent, son of John Child, was born in 1613, and matriculated in the University of Cambridge pensioner from Corpus Christi College in Easter term 1628; B.A. 1631-32; M.A. 1635. Entered the University of Leyden as a student of medicine 23 May 1635. Proceeded to Padua and took an M.D. 13 August 1638. Visited New England in 1639 and emigrated in 1645; invested in land, iron works, the fur trade, and wine growing; headed the Remonstrance of 1646 against the Bay authorities and appealed to Parliament for toleration to Presbyterians; fined £250 and returned to England in 1647, after which his proposed reforms in the Massachusetts government, including a body of definite laws, were adopted; became a member of the London scientific group which later founded the Royal Society, dabbled in alchemy and scientific agriculture, removed to Ireland as agricultural expert about 1651, and died *c.* March, 1654. G. L. Kittredge in *C.S.M.*, XXI. 1–146; S. E. Morison, *Builders of the Bay.*

THOMAS COBBETT, the son of Thomas of Newbury, Berks, matriculated as a commoner's son in the University of Oxford from Trinity College, 12 October 1627, aged 19. One of the same name and college took his B.A. 11 February 1627–28; a Thomas Cobbett took his M.A. from St. Mary Hall 26 June 1632; but this may not be the same man, since Mather says that Cobbett removed from Oxford 'in the time of a plague raging there,' and continued his studies with Dr. Twisse at Newbury. Preached 'at a small place in Lincolnshire'; emigrated *c.* 1637, admitted freeman 2 May 1638; served as teacher of the church at Lynn, as colleague to an old friend, Samuel Whiting. Upon the death of Nathaniel Rogers in 1655, Cobbett became minister of Ipswich, and there continued until his death 5 November 1685. A man mighty in prayer, according to Cotton Mather. Author of a treatise on church and state, *The Civil Magistrates Power in matters of Religion Modestly Debated* (London, 1653), of a controversial work on the halfway covenant, and other tracts. Overseer of Harvard College. Samuel Cobbett (A.B. 1663) was his son. *Magnalia;* Lewis & Newhall, *Lynn.*

GEORGE COOKE, third son of Thomas Cooke, a country gentleman of Yeldham, Essex, born *c.* 1610, matriculated in the University of Cambridge as pensioner of St. John's College, Michaelmas term 1626. With his brother Joseph of Earl's Colne, a friend of Thomas Shepard, he accompanied Shepard to Newtown (Cambridge) in 1635, and became prominent in military and civil affairs. Captain of the first militia company of Cambridge, of the Artillery Company of Boston 1643, and of the company which fetched the Gortonites to Boston. Deputy to the General Court 1642–45; Speaker of the House 1645. Near the end of that year he returned to England, became a colonel in Cromwell's army, and was killed in action near Dublin, 1652. President Dunster was appointed an administrator of his property, which was large. Joseph Cooke (A.B. 1661) was his nephew. Paige, *Cambridge*, p. 513; Winthrop; *W.W.P.*

ELIJAH CORLET was the son of Henry Corlet of London, wax chandler. An exhibitioner at Christ's Hospital; matriculated in the University of Oxford 16 March 1626–27 from Lincoln College, aged 17; B.A. probably 1631; migrated to Cambridge and incorporated *ad eundem* 1634; M.A. from Pembroke College, Cambridge, 1638. Ordained deacon 22 September 1633. Schoolmaster at Framlingham, Suffolk, and master of Halstead grammar school, Essex. It is not known when he emigrated. Master of the Grammar School at Cambridge by 1642; and so continued until his death, 24 February 1687–88. Ammi Ruhamah Corlet (A.B. 1670) was his son. W. C. Lane in *Proceedings Cambridge Hist. Soc.*, II; G. E. Littlefield in *C.S.M.*, XVII. 131–141.

JOHN COTTON, son of Roland Cotton, an attorney of Derby, was born there 4 December 1584. Entered the University of Cambridge from Derby Grammar School; matriculated sizar from Trinity College 1598; admitted scholar 16 April 1602; B.A. 1602–03 or 1603–04. Migrated to Emmanuel; M.A. 1606; became fellow and head lecturer of the College; ordained 1610; vicar of St. Botolph's, Boston, 1612; B.D. 1613. His fame as preacher and theologian, already great at Cambridge, increased at Boston; Bishop Williams protected him from the consequences of non-conformity and Archbishop Ussher consulted him on theology; the Master of Emmanuel sent him divinity students to complete their studies. Preached farewell sermon to Winthrop's fleet at Southampton, 1630; resigned vicarage 8 July 1633, owing to unwillingness to conform, and emigrated in the *Griffin* with Hooker and Stone. Ordained in October, 1633, as colleague to John Wilson; teacher of the First Church, Boston, from 1633; Overseer of Harvard College from 1637 to his death on 23 December 1652, which took place in consequence of catching cold while preaching to Harvard students. Cotton, Hooker, and Davenport were the ecclesiastical statesmen of New England; their works on church polity, notably Cotton's *Way of the Churches* and Hooker's *Survey*, were of the first importance in defining Congregational polity; their homilies and catechisms, such as Cotton's *Milk for Babes*, were read long after their deaths; their presence and counsel at the Westminster Assembly, were sought by the Independents of England. Seaborn (A.B. Harvard 1651) and John Cotton (A.B. 1657) were John Cotton's sons; his daughter Maria married Increase Mather. *Magnalia; D.A.B.; D.N.B.* (supplement).

TIMOTHY DALTON, probably son of Philemon Dalton, linen-weaver, was born *c.* 1588, matriculated in the University of Cambridge sizar from St. John's at Michaelmas, 1610; B.A. 1613–14; ordained 1614. Vicar of Woolverstone, Suffolk, 1615–36, and part of the time also rector of Flowton. Suspended by Bishop Wren; emigrated in 1636, and resided at Watertown and Dedham. Admitted freeman 7 September 1637. A founder of Hampton in 1639, he became teacher of the church as colleague to Stephen Bachiler. His wife, Ruth, was a kinswoman of Bachiler, but the town divided into two factions under the ministers, 'both men very passionate, and wanting discretion and moderation' (Winthrop). Johnson (*W.W.P.*) calls Dalton 'reverend, grave, and gracious.' After Bachiler's departure, Dalton remained sole minister of Hampton until his death on 28 December 1661.

FRANCIS DANE, son of John and Frances Dane, was baptized at Bishop's Stortford, 20 November 1615. He matriculated in the University of Cambridge sizar from King's College in Easter term, 1633. Emigrated with his parents about 1636, and in 1648, in succession to John Woodbridge, became the minister of Andover, where he died 17 February 1696–97, having barely escaped being a victim of the witchcraft delusion of 1692 — a delusion which he did not share.

JOHN DAVENPORT, son of John Davenport, alderman of Coventry, and Winifred Barnabit, was baptized at Coventry 9 April 1597. Attended Coventry Grammar School; entered Merton College, Oxford, as a batteler in 1613; migrated to Magdalen Hall, remaining but a short time; returned to take a B.D. in 1625. Curate of St. Lawrence Jewry, 1619; vicar of St. Stephen's Church, Coleman Street, 1624; spiritual adviser to Lady Mary Vere, and one of the feoffees of impropriations. An original stockholder of the Massachusetts Bay Company. Fled to Holland in 1633; supported Ames's polity of non-separating congregationalism and engaged in a spirited pamphlet war with John Paget, his colleague minister of the English church at Amsterdam. Returned to England in 1635 and emigrated with Theophilus Eaton and other former parishioners. First settled in Boston, and on 20 November 1637 appointed to the first governing board of Harvard College, the only Oxonian on it. Davenport and his group left the Bay Colony in April 1638 and founded the town and colony of New Haven, Davenport being the principal pillar of the state and pastor of the church. Refused an invitation to attend the Westminster Assembly in 1642. After the absorption of the New Haven colony in Connecticut, he accepted, in 1667, a call to the First Church in Boston, where his ordination (9 December 1668) precipitated a church quarrel which shortened his life. He died in March 1669–70. Author of numerous tracts on doctrine and polity. Grandfather of John Davenport (A.B. Harvard 1687). *D.A.B.; D.N.B.; Magnalia;* Wood, *Athenae Oxon.* (1721), II. 650; R. P. Stearns, in *N.E.Q.*, VI. 778–86.

 DANIEL DENISON, the son of William and Margaret (Chandler) Denison of Bishop's Stortford, Herts, was baptized there 18 October 1612. Matriculated in the University of Cambridge from King's College 18 October 1625; migrated to Emmanuel 1626; B.A. 1629–30. Emigrated, 1631, with his younger brother John and his parents, who brought 'a very good estate' and settled in Roxbury, where said estate was 'somewhat weakened.' On 18 October 1632 he married Patience, daughter of Governor Dudley and sister of Mrs. Simon Bradstreet and Mrs. John Woodbridge. Lived at Cambridge from that time to 1635, when he removed to Ipswich with the first settlers of that remarkable pioneer community. Town clerk and local magistrate; deputy to the General Court from Ipswich 1635–38, and on six later occasions; thrice Speaker of the House. Commissioner of the United Colonies, 1655–63. In military affairs, Denison rose from captain of the trained band to major of the Essex regiment, and Major General of the Colonial forces; Assistant of the Colony from 1653 to his death on 20 September 1682, and as such, Overseer of Harvard College. Author of an interesting hortatory tract called 'Irenicon, or a Salve for New England's Sore,' which is printed as an appendix to William Hubbard's funeral sermon on 'the Worshipful Major General Denison' (Boston, 1684). His daughter Elizabeth married President Rogers; their daughter Margaret married President Leverett. His son John married the daughter of Deputy-Governor Symonds; their son was John Denison (A.B. 1684). There is a full account of his family and connections in an autobiographical fragment written for his grandchildren, printed in *N.E.H.G.R.*, XLVI. 127–33; articles by D. D. Slade, *ibid.*, XXIII. 312–35, and *C.S.M.*, I. 116–32.

RICHARD DENTON, born 1603 in Yorkshire, matriculated in the University of Cambridge sizar from St. Catharine's, Easter term 1621; B.A. 1623–24; ordained 1623. Curate of Coley Chapel, Halifax, Yorks. Emigrated to New England *c.* 1638; successively minister at Wethersfield, Conn., and Stamford, whence he withdrew in 1644 on account of his Presbyterian views; and became minister of Hempstead, Long Island, in the Colony of New Netherlands, in association with Robert Fordham. A number of his English parishioners followed him through all these removes. Returned to England 1659, and is said to have died at Hempstead, Essex, in 1663. 'A little man . . . blind of one eye,' wrote Mather, 'his well accomplished Mind, in his lesser Body, was an Iliad in a Nut-Shell.' *Magnalia;* Trumbull, *Connecticut* (1898 ed.), I. 421; B. F. Thompson, *Long Island* (1843), II. 19–22.

EMMANUEL DOWNING, son of George Downing of Ipswich, was baptized there 12 August 1585, and admitted scholar at Trinity Hall, Cambridge, 16 December 1602. Married as second wife Lucy, sister of John Winthrop, 10 April 1622; lived for a time in Dublin. An attorney with John Winthrop of the Court of Wards and Liveries; admitted of the Inner Temple with Winthrop, 29 June 1628. An early member of the Massachusetts Bay Company, he emigrated in 1638, when he settled at Salem, engaged in mercantile business, and served as deputy in the General Court. Returned to England in 1654; died at Edinburgh about 1660. Father of Sir George Downing. *Winthrop Papers.*

SAMUEL DUDLEY, son of Governor Thomas Dudley, was baptized at Northampton 30 November 1608. Admitted pensioner at Emmanuel College, Cambridge, Easter term 1626. Emigrated in the Winthrop fleet with his father and family, 1630, and after five years' residence at Cambridge (where he married Mary, daughter of Governor Winthrop), joined his brother-in-law, Simon Bradstreet, at Ipswich; in 1637 took up a farm at Salisbury. In 1650 he was settled minister of Exeter, New Hampshire, in succession to John Wheelwright; lived there until his death on 10 February 1682–83; a great power in the community. Father of Thomas Dudley (A.B. 1651), the only one of nineteen children to attend college. C. H. Bell, *Exeter,* pp. 159–69.

HENRY DUNSTER, son of Henry Dunster, yeoman of Bury, Lancs; baptized there 26 November 1609. Matriculated in the University of Cambridge sizar from Magdalene in Easter term, 1627; B.A. 1630–31; M.A. 1634. Taught school at Bury; and curate of the church there. Emigrated in the summer of 1640; elected President of Harvard College 27 August 1640; resigned 24 October 1654. In the spring of

1655 removed to Charlestown and in the fall to Scituate, where he preached until his death, 27 February 1658–59. Married (1) Elizabeth (Harris), widow of Jose Glover; (2) Elizabeth Atkinson. See Index to this volume, and to *H. C. S. C.*

NATHANIEL EATON was the fifth son of Richard Eaton, vicar successively of Trinity parish, Coventry, and Great Budworth, Cheshire, and claimed by both Venn and Foster as a graduate of their respective universities. Nathaniel was born *c.* 1610; attended Westminster School, and thence elected scholar to Trinity College, Cambridge; matriculated as pensioner, Hilary term, 1629–30. Leaving Cambridge in 1632, he resided at London with his brother Theophilus Eaton (Deputy Governor of the Eastland Company; afterwards Governor of New Haven Colony), and the same year obtained a license to pass to Leyden. For a short time he studied at Franeker under William Ames, and published there a Latin pamphlet on Sabbatarian doctrines in 1633. Returned to England and taught school at two different places. Emigrated to New England with his brothers Theophilus and Samuel in 1637. The first head of Harvard College; removed from office September 1639, fled to Virginia, became assistant rector of Hungar's parish, Northampton County; returned to England 1646; took degrees of PH.D. and M.D. at Padua in 1647; vicar of Bishop's Castle, Shropshire, 1661; rector of Bideford, Devon, in 1668; arrested for debt and died in King's Bench prison, Southwark, 1674. See Index to this volume.

SAMUEL EATON, third son of Richard, and brother of Nathaniel Eaton (*q.v.*), was born at Crowley, Great Budworth, Cheshire, *c.* 1596. Matriculated in the University of Cambridge as sizar from Magdalene College, Hilary term 1620–21; B.A. 1624–25; ordained 1625; M.A. 1628. Emigrated with his two brothers, and settled at New Haven, where his brother Theophilus became governor and he teacher of the church, John Davenport being the pastor. Protested against church-membership franchise. Returned to England in 1640 or 1641, in order to procure colonists for a new settlement, but decided to remain; assisted the parliamentary commissioners of Cheshire; Congregational minister of Stopford and Dukinfield, Cheshire, *c.* 1644; ejected 1662; a prolific writer on religious topics. Died 9 January 1664–65 at Denton, Lancs, 'aged 68.' Samuel Eaton (A.B. Harvard 1649), son of the Governor, was his nephew. *D.A.B.*; *D.N.B.*; Calamy; Anthony Wood, *Athenae Oxon.* (Wood being under the impression that Eaton was an Oxonian).

JOHN ELIOT, son of Bennett and Lettice (Aggar) Eliot, was baptized at Widford, Herts, 5 August 1604. Matriculated in the University of Cambridge 20 March 1618–19 pensioner of Jesus College; B.A. 1622. Lived in the family of Thomas Hooker (*q.v.*) near Chelmsford, and taught in his school. Emigrated in 1631, and the next year became teacher of the church at Roxbury, and its sole minister after the departure of Thomas Weld in 1641. An Overseer of Harvard College from 1642 to 1685. In 1646 began his missionary work to the Indians, and in 1650 his translation of the Bible. His many activities terminated only with his death, 21 May 1690. John Eliot (A.B. Harvard 1656), Joseph Eliot (A.B. 1658), Samuel Eliot (A.B. 1660), and Benjamin Eliot (A.B. 1665) were his sons. *Magnalia; D.A.B.; N. E. H. G. R.*, XLVIII. 80; S. E. Morison, *Builders of the Bay.*

GEORGE FENWICK, son and heir of George Fenwick, Esq., of Brinkburn, Northumberland, was born there around 1603. Matriculated in the University of Cambridge, fellow-commoner from Queens' College, Easter term 1619; admitted to Gray's Inn 11 February 1621–22, and called to the bar 21 November 1631. One of the 'lords and gentlemen' to whom the Earl of Warwick made the Saybrook grant in 1632. Visited Boston and Saybrook Fort 1636; returned to England and married Alice, daughter of Sir Edward Apsley; emigrated with his family 1639 and resided at Saybrook; magistrate of Connecticut and Commissioner of the United Colonies. Returned to England in 1645; elected M.P. for Morpeth, 1645–53; and for Berwick on Tweed, 1654–56. Colonel of a northern regiment in the second civil war, where he distinguished himself; military governor of Edinburgh Castle and Leigh, and of Teignmouth Castle. Died 15 March 1656–57. *D.N.B.; D.A.B.*

GILES FIRMIN, son of Giles Firmin, apothecary of Sudbury, was born *c*. 1615; converted by John Rogers of Dedham. Admitted pensioner at Emmanuel College, Cambridge, 24 September 1629. Emigrated 1632; ordained deacon of the First Church, Boston, 10 October 1633, when John Cotton was ordained teacher. In England, 1633, studying medicine; settled as farmer and physician at Ipswich, 1637 or 1638 (his wife being a daughter of Nathaniel Ward), and 'performed an anatomy' (dissection of a cadaver) for such medical students as were interested. Returned to England *c*. 1647, and was ordained presbyter of Shalford, Essex, 1649; ejected 1662. His house was licensed for Presbyterian worship in 1672. He also practised medicine in England, and wrote sundry controversial religious tracts, mostly against the Baptists and Quakers; carried on a friendly controversy with Richard Baxter. Died at Shalford in April 1697. *D.N.B.*

JOHN FISKE, son of John Fiske of St. James' parish, South Elmham, Suffolk, was baptized there 20 March 1607–08. Admitted sizar at Peterhouse, Cambridge, 2 July 1625; B.A. 1628–29, and married the same year. Preached, studied medicine, and received a licence to practice. Emigrated with his wife and John Allen in 1637; Fiske and Allen 'entertained the passengers with two sermons every day, besides other agreeable devotions.' A disgruntled passenger complained 'he did not know when the Lord's day was . . . they did nothing but pray and preach all the week long' (*Magnalia*). Fiske was admitted freeman of the colony with John Harvard on 2 November 1637. He taught the grammar school at Salem, and when a group of Salemites founded Wenham, 'the godly and reverend Mr. John Fisk went thither with them, at first settling down as a planter among them, yet withal he became helpful in preaching the Word' (*W.W.P.*), and was ordained their minister 8 October 1644. With a majority of the Wenham church he removed to Chelmsford in 1656, and there remained minister to his death, 14 January 1676–77. Practised medicine in addition to his clerical duties. Father of Moses Fiske (A.B. 1662). *Magnalia; Fiske Family Papers; N. E. H. G. R.*, LXXXVIII. 272–73.

ROBERT FORDHAM, son of Philip Fordham, a husbandman of Sacomb, Hertfordshire, attended Watton School; was admitted sizar at Caius College, Cambridge, 3 July 1622, aged 19; B.A. 1625–26; M.A. 1629. Vicar of Flamstead, Herts, 1628–38, when he emigrated. Lived first in Cambridge; a founder of Sudbury, where he lived as planter until 1643 or 1644, when in association with Richard Denton and others he obtained a grant from the Dutch Governor Kieft, and founded Hempstead, Long Island. In 1649 or 1650 he accepted a call to the church at Southampton, L. I., and died there in September or November, 1674. Left an estate appraised at £1164, of which £53 represented his library. Jonah Fordham (A.B. Harvard 1658) was his son. Venn, *Biog. Hist. Gonville & Caius College*, I. 259; B. F. Thompson, *Long Island*, I. 337–338.

JOSE[1] GLOVER, eldest son of Roger Glover, merchant of London, is probably identical with the 'Joseph' Glover of London, son of a commoner, who matriculated in the University of Oxford from St. John's College 4 July 1609, aged 14; B.A. 1612; M.A. 1615. Jose

1. Also spelt Joas and Josse. A dialect form of Joseph; pronounced *Jōze.*

Glover became rector of Sutton, in Surrey, May 1624; suspended in 1634 for refusing to publish the Book of Sports, he resigned the benefice about 1 June 1636, 'much lamented of the most, if not of all' his parishioners, as reads the opening entry of the Sutton Parish register. In 1638 he emigrated with his wife and children, a large amount of personal property, and a printing press and font of type. The parson died on the voyage; but the press was promptly set up, and the widow Glover married President Dunster. Father of John Glover (A.B. Harvard 1650). J. H. Trumbull in *Proceedings Amer. Antiq. Soc.*, April 1875; *C.S.M.*, VIII. 333; Thomas Lechford, *Note-Book*; see Index to this volume.

HENRY GREEN, baptized at Great Bromely, Essex, 20 January 1618–19, admitted pensioner at Emmanuel College, Cambridge, 2 July 1634, is probably identical with the Henry Green of Ipswich who was admitted freeman of the Bay Colony 13 May 1642. This 'young man, one Mr. Green, a scholar,' refused an invitation to Martha's Vineyard as minister in 1643 (Winthrop); the same 'young man of good abilities to preach the Word, and of very humble behaviour, named Mr. Green' (*W.W.P.*, p. 226), was ordained first pastor of the church at Reading 5 November 1645. He died there 11 October 1648.

JOHN HARVARD, son of Robert Harvard, butcher of Southwark, and Katherine Rogers of Stratford-on-Avon, was baptized 29 November 1607 at St. Saviour's, Southwark. Admitted pensioner at Emmanuel College, Cambridge, 19 December 1627 (Emmanuel MS. Records; the date 17 April 1628 sometimes found is erroneous); B.A. 1631–32; M.A. 1635; married Ann, d. of the Rev. John Sadler, at South Malling 19 April 1636. Emigrated in May or June 1637 with his wife; settled at Charlestown; admitted freeman of the Bay Colony 2 November 1637; preached at Charlestown; died 14 September 1638. The little that is known of his career is related elsewhere in this volume. *D.A.B.*

 FRANCIS HIGGINSON, son of John Higginson, vicar of Claybrook, Leics, was baptized there 6 August 1586. Matriculated in the University of Cambridge sizar from St. John's, Michaelmas term 1602; migrated to Jesus College; B.A. 1609–10; M.A. 1613; ordained 1614; vicar of Claybrook 1615; lecturer at St. Nicholas', Leics, 1617 to 1627, when deprived for non-conformity. Engaged by the Massachusetts Bay Company for their plantation at Salem; emigrated with Skelton, in 1629, and at the organization of the first church of Salem became teacher by Congregational ordination. Died 6 August 1630. Author of *New Englands Plantation* (London, 1630), and of a Journal or 'True Relacion' of the voyage over. Grandfather of Nathaniel Higginson (A.B. 1670). *Magnalia; D.N.B.; D.A.B.*

THOMAS HINCKLEY, son of Samuel Hinkley, yeoman, of Tenterden, Kent, was baptized at Hawkhurst, 19 March 1619–20. Matriculated in the University of Cambridge sizar of Trinity College Easter term 1633. Emigrated with his parents in 1635, settling first at Scituate and in 1640 at Barnstable. Practised law and became a pillar of the Pilgrim Colony, serving as Assistant, Deputy Governor, and Governor of New Plymouth Colony until its absorption into Massachusetts Bay in 1692. Named councillor in the Province Charter of 1691. Died at Barnstable 16 April 1705, the last survivor of this group. 4 *Coll. M.H.S.*, V; *N.E.H.G.R.*, LXV, *passim*.

PETER HOBART, or HUBBERD, son of Edmund and Margaret (Dewey) Hobart, puritans of Hingham, Norfolk, was baptized there 14 October 1604. Prepared at the Free School, Kings Lynn. Admitted to Queens' College, Cambridge, 1 December 1621; migrated to Magdalene in 1623; B.A. 1625–26; ordained 1627; M.A. 1629; curate at Haverhill. Emigrated 1635, following his parents and many fellow-townsmen who founded Hingham, Massachusetts, of which he was pastor from September, 1635, until his death 20 January 1678–79. An autocrat in his own village, and preferring the Presbyterian church discipline, he stoutly defended local and personal liberties in the famous Hingham militia affair, and was probably in sympathy with the Child remonstrance against the oligarchy. As father of Harvard graduates, Peter Hobart was second only to Charles Chauncy: two sons, Joshua and Jeremiah, graduated in 1650, and three others, Gershom, Japhet and Nehemiah, made up almost half the class of 1667. All but one became clergymen, and that one, Japhet, is rumored to have become a Catholic priest. *Magnalia; History of Hingham, Mass.* (1893), I. part II. 1–21; Brook, *Lives of Puritans*.

WILLIAM HOOKE of Southampton matriculated as a gentleman's son in the University of Oxford 19 May 1620 from Trinity College, aged 19 (having probably resided there since 1616); B.A. 28 June 1620; M.A. 26 May 1623; ordained. Successively rector of Upper Clatford, Hants, and vicar of Axmouth, Devon, from which place he was forced to depart because of nonconformity. Married Jane, sister to Edward Whalley the regicide, the lady whom Roger Williams wished to marry when he was chap-

lain to Sir William Masham. Emigrated *c.* 1639 and became minister
at Taunton, where he preached a famous sermon, *New England's
Teares for Old England's Feares,* which was published (London, 1641).
About 1645 became teacher of the church of New Haven as colleague
to John Davenport, in collaboration with whom he drew up a catechism. Corresponded with Cromwell. Returned to England *c.* 1656;
restored to his former vicarage; chaplain to Cromwell and court
preacher of the Protectorate; wrote several religious treatises and
said to have been Master of the Savoy (*Magnalia*). Died in or near
London 21 March 1676–77, aged 77. His sons John and Walter were
members of the Harvard classes of 1655 and 1656 respectively, but
before graduating went to England. John became rector of King's
Worthy, Hants, chaplain of the Savoy, and minister of Basingstoke;
and Walter, admitted sizar at Pembroke College, Cambridge, late in
1654, B.A. 1656–57, became chaplain to the East India Company's
factory at Masulipatam, where he died in 1670. *D.N.B.;* Tyler, *Hist.
of American Literature,* II; Mss. Camb. Univ. Registry; *Notes &
Queries,* 10th ser. IX. 421–22; *Calamy Revised.*

THOMAS HOOKER, born *c.* 7 July 1586, was the son of Thomas Hooker,
described in the records both as gentleman and yeoman, of Marfield,
Leicestershire. His grandfather was steward of the Kenelm Digbys.
Attended Market Bosworth grammar school; matriculated in the
University of Cambridge sizar from Queens' College, Easter term
1604; soon migrated to Emmanuel; scholar 1604–09; fellow 1609–
18; dean 1616–17; B.A. 1607–08; M.A. 1611. As Curate of Esher,
Surrey, and lecturer at Chelmsford, Essex, he became widely known
as a puritan, and of the Congregationalist wing. Silenced in 1629, he
kept a private school near by at Little Baddow. In 1630 he escaped
to Holland; preached at Delft and assisted Hugh Peter in ministering to the English church at Rotterdam; emigrated in the *Griffin,*
1633, to New England. He and Samuel Stone organized the church at
Newtown (Cambridge), the members of which removed to Hartford,
making way for Thomas Shepard's followers. Hooker was pastor of
the Hartford church and a power in the government of Connecticut,
until his death on 7 July 1647. Most of his many works were on the
psychology of conversion; his *Summe of Church Discipline,* printed
posthumously, still stands as the greatest exposition of Congregational polity. Certain phrases of his, taken out of their context by
later writers, have been used to build up a false picture of him as a
democrat; Hooker, on his political side, was essentially a medieval
church autocrat. Father of Samuel Hooker (A.B. Harvard 1653);
of Sarah, who married John Wilson (A.B. 1642); and of Joanna,
who married Thomas Shepard. *Magnalia; D.A.B.; D.N.B.;* G. L.

Walker, *Thomas Hooker* (1891); P. G. Miller, in *New England Quarterly*, IV. 663–712; *N.Y. Gen. & Biog. Record*, XLVIII. 393–98.

EPHRAIM HUET, Huitt, or Hewett, matriculated in the University of Cambridge as sizar from St. John's in Easter term 1611. Curate in Cheshire and at Knowle and Wroxhall, Warwickshire; silenced by Laud. Emigrated in 1639; teacher of the church at Windsor, Connecticut, as colleague of John Warham until his death, 4 September 1644. Author of *The Whole Prophecie of Daniel Explained* (London, 1644).

JOSEPH HULL matriculated in the University of Oxford as a commoner's son from St. Mary Hall 22 May 1612, aged 17; B.A. 1614; rector of Northleigh, Devon, 1621. Sailed from Weymouth, Dorset, as leader of twenty-one Somersetshire families, in March 1635. They revived the plantation of Wessaguscus, and renamed it Weymouth (Banks, *Planters of Comm.*, p. 125). Hull was their minister and also deputy to the General Court, 1638–39; that year he went to Barnstable. Excommunicated by Barnstable church for having accepted a call to Yarmouth without their permission. Thence, *c.* 1643, to Agamenticus (York, Maine), where his kind reception by the people, as minister, furnished an excuse for the exclusion of Maine from the New England Confederacy (Winthrop). Returned to England, 1659, rector of St. Buryan, Cornwall; ejected 1662, returned to New England, and in 1662 was minister of Oyster River (Durham, N. H.), whence he was driven by the Quakers. At intervals since 1641 he had preached to the fishermen at the Isles of Shoals (*Proc. M.H.S.*, XIV. 144, n.), where he died 19 November 1665. Libby, *Province Records of Maine*, I. 269–70; Gilbert Nash, *Weymouth*, pp. 158–59.

JOHN HUMFREY or HUMPHREY, born *c.* 1593, was the son of Michael Humfrey, steward of an estate at Chaldon, Dorset. Matriculated in the University of Cambridge from Trinity College, Easter term 1613; scholar of Trinity 1614. Admitted to Lincoln's Inn 1615. Resided at Dorchester, Dorset, where he came under the influence of John White. Treasurer of the Dorchester Company (1624), the nucleus of the Massachusetts Bay Company, of which he was one of the principal organizers. Named patentee and Assistant in the royal charter, he was elected Deputy-Governor in 1629 and Assistant 1632–42. His second wife was Elizabeth, daughter of Herbert Pelham and granddaughter of the second Lord de la Warr; his third wife was the Lady Susan, daughter of

Thomas Clinton Fiennes, Earl of Lincoln, and sister to the Lady Arabella Johnson. Decided at the last minute not to emigrate with Winthrop, but active in obtaining money and supplies for the colony. Emigrated in 1634 with his family and settled in Lynn; a member of the first Board of Overseers of the College, 1637; and 'fell foul upon Mr. Endecott in the open assembly at Salem' for opposing the Weld-Peter mission to England. Humfrey is described by Winthrop as 'a gentleman of especial parts, of learning and activity, and a godly man'; but he disliked the climate of New England, urged the transference of the settlement further south, and on 20 November 1641 returned to England with the promise from Lord Saye and Sele of the governorship of Old Providence in the Caribbean. As that island had already been captured by Spain, Humfrey remained in England, and served as Colonel in the parliamentary army. Died c. 1652. His son John, also Colonel, bore the sword of state at the trial of Charles I, and took part in the conquest of Jamaica; Pelham Humfrey the composer was probably his grandson. Frances Rose-Troup, in *Essex Inst. Hist. Colls.*, LXV. 293–308; A. P. Newton, *Colonizing Activities of English Puritans*.

THOMAS JAMES, baptized at Boston 5 October 1595, was the son of John James, rector of Skirbeck. Matriculated in the University of Cambridge pensioner from Emmanuel in Easter term 1611; B.A. 1614–15; M.A. 1618; ordained 1616–17. Emigrated in 1632, and became first pastor of the church at Charlestown, 'A very melancholick man, and full of causeles jealousies' (Winthrop), he quarrelled with his church, resigned or was expelled c. 1636, and settled in New Haven as a planter. In 1643 James was sent to Virginia with John Knowles and William Tompson, upon the request of Richard Bennett and other puritans of Nansemond County. He remained in Virginia until banished by Governor Berkeley; then returned to New Haven, and to England c. 1648. Minister at Needham Market, Suffolk; ejected in 1662; died at Needham Market in February 1682–83. Frothingham, *Charlestown; Calamy Revised;* P. A. Bruce, *Institutional History of Virginia*, I. 253–54.

THOMAS JENNER, the son of Thomas Jenner, a farmer of Fordham, Essex, was admitted sizar at Christ's College, Cambridge, February 1623–24, aged 17. Emigrated 1635 with wife and family; minister of Weymouth in succession to Joseph Hull, but 'not liking the place, repaired to the Eastern English' (Johnson, *W.W.P.*, p. 181) at Saco, Maine, before 1641. It was probably his son Thomas who lived at Charlestown after 1646. Our Thomas returned to England in 1650, served as Minister at Coltishall, Norfolk, 1652–58, and died *c.* 1676. Author of *Quakerism Anatomiz'd and Confuted* (1670). A catalogue of the 200 titles in his library is in *C.S.M.*, xxviii. 113–35.

 Isaac Johnson, son of Abraham Johnson of South Luffenham, Rutland (matriculated at Emmanuel 1591) and Anne Meadows; grandson and principal heir of Archdeacon Robert Johnson, Fellow of Trinity; step-grandson of Laurence Chaderton, Master of Emmanuel. Born at Stamford, Lincolnshire, *c.* 1600; admitted sizar at Emmanuel in 1616; later pensioner; b.a. 1617–18; m.a. 1621; admitted to Gray's Inn 31 January 1620–21; ordained priest 27 May 1621, but never had a cure. An original patentee and assistant of the Massachusetts Bay Company, and signer of the Cambridge agreement. Married 1623 the Lady Arabella, daughter of Thomas Clinton Fiennes, Earl of Lincoln, and emigrated with her in 1630. She died at Salem in August; he on 30 September, 1630, and was buried at Boston, of which he was probably the first puritan settler. 'He was a holy man and wise, and died in sweet peace, leaving some part of his substance to the colony,' wrote Winthrop. The wealthiest and most generous of the founders of the colony, 'in which expedition,' his father complained, 'he spent from £5,000 to £6,000. And was so sett upon it, that had he again come over, as he intended the spring after, he had sold every foot of land his grandfather left him . . .' *N.E.H.G.R.*, viii. 358; Waters, *G.G.E.*, ii. 1033; M. J. Canavan, in *C.S.M.*, xxvii. 272–85; *Winthrop Papers*, ii. 49–56 *et passim*.

John Jones of Northampton, born *c.* 1592, matriculated in the University of Cambridge sizar from Queens' College, Michaelmas term 1608; b.a. 1612–13; m.a. 1616; ordained 1613. Probably rector of Abbots Ripton, Hunts, 1619–30, when he was deprived. Emigrated on the *Defence* with his wife and children and with Thomas Shepard, in 1635. Jones and Peter Bulkeley were leaders in the settlement of Concord, and colleague ministers of the church there. Jones, with a part of the flock, migrated in 1644 to Fairfield, Connecticut, and served as pastor until his death in January 1664–65. Father of John Jones (a.b. Harvard 1643).

William Knight, the son of William Knight of the parish of St. Olave's, Southwark, and Elizabeth, widow of Thomas Stoughton, was a neighbor of John Harvard and his contemporary at Emmanuel College, Cambridge. He was admitted pensioner there 31 January

1626–27, but did not graduate. Emigrated in 1637, received a grant in that part of Ipswich which later became Topsfield, and preached to the people there. Returned to England in 1643 with his half-brother Israel Stoughton. Presented by Cromwell with the living at St. Matthew's, Ipswich, 11 July 1655. Curate of St. Mary-at-Elms; later conformed, and held his livings until his death in early January 1694–95. Uncle of Lieut.-Gov. William Stoughton (A.B. Harvard 1650).

HANSERD KNOLLYS, born at Caukwell or Calkwell, Lincolnshire, *c.* 1599; attended the free school at Grymby; matriculated in the University of Cambridge pensioner from St. Catharine's in Easter term 1629; ordained this same year and in 1631 was vicar of Humberston, Lincolnshire. Partly through the influence of John Wheelwright he renounced his orders and resigned his living. Taught school and preached at various places, for which he was imprisoned. Escaped, and after lying hidden in London until his funds were down to '6 brass farthings,' took ship *c.* 1638 with his wife and one child. Finding himself suspected of Antinomianism in Boston, he went to New Hampshire; preached at Portsmouth, but was ousted by George Burdett (*q.v.*); then at Cocheco (Dover), whence ousted by Thomas Larkham (*q.v.*), who accused him of a 'pope-like carriage' in the church. Returned to England in 1641, and became successively schoolmaster, army chaplain, and Baptist clergyman in London. Died 19 September 1691. Author of a Hebrew Grammar, of many religious tracts, and of an autobiography, which was published posthumously as *The Life and Death of Mr. Hanserd Knollys* (London, 1692; copy in Congregational Library, Boston). *D.N.B.*; Backus, *History of the Baptists;* Winthrop; 5 *Coll. M.H.S.*, I. 280, 313–17.

JOHN KNOWLES of Lincolnshire, born *c.* 1606, matriculated pensioner in the University of Cambridge from Magdalene, Easter term 1620. In college was chamber-fellow of Richard Vines, and regarded as one of the most learned undergraduates. Scholar in 1621, and stood 18th in the *ordo senioritatis*. He took his B.A. 1623–24; M.A. 1627. Fellow of St. Catharine's, 1627, but not of Emmanuel as Cotton Mather states (*Magnalia*, Bk. III. 216). Ordained 1627; lecturer at Colchester 1635–37; emigrated 1639. Winthrop records, 9 December 1640, 'The church of Watertown ordained Mr. Knolles, a godly man and a prime scholar, pastor, and so they had now two pastors and no teacher.' His colleague was George Phillips. In 1642–43 Knowles was in Virginia on the missionary enterprise, with Tompson and James. After the death of Phillips in 1644, he became sole pastor of the church at Watertown, and presumably a member of the Board of

Overseers. Returned to England 1651; lecturer at Bristol Cathedral 1653–58; silenced in 1662. Knowles continued his interest in the College; and in 1672, when minister of a Congregational church in London, he was proposed for the presidency by Richard Saltonstall and others, but probably declined to be considered. Died 10 April 1685. Magdalene College Register (MS.); *D.N.B.; C.S.M.,* VIII. 194–99; *Calamy Revised.*

THOMAS LARKHAM, born at Lyme Regis, Dorset, 17 August 1602, matriculated in the University of Cambridge sizar from Trinity College in Michaelmas term 1619; B.A. Trinity Hall 1621–22; M.A. 1626; ordained 1624. Vicar of Northam, Devon, 1626–39; deprived; emigrated to New England 1640, and went to Cocheco (Dover, N. H.), where 'being a man of good parts and wealthy, the people were soon taken with him . . . cast off Mr. Knollys their pastor . . . to choose him.' Knollys (*q.v.*) excommunicated Larkham, who laid violent hands on Knollys; the latter raised an armed party, led by Captain John Underhill with a Bible upon a staff in lieu of ensign. The Bay Colony sent Simon Bradstreet, Hugh Peter, and Timothy Dalton as a commission to restore the peace, and they awarded the decision to Larkham. Nevertheless he returned to England in 1642, and became successively army chaplain (whence ousted by court martial) and vicar of Tavistock, Devon, 1648; where he quarrelled with his parish, and with all neighboring ministers, and resigned 1660. Imprisoned at the Restoration; released and became apothecary in Tavistock, where he was buried, 23 December 1669. *D.N.B.;* Winthrop; Palfrey, *Hist. of New England; Calamy Revised.*

ROBERT LENTHALL of Oxfordshire, a minister's son, matriculated in the University of Oxford from Oriel College 17 October 1616, aged 14; B.A. from All Souls' 8 July 1619. Rector of Aston Sandford, Bucks, in 1627; and of Great Hampden, Bucks, 1643. In 1638 he arrived at Weymouth, Massachusetts, on an invitation to become the minister. Committed the political error of 'standing upon his ministery as of the Church of England.' After a long controversy with a party in the town who preferred Joseph Hull and Thomas Jenner, Lenthall was forced out by the authorities for alleged Antinomian opinions, and fined £20. Removed to Newport, R. I., 1640, and taught school there; returned to England in 1642. *Magnalia;* Winthrop; Lechford, *Plain Dealing.*

WILLIAM LEVERITCH, born 1603, was admitted sizar at Emmanuel College, Cambridge, 28 March 1623; B.A. 1625–26; M.A. 1631; ordained 1626–27. In 1631 he was rector of Great Livermere, Suffolk.

Emigrated 1633; minister at Dover, N. H. Removed to Boston in 1635. About 1637 became colleague minister to Ralph Partridge at Duxbury; and in 1639 the first pastor of Sandwich on Cape Cod. Removed to Long Island in 1651; minister at Oyster Bay *c.* 1653–58 and at Huntington for about ten years. Removed to Newtown, L. I., in 1669; and served as pastor there till his death in 1677. Praised by Johnson for labors among the Indians of Cape Cod.

JOHN LOTHROP, son of Thomas Lothrop of Cherry Burton and Etton, Yorkshire, was baptized there 20 December 1584. He matriculated as a commoner's son 15 October 1602 in the University of Oxford from Christ Church, where he was sizar to Dr. John King, who became Dean of Christ Church in 1605. Lothrop removed to Cambridge and took his B.A. from Queens' College in 1607; ordained the same year and took his M.A. 1609. Married in 1610 Hannah, d. of Rev. John Howes of Eastwell, Kent. Successively curate of Bennington, Herts, and of Egerton, Kent, he left the Church of England to become pastor of the independent Congregational church at Southwark. Imprisoned for non-conformity 1632; released and emigrated 1634; gathered a church in Scituate, January, 1635, and from 1639 served as minister at Barnstable until his death, 8 November 1653. 'A man of learning, and of a meek and quiet spirit.' *D. N. B.; Calamy Revised;* Dean, *Scituate,* p. 168; *N.E.H.G.R.,* LXVI. 357; LXXXIV. 438.

ROGER LUDLOW, son of Thomas Ludlow, Esq., of Hill Deverill, Warminster, Wilts (great-uncle of General Edmund Ludlow), baptized at Dinton March 7, 1590. Matriculated as gentleman's son at Balliol College, Oxford, June 16, 1610; perhaps entered Inner Temple, November, 1612. Assistant of the Massachusetts Bay Company, 1630; emigrated in the *Mary and John* to Dorchester; Deputy-Governor, 1633. To Windsor, Connecticut, 1635; drafted Fundamental Orders and Law Code of 1650; settled Fairfield; Assistant and Deputy-Governor of Connecticut; emigrated to Ireland, 1654; member of commission on forfeited lands until 1660. *D.N.B.; D.A.B.;* R. V. Coleman, *Roger Ludlow in Chancery* (1934).

RICHARD MATHER, son of Thomas Mather, yeoman, born at Lowton, Lancs, 1596, was admitted to Brasenose College, Oxford, 9 May 1618; took holy orders 1619; minister at Toxteth near Liverpool. In 1634 he was suspended and the next year emigrated to New England, where he became teacher of the Church at Dorchester in 1636, and as such Overseer of Harvard College from 1642 until his death 22 April 1669. Author of the Cambridge platform of discipline of the New England churches. Married (1) in 1625 Katherine Holt of Bury.

Their four sons were Samuel (A.B. Harvard 1643), Nathaniel (A.B. 1647), Eleazer (A.B. 1656) and Increase (A.B. 1656), later President of the College. Married (2) in 1656 the widow of John Cotton. Anonymous biography printed in 1670; *D.A.B.; D.N.B.;* Wood, *Athenae Oxon.* (1721 ed.), II. 427; published *Journal* of his voyage; and K. B. Murdock, in *Old Time New England*, xv. 51–57.

MARMADUKE MATTHEWS, son of Matthew Matthews of Swansea, Wales, matriculated in the University of Oxford as a commoner's son from All Souls' 20 February 1623–24, aged 18; B.A. 1624–25; M.A. 1627. Vicar of St. John's, Swansea. Emigrated in 1638, first to the West Indies, and then to New England. Successively minister at Yarmouth, Hull and Malden (1650), whence, though much beloved, he was removed by pressure from the authorities for alleged heretical opinions. Returned to Swansea *c.* 1654, 'depending wholly upon Providence for the support of himself and his family,' preaching in a little chapel, and making house-to-house visits for spiritual discourse. Died there *c.* 1683. Mordecai Matthews (A.B. Harvard 1655), and Manasseh Matthews of the same class, were his sons. G. L. Turner, *Orig. Recs. Early Nonconformity*, i. 623, iii. 341, 344.

DANIEL MAUDE, baptized at Halifax, Yorks, 9 October 1586. Admitted sizar at Emmanuel College, Cambridge, 23 April 1603, became scholar; B.A. 1606–07; M.A. 1610. Emigrated with Richard Mather in 1635. Appointed master of the Grammar School at Boston — subsequently the Boston Latin School — 12 August 1636; freeman and church member. In 1643 he became pastor of the church at Dover, N. H., where he remained until his death in 1655. 'A good man, and of a serious spirit, and of a peaceable and quiet disposition,' writes Hubbard. H. F. Jenks, *Hist. Sketch Boston Latin School* (1886).

JOHN MAVERICK, son of Peter Maverick, vicar of Awliscombe, Devon, was baptized there 28 December 1578, and matriculated in the University of Oxford from Exeter College, 24 October 1595; ordained 29 July 1597; B.A. 1599; M.A. 1603. Curate to his uncle Radford Maverick, vicar of Islington; Rector of Beaworthy, Devon, 1615–30. Emigrated to New England on the *Mary and John*, 1630, with John Warham and the group of west countrymen who settled Dorchester, Massachusetts. The church there was probably formed at Plymouth before sailing; Maverick was teacher of it until his death, 2 February 1635–36. He was a 'man of very humble spirit, and faithful in furthering the work of the Lord here, both in the churches and civil state' (Winthrop). Father of Samuel Maverick, the pioneer planter of East Boston. *N.E.H.G.R.*, LXIX. 146–59.

John Mayo of Northamptonshire, who matriculated in the University of Oxford as a commoner's son from Magdalen Hall 28 April 1615, aged 17, but took no degree, was probably identical with the emigrant of that name who became colleague minister to John Lothrop at Barnstable in 1640, first pastor of Eastham in 1646, and first minister of the Second (North) Church in Boston 9 November 1655. Increase Mather was his colleague. Overseer of Harvard College. Dismissed in 1673 on account of age; died at Yarmouth in May 1676.

Edward Mellowes or Mellhouse, son of Abraham Mellowes of Lincolnshire, who adventured £50 in the Massachusetts Bay Company, was admitted pensioner at Emmanuel College, Cambridge, 1 July 1627. Emigrated with his parents in 1633; admitted freeman 4 March 1634; constable, town clerk and selectman of Charlestown, where he died 5 May 1650. Thomas Lechford, *Note-Book*, p. 410.

 William Mildmay, born 1622, was the eldest son of Sir Henry Mildmay (the regicide) of Wanstead, and great-grandson of the founder of Emmanuel College, Cambridge, where he was admitted fellow-commoner 26 September 1640. In 1644 he went to New England with his tutor, Richard Lyon, took his A.B. from Harvard as of the Class of 1647, A.M. 1650, and resided at the College until 1651, when he returned to England. Died 1 June 1682. Sibley, I. 164–65; *C.S.M.*, xv. cxl *n*.

John Miller, son of Martin Miller, weaver, was baptized at Ashford, Kent, 21 October 1604 and attended school there. Admitted sizar at Caius College, Cambridge, 20 May 1624, 'aged 18'; B.A. 1627–28. Emigrated 1638; lived at Dorchester, Roxbury, and Rowley, where he was town clerk. In 1641 invited to Virginia, but his 'Bodily Weaknesses caused him also to Decline the Voyage' (*Magnalia*). In 1646 he became pastor of Yarmouth, and in 1662–63 of Groton, where he died in June, 1663. Venn, *Biogr. Hist. Gonville & Caius College*, I. 266.

George Moxon, son of James, husbandman, was baptized at Wakefield, Yorkshire, 28 April 1602. Admitted sizar at Sidney Sussex College, Cambridge, 6 June 1620; B.A. 1623–24; ordained 1626. Chaplain to Sir William Brereton; curate of St. Helen's, Chester. Having been cited for non-conformity, he fled to New England in 1637, and first settled at Dorchester; admitted freeman 7 September 1637. A good lyric poet and successful imitator of Horace, he was withal a man of 'strong and able parts,' and by William Pynchon was selected to be pastor of the trading post at Springfield in 1637. There he remained until 1652, returning to England with Pynchon, whose heretical views on the atonement he probably shared. In England he occupied various pulpits until his death on 15 September 1687. Burt, *History of Springfield;* MS. records of Sidney Sussex College; Calamy.

SAMUEL NEWMAN, son of Richard Newman, was born at Banbury in 1600 (Foster), and baptized 24 May 1602. Entered Magdalen College, Oxford, 1616, and matriculated as a commoner's son 3 March 1619–20; B.A. from St. Edmund Hall 17 October 1620. Minister in Ecclesfield, Yorks, 1625–35. Emigrating to New England, *c.* 1636, he lived for a time at Weymouth, and in 1644 became the first minister of Rehoboth. 'A very lively preacher and a very preaching liver,' according to Mather, he bestowed much 'toyl and oyl' upon his Concordance of the Bible (London, 1643), which held its own until superseded by Cruden's. He died 5 July 1663, having predicted the exact moment of his death, when he summoned the angels, 'Come do your office!' (as my Lord Crew related to Mr. Pepys). Henry Newman (A.B. Harvard 1687) was his grandson. S. C. Newman, *Rehoboth in the Past; Magnalia;* Wood, *Athenae Oxon.;* Pepys's *Diary* (Wheatley ed.), VII. 163, 287–88.

ROGER NEWTON matriculated sizar in the University of Cambridge from King's College in Easter term 1636, and emigrated *c.* 1638. Continued his studies at Hartford under Thomas Hooker, whose daughter Mary he married in 1645. Ordained 13 October 1652 the first pastor of Farmington, Connecticut. Left there in 1657, intending for England, but the ship was so delayed in Nantasket Roads by head winds that the master set Newton ashore as a Jonah, and he returned to Connecticut. A pulpit was found for him at Milford in 1659, and there he remained until his death, 7 June 1683.

NATHANIEL NORCROSS of London was admitted pensioner at St. Catharine's Hall, Cambridge, 1632; B.A. 1636–37; emigrated 1638. He joined the church of Salem in 1641, but removed to Watertown the following year. The organizers of the plantation of Nashaway (Lancaster, Mass.) chose him to be their pastor in 1644, but the authorities opposed the projected settlement, and Norcross after declining a call to New Hampshire returned to England in 1650, where he became vicar of Walsingham, Norfolk. Ejected in 1660, he died at St. Dunstan-in-the-East, London, 10 August 1662.

EDWARD NORRIS of Gloucestershire matriculated as a clergyman's son in the University of Oxford from Balliol College, 30 March 1599, aged 15; B.A. from Magdalen Hall 23 January 1606–07; M.A. 1609. Rector of Anmer, Norfolk, 1624; also taught and preached at Tetbury and Horsley, Gloucester; emigrated *c.* 1639, and first settled in Boston. 'Yong Mr. Norris was chosen to teach skoole' at Salem in January, 1639–40, and on 18 March was ordained teacher of the church. Winthrop in 1642 characterized him as 'a grave and judicious elder.' Died 23 December 1659. His son Edward was the schoolmaster at Salem for many years. Hubbard, *New England* (1848), p. 276; *Essex Inst. Hist. Coll.,* IX. 97; John Hull, *Diary.*

 JOHN NORTON, son of William Norton, was born at Bishop's Stortford, Herts, 6 May 1606. Admitted pensioner at Peterhouse, Cambridge, 1620; scholar; B.A. 1623–24; M.A. 1627; declined fellowship at St. Catharine's. Curate at Bishop's Stortford; emigrated in 1635; several families of his parish accompanied him. Shortly after arriving at Plymouth he removed to Ipswich, where he assisted and succeeded Nathaniel Ward; in 1653 he succeeded John Cotton as colleague to John Wilson in the Boston church, and appointed Overseer of Harvard College; and after a vexatious diplomatic mission to England, died at Boston 5 April 1663. 'Vast was the treasure of learning in this reverend man' (*Magnalia*). One of the leaders of the New England churches, active in church synods, and a vigorous persecutor of Quakers and other heretics, Norton came nearer to the popular notion of a 'grim puritan' than any other of this group. His best-known writings were *Responsio ad syllogen a Guilielmo Apollonio propositam* (London, 1648); *The Orthodox Evangelist* (1654); and the *Heart of New England rent at the Blasphemies of the Present Generation* (1659). Uncle of John Norton (A.B. Harvard 1671). A.B. Ellis, *First Church in Boston.*

JAMES NOYES, son of the Rev. William Noyes (B.A. from University College, Oxford, 1592) and Sara, sister of Robert Parker the theologian, was born in 1608 in Choulderton, Wiltshire. Admitted to Brasenose College, Oxford, 22 August 1627, aged 18 (B.N.C. *Register*, I. 154); received grace for B.A. 7 May 1629, but apparently did not take the degree. Assisted his cousin Thomas Parker at the Free School, Newbury; they emigrated in March 1633–34 with Noyes's wife and younger brother Nicholas, in the *Mary and John*. Preached for a time at Medford, but on the gathering of a church at Newbury came there as teacher with Parker, and 'continued painful and successful in that station something about twenty years,' until his death on 21 October 1656. 'There was the greatest amity, intimacy, unanimity, yea, unity imaginable between Mr. Parker and Mr. Noyes. . . . They taught in one School; came over in one Ship; were Pastor and Teacher of one Church; and Mr. Parker continuing always in Celibacy, they lived in one House' (*Magnalia*). Father of James and Moses Noyes, both A.B. Harvard 1659; uncle of Nicholas Noyes, A.B. 1667, who wrote the memoir which is printed in the *Magnalia*, Bk. III, chap. xxv.

THOMAS PARKER, only son of Robert Parker (1564–1614), the eminent puritan divine, was born at Stanton St. Bernard, Wilts, 8 June 1595. Matriculated sizar at Trinity College, Dublin, Michaelmas term 1610. Matriculated in the University of Oxford, probably from Magdalen College, 23 April 1613. Registered as student of theology at the University of Leyden 15 July 1614. Proceeded to the University of Franeker to study under his father's friend William Ames, and there took the degree of M.A. or M.PHIL. 1 April 1617. Engaged in a theological controversy there. Returned to Newbury as schoolmaster, and assistant to the minister, Dr. William Twisse. Emigrated in 1633–34 in the *Mary and John*; settled at Ipswich; and in 1635 with his cousin James Noyes and nephew John Woodbridge (*qq.v.*) founded Newbury, becoming pastor of the church. Leaned toward Presbyterianism, which involved him in controversy with his church, the members of which were devoted to him personally. Prepared boys for Harvard College, and published several theological tracts. Died at Newbury, unmarried, 24 April 1677. *D.A.B.; Magnalia;* S. E. Morison, in *C.S.M.*, XXVIII. 261–67.

RALPH PARTRIDGE, son of Thomas Partridge, clerk, was baptized at Sutton Valence, Kent, 12 April 1579. Matriculated in the University of Cambridge sizar from Trinity College *c.* 1595; B.A. 1599–1600; M.A. 1603. Curate of Sutton-by-Dover, Kent, 1619–25. Arriving in Boston in November 1636, he removed to the Plymouth Colony, and became pastor of Duxbury, 1638. 'Notwithstanding the paucity and poverty of his flock, he continued in his work amongst them to the end,' dying *c.* 1 May 1658. His daughter Elizabeth married Thomas Thacher, minister of the Old South Church, Boston; Peter Thacher (A.B. Harvard 1671) was their son. Will abstracted in *Mayflower Descendant*, XIV. 228–30.

ROBERT PECK, son of Robert Peck of Beccles, Suffolk, was born there in 1580; B.A. from St. Catharine's, Cambridge, 1598–99; M.A. from Magdalene College 1603. Ordained 1604–05, aged 25. Curate of Oulton; rector of Hingham, Norfolk, until 1638, when deprived, and emigrated to Hingham, Massachusetts, founded by his parishioners. Teacher of the church there. 'A Great Person for Stature, yet a Greater for Spirit' (*Magnalia*). Returned to England 27 October 1641, and in 1646 was reinstated in his former English rectory, where he died in 1658. His son Jeremiah was of the Harvard Class of 1657. *History of Hingham, Mass.* (1893), I. pt. ii; Sibley, I. 569.

WILLIAM PELHAM was one of sixteen children of Herbert Pelham Esq. of Hastings and Boston, and Penelope, daughter of Thomas West, second Lord de la Warr. Matriculated in the University of Cambridge fellow-commoner from Emmanuel in Michaelmas term 1615. Probably became an attorney in London. Emigrated 1630 in the Winthrop fleet. One of the founders of Sudbury; selectman, captain of the trained band, and deputy to the General Court. Returned to England before 1653 and died unmarried in 1667, leaving his property to his brother Herbert, the first Treasurer of Harvard College. His sister Penelope married Governor Bellingham. David McLean, in *Sussex County Magazine*, IV. 357–68.

WILLIAM PERKINS, son of William Perkins, a merchant tailor of London who subscribed £50 to the Massachusetts Bay Company, was born 25 August 1607. Versatile and restless as boy and man, he was admitted to Emmanuel College, Cambridge, 1624; migrated to Christ's 15 November 1626; B.A. 1627–28. Emigrated 1632, residing first at Roxbury where he married Elizabeth Wooton in 1636; freeman of the Colony and member of the Artillery Company. In 1643 removed to Weymouth where he served as captain of the trained band and deputy to the General Court. Removed to Gloucester *c.* 1650; again captain and also taught school and succeeded Richard Blinman in the ministry. Removed to Topsfield in 1655, and took charge of the church there after the minister had been dismissed for habitual drunkenness. Died 21 May 1682. J. J. Babson, *History of Gloucester*; *N.E.H.G.R.*, LXXVI. 223–32.

HUGH PETER, baptized 11 June 1598 at Fowey, Cornwall, was the son of Thomas Dickwood, who in 1600 changed his name to Peter, and

Martha Treffry. At Cambridge University he matriculated sizar from Trinity College in Michaelmas term 1613; B.A. 1617–18; taught school at Langdon, Essex; ordained 1621; M.A. 1622. Curate at Rayleigh, Essex; suspended, 1627, for some sermons that he preached, and that year emigrated to the Netherlands. Subscribed £50 to the Massachusetts Bay Company, and was present at a meeting in London 11 May 1629. Returned to the Continent; travelled; minister of the English church at Rotterdam 1630. Emigrated to New England 1635; pastor of Salem church, active in politics and industrial promotion, member of the first Harvard Board of Overseers. Returning to England in 1641, partly in order to raise money for the College, he took an active part in the Civil War, and became one of the best-known figures in England. Executed 16 October 1660. Sir Charles Firth in *D.N.B.; Proc. M.H.S.,* LXIV; bibliography in *Harv. Grads. Mag.,* XXXIX. 130–40; *N.Y. Gen. & Biog. Mag.,* XLVIII. 75, 180; Ms. doctoral dissertation by Raymond P. Stearns.

THOMAS PETERS, elder brother of Hugh Peter, baptized 1 June, 1697, took his B.A. from Brasenose College, Oxford, 1614; M.A. 1625. Vicar of Mylor, Cornwall, 1628. Driven out by the cavaliers 1643; emigrated in 1644. Preached at Saybrook, Connecticut, and in 1646 was engaged by John Winthrop, Jr., to be minister of New London, whence he wrote to Governor Winthrop soliciting aid for Uncas against the Narragansetts. Shortly after, invited by his former parish, he returned to Mylor, and died there in 1654.

JOHN PHILIP or PHILLIPS was admitted sizar at Emmanuel College, Cambridge, 27 June 1600; B.A. 1603–04; M.A. 1607; ordained 1609, aged 24. Rector of Wrentham, Suffolk, 1609–38. Married there 6 January 1611–12 Elizabeth, sister of the great William Ames. Deprived in 1638 and emigrated to Salem. Invited to be pastor of the church at Dedham, and also to be Ezekiel Rogers' colleague at Rowley; but in the summer of 1639 removed to Cambridge. On 24 May 1640 he was admitted to the church at Dedham, and lived there until October 1641, when he returned to England, recovered his rectory, and reorganized the church on Congregational principles. Philip's nephew William Ames (A.B. Harvard 1645), concerning whom he corresponded with President Dunster, became his colleague minister in the Wrentham church. Philip was ejected in 1662. Sibley, I. 108; Dunster Notebook, *M.H.S.;* Calamy; J. H. Tuttle in *C.S.M.,* XVII. 208–15.

GEORGE PHILLIPS, son of Christopher Phillips 'mediocris fortunae' of South Rainham, Norfolk, prepared at Tivetshall School. Admitted sizar at Caius College, Cambridge, 10 April 1610, aged 17;

B.A. 1613–14; curate of Boxted, Essex, *c.* 1615; M.A. 1617; resided at Wrentham. Emigrated with his wife and children in 1630 in the Winthrop fleet; possibly author of the *Humble Address*, which he signed. With Sir Richard Saltonstall, Phillips founded Watertown, became first pastor of the church there, and an Overseer of Harvard College from 1642 until his death on 1 July 1644. One of the most intellectually gifted of the New England clergy, and one of the most independent in politics and theology. His books were valued at £71 9*s* 9*d* at his death. *D.N.B.*; H. W. Foote, in *Proc. M.H.S.*, LXIII. 193–227.

ABRAHAM PIERSON of Yorkshire matriculated in the University of Cambridge pensioner from Trinity College in Michaelmas term 1629; B.A. 1632; ordained 1632; emigrated 1639; minister at Southampton, Long Island, 1640–44, having gone thither with a group from Lynn. In 1644, with part of the congregation, he crossed the Sound to become minister of Branford, and also preached to the Indians in their own language. 'Mr. Pierson and almost his whole church and congregation were so displeased' at the union of New Haven and Connecticut, writes Trumbull, 'that they soon removed into Newark, in New Jersey.' There Pierson was a dominant figure in civil life, and continued his ministrations until his death, 9 August 1678. Abraham Pierson (A.B. Harvard 1668), the first Rector of Yale College, was his son. *D.N.B.*

 WILLIAM POLE, fourth son of Sir William Pole, a well-known antiquary of Colyton, Devon, and Mary, d. of Sir William Periham, Chief Baron of the Exchequer, was baptized 4 December 1593. The family originated in Cheshire. Pole matriculated at Oxford from Oriel College 1609–10, aged 16; B.A. 1612. A Latin poem by him is no. 221 in the *Epithalamia* printed at Oxford in 1613 upon the occasion of Princess Elizabeth's marriage to Frederick Count Palatine. Member of the Inner Temple in 1616. With his sister Elizabeth, he migrated to New England and founded Taunton. Winthrop records in 1637: 'This year a plantation was begun at Tecticutt by a gentlewoman, an ancient maid, one Mrs. Poole. She went late thither, and endured much hardship, and lost much cattle. Called, after, Taunton.' William Pole died at Taunton 24 February 1674. *D.N.B.*; W. H. H. Rogers, *Memorials of the West*, 351–60.

PETER PRUDDEN, born *c.* 1600, was admitted sizar at Emmanuel College, Cambridge, 20 June 1620. After declining a pulpit in the Bahamas, he emigrated with his wife to New England in 1637 as part of the Eaton-Davenport company, with which he went to found New Haven in 1638. Withdrew in 1639 to found Milford, where he organized a church of 'seven pillars' on the New Haven model, and served as pastor from 1640 to his death in 1656, aged 56. John Prudden (A.B. Harvard 1668) was his son.

THOMAS RASHLEY, exhibitioner from Charterhouse 1629, matriculated in the University of Cambridge pensioner from Trinity College in Easter term of that year; scholar 1631; B.A. 1632–33; fellow 1633; M.A. 1636. Emigrated c. 1639; admitted 'a studyent' to Boston Church 8 March 1639–40. Shortly after 'at Cape Anne, where fishing is set forward, and some stages builded, there one master Rashley is Chaplain: for it is farre off from any Church' (Lechford's *Plain Dealing*, 106–07). Moved to Exeter, N. H. in the spring of 1643 with the expectation of becoming minister as successor to John Wheelwright; but remained only a year. In Boston 1645; returned to England c. 1646; successively minister at Bishopstoke, Hants; Barford, Wilts; and at Salisbury Cathedral. Ejected in 1662, and lived at Abrey near Marlborough.

JOHN RAYNER, son of Humfrey Rayner, a considerable landowner at Gildersome, near Batley, Yorks, matriculated in the University of Cambridge pensioner from Magdalene College in Easter term 1622; B.A. 1625–26. Married a local heiress named Boyes, sister to Peter Prudden's wife, and lived on his estate at Gildersome. Emigrated with his wife and brother Humfrey in 1635, and the same year was chosen pastor of the church at Plymouth, in succession to Ralph Smith. A controversy over baptism with the teacher of the church, Charles Chauncy, ended in the latter removing to Duxbury. In consequence of some other 'unhappy difference' with the people, Rayner resigned and left Plymouth in November 1654 for Dover, N. H., where he ministered during the remaining fourteen years of his life. The church historians of Plymouth characterized him as an 'able faithfull laboriouse preacher of the Gospell, and a wise order of the affaires of the Church'; his departure was followed by 'ignorance . . . amongst the voulgare and alsoe much lysensiousness and prophanes amongst the younger sort.' Died at Dover in April 1669. Father of John Rayner (A.B. Harvard 1663). *C.S.M.*, XXII, XXIII.

EZEKIEL ROGERS, son of Richard Rogers (M.A. 1574), lecturer at Wethersfield, Essex, and author of the *Seven Treatises*, took his B.A. from Christ's College, Cambridge, 1604–05; M.A. 1608. Chaplain to Sir Francis Barrington of Hatfield, Broad Oak, Essex; rector in 1621 of Rowley St. Peter, Yorkshire, a benefice with £240 per annum, and 'favored both for subscription and ceremonies' by the Archbishop of York; but resigned and emigrated with his wife in 1638 rather than read the Book of Sports. Founded the town of Rowley in Massachusetts, and became its first pastor, with a salary of £60. Eaton and Davenport 'laboured by all means to draw' Rogers to New Haven, but he 'went on with his plantation' at Rowley, and died there in 1660. Married thrice (the second wife being a daughter of John Wilson), but remained childless. A masterful man of strong opinions, he refused to make his cousin and namesake, Ezekiel Rogers (A.B. Harvard 1659), his chief legatee, because he insisted on wearing long hair; and left most of his books, valued at £73, and the reversion of 'sundry parcels of land of great value' to the College. In 1735 the College Corporation proposed to defray half the cost of a 'suitable stone and proper inscription' over Rogers' grave at Rowley, provided the town would pay the other half, but it does not appear that this offer was accepted. Sibley, II. 41; *D.N.B.*; *C.S.M.*, XII, XV, XVI.

NATHANIEL ROGERS, born at Haverhill, Suffolk, 1598, the second son of 'Roaring John' Rogers (B.A. 1592, lecturer at Dedham and author of *Doctrine of Faith*) by his first wife, Bridget Ray. John's father was brother to Richard Rogers, father of Ezekiel (*q.v.*). Admitted sizar at Emmanuel College, Cambridge, 1614; scholar; B.A. 1617–18; M.A. 1621; ordained 1619; curate at Bocking, Essex; rector of Assington, Suffolk, 1630. Emigrating with his wife in 1636, in the same ship with Ralph Partridge, he succeeded Nathaniel Ward as pastor of the church of Ipswich in 1638; John Norton was his colleague. 'An able disputant, whose mouth the Lord was pleased to fill with many arguments for the defence of his truth' (Johnson, *W.W.P.*, p. 88). Died July 3, 1655. Father of President John Rogers (A.B. Harvard 1649), Ezekiel Rogers (A.B. 1659), and Mary, who married William Hubbard (A.B. 1642). Waters, *G.G.E.*, I. 209–36.

RICHARD SADLER, son of Richard Sadler of Worcester, born there around 1620, admitted pensioner at Emmanuel College, Cambridge, 30 December 1636. In 1638, emigrated with his parents who settled at Lynn, the father being a farmer. Either the son or the father was member of the Salem Court and clerk of the writs in 1640–41. The son returned to England in 1646, preached at Whixall, Salop, 1648; and at Ludlow; ejected 1662. Retired to Whixall, and there died in 1675. 'He had a wife and many children, and very little to live on, but was chearful and hearty.' Calamy.

SIR RICHARD SALTONSTALL, the son of Samuel of Halifax, Yorkshire, and nephew of Sir Richard, Lord Mayor of London, was baptized 4 April 1586. Matriculated in the University of Cambridge pensioner from Clare in Easter term 1603; admitted to the Middle Temple 24 February 1605–06. Justice of the peace for West Riding, Yorks; knighted 23 November 1618. An original patentee and assistant of the Massachusetts Bay Company, he migrated with the Winthrop fleet in 1630, founded Watertown, but returned to England the following year. His letter of 1651, remonstrating with Cotton and Wilson over the persecution of Quakers, has often been quoted as proof of his wisdom and tolerance. The Saltonstalls have the singular distinction of having sent nine successive generations, all in the male line, to Harvard College. Sir Richard was the father of Henry Saltonstall (A.B. 1642), and the grandfather of Nathaniel (A.B. 1659); the rest are Richard (A.B. 1695), Richard (A.B. 1722), Nathaniel (A.B. 1766), Leverett (A.B. 1802), Leverett (A.B. 1844), Richard Middlecott (A.B. 1880), and Leverett (A.B. 1914). *D.N.B.*; Sibley, II. 8.

RICHARD SALTONSTALL, son of Sir Richard (*q.v.*) and Grace (Kaye) Saltonstall, was baptized at Woodsome, Almondbury, 1 October 1610. Admitted fellow-commoner at Emmanuel College 28 April 1627. Emigrated with his father in 1630. He made four subsequent visits to England and died there 29 April 1694, but passed the greater part of his life at Ipswich in Massachusetts. Assistant of the Bay Colony from 1637 to 1649, and again in 1664 and 1680–82; at the same time was Overseer of the College and took a keen interest in its welfare. Saltonstall led the opposition to the somewhat arbitrary methods of Winthrop, Dudley, and Endicott, and protested in vain against the slave trade. Father of Nathaniel Saltonstall (A.B. 1659). *D.A.B.*; *D.N.B.*; Winthrop.

PETER SAXTON, perhaps son of Christopher Saxton the map-maker, was born at Bramley, Leeds; matriculated in the University of Cambridge sizar from Trinity College *c.* 1595; B.A. 1595–96; M.A. 1603; ordained 1611. Rector of Edlington, Yorkshire, 1614–40, when he migrated to New England, and succeeded John Lothrop as minister at Scituate, but returned to England in 1641, probably intending for Old Providence with John Humfrey. Vicar of Leeds from 1646 to his death on 1 October 1651. Mather calls him 'a studious and a learned person, a great Hebrician.' *Magnalia.*

THOMAS SHEPARD, son of William Shepard, grocer of Towcester, Northants, was born there 5 November 1605. Admitted pensioner at Emmanuel College, Cambridge, 1619–20; B.A. 1623–24; M.A. and ordained 1627. Lecturer at Earls Colne, Essex; reprimanded by Laud, and suspended. Chaplain to Sir Richard Darley of Buttercrambe, Yorks. A friend of Hooker, Stone, and Weld, he emigrated with several followers in 1635 and became pastor of the church organized at Cambridge before the departure of Thomas Hooker's company. 'The Character of his daily Conversation was a Trembling Walk with God' (*Magnalia*, 1702); but this 'poore weake pale complectioned man' (*W.W.P.*, p. 136) was the most noted evangelist in early New England, and one of the leading theologians, whose works were reprinted in the 19th century. Overseer of Harvard College from 1637 to his death on 29 August 1649. His first wife bore to him Thomas Shepard (A.B. Harvard 1653); his second (a daughter of Thomas Hooker) was the mother of Samuel Shepard (A.B. 1658); and Jeremiah Shepard (A.B. 1669) was his son by a third wife. S. E. Morison, *Builders of the Bay*; autobiography reprinted in *C.S.M.*, XXVII. 352–400.

JOHN SHERMAN, born at Dedham, Essex, 1613, matriculated sizar in the University of Cambridge from St. Catharine's, 1631, but declined to subscribe for his degree. Emigrated *c.* 1635, and after preaching in Connecticut succeeded George Phillips as minister of Watertown in 1647. Overseer of Harvard College from that date, and Fellow of the Corporation from 1678 to his death, 8 August 1685. An amateur astronomer, also compiled almanacs. 'Such keenness of wit, such soundness of judgment, such fulness of matter, and such vigour of language, is rarely seen in old age, as was to be seen in him when he was old' (*Magnalia*). Father of Bezaleel Sherman (A.B. 1661), ancestor of Roger Sherman.

SAMUEL SKELTON was baptized at Coningsby, Lincolnshire, 26 February 1592–93. Matriculated in the University of Cambridge sizar from Clare 1608; B.A. 1611–12; M.A. 1615. Rector of Sempringham from about 1615 to 1620; probably chaplain to the Earl of Lincoln, brother to Lady Arabella Johnson. As one of the ministers engaged by the Massachusetts Bay Company for its plantation, he crossed in 1628–29 with his family and library of fifty-five volumes, on the same ship as Francis Higginson, and became pastor of the First Church of Salem, of which Higginson was teacher: the pioneer Congregational church of the Bay Colony. Died 2 August 1634.

HENRY SMITH, who matriculated in the University of Cambridge as sizar from Magdalene in Easter term 1618, B.A. 1621–22, M.A. 1625, ordained 1623, is probably identical with the Henry Smith who emigrated to New England in 1636, and who was described by his son as 'educated at Cambridge.' He lived at Watertown for a time, but later removed to Wethersfield, Connecticut, where he became pastor in 1641, succeeding Peter Prudden, and died in 1648, leaving an estate valued at £370, including many books. *Conn. Col. Records*, I.

RALPH SMITH matriculated in the University of Cambridge sizar from Christ's July 1610; scholar, 1610–14; B.A. 1613–14. Emigrated with his family 1628–29 in the same ship with Higginson and Skelton; became the first regularly ordained minister of the Pilgrim church at Plymouth *c.* July 1629. Apparently incompetent; and resigned in 1636 to make way for John Norton, who did not stay; preached at Manchester, 1645, and finally settled in Boston, where he died 1 March 1660–61.

SAMUEL STONE, baptized at Hertford 30 July 1602, matriculated in the University of Cambridge sizar from Emmanuel in 1620; B.A. 1623–24; M.A. 1627; ordained 1626. Curate at Stisted, Essex, and Lecturer at Taventer; suspended for non-conformity. Having by his ready wit and a white lie saved Thomas Hooker from arrest in 1633, Stone became the inseparable companion and colleague of that 'son of thunder': — teacher of the church at Newtown, founder of Connecticut, and teacher of the church at Hartford, which was named after his birthplace. After Hooker's death, a violent controversy between Stone and the ruling elder, William Goodwin, divided the church, the town, and the colony. Although a man of wit, he was also 'a man of principles, and in the management of those principles he was both a Load-Stone and a Flint-Stone' (*Magnalia*). He died at Hartford 20 July 1663. John Stone (A.B. Harvard 1653) and Samuel Stone (class of 1662) were his sons. *D.A.B.*

NICHOLAS STREET of Somerset matriculated in the University of Oxford 2 November 1621 from Pembroke College, aged 18; B.A. 1624–25. He then migrated to Cambridge and took his M.A. from Emmanuel in 1636. Emigrating probably with the Poles in 1637, he and William Hooke were ordained respectively teacher and pastor of the church of Taunton on the same day. When Hooke went to New Haven, Streete succeeded to his pastorate at Taunton, and later took Hooke's place in the New Haven church in 1659, as colleague to John Davenport. Davenport removed to Boston, and Street be-

came the sole minister of the church in New Haven, where he died
22 April 1678. Samuel Street (A.B. Harvard 1664) was his son. Bradford, *Plimmoth Plantation* (1912 ed.), II. 262; Trumbull, *Connecticut*,
I. 247.

ZECHARIAH SYMMES, born at Canterbury 5 April 1599, was son of the
Rev. William Symmes, B.D. Admitted pensioner at Emmanuel College, Cambridge, 1617; B.A. 1620–21; M.A. 1624. Lecturer at St.
Antholin's, London, 1621–25; resigned owing to pressure on him as
a puritan; rector of Dunstable 1625–32. Emigrated in 1634 with his
family to Charlestown, where he was ordained teacher of the church
22 December 1634. After the resignation of Thomas James (*q.v.*)
Symmes became pastor, and so remained until his death, 28 January
1671–72. During a large part of this period he was Overseer of
Harvard College. Zechariah Symmes (A.B. Harvard 1657) was his
son. *Magnalia.*

WILLIAM TOMPSON, of Lancashire, matriculated in the University
of Oxford from Brasenose College as a commoner's son 28 January
1619–20, aged 22; B.A. 1621–22. Emigrated in 1637; preached for
a time at Agamenticus (York, Maine); and in 1639 became minister of Braintree. One of the puritan clergy in Virginia in 1642–43.
Although 'a very powerful and successful preacher,' 'he fell into that
Balneum Diaboli, a black *Melancholy*, which for divers Years almost
wholly disabled him for the Exercise of his Ministry' (*Magnalia*),
and died 10 December 1666. William Tompson (A.B. Harvard 1653),
Benjamin Tompson (A.B. 1662), the 'first native-born poet' of the
English colonies, and Joseph Tompson, also a poet but not a graduate,
were his sons. K. B. Murdock, *Handkerchiefs from Paul.*

 SIR HENRY VANE, eldest son of Sir Henry Vane (1589–
1655) and Frances Darcy, was baptized 26 May 1613
at Debden near Newport, Essex. He was educated at
Westminster School, was converted to puritanism at
the age of 15, and in 1629 was admitted gentleman
commoner at Magdalen Hall, Oxford, and remained
there for some time; but refused to matriculate in the
university on account of the required oaths. After leaving Oxford
he spent some time at Geneva and Leyden, and went to Vienna in the
suite of the English ambassador 1631. Emigrated in the *Abigail*,
1635, was given magisterial duties within two months of his arrival
at Boston, and on 25 May 1636 was elected Governor of the Massachusetts Bay. As such, member and presiding officer of the General
Court whose appropriation of £400 for a 'schoale or colledge' on Oc-

tober 28, 1636, founded Harvard. Defeated for the governorship in 1637 by reason of his support of the Antinomian party, Vane sailed for England 3 August 1637. Knighted in 1640. His subsequent career belongs to English history, although he always 'showed himself a true friend to New England and a man of noble and generous mind.' (Winthrop.) Sir Charles Firth in *D.N.B.*; J. K. Hosmer, *Sir Harry Vane*; Anthony Wood, *Athenae Oxon.* (ed. Bliss), III. 578; George Sikes, *Life and Death of Sir Henry Vane* (1662).

WILLIAM WALTON, of Seaton, Devonshire, was admitted sizar at Emmanuel College, Cambridge, in 1618; B.A. 1621–22; M.A. 1625; ordained 1621. Vicar or curate of Seaton; married Elizabeth Cooke, niece of the Rev. John White, and with her emigrated *c.* 1635. Settled first at Hingham, then at Weymouth, and in 1637 at Marblehead, where he ministered to the fishermen's church until his death, early in November 1668.

JOHN WARD, son of Nathaniel Ward (*q.v.*), was born at Haverhill in Essex 5 November 1606; admitted pensioner at Emmanuel College, Cambridge, 30 August 1622; B.A. 1626–27; M.A. 1630. Rector of Hadleigh, Essex, 1633–39. Emigrated to New England, preached at Kittery and at York, Maine, in 1641, and the same year was ordained pastor of the new church at Haverhill. 'A person of quick apprehension, a clear understanding, a strong memory, a facetious conversation' (*Magnalia*). His last sermon was preached in his eighty-eighth year, shortly before his death on 27 December 1693.

NATHANIEL WARD, the 'simple Cobler of Aggawam,' son of John Ward, 'painful minister' of Haverhill in Essex, was born there in 1578. Admitted sizar at Emmanuel College, Cambridge, 15 April 1596; B.A. 1599–1600; M.A. 1603. Studied and practised law, travelled on the Continent, was converted by David Pareus, and became chaplain to the English factory at Ebling. Returning to England about 1624, he was successively curate of St. James's, Piccadilly, and rector of Stondon Massey, Essex, 1628–33. Suspended by Laud, he emigrated in 1634, and served as minister of Ipswich (Agawam) until 1636, when he resigned. Compiled the famous Body of Liberties of 1641, as a check on arbitrary government; and led an opposition movement to Governor Winthrop. His famous pamphlet, *The Simple Cobler of Aggawam*, written in 1645–46, was published in London in 1647, after his return to England, where he championed the cause of Charles I and indulged in a pamphlet controversy with Hugh Peter. From 1648 to his death in 1652 he was minister of

Shenfield, Essex. John Ward (above) and James Ward (A.B. Harvard 1645) were his sons. S. E. Morison, *Builders of the Bay*; J. W. Dean, *Nathaniel Ward* (1868); *N.E.H.G.R.*, xvi. 365, xli. 282.

JOHN WARHAM, a west-countryman, took his B.A. in the University of Oxford from St. Mary Hall, 14 November 1614, and his M.A. in 1618. Minister of Crewkerne, Somerset, forced to resign by Laud, then Bishop of Bath and Wells; obtained a living at St. Sidwell's by Exeter. Emigrated in 1630 in the *Mary and John* with his wife, John Maverick, and the west-countrymen who settled Dorchester, Warham and Maverick becoming their pastor and teacher. Emigrated with a part of his flock to Windsor, Connecticut, in 1635, and ministered to them until his death, 19 April 1670, although the parish had long wished to be rid of him on account of his melancholy disposition. *Magnalia;* Frances Rose-Troup, *John White.*

THOMAS WATERHOUSE, son of Edward Waterhouse, barber-chirurgeon of London, was admitted pensioner from Charterhouse at Emmanuel College, Cambridge, 15 July 1631; B.A. 1634–35. Beneficed in Hertfordshire; emigrated 1639; schoolmaster at Dorchester until 1642, when he returned to England. Taught school and enjoyed various benefices until his ejection in 1662. Died at West Creeting, Suffolk, August 20, 1680. *Calamy Revised.*

THOMAS WELD, son of Edmund Weld, a mercer of Sudbury, Suffolk, was baptized 15 July 1595. Matriculated in the University of Cambridge pensioner from Trinity College in 1611; B.A. 1613–14; M.A. 1618; ordained the same year. Vicar of Haverhill, Suffolk, and of Terling, Essex; a warm friend of Hooker and Eliot. Ejected for non-conformity, emigrated in 1632 and became pastor of the church at Roxbury. Joint author of the Bay Psalm Book, and a bitter opponent of the Antinomians. A member of the first Harvard Board of Overseers, he returned to England with Hugh Peter in 1641, as agent of the Colony, and collected sundry moneys for the College. Joint author of *New Englands First Fruits;* author of *A Brief Narration of the Opinions and Practices of the Churches in New England* (1645) and of other tracts. Rector of St. Mary, Gateshead, Durham, 1649–60. Died 23 March 1661. Edmund Weld (A.B. Harvard 1650) was his son. *D.N.B.;* introduction to C. F. Adams, *Antinomianism; N.E.H.G.R.*, xxxvi. *passim;* catalogue of his library, *C.S.M.*, xxviii. 136–56.

WILLIAM WETHERELL or WITHERELL, born about 1600, matriculated in the University of Cambridge sizar from Corpus Christi College in Easter term 1619; B.A. 1622–23; M.A. 1626. Schoolmaster at Maidstone, Kent. Emigrated with his family in the *Hercules*, 1635, with a certificate of proficiency from the mayor of Maidstone. Taught school probably first at Cambridge, and certainly at Charlestown, where he resided from June 1636 until late in 1638, when he migrated to Duxbury. Finally settled in Scituate, where he was ordained pastor of the Second Church 2 September 1645, the choice of the party who objected to Chauncy's views on baptism. Under his long pastorate, ending with his death 9 April 1684, the bitter church quarrels of Scituate were composed, and a new meeting-house erected. Wrote elegiac verse. Frothingham, *Charlestown*, p. 65; Dean, *Scituate*, pp. 190–94, 295–397; M. W. Jernegan, in *School Review*, XXIII. 367.

RALPH WHEELOCK, born in Shropshire 1600, was probably brother to the orientalist Abraham Wheelock (1593–1653). Matriculated in the University of Cambridge sizar from Clare in Easter term 1623; B.A. 1626–27; ordained 1629; M.A. 1631. Emigrated with his wife in 1637, settled first at Watertown, then at Dedham, where he and John Allin organized the first church; presided over the town-meeting which early in 1645 established a public school, of which he was probably master. Clerk of the writs 1642–47, and twice deputy to the General Court. In 1651 he became one of the principal founders of Medfield, where again he acted as schoolmaster and deputy to the General Court. Died 11 January 1683–84. D. G. Hill (ed.), *Dedham Records*; C. Slafter, *Schools and Teachers of Dedham*.

JOHN WHEELWRIGHT, son of Robert Wheelwright, yeoman of Saleby, Lincolnshire, was born there about 1592. Admitted sizar at Sidney Sussex College, Cambridge, 28 April 1611, became scholar, and 'noted for more than ordinary stroke at wrestling'; B.A. 1614–15; M.A. 1618 (ranked 104th out of 209 in the *ordo senioritatis*); ordained 1619. Vicar of Bilsby, Lincolnshire 1623, which benefice escheated to the Crown in 1632 'per pravitatem simoniae,' Wheelwright probably having promised to resign it for a consideration. Subsequently preached at Belleau, Lincolnshire, where young Harry Vane had a seat. Married (1) Mary Storre; (2) Mary, d. of Edward Hutchinson. Emigrated with her in 1636 and became minister of Wollaston, then a part of Boston. Owing to the over-enthusiastic advocacy of him by his sister in-law, Anne Hutchinson, as well as to his independent speaking, he was banished from the colony in March 1636–37, founded Exeter, N. H., and became minister of that and other frontier settlements in Maine and New Hampshire. In England 1656–62.

The sentence of banishment having been long since revoked, he returned to the Bay Colony in 1662 as minister of Salisbury, and died there 15 November 1679. John Heard, Jr., *John Wheelwright* (Boston, 1930); C. H. Bell, *Memoir of John Wheelwright* (Cambridge, 1876); Belknap, *New Hampshire* (1792), III. 335–40.

HENRY WHITEFIELD, son of Thomas Whitefield, Esq., an attorney of Mortlake, Surrey, and of Mildred, daughter of Henry Manning, Esq., of Greenwich, matriculated in the University of Oxford from New College, 16 June 1610, aged 19. There is no record of his taking a degree, unless he is identical with the Henry Whitfield who took a B.D. at Cambridge in 1631–32. Cotton Mather states that he was at the Inns of Court. Rector of Ockley, Surrey, 1618–38. A gentleman and a scholar, charitable and hospitable, he was the most popular and beloved minister in the diocese. Entertained and sometimes sheltered nonconformists such as Cotton, Hooker and Davenport. Resigned his cure, sold his personal estate, and emigrated with his family in 1639, taking sundry poor families at his own expense. Aboard ship, Whitefield and other responsible emigrants drew up a plantation covenant, which became the basis of the town of Guilford, Connecticut, Whitefield purchasing the land from the Indians, and serving as minister without pay for eleven years. Finding the climate and life too rigorous, and solicited by his English friends, he returned to England in 1650. 'The whole Town accompanied him unto the Water-side, with a Spring Tide of Tears.' Took charge of a parish at Winchester; advertised New England's missionary efforts among the Indians in two tracts, *The Light appearing more and more* (1651) and *Strength out of Weaknesse* (1652) and was instrumental in founding the corporation which supported John Eliot's work. Died in September 1657. *Magnalia*; B. C. Steiner, *Guilford* (1897).

SAMUEL WHITING, son of John Whiting, mayor of Boston, was baptized 21 November 1597; admitted pensioner at Emmanuel College, Cambridge, 4 June 1613; B.A. 1616–17; M.A. 1620; ordained 1621. Successively chaplain to Sir Roger Townshend and to Sir Nathaniel Bacon; curate of Lynn Regis and rector of Skirbeck, Lincolnshire. Emigrated in 1636, and organized with some of his old parishioners a church at Lynn, of which he was pastor from 1636 until his death 11 December 1679. Overseer of Harvard College. Whiting was first cousin of Anthony Tuckney the theologian, later Master of Emmanuel. 'They were School Fellows at Boston, and Chamber Mates at Cambridge . . . and they continued an intimate friendship . . .

when they were a thousand Leagues assunder' (*Magnalia*). His second wife was Elizabeth, sister to Oliver St. John, and cousin to Peter Bulkeley. Samuel Whiting (A.B. Harvard 1653), John Whiting (A.B. 1657), and Joseph Whiting (A.B. 1661) were their sons.

ROGER WILLIAMS, son of James Williams, merchant tailor of London, and Alice Pemberton (great-aunt of Lord Chief Justice Pemberton), was born c. 1603. Admitted pensioner at Pembroke College, Cambridge, 29 June 1623; B.A. 1626–27; emigrated 1630. His long and remarkable career in Old and New England, his founding of the Colony of Rhode Island on the basis of religious liberty, his consistent practice of that revolutionary principle, and his influence on political and religious theory are too well known to be repeated here. It may be noted, however, that he was successively assistant to Samuel Skelton at Salem, assistant to Ralph Smith at Plymouth, and teacher of the church of Salem after Skelton's death, before leaving the Bay Colony by request in 1636. Died at Providence in April 1683. *D.N.B.* and sundry biographies; articles by James Ernst in *R. I. Hist. Soc. Collections*, 1929–31.

 THOMAS WILLIS, the 'famous schoolmaster of Isleworth,' 'whom some pedagogical writers call Volentius' (Wood), was the son of Richard Willis of Fenny Compton, Warwickshire, where he was born in 1582 or 1583. Matriculated in the University of Oxford as a commoner's son from St. John's College, 11 June 1602, aged 19; B.A. 3 June 1606; M.A. 1609; incorporated M.A. Cambridge 1619. Schoolmaster at Isleworth, Middlesex, c. 1610 to c. 1633, when he emigrated to Lynn, Massachusetts, with his wife (Mary Tomlyn of Isleworth). Deputy to the General Court in 1634 and schoolmaster of Lynn (5 *Coll. M.H.S.*, I. 320). Admitted freeman 14 March 1638–39. In the town's land division of 1638 he received 500 acres, only two of the 102 grantees obtaining more. Annually appointed special magistrate of the Salem Court, 1639–41. Late in 1641 or early in 1642 he returned to England, resumed his former position at Isleworth, and became well known in educational circles for his *Vestibulum Linguae Latinae* (1651) and *Proteus Vinctus* (1655), an Anglo-Latin phrase-book. Buried 15 October 1666. Willis's daughter Elizabeth married John Knowles (*q.v.*). Governor George Willis or Wyllys of Connecticut, father of Samuel Willis (A.B. Harvard 1653), was his cousin. *D.N.B.*; Wood, *Athenae Oxon.* (Bliss ed.), III. 406. Neither of these authorities mentions his transatlantic sojourn; but a positive identification of the Lynn man with the Isle-

worth schoolmaster will be found in Waters, *Gen. Gleanings*, I. 599; *Geneal. Quart.*, III. 162–63; *Quart. Courts Essex County*, I. 21, 45; *N.E.H.G.R.*, XXX. 463.

JOHN WILSON, born at Windsor *c.* December 1588 (Bartlett), the son of William Wilson, D.D. (*c.* 1542–1615), an Oxford man who was then canon of Windsor, and a successful pluralist. His mother, Isabel (Woodhall), was niece to Edmund Grindal, Archbishop of Canterbury. As scholar from Eton, Wilson was admitted to King's College, Cambridge, 23 August 1605, 'aged 14'; Fellow of King's 1608–10; B.A. 1609–10; possibly admitted to the Inner Temple 1610; M.A. 1613; possibly Fellow of Emmanuel. Married Elizabeth, daughter to John Mansfield, Esq., and sister to the wife of Robert Keayne. Lecturer at All Saints', Sudbury; in trouble for non-conformity. Emigrated in 1630; teacher and then pastor of the church in Boston, and member of the first Harvard Board of Overseers. Died 7 August 1667. His brother Edmund Wilson, M.D., F.R.C.P., gave £1000 to the Massachusetts Bay Company; his sister Margaret married David Rawson, merchant of London; their son Edward was secretary of the Bay Colony; Edward Rawson (A.B. Harvard 1653) and Grindall Rawson (A.B. 1678) were their grandsons; his brother Thomas Wilson, D.D., became a canon of St. Paul's; his daughter Mary married Samuel Danforth (A.B. 1643). J. G. Bartlett, in *N.E.H.G.R.*, LXI. 36–41, 127–33; C. Mather, *Memoria Wilsoniana* (1695), reprinted in *Magnalia.* See Index to this volume.

JOHN WINTHROP, the son of Adam Winthrop (a former student of Magdalene College, and auditor of Trinity and St. John's) and Anne Brown, was born at Edwardstone, Suffolk, 12 January 1587–88. Entered Trinity College, Cambridge, as a pensioner early in March, 1603, and remained less than two years (*Winthrop Papers*, I. 155 *n*, 88), his first marriage, to Mary Forth, taking place on 16 April 1605. His part in the founding of New England and career as Governor of Massachusetts Bay are too well known to be repeated here. From 1637 until his death, 26 March 1649, Governor Winthrop was an Overseer of Harvard College. Thirty of his name, all descendants, have since graduated from Harvard. See Index to this volume.

JOHN WINTHROP, Junior, the eldest son of Governor Winthrop, was born at Groton, Suffolk, 12 February 1605–06, attended the grammar school at Bury St. Edmunds, and entered Trinity College, Dublin, about July 1622. There he remained about two years, and was admitted to the Inner Temple in November 1624 (*Winthrop Papers*, I. 271, 313, 318 *n*.). Travelled to Italy and the Near East, and emigrated to New England in 1631. His career as scientist, industrial pioneer, physician, magistrate, founder of Ipswich and of New London, and governor of Connecticut is too well known to be repeated here. Elected Fellow of the Royal Society in 1663. As Assistant of the Bay Colony he was Overseer of the College from 1642 to 1650, and one of its benefactors. Died at Boston 5 April 1676. Father of Wait Still Winthrop, of the Harvard class of 1662. S. E. Morison, *Builders of the Bay*.

BENJAMIN WOODBRIDGE of Stanton, Wilts, younger brother of John Woodbridge (*q.v.*), was born in 1622, and entered Magdalen Hall, Oxford, as batteler or commoner in Michaelmas term 1638. A nephew of Thomas Parker, he emigrated to New England in 1641 or early in 1642, joined the Senior Sophister class at Harvard College, and received his B.A. at the first commencement in 1642, at the head of the class. Returning to England shortly after, he resumed residence at Magdalen Hall, took his M.A. in 1648, became minister of Newbury, and a well-known writer on theology. Chaplain to Charles II, 1660; commissioner to the Savoy Conference 1661; ejected 1662. Died at Inglefield, Berks, 1 November 1684. Sibley, I. 20–27; *D.N.B.*; Wood, *Athenae Oxon.*; *Magnalia*.

JOHN WOODBRIDGE, son of John Woodbridge (M.A. Oxford 1606), minister of Stanton near Highworth, Wilts, and Sara, daughter of Robert Parker, was born at Stanton in 1613. Cotton Mather states (*Magnalia*, Bk. III. p. 219) that Woodbridge was 'sent unto Oxford . . . and kept at Oxford, until the Oath of Conformity came to be required of him, which neither his Father nor his Conscience approving, he removed from thence.' Doubtless the stumbling block was the subscription to the Three Articles required before matriculation, which would explain the absence of Woodbridge's name from existing university records. His college was probably Magdalen Hall, that of his brother and of Henry Vane, who left for the same reason. He emigrated in 1633–34 with his uncle Thomas Parker and James Noyes, and with them settled in Newbury, which he represented thrice in the General Court. Married *c.* 1639 Mercy, daughter of Governor Dudley. Possibly master of the Boston Latin School in 1643. Ordained about 1645 first minister of the new town of Andover, for the purchase of which he negotiated with the Indians. Returned to England, 1647; chaplain to the Parliamentary commission which treated with the King at the Isle of Wight. Minister at Andover, Hants, and Barford St. Martins, Wilts. After being ejected, he returned in 1663 to Newbury, Mass. and became a large landowner and man of substance. In succession to James Noyes, he assisted his uncle Parker, whose Presbyterian tendencies he apparently strengthened to the point where the town and church were split, and Woodbridge was dismissed from church office, *c.* 1670. Elected Assistant of the Colony 1683 and 1684. Died 17 March 1695. Father of John Woodbridge (A.B. Harvard 1664) and Timothy Woodbridge (A.B. 1675). *Magnalia;* Calamy; *D.N.B.;* Louis Mitchell, *Woodbridge Record;* Joshua Coffin, *Newbury; N.E.H.G.R.,* XXXII. 292.

ROBERT WOODMANCY matriculated in the University of Cambridge sizar from St. John's in Easter term 1609; B.A. from Magdalene 1612–13; M.A. 1616. Emigrated in 1635 and settled as a planter at Ipswich; removed to Boston 1644; headmaster of the Latin School from *c.* 1650 to his death, 13 August 1667. His widow refused to remove from the schoolhouse until granted £8 per annum by the town. *Boston Town Records;* Jenks, *Hist. Sketch Boston Latin School.*

WILLIAM WORCESTER was the son of William Worcester, vicar of Watford, Northamphire, where he was baptized 5 October 1595. Matriculated in the University of Cambridge sizar from St. John's at Easter term 1620; ordained 1622. Vicar of Olney, Bucks, 1624–36, when he emigrated. Became the first minister of Salisbury, where he died 28 October 1662.

JOHN YONGES or YONG, son of Christopher Yonges (M.A. Cantab. 1600), vicar of Southwold, was born 1602 and admitted sizar at Emmanuel College, Cambridge, 3 June 1620; B.A. from St. Catharine's 1623. Minister at St. Margaret's, Suffolk. Married Mary, d. of Thomas Warren of Southwold, merchant; emigrated with her to Salem, 1637. Removed to Long Island, founded the town of Southold; Minister there from 1641 until his death 24 February 1671–72. 'Distinguished for his general intelligence, learning and prudence.' B. F. Thompson, *Long Island.*

APPENDIX C

WAS HARVARD THE EARLIEST COLONIAL COLLEGE NORTH OF MEXICO?

1. The Proposed University and Indian College in Virginia

In the promotion literature for Virginia and New England, a prominent place was given to the conversion of the natives as an object which should attract the support of all good and faithful people. The Virginia Company, taking this obligation more seriously than did later colonizing companies, initiated in 1617 a movement for converting the heathen by the typical English method of a college education. In that year King James ordered his bishops to take a collection in every parish for 'the erecting of some Churches and Schooles for the education of the children of those Barbarians.'[1] In its instructions, dated November 18, 1618, to Governor Sir George Yeardley (who was cousin to John Harvard's stepfather), the Company gave the following directions on educational matters:

Whereas by a special grant and license from his majesty a general contribution over this Realm hath been made for the building and planting of a college for the training up of the children of those Infidels in true Religion moral virtue and civility and for other Godly uses. We do therefore according to a former grant and order hereby ratify, confirm and ordain that a convenient place be chosen and set out for the planting of a University at the said Henrico in time to come, and that in the mean time preparation be there made for the building the said college for the children of the Infidels according to such Instructions as we shall deliver. And we will and ordain that ten Thousand

---

1. Edward D. Neill, *Virginia Vestuta*, p. 167. Mr. W. Gordon McCabe, in an address entitled 'The First University in America' (*Virginia Magazine of History and Biography*, xxx. 133–56), attributes this pious initiative to Pocahontas: 'No doubt, she herself, in her half-shy, half-direct, manner, had spoken with the King about this matter that lay so close to her heart.' A letter from the Virginia Company to the mayor of Salisbury 'concerning a college for Virginia' is calendared in S. M. Kingsbury's *Records of the Virginia Company of London*, i. 129, and referred, without volume or page, to the *N. E. H. G. R.*, where it cannot be found.

acres partly of the Lands they impaled and partly of other Land within the
territory of the said Henrico be allotted and set out for the Endowing of the
said University and college with sufficient possessions.[1]

These lands — 10,000 acres 'for the vniuersity . . . of which 1000 for
the Colledge'— were duly laid out[2] on the north side of the James, at
Henricopolis,[3] and the first Virginia Assembly petitioned the Company in 1619 to send over 'towards the erecting of the university and
college . . . workmen of all sortes, fitt for that purpose.'[4] With one
exception noted hereinafter, these are the only mentions in contemporary records of any project for a university or other institution of
higher learning for the *English* in Virginia.

 The movement for an Indian College went con-
siderably further, though not to the point of gather-
ing pupils and beginning instruction. On May 26,
1619, the Treasurer of the Virginia Company, Sir
Edwin Sandys, D.C.L. (a former fellow of Corpus
Christi College, Oxford), reported to the General Court
of the Company that £1500 had already been collected
under the King's letters 'to erect and build a Colledge in Virginia for
the trayning and bringing vp of Infidells children to the true knowledge of God & vnderstanding of righteousnes.'[5] These diocesan collections actually realized £1400. In addition, £550 in gold, a communion service, altar furniture, St. Augustine's 'City of God,' and the
collected works of Dr. William ('Painful') Perkins were donated
by individuals in 1619 and 1620 for the use of the Indian College.[6]
Unfortunately the Company at this time was in pressing need of
money for promoting the policy of Sir Edwin Sandys to increase the
population and diversify the industries of Virginia. Hence, instead of
using this large sum in hand — almost five-fold the original grant to
Harvard College — to put up a building and hire a master, the Company decided to 'forbeare a while' and invest the money in enterprises
of immediate value to the Colony, reserving to the College a share in
the anticipated revenue. A large part of the college fund was used to

---

1. *Va. Mag. Hist. and Biog.*, II. 158–59.
2. The evidence is in a list of titles and landowners in 1625. *Va. Mag.*, XVI. 8–15;
William and Mary College Quarterly, XXIV. 123. The instruction is referred to as having
been carried out in *Records Va. Co.*, I. 268. Cf. *Works of Captain John Smith* (Arber
ed.), II. 542.
3. Now called Dutch Gap.
4. *Va. Mag.*, II. 63.
5. *Records Va. Co.*, I. 220.
6. *Id.*, I. 247–48, 257, 263, 307–08, 313–14, 421. The communion service has been
traced to St. Anne's Hampton. *Va. Mag.*, XXIX. 301–02.

send over tenants to the college lands, providing that half their production should be used as 'an Annuall revennue ' out of which 'to begin the ereccion of the said Colledge.' [1] The first fifty tenants arrived in December, 1619, in charge of George Thorpe, a gentleman sincerely interested in the conversion of Indians.[2] Another fund of £550, which had been given 'for the conversion of Infidelles Children,' was used to erect ironworks at Falling Creek, and to send out eight workmen to operate it — the net proceeds being promised 'for the educatinge of 30 of the Infidelles Children.' [3] Consequently, the erection of a college had to be postponed until these investments brought in revenue. 'A Comittie of choice Gentlemen' of London was appointed by the Company on June 14, 1619, to be Overseers of the Indian College; [4] but they were inactive for three years.

There is no suggestion in the records before 1621 that this proposed college was for any other purpose than teaching and converting young Indians. William Stith, writing over a century later, stated that the contributions and land were 'intended as well for the College for the Education of Indians as also to lay the Foundation of a Seminary of learning for the English.' This intention either developed out of the Indian College plan, or was a revival, under the more modest name of college, of the university portended in the instructions of 1618. Patrick Copland, returning to England from India on the *Royal James* in 1621, took up a collection of £70 from the 'Gentlemen and Marriners' for a free grammar school in Virginia.[5] This was reported to the executive committee of the Company, which on October 30, 1621, recommended that the 'East Indy Schoole,' a Latin school for planters' sons, be established in Charles City, as a feeder to the College, 'which should be made capable to receaue Schollers from the Schole into such Scollershipps and fellowshipps as the Said Colledge shalbe endowed withall.' [6] This particular condition was not accepted

1. *Records Va. Co.*, I. 220–21. In addition, £800 were borrowed by the Company from the college funds, but apparently returned (p. 263).

2. *Id.*, pp. 255, 268, 332; Alex. Brown, *First Republic*, pp. 370, 376; *Works of Captain John Smith* (Arber ed.), II. 574.

3. *Records Va. Co.*, I. 585–89. It is a fair inference from the records that the Sandys régime was embarrassed for want of funds to carry out its ambitious and worthy projects, and too easily found good reasons for spending charitable funds on non-educational enterprises. Cf. Wesley F. Craven, *Dissolution of the Virginia Company* (1932), esp. chap. VI.

4. *Records Va. Co.*, I. 231. The committee, composed mostly of Oxford and Cambridge men, included John Ferrar, brother to and biographer of Nicholas Ferrar of Little Gidding; Sir Dudley Digges, the diplomatist and parliamentary leader; and Sir John Danvers, the future regicide.

5. P. A. Bruce, *Institutional Hist. of Virginia*, I. 347–49. For Copland see above, pp. 129 n., 346; *H. C. S. C.*, Chapter III; and E. D. Neill in *Macalester College Contributions*, 2d. ser. (St. Paul, 1892), pp. 61–88.

6. *Records Va. Co.*, I. 540.

by the Company, and nothing was said about the College when, a month later, the Company founded the 'East Indy Schoole.' [1] Patrick Copland apparently assumed that the project had gone through, and that 'Henrico Colledge' would open her doors to 'East Indy' graduates; [2] but the Company certainly lent no countenance to this assumption when on July 22, 1622, it appointed Master Copland 'Rector of the Intended Colledge in Virginia for the Conversion of the Infidelles.' [3]

In 1621–22 there were other signs of activity concerning the 'intended Colledge.' More tenants were sent out, and workmen to erect a college building. A contract had been made, it is said, for the bricks, when the Indian massacre of 1622 occurred. Seventeen of the tenants and their superintendent George Thorpe were killed. But it was not this disaster that prevented the College from being erected, as has often been stated. The majority of tenants returned to the college lands in 1623; [4] the Company ordered the bricklayers to carry out their contract, [5] and declared a firm intention to go through with the work. Whether they could have found the money for an Indian College, after what had occurred, or revived the university project after their unwise investment of the contributions, may be doubted; but the revocation of the Virginia charter in 1624 ended everything. These public-spirited Englishmen who had hitherto promoted Indian education in Virginia no longer had the power to effect their benevolent scheme; and the Virginians themselves are to be pardoned for having lost whatever interest they may ever have had in providing a college for the natives. The university was completely forgotten.

1. *Id.*, p. 559, and *Voyage of Thomas Best* (Hakluyt Society, 1934), see index.

2. 'Likewise the said honorable *Virginia* Court . . . thought fit also, that this (as a Collegiat or free Schoole) should haue dependance on *Henrico* Colledge in *Virginia*, which should be made capable to receiue Schollers from the [East India] Schoole, into such Schollerships and Fellowships as the said Colledge shall be endowed withall, for the aduancement of Schollers, as they shall rise by degrees and desert in learning.' Copland, *A Declaration how the monies were disposed* (7 pp., London, 1622; No. 87 of the M. H. S. *Americana* series).

3. *Records Va. Co.*, II. 76; and cf. p. 91: 'Rector of the intended Colledge there for the Conuersion of the Infidelles.'

4. *Id.*, II. 395. The contemporary detailed 'List of the Livinge & Dead in Virginia, Feb. 16, 1623' gives the names of twenty-nine men, some of them already married, living on the college lands, and the names of seventeen who were slain. *Wm. and Mary College Quart.*, XXIV. 123–26.

5. E. D. Neill, *Virginia Company of London*, p. 330.

At least one free grammar school was established in Virginia before 1647, and on local initiative; [1] but no plans for higher education were developed until 1660, when the population of Virginia was about 33,000.[2] The Virginia Assembly then proposed to establish 'a college of students of the liberal arts.' [3] Nothing, however, was done in this direction until 1693, when the College of William and Mary was founded. Profiting by the errors of their predecessors (and, may one suggest, the example of Harvard?), the authorities then fixed their college near the center of population instead of on the frontier; and, instead of investing their funds, used them to erect a magnificent building, to secure masters, and to open the college.

2. The Proposed Indian College in New England
(Document found in Dr. Stoughton's Study) [4]

The Providence of god having caried many of our brethren into NE. and by that meanes put an opportunity into their hands for the advancement of his glory and propagating the Knowledge and Kingdome of Christ and an engagment lyeing upon them in Conscience to doe it and on all good Christians to further soe glorious a worke the expectacions of all concurring this way though the worke hitherto hath bene neglected through the manyfold necessityes of the Plantacion and seeinge they cannot of themselves lay that Foundacion (for matter of charge) upon which the future superstruccion might by the blessing of god be raised The way of furthering this worke being by erecting a place where Some may be maintained for learninge the language and instructing heathen and our owne and breeding up as many of the Indians children as providence shall bringe unto our hands and the abilityes of the Plantacion assisted by the pious charity of godly men will releive As alsoe by furnishing them with a competent library and meanes to maintaine it and them with all things necessary for theire sustenance and defence against such attempts of the Indians as the Divell is not unlike to stire them up to for the disturbance of this worke intended for the overthrow of his Kingdome in them and making the lord Christ glorious in his gospell amonge them.

1. P. A. Bruce, *Institutional Hist. of Va.*, I. 350–56, where it is pointed out that Benjamin Symmes' bequest of the income from two hundred acres of land and eight cows for a free primary and grammar school antedates John Harvard's benefaction by three years. Mr. Bruce gives a full and accurate account of the Indian College project on pp. 362–79; and there is a shorter account in Mrs. Mary Newton Stanard's *Story of Virginia's First Century*, chap. xv.

2. *A Century of Population Growth* (1909), p. 9.

3. Bruce, *op. cit.*, I. 375.

4. Public Record Office, C. O. 1/8 (Colonial Papers, 1634–35), No. 41. See above, p. 161, and cf. Frances Rose-Troup, *John White*, p. 298 n. The date cannot be earlier than 1634 or later than March, 1636.

We therfore whose names are under written; haveing ourselves tasted the sweetnes of that gospell and not Knowing how to evidence better unto our selves and others the love of Christ and the power of it, being offred (with this opportunity of doeing good) the libertyes and allotments of lands answerable to other mens formerly for the like Somes by them put in, doe promise to pay in upon the tearmes and tymes expressed the severall sumes subscribed upon demaund made therof by such as are desired by the well willers of the cause to require it.

[Endorsed:] found amongest D. Stoughtons

A forme of project for the setting the profession of the ghospell of Christ in Newe England to be signed by benefactores to that plantacion.

[In another hand:] This letter containeth an undue way of gathering monyes without Authority for the plantation in New England.

3. The Jesuit College of Quebec

The other rival to Harvard's priority in the field of higher education north of Mexico is the Jesuit College of Quebec. Francis Parkman wrote, 'In 1637, a year before the building of Harvard College, the Jesuits began a wooden structure in the rear of the fort; and here, within one enclosure, was the Huron seminary and the college for French boys.' [1] 'Their college of Quebec was three years older than Harvard.' [2]

Unfortunately, comparatively little is known of the history of this college, but that little is told candidly and without exaggeration by two leading historians of French Canada.[3] The Jesuit College at Quebec was planned or founded as early as 1626, when the Marquis de Gamaches donated 16,000 écus and an annual income of 3000 livres for that purpose. Père le Jeune caused the first college building to be constructed shortly after his return to Quebec in 1633. The exact date of the opening is not known, but Le Jeune's correspondence shows that as early as August, 1635, he was teaching the catechism and the first elements of letters to the children of French residents. Instruction in Latin began not later than 1637. Up to 1650 there was one 'regent' or 'professor,' who taught reading, writing, and the elements of Latin. In that year two more regents were added, one of mathematics and the other of grammar, and the number of students who took these courses was sixteen.[4] In 1655 a fourth regent, to teach rhetoric and the humanities, was appointed. Up to that time the College was an institution corresponding roughly to the con-

---

1. *Jesuits in North America* (Boston, 1909), p. 260.

2. *The Old Régime in Canada* (Boston, 1908), p. 425.

3. Notably in Camille de Rochemonteix, *Les Jésuites et la Nouvelle-France* (1895), 1. 205 ff., and Amédée Gosselin, *L'Instruction au Canada sous le régime français* (1911), pp. 247–346.

4. Rochemonteix, *op. cit.*, 1. 220 n.

temporary grammar schools of England and New England. It took boys at the age of seven or thereabouts, and finished with them at fourteen. Owing to the interest and patronage of Mgr. de Laval, the Apostolic Vicar who came out to Quebec in 1659, the College brought her curriculum up to university standards. One cannot fix an exact date, as the change was gradual; but not later than 1665 instruction in philosophy and scholastic theology was established. In 1666 took place the first public disputations on logical theses, one of the respondents being Louis Joliet, the discoverer of the Mississippi. By 1670 there were fifty or sixty students in the College — many of them in the grammar grades — and five or six graduates had already taken orders. In accordance with Jesuit practice, the College of Quebec did not grant degrees, and did not pretend to the name or the privileges of a university; but in view of the Jesuits' pedagogical efficiency, systematic curriculum, and independence of local financial support, it is probable that during the half-century after 1665 the College of Quebec had standards at least as high as Harvard's. The Superior of Quebec wrote to his Provincial in 1711: 'Toutes choses y sont ou se font comme dans nos collèges d'Europe, et peut-être avec plus de regularité d'exactitude et de fruit que dans plusieurs de nos collèges de France. On y enseigne les classes de grammaire, d'humanité, de rhétorique et de mathématiques.' [1]

During the second half of the eighteenth century the College of Quebec declined,[2] and in 1768, after the English conquest, it was closed for lack of interest. Laval University later inherited the library. The social organization of Canada was such that the advantages of the College were little appreciated, except by boys destined to the priesthood. De la Tour wrote that young Canadians were naturally intelligent but frivolous; their inherited taste for a free life of action and adventure was such that they could not or would not concentrate on book learning.[3] Bougainville in 1757, and the intendant Hocquart in 1736, agreed that 'even the children of officers and gentlemen scarcely know how to read and write.' [4]

*   *   *   *   *

1. *Jesuit Relations* (ed. Thwaites), LXVI. 208. A class in hydrography and cartography was founded shortly after.

2. The College should not be confused with the *Grand Séminaire* for training priests which de Laval established, nor with the Jesuits' *séminaire* for Indian children, opened in 1635, which lasted only five years: 'L'insuccès était notoire; il fallait en chercher la cause dans le génie du jeune sauvage.' Rochemonteix, I. 284; cf. Parkman, *Old Régime* (1908 ed.), p. 223.

3. Gosselin, *op. cit.*, 2ᵉ partie, chapitres II-IV, which have also some interesting details on the collegians' recreations. It appears that they were allowed to play tragedies of Racine and Corneille, but that *Tartuffe* was forbidden by the bishop.

4. J. B. A. Ferland, *Cours d'histoire du Canada*, II. 64-65; Gosselin, *op. cit.*, p. 297; Parkman, *Old Régime* (1908 ed.), p. 432.

The answer to this question as to which college was 'first' depends on one's definition of a college. That word has acquired in the United States and Canada a connotation of higher learning, of university standards. But in England around 1630 it meant merely an educational institution of any grade which had a corporate individuality or government; and in France it was used mainly for secondary schools maintained by religious bodies. The Jesuit College at Quebec was the first college in that sense to be established north of Mexico; but it did not attain university standards until around 1660. A Virginian university and Indian college were planned as early as 1617, but never established. Harvard, as the earliest institution in this area to offer a fairly complete course in the Liberal Arts, the Three Philosophies, and *bonae litterae*, and to confer the traditional degrees in Arts, may justly be called the first college in the modern sense.

APPENDIX D

ALTHOUGH 'New Englands First Fruits' is a mine of information about the College, the Indians, and the resources of New England in 1642, it has only once been completely reprinted — in Sabin's Reprints, Quarto Series, no. vii (New York, 1865). The present line-for-line and word-for-word reprint is from the copy in the Pierpont Morgan Library of New York, by kind permission of the Trustees.

Data on the circumstances of publication and a discussion of the authorship will be found on pp. 304–05 of this volume. Mr. Worthington C. Ford, to whose study of the authorship [1] I am much indebted, points out that the printers' initials stand for Richard Oulton and Gregory Dexter, who printed Roger Williams's 'Key into the Language of America,' John Cotton's 'Churches Resurrection' and 'Modest and Cleare Answer,' and Richard Mather's 'Church-Government and Church-Covenant Discussed' in 1642 and 1643. Henry Overton was a London bookseller who published these two works of Cotton and several other tracts by New Englanders. He was also patronized by English puritans, such as Dr. John Stoughton, whose plan for an Indian College is in Appendix C.

Such errata as are indicated on the contemporary list at the end of the pamphlet (wanting in some copies and in the Sabin reprint), I have corrected in this edition.[2] A few obvious printer's errors, such as 'eath' for 'hath' and 'doe' for 'done,' have also been corrected. The original pagination, which is highly erratic from pages 6 to 12 inclusive (6–15–8–9–18–19–12–13–22–15), is preserved by arabic numerals in parentheses. The Greek on page 19 includes certain ligatures not found in modern Greek fonts. I have altered no punctuation, having observed that in sundry quotations from the opening paragraph on the College (page 12), the change of a semicolon to a comma at the end of 'Posterity' on line 6 materially alters the sense. In the H. C. L. copy, a contemporary hand has shifted the parenthesis from the end of the next to the last line on page 12 to the end of the word following, and inserted 'and' before 'Exercises.' On page 16, line 4, 'The first houre' is almost certainly a misprint for 'The first yeare,' but as it is not corrected in the errata list, I have let it stand.

1. *Proc. M. H. S.*, XLII. 259–66.
2. The last *erratum* is itself an error; the 'first' to be 'put out' is evidently the 'first' between 'space' and 'the' on line 4, not line 2, p. 25. The H. C. L. copy is so corrected.

NEVV
ENGLANDS
FIRST FRUITS;

IN RESPECT,

First of the ⎰ Converfion of fome, ⎱ of the *Indians*.
⎰ Conviction of divers, ⎱
⎰ Preparation of fundry ⎱

2. Of the progreffe of *Learning*, in the *Colledge* at
CAMBRIDGE, in *Maſſacuſets* Bay.

WITH

Divers other fpeciall Matters concerning that *Countrey*.

Publiſhed by the inftant requeft of fundry Friends, who defire
to be fatisfied in thefe points by many *New-England* Men
who are here prefent, and were eye or eare-
witneffes of the fame.

Who hath defpifed the Day of fmall things. Zach. 4. 10.

*If thou wert pure and upright, furely now he will awake for thee: -- And though
thy beginnings be fmall, thy latter end fhall greatly encreafe.* Iob. 8 6,7.

LONDON,

Printed by R. *O.* and *G. D.* for *Henry Overton*, and are to be
fold at his Shop in *Popes-head-Alley.* 1 6 4 3.

(1.)

NEW
ENGLANDS
FIRST FRUITS:

1. In refpect of the INDIANS, &c.

He Lord, who ufeth not to be wanting to the defires of his Servants, as he hath not fruftrated the ends of our Tranfplanting in fundry other refpects; fo neither in the giving fome light to thofe poore *Indians*, who have ever fate in hellifh darkneffe, adoring the *Divell* himfelfe for their *GOD:* but hath given us fome teftimony of his gracious acceptance of our poore endeavours towards them, and of our groanes to himfelfe for mercy upon thofe miferable Soules (the very Ruines of Mankind) there amongft us; our very bowels yerning within us to fee them goe downe to Hell by fwarmes without remedy.

Wherefore we judged it our duty no longer to conceale, but to declare (to the praife of his owne free grace) what *firft Fruits* he hath begun to gather in amongft them, as a fure pledge (we are confident) of a greater *Harveft* in his owne time. And wonder not that wee mention no more inftances at prefent: but confider, Firft, their infinite diftance from Chriftianity, having never been prepared thereunto by any Civility at all. Secondly, the difficulty of their Language to us, and of ours to them; there being no Rules to learne either by. Thirdly, the diverfity of their owne Language to it felfe;

A 2   every

(2.)

every part of that Countrey having its own Dialect, differing much from the other; all which make their comming into the Gofpel the more flow. But what God hath done for fome of them, we will declare.

1. MAny years fince at *Plimmouth* Plantation, when the Church did faft and pray for Raine in extreame Drought; it being a very hot and cleare fun-fhine day, all the former part thereof; An *Indian* of good quality, being prefent, and feeing what they were a-bout, fell a wondring at them for praying for raine in a day fo un-likely, when all Sunne and no Clouds appeared; and thought that their God was not able to give Raine at fuch a time as that: but this poore wretch feeing them ftill to continue in their Prayers, and be-holding that at laft the Clouds began to rife, and by that time they had ended their Duty, the Raine fell in a moft fweet, conftant, foaking fhowre, fell into wonderment at the power that the Englifh had with their God, and the greatneffe and goodneffe of that God whom they ferved, and was fmitten with terror that he had abufed them and their God by his former hard thoughts of them; and re-folved from that day not to reft till he did know this great good *God*, and for that end to forfake the *Indians*, and cleave to the Englifh, which he prefently did, and laboured by all publique and private meanes to fuck in more and more of the knowledge of God, and his wayes. And as he increafed in knowledge fo in affection, and alfo in his practice, reforming and conforming himfelfe accordingly: and (though he was much tempted by inticements, fcoffes and fcornes from the *Indians*) yet, could he never be gotten from the *Englifh*, nor from feeking after their God, but died amongft them, leaving fome good hopes in their hearts, that his foule went to reft.

2. *Sagamore Iohn*, Prince of *Maffaquefers*, was from our very firft landing more courteous, ingenious, and to the Englifh more loving then others of them; he defired to learne and fpeake our Language, and loved to imitate us in our behaviour and apparrell and began to hearken after our God and his wayes, and would much commend Englifh-men and their God; faying (*Much good men, much good God*) and being convinced that our condition and wayes were better farre then theirs, did refolve and promife to leave the *Indians*, and come live with us; but yet kept downe by feare of the fcoffes of the *Indi-ans*, had not power to make good his purpofe; yet went on not with-

out

(3.)

out fome trouble of mind, and fecret plucks of Confcience, as the fequel declares: for being ftruck with death, fearfully cryed out of himfelfe that he had not come to live with us, to have knowne our ,, God better: *But now* (faid he) *I muft die, the God of the Englifh is* ,, *much angry with me, and will deftroy me; ah,* I *was affraid of the fcoffes of* ,, *thefe wicked* Indians; *yet my Child fhall live with the* Englifh, *and learne* ,, *to know their God when I am dead; Ile give him to Mr.* Wilfon, *he is a* ,, *much Good man, and much loved me:* fo fent for Mr. *Wilfon* to come to him, and committed his onely Child to his care, and fo died.

3. Divers of the *Indians* Children, Boyes and Girles we have received into our houfes, who are long fince civilized, and in fubjection to us, painfull and handy in their bufineffe, and can fpeak our language familiarly; divers of whom can read Englifh, and begin to underftand in their meafure, the grounds of Chriftian Religion; fome of them are able to give us account of the Sermons they heare, and of the word read and expounded in our Families, and are convinced of their finfull and miferable Eftates, and affected with the fenfe of Gods difpleafure, and the thoughts of Eternity, and will fometimes tremble and melt into teares at our opening and preffing the Word upon their Confciences; and as farre as we can difcerne, fome of them ufe to pray in fecret, and are much in love with us, and cannot indure to returne any more to the *Indians*.

Some of them will not be abfent from a Sermon or Family duties if they can help it; and we have knowne fome would ufe to weep and cry when detained by occafion from the Sermon.

Others of them are very inquifitive after God and his wayes; and being themfelves induftrious in their Calling, will much complaine of other fervants idleneffe, and reprove them.

One of them, who for fome mifdemeanour that laid him open to publique punifhment, ran away; and being gone, God fo followed him, that of his owne accord he returned home, rendred himfelfe to Juftice, and was willing to fubmit himfelfe, though he might have efcaped.

An *Indian* Maid at *Salem*, would often come from the Word, crying out with abundance of teares, concluding that fhe muft burne when fhe die, and would fay, fhe knew her felfe naught for prefent, and like to be miferable for ever, unleffe free Grace fhould prevent it, and after this grew very carefull of her carriage, proved induftrious in her place, and fo continued.

Another

(4.)

Another often frequenting the Houſe of one of the Miniſters at *Salem*, would tell him the Story of the Bible, even to his admiration, and that he attended upon the Word preached, and loved it; and how he could tell all the Commandements, and in particular each Commandement by itſelfe, and how he laboured to keep them all; and yet for all this (ſaid he) [*Me die, and walke in fire*] that is, when I die, I muſt to Hell: That Miniſter asked him why? he anſwered, becauſe I know not *Ieſus Chriſt*, and pray'd him earneſtly to teach him *Ieſus Chriſt*, and after went out amongſt the *Indians*, and called upon them to put away all their wives ſave one becauſe it was a ſinne againſt Engliſh-mans Saviour

Another *Indian* comming by, and ſeeing one of the Engliſh (who was remote from our juriſdiction, prophaning the Lords day, by felling of a tree, ſaid to him, ,, *Doe you not know that this is the Lords day*, in *Maſſaquſetts*? *much machet man*, that is *very wicked man, what, breake you Gods Day*?

The ſame man comming into an houſe in thoſe parts where a man and his wife were chiding, and they bidding him ſit downe, he was welcome; he anſwered, ,, *He would not ſtay there, God did not dwell there, Hobamook*, (that is *the Devill*) *was there*, and ſo departed.

One of the *Sagamores*, having complaint made to him by ſome of the Engliſh, that his men did uſe to kill Pigeons upon the Lords day, thereupon forbad them to doe ſo any more; yet afterwards ſome of them did attempt it, and climbing the high trees (upon which Pigeons in that Countrey uſe to make their neſts) one of them fell down from off the tree and brake his neck, and another fell down and brake ſome of his limbs: thereupon the *Sagamores* ſent two grave old men to proclaime it amongſt his *Indians*, that none of them ſhould kill Pigeons upon the Sabboth day any more.

Another *Indian* hearing of the fame of the *Engliſh*, and their God came from a far to ſee them, and ſuch was this mans love to the *Engliſh* and their wayes after he came acquainted with them, that he laboured to transform himſelfe into the *Engliſh* manners and practiſes, as if he had been an Engliſh man indeed; he would be called no more by his *Indian* name, but would be named *William*; he would not goe naked like the *Indians*, but cloathed juſt as one of our ſelves; he abhorred to dwell with the *Indians* any longer; but forſaking all his friends and Kindred dwelt wholly with us; when he ſate downe to meat with us, if thanks were given before he came in, or if he did eat

by

(5.)

by himfelfe, conftantly he would give thanks reverently and grave-
ly, he frequented the word and family duties where he came, and gat
a good meafure of knowledge beyond ordinary, being a man of fin-
gular parts, and would complaine that he knew not Chrift, and without him, he faid, all he did was nothing; hee was fo zealous for the
Lords day, that (as it was obferved) if he faw any profaning it, he
would rebuke them, and threaten them to carry them to the Governour.

All which things weighed, we dare not but hope, that many of
them, doe belong to the Kingdome of God; and what further time
may produce, we leave it to him that is excellent in Counfell, and
wonderfull in working.

4. There is alfo a Blackmore maid, that hath long lived at *Dorche-
fter* in *New England*, unto whom God hath fo bleffed the publique
and private means of Grace, that fhe is not only indued with a competent meafure of knowledge in the myfteries of God, and conviction of her miferable eftate by finne; but hath alfo experience of a
faving work of grace in her heart, and a fweet favour of Christ brea-
thing in her; infomuch that her foule hath longed to enjoy Church-
fellowfhip with the Saints there, and having propounded her defire
to the Elders of the Church after fome triall of her taken in private,
fhe was called before the whole Church, and there did make confef-
fion of her knowledge in the Myfteries of Chrift and of the work of
Converfion upon her Soule: And after that there was fuch a tefti-
mony given of her blameleffe and godly Converfation, that fhe was
admitted a member by the joynt confent of the Church with great
joy to all their hearts. Since which time, we have heard her much
admiring Gods free grace to fuch a poore wretch as fhe was; that
God leaving all her friends and Kindred ftill in their finnes, fhould
caft an eye upon her, to make her a member of Chrift, and of the
Church alfo: and hath with teares exhorted fome other of the *Indians* that live with us to embrace *Iefus Chrift*, declaring how willing
he would be to receive them, even as he had received her.

5. The laft inftance we will give fhall be of that famous Indian
Wequafh, who was a Captaine, a proper man of perfon, and of a very
grave and fober fpirit; the Story of which comming to our hands
very lately, was indeed the occafion of writing all the reft: This
man a few yeares fince, feeing and beholding the mighty power of
God in our Englifh Forces, how they fell upon the *Pequits*, where
divers

(6.)

divers hundreds of them were flaine in an houre: The Lord, as a
God of glory in great terrour did appeare unto the Soule and Confcience of this poore Wretch, in that very act; and though before
that time he had low apprehenfions of our God, having conceived
him to be (as he faid) but a *Musketto* God, or a God like unto a flye;
and as meane thoughts of the Englifh that ferved this God, that they
were filly weake men; yet from that time he was convinced and per-
fwaded that our God was a moft dreadfull God; and that one *Englifh* man by the help of his God was able to flay and put to flight an
hundred *Indians*.

This conviction did purfue and follow him night and day, fo that
he could have no reft or quiet becaufe hee was ignorant of the *Englifh mans God:* he went up and down bemoaning his condition, and
filling every place where he came with fighes and groanes.

Afterward it pleafed the Lord that fome *Englifh* (well acquainted
with his Language) did meet with him; thereupon as a Hart pan-
ting after the water Brookes, he enquired after God with fuch incef-
fant diligence, that they were conftrained conftantly for his fatisfa-
ction to fpend more then halfe the night in converfing with him.

Afterwards he came to dwell amongft the Englifh at *Connecticut*,
ftill travelling with all his might, and lamenting after the Lord: his
manner was to fmite his hand on his breaft, and to complaine fadly
of his heart, faying it was *much machet*, (that is, very evill) and when
any fpake with him, he would fay, *Wequafh, no God, Wequafh no know
Chrift*. It pleafed the Lord, that in the ufe of the meanes, he grew
greatly in the knowledge of Chrift, and in the Principles of Religion, and became thorowly reformed according to his light, hating
and loathing himfelfe for his deareft finnes, which were efpecially
thefe two *Luft* and *Revenge*, this repentance for the former was teftified by his temperance and abftinence from all occafions, or matter of provocation thereunto. Secondly, by putting away all his
Wives, faving the firft, to whom he had moft right.

His repentance for the latter was teftified by an eminent degree of
meekneffe and patience, that now, if any did abufe him, he could lie
downe at their feet, and if any did fmite him on the one cheeke, he
would rather turne the other, than offend them: many trialls hee
had from the *Jndians* in this cafe. Thirdly, by going up and downe
to thofe hee had offered violence or wrong unto, confeffing it, and
making reftitution.

Afterwards

(15)

Afterwards he went amongſt the Indians, like that poore Woman of *Samaria*, proclaiming *Chriſt*, and telling them what a Treaſure he had found, inſtructing them in the knowledge of the true *God:* and this he did with a grave and ſerious ſpirit, warning them with all faithfullneſſe to flee from the wrath to come, by breaking off their ſinnes and wickedneſſe.

This courſe of his did ſo diſturb the Devill, that ere long ſome of the Indians, whoſe hearts Satan had filled, did ſecretly give him poy-ſon, which he tooke without ſuſpition: and when he lay upon his death bed, ſome Indians who were by him, wiſhed him according to the Indian manner, to ſend for *Powow* (that is to ſay) a Wizzard; he told them, *If Ieſus Chriſt ſay that Wequaſh ſhall live, then Wequaſh muſt live; if Ieſus Chriſt ſay, that Wequaſh ſhall dye, then Wequaſh is willing to dye, and will not lengthen out his life by any ſuch meanes.* Before he dyed, he did bequeath his Child to the godly care of the Engliſh for education and inſtruction and ſo yielded up his ſoule into *Chriſt* his hands.

I cannot omit the teſtimony of Mr. *Sh* a godly Miniſter in the *Bay*, that wrote to his Friend in *London* concerning this Story, his lines are full plain and pithy his words theſe,

Wequaſh the famous Indian at the Rivers mouth is dead, and certainly in heaven; glorioufly did the Grace of Chriſt *ſhine forth in his converſation, a yeare and a halfe before his death he knew Chriſt; he loved Chriſt, he prea-ched Chriſt up and down, and then ſuffered Martyrdome for Chriſt; and when he dyed, he gave his ſoule to Chriſt, and his only child to the Engliſh, rejoycing in this hope, that the child ſhould know more of Chriſt then its poore Father ever did.*

Thus we have given you a little taſt of the ſprincklings of Gods ſpirit, upon a few Indians, but one may eaſily imagine, that here are not all that may be produced: for if a very few of us here preſent, upon very ſudden thoughts, have ſnatcht up only ſuch inſtances which came at preſent to hand you may conceive, that if all in our Plantations (which are farre and wide) ſhould ſet themſelves to bring in the confluence of all their Obſervations together, much more might be added.

We beleeve one mean amongſt others, that hath thus farre wonne theſe poore wretches to looke after the Goſpell, hath been the deal-ings and carriages, which God hath guided the Engliſh in our Pa-tent, to exerciſe towards them: For,

B   1. At

(8)

1. At our entrance upon the Land, it was not with violence and intrufion, but free and faire, with their confents and allowance the chief Sagamores of all that part of the Countrey, entertaining us heartily, and profeffed we were all much welcome.

2. When any of them had poffeffion of, or right unto any Land we were to plant upon, none were fuffered, (to our knowledge) to take one acre from them, but do ufe to compound with them to content.

3. They have had juftice truly exercifed towards them in all other particular acts; that as we expect right dealing from them, in cafe any of them fhall trefpaffe us, we fend to their Sagamore, and he prefently rights us, or elfe we fummon them to our Court to anfwer it; fo if any of our men offend them and complaint and proofe be made to any of our Magiftrates, or the publique Court (they know) they are fure to be righted to the utmoft, by us.

4. The humanity of the Englifh towards them doth much gaine upon them, we being generally wary, and tender in giving them offenfive or harfh language, or carriage, but ufe them fairly and courteoufly, with loving termes, good looks and kind falutes.

Thus they having firft a good efteem of our Perfons, (fuch of them as God intends good unto) are the fooner brought to hearken to our words, and then to ferve our God: wheras on the contrary, the wicked, injurious and fcandalous carriages of fome other Plantations, have bin a mean to harden thofe poore wofull foules againft the Englifh, and all Religion for their fakes; and feale them up under perdition.

Yet (miftake us not) we are wont to keep them at fuch a diftance, (knowing they ferve the Devill and are led by him) as not to imbolden them too much, or truft them too farre; though we do them what good we can. And the truth is, God hath fo kept them, (excepting that act of the Pequits, long fince, to fome few of our men) that we never found any hurt from them, nor could ever prove any reall intentions of evill againft us: And if there fhould be fuch intentions and that they all fhould combine together againft us with all their ftrength that they can raife, we fee no probable ground at all to feare any hurt from them, they being naked men, and the number of them that be amongft us not confiderable.

Let us here give a touch alfo of what God hath done and is further about to doe, to divers Plantations of the Englifh, which before that
time

(9)

time that God fent light into our coafts, were almoft as darke and rude as the Indians themfelves.

1. Firft at *Agamenticus* (a Plantation out of our jurifdiction) to which one of our Preachers comming and labouring amongft them, was a meanes under God, not only to fparkle heavenly knowledge, and worke conviction and reformation in divers of them, but converfion alfo to Chrift in fome of them, that bleffe God to this day, that ever he came thither.

2. Then after that, at *Sauco* Plantation, which is an hundred miles from us, divers of that place comming often into our coafts and hearing the Word preached, and feeing Gods goings amongft his people there, being much affected went home and lamented amongft their neighbours their own wofull condition, that lived like heathens without the Gofpel, when others injoyed it in great plenty: hereupon with joynt confent two of their chiefe men were fent in all their names earneftly to intreat us to fend a godly Minifter to preach the Word unto them; which was done accordingly, not without good fucceffe to the people there, and divers places about them.

3. After this, towards the end of laft Summer, foure more Plantations fome of which are divers hundred miles; others of them many hundred leagues from our Plantation) hearing of the goodneffe of God to his people in our parts, and of the light of the Gofpel there fhining; have done even as *Jacob* did in the Famine time, when he heard there was bread in *Egypt*, he hafted away his Sonnes for Corn, that they might live and not die: in like manner three feverall Towns in *Virginia*, as alfo *Barbados*, *Chriftophers*, and *Antego*, all of them much about the fame time, as if they had known the minds of each other, did fend Letters and Meffengers, crying out unto us, as the man of *Macedonia* to *Paul, Come and help us*, and that with fuch earneftneffe, as men hunger-ftarved and ready to die, cry for bread; fo they cry out unto us in the bowels of compasfion, for the Lord Jefus fake to fend them fome helpe. They tell us in fome of their Letters, that from the one end of the Land to the other, there is none to break the *bread* of *life* unto the *hungry*; and thofe that fhould doe it, are fo vile, that even drunkards and fwearers, cry fhame on them.

We had thought (but only for the fwelling of our Difcourfe) to have fet down their Letters at large, which they wrote to all our Churches, which fpake with fuch ftrength of reafon and affection, that when they were read in our Congregations, they prevailed with

B 2   us

(18)

us, that for their necesfity, we fpared the bread from our own mouths
to fave their lives, and fent two of our Minifters for the prefent to
Virginia; and when the Ships came away from them they left them in
ferious confultation, whom to give up to the worke of Chrift in the
other three places alfo.

We heare moreover that the Indians themfelves in fome of the
places named, did joyne with them in this their fuit.

Now from what hath bin faid, fee the riches of Gods free Grace
in Chrift, that is willing to impart mercy even to the worft of men,
and fuch as are furtheft off, cry out with *Paul, Oh the depths, &c.* and
let heaven and earth be filled with the glorious praifes of God for
the fame.

And if fuch as are afarre off, why fhould not we that are nearer
prefle in for a fhare therin, and cry out, as *Efau* did with teares to his
Father, when he faw the blefling going away to his younger brother,
and himfelfe, like to lofe it: [*Oh my Father haft thou but one blefling,
bleffe me alfo, even me thy firft borne, bleffe me, oh my Father.*] Elfe thefe
poore Indians will certainly rife up againft us, and with great bold-
neffe condemn us in the great day of our accompts, when many of
us here under great light, fhall fee men come from the Eaft and from
the West, and fit down in the Kingdome of God, and our felves caft
out.

2. Let the world know, that God led not fo many thoufands of
his people into the Wildernefle, to fee a reed fhaken with the wind,
but amongft many other fpeciall ends, this was none of the leaft, to
fpread the light of his bleffed Gofpel, to fuch as never heard the
found of it. To ftop the mouths of the profane that calumniate the
work of God in our hands, and to fatisfie the hearts of the Saints
herin that God had fome fpeciall fervice for his people there to doe,
which in part already we begin to fee, and wait upon *Divine Wifdome*,
to difcover more of his pleafure herin, and upon his Grace to effect,
which we beleeve in his time he will fo doe, that men fhall fee and
know the wifdome and power of God herin.

3. Shall we touch here upon that apprehenfion which many godly and wife have conceived, and that from fome Scriptures compared, and from other grounds, and paffages of Providence collected
that (as it's very probable) God meanes to carry his Gofpel weftward, in thefe latter times of the world; and have thought, as the
Sunne in the afternoon of the day, ftill declines more and more to
the

(19)

the Weft, and then fets: fo the Gofpel (that great light of the world) though it rofe in the Eaft, and in former ages, hath lightened it with his beames; yet in the latter ages of the world will bend Weftward, and before its fetting, brighten thefe parts, with his glorious luftre alfo.

4. See how Gods wifdome produceth glorious effeɗs, from un-likely meanes, and make ftreight works by crooked inftruments: for who would have thought, that the chafing away hence fo many godly Minifters, fhould fo farre have promoted the praifes of God, and fhould be a meane to fpread the Gofpel, when they intended to ruine it: they blew out their lights and they burn clearer: their filencing Minifters have opened their mouths fo wide, as to found out his glorious praifes, to the uttermoft parts of the earth; fay with the Pfalmift, *This is the Lords doing, and it is marvelous in our eyes.*

5. Defpife not the day of fmall things; let none fay of us as thofe fcoffers did of their building *Ierufalem, What will thefe weak Iewes doe?* but learne to adore God in all his Providence, and wait to fee his ends.

6. Lend us, we befeech you (all you that love *Zion*) your prayers and helpe in heaven and earth for the furtherance of this great and glorious worke in our hands; great works need many hands, many prayers, many teares: And defire the Lord to ftirre up the bowels of fome godly minded, to pitty thofe poore Heathen that are bleeding to death to eternall death, and to reach forth an hand of foule-mercy, to fave fome of them from the fire of hell by affording fome means to maintain fome fit inftruments on purpofe to fpend their time, and give themfelves wholly to preach to thefe poore wretches, that as the tender *Samaritan* did to the wounded man, they may pitty them, and get them healed, that even their bowels may bleffe them in the day of their vifitation, and Chrifts bowels refrefhed by their love, may fet it on his own fcore, and pay them all againe in the day of their accompts.

B 3 NEW

(12)

NEW
ENGLANDS
FIRST FRUITS:

2. In refpect of the Colledge, and the

proceedings of *Learning* therein.

1.   Fter God had carried us fafe to *New England*, and wee had builded our houfes, provided neceffaries for our liveli-hood, rear'd convenient places for Gods worfhip, and fetled the Civill Government: One of the next things we longed for, and looked after was to advance *Learning* and perpetuate it to Pofterity; dreading to leave an illiterate Miniftery to the Churches, when our prefent Minifters fhall lie in the Duft. And as wee were thinking and confulting how to effect this great Work; it pleafed God to ftir up the heart of one Mr. *Harvard* (a godly Gentleman, and a lover of Learning, there living amongft us) to give the one halfe of his Eftate (it being in all about 1700. l.) towards the erecting of a Colledge: and all his Library: after him another gave 300. l. others after them caft in more, and the publique hand of the State added the reft: the Colledge was, by common confent, appointed to be at *Cambridge*, (a place very pleafant and accommodate) and is called (according to the name of the firft founder) *Harvard Colledge*.

The Edifice is very faire and comely within and without, having in it a fpacious Hall; (where they daily meet at Commons, Lectures) Exercifes, and a large Library with fome Bookes to it, the gifts of

diverfe

(13)

diverfe of our friends, their Chambers and ftudies alfo fitted for, and poffeffed by the Students, and all other roomes of Office neceffary and convenient, with all needfull Offices thereto belonging: And by the fide of the Colledge a faire *Grammar* Schoole, for the training up of young Schollars, and fitting of them for *Academicall Learning*, that ftill as they are judged ripe, they may be received into the Colledge of this Schoole: Mafter *Corlet* is the Mr., who hath very well approved himfelfe for his abilities, dexterity and painfulneffe in teaching and education of the youth under him.

Over the Colledge is mafter *Dunfter* placed, as Prefident, a learned confcionable and induftrious man, who hath fo trained up, his Pupills in the tongues and Arts, and fo feafoned them with the principles of Divinity and Chriftianity, that we have to our great comfort, (and in truth) beyond our hopes, beheld their progreffe in Learning and godlineffe alfo; the former of thefe hath appeared in their publique declamations in *Latine* and *Greeke*, and Difputations Logicall and Philofophicall, which they have beene wonted (befides their ordinary Exercifes in the Colledge-Hall) in the audience of the Magiftrates, Minifters, and other Schollars, for the probation of their growth in Learning, upon fet dayes, conftantly once every moneth to make and uphold: The latter hath been manifefted in fundry of them, by the favoury breathings of their Spirits in their godly converfation. Infomuch that we are confident, if thefe early bloffomes may be cherifhed and warmed with the influence of the friends of Learning, and lovers of this pious worke, they will by the help of God, come to happy maturity in a fhort time.

Over the Colledge are twelve Overfeers chofen by the generall Court, fix of them are of the Magiftrates, the other fix of the Minifters, who are to promote the beft good of it and (having a power of influence into all perfons in it) are to fee that every one be diligent and proficient in his proper place.

2. *Rules, and Precepts that are obferved in the Colledge.*

1. VVHen any Schollar is able to underftand *Tully*, or fuch like clafficall Latine Author *extempore*, and make and fpeake true Latine in Verfe and Profe, *fuo ut aiunt Marte*; And decline perfectly the Paradigm's of *Nounes* and *Verbes* in the *Greek* tongue: Let him then and not before be capable of admiffion into the Colledge.

2. Let

(22)

2. Let every Student be plainly inſtructed, and earneſtly preſſed to conſider well, the maine end of his life and ſtudies is, *to know God and Ieſus Chriſt which is eternall life*, Joh. 17. 3. and therefore to lay *Chriſt* in the bottome, as the only foundation of all ſound knowledge and Learning.

And ſeeing the Lord only giveth wiſedome, Let every one ſeriouſly ſet himſelfe by prayer in ſecret to ſeeke it of him *Prov* 2, 3.

3. Every one ſhall ſo exerciſe himſelfe in reading the Scriptures twice a day, that he ſhall be ready to give ſuch an account of his proficiency therein, both in *Theoreticall* obſervations of the Language, and *Logick*, and in *Practicall* and ſpirituall truths, as his Tutor ſhall require, according to his ability; ſeeing *the entrance of the word giveth light, it giveth underſtanding to the ſimple*, Pſalm. 119. 130.

4. That they eſhewing all profanation of Gods Name, Attributes, Word, Ordinances, and times of Worſhip, doe ſtudie with good conſcience, carefully to retaine God, and the love of his truth in their mindes, elſe let them know, that (notwithſtanding their Learning) God may give them up *to ſtrong deluſions*, and in the end *to a reprobate minde*, 2 Theſ. 2. 11, 12. Rom. 1. 28.

5. That they ſtudiouſly redeeme the time; obſerve the generall houres appointed for all the Students, and the ſpeciall houres for their owne *Claſſis*: and then diligently attend the Lectures, without any diſturbance by word or geſture. And if in any thing they doubt, they ſhall enquire, as of their fellowes, ſo, (in caſe of *Non ſatisfaction*) modeſtly of their Tutors.

6. None ſhall under any pretence whatſoever, frequent the company and ſociety of ſuch men as lead an unfit, and diſſolute life.

Nor ſhall any without his Tutors leave, or (in his abſence) the call of Parents or Guardians, goe abroad to other Townes.

7. Every Schollar ſhall be preſent in his Tutors chamber at the 7th. houre in the morning, immediately after the ſound of the Bell at his opening the Scripture and prayer, ſo alſo at the 5th. houre at night, and then give account of his owne private reading, as aforeſaid in Particular the third, and conſtantly attend Lectures in the Hall at the houres appointed? But if any (without neceſſary impediment) ſhall abſent himſelf from prayer or Lectures, he ſhall bee lyable to Admonition, if he offend above once a weeke.

8. If any Schollar ſhall be found to tranſgreſſe any of the Lawes of God, or the Schoole, after twice Admonition, he ſhall be lyable,

if

(15)

if not *adultus*, to correction, if *adultus*, his name fhall be given up to the Overfeers of the Colledge, that he may bee admonifhed at the publick monethly Act.

3. *The times and order of their Studies, unleffe experience fhall fhew caufe to alter.*

THe fecond and third day of the weeke, read Lectures, as follow-eth.

To the firft yeare at 8th. of the clock in the morning *Logick*, the firft three quarters, *Phyficks* the laft quarter.

To the fecond yeare, at the 9th. houre, *Ethicks* and *Politicks*, at con-venient diftances of time.

To the third yeare at the 10th. *Arithmetick* and *Geometry*, the three firft quarters, *Aftronomy* the laft.

Afternoone,

The firft yeare difputes at the fecond houre.

The 2d. yeare at the 3d. houre.

The 3d. yeare at the 4th. every one in his Art.

The 4th. day reads Greeke.

To the firft yeare the *Etymologie* and *Syntax* at the eigth houre.

To the 2d. at the 9th. houre, *Profodia* and *Dialects*.

Afternoone.

The firft yeare at 2d houre practice the precepts of *Grammar* in fuch Authors as have variety of words.

The 2d. yeare at 3d. houre practice in *Poëfy*, *Nonnus*, *Duport*, or the like.

The 3d. yeare perfect their *Theory* before noone, and exercife *Style*, *Compofition*, *Imitation*, *Epitome*, both in Profe and Verfe, afternoone.

The fift day reads Hebrew, and the Eafterne Tongues.

Grammar to the firft yeare houre the 8th.

To the 2d. *Chaldee* at the 9th. houre.

To the 3d. *Syriack* at the 10th. houre.

Afternoone.

The firft yeare practice in the Bible at the 2d. houre.

The 2d. in *Ezra* and *Danel* at the 3d. houre.

The 3d. at the 4th. houre in *Troftius* New Teftament.

The 6th. day reads Rhetorick to all at the 8th. houre.

Declamations at the 9th. So ordered that every Scholler may de-

C   claime

(16)

claime once a moneth. The reſt of the day *vacat Rhetoricis ſtudiis.*
*The 7th..day reads Divinity Catecheticall at the 8th. houre, Common places
at the 9th. houre.   Afternoone.*

The firſt houre reads hiſtory in the Winter,
The nature of plants in the Summer

The ſumme of every Lecture ſhall be examined, before the new Lecture be read.

Every Schollar, that on proofe is found able to read the Originalls of the *Old* and *New Teſtament* into the Latine tongue, and to reſolve them *Logically*; withall being of godly life and converſation; And at any publick Act hath the Approbation of the Overſeers and Maſter of the Colledge, is fit to be dignified with his firſt Degree.

Every Schollar that giveth up in writing a *Syſtem,* or *Synopſis,* or ſumme of *Logick,* Naturall and Morall *Phyloſophy, Arithmetick, Geometry* and *Aſtronomy*: and is ready to defend his *Theſes* or poſitions: withall ſkilled in the Originalls as aboveſaid: and of godly life & converſation: and ſo approved by the Overſeers and Maſter of the Colledge, at any publique *Act,* is fit to be dignified with his 2d. Degree.

---

4. *The manner of the late Commencement, expreſſed in
    a Letter ſent over from the Governour, and diverſe
    of the Miniſters, their own words theſe.*

T H E *Students of the firſt Claſſis that have beene theſe foure yeeres
trained up in* Univerſity-Learning *(for their ripening in the knowledge of the Tongues, and Arts) and are approved for their manner-
as they have kept their publick Acts in former yeares, our ſelves being preſent,
at them; ſo have they lately kept two ſolemne Acts for their Commencement,
when the Governour, Magiſtrates, and the Miniſters from all parts, with
all ſorts of Schollars, and others in great numbers were preſent, and did heare
their Exerciſes; which were Latine and Greeke Orations, and Declamations, and Hebrew Analaſis, Grammaticall, Logicall & Rhetoricall of the Pſalms:
And their Anſwers and Diſputations in Logicall, Ethicall, Phyſicall and Me-
taphyſicall Queſtions; and ſo were found worthy of the firſt degree, (commonly called* Batchelour) pro more Academiarum in Anglia: *Being firſt pre-
ſented by the Preſident to the Magiſtrates and Miniſters, and by him, upon
their Approbation, ſolemnly admitted unto the ſame degree, and a Booke of*
Arts

(17)

Arts delivered into each of their hands, and power given them to read Le-
ctures in the Hall upon any of the Arts, when they shall be thereunto called, and
a liberty of studying in the Library.

All things in the Colledge are at present, like to proceed even as wee can
wish, may it but please the Lord to goe on with his blessing in Christ, and stir
up the hearts of his faithfull, and able Servants in our owne Native Coun-
try, and here, (as he hath graciously begun) to advance this Honourable and
most hopefull worke. The beginnings whereof and progresse hitherto (gene-
rally) doe fill our hearts with comfort, and raise them up to much more expe-
ctation, of the Lords goodnesse for hereafter, for the good of posterity, and the
Churches of Christ Iesus.

B o s t o n in New-England,

September the 26.

1 6 4 2.
Your very loving

friends, *&c.*

A Copie of the Queſtions given and maintained by the
Commencers in their publick Acts, printed in *Cam-*
bridge in *New-England*, and reprinted here *verbatim*,
as followeth.

C 2 *SPECTATISSIMIS*

(18)

Spectatisfimis Pietate, et Illuftrisfimis Eximia
Virtute Viris, D. *Iohanni Winthropo*, inclytæ Maffachu-
fetti Coloniæ Gubernator*i*, D. *Johanni Endicotto* Vice-
Gubernatori, D. *Thom. Dudleo*, D. *Rich. Bellinghamo*,
D. *Ioan. Humphrydo*, D. *Ifrael. Stoughtono*.

Nec non Reverendis pientiffimifque viris *Ioanni Cottono*,*Ioan. Wilfono*,
Ioan. Davenport, *Tho. Weldo*. *Hugoni Petro*, *Tho. Shepardo*, Collegij
Harvardenfis nov. *Cantabr.* infpectoribus fideliffimis, cæterifq;
Magiftratibus, & Ecclefiarum ejufdem Coloniæ Pref-
byteris vigilantiffimis,

Has Thefes Philologicas, & Philofophicas, quas Deo duce, Præfide
Henrico Dunftero palam pro virili propugnare conabuntur, (honoris & obfervantiæ gratia) dicant confecrantque in artibus
liberalibus initiati Adolefcentes.

Benjamin Woodbrigius.	*Henricus Saltonftall.*	*Nathaniel Brufterus.*
Georgius Downingus.	*Iohannes Bulkleius.*	*Samuel Belinghamus.*
Gulielmus Hubbardus.	*Iohannes Wilfonus.*	*Tobias Bernardus.*

Thefes Philologicas.

GRAMMATICAS.

Inguarum Scientia eft utiliffima.
Literæ non exprimunt quantum vocis Organa efferunt.
3 Hæbræa eft Linguarum Mater.
4. Confonantes & vocales Hæbreorum funt coætaneæ.
5. Punctationes chatephatæ fyllabam proprie non efficunt.
6. Linguarum Græca eft copiofiffima
7. Lingua Græca eft ad accentus pronuntianda.
8. Lingua Latina eft eloquentiffima.

RHETO-

(19)

RHETORICAS.

R Hetorica fpecie differt a Logica.
In Elocutione perfpicuitati cedit ornatus, ornatui copia.
3. Actio primas tenet in pronuntiotione.
4. Oratoris eft celare Artem.

LOGICAS.

U Niverfalia non funt extra intellectum.
Omnia Argumenta funt relata.
3. Caufa *fine qua non* non eft peculiaris caufa a quatuor reliquis generalibus,
4. Caufa & Effectus funt fimul tempore.
5. Diffentanea funt æque nota.
6. Contrarietas eft tantum inter duo,
7. Sublato relato tollitur correlatum.
8. Genus perfectum æqualiter communicatur fpeciebus.
9. Teftimonium valet quantum teftis.
10. Elenchorum doctrina in Logica non eft neceffaria.
11. Axioma contingens eft, quod ita verum eft, ut aliquando falfum
    effe poffit.
12. Præcepta Artium debent effe Κατὰ πάντος, καθ' αὐτὸ, καθ' ὅλου
    πρῶτον.

Theses Philofophicas.

ETHICAS.

P Hilofophia practica eft eruditionis meta.
Actio virtutis habitum antecellit.
3. Voluntas eft virtutis moralis fubjectum.
4. Voluntas eft formaliter libera.
5. Prudentia virtutum difficillima.
6. Prudentia eft virtus intellectualis & moralis.
7. Juftitia mater omnium virtutum.
8. Mors potius fubeunda quam aliquid culpæ perpetrandum.
9. Non injufte agit nifi qui libens agit.
10. Mentiri poteft qui verum dicit.
11. Juveni modeftia fummum Ornamentum.

PHYSI-

(20)

PHYSICAS,

COrpus naturale mobile eft fubjectum Phificæ.
Materia fecunda non poteft exiftere fine forma.
3. Forma eft accidens.
4. Unius rei non eft nifi unica forma conftitutiva.
5. Forma eft principium individuationis.
6. Privatio non eft principium internum.
7. Ex meris accidentibus non fit fubftantia.
8. Quicquid movetur ab alio movetur.
9. In omni motu movens fimul eft cum mobili.
10. Cœlum non movetur ab intelligentijs.
11. Non dantur orbes in cœlo.
12. Quodlibet Elementum habet unam ex primis qualitatibus fibi maxime propriam.
13. Putredo in humido fit a calore externo.
14. Anima non fit ex traduce.
15. Vehemens fenfibile deftruit fenfum.

METAPHISICAS.

OMne ens eft bonum.
Omne creatum eft concretum.
3. Quicquid æternum idem & immenfum.
4. Bonum Metaphyficum non fufcipit gradus.

Thus farre hath the good hand of God favoured our beginnings: fee whether he hath not engaged us to wait ftill upon his goodneffe for the future, by fuch further remarkable paffages of his providence to our Plantation in fuch things as thefe:

1. In fweeping away great multitudes of the Natives by the fmall Pox, a little before we went thither, that he might make room for us there.

2. In giving fuch merveilous fafe Paffage from firft to laft, to fo many thoufands that went thither, the like hath hardly been ever obferved in any Sea-voyages.

3. In blesfing us generally with health and ftrength, as much as ever (we might truly fay) more then ever in our Native Land; many that were tender and fickly here, are ftronger and heartier there. That wheras diverfe other Plantations have been the graves of their

Inha

(21)

Inhabitants, and their numbers much decreafed: God hath fo prof-pered the climate to us, that our bodies are hailer, and Children there born ftronger, wherby our number is exceedingly increafed.

4. In giving us fuch peace and freedome from enemies, when al-moft all the world is on a fire that (excepting that fhort trouble with the Pequits) we never heard of any found of Warres to this day. And in that Warre which we made againft them, Gods hand from heaven was fo manifefted, that a very few of our men, in a fhort time, purfu-ed through the Wildernefle, flew and took prifoners about 1400 of them, even all they could find, to the great terrour and amazement of all the Indians to this day: fo that the name of the Pequits (as of *Amaleck*.) is blotted out from under heaven, there being not one that is, or, (at leaft) dare call himfelfe a Pequit.

5. In fubduing thofe erronious opinions carryed over from hence by fome of the Paffengers, which for a time infefted our Churches peace but (through the goodneffe of God) by conference preaching, a generall affembly of learned men, Magiftrates timely care, and laftly, by Gods own hand from heaven, in moft remarkable ftroaks upon fome of the chief fomenters of them; the matter came to fuch an happie conclufion, that moft of the feduced came humbly and confefled their Errours in our publique Affemblies and abide to this day conftant in the Truth; the reft (that remained obftinate) finding no fit market there to vent their wares, departed from us to an Iland farre off; fome of whom alfo fince that time, have repented and re-turned to us, and are received againe into our bofomes. And from that time not any unfound, unfavourie and giddie fancie have dared to lift up his head, or abide the light amongft us.

6. In fettling and bringing civil matters to fuch a maturity in a fhort time amongft us having planted 50. Townes and Villages, built 30. or 40. Churches, and more Minifters houfes; a Caftle, a Colledge, Prifons, Forts, Cartwaies, Caufies many, and all thefe upon our owne charges, no publique hand reaching out any helpe: having comfort-able Houfes, Gardens, Orchards, Grounds fenced, Corne fields &c. and fuch a forme and face of a Common wealth appearing in all the Plantation, that Strangers from other parts, feeing how much is done in fo few yeares, have wondred at Gods blesfing on our indea-vours.

7. In giving fuch plenty of all manner of Food in a Wildernefle infomuch, that all kinds of Flefh, amongft the reft, ftore of Venifon

in

(22)

in its feason. Fifh, both from Sea and Fresh water. Fowle of all kinds, wild & tame; ftore of Whitemeate, together with all forts of Englifh Graine, afwell as Indian, are plentifull amongft us; as alfo Rootes, Herbs and Fruit, which being better digefted by the Sun, are farre more faire pleafant and wholfome then here.

8. In profpering Hempe and Flaxe fo well, that its frequently fowen, fpun, and woven into linnen Cloath: (and in a fhort time may ferve for Cordage) and fo with Cotton-wooll, (which we may have at very reafonable rates from the Ilands) and our linnen Yarne, we can make Dimittees and Fuftions for our Summer cloathing. And having a matter of a 1000. Sheep, which profper well, to begin withall, in a competent time we hope to have wollen Cloath there made. And great and fmall Cattel, being now very frequently killd for food; their skins will afford us Leather for Boots and Shoes, and other ufes: fo that God is leading us by the hand into a way of cloathing.

9. In affording us many materialls, (which in part already are, and will in time further be improved) for Staple commodities, to fupply all other defects: As

1. Furres, Bever, Otter, &c.
2. Clapboord, Hoops, Pipeftaves, Mafts.
3. Englifh Wheat and other graine for *Spaine* and Weft Indies; and all other provifions for Victualling of Shippes
4. Fifh, as Cod, Haddock, Herrings, Mackerill, Baffe, Sturgeon, Seales, Whales, Sea-horfe.
5. Oyle of fundry forts, of Whale, Sea-horfe, &c.
6. Pitch and Tarre, Rofen and Turpentine, having Pines, Spruce, and Pitch-trees in our Countrey to make thefe on.
7. Hempe and Flaxe.
8 Mineralls difcovered and proved, as of Iron in fundry places, Black-lead (many other in hopes) for the improving of which, we are now about to carry over Servants and inftruments with us,
9. (Befides many Boates, Shallops, Hoyes, Lighters, Pinnaces) we are in a way of building Shippes, of an 100, 200, 300. 400. tunne, five of them are already at Sea; many more in hand at this prefent, we being much incouraged herein by reafon of the plenty and excellencie of our Timber for that purpofe, and feeing all the materialls will be had there in fhort time.

10. In

(23)

10. In giving of fuch Magiftrates, as are all of them godly men, and members of our Churches, who countenance thofe that be good, and punifh evill doers, that a vile perfon dares not lift up his head; nor need a godly man to hang it down, that (to Gods praife be it fpoken) one may live there from yeare to yeare, and not fee a drunkard, heare an oath, or meet a begger. Now where finne is punifhed, and judgement executed, God is wont to bleffe that place, and protect it, *Pfal.* 106. 30, *Ier.* 5. 1, *Iof.* 7. 25 with 8. 1. *e contra Efa.* 20 21.

11. In ftoring that place with very many of his own people, and diverfe of them eminent for godlineffe. Now where his people are, there is his prefence, and Promife *to be in the middeft of them, a mighty God to fave, and to joy over them with finging,* Zeph. 3. 17.

12. Above all our other blesfings, in planting *his own Name,* and *precious Ordinances* among us; (we fpeak it humbly, and in his feare) our indeavour is to have all his own Inftitutions, and no more then his own and all thofe in their native fimplicity without any humane dresfings; having a liberty to injoy all that God Commands, and yet urged to nothing more then he Commands. Now *Where foever he records his Name, thither he will come and bleffe,* Ex. 20. 24.

Which promife he hath already performed to very many foules, in their effectuall converfion to Chrift, and the edification of others in their holy Faith who daily bleffe God that ever he carried them into thofe parts.

All which blesfings named we looke upon, as an earneft-penny of more to come. If we feeke his face, and ferve his Providence, wee have no caufe to doubt, that he for his part will faile to make feafonable fupplies unto us.

1. By fome meanes to carry on to their perfection our ftaple trades begun.

2. By Additions of Ammunition and Powder.

3. By maintenance of Schooles of Learning efpecially the Colledge, as alfo additions of building to it, and furnifhing the Library.

4. By ftirring up fome well-minded to cloath and tranfport over poore children Boyes and Girles, which may be a great mercy to their bodies and foules, and a help to us, they being fuper abundant here, and we wanting hands to carry on our trades, manufacture and husbandry there.

5. By ftirring up fome to fhew mercy to the *Indians,* in affording maintenance to fome of our godly active young Schollars, there to
D   make

(24.)

make it their worke to ftudie their Language converfe with them and carry light amongft them, that fo the Gofpell might be fpread into thofe darke parts of the world.

Ob. But all your own coft and ours alfo will be loft, becaufe there can be no fubfiftence there for any long time. For,

1. Your ground is barren,

Anfw. 1. If you fhould fee our goodly Corne-fields, neere harveft, you would anfwer this your felfe. Secondly, how could it be thin, that we fhould have *Englifh* Wheat at 4. *s. per* bufhell, and *Indian* at 2.8. and this not only for ready money, but in way of exchange. Thirdly, that in a wildernefle in fo few yeares, we fhould have corne enough for our felves and our friends that come over, and much to fpare.

2 *Obj.* Your ground will not continue above 3. or 4 yeares to beare corne.

Anfw. Our ground hath been fowne and planted with corne thefe 7. 10. 12. yeares already by our felves, and (which is more than can be faid here of *Englifh* Land) never yet fummer tild: but have borne corne, every yeare fince we firft went, and the fame ground planted as long by the *Indians* before, and yet have good crops upon it ftill, and is like to continue as ever: But this is, (as many other flanders againft that good Land) againft all fenfe, reafon and experience.

3. *Obj.* But you have no money there.

Anfw. It's true we have not much, though fome there is, but wee having thofe ftaple commodities named, they will (ftill as they are improved) fetch money from other parts. Ships, Fifh, Iron, Pipeftaves, Corn, Bever, Oyle, &c. will help us with money and other things alfo.

2 Little money is raifed in coyne in *England*, how then comes it to abound, but by this meane?

3. We can trade amongft our felves by way of exchange, one commodity for another, and fo doe ufually.

4. *Obj.* You are like to want clothes hereafter.

Anfw. 1. Linnen Fuftians Dimettees we are making already. Secondly, Sheepe are comming on for woollen cloath. Thirdly, in meane time we may be fupplied by way of trade to other parts. 4th. Cordevant, Deere, Seale; and Moofe Skins (which are beafts as big as Oxen, and their skins are buffe) are there to be had plentifully, which will help this way, efpecially for fervants cloathing.

5. *Ob.*

(25.)

5. *Obj.* Your Winters are cold.

Anſw. True, at ſometimes when the wind blowes ſtrong at *Nor-Weſt*: but it holds not long together and then it uſeth to be very moderate for a good ſpace, the coldneſſe being not naturall (that place being 42. degrees) but accidentall. Secondly, The cold there is no impediment to health, but very wholſome for our bodies, inſomuch that all ſorts generally, weake and ſtrong had ſcarce ever ſuch meaſure of health in all their lives as there. Thirdly, Its not a moiſt and foggie cold, as in *Holland*, and ſome parts of *England*, but bright, cleare, and faire wether, that men are ſeldome troubled in Winter with coughes and Rheumes. Fourthly, it hinders not our imployment, for people are able to worke or travell uſually all the Winter long, ſo there is no loſſe of time, ſimply in reſpect of the cold. Fiftly good fires (wood being ſo plentifull) will make amends.

6. *Ob.* Many are growne weaker in their eſtates ſince they went over.

Anſ. Are not diverſe in *London* broken in their Eſtates? and many in *England* are growne poore, and thouſands goe a begging (yet wee never ſaw a beggar there) and will any taxe the City or Kingdome, and ſay they are unſubſiſtable places?

Secondly their Eſtates now lie in houſes, Lands, Horſes, Cattel, Corne, &c. though they have not ſo much money as they had here, and ſo cannot make appearance of their wealth to thoſe in *England*, yet they have it ſtill, ſo that their Eſtates are not loſt but changed.

3. Some mens Eſtates may be weaker through great and vaſt common charges, which the firſt planters eſpecially have bin at in making the place ſubſiſtable and comfortable, which now others reape the fruit of, unknowne ſummes lye buried underground in ſuch a worke as that is.

4. Some may be poore, (ſo we are ſure) many are rich, that carried nothing at all, that now have Houſe, Land, Corne, Cattel, &c and ſuch as carry ſomething are much encreaſed.

7. *Ob.* Many ſpeake evill of the place.

Anſ. Did not ſome doe ſo of the Land of *Canaan* it ſelfe, yet *Canaan* was never the worſe and themſelves ſmarted for ſo doing. Secondly, ſome have been puniſhed there for their Delinquencies, or reſtrained from their exorbitances; or diſcountenanced for their ill opinions and not ſufferd to vent their ſtuffe: and hence being diſpleaſed take revenge by ſlanderous report. Thirdly, Let ſuch if any ſuch there be as have ought to alleadge, deale fairely and above board, and

D 2   come

(26.)

come and juftifie any thing againft the Country to our faces while we are here to anfwer, but fuch never yet appeared in any of our prefence to avouch any thing in this kinde, nor (we beleive) dare do it without blufhing.

8. *Ob.* Why doe many come away from thence?

Anfw. Doe not many remove from one Country to another, and yet none likes the Country the leffe becaufe fome depart from it? Secondly, few that we know of intend to abide here, but doe come on fome fpeciall bufines, and purpofe to returne. Thirdly of them that are come hither to ftay, (on our knowledge) fome of the wifeft repent them already, and wifh themfelves there againe. Fourthly as fome went thither upon fudden undigefted grounds, and faw not God leading them in their way, but were carryed by an unftayed fpirit, fo have they returned upon as fleight, headleffe, unworthy reafons as they went. Fiftly, others muft have elbow-roome, and cannot abide to be fo pinioned with the ftrict Government in the *Common-wealth*, or Difcipline in the Church, now why fhould fuch live there; as *Ireland* will not brooke venemous beafts, fo will not that Land vile perfons, and loofe livers. Sixtly, though fome few have removed from them, yet (we may truly fay) thoufands as wife as themfelves would not change their place for any other in the World.

FINIS.

Errata.

For *common* read *commons*, with a comma, pag. 12. line laſt ſave one. At Colledge, put a Colon : for *whitemeale*, read *whitemeate*, *pag.* 22. *line* 2. for *Howes* read *Hoyes*. put out *firſt*, p. 25. *line* 2.

APPENDIX E

DUNSTER'S MEMORANDUM OF DECEMBER, 1653 [1]

To the honoured Commissioners for the Colledg, the honoured
Mr Increase Nowel, Mr Daniel Gookin Ma[gistra]ts
Mr Edward Johnson Captain and Mr Edward Jacson
  These.

Honoured and respected gentlemen

The 27 of 6 m[onth] 1640 About 10 magistrates and 16 Elders
cald mee (arrived som 3 weeks before and a meer stranger in the
Country) to undertake the instructing of the youth of riper years and
literature after they came from grammer schools, and Mr Eliot fully
wittness[eth] that they then promissed [that] which I demand[ed], yea
with suitable advance of the stipend in case I should marry: which to
my satisfaction was payd mee the first year. No further care or distraction was imposed on mee or expected from mee but to instruct.
For the building was committed to Mr Hugh Peeter, Mr Sam. Shepheard, and Mr Joseph Cook, who prudently declined the troble and
left it to the two first. They also when they had finished the Hall (yet
without skreen table form or bench) went for England leaving the
work in the Carpenters and masons hands without Guide or further
director, no floar besides in and aboue the hall layd, no inside separating wall made nor any one study erected throughout the house. Thus
fell the work upon mee, 3d October 1641: which by the Lords assistance was so far furthered that the students dispersed in the town and
miserably distracted in their times of concourse came into commons
into one house September 1642, and with them a 3d burthen upon my
shoulders, to bee their steward, and to Direct their brewer, baker,
buttler, Cook, how to proportion their commons. A work then
acceptable to all sides easing aswell their parents a third part of their
charges as the students of endless distractions. Under these 3 works,

---

1. Dunster's own copy, in his handwriting, now in Dunster Mss., H. U. Archives.
It descended to Miss Theodora Willard of Cambridge, from her ancestor Major Simon
Willard of Concord, who married for second wife Elizabeth, sister of President Dunster,
and for third wife Mary Dunster, the President's niece or second cousin (*N. E. H. G. R.*,
LXXX. 93). Printed with facsimile in *C. S. M.*, III. 418–23, and also separately, as *A
Letter of Henry Dunster with Notes and Remarks by Henry Herbert Edes* (Cambridge,
1897). The letter is printed here on account of the autobiographical data that it contains; the financial investigation of the College, to which it especially refers, will be
described, and other documents on the same subject printed, in *H. C. S. C.*

viz The education of youth; the building, reparing, and purchasing of suitable housing for us; And the regulating the servants in their work wages and accounts: The Lord hath supported us from the beginning; to the end of the year 1652. And that without burthening the Colony any penny (1) given (2) askt or (3) bestowed at my motion to the carrying on of the Coll: work but that which was before my time already the Coll. own estate, or since hath from benefactors from abroad been bestowed, of which wee give account how it is bestowed and not spent; so that wee are at an hours warning ready to shew what and where every gift is not ingulfed but visibly by Gods blessing extant.

Petitond I confess many times haue I, (1) for repar[ati]on and inlargement of building as our good God hath increast the Number of students, when wee haue not had where to bestow them: And when the Colony could not relieve us, God hath sent supplies even from poor Cyguotea [1] to inlarge our room.

(2) And of late when Mr Shepheards motion of beneficence [2] fell to grownd which was the grownd wheron fellowships weer erected: That therfore as the Country had constituted such fellowships they would direct how they should bee mentaind I~petitioned. For whilest that they in an arbitrary way only read to som students; and at their parents and own pleasure come and go tyed to no residence, being so unsetled, and so often changed, that ever and anon all the work committed unto them falleth agen on my shoulders: where the students friends leaue it under God committing their children to mee only, faithfully to bee looked unto. I say whilest the case stands thus the Honoured and reverend overseers of the Coll: never yet thought it just or expedient to state [3] the tuitions on such as yet never would undertake to bee tutors through their pupils time, nor ever did or weer desired to admitt any students under themselves. Besides fellowships haue been promissed us otherwise to bee mentaind viz. 20*ll* a year for Mr Oks from our Christian Brethren of Charlstown; as much from Harford Colony for another fellow too much I confess for single towns to undertake, if all Massachusets Colony find that the 3d 20*li* (besides the ferry) is too heavy to contribute to myself, to make good the word and promiss of the Honoured magistrates and reverend Elders for their faithful and fatherly care to the country in referrence to the education of youth for their present and future weal in the Churches and Commonwealth: But the fault is ours whose seldom and modest demand, hath made it fall out of mind that any such thing is due.

---

1. The Eleuthera donation, with which the Goffe property (IV) and possibly the Bradish lot (B) were purchased. See *H. C. S. C.*, Chapter III.

2. The College Corn. See above, Chapter XXI.

3. I. e., settle upon. See *N. E. D.* 'State,' *v.* 4b.

neither haue I been buisy to seek wittness only you may inquire of Mr Eliot if you see good; to the Elders of Lin or any that way I haue not spoken, nor can I tel that I shal: for verily this is a burthen, which henceforth I shal discharge my support off when I haue cleared my innocency that I haue not faigned a false claime. And when the contry truely understands the case, which in sum is This.

Of all that the country from first, to the last December 1652 hath betrusted to my fidelity and care to manage for them in refference to the Coll: I haue given them [1] an account presented to the Honoured Overseers March the last $165\frac{2}{3}$ nothing lost wasted or diminished by mee but which I do undertake to make good all being extant by Gods mercy while under my sole stewardship all was.

2 Of some hundreds of pounds gifts from other places theron also you haue the like account.

3ly Of the work the contry cald mee unto and what further Gods inevitable providences hath put mee upon you theer and Heer haue. . . .

4 By virtue of your commission you haue taken som account of the personall Talents the Lord himself hath betrusted to mee: I mean what hath been cast in upon mee from sundry persons coming out of other Colonies, Ilands, and countries, whether England itself or others. To the inhabitants of which places wee are also justly liable to make account for what hath been from theirs received, and why — which their wisdoms will weigh. And how it wil stand with Gods and this countries honour, to make good their promis by others bounty.

5 All menial servants and other workmen for the Coll: are so satis-fyed and payd that none of them shal ask any thing saue of ourselves within the house so that wee haue not run the country in debt, nor the Colledge; but dues therunto being payd shal leaue it before hand aboue 100*ll* besides all manner of gifts whatever mentioned in accounts.

The premisses considered, Honoured Gentlemen and faithful Commissioners,

I haue these few requests which I humbly pray you further

1 To inform mee faithfully if you see or suspect any injury don by mee to any person or society in reference to the case in hand, or of my demand.

2 To Represent the Case to the court according to your wisdom and faithfulness that neither the Colony may suffer dishonour nor myself bee overburthened, and that wee may never bee put to speake more in the face of the court for a pecuniary interest

3ly That if you can propound matter of settling a Convenient revenue upon the Coll. you wilbee pleased to take in the advise of

---

1. A 'y' with an indeterminate superior letter; possibly 'you' should be read.

Accademical persons [1] as Norton etc for the forming therof, unless for the present Now.[2] Or els at least hear such as haue been fellows in the Coll:.

4 That your wisdoms will advise about a setled way to set and keep the buildings in repair, and how for the present or whence wee may haue suply to procure pay for the necessary repayrs wee haue ingaged for, in reference to bord, shingle, glass, nayles etc

5 That besydes myself some other at least one may bee joynd to look to these country accounts and that from year to year giving them up to the honoured Magistrats at our country courts there may bee an issue of them henceforth. So shal I rest

yours chearfully to serve in the Lord while hee sees good

HENRY DUNSTER.

The main of the premisses presented in December 1653.

1. University alumni. There were none such on the Commission.
2. Cf. Nicholas Rowe, *Jane Shore*, act iii: 'this present now, some matters of the State detain our leisure.'

INDEX

INDEX